THE STRUCTURE OF PAUL'S THEOLOGY

"The Truth Which Is the Gospel"

THE STRUCTURE
OF PAUL'S THEOLOGY

"The Truth Which Is the Gospel"

Christopher A. Davis

MELLEN BIBLICAL PRESS

Lewiston/Lampeter/Queenston

Library of Congress Cataloging-in-Publication Data

Davis, Christopher A. 1958-
   The structure of Paul's theology : "the truth which is the Gospel"
/ Christopher A. Davis.
     p.   cm.
   Includes bibliographical references and index.
   ISBN 0-7734-2422-9 (alk. paper)
    1. Bible. N.T. Epistles of Paul--Criticism, interpretation, etc.
   2. Theology, Doctrinal--History--early church, ca. 30-600.
   I. Title.
   BS2651.D33   1995
   227'.06--dc20   94-48472
                                                 CIP

A CIP catalog record for this book is available from the British Library.

All rights reserved. For information contact

The Edwin Mellen Press   The Edwin Mellen Press
Box 450   Box 67
Lewiston, New York   Queenston, Ontario
USA 14092-0450   CANADA L0S 1L0

The Edwin Mellen Press, Ltd.
Lampeter, Dyfed, Wales
UNITED KINGDOM SA48 7DY

Printed in the United States of America

To Cathy

ἀσθενοῦσα δυναμωθήσεται
πάσχουσα δοξασθήσεται
ἀποθνήσκουσα ζῳοποιηθήσεται

TABLE OF CONTENTS

ILLUSTRATIONS

PREFACE

The following analysis of Paul's theology is based on the twenty-sixth edition of the Nestle-Aland *Novum Testamentum Graece* (Stuttgart: Deutsche Bibelstiftung, 1979). Old Testament citations are taken from (1) *Biblia Hebraica Stuttgartensia*, edited by K. Elliger and W. Rudolph (Stuttgart: Deutsche Bibelgesellschaft, 1977), and (2) *The Septuagint With Apocrypha: Greek and English*, edited and translated by Lancelot C. L. Brenton (Grand Rapids: Zondervan Publishing House, 1851). The texts and critical apparatus of three other editions of the Septuagint were also consulted: (1) *Septuaginta: Vetus Testamentum Graecum Auctoritate Academiae Scientiarum Gottingensis editum* (Göttingen: Vandenhoeck & Ruprecht, 1931-[86]), (2) *Septuaginta; id est Vetus Testamentum graece iuxta LXX interpretes*, 2 vols., edited by Alfred Rahlfs (Stuttgart: Privilegierte Württembergische Bibelanstalt, 1935), and (3) *The Old Testament in Greek: According to the Text of Codex Vaticanus, Supplemented from Other Uncial Manuscripts* . . . , 2 vols., edited by Alan England Brooke and Norman McLean (Cambridge: The University Press, 1917). English translations of these biblical writings (i.e., Paul's letters, other New Testament documents, the Hebrew Old Testament, and the Septuagint) are the work of the author and reflect his exegetical decisions.

Translations of Old Testament pseudepigraphical writings generally follow *The Old Testament Pseudepigrapha*, 2 vols., edited by James H. Charlesworth (Garden City, NY: Doubleday & Company, Inc., 1983). Some corrections or alterations have been made by the author on the basis of the "Corpus des Textes" found on pages 813-925 of *Concordance Grecque des Pseudépigraphes D'Ancien Testament*, by Albert-Marie Denis (Louvain-la-Neuve: Université Catholique de Louvain, Institut Orientaliste, 1987). *The Apocrypha and Pseudepigrapha of the Old Testament in English*, a two-volume work edited by R. H. Charles (Oxford: The Clarendon Press, 1913), was also consulted.

ACKNOWLEDGMENTS

This book began as a dissertation prepared in partial fulfilment of the requirements for the degree Doctor of Philosophy from Union Theological Seminary in Richmond, Virginia. It was completed with the help and support of many people. I gratefully acknowledge the contributions made by the following:

Dr. Paul J. Achtemeier supervised the project, providing many helpful insights and suggestions. He has proved to be not only a master teacher but also a good friend. Standing on his shoulders, I can see much farther than I could have seen on my own.

Professors Jack Dean Kingsbury and Peter Lampe also served on my doctoral committee, offering their counsel and encouragement.

During my years at the seminary, I enjoyed the benefit of studying under an excellent biblical faculty. In addition to Professors Achtemeier, Kingsbury, and Lampe, it was my privilege to work with Mathias Rissi, James Luther Mays, Patrick D. Miller, W. Sibley Towner and S. Dean McBride. They provided a model of careful, responsible scholarship in the service of the Church.

The faculty, administration, staff and friends of Union Theological Seminary showed great kindness in the form of advice and instruction, along with finances, housing and other services prerequisite to any scholarly pursuit.

The library staff put the world at my fingertips. Sophie Ann White, Patsy Verrault, Elaine Christensen, Hobbie Bryant, Kristin Strong and Linda Quinn helped to locate resources--whether they were in Scotland, or France, or on my own desk! Robert Benedetto and Martha Aycock Sugg read the manuscript and offered direction concerning its form.

Through his book on *Paul the Apostle: The Triumph of God in Life and Thought,* J. Christiaan Beker challenged me to search out the "coherent center" of Paul's theology and convinced me that it took the form of an "apocalyptic interpretation of the Christ-event." He laid much of the foundation upon which I have built.

The friendship and humor of my colleagues at Union (especially Bruce Schuchard, Jim and Kathy Fladland, Liz Yates, Roy Harrisville, Ray Jones, Jeff Gibbs, Kevin O'Brien, Chuck Aaron, Michael Brooks, Frank Norris, John Strong, Nelson Kraybill, David Handy, Jerome Creach, Rich Christensen and Larry Toney) helped me through the highs and lows of a long and (finally) extinguished seminary career. I leave them one more book to read--which, considering their "high tolerance for pain," should not prove too great a burden.

Throughout the process of research and writing, I received constant support and encouragement from my parents, Jerry and Margie Davis; my family; my minister, Kenneth McCrickard; and my church, the Parham Hills Christian Church of Richmond, Virginia. I hope that this study will serve as a partial repayment of the debt I owe to them.

My students and colleagues on the faculty and staff of Minnesota Bible College provided encouragement and support as I updated and revised the work. Professor Ruth Picker read the entire manuscript and offered many suggestions which have improved its quality. My student assistant, Thomas Manzke, prepared portions of the index.

Finally, my wife Cathy has persevered through thirteen years of graduate school, comprehensive exams, a master's thesis, a doctoral dissertation, and the struggles of a new professor. She has worked to support our family, and has sustained me both physically and emotionally and spiritually. She has read through multiple drafts of this study, and our discussions have clarified the issues and shaped their presentation. She has demonstrated daily what Paul means by "dying with Christ;" she has willingly and joyfully borne on her body "the marks of Jesus." Cathy has made this book possible. It is with love, and respect, and gratitude that I dedicate it to her.

ABBREVIATIONS

AnBib	*Analecta biblica*
ATJ	*Ashland Theological Journal*
AusBR	*Australian Biblical Review*
BA	*Biblical Archaeologist*
BAG	Bauer, Arndt, and Gingrich, *A Greek-English Lexicon of the New Testament and Other Early Christian Literature*
BB	*Bible Bhashyam: An Indian Biblical Quarterly*
BBR	*Bulletin for Biblical Research*
BDB	Brown, Driver, and Briggs, *A Hebrew and English Lexicon of the Old Testament*
BeO	*Bibbia e Oriente*
Bib	*Biblica*
BibR	*Bible Review*
BHS	*Biblia Hebraica Stuttgartensia*
BJRL	*Bulletin of the John Rylands University Library of Manchester*
BSac	*Bibliotheca sacra*
BTB	*Biblical Theology Bulletin*
BZ	*Biblische Zeitschrift*
CBQ	*The Catholic Biblical Quarterly*
Coll	*Colloquium*
CT	*Christianity Today*
CTQ	*Concordia Theological Quarterly*
ER	*Epworth Review*
ETL	*Ephemerides theologicae Lovanienses*
ETR	*Etudes theologiques et religieuses*
EvQ	*The Evangelical Quarterly*
EvT	*Evangelische Theologie*
ExpTim	*Expository Times*
FV	*Foi et Vie*

GOTR	*The Greek Orthodox Theological Review*
GTJ	*Grace Theological Journal*
HBT	*Horizons in Biblical Theology*
HeyJ	*The Heythrop Journal*
HTR	*Harvard Theological Review*
IBS	*Irish Biblical Studies*
IDB	*The Interpreter's Dictionary of the Bible*
IDBSup	*The Interpreter's Dictionary of the Bible, Supplementary Volume*
Int	*Interpretation*
IRM	*The International Review of Mission*
ITQ	*The Irish Theological Quarterly*
JAAR	*Journal of the American Academy of Religion*
JBL	*Journal of Biblical Literature*
JBR	*The Journal of Bible and Religion*
JETS	*Journal of the Evangelical Theological Society*
JJS	*Journal of Jewish Studies*
JSNT	*Journal for the Study of the New Testament*
JTS	*The Journal of Theological Studies*
KD	*Kerygma und Dogma*
KTR	*King's Theological Review*
LouvS	*Louvain Studies*
LS	Liddell and Scott, *A Greek-English Lexicon*
LXX	Septuagint
MT	Masoretic Text
NEB	The New English Bible
Neot	*Neotestamentica*
NJB	The New Jerusalem Bible
NovT	*Novum Testamentum*
NT	New Testament
NTS	*New Testament Studies*

OT	Old Testament
RB	*Revue Biblique*
RelSRev	*Religious Studies Review*
RestQ	*Restoration Quarterly*
RevExp	*Review and Expositor*
RevQ	*Revue de Qumran*
RevR	*Review for Religious*
RSV	Revised Standard Version
RTR	*Reformed Theological Review*
SBS	*Stuttgarter Bibelstudien*
ScEs	*Science et Esprit*
SEA	*Svensk Exegetisk Årsbok*
Sem	*Semeia*
SJT	*Scottish Journal of Theology*
SR	*Studies in Religion/Sciences Religieuses*
StTh	*Studia Theologica (Scandinavian Journal of Theology)*
SWJT	*Southwestern Journal of Theology*
TB	*Tyndale Bulletin*
TDNT	*Theological Dictionary of the New Testament*
Them	*Themelios*
TJ	*Trinity Journal*
TS	*Theological Studies*
TSFB	*TSF [Theological Students Fellowship] Bulletin*
TZ	*Theologische Zeitschrift*
USQR	*Union Seminary Quarterly Review*
WTJ	*The Westminster Theological Journal*
WW	*Word & World*
ZAW	*Zeitschrift für die alttestamentliche Wissenschaft*
ZNW	*Zeitschrift für did neutestamentliche Wissenschaft*

CHAPTER ONE

THE COHERENT CENTER OF PAUL'S THEOLOGY:
A PROPOSAL

During the Society of Biblical Literature's 1986 meeting in Atlanta,
Georgia, Hendrikus Boers pointed to the identification of a theological center
that "integrates the diversity of the apostle's thinking into a coherent whole"
as "the most fundamental problem in Pauline interpretation."[1] The Church
has wrestled with this problem for as long as it has considered Paul's epistles
"scripture"--i.e., from the time that Christians first sought to release Paul's
letters from the limitations of particularity in order to mine from them an
authoritative word to the Church universal.[2] Scholars have advanced many
different models for understanding the Apostle's thought, but a consensus
regarding the nature and content of Paul's "coherent center" has not yet

---

[1]Hendrikus Boers, "Proposal for SBL Meeting, Atlanta, 1986," 2, quoted in J. Christiaan
Beker, "Paul the Theologian: Major Motifs in Pauline Theology," *Int* 43 (1989): 354.

[2]That this was already beginning to take place in the first century is shown by 2 Pet 3:15-16,
which (1) places the collection of Paul's "epistles" in the same category with the "other scriptures," and (2) views those epistles as the common property of all the churches. See also Nils
Alstrup Dahl, "The Particularity of the Pauline Epistles as a Problem in the Ancient Church,"
in *Neotestamentica et Patristica: Eine Freundesgabe, Herrn Professor Dr. Oscar Cullmann zu
seinem 60. Geburtstag Überreicht,* ed. E. Earle Ellis and Max Wilcox (Leiden: E. J. Brill, 1962),
261-71.

2

emerged.[3] This study attempts to move the discussion forward by offering a new proposal based on evidence from the Pauline epistles not fully appreciated in the past.

The Notion of the "Center"

"Paul's theology" as "the truth." We begin by defining precisely what we mean by "the coherent center of Paul's theology." By "Paul's theology" we mean his understanding of God's Person and God's actions in their significance for God's Creation. When Paul articulates his "theology," or his understanding of how God has acted--and will continue to act--in order to shape reality, he views himself as simply speaking the "truth," or "the truth

---

[3]The following scholars provide historical surveys of attempts to locate Paul's theological center: (1) J. Christiaan Beker in (a) "Contingency and Coherence in the Letters of Paul," *USQR* 33 (1978): 141-51, (b) *Paul the Apostle: The Triumph of God in Life and Thought* (Philadelphia: Fortress Press, 1980), 13-15, 27-33, (c) "The Method of Recasting Pauline Theology: The Coherence-Contingency Scheme as Interpretive Model," in *Society of Biblical Literature 1986 Seminar Papers,* ed. Kent Harold Richards (Atlanta: Scholars Press, 1986), 600-01, (d) "Paul's Theology: Consistent or Inconsistent?" *NTS* 34 (1988): 364-67, (e) "Paul the Theologian," 354-55, (f) *The Triumph of God: The Essence of Paul's Thought,* trans. Loren T. Stuckenbruck (Minneapolis: Fortress Press, 1990) (an abridged version of *Paul the Apostle,* which first appeared in German as *Der Sieg Gottes: Eine Untersuchung zur Struktur des paulinischen Denkens* [1988]), 3-14; (2) Hendrikus Boers in "The Foundations of Paul's Thought: A Methodological Investigation--The Problem of the Coherent Center of Paul's Thought," *StTh* 42 (1988): 55-58; (3) Victor Paul Furnish in "On Putting Paul in His Place," *JBL* 113 (1994): 3-17; (4) Don N. Howell, Jr., in "Pauline Thought in the History of Interpretation," *BSac* 150 (1993): 303-26; and (5) Joseph Plevnik in "The Center of Pauline Theology," *CBQ* 51 (1989): 461-67, 69-76. Plevnik offers an incisive critique of the solutions to the problem of the Pauline center offered by Davies, Stendahl, Dahl, Sanders, Beker, Reumann, and R. B. Hays. Boers focuses on the work of Barth, Bultmann, Käsemann, Beker and Patte.

For summaries that focus primarily on whether or not the doctrine of justification by faith forms the center of Pauline theology, see (1) Hans Conzelmann, "Current Problems in Pauline Research," *Int* 22 (1968): 171-86, (2) John Reumann, Joseph A. Fitzmyer, and Jerome D. Quinn, *"Righteousness" in the New Testament: "Justification" in the United States Lutheran-Roman Catholic Dialogue* (Philadelphia: Fortress Press, 1982), 105-20, and (3) E. P. Sanders, *Paul and Palestinian Judaism: A Comparison of Patterns of Religion* (Philadelphia: Fortress Press, 1977), 434-42.

In recent years, the team of international scholars who form the Society of Biblical Literature's Pauline Theology Group have addressed the question of the Pauline center. As of this writing, they have published two insightful volumes detailing the results of their work: (1) Jouette M. Bassler, ed., *Pauline Theology, Volume I: Thessalonians, Philippians, Galatians, Philemon* (Minneapolis: Fortress Press, 1991), and (2) David M. Hay, ed., *Pauline Theology, Volume II: 1 & 2 Corinthians* (Minneapolis: Fortress Press, 1993). See also James D. G. Dunn, "Prolegomena to a Theology of Paul," *NTS* 40 (1994): 407-32.

about God" (ἡ ἀλήθεια θεοῦ).[4] The Apostle refers to his "personal way of summing up" the truth as "the gospel" (τὸ εὐαγγέλιον, lit. "the good news"),[5] or "the truth which is the gospel" (ἡ ἀλήθεια τοῦ εὐαγγελίου).[6] In exploring "Paul's theology," then, we are attempting to think the Apostle's thoughts after him, to "hear" his gospel, to grasp his conception of what is "true" about God.

The "coherent center" of "Paul's theology." As J. Christiaan Beker has so ably pointed out, Paul did not leave us a "systematic theology," or a complete and orderly presentation of the gospel message. Instead, we possess only a collection of letters in which the Apostle speaks to his readers a "word on target" that is both appropriate for their particular situation and grounded in the universal "truth which is the gospel."[7] When we speak of the "coherent

---

[4]See, e.g., Rom 1:18, 25 ("the truth about God," ἡ ἀλήθεια τοῦ θεοῦ); 2:8; 2 Cor 4:2 ("the open announcement of the truth," ἡ φανέρωσις τῆς ἀληθείας); 6:7 ("the word which is truth," ὁ λόγος ἀληθείας); 7:14; 11:10 ("the truth about Christ," ἡ ἀλήθεια Χριστοῦ); 13:8; Gal 5:7.

[5]For Paul's use of this term, see (1) Joseph A. Fitzmyer, "The Gospel in the Theology of Paul," *Int* 33 (1979): 339-50, and (2) A. J. Spallek, "The Origin and Meaning of Εὐαγγέλιον in the Pauline Corpus," *CTQ* 57 (1993): 177-90.

[6]See Gal 2:5, 14.

[7]See the list of studies mentioned in note 3, along with "Recasting Pauline Theology: The Coherence-Contingency Scheme as Interpretive Model," in *Pauline Theology, Volume I: Thessalonians, Philippians, Galatians, Philemon,* ed. Jouette M. Bassler (Minneapolis: Fortress Press, 1991), 15-24. Note also Hans Hübner's assessment of Beker's coherence-contingency scheme in "Methodologie und Theologie: Zu neuen methodischen Ansätzen in der Paulusforschung. Teil I," *KD* 33 (1987): 150-76.
  In his work, Beker calls attention to the presence of both contingency and coherence in Paul's thought. By "contingency" he means "the variable element, i.e., the variety and particularity of sociological, economic and psychological situations which Paul faces in his churches and on the mission field" ("Paul's Theology," 368). By "coherence" he means "the stable, constant, cohesive element which expresses the convictional basis of Paul's proclamation of the gospel, i.e., 'the truth of the gospel' (Gal 2:5, 14), apostasy from which constitutes an apocalyptic curse (Gal 1:8, 9; cf. also Phil 1:27)" (368). According to Beker, Paul's distinctive hermeneutic--his special genius as an interpreter of the gospel--is marked by "a continuous interaction . . . between the constant elements of the gospel and the variable elements of the situation, so that in each new situation the gospel comes to speech again" as a "word on target" for that situation ("Contingency and Coherence," 148). "Paul's hermeneutic not only distills a specific core out of the variety of gospel traditions in the early church but also 'incarnates' that core into the particularity of historical occasions and contexts" (*Paul the Apostle,* 351). This hermeneutic is "Paul's particular contribution to theology" ("Contingency and Coherence," 150).

center" of Paul's theology, we are referring to the Apostle's most basic and fundamental convictions concerning the "truth"--the "core convictions" underlying all the various contingent expressions of the gospel found in his letters. In searching for that "center," we are attempting to look beyond the purely contingent concerns of his letters in order to discover the essential and unchanging elements of Paul's gospel in their proper relationship to one another.

Response to objections raised by Beker. Beker maintains that this cannot be done because "[the gospel] tradition for Paul is always interpreted tradition."[8] The "coherent center" of Paul's gospel "is never an abstraction away from its 'address' and audience,"[9] but is "inseparably related to its contingent expressions."[10] The "gospel of 'Christ crucified' ceases to be gospel unless it lights up the particular world to which it is addressed."[11] For this reason, we cannot separate out the "center" of Paul's gospel from its contingent expressions in his letters without destroying the gospel itself. Is this argument valid?

Beker is certainly correct to say that Paul never abstracts the gospel away from the contingent situation in his letters. Yet he seems to overlook the fact that Paul's letter-writing activity was only one aspect of a very long and eventful apostolic ministry. Beker has increased our appreciation for Paul's skill as an "interpreter of the gospel," but Paul the "interpreter of the gospel" is not Paul in his totality.

The letters we possess only show us Paul in his dealings with other Christians.[12] Since the intended readers (with the possible exception of some

---

[8]Beker, "Contingency and Coherence," 148.

[9]Beker, "Contingency and Coherence," 142.

[10]Beker, "Paul's Theology," 369.

[11]Beker, *Paul the Apostle,* 352.

[12]On this point, see Plevnik, "The Center," 467-68.

members of the church at Rome) are already acquainted with the basic outlines of his gospel, the Apostle can immediately proceed to develop the
further implications of that message for their present situation.[13] However,
passages such as Gal 1:6-9 ("the gospel . . . which we preached to you") 1 Cor
11:23-25 ("I myself received from the Lord what I also delivered to you"), and
1 Cor 15:3-8 ("I delivered to you at the first what I also received") open a win-
dow to another side of Paul's apostolic labors. They show that, in his initial
contacts with non-Christians or new Christians, the Apostle sometimes played
the role of proclaimer of the gospel, or transmitter of authoritative gospel traditions. On these occasions, Paul apparently did hand down a more or less
fixed doctrinal "core," which embodied the heart of his message, and which
was no more (or less) relevant to one contingent situation than another.

The text which proves most instructive on this point is 1 Cor 4:17, in
which the Apostle says:

> For this [very] reason I sent to you Timothy, who is my beloved and trust-
> worthy child in the Lord. He will remind you of my ways in Christ Jesus,
> as I customarily teach them everywhere in every church.

Concerning this passage, J. Paul Sampley writes:

> From this we know that there was a core representation of Paul's teaching,
> that it was possible for someone--like Timothy here--to grasp it and to
> communicate it on a visit, and that this same communication was at the
> core of what every church everywhere was taught by Paul. If we could
> have access to Timothy, our enterprise [i.e., synthesizing the theology of
> the various Pauline letters] would not be necessary! As it is, we have
> reason to search the Pauline letters in the hope that we can reconstruct
> the core communication, but seeking that in highly situational letters will

---

[13]Much of what Paul writes is comprehensible only on the basis of one's having prior knowledge of the gospel message. This explains the difficulty we experience in our efforts to work
backwards, through the letters, to that message.

be a much more delicate and difficult task than quizzing Timothy would have been.[14]

Criteria for identifying the "center." If it is indeed possible to "recon-struct" Paul's "core communication" from the evidence preserved in his letters, then how do we distinguish which elements of the Apostle's thought belong to that "core"? In his article on "The Center of Pauline Theology," Joseph Plevnik (building on the earlier work of Wrede, Schweitzer, Sanders and Reumann) lays down the following criteria:[15]

First, we must limit our search for the "core" or "coherent center" of Paul's theology to the epistles that Paul himself certainly authored. For this purpose, we accept only the seven undisputed letters--namely, Romans, 1 Cor-inthians, 2 Corinthians, Galatians, Philippians, 1 Thessalonians, and Philemon.

Second, we are not searching for what is unique in Paul's theology, but what is central in Paul's theology. Therefore, when the Apostle takes over earlier traditions (such as the "Kenosis Hymn" of Phil 2:6-11) and makes them his own, we will treat those traditions as accurate expressions of Paul's own convictions.

Third, "the center cannot be what is affirmed solely with respect to a particular historical situation in the past." Whatever "is of merely temporal, contingent significance cannot be the center."[16]

Fourth, Plevnik maintains that "anything . . . derived from something else in Pauline theology is not the center."[17] This statement could be misleading. If the Pauline center should happen to be a "network of convictions" (as

---

[14]J. Paul Sampley, "Overcoming Traditional Methods by Synthesizing the Theology of Indi-vidual Letters," in *Society of Biblical Literature 1986 Seminar Papers,* ed. Kent Harold Richards (Atlanta: Scholars Press, 1986), 605.

[15]See Plevnik, "The Center, 464-66.

[16]Plevnik, "The Center," 465.

[17]Plevnik, "The Center," 466.

Daniel Patte suggests[18]), then it may be that some of those convictions are dependent upon, or "derived from," other convictions. At the same time, Paul could consider those "secondary" convictions "essential" and condemn their removal as a denial of "the truth which is the gospel." If this is the case, then it would be more accurate to say that anything derived from this "network of convictions" (viewed as a whole) cannot be the "center" of Paul's theology.

Finally, in order for a particular conviction or "network of convictions" to qualify as Paul's "coherent center," we must be able to derive all major aspects of the Apostle's theology from it. The "center" must take in, for example, both the objective events of God's action in Christ and the subjective appropriation of those events by the believer.

The Content of Paul's "Coherent Center"

With these criteria in mind, we now take up the question of greatest importance: What is "the truth"? What, precisely, is the content of the "coherent center" of Paul's theology?

Pauline "summary statements." We begin with an observation: Scattered throughout the Pauline letters we find a series of passages in which the Apostle communicates four specific ideas, and always in the same relationship to one another. The Apostle's language and mode of expression may vary, but four ideas remain constant and ever-present: (A) Christ's death, (B) Christ's resurrection/"eschatological life," (C) the Christian's "death" with Christ, and (D) the Christian's resurrection/"eschatological life" with Christ. All four ideas (marked A, B, C, and D) appear together in the five passages examined below.[19]

---

[18]See Daniel Patte, *Paul's Faith and the Power of the Gospel: A Structural Introduction to the Pauline Letters* (Philadelphia: Fortress Press, 1983). For a critique of Patte's work on Paul, see Hübner, "Methodologie."

[19]We will examine these texts more closely in later chapters.

First, Rom 6:3-11 reads as follows:

(C)   Or do you not realize that as many of us as have been baptized into Christ Jesus have been baptized into [A] his death? We, then, have been buried together with him, by means of baptism, into "death," in order that,

(B)   just as Christ has been raised from the dead by the Glory who is the Father,

(D)   so might we also live a new life.

(C)   For if we have been planted together [with one another] in [a "death"] like [A] his death,

(D)   [then] we will certainly also [participate in a resurrection like his] [B] resurrection.

(C)   This we know: Our old self has been crucified together with [Christ], in order that the body [ruled by] Sin might pass away, with the result that we are no longer enslaved to Sin. For the person who has [thus] "died" has been reckoned righteous; [s/he is] apart from Sin. Now if we have "died" with Christ,

(D)   [then] we trust that we will also come to life with him.

(B)   [We] know that since Christ has been raised from the dead, he dies no more. Death is his lord no longer.

(A)   For [the death] which [Christ] died he died to Sin, once for all time;

(B)   but [the life] which [Christ] lives he lives to God.

(C)   In the same way, reckon yourselves to be dead to Sin,

(D)   but alive to God within [the sphere where] Christ Jesus [rules].

Second, Paul speaks of the Christian's "death" and resurrection with Christ in terms of "suffering" and "glory" in Rom 8:17:

But if we are God's children, then we are also heirs--on the one hand God's heirs, and on the other hand fellow-heirs with Christ--

(C)   provided that we suffer together with [A] him,

(D)   in order that we may also be glorified together with [B] him.

Third, the Apostle reviews his own experience in Phil 3:10-11:

[I have been caused to lose all things] in order that I may know him,

(D)   and the strength [of God which effected] [B] his resurrection,

(C)   and fellowship [with him] in [A] his sufferings, being conformed with [him] in [A] his death,

(D)   [so that] if at all possible I may attain to the Resurrection of the dead.

Fourth, Paul makes this statement in 2 Cor 4:10-11:

(C)   We are always carrying about in our body [A] the death of Jesus,

(D)   in order that [B] the life of Jesus might also be manifested in our body.

(C)   For we who are alive are continually being delivered over to death for the sake of Jesus,

(D)   in order that [B] the life of Jesus might also be manifested in our mortal flesh.

Finally, Paul speaks of "death" and resurrection in terms of "weakness" and "strength" in 2 Cor 13:4-5a:

(A)   For [Christ] was indeed crucified because of "weakness,"

(B)   but he is alive because of God's strength . . .

(C)   we ourselves are now "weak" within [the sphere ruled by] him--

(D)   but we will live along with [B] him because of the strength God will demonstrate toward you.

(C)   Test yourselves [to determine] whether you are within [the sphere where] trust [is the rule].

Alongside the five passages already cited, there are a number of other Pauline texts in which two or three of the four ideas under consideration appear together. First, Paul treats (A) Christ's death, (B) Christ's "life," and (C) the Christian's "death" together in 2 Cor 5:14-15:

(A)   For Christ's expression of his love compels us, since we have judged this--namely, that one has died for all;

(C)   therefore all have died.

(A)   And he died for all

(C)   in order that those who are alive might no longer live for themselves, but for the [one]

(A)   who died for them,

(B)   and who was raised.

It is important to notice that, according to this passage, Christians "die" only because Christ first died "for them."[20]

Second, Christ's death and "life" also appear alongside the Christian's "death" in Phil 2:5-11:

(C)   Have this mind-set in you which was also in Christ Jesus,

(A)   Who, although [he] was in the form of God, did not consider equality with God something to be seized. Instead, he emptied himself by taking the form of a slave, by being [born] in the likeness of men. And after he was found in outward form as a man, he humbled himself by being obedient to the point of death--even the death which is the cross.

(B)   For this very reason God super-exalted him and gave to him the Name which is above every name, in order that, at the nam[ing] of Jesus, every knee should bow--of heavenly [beings] and of earthly [beings] and of [beings] under the earth--and every tongue should confess, "Jesus Christ [is] Lord," to the glory of God the Father.

Paul here links ("for this very reason," διὸ καὶ) God's decision to (raise Christ from the dead and) exalt him to Christ's acceptance of the cross.

Third, Paul lays (A) Christ's death alongside (C) the Christian's "death" in Gal 2:19-20:

(C)   For, by means of the Law, I have died to the Law, in order that I may live to God. I have been crucified with [A] Christ. I myself no longer live. Instead, Christ lives in me. The life which I am

---

[20]Note Paul's use of the conjunctions ἄρα ("therefore") and ἵνα ("in order that").

now living in the flesh, I am living within [the sphere where] trust [is the rule--namely], the [trust of]

(A)   the Son of God, who loved me and who delivered himself over [to death] for me.

Fourth, Paul speaks of (A) Christ's death in relationship to (C) the Christian's "death" and (D) "life" in 2 Cor 12:9-10:

(A)   Then He has said to me, "My expression of my goodwill is enough for you,

(D)   for strength achieves its intended end

(C)   within [the sphere where] 'weakness' [is the rule]." Most gladly, therefore, will I boast all the more within [the sphere where] my "weaknesses" [are the rule],

(D)   so that the strength [which is] Christ may "pitch its tent" upon me.

(C)   For whenever I am "weak,"

(D)   then am I "strong"!

Again, the Christian's resurrection depends upon his/her first "dying" with Christ.[21]

Fifth, Paul points to (A) Christ's death as the means by which (D) the Christian enjoys "life" in 2 Cor 8:9:

(A)   For you know our Lord Jesus Christ's expression of his goodwill: Although rich, he became poor for us,

(D)   in order that you yourselves, by means of [A] his poverty, might become rich.

Sixth, we gain insight into Paul's conception of (B) Christ's resurrection, (C) the Christian's "death," and (D) the Christian's "life" in Phil 3:21:

(D)   He will transform [C] our body of humiliation, so that it will be in conformity with [B] his body of glory . . . .

---

[21]Note God's assurance that His "strength achieves its intended end [only] within the domain where 'weakness' is the rule," along with Paul's use of ἵνα ("in order that") and ὅταν . . . τότε ("whenever . . . then").

Seventh, Rom 8:13b again highlights the necessary connection between the Christian's "death" and "life":

(C)   . . . if, by means of the Spirit, you are putting to death the deeds of the body [as determined by the flesh],

(D)   then you will come to life.

Eighth, we see the same connection made in 2 Cor 4:17b:

(C)   For our momentary, insignificant suffering is preparing for us

(D)   an eternal weight of eschatological glory, transcendent beyond measure.

Finally, Paul refers once more to the Christian's "death" and "life" in 2 Cor 7:3b:

(C)   . . . you are continally in our hearts, toward the end of our dying together

(D)   and our living together.

Behind the Apostle's variety of expression, and amid his shifting concerns, we see Paul returning again and again to (A) Christ's death and (B) resurrection, and to (C) the Christian's "death" (D) and resurrection with Christ. On each occasion, the Apostle insists on maintaining a specific network of temporal and conditional relationships between these four events: Christ's death always belongs to the past, while his resurrection/"eschatological life" continues into the present. The Christian's "death" with Christ belongs to the present, while his/her resurrection/"eschatolological life" with Christ remains in the future. Furthermore, the Christian's resurrection with Christ is somehow dependent upon, or conditioned upon, his/her first "dying" with Christ.[22]

---

[22]See, e.g., Rom 6:4-5 ("We, then, have been buried together with him, by means of baptism, into 'death,' in order that [ἵνα], just as Christ has been raised from the dead by the Glory who is the Father, so might we also live a new life. For if [εἰ] we have been planted together with one another in a 'death' like his death, then we will certainly also participate in a resurrection like his resurrection."), 8 ("Now if [εἰ] we have died with Christ, then we trust that we will also

These four ideas permeate Paul's correspondence with all his church-es.[23] When taken together (and when properly understood), they form the basis for every major aspect of Paul's theology, including, for example, his christology, soteriology, eschatology, ecclesiology, nomology, and ethics--along with both his doctrine of "righteousness through trust" and his doctrine of "participation in Christ." For this reason, we propose that the passages mentioned above represent "summary statements" in which Paul himself sets forth --in abbreviated fashion--the "coherent center" of his theology, or "the truth which is the gospel."

Thesis. Building on this insight, we will, in the chapters that follow, undertake to prove the following thesis:

The content of the "coherent center" of Paul's theology consists of a net-work of fourteen "core convictions" revolving around four ideas--namely,

(A) Christ's death, which Paul understands as
    (1) the sacrifice for sins which established the "new covenant,"
    (2) God's expression of His righteousness toward both Abraham and all nations, and
    (3) Christ's expression of trust in, or self-humiliation before God;

(B) Christ's resurrection to "eschatological life," which Paul understands as
    (4) an act of God,

---

come to life with him."); 8:17 (". . . we suffer together with him, in order that [ἵνα] we may also be glorified together with him."); 2 Cor 4:10-11 (". . . always carrying about in our body the death of Jesus, in order that [ἵνα] the life of Jesus might also be manifested in our body . . . continually being delivered over to death for the sake of Jesus, in order that [ἵνα] the life of Jesus might also be manifested in our mortal flesh.").

[23]The passages quoted above represent Romans and Corinthians, Galatians and Philippians. In Galatians, Paul focuses primarily on (A) Christ's death and (C) the Christian's "death" with Christ. However, (B) Christ's resurrection, along with (D) the Christian's resurrection with Christ, are mentioned in Gal 1:1, 4. In 1 Thessalonians, Paul directs his attention primarily to-ward (C) the Christian's "death" with Christ. However, (A) Christ's death is mentioned in 2:15, 4:14, and 5:10, while (B) the resurrection of Christ and (D) of Christians takes center stage in 1:10 and 4:13-5:11. Philemon, by reason of its nature and brevity, does not speak directly to these themes. However, we detect faint echoes concerning the Christian's "death" with Christ behind, for example, vv. 1, 5-6, 9-10, 13.

(5) the beginning of the eschatological age and the general Resurrection of the righteous,

(6) Christ's entrance into "eschatological life," which is characterized
by glory and immortality, and

(7) God's exaltation of the humble, trusting Jesus;

(C) the Christian's "death" with Christ, which Paul understands as his/her

(8) trust in, or self-humiliation before God,

(9) participation in the "new covenant," or in the "righteousness" that
is based on trust, and (in the case of many Christians)

(10) suffering for Christ's sake; and

(D) the Christian's resurrection to "eschatological life" with Christ, which
Paul understands as

(11) an act of God,

(12) his/her future participation in the general Resurrection of the
righteous,

(13) his/her future entrance into "eschatological life," which is characterized by glory and immortality, and

(14) God's future exaltation of the humble, trusting Christian.[24]

Outline. In defending our thesis, we will proceed according to the
following plan:

We will devote chapters 2, 3, and 6, to an examination of particular key
texts--namely, (1) Rom 3:21-26, (2) Rom 5:12-21 and 1 Cor 15:20-23, 44-49,
and (3) Rom 6:1-14, respectively. These portions of our study will introduce
certain pivotal concepts in Pauline thought (such as "righteousness," "covenant," "sin," "glory," "goodwill" [χάρις], "trust," "Law," and "dying with Christ"),
and will serve to correct common misunderstandings of the Apostle's meaning.

In chapters 4, 5, 7, and 8, we will examine the evidence for, and the
meaning of, Paul's "core convictions" concerning (1) Christ's death, (2) Christ's
resurrection to "eschatological life," (3) the Christian's "death" with Christ, and
(4) the Christian's resurrection to "eschatological life" with Christ, respectively.

---

[24]A glance at this thesis statement reveals that Beker is essentially correct to identify the
"coherent center" of Paul's theology as "the apocalyptic interpretation of the Christ-event" (*Paul
the Apostle*, 135). Beker characterizes the apocalyptic world view as revolving around "three
basic ideas: (1) historical dualism, (2) universal cosmic expectation, and (3) the imminent end
of the world" (136). We will discuss Paul's apocalyptic world view in chapter 2.

Finally, in chapter 9, we will summarize the results of our study and offer a brief description of the "coherent center" of Paul's theology.

The Aim of This Study

Not all aspects of Paul's theology are available to us through his letters. However, the "summary statements" discussed above offer hope that we can at least reconstruct Paul's "core communication," or the network of fundamental "core convictions" which together formed the "coherent center" of his theology. The present study aims to accomplish that goal.

Yet even if our efforts prove successful, a more important task awaits. Beker (quoting Bultmann) reminds us that

> the task of New Testament theology is not the "reconstruction of past history" but rather the "interpretation of the New Testament writings"; thus "reconstruction stands in the service of the interpretation of the New Testament under the presupposition that they have something to say to the present."[25]

Interpreting "the truth which is the gospel" for the contemporary world requires a clear understanding of the "coherent center" of that gospel. The present study therefore represents a necessary beginning--but only a beginning. The task is not complete until Christians proclaim the gospel into each particular human situation and all nations respond with "the obedience which proceeds from trust."[26] Paul would have accepted nothing less. May this study serve to advance his apostolic witness.

---

[25] Beker, "Paul the Theologian," 352.

[26] See Rom 1:5; 16:26.

CHAPTER TWO

ROMANS 3:21-26

Paul brings together many key elements of his thought in Rom 3:21-26. Here the Apostle speaks of God's "righteousness" (δικαιοσύνη) revealed, "the present time" (ὁ νῦν καιρός), "sin" (ἁμαρτία) and "glory" (δόξα), "goodwill" (χάρις[1]) and "sacrifice" (ἱλαστήριον[2]), "trust" (πίστις) and "Law" (νόμος). In the following pages, we will examine these terms in an effort to uncover the meaning of this important Pauline text.

I. Ο ΝΥΝ ΚΑΙΡΟΣ ("THE PRESENT TIME")

In Rom 3:21-26, Paul says that Christ's death serves as the demonstration of God's righteousness in the "present" (νῦνι, v. 21), or in "the present time" (ὁ νῦν καιρός, v. 26). To understand what Paul means by "the present

---

[1]Throughout this study, we will translate the Pauline term χάρις as "goodwill," rather than as the more ambiguous term "grace." For a full explanation, see note 174.

[2]In Rom 3:25, the term ἱλαστήριον communicates the idea of "a sacrifice which purifies from sin." See note 178.

time," we must view the Apostle within the context of Jewish apocalyptic expectation.[3]

The Two Ages

"The present evil age." Before he became a Christian, Paul the Pharisee was, in all likelihood, an apocalypticist.[4] This means that he understood reality in terms of two "ages," which we will term (1) "the present historical age," and (2) "the future eschatological age" (i.e., the "last" age, from the Greek term ἔσχατος). Paul believed that "in the beginning, God created the heavens and the earth" so that they conformed perfectly to His will. "When God saw everything He had created, it was very good."[5] Creation, however, soon "fell away" from its original "goodness," inasmuch as God's creatures--beginning with the serpent (whom Paul seems identifies as Satan in 2 Cor 11:3, 14) and continuing with Adam and Eve and their descendants--rebelled against Him. God responded not by destroying the universe, but by mercifully tolerating the presence of evil in His "good" Creation for a period of time. During the historical age, God allows His enemies--whom Paul collectively refers to as "Sin" (see below)--to exist and to exercise some degree of influence or "rule" (βασιλεία) within His Creation. As a result, the present age is characterized by wickedness and all its terrible consequences, including pain, hardship, broken relationships, decay and death.[6] Paul accordingly

---

[3]For an introduction to Jewish apocalyptic, see the studies in the bibliography by Collins, Funk, P. D. Hanson, Morris. For a discussion of early Christian apocalyptic, see the essays by Käsemann and Court. On the relationship between Paul and Jewish apocalyptic theology, see the pertinent works by Keck, Boer, Beker, Branick, Howell, Sturm and Schade. For further reading, see Christopher Rowland, "Books on Apocalyptic," *ER* 16 (1989): 86-90.

[4]For further discussion of Paul's background, see part II of chapter 5.

[5]See Gen 1:1, 31.

[6]See Gen 2:15-17; 3:1-24. For further discussion of Adam's sin and its consequences, see chapter 3.

refs to the historical age as "the present *evil* age" (ὁ αἰὼν ὁ ἐνεστηκὼς πονηρός) in Gal 1:4.[7]

The eschatological age. As an apocalypticist, Paul the Pharisee anticipated that God, in the near future, would suddenly bring an end to this "present evil age" and inaugurate the eschatological age. In the eschatological age God would subdue or destroy His enemies (= the Final Judgment), cleanse and renew His Creation, raise up the righteous dead to "eschatological life" (= "salvation," σωτηρία), and establish His own eschatological "Kingdom" or "Rule" (βασιλεία).[8] While the present historical age may be fairly characterized as the kingdom/rule of "Sin," Paul and other apocalypticists expected the future eschatological age to be "the Kingdom/Rule of God" (ἡ βασιλεία τοῦ θεοῦ)[9] (see Fig. 1).

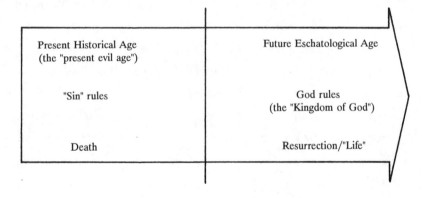

Present Historical Age (the "present evil age")	Future Eschatological Age
"Sin" rules	God rules (the "Kingdom of God")
Death	Resurrection/"Life"

Fig. 1. The "two ages" in Jewish apocalyptic

---

[7]Paul refers to "the present evil age" as "this age" (αἰὼν οὗτος) in Rom 12:2; 1 Cor 1:20; 2:6, 8; 3:18; and 2 Cor 4:4. Cf. 1 Cor 2:7, which speaks of God's sovereign decree issued "before the ages" (πρὸ τῶν αἰώνων).

[8]See part II of chapter 5, which describes "The View of the Resurrection Held By Paul the Pharisee."

[9]Paul speaks of the eschatological "Rule of God" in Rom 14:17; 1 Cor 4:20; 6:9-10; 15:24, 50; Gal 5:21; and 1 Thess 2:12.

The "overlap" of the ages. As a Christian, Paul came to believe that the transition from the historical age to the eschatological age would not be so abrupt.[10] He altered the apocalyptic scenario to include an intermediate period in which the two ages "overlap." During this intermediate period human beings still die; Sin's rule has not entirely ended. At the same time, "God's Rule" is proleptically present; the Resurrection to "eschatological life" has already begun with the resurrection of Jesus Christ.[11] Paul the Christian believes that the eschatological "Kingdom of God" has already broken into history,[12] but it has not yet arrived in all its fullness. He thinks in terms of the past (i.e., the portion of the historical age, or "present evil age," when Sin or evil was at the height of its power), the present (i.e., the intermediate period, when the historical age is fading and the eschatological age dawns), and the future (i.e., the portion of the eschatological age when the "Rule of God" has come in all its fullness) (see Fig. 2).

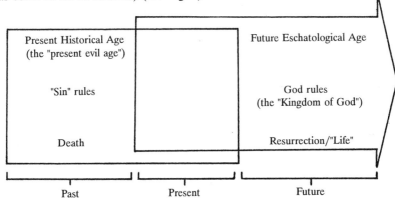

Fig. 2. Paul's altered apocalyptic scenario

---

[10]For a discussion of how Paul arrived at this view, see chapter 5 under "The present time."

[11]For a discussion of this interpretation of Christ's resurrection, see the discussion of "core conviction" 5 in Part III of chapter 5.

[12]Paul thus refers to Christians as persons "to whom the end of the ages has already come" in 1 Cor 10:11.

The "Times" and "the Present Time"

Καιρός *("time").* Within this historical-eschatological scheme, Paul identifies several different καιροί ("times") as holding special significance. Oscar Cullmann examines the Greek term καιρός ("time") in his classic study on *Christ and Time.* He writes:

> The characteristic thing about *kairos* ["time"] is that it has to do with a definite point of time which has a fixed content . . .
> *Kairos* in secular usage is the moment in time which is especially favorable for an undertaking . . . It is human considerations that cause a point of time to appear especially adapted for the execution of this or that plan, and thus make it a *kairos.* In this secular sense Felix says to Paul: "When I have a convenient season [καιρός], I will call for thee" (Acts 24: 25).[13]
> The New Testament usage with reference to redemptive history is the same. Here, however, it is not human deliberations but a divine decision[14] that makes this or that date a *kairos,* a point of time that has a special place in the execution of God's plan of salvation.[15]

Three "times" in Paul's letters. Paul singles out three such καιροί ("times") in his letters. First, Rom 5:6 speaks of the "time" when "Christ died for the ungodly" as a decisive moment in "salvation history"--the moment when God chose to demonstrate His love for sinners. Second, Paul identifies Christ's coming Parousia (i.e., "the Day of the Lord"[16] or Christ's "Second

---

[13]In Paul's writings we observe this "secular" use of καιρός in, for example, (1) 1 Cor 7:5, which speaks of a "time" set apart by a married couple for prayer, and (2) Gal 4:10, which speaks of certain "days and months and times (καιροί) and years" which the Judaizers have encouraged the Galatians to observe.

[14]See Rom 9:9, which speaks of God's choosing the "time" (καιρός) for Isaac's birth. Paul here refers to Gen 18:10 and 14.

[15]Oscar Cullmann, *Christ and Time: The Primitive Christian Conception of Time and History,* trans. Floyd V. Filson (London: SCM Press Ltd., 1951), 39. Cullmann focuses on the meaning of καιρός ("time") on pp. 39-44. For further discussion, see (1) *Harper's Bible Dictionary,* ed. Paul J. Achtemeier (San Francisco: Harper & Row, Publishers, 1985), s.v. "Time," by Jeremiah Unterman and Paul J. Achtemeier, 1072-73, and (2) *Theological Dictionary of the New Testament,* trans. and ed. Geoffrey W. Bromiley (Grand Rapids: Wm. B. Eerdmans Publishing Company, 1964), s.v. "Καιρός," by Gerhard Delling, 3:455-64.

[16]See 1 Thess 5:1-2.

Coming") as the "time" of the Resurrection,[17] the Judgment,[18] and the final Consummation of God's eschatological Rule. Third, Paul often speaks of "the present time" (ὁ νῦν καιρός), or simply "the present" ("now," νῦν or the emphatic νυνί). It begins after Christ's death on the cross,[19] at the moment of his resurrection from the dead.[20] It will not end until Christ's Parousia, when the eschatological age of "glory" (δόξα, see below) arrives in all its fullness.[21] "The present time" is, quite literally, the "time (καιρός) between the times" (i.e., the καιρός ["time"] of Christ's death and the καιρός ["time"] of Christ's Parousia). Romans 13:11-14 shows that "the present time" (ὁ νῦν καιρός) is Paul's designation for the "intermediate period" in his historical-eschatological scenario (see above). The Apostle writes: "[You] know the [present] time (ὁ [νῦν] καιρός) . . . the night [i.e., the historical age, the 'present evil age'] is fading away;[22] the day [i.e., the eschatological age] has dawned."

"The present time." As we examine Paul's letters, we will see that this "intermediate period"--this "present time"--occupies an important place in "salvation history" alongside the "time" of Christ's death and the "time" of his glorious return. In 2 Cor 6:2 Paul characterizes "the present time" as "the day

---

[17]See Gal 6:8-9.

[18]See 1 Cor 4:4-5.

[19]See Rom 3:21, where Paul identifies "the present" (νῦν) as the "time" when "God's expression of His righteousness" in the sacrificial death of Christ has *already* "been revealed apart from the Law" (cf. v. 26).

[20]See 1 Cor 15:20: "But now (νυνί) Christ has been raised from the dead [as] the first-fruits of those who have fallen asleep."

[21]See Rom 8:18, which speaks of "the present time" (ὁ νῦν καιρός) as present, and "the glory which is going to be revealed" as future.

[22]Cf. 1 Cor 7:29, 31: "The time (καιρός) grows short; . . . the form of this world is passing away."

of salvation" (ἡ ἡμέρα σωτηρίας).[23] During this "time" Christians preach the gospel and urge persons "to accept God's expression of His goodwill" (τὴν χάριν τοῦ θεοῦ δέχεσθαι)[24]--to embrace the Cross of Christ[25] that brings "salvation" to those who trust.[26] During this "time" both Jews and Gentiles are "reckoned righteous," "apart from the Law," through participation in the "new covenant" based on trust.[27] During this "time" believers endure suffering and persecution as they struggle against the demonic powers of "Sin," which resist the emerging "Rule of God."[28] During this "time" Christians adopt behavior that is appropriate for persons who trust in God and who welcome His eschatological Rule.[29]

---

[23]Paul here cites Isa 49:8 (LXX). Note that, in this context, Isaiah links the promised "salvation" (σωτηρία) to "a covenant of the nations" (διαθήκη ἐθνῶν), which we will discuss in part III of this chapter.

[24]See Rom 11:5: "In the present time (ὁ νῦν καιρός) a remnant has been [chosen], according to the election of [God's] goodwill."

[25]On the Cross as "God's expression of His goodwill," see, e.g., Rom 3:24, which we will discuss later in this chapter.

[26]See, e.g., 1 Cor 1:17-18.

[27]See Rom 3:21 ("in the present [νῦν] God's expression of His righteousness has been revealed apart from the Law"), 26 ("the demonstration of His righteousness, in the present time [ὁ νῦν καιρός], so that [God] Himself might be . . . the One who reckons righteous the person grounded in Jesus' act of trust"); 5:9 ("now [νῦν] reckoned righteous at the cost of his blood"); 7:6 ("now [νῦν] we have been released from the Law"); 1 Cor 13:13 ("now [νῦν] remain trust, hope, love"); Gal 2:20 ("the life which I am now [νῦν] living in the flesh, I am living within [the sphere where] trust [is the rule]"); cf. Rom 5:11 ("we have now [νῦν] received the reconciliation"); 8:1 ("[there is] now [νῦν] no condemnation for those within [the sphere of] Christ Jesus' [rule]").

[28]See, e.g., Rom 8:18 ("the sufferings of the present time [ὁ νῦν καιρός]"; cf. Phil 1:30, "having the same sort of struggle which you have seen in me, and which you are now [νῦν] hearing in me") and Gal 4:29 ("As in that time the one fathered according to the flesh kept on persecuting the [one fathered] according to the Spirit, so [is it] now [νῦν]").

[29]See, e.g., Rom 6:19 ("just as you once yielded your members as slaves to impurity and to greater and greater lawlessness, so now [νῦν] yield your members as slaves to righteousness which leads to holiness"), 22 ("now [νῦν] . . . you have been set free from Sin and enslaved to God"); 13:11-14 ("[You] know the time [καιρός] . . . Let us therefore put off the works of darkness and put on the weapons of light. Let us conduct ourselves appropriately, as in the day

Summary. To summarize: Paul the Christian thinks in terms of the past, "the present time," and the future. The "past" represents that portion of the historical age, or "present evil age," when Sin was at the height of its power. The "time" (καιρός) of Christ's sacrificial death on the cross occurred in the "past." "The present time" (ὁ νῦν καιρός) represents the "intermediate period," in which the historical age is fading away and the eschatological age dawns. It began at the moment of Christ's resurrection and will end at the "time" of his Parousia. During this "time between the times," persons hear the gospel and respond by putting their trust in God. The "future" represents the portion of the eschatological age following the Consummation of the "Rule of God." It begins with Christ's Second Coming, the general Resurrection of the righteous, the Judgment, and God's final Triumph over all who oppose Him. God's eschatological "future" will have no end (see Fig. 3).

Throughout the remainder of this study, we will speak of events Paul locates in the past (e.g., God's promise to Abraham, Christ's death), the present (e.g., Christ's resurrection, the Christian's "death" with Christ, Paul's Gentile mission), and the future (e.g., the Christian's resurrection with Christ, "eschatological life"). The reader should understand such temporal relationships in terms of the "past," "the present time," and the "future," as defined here in chapter 2.

. . ."); 1 Cor 7:29-31 ("the time [καιρός] grows short; from now on, let . . . those who have dealings with the world live as persons who do not have dealings [with the world]"); Gal 6:10 ("as long as we have the time [καιρός], let us do good to all persons--especially to those belonging to the household of trust"). Cf. Rom 12:11, the Western variant of which reads "serve the 'time' (καιρός)." The text appears to express the same sort of idea found in Col 4:5, where the writer urges believers to recognize "the present time" as ordained by God and to put themselves at the "service" of this "time" by behaving in a manner appropriate for this "time" (see Cullmann, *Christ and Time*, 42, 225).

24

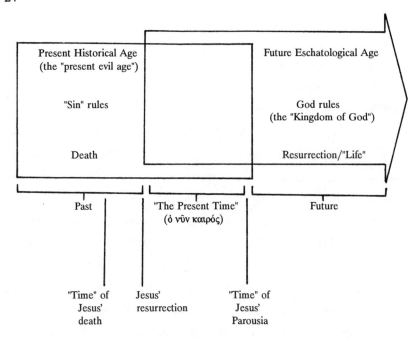

Fig. 3. Three "times" in Paul's apocalyptic scenario

II. ΑΜΑΡΤΙΑ ("SIN") VERSUS ΔΟΞΑ ("GLORY")

We will now examine two terms Paul places side-by-side in Rom 3:23--namely, "sin" and "glory."

Ἀμαρτία ("Sin")

Sin as "wrong deeds." Paul's ἁμαρτία ("sin") language is rooted in the Septuagint (LXX).[30] This Greek translation of the Old Testament uses such

---

[30]On Paul's knowledge of the Scriptures and his exegetical method, see the studies by Dinter, Ellis, Hays, Hooker, Koch, Longenecker, and D. M. Smith, listed in the bibliography.

terminology in order to refer to wrongdoing of all kinds, but predominantly to moral wrong committed in conscious opposition to God. Ἀμαρτία carries this general sense of "wrong deeds" in Paul's writings when the Apostle (1) quotes the LXX, (2) draws on early Christian tradition interpreting Christ's death as a sacrifice for sins, or (3) uses "sin" as a synonym for terms such as ἀδικία ("unrighteousness"), ἀκαθαρσία ("impurity"), ἀνομία ("lawlessness"), κακός ("evil"), παράβασις ("transgression"), παρακοή ("disobedience"), and πορνεία ("sexual immorality").

Paul most often employs ἁμαρτία ("sin") to refer to conduct characteristic of persons outside of Christ. However, the Apostle clearly believes that Christians, too, in this "overlap of the ages," retain the potential for engaging in this kind of "sinful" behavior (a fact which some of Paul's converts seem all too eager to demonstrate!). He repeatedly forbids his readers to participate in conduct unbecoming of Christ and, when the potential for Christian misbehavior does become a reality (as in 1 Cor 15:34, where the present imperative μὴ ἁμαρτάνετε ["Stop sinning!"] marks a clear instance of Christian "sin"), he demands that such conduct immediately cease.

Sin as a "power." While the Apostle does sometimes employ ἁμαρτία ("sin") to refer to wrongful "deeds" committed by believers or unbelievers, the most characteristically Pauline usage of the term depicts sin as "Sin"--as the "power" which entered the world through Adam and then spread throughout the entire human race. In what sense does Paul conceive of "Sin" as a "power"?

In accordance with the Jewish scriptures, Paul believes that God created the world[31] and that, as Creator, He alone is rightful Lord or Ruler over Creation, with authority to determine what should be and what should not be

---

[31]See, e.g., Rom 1:25; cf. Gen 1:1.

(i.e., "good and evil").[32] Genesis 3 describes the sin of the first man, Adam, as the refusal of a creature of God to relate to his Creator as the Person He truly is--namely, as Creator and Lord and God.[33] Instead, Adam sought to lay hold of the serpent's promise: "You will be as gods" (v. 5 [6, LXX]). He seized "the knowledge of good and evil" and thereby made himself, in a very real sense, his own "creator" and "lord."[34]

For Paul, the scriptural account of Adam's Fall provides a paradigm for human "sin" as the attempt to usurp God's throne, to put some other per- son--some other "power"--in God's rightful place. We see this, for example, in Rom 1:18-21 and 1 Cor 8:4-6. In the first text, Paul maintains that the whole of humanity has followed Adam in suppressing the truth about God's real identity by substituting the created thing for the true Creator and Lord of all. Likewise, in the second text, Paul acknowledges that "there are many 'gods' and many 'lords'" in the world, whether they be individual human beings seeking to determine their own existence apart from their Creator, or other human "powers" who claim for themselves the prerogatives of deity (e.g., some of the Caesars of Paul's own era), or even angelic beings seeking to exercise control over what rightfully belongs to God. Paul rejects all these rival "gods" as illegitimate frauds and pretenders on the grounds that humanity's rightful Master is the true Creator and Lord, the God who presently exercises His Rule through Jesus Christ.[35] He insists that, for Christians, "there is one

---

[32]See, e.g., Rom 9:19-29, wherein the Apostle proves from the OT that God has the same right to shape Creation according to His will that a potter has over clay.

[33]Paul shares this interpretation of Genesis 3 with the author of the Second (Syriac) Apocalypse of Baruch. See chapter 3 under "Adam as the first sinner" (in 2 Apoc. Bar.) and "Adam as the first sinner" (in Paul). For a more detailed discussion of Paul's views concerning Adam and his sin, see chapter 3.

[34]In this sense, "sin" is "idolatry," or the putting of some other person or thing in the place of God.

[35]For a discussion of Christ's "Rule," see the portion of chapter 5 marked "The Name which is above every name."

God, the Father, from whom are all things and for whom we exist, and one Lord, Jesus Christ, through whom are all things and through whom we exist."[36]

According to Paul's way of thinking, then, a "sinner" (ἁμαρτωλός) is a person under the dominion or lordship of some "power" other than the Creator, the Father of Jesus Christ. Since Paul conceives of "sin" in these terms, he often collectively personifies all "powers" opposed to God as "Sin." This enables him to speak of "Sin" as a power which "reigns,"[37] "exercises lordship,"[38] "enslaves,"[39] or even "owns" a person,[40] so that that person is "within [the sphere ruled/determined by] Sin" (ἐν ἁμαρτία),[41] or "under [the dominion of] Sin" (ὑφ' ἁμαρτίαν).[42] Accordingly, when Paul speaks of deliverance from Sin, he does not have in mind a deliverance from all bondage, but a release from one lordship into another--a transfer from the dominion of "Sin" (i.e., some "power[s]" or "lord[s]" other than God) to the dominion of God in Christ. Set free from slavery to "Sin," the "sinner" becomes, like Paul, a "slave of God/Christ."[43]

Human beings, however, can no more effect their own release from Sin by a mere act of the will than the American colonists could remove them-

---

[36]See 1 Cor 8:4-6.

[37]See Rom 5:21; 6:12.

[38]See Rom 6:14.

[39]See Rom 6:6, 16-17, 20; cf. Gal 4:3, 8.

[40]This may be the meaning of τὸ σῶμα τῆς ἁμαρτίας ("the body [owned by] Sin," or perhaps "the body [ruled by] Sin") in Rom 6:6. See the discussion of this verse in chapter 6.

[41]See Rom 6:1-2; 1 Cor 15:17. The locative of sphere in Paul often functions as "dominion language." See note 176.

[42]See Rom 3:9.

[43]See, e.g., Rom 1:1; 6:16-18, 20, 22; 1 Cor 7:22; Gal 1:10; Phil 1:1; cf. Rom 12:11; 14:18; 1 Thess 1:9. For further discussion, see chapter 6 under "The lordship of Sin and the lordship of God."

selves from the influence of the British Crown by the mere act of issuing a Declaration of Independence. They had to fight a war! They had to break the existing rule of England and establish the new authority of an American government. Before they accomplished this change in lordship, the American colonists had no choice but to live as British citizens, doing "British" deeds. Even in their words of protest and their deeds of rebellion, they were acting as subjects (albeit unwilling subjects) of King George III!

In the same way, Paul believes that persons under the dominion of Sin cannot cease to be "sinners" (i.e., Creation's "Fall" into evil cannot be undone) until the Creator breaks the existing rule of Sin and establishes the "Kingdom" or "Rule" or lordship of God (ἡ βασιλεία τοῦ θεοῦ); for until God makes Himself King, human beings have no choice other than to sin.[44] Even their "good deeds" are done by persons who are "sinners"--subjects of "Sin"--so that, in the final analysis, even their acts of kindness must still be judged as "sinful."

In Romans 7, Paul describes the terrible plight of the sinner (specifically the non-Christian Jew under the Law) from his new perspective in Christ. In v. 15 he pictures the sinner saying, "I do not do what I want to do; instead, I do what I hate." Like Paul the Pharisee, who demonstrated such zeal for God's good Law, the sinner may not wish to live in bondage to Sin; s/he may not want to do "evil deeds." S/he may instead desire to do "good deeds," and may even put that desire into action by performing "good deeds." Nevertheless, whatever deeds s/he does are still the deeds of a sinner--"sinful deeds"--inasmuch as the Apostle Paul views "sin" not so much in terms of wrong actions as in terms of being under the wrong lordship. Until God establishes His lordship, the sinner has no choice but to remain under the sovereignty of Sin. Since only God Himself can establish His Rule, the sinner can do nothing to effect his/her own release from Sin. "But thanks be to

---

[44] In Augustine's terms, life outside Christ's lordship is *non posse non peccare* ("the impossibility not to sin").

God! [Deliverance comes] through Jesus Christ our Lord!"[45] Paul proclaims the "good news" that, in recent history, God Himself--the Creator and only rightful Lord--has indeed acted to redeem sinners by establishing His lordship, His Rule (βασιλεία), through the Cross of Jesus Christ.[46]

We may also express this aspect of the Apostle's theology in another manner: For Paul, a "sinner" is a person trapped in a "fallen" world not completely under the lordship of God--i.e. trapped in "the present evil age" (see above). Accordingly, Paul conceives of "forgiveness" of sins as more than pardon for wrong behavior. It is also "rescue from out of the present evil age" (Gal 1:4) into the Kingdom/Rule (Βασιλεία) of God. Col 1:13-14 communicates this idea quite well:

> [God] has rescued us from the authority of darkness and transferred [us] to the Kingdom/Rule of His beloved Son, in [the dominion of] whom we have the deliverance, [even] the forgiveness of sins."

"Sinners" and "saints." In Rom 6:22, Paul declares that, through Christ's death on the cross, Christians "have been set free from Sin and have become slaves of God." How can the Apostle pronounce believers "free from Sin" in one place, and then accuse them of "sinning" in another (see above under "Sin as 'wrong deeds'")?

The American colonists experienced a change of lordship when they threw off British rule and came under the jurisdiction of the new United States government. At the same time, individual Americans remained entirely capable of behaving in a manner contrary to that rule, while continued violations could endanger even their rights of citizenship. In the same way, Paul maintains that, through Christ, God has freed Christians from bondage to Sin

---

[45]Rom 7:25.

[46]For a discussion of precisely how God effects this redemption, see chapter 4, parts I and II.

and is calling them "into His Kingdom/Rule."[47] Even now, at least in a pro-
visional sense, they enjoy the benefits of His Reign of goodwill. Since God
has delivered Christians from Sin's dominion, Sin no longer determines their
existence. God has opened to them the possibility of not sinning.[48] In fact,
Christians cannot "sin" in the sense that persons under the lordship of God
cannot, at the same time, be under the lordship of Sin.

For this reason, Paul never calls believers ἁμαρτωλοί ("sinners"); he
prefers instead to call them ἅγιοι ("saints," or "persons set apart for God's
service").[49] As long as "the present time" endures, such "saints" are indeed
capable of committing "sins," or deeds more becoming of a person "under [the
dominion of] Sin" than a person "under [the dominion of] Christ." (Paul interprets willful persistence in such behavior as rejection of God's lordship in
Christ, and thus a return to life under the dominion of Sin.[50]) Since this kind
of behavior is inconsistent with the believers' calling, Paul demands that it
immediately cease; for "how can we who have died to Sin still live within [the
sphere where] it [rules] (ἐν αὐτῇ)?"[51] Nevertheless, for Paul, one error or
one transgression does not make a "saint" a "sinner." The apostle can speak
of Christians sometimes committing "sins" without, at the same time, implying
that they are still "within [the sphere determined by] Sin."

---

[47]See 1 Thess 2:12.

[48]In Augustine's terms, Christian existence is marked by *posse non peccare* ("the possibility
not to sin").

[49]Note, for example, the manner in which Paul addresses his readers in Rom 1:7; 1 Cor 1:2;
2 Cor 1:1 and Phil 1:1.

[50]To illustrate: Paul accuses some of the Galatian believers of being "severed from Christ"
and "fallen away from [God's] goodwill" (Gal 5:4) because, by observing "days and months and
times and years" (4:10) in an effort to be "reckoned righteous on the basis of the Law," they are
"deserting" God (1:6) and turning back to slavery under other powers, namely, "the weak and
inferior elemental powers" (4:8-9).

[51]Rom 6:2.

Δόξα ("Glory")

Basic meanings of δόξα *("glory")*. Next, we examine the Pauline concept of "glory" (δόξα). The Greek-speaking world of Paul's time used the
term δόξα ("glory") to express a number of different nuances of meaning. In
accordance with its philogical relationship to δοκεῖν ("to think"), the noun δόξα
originally expressed the idea of "a thought, an opinion." Accordingly, the verb
δοξάζειν ("to glorify") meant "to think, to hold an opinion."

Over time, δόξα ("glory") also came to refer to a particular kind of
opinion, namely, a "favorable opinion," or "high opinion." The LXX and other
Jewish literature of the intertestamental period reflect this development when
they use δόξα ("glory") to signify (1) "fame" or "reputation," (2) "honor," and
(3) "praise." From this point, it is only a small step to move to an understanding of "glory" as (1) "that which brings honor," or (2) "that which signifies
honor."

Most of these variations in meaning for δόξα ("glory") occur in Paul's
writings as well. By way of illustration, the δόξα ("glory") terminology expresses (at least) the idea of "honor" in Paul's description of the Resurrection
of the righteous dead in 1 Cor 15:43: "[The body (σῶμα)] is sown in dishonor
(ἀτιμία); it is raised in glory (δόξα)." Paul clearly employs the terminology of
"glory" to express the idea of "praise," or a verbal expression of honor, in Rom
15:6: ". . . in order that together, with one voice, you may glorify the God and
Father of our Lord Jesus Christ." Furthermore, when Paul refers to the
Thessalonians as "our glory" (ἡ δόξα ἡμῶν) and "crown of boasting" (στέφανος
καυχήσεως) in 1 Thess 2:19-20, he means that they are "persons who bring
honor" to him and his companions.

However, the ideas of "honor" and "praise" do not exhaust the meaning
of δόξα ("glory") for Paul. Building on the work of Greek-speaking Jews who
came before him, the Apostle utilizes the terminology of "glory" to express
four other ideas of particular significance for his thought--namely, (1) the
visible, radiant presence of God, (2) the radiance taken from Adam at the

Fall and restored to the righteous at the Eschaton, (3) exaltation, and (4) the "image of God."

Δόξα ("glory") as the visible, radiant presence of God. The LXX frequently uses δόξα ("glory") to translate the Hebrew כָּבוֹד ("heaviness," and thus "importance, honor, something impressive"), which often refers to the visible presence of God. Jewish tradition seems to envision God's "glory" as taking the form of a bright light, or radiance, or fire,[52] which was sometimes partially hidden by a cloud. The LXX describes how such theophanies appeared (1) in a cloud in the wilderness, (2) in a cloud and "burning fire" on Mount Sinai, (3) in or on Israel's Tabernacle or (4) the Temple built by Solomon, and especially (5) between the golden cherubim on the ἱλαστήριον (sometimes translated "mercy seat," see note 178), or the slab of gold resting upon the ark of the covenant.[53] Exodus 34 relates how Moses ascended Mount Sinai, stood face-to-face with the Lord in His "glory," and received God's covenant with Israel. When he came down from the mountain, the people saw that Moses' face was "glorified," i.e., it shone with light reflected from God's own "glory."

Paul shares with his ancestors the notion of δόξα ("glory") as a radiant light, whether it be, for example, the illumination of the night by the heavenly bodies,[54] or the light of God's presence made manifest to Israel.[55] In 2 Cor 3:7-4:6 the Apostle recalls the story of Moses' "glorification" on Mount Sinai

---

[52]See, e.g., Isa 60:1-3; Ezek 10:4; cf. 4 Ezra 7:42 [112]. For δόξα as a radiant light, see also 3 (Greek) Apoc. Bar. 7:1-5; T. Job 31:5; 43:5-6; T. Abra. 16:10.

[53]See (1) Exod 16:10; (2) Exod 24:16-17; cf. Deut 5:24; (3) Exod 40:34-38; Num 14:10; 16:42; 20:6; (4) 1 Kgs (3 Kgs, LXX) 8:11; 2 Chr 7:1-3; and (5) Ps 80(79):1; cf. Exod 25:21-22; 1 Sam (1 Kgs, LXX) 4:22.

[54]See 1 Cor 15:40-41.

[55]This is probably what Paul means by "glory" in Rom 9:4. The reader should also compare (1) Rom 1:23, where "the glory of God" seems to emphasize not so much "God in His visible presence" as "God in His Person," and (2) Rom 6:4 and Phil 4:19, where the focus seems to be on "God in His power." Many LXX passages express similar ideas.

in discussing how (1) God's "glory" is reflected in the face of the Christ of Paul's gospel, so that, through the Spirit of Christ, believers enjoy a deeper understanding of God and His workings in history than do "veiled" Jews who read the Law outside of Christ, (2) believers are being "glorified" by the Spirit of Christ (see below), and (3) the greater, permanent "glory" of the "ministration of the Spirit" and "righteousness" (i.e. of the "new covenant") demonstrates its superiority over the "ministration of death" and "condemnation" (i.e. of the "old," Mosaic covenant) with its fading "glory."

The "glory" (δόξα) taken from Adam at the Fall and restored to the righteous at the Eschaton. According to the Psalmist, God created human beings to share His glory: "You made him a little lower than the angels; you crowned him with glory and honor."[56] Later (mostly apocalyptic) writers built on this notion with the result that, by the Apostle Paul's day, one common view held that Adam originally reflected God's radiant glory, but that he lost this gift in the Fall. To illustrate: The first century Greek version of the Life of Adam and Eve (otherwise known as the Apocalypse of Moses) relates how, after eating the forbidden fruit offered by his wife, Adam cried out, "O evil woman! Why have you wrought destruction among us? You have estranged me from the glory of God."[57]

Many of these writers anticipated that God would restore His glory to the righteous in the coming Resurrection of the dead,[58] so that they would

---

[56]Ps 8:5 (LXX); cf. Isa 43:7, which seems to reserve a share in God's glory for Israel only, rather than for humankind in general.

[57](Greek) Life of Adam and Eve 21:6; cf. 20:1-2 (which seems to spiritualize δόξα to mean "righteousness" rather than "radiance; cf. Bar 5:1-2); 21:1-2; 3 (Greek) Apoc. Bar. 4:16. This notion of mankind's lost "glory" also appeared in rabbinical circles, as testified to by the midrash on Gen 2:4, which includes "glory" in a list of six things taken from Adam in the Fall (*Gen. Rab.* XII.vi).

[58]On the Resurrection, see the portion of chapter 5 dealing with "Views of the Resurrection Prior to Paul."

"shine like the shining of the firmament . . . like the stars for ever and ever."[59] 1 Enoch 50:1, for example, reads as follows: "In those days, there will be a change for the holy and the righteous ones and the light of days shall rest upon them; and glory and honor shall be given back to the holy ones, on the day of weariness."[60]

Like many of his contemporaries, Paul believes that humankind was created to reflect the glory of God,[61] but that, like Adam, "all have sinned and [thus] lack the glory of God."[62] The Apostle is confident, however, that the "righteous" in Christ are presently "being transformed into his image from one degree of glory to another,"[63] and that this process of change will culminate at the Resurrection, when Christ returns. Paul encourages the Philippians with this thought:

> Our homeland is in the heavens, from whence we are also awaiting a Savior, even the Lord Jesus Christ. He will transform our body (σῶμα) of humiliation, so that it will be in conformity with his body (σῶμα) of glory (δόξα) . . . .[64]

---

[59]See Dan 12:3 (LXX); cf. 4 Ezra 7:55 [125].

[60]Cf. T. Benj. 10:8; 2 (Syriac) Apoc. Bar. 51:1-3; 3 (Slavonic) Apoc. Bar. 16:4; (Greek) Life of Adam and Eve 39. The sectarians at Qumran clung to a similar hope, as shown by the following passage from column IV of The Community Rule: "God has chosen them [i.e., 'the perfect of way'] for an everlasting Covenant and all the glory of Adam shall be theirs." (G. Vermes, *The Dead Sea Scrolls in English*, 2d ed. [New York: Penguin Books, 1975], 78. Cf. the last few lines in col. III of The Damascus Rule [Vermes, p. 100] and the last line of hymn 23 in The Hymns Scroll [Vermes, p. 198].)

[61]A. M. Hunter (*The Epistle to the Romans: Introduction and Commentary*, Torch Bible Commentaries [London: SCM Press, 1955], 46) cites 1 Cor 11:7 in support of this point.

[62]Rom 3:23 (see below).

[63]See 2 Cor 3:18; cf. Rom 8:30.

[64]Phil 3:20-21; cf. Rom 2:7; 5:2; 8:18-21; 9:22-24; 1 Cor 2:7-8; 2 Cor 4:17; 1 Thess 2:12. For a discussion of the believer's resurrection "glory," see chapter 8.

Δόξα *as exaltation.* Since one of the basic concepts expressed by the term δόξα ("glory") is "honor," it comes as no surprise that pre-Christian Jewish writings often (1) link δόξα ("glory") with the idea of "exaltation," or of being lifted from a position of humility to one of stature,[65] and (2) conceive of the future "glorification" of the righteous as such an exaltation.[66] It will become increasingly clear throughout the remainder of this study that Paul, in like manner, conceives of the "glorification" of Christ, and of those who trust in him, as a great "exaltation." He views Christ's resurrection to "eschatological life"--in which Christians will one day share--as a movement upward from suffering, humility and servanthood, to honor and "glory" and reign.[67]

The "glory of God" and the "image (εἰκών) of God." According to Gen 1:27 (LXX), "God made man[kind]. He made him according to the image (εἰκών) of God. He made them male and female." The fact that the LXX uses εἰκών ("image") almost exclusively of idol-images could easily lead us to understand this writer to mean that human beings resemble God in their outward appearance.[68] However, the preceding verse ("Let us make man[kind] according to our image and likeness, and let them rule over . . . all the earth") may offer a different interpretation--namely, that God created mankind in His "image" or "likeness" (ὁμοίωσις) in the sense that He intended for human

---

[65]See, e.g., Esth 4:17 and 5:1-2 (LXX), which contrast "glorious garments" with garments of humility and mourning and servanthood; 6:3-11, where δόξα appears as a synonym for χάρις (see below); Prov 29:23, which contrasts "glory" with being "humbled;" Isa 52:13, which speaks of the "exaltation" and "glorification" of the Servant of the Lord; and 1 Esdr 4:59, which contrasts "glorification" with being a house-slave. Cf. Isa 3:9, 16-26, wherein God describes how He will bring down the "glory" of the daughters of Zion to humiliation.

[66]See, e.g., 2 Apoc. Bar. 51:5.

[67]For further discussion, see chapters 5 and 8.

[68]See Deut 4:16; 2 Kgs (4 Kgs, LXX) 11:18; 2 Chr 33:7; Wis 13:13, 16; 14:15, 17; 15:5; Hos 13:2; Isa 40:19-20 (εἰκών as a synonym of ὁμοίωμα ["likeness"]); Ezek 7:20; 16:17; Dan 2:31; 3:1-18. Cf. Ezek 23:14, which speaks of "images" of the Chaldeans painted upon a wall, and Gen 5:3, wherein Adam fathers Seth "according to his own image."

beings to rule over the rest of Creation with Him. The Wisdom of Solomon shows that, by Paul's time, some Jews also understood "the image of God" in terms of "immortality."[69]

Paul himself makes the unprecedented move of equating "the image of God" with Adam's lost "glory," which the resurrected righteous regain in Christ. He calls the raised and "glorified" Christ "the image of God,"[70] and maintains that the Spirit is presently transforming believers into Christ's image "from one degree of glory to another"--a process which will culminate at the future Resurrection of the righteous.[71] Since the Apostle characterizes this "image" as "spiritual" and "imperishable" in 1 Cor 15:44-50, "immortality" also marks the full "glory," or "image of the man of heaven" (i.e., Christ, the "Eschatological Adam"[72]), which Paul anticipates the "righteous" will receive at the Lord's return.

III. ΔΙΚΑΙΟΣΥΝΗ ("RIGHTEOUSNESS") AND ΔΙΑΘΗΚΗ ("COVENANT")

Scholars have debated for centuries what Paul meant by δικαιοσύνη ("righteousness") and, more specifically, δικαιοσύνη θεοῦ ("the righteousness of God"). The Apostle's views were shaped by an ancient Jewish tradition, to which we now turn.

---

[69] See Wis 2:23; cf. 7:26, which describes Wisdom as "the image of His goodness."

[70] See 2 Cor 3:18; 4:4; cf. Col 1:15.

[71] See Rom 8:29, 1 Cor 15:49, and 2 Cor 3:18, wherein the end result of believers' "glorification" is "the image of Christ." Paul believes that God created humankind in His own "image" (1 Cor 11:7). By consistently saying that Christians are being transformed into the image of Christ, rather than "the image of God" (as in Col 3:10), the Apostle probably intends both to stress Christ's role as the "Eschatological Adam" (see chapter 3), and to make the "image of God" in redeemed humans one step removed from "the image of God" in the Lord Christ.

[72] See chapter 3.

Δικαιοσύνη ("Righteousness") in the Jewish Scriptures

In its oldest known usage, the Greek δικαιοσύνη ("righteousness") ter-minology expressed the idea of what is "customary," and therefore what society considered "right," or "normal," or "appropriate" behavior.[73] From this basic idea a whole range of meaning developed--particularly in the areas of the law-court and the "setting right" or "avenging" of wrongs.

The LXX uses δικαιοσύνη ("righteousness") language to translate a number of different Hebrew terms--especially the word-group represented by צֶדֶק ("righteousness"), which has less to do with societal norms than it does with fulfilling the demands of a given relationship.[74] Below, we will briefly examine how the Greek terminology of "righteousness" came to function in its new Jewish setting.

"Righteousness" as a forensic term. Like the Greeks before them, Greek-speaking Jews employ "righteousness" terminology when describing the proceedings of a law-court. In this forensic context, the adjective "righteous" (δίκαιος) describes the man or woman who is "innocent" of wrongdoing or, in other words, who behaves "appropriately" in the eyes of Jewish society (as that society's norms are interpreted by its judges). For example, Job pictures him-self as standing before the judgment-seat of God when he says: "Behold, I am near my judgment. I know I will be shown to be righteous (δίκαιος)"--i.e., "innocent" of any wrongdoing.[75]

---

[73]We can trace the word group as far back as the 8th century B.C., where two surviving works by Hesiod (*Theogony* and *Works and Days*) describe how the new δίκη of the victorious Olympian, Zeus, has replaced the δίκη ("the way of things") of Gaea, or "Mother Earth." 4 Macc 6:34 (cf. 9:6) provides a later example of the basic sense of δίκαιος: "And it is appropriate (δίκαιος) that we admit that the power belongs to reasoning . . . ."

[74]See *The Interpreter's Dictionary of the Bible: An Illustrated Encyclopedia,* ed. George Arthur Buttrick (New York: Abingdon Press, 1962), s.v. "Righteousness in the OT," by E. R. Achtemeier, 4:80-85.

[75]Job 13:18; cf. 32:1.

In Israel, when someone acting as a "judge" determined that a person accused of wrongdoing, or "unrighteousness," was actually "innocent," or "righteous," then that man or woman was said to have been "judged righteous" or "reckoned righteous" (δικαιοῦν), and thus "vindicated." Genesis 44:16 offers a negative illustration in that Joseph's brothers do not expect to be "reckoned righteous" (or "judged to have behaved 'appropriately' or 'innocently'") when they are caught with Joseph's stolen cup.

The biblical writers also speak of "righteous judges," by which they mean judges who render "appropriate" judgments. The several books of the Maccabbees call a judgment "appropriate," or "righteous," if it fits the crime;[76] but 1 Kgs (3 Kgs, LXX) 3:9 describes what the LXX most often means by "righteous judgments" when it has Solomon define "judging in righteousness" (διακρίνειν ἐν δικαιοσύνῃ) as "discerning between good and evil." A "righteous" judge is one who consistently, and without partiality, "reckons righteous" those who are actually "righteous" and condemns those actually guilty of sin. In contrast, "the one who judges the righteous to be unrighteous, and judges the unrighteous to be righteous, is unclean and abominable before God."[77] We may also state the matter in a different manner: The person who judges "righteously" judges "truly," or in accordance with the truth. Isaiah predicts that the "rod" who will come forth out of the root of Jesse will be such a judge: "He will not judge according to glory [i.e., according to social

---

[76]We find examples of such "poetic righteousness" in (1) 2 Macc 9:6, where God "righteously" afflicts Antiochus with a terrible bowel disease "since he had tormented others' bowels with many unusual calamities," and (2) 13:7, where Menelaus smothers in a tower full of ashes "inasmuch as he had committed many sins about the altar, whose fire and ashes were holy." Cf. 3 Macc 2:21-22.

[77]Prov 17:15; cf. 24:23-26; Exod 23:2-3, 6-8; Lev 19:15; Deut 1:16-17; 16:18-20; 25:1.

status] . . . He will gird his thigh with righteousness, and wrap his sides with truth."[78]

Early Jewish writers often speak of God as "the One who judges the earth."[79] As such, He is the "righteous" Judge, who renders "true" judgments[80] by punishing the wicked and vindicating the righteous.[81] To illustrate: Testament of Job 43:13 declares: "Righteous is the Lord; true are his judgments. With Him there is no favoritism."

"Righteousness" as God's salvation and God's condemnation. Since Israel celebrated the Lord as a "Righteous Judge," who condemns the guilty and defends the innocent, it is quite understandable that some Jewish writings should describe God's "righteousness" in terms of His "saving" righteous human beings from their enemies, or punishing the unrighteous for their sins. Samuel acknowledges both aspects of God's "righteousness" in 1 Sam (1 Kgs, LXX) 12:6-12. Here the prophet says to the people, "I will relate to you all the righteousness of the Lord." Then he goes on to describe not only how God saved Israel from the Egyptians when they called upon Him, but how God punished them through Sisera, the Philistines and the Moabites when Israel "forgot the Lord their God."[82]

---

[78]Isa 11:3, 5; cf. 26:2; 45:19. The adjective "righteous" likewise carries the sense of "true" when the LXX speaks, for example, of "righteous" weights and measures in Lev 19:35-36 and Deut 25:15.

[79]See, e.g., Gen 18:25; Ps 94(93):2; cf. Judg 11:27; 1 Sam (1 Kgs, LXX) 2:10; Ps 9:7-8; 58(57):11; 82(81):8; Joel 3:12; Mic 4:3; Pss. Sol. 8:24; T. Abra. (resc. A) 13:7; T. Benj. 10:8-9. Apocalyptic writers, in particular, predict a final Day on which God will judge both the righteous and sinners alike (see, e.g., 1 Enoch 1:7-9).

[80]See Ps 119(118):75; Tob 3:2.

[81]See Gen 18:23; 1 Kgs (3 Kgs, LXX) 8:31-32 // 2 Chr 6:22-23; Job 8:3-4; Ps 58(57):10-11; cf. Pss. Sol. 2:18.

[82]Here the biblical writer may intend for the reader to interpret God's "righteousness" covenantally (see below), even though the Mosaic covenant had not yet been formally established when God saved Israel from the Egyptians. (note continued on next page)

Passages such as David's prayer in Ps 51(50):14 are more difficult to understand. The text reads: "Rescue me from bloodguiltiness, O God, the God of my salvation, [and] my tongue will joyfully declare your righteousness." How can the transgressor expect a "righteous" God, who Himself declares that He "will not cleanse the guilty,"[83] to deliver him from sin? For the answer to this question we must turn to an examination of how Jewish writers employed "righteousness" terminology in relational or covenantal contexts.

"Righteousness" as a relational term. In addition to the forensic use, Greek-speaking Jews employed the language of "righteousness" (δικαιοσύνη) when discussing "appropriate" behavior within the bounds of personal relationships. For example, when God threatens to kill Abimelech for unknowingly taking a married woman to be his wife, the king protests: "I have done this with a pure heart and in the righteousness of [my] hands."[84] In other words, Abimelech had tried to act "appropriately," in accordance with the norms then governing marital relationships.

In the context of personal relationships, then, the "righteous" (δίκαιος) man or woman is the one who fulfils the demands of the particular relationship in question. "Righteousness" (δικαιοσύνη) refers to (1) the sum-total of those responsibilities which the person entering into the relationship takes upon him/herself, and also to (2) the attribute possessed by the person who carries out those responsibilities.[85] To say that someone has been "reckoned

---

Those who describe God's eschatological judgment as a Day of "wrath" against the unrighteous likewise call attention to the negative side of the Lord's "righteousness." See, e.g., Isa 13:9, 13; Zeph 1:14-2:3; 3:8; Dan 8:19; 1 Enoch 84:4 (wherein God's "wrath" already rests upon the earth in the present); 91:7-11.

[83]See Exod 34:7.

[84]Gen 20:3-5.

[85]Ps 15(14):2 illustrates the first meaning when it speaks of "the one who lives blamelessly and works righteousness," while we find an example of the second sense of δικαιοσύνη ("righteousness") in Prov 11:6, which says that "the righteousness of upright men delivers them."

righteous" (δικαιοῦν) with regard to a particular relationship means that others acknowledge that that man or woman acts "appropriately," or "righteously," by fulfilling the demands placed upon him/her by that relationship. The Epistle of Aristeas 168-169 argues that the aim of the Mosaic Law is to promote this kind of "relational" righteousness:

> . . . all the regulations have been made with righteousness in mind, and . . . no ordinances have been made in scripture without purpose or fancifully, but to the intent that through the whole of our lives we may also practice righteousness toward all humankind in our acts, remembering the all-sovereign God . . . the whole underlying rationale is directed toward righteousness and righteous human relationships.

"Righteousness" as a covenantal term. In the ancient Near East, a formal relationship established between two parties was termed a "covenant" (בְּרִית, διαθήκη).[86] The demands placed upon the participants in a covenant-- i.e., the content of "righteousness"--varied from covenant to covenant. For example, the book of Genesis relates how God entered into a covenant with the patriarch Abraham. Under this covenant, God promised to provide Abraham with land, descendants, and other benefits (see below), while Abraham committed himself to God in trust. God fulfilled "righteousness" under this covenant by keeping His promises,[87] while "Abraham trusted God, and it [i.e., Abraham's trust] was reckoned to him as righteousness (ἐλογίσθη

---

[86]The Jewish scriptures describe a number of covenants between human beings (e.g., Abraham and Abimelech in Gen 21:22-32 [LXX], Isaac and Abimelech in Gen 26:26-31, Jacob and Laban in Gen 31:43-54, and Jonathan and David in 1 Sam [1 Kgs, LXX] 20:8; 23:18), and also between God and human beings (e.g., God and Adam in [Greek] Life of Adam and Eve 8:2, God and Noah in Gen 9:8-17, God and Abraham in Gen 15:1-21; 17:1-22, God and Israel [the "Mosaic covenant"] in Exod 19-24, God and Phineas in Num 25:10-15, and God and David in 2 Kgs 7:8-16; 23:5). Some prophets also anticipate the establishment of a new, eschatological covenant between God and Israel (see, e.g., Isa 59:20-21; 61:8; Jer 31[38]:31-36; Hos 2:15-23).

[87]See Neh 9:7-8, in which Ezra praises God as "righteous" because He had, in fact, done what he told Abraham He would do.

αὐτῷ εἰς δικαιοσύνην)."[88] In contrast to this friendly association, the covenant between Jacob and Laban in Gen 31:43-54 placed each under the "righteous" obligation to stay away from the other!

The covenant which Moses mediated between God and Israel is, by far, the most significant covenant discussed in the Jewish scriptures. Under this covenant, the God who had given promises to Abraham, Isaac and Jacob, and who had brought their descendants out of bondage in Egypt, now committed Himself to being Israel's God; while Israel, in turn, committed itself to being God's people.[89]

How does Israel fulfil this covenant-commitment? How does Israel act as the "people of God"? Israel maintains its covenant relationship with the Lord by forsaking all other gods in order to serve Him alone.[90] This involves adherence to the Law, through which God exercises His rule over all aspects of life within the covenant community.[91] The "works of the Law" define the content of "righteousness" for the Jewish people under the Mosaic covenant.[92]

It is important to note that, in the context of a covenant with God, human "sin" is equivalent to "unrighteousness"--i.e., the refusal to participate in/uphold the covenant which God has established, and through which He

---

[88]Gen 15:6; cf. 1 Macc 2:52. In like manner, Ps 106(105):28-31 recalls that when the priest Phineas (apparently in the context of an everlasting covenant of priesthood made with Aaron and his descendants--see Exod 40:15; Sir 45:24-25) killed the worshippers of the Baal of Peor, it was not his trust but his act of atonement which was "reckoned to him as righteousness, for generation upon generation forever" (see Num 25:1-13; cf. Sir 45:23-25; 1 Macc 2:51-54).

[89]This forms the thrust of both the first lines of the Decalogue ("I am the Lord your God . . . You shall have no other gods beside me," Exod 20:2-3) and the "Shema" of Deut 6:4-5 ("Hear, O Israel, the Lord [is] our God; the Lord [is] one. And you shall love the Lord your God with your whole mind, and with your whole soul, and with your whole strength.").

[90]See, e.g., Josh 24:14-15.

[91]See, e.g., Exod 20:1-17 and Deut 30:15-16.

[92]See, e.g., 2 Sam (2 Kgs, LXX) 22:21-25.

exercises His lordship. The Israelites call themselves "the righteous," and thus distinguish their nation from the other "sinner" nations,[93] not because God has freed them from every moral peccadillo, but because God has entered into covenant with them.

How does God fulfil His covenant-commitment? How does God act as "the God of Israel"? The Jewish scriptures constantly proclaim God's "righteousness," or His faithfulness to the Mosaic covenant, which they recognize, for example, in (1) His giving Israel the Law, the land promised to their fathers, deliverance from their enemies, abundant food and material possessions, and guidance through the prophets, and in (2) His seeking to uphold even Israel's own "righteousness" by punishing the nation when it sins (e.g., unfaithful Judah in the Babylonian Exile), but forgiving the penitent (e.g., David in the Psalm mentioned above).[94] Such actions define the content of "righteousness" for God under the Mosaic covenant.

It is particularly important to note that, under the Mosaic covenant, God does forgive persons who transgress (if they repent and return to the Lord, which often involves offering one of the atoning blood-sacrifices that God, out of His goodwill, provides for that purpose[95]). This means that God's "righteousness" (or what action is "appropriate" for God) within the context of the covenant differs from His "righteousness" toward those outside the covenant. Those who transgress outside the covenant experience God as a "righteous" (in the sense that He renders "true" judgments--see above) and unyielding Judge; but those within the covenant know Him as a "righteous" (in the sense that God seeks to maintain His covenant relationship with His

---

[93]To illustrate: In Esth 1:1, Mordecai dreams of all the nations of the earth preparing for battle against "the righteous nation," or Israel. Compare Paul's contrast of "[righteous] Jews" with "Gentile sinners" in Gal 2:15.

[94]Ezra mentions all these manifestations of God's "righteousness" in the prayer found in Neh 9:6-38.

[95]See the discussion of sacrifice found in part I of chapter 4.

people in spite of their sin), merciful and forgiving Judge.[96] As the Lord says to Israel in Deut 7:9-10,

> You shall know that the Lord your God, He [is] God, a faithful God, who upholds covenant and mercy for those who love Him, and for those who uphold His commandments, to a thousand generations; but who recompenses those who hate [Him] to [their] face, toward the end of utterly destroying them.[97]

We cannot account for the "righteousness" by which God forgives sinners, "saving" them from guilt, solely on the basis of a forensic understanding of δικαιοσύνη θεοῦ ("the righteousness of God"); for in the context of the courtroom, the judge who pardons the guilty is not a "righteous" judge! When viewed as a whole, the evidence suggests that we must instead interpret the vast majority of pre-Christian Jewish statements concerning "the righteousness of God" and the "righteousness" of Israel against the background of the Mosaic covenant.[98] Israel practices forensic "righteousness" in the courts because the Lord of the covenant demands it; "forensic righteousness" is part of the content of "covenantal righteousness" for the Jews.[99] Israelites seek to maintain "relational righteousness" with their neighbors because their relationship with God, under the covenant, requires it. Jews refer to themselves as "the righteous" not because they are free from all moral guilt, but because they have entered into covenant with God. The Lord saves sinners not because He despises "forensic righteousness," but because He upholds "covenantal righteousness" with Israel.

---

[96]See, e.g., Ps 143(142):1-2; Isa 43:26.

[97]Cf. Exod 34:6-7; Pss. Sol. 2:33-37. Note also the series of blessings and curses attached to the covenant in Deut 27-28.

[98]Since none of the Jewish scriptures received their final form until after the giving of the Mosaic covenant, all the biblical writers (or editors) assume the existence and the terms of that covenant.

[99]See Ezek 18:5-9.

Δικαιοσύνη *("Righteousness") in the Writings of Paul*

Three interpretations of "righteousness" in Paul. For centuries a fierce debate has raged over the correct understanding of the δικαιοσύνη ("righteousness") word group in Paul's epistles.[100] Today, the majority of Pauline scholars agree that the Apostle employs "righteousness" in order to evoke not one, but a broad range of meanings associated with that term in pre-Christian Jewish literature, including (1) forensic ideas, (2) images of God's "salvation," "vindication," or "forgiveness" of sins, and (3) relational or covenantal concepts.[101] However, most scholars identify one or the other of these ideas

---

[100]Several writers provide us with brief summaries of the history of the interpretation of δικαιοσύνη and δικαιοσύνη θεοῦ in Paul, including (1) Manfred T. Brauch, "Perspectives on 'God's righteousness' in recent German discussion," in E. P. Sanders, *Paul and Palestinian Judaism*, 523-42, (2) Christian Müller, *Gottes Gerechtigkeit und Gottes Volk: Eine Untersuchung zu Römer 9-11* (Göttingen: Vandenhoeck & Ruprecht, 1964), 5-27, (3) Marion L. Soards, "Once Again 'Righteousness of God' in the Writings of the Apostle Paul," *BB* 17 (1991): 16-23 (an expanded and updated version of "The Righteousness of God in the Writings of the Apostle Paul," *BTB* 15 [1985]: 104-107), (4) Peter Stuhlmacher, *Gerechtigkeit Gottes bei Paulus* (Göttingen: Vandenhoeck & Ruprecht, 1965), 11-73, and (5) J. A. Ziesler, *The Meaning of Righteousness in Paul: A Linguistic and Theological Enquiry* (Cambridge: The University Press, 1972), 1-14.

Recent studies worthy of mention include those by (1) Ronald Y. K. Fung ("The Status of Justification by Faith in Paul's Thought: A Brief Survey of a Modern Debate," *Them* 6 [1981]: 4-11); and "Justification by Faith in 1 & 2 Corinthians," in *Pauline Studies: Essays Presented to Professor F. F. Bruce on His 70th Birthday*, ed. Donald A. Hagner and Murray J. Harris [Grand Rapids: The Paternoster Press and William B. Eerdmans Publishing Company, 1980], 246-61), (2) Richard B. Hays ("Psalm 143 and the Logic of Romans 3," *JBL* 99 [1980]: 107-15), who asserts that, against the background of Ps 143, we must understand Paul's conception of "the righteousness of God" in Rom 3 as God's salvation-creating power, (3) Sam K. Williams ("The 'Righteousness of God' in Romans," *JBL* 99 [1980]: 241-90), who understands δικαιοσύνη θεοῦ in Paul to refer to God's fidelity to his promise to Abraham, (4) John Piper ("The Demonstration of the Righteousness of God in Romans 3:25, 26," *JSNT* 7 [1980]: 2-32), who maintains that δικαιοσύνη θεοῦ in Rom 3:21 refers to God's commitment to act for His own Name's sake, (5) John Reumann (*"Righteousness" in the New Testament: "Justification" in the United States Lutheran-Roman Catholic Dialogue* [Philadelphia: Fortress Press, 1982], which includes responses by Joseph A. Fitzmyer and Jerome D. Quinn), who defends the centrality given to the Pauline doctrine of justification by confessional Lutheranism, and (6) J. H. Roberts ("Righteousness in Romans With Special Reference to Romans 3:19-31," *Neot* 15 [1981]: 12-33), who identifies six senses in which Paul uses the term "righteousness," four of which appear in Romans.

[101]The Apostle uses δικαιοσύνη ("righteousness") language in its most basic sense to speak of "right" or "appropriate" thinking in 1 Cor 15:34 and Phil 1:7. We observe its forensic meaning when, for example, Paul (1) discusses the coming Day of God's Judgment (see Rom 2:5-16; 1 Cor 4:3-5) and (2) uses δίκαιος ("righteous") as a synonym for terms such as ἀγαθός ("good"

46

as dominant, providing the framework within which Paul understands the others.[102]

A juridical interpretation of δικαιοσύνη ("righteousness") fails to capture Paul's meaning in most contexts; for no "righteous" judge acquits the guilty, but Paul's "righteous" God does just that through the Cross of Jesus Christ.[103] Likewise, the suggestion that Paul conceives of "righteousness" in terms of "salvation" proves inadequate; for while the Apostle does closely link these two ideas, he refuses to simply equate them.[104] Instead, Paul follows the LXX in using δικαιοσύνη ("righteousness") as a predominantly covenantal

---

[Rom 5:7; 7:12]), ἀληθής ("true" [Phil 4:8]), and ἄμεμπτος ("blameless" [1 Thess 2:10]), or as an antonym for ἀνομία ("lawlessness" [2 Cor 6:14]). As in Isaiah and the Psalms, Paul links God's "righteousness" both with His "saving" the righteous (see, e.g., Rom 1:16-17; 10:1-4, 9-10) and His "condemning" sinners in His "wrath" (see, e.g., Rom 1:17-18; 2:5). "Righteousness" denotes the demands dictated by human relationships in 1 Thess 2:10-11, where Paul compares his behavior toward the Thessalonians with that of "a father [toward] his children" (cf. Col 4:1, where the writer exhorts masters to treat their slaves "righteously"). Finally, Paul is well-acquainted with "righteousness" as a covenantal concept, as his use of δικαιοσύνη ("righteousness") terminology in discussing the Abrahamic (Rom 4; Gal 3) and Mosaic (e.g., Rom 2:12-13; 9:31; 10:3, 5; Gal 5:4; Phil 3:5-6, 9) covenants clearly shows.

[102]Scholars who tend to interpret "righteousness" in Paul as, first and foremost, the language of the law-court include, for example, Barrett, Bornkamm, Bruce, Calvin, Cranfield, Ladd, Ridderbos, Sanday and Headlam. Those who appeal to Isaiah, Psalms, and the Qumran literature in order to argue that Paul virtually equates God's "righteousness" with His "saving" and/or "forgiving" His people include Best, Dodd, Fitzmyer, Hunter and Kümmel. Writers who point to Jewish relational or covenantal concepts as the key to understanding "righteousness" terminology in Paul include Achtemeier, Dunn, Hill, Leenhardt, Nygren, J. L. Price and Ziesler. See the bibliography at the end of this book.

[103]Unable to overcome this insurmountable problem with their position, William Sanday and Arthur C. Headlam conclude that "The Christian life is made to have its beginning in a fiction" (A Critical and Exegetical Commentary on the Epistle to the Romans, 5th ed., The International Critical Commentary [Edinburgh: T. & T. Clark, 1902], 36). Unwilling for God to live a lie, C. K. Barrett suggests that "Justification . . . means no legal fiction but an act of forgiveness on God's part, described in terms of the proceedings of a law court" (A Commentary on the Epistle to the Romans, Harper's New Testament Commentaries [New York: Harper & Row, Publishers, 1957], 76). However, by giving "righteousness" a meaning unheard of in a law court (i.e., acquittal of sinners), he admits that, in Paul, the term has ceased to express a forensic idea!

[104]To illustrate: Romans 5:9 ("Since we have now been reckoned righteous by means of his blood; [how] much more, then, will we be saved from the Wrath [of God] by means of it!") shows that, for Paul, "righteousness" denotes the believer's present experience, while "salvation" designates his/her future hope.

term, so that the saving activity of a "righteous" God, along with the "righteousness" of humans, become manifestations of their faithfulness to a covenant. We must emphasize this point: When Paul employs the language of "righteousness," he almost always refers to a covenant. What covenant determines the content of "righteousness" for Paul?

In his letters, Paul speaks of three specific covenants (διαθῆκαι): (1) God's covenant with Abraham and his descendants, (2) the covenant God established with Israel at Sinai through Moses, and (3) the "new covenant" (καινὴ διαθήκη) God makes with Jews and Gentiles alike through the blood of Christ.[105] One of these covenants dictates the content of "righteousness" in almost every context where Paul employs the δικαιοσύνη ("righteousness") word group. We will discuss briefly Paul's understanding of these covenants in the following paragraphs.

The Abrahamic covenant. We have already noted how God showed goodwill toward Abraham by making a covenant with him. God promised, among other things, to give Abraham many descendants through his wife Sarah, and to provide them with the land of Canaan for their home.[106] Within the bounds of this covenant, "righteousness" on God's part involved fulfilling His promises to Abraham; while the content of Abraham's "righteousness" was simply entrusting himself to God.

As the Apostle to the Gentiles, Paul shows particular interest in one promise, or one aspect of "the righteousness of God," which pertains not only to Abraham's physical descendants, but to Gentiles as well. In Gal 3:8 he recalls that, after the Lord told Abraham, "I will bless you," He added the

---

[105]Paul mentions (1) the Abrahamic covenant in Rom 9:4; Gal 3:17; 4:24, (2) the Mosaic covenant in Rom 9:4; 2 Cor 3:14 (where the Apostle calls it "the old covenant" in contrast to the "new"); Gal 4:24, and (3) "human covenants" in general in Gal 3:15. On the "new covenant," see below.

[106]See Gen 12:1-3, 7; 13:14-17; 15:1-21; 17:1-22; 18:1-15; 22:15-18.

additional promise that "all the Gentiles (or "nations," τὰ ἔθνη) will be blessed in you."[107] What form would this "blessing" for the Gentiles take?

According to Paul, it has taken the form of a covenant with God, under which the content of "righteousness" is trust (πίστις)! Paul's gospel proclaims that God is now fulfilling His promise to Abraham by reckoning both Jews and Gentiles "righteous"--or, in other words, establishing a covenant relation-ship with them--on the basis of trust. He explains to the Galatians that

> [It is] just as [it is written]: "Abraham trusted in God, and it [i.e., his trust] was reckoned to him as righteousness." Consequently [i.e., since "Abraham trusted in God"], you know that those [who live] on the basis of trust (οἱ ἐκ πίστεως)--they are the children (υἱοί) of Abraham.[108]
> The scripture foresaw that God would reckon the Gentiles right-eous on the basis of trust (ἐκ πίστεως), and it proclaimed the gospel to Abraham in advance (προευηγγελίσατο τῷ 'Αβραάμ): "All the Gentiles with-in [the sphere of] you (ἐν σοί, i.e., within the sphere of "trusting Abraham" [v. 9], or within the sphere of Abraham's trust [vv. 6-7]) will be blessed." Therefore those [who live] on the basis of trust (οἱ ἐκ πίστεως) are blessed along with trusting Abraham. (Gal 3:6-9)[109]

We may summarize Paul's view as follows: God established with Abraham a covenant, to which He attached a number of promises. Under this covenant, Abraham's "righteousness" (or what was required of Abraham in order to maintain the covenant relationship) consisted of mere trust (πίστις) in God; while "the righteousness of God" involved His fulfilling His promises--notably the promise to bring "blessing" to all nations by means of Abraham and his descendants. Through the writers of scripture, God made known in advance His decision to fulfil this promise (and thus to do

---

[107]Cf. Gen 12:2-3; 18:18.

[108]This recalls a second promise of special significance for Paul--namely, God's assurance that Abraham would be "heir of the world," which the Apostle interprets to mean that he would become not only patriarch of the Jewish nation, but "the father of many nations," because he is "father of all who trust," both Jews and Gentiles alike. See Rom 4:11-13, 17-18; cf. Gen 15:5; 17:5; 22:17; Sir 44:19, 21.

[109]For a more complete discussion of this text, see chapter 4 under "Galatians 3:13."

"righteousness" toward Abraham) by establishing another covenant, under which He would reckon "righteous" Jews and Gentiles alike on the basis of Abraham-like trust. This later covenant of "blessing" would be distinct from the Lord's original covenant with Abraham, but God would give it in fulfilment of His covenant obligations to Abraham as an expression of "the righteousness of God" toward His faithful servant. It is this long-awaited covenant of "blessing," now at last made real through Christ, which Paul sometimes refers to in his letters as the "new covenant."

Ἡ καινὴ διαθήκη ("the new covenant"). Paul employs the phrase καινὴ διαθήκη ("new covenant") only in 1 Cor 11:25 and 2 Cor 3:6.[110] Nevertheless, the Apostle's free use of "righteousness" terminology throughout his epistles shows that this "new covenant" constantly fills his thoughts.

The broad outlines of the "new covenant" began to come into focus during our earlier discussion of the "blessing" for all nations promised under the Abrahamic covenant (see above). We will also devote major portions of chapters 4 and 7 to exploring Paul's "core convictions" concerning the Christian's covenant relationship with God in Christ. For now, let it suffice to say that the Apostle views the "new covenant" as a free gift of God's goodwill (χάρις), given through the bloody sacrificial death of Christ, as "God's expression of His righteousness" (δικαιοσύνη θεοῦ) toward Abraham (in the sense that He gives the "new covenant" in fulfilment of His covenant obligation to Abraham) and toward those Jews and Gentiles who enter into covenant with

---

[110]In the first text, ἡ καινὴ διαθήκη ("the new covenant") appears on the lips of Jesus in a traditional eucharistic formula ("This cup is the new covenant in my blood"). In 2 Corinthians 3, the Apostle contrasts "the ministration of the Spirit" or "righteousness" (ἡ διακονία τοῦ πνεύματος, τῆς δικαιοσύνης)--namely, the "new covenant"--with the "ministration of death" or "condemnation" (ἡ διακονία τοῦ θανάτου, τῆς κατακρίσεως), by which he means the Mosaic, or "old covenant" (ἡ παλαιὰ διαθήκη--see below). Compare also (1) Gal 4:21-31, where Paul contrasts the "old" Mosaic covenant (represented by Hagar) with the "new covenant" (represented by Sarah), and (2) Rom 11:27, where the Apostle seems to combine ideas from Isa 27:9 and Jer 31(38):31-36 in order to describe how God's "new covenant" will provide for the salvation of "all Israel" in the end.

Him (in the sense that God establishes and maintains this covenant with them).[111]

We saw above that Abraham-like "trust" (πίστις) defines the content of human "righteousness" under the "new covenant." Paul accordingly refers to his gospel (which proclaims the recent revelation in Christ of "the righteous-ness [or covenant relationship] from God based on trust" [ἡ ἐκ θεοῦ δικαιοσύνη ἐπὶ τῇ πίστει][112]) as "the message which calls for trust" (τὸ ῥῆμα τῆς πίστεως),[113] and to Christians (who have received his gospel and therefore participate in the "new covenant") as "persons who trust" (οἱ πιστεύοντες),[114] or persons who live "within the sphere determined by trust" (ἐν πίστει).[115] When Paul speaks of God's "reckoning righteous" (δικαιοῦν) those who trust, he does not ground the "new covenant" in a "fiction" (as Sanday and Headlam have claimed[116]), so that God treats persons who are not really "righteous"

---

[111]Paul employs the terms δικαιοσύνη θεοῦ ("the righteousness of God") or δικαιοσύνη αὐτου ("His righteousness", where the pronoun αὐτοῦ ["his"] refers to God) in Rom 1:17; 3:5, 21, 22, 25, 26; 10:3 (twice); 2 Cor 5:21; and 9:9. Apart from 2 Cor 9:9 (where the Apostle quotes Ps 112[111]:9) and Rom 3:5 (where the phrase refers specifically to "God's expression of His faithfulness" [ἡ πίστις τοῦ θεοῦ--see v. 3] to His covenant with Abraham, in contrast to the un-faithfulness of Abraham's Jewish descendants), the Apostle consistently employs these phrases to refer to God's action to uphold the "new covenant" in righteous fulfilment of His promise under the Abrahamic covenant.

[112]See Rom 1:17 and Phil 3:9.

[113]See Rom 10:8; cf. 10:17; 1 Cor 15:11; Phil 1:27. Sam K. Williams ("The Hearing of Faith: ἀκοὴ πίστεως in Galatians 3," NTS 35 [1989]: 82-93) correctly argues that ἡ ἀκοὴ πίστεως in Gal 3:2, 5 refers not to "the message of trust," but to trust itself--i.e., "that 'hearing' which Christians call faith" (p. 90). H. Wayne Johnson ("The Paradigm of Abraham in Galatians 3:6-9," TJ 8 n.s. [1987]: 179-99) likewise interprets the phrase to refer to "the message (as it is heard) which leads to πίστις ['trust']" (p. 187).

[114]See Rom 3:22; 4:11-12; 1 Cor 14:22; 1 Thess 1:7; 2:10, 13; cf. Rom 1:8, 12; 2 Cor 6:15; Gal 3:9; 6:10 ("the household of trust"); 1 Thess 3:5. Contrast Paul's talk of "unbelievers," or "un-trusting persons," in 1 Cor 6:6; 7:12-15; 10:27; 14:22-24; 2 Cor 4:4; 6:14-15.

[115]See 2 Cor 13:5; Gal 2:20.

[116]See note 103.

as if they were. Under the terms of this covenant, those who entrust them-selves to God as Lord truly are "righteous" in His sight.

What precisely does the Apostle mean by "trust" (πίστις)? When Paul speaks of "trust" as the content of "righteousness" under the "new covenant," he does not mean simply a "trusting" attitude of mind with no specific direc-tion or focus. Instead, Paul calls upon men and women everywhere to "trust in," or "entrust" themselves to,[117] a particular Person--namely, the Covenant-Maker, the God who made promises to Abraham and then acted to fulfil those promises in Christ.[118] For Paul, the essence of "trust" (πίστις) is commitment or submission to the God of the covenant as Lord of one's life.

Paul does not equate "trust" with "obedience," so that the lack of perfect obedience immediately makes a person a "sinner," standing outside the "new covenant" based on trust.[119] However, he fully expects that such "trust" will seek to manifest itself in obedience, or in behavior that is consistent with the Lord's known will and becoming of a person living under His lordship.[120]

---

[117]Πιστεύειν ("to trust") clearly communicates this idea in, e.g., Rom 3:2; 1 Cor 9:17; Gal 2:7; 1 Thess 2:4.

[118]Hence, Paul speaks of (1) trust in God (1 Thess 1:8), the Creator (Rom 4:17), who sent Jesus to die as a sacrifice for our sins (Rom 4:24-25), and then raised him from the dead (Rom 10:9; 1 Cor 15:14-17; 2 Cor 4:13-14) in order to effect our "righteousness," or covenant with Him (Rom 4:5, 24-25; cf. 1 Cor 2:2, 5), and our salvation (1 Cor 15:1-11), or (2) trust in His agent, Jesus Christ (Gal 2:16; Phil 1:29), the Son of God who, out of love, delivered himself over to death for us as an expression of God's goodwill and for the purpose of effecting "right-eousness," or a covenant relationship with God, for humankind (Gal 2:16, 20-21), so that we might share in his resurrection and glory (Rom 6:8; 1 Thess 4:14-18; cf. Rom 4:17). As D. H. van Daalen ("'Faith' According to Paul," *ExpTim* 87 [1975]: 85) writes: ". . . without God's act of salvation it [πίστις, 'trust'] simply does not exist." Cf. Gal 3:23 ("Before trust came . . .").

[119]See above, under "'Sinners' and 'saints.'"

[120]See, e.g., Rom 1:5 (ὑπακοὴ πίστεως ["the obedience which proceeds from trust"], an ablative of source); 6:13, 16-19; 14:23; 16:26 (compare 1:5); 2 Cor 9:10; Gal 5:6; Phil 1:11, 25; 1 Thess 1:3. Note also that Paul views Christian trust as a matter of degrees; it can grow in strength and commitment (see Rom 12:3, 6; 14:1; 1 Cor 13:2; 2 Cor 10:15; 1 Thess 3:5). For a discussion of πίστις as "action-modifying trust in God" in classical and hellenistic Greek literature, the LXX, and the NT, see (1) Dennis R. Lindsay, "The Roots and Development of the πιστ- Word Group as Faith Terminology," *JSNT* 49 (1993): 103-18; and (2) Dieter Lührmann, "*Pistis* in Judentum," *ZNW* 64 (1973): 19-38. For further discussion of the

Since the "new covenant" is based on "trust" in God, we may characterize it as a relationship of creatures to their Creator, of servants to their
rightful Lord. Entering the "new covenant" therefore involves deliverance
from the dominion of Sin and transfer into the dominion of the God who gave
promises to Abraham and then fulfilled them in Christ. To fulfil "righteousness" under this "new covenant" (i.e., to entrust oneself to God as Lord) is to
embrace the emerging "Rule" or "Kingdom of God" (βασιλεία τοῦ θεοῦ).[121]

The Mosaic covenant. Finally, we come to the Mosaic covenant, which
we introduced in our earlier discussion of "'Righteousness' as a covenantal
term." Several aspects of Paul's understanding of this covenant demand further development here.

Whereas God offers the "new covenant" to Jews and Gentiles alike,
Paul and his Jewish contemporaries view the Abrahamic and Mosaic covenants as gifts given specifically to Abraham and his descendants, to the people
of Israel. They are "Jewish covenants," in which only Jews participate. Paul
has these two covenants (as well as the "new covenant") in mind in Rom 9:4,
where he writes: "They are Israelites, to whom belong . . . the covenants, and
the giving of the Law, and . . . the patriarchs."

Paul likewise holds the traditional Jewish view that, when the Lord
entered into covenant with Israel at Sinai, He showed goodwill to His people

---

relationship between "faith" and "obedience" in Paul's letters, see (1) A. B. du Toit, "Faith and
Obedience in Paul," *Neot* 25 (1991): 65-74, and (2) D. B. Garlington's insightful, multi-part
study of "The Obedience of Faith in the Letter to the Romans": (a) "Part I: The Meaning of
ὑπακοὴ πίστεως (Rom 1:5; 16:26)," *WTJ* 52 (1990): 201-24, (b) "Part II: The Obedience of Faith
and Judgment by Works," *WTJ* 53 (1991): 47-72, (c) "Part III: The Obedience of Christ and the
Obedience of the Christian," *WTJ* 55 (1993): 87-112, and (d) "Part III: The Obedience of Christ
and the Obedience of the Christian (continued)," *WTJ* 55 (1993): 281-97.

[121]See Rom 14:17 and 1 Cor 6:9-11, along with our earlier discussions of "Sin as a 'power'"
and "the present time" (ὁ νῦν καιρός).

by giving them the Law,[122] in order to instruct them in how to maintain their newly-formed relationship with Him. The content of Israel's "righteousness" under the Mosaic covenant is Law-keeping. As Paul says in Rom 2:13, "the hearers of the Law [are] not righteous before God [under the Mosaic covenant]; instead, the doers of the Law will be reckoned righteous."[123]

Since the Law embodies the terms of the Mosaic covenant, and since only Jews participate in that covenant, Paul (like his Jewish contemporaries) views the Law and Law-keeping as distinctive marks of "Jewishness": "To them belong . . . the giving of the Law."[124] When, therefore, Paul speaks of persons "under the Law" (ὑπὸ νόμον), or persons "within [the sphere determined by] the Law" (ἐν τῷ νόμῳ), he is referring to Jews under the Mosaic covenant and not to humanity as a whole.[125] Since Gentiles are excluded from this covenant (unless they become "Jews" by accepting circumcision [the outward mark of "Jewishness"/participation in the Jewish covenants] and the "yoke" of the Law), they are, by definition, "Law-less" (ἄνομος); they are "persons who

---

[122]By "Law" (νόμος), Paul consistently means the "Jewish Law" as contained in scripture, rather than civil law or an abstract "principle." The Apostle takes a rather broad view as to which scriptures represent the "Law," as shown by the fact that he quotes as "Law" not only the Decalogue (Rom 7:7; cf. Gal 3:17) and the Pentateuch (1 Cor 9:8; 14:34; Gal 3:10-13, 21; 4:21), but also the Prophets (1 Cor 14:21). Furthermore, his frequent use of the Psalms (which belong to the third major division of the Jewish corpus, the "Writings") confirms the view of Barrett (*Romans,* 73) and others that what Paul means by "the Law," or "the Law and the Prophets" (see Rom 1:2; 16:26), is "the Old Testament as a whole."

Two writers offer excellent surveys of scholarship regarding Paul's view of the Law: (1) Douglas Moo, in "Paul and the Law in the Last Ten Years," *SJT* 40 (1987): 287-307, and (2) Stephen Westerholm, in *Israel's Law and the Church's Faith: Paul and His Recent Interpreters* (Grand Rapids: William B. Eerdmans Publishing Company, 1988). Daniel G. Reid offers a fine summary of the contributions made by E. P. Sanders, James Dunn and Stephen Westerholm in "The Misunderstood Apostle," *CT* 34 (1990): 25-27.

[123]Cf. Rom 10:5; Gal 3:10, 12; 5:3.

[124]See Rom 9:4; cf. 2:17-20, 23; 3:28-29; 1 Cor 9:20-21.

[125]See Rom 3:19; 1 Cor 9:20-21; Gal 4:4-5, 21.

do not have the Law," who consequently cannot do "the works required by the Law" (ἔργα νόμου).[126]

Paul does not deny that there is such a thing as "righteousness" under the Mosaic covenant. What he does deny is that persons can be "reckoned righteous" under the "new covenant" through doing the "righteousness" of the "old." The Apostle states his position very clearly in Rom 3:28:

> We maintain [that] a person is reckoned righteous [under the "new cove-nant"] by means of trust, apart from the works of the Law [which form the content of righteousness under the Mosaic covenant].

Note that, when Paul sets "trust" in opposition to "the works of the Law," he is not contrasting reliance on human effort ("works") with reliance on divine effort ("trust"). Instead, he is contrasting two very different covenants--namely, the "new covenant" based on trust and the Mosaic cove-nant based on "the works of the Law." The Mosaic Law may be "holy and righteous and good,"[127] but it has nothing whatsoever to do with fulfilling "righteousness" under the "new covenant" based on trust.

As a Pharisee, Paul himself had been very careful to fulfil his obliga-tions under the Mosaic covenant. He recalls in Phil 3:6b that, "with regard to the righteousness which [is] within [the sphere determined by] the Law, I was faultless." However, the decisive reality for Paul the Christian is not the Mosaic covenant, but the "new covenant" of "blessing" promised to Abraham and later instituted by God through the Cross of Christ. Paul composes one of the most moving passages in scripture as he seeks to impress this point up-on the Christians at Philippi:

---

[126]See Rom 2:14 and 1 Cor 9:21. Paul J. Achtemeier ("'Some Things in Them Hard to Un-derstand': Reflections on an Approach to Paul," *Int* 38 [1984]: 254-67) shows that, in the first text, "Paul is describing Gentiles as a people who by nature do not have the law, rather than as people who by nature do the law" (258).

[127]See Rom 7:12.

. . . with regard to the righteousness which [is] within [the sphere determined by] the Law, [I was] faultless.[128] But what used to be gain, I have come to consider loss because of Christ. Indeed, I consider all things loss because of the superior thing, [which is] knowing Christ Jesus my Lord. Because of him, I have been caused to lose all things. I consider [them mere] dung, in order that I may gain Christ, and may be found within [the sphere determined by] him--not having my own righteousness [under the Mosaic covenant], which [is] based on the Law, but that which [is] through Christ's act of trust [i.e., Christ's sacrificial death which established the "new covenant"[129]], [namely,] the righteousness from God [under the "new covenant"] based on trust. (Phil 3:6b-9)

Paul, the former Pharisee, has given up one covenant for another. Why? Because he has seen the crucified Christ raised from the dead, and has himself witnessed that God is presently fulfilling His promise of "blessing" for the Gentiles through him, rather than through the Law of Moses.[130] He has come to the conclusion that "the Law, which came four hundred and thirty years after [God made His covenant of promise with Abraham], does not nullify the [Abrahamic] covenant which had previously been ratified by God, so as to cancel the promise [of a 'blessing' for all nations which takes the form of a 'new covenant' based on trust]."[131] Most importantly, he has come to the realization that it is "the [person reckoned] righteous on the basis of trust" (i.e., those who participate in the "new covenant")--rather than the person reckoned righteous on the basis of the Law/"Jewishness" (i.e., those who

---

[128]In other words, Paul had fulfilled the demands of "righteousness" under the Mosaic covenant by doing the Law.

[129]See below under "Verse 22a." See also chapter 4 under "Christ's death as the sacrifice which established the 'new covenant'" and "Jesus' Act of Trust."

[130]As Paul says to his converts in Gal 3:2, "Did you receive the Spirit [a manifestation of the close fellowship with God believers enjoy during the 'eschatological age' (see above) within the bounds of the covenant of 'blessing'] on the basis of the Law, or on the basis of the message which calls for trust?"

[131]Gal 3:17; cf. Rom 4:13-14.

participate in the Mosaic covenant)--who "will live ['eschatological life']"[132] in the coming Resurrection of the righteous, when God consummates His eschatological Rule.[133] Two thousand years before, the Lord of the universe made a promise to a "wandering Aramean"[134] who, in trust, entered into a covenant with Him. Now, in Paul's own day, God had acted in Jesus Christ to fulfil that promise by establishing a "new covenant" in his blood. Paul relates the Abrahamic covenant to the "new covenant" as promise to fulfilment, and he pushes aside a third covenant--the Mosaic covenant--as secondary.

Why, then, did God give the Mosaic covenant at all? "Why, then, the Law?"[135] Paul, at one point or another, says that (1) "knowledge of sin [comes] by means of the Law," (2) "God's expression of His righteousness . . . is witnessed to by the Law and the Prophets," (3) "the Law entered in order to increase the trespass," (4) "the Law . . . was added on account of transgressions" and "imprisoned all things under Sin," and (5) "the Law was our pedagogue until Christ [came] for the purpose of our being reckoned righteous on the basis of trust."[136] A detailed analysis of each of these statements is beyond the scope of this study, but together they show that Paul views the Law as something intended by God to play a positive role--though not the central role--in the working out of His grand design.

---

[132]Hab 2:4, quoted by Paul in Rom 1:17 and Gal 3:11.

[133]For a discussion of the Resurrection of the "righteous" and God's eschatological Reign, see part I of this chapter, along with the more detailed explanations given in chapters 5 and 8.

[134]See Deut 26:5.

[135]See Gal 3:19.

[136]See (1) Rom 3:20; cf. 7:7-8; (2) Rom 3:21; cf. 1:1-2; 3:27-28, 31; 16:25-26; (3) Rom 5:20; (4) Gal 3:19, 22; and (5) Gal 3:23-24; cf. Rom 10:4. On the "pedagogue" (παιδαγωγός) metaphor, see two studies by Norman H. Young: (1) "*Paidagōgos*: The Social Setting of a Pauline Metaphor," *NovT* 29 (1987): 150-76, and (2) "The Figure of the *Paidagōgos* in Art and Literature," *BA* 53 (1990): 80-86.

IV. ROMANS 3:21-26

Having surveyed Paul's views concerning sin and glory, righteousness and covenant, trust and the Law, we now turn to Romans 3:21-26, where the Apostle places these ideas in relationship to God's demonstration of His goodwill in the Cross of Jesus Christ.

Context

Occasion. As the Jewish "minister of Christ Jesus to the Gentiles"[137] writes his epistle to the Christians at Rome, the future of the Church and of the gospel fills his thoughts. Paul has preached his Law-less message "from Jerusalem and as far round as Illyricum,"[138] winning many converts to Christ. "No longer having any room in these regions," he hopes the Romans will soon aid him in a journey to Spain, so that he might reap some "fruit" from among the Gentiles there as well.[139] Yet he may never have the opportunity, for the Jewish element in the Church, centered in Jerusalem, has vacillated over whether or not to accept believing Gentiles as full and unconditional partici- pants in the body of Christ (a conflict typified in Paul's confrontation with Cephas at Antioch[140]). By insisting that Gentiles must become Jews (through circumcision and Law-keeping) in order to participate in the benefits wrought by Christ, the "judaizing" party has called into question Paul's gospel, his "apostleship for the Gentiles,"[141] and his entire missionary enterprise.[142] Paul therefore feels compelled to journey first to Jerusalem--before he goes

---

[137]See Rom 15:16.

[138]See Rom 15:19.

[139]See Rom 15:23-24; cf. 1:13.

[140]See Gal 2:11-14.

[141]See Gal 2:8.

[142]For further discussion of the "Judaizers," see chapter 4 under "Galatians 3:13."

58

to Rome--in order to deliver a collection from the churches of Asia Minor, Macedonia and Achaia "for the poor among the saints at Jerusalem."[143] The Apostle hopes that the Christians there will confirm the truth of his "gospel for the uncircumcision"[144] by accepting this gift as a symbol of unity between Jews and Gentiles in the Church.[145] Accordingly, Paul writes Romans in order to (1) explain the place of his gospel and the Gentile mission in the eternal purpose of God, and to thereby (2) impress upon an increasingly important church the significance of the collection for the Jerusalem saints, in the hope that he may (3) win their approval of his past evangelistic activity as well as their support for the work he plans to do in Spain.[146]

Romans 1:18-3:20. Whereas the Jews traditionally looked upon the Gentiles as "sinners" outside the bounds of God's goodwill, they reckoned themselves "righteous" because they alone possessed the Mosaic covenant and the Mosaic Law. In Rom 1:18-3:20, Paul agrees with the Jews that the Gentiles are "sinners" who "have worshipped and served the creature rather than the Creator."[147] However, he takes issue with the Jewish claim to "righteousness" by reminding his readers that, under the Mosaic covenant, it is "not

---

[143]See Rom 15:25-32; cf. 1 Cor 16:1-4; 2 Cor 8:1-15; 9:1-15; Gal 2:10.

[144]See Gal 2:7.

[145]See Rom 15:30-32. Paul Achtemeier offers a compelling reconstruction of these events in *The Quest for Unity in the New Testament Church: A Study in Paul and Acts* (Philadelphia: Fortress Press, 1987). See also Günther Bornkamm's discussion of the meaning of the collection for the Jerusalem saints in *Paul* (New York: Harper & Row, Publishers, 1971), 40-41, 58, 92-93.

[146]In an article entitled "Rome (and Jerusalem): The Contingency of Romans 3:21-26" (*IBS* 11 [1989]: 54-68), Warren C. Carter argues that "Romans was composed from a convergence of motivations related to both the Roman church and to Paul's larger mission. A common factor in these situations was tension in the relationships of Jewish and Gentile Christians" (pp. 64-65). Paul seeks to resolve these tensions by stressing three themes, which appear in Rom 3:21-26--namely, (1) "the equality of Jew and Gentile before God" (pp. 58-61), (2) "Jewish temporal priority" (pp. 61-63), and (3) "the visibility of God's Acts" (pp. 63-65).

[147]See Rom 1:25, along with our earlier discussion of "Sin as a 'power.'"

the hearers of the Law [who are] righteous before God; instead, the doers of the Law will be reckoned righteous."[148] Since the Jews have not faithfully observed God's Law, Paul insists that "both Jews and Greeks alike are under [the dominion of] Sin."[149] The Law itself supports this contention when it declares that "none is righteous, not even one."[150] The Law, then, has not brought Jewish "righteousness," but only the "knowledge of [universal human] sin."[151] The logical implication of this whole discussion is that Jewish Christians who seek to impose circumcision and Law-keeping (i.e., "Jewishness") on Gentile believers are requiring something that will bring the Gentiles no advantage whatsoever.

The only "advantage" Paul will grant to the Jews is that "they have been entrusted with the oracles of God," or the promises given to Abraham by God when He established His covenant with the Jewish patriarch and his descendants.[152] Although the Jews hold them in trust, these promises pledge "blessing" not for Jews only, but for all the peoples of the earth. Paul has come to the realization that, even if Abraham's descendants have not always been faithful in their relationship to the Lord, God has remained faithful to His covenant with Abraham and has acted "righteously" to fulfil His promises

---

[148]See Rom 2:13.

[149]See Rom 3:9. The Apostle makes such an argument in order to break down Jewish pretensions. Yet even if the Jews had followed Moses' commands (as Paul himself claims to have done in Phil 3:6), Paul's gospel would still stand; for release from Sin and participation in the "new covenant" of "blessing" comes through trust, rather than through doing "the works of the Law." See above under "The Mosaic covenant."

[150]See Rom 3:10.

[151]See Rom 3:20.

[152]See Rom 3:1-2. Williams argues that τὰ λόγια ("the oracles") refers to the Abrahamic promises in "The 'Righteousness of God,'" 266-67. Paul sometimes speaks in a similar fashion of God's "entrusting" him and his fellow-workers with the gospel, which proclaims God's fulfilment of His promises to Abraham in Christ (see 1 Cor 9:16-17; Gal 2:7; 1 Thess 2:4).

through Jesus Christ.[153] Therefore, the Apostle proceeds to proclaim the "good news" concerning how God has kept His word, and what form those promises have taken, in Rom 3:21-26.

Translation

(21) But in the present God's expression of His righteousness (δικαιοσύνη θεοῦ) has been revealed apart from the Law--although it is witnessed to by the Law and the Prophets. (22) [I am speaking of] the righteousness of God expressed (δικαιοσύνη θεοῦ), through Jesus Christ's act of trust (πίστις Ἰησοῦ Χριστοῦ), toward all who trust. [I say "all" who trust] because there is no distinction. (23) [There is no distinction between Jews and Gentiles under this expression of God's righteousness] because all have sinned and lack the glory of God, (24) and [all] are freely reckoned righteous by His goodwill (χάρις), through the deliverance (ἀπο-λύτρωσις) which [is] within [the sphere of] Christ Jesus[' rule] (ἐν Χριστῷ Ἰησοῦ). (25) God publicly displayed him [as] a sacrifice which purifies from sin (ἱλαστήριον), through [Jesus'] act of trust,[154] at the cost of his blood (ἐν τῷ αὐτοῦ αἵματι). [God publicly displayed him] as the demonstration of His righteousness because of the remission of the former sins [committed] (26) during the period of God's forbearance (ἐν τῇ ἀνοχῇ τοῦ θεοῦ). [God publicly displayed him] in order to [serve as] the demonstration of His righteousness, in the present time (ὁ νῦν καιρός), so that [God] Himself might be righteous by [the] very [act of His] reckoning righteous the person grounded in Jesus' act of trust (τὸν ἐκ πίστεως Ἰησοῦ).

Interpretation

Verse 21. In this passage, Paul proclaims the recent revelation, in history, of δικαιοσύνη θεοῦ ("the righteousness of God" or "God's expression of His righteousness"). Earlier in this chapter we argued that Paul consistently employs "righteousness" as a covenantal term. Within the covenantal context, δικαιοσύνη θεοῦ ("the righteousness of God") can refer either to (1) the "righteousness" God does, i.e., God's action to uphold His covenant

---

[153]See Rom 3:3-4.

[154]Bruce W. Longenecker shows that διὰ [τῆς] πίστεως here refers to Jesus' "act of trust" in "Πίστις in Romans 3:25: Neglected Evidence for the 'Faithfulness of Christ'?" *NTS* 39 (1993): 478-80.

obligations, or (2) "righteousness" as the quality possessed by God, inasmuch as He fulfils His covenant obligations.[155]   In our judgment, Paul intends for the term to communicate both God's action ("God's expression of . . . righteousness") and His attribute ("His righteousness"), or, in other words, God's attribute as expressed in His action. We have therefore attempted to capture both senses of the phrase by translating δικαιοσύνη θεοῦ as "God's expression of His righteousness."[156]

If Paul means to say that God has acted to uphold a covenant, then what covenant does the Apostle have in mind? What covenant specifies the content of the "righteousness" God has fulfilled? We should eliminate the Mosaic covenant from the start; for Paul says that the "expression of God's righteousness" in question is "apart from," or "independent of the Law" (χωρὶς νόμου, v 21). The Apostle does not speak of the Abrahamic covenant, for here God directs His righteous action toward "all who trust"--without "distinction" between Jews and Gentiles (vv. 22-23)--rather than toward Abraham and his Jewish descendants alone. Paul instead refers to the third covenant occupying a central place in his thought--namely, the "new covenant" God has given in fulfilment of His promise to Abraham. This is confirmed by the fact that Paul's description of "God's expression of His righteousness" in Rom 3:21-26 is consistent with what the Apostle says elsewhere in his letters concerning that "new covenant": It is "witnessed to by the Law and the

---

[155]See R. K. Moore, "Issues Involved in the Interpretation of δικαιοσύνη θεοῦ in the Pauline Corpus," *Coll* 23 (1991): 59-70.

[156]In other words, the term θεοῦ ("of God") in δικαιοσύνη θεοῦ ("the righteousness of God") functions as a subjective genitive (in the sense that "God does righteousness") or an adjectival genitive ("the righteousness characteristic of God"). We reject the opinion, put forth by Bultmann and others, that what we have here is a genitive of authorship; for when Paul wishes to speak of "the righteousness which comes from God," he uses the expression δικαιοσύνη ἐκ θεοῦ, as in Phil 3:9.

Prophets" (v. 21),[157] initiated by God's goodwill toward sinners (v. 24), instituted by Christ's sacrificial death (v. 25), and open to "all who trust" (vv. 22, 25).[158]

Since God gives the "new covenant" in righteous fulfilment of His promise under the Abrahamic covenant, "God's expression of His righteousness" in establishing and upholding that "new covenant" can be distinguished--but never entirely separated--from His "righteousness" toward Abraham.[159] Therefore, when Paul proclaims the revelation of "God's expression of His righteousness" in Rom 3:21-26, he means "God's action to establish and maintain the 'new covenant' in an effort to uphold His earlier covenant with Abraham."[160] The following paraphrase of Rom 3:21 captures the Apostle's intent:

> In "the present time" (νῦν, "now"),[161] we have already seen (πεφανέρωται, "it has been revealed") God establish a "new covenant" in fulfilment of His promise under the Abrahamic covenant (δικαιοσύνη θεοῦ, "God's expression of His righteousness"). This "new covenant" is totally independent of the Mosaic covenant with its righteousness based on Law-keeping (χωρὶς νόμου, "apart from the Law"), although the Law and the Prophets do witness to it.

Verse 22a. During the last two decades, scholars have devoted much energy to the question of whether πίστις Ἰησοῦ Χριστοῦ ("the trust of Jesus

---

[157]We find several outstanding illustrations of how the Law "witnesses" to the "new covenant" in this very context, including Paul's citation of Hab 2:4 in Rom 1:17, and his use of Gen 15:6 and Ps 32(31):1 in Rom 4.

[158]See above under "Η καινὴ διαθήκη ('the new covenant')."

[159]See above under "The Abrahamic covenant."

[160]This suggestion receives support from the fact that Paul has already identified the Abrahamic covenant as the covenant under which the "new covenant" was promised in Rom 3:1-4 (see note 152). He will revisit this idea in Romans 4.

[161]The word νῦν ("now") in Rom 3:21 is an abbreviated form of ὁ νῦν καιρός ("the now time" or "the present time"). See part I of this chapter.

Christ") in Rom 3:22[162] functions as an objective genitive ("trust in Jesus Christ") or a subjective genitive ("the trust shown by Jesus Christ," or "Jesus Christ's act of trust").[163] Four arguments, when taken together, speak decisively in favor of the latter alternative.

First, Paul uses this construction (i.e., πίστις followed by a genitive of person, or personal pronoun) to speak not only of "the trust of Jesus Christ," but also "the trust of" (1) God, (2) Abraham, (3) Christians, and (4) the person whose trust rests upon God.[164] In every case, the Apostle speaks not of trust in that person(s), but of the trust exercised by that person(s). This suggests that when Paul uses the phrase πίστις Ἰησοῦ Χριστοῦ ("the trust of Jesus Christ"), he likewise does not mean "trust in Jesus Christ" (objective genitive), but "Jesus Christ's act of trust" (subjective genitive).

A second observation adds weight to this interpretation: Paul does speak of "trust in" someone, or something, in a great number of contexts. When he does so, he avoids the ambiguous genitive construction by employing

---

[162]Πίστις ("trust") also appears with the genitives Ἰησοῦ ("of Jesus") or Χριστοῦ ("of Christ")--or some combination of the two--in Rom 3:26; Gal 2:16; 3:22; and Phil 3:9. John W. Pryor ("Paul's Use of Iēsous--A Clue for the Translation of Romans 3:26?" *Coll* 16 [1983]: 31-45) shows that Paul uses the appellations Ἰησοῦς ("Jesus") and Χριστός ("Christ") interchangeably. Since Ἰησοῦ alone may, on the basis of form, function as either a genitive ("of Jesus") or dative ("in Jesus"), the reader could conceivably understand the word in Rom 3:26 as a dative denoting the object of trust ("the person grounded in trust in Jesus"). However, its appearance with the genitive Χριστοῦ ("of Christ") in most of the other passages mentioned above removes the ambiguity and suggests that Ἰησοῦ is a genitive ("the person grounded in Jesus' act of trust") in this verse as well.

[163]Scholars who argue for the objective reading include Barrett, Bruce, Cranfield, Dunn, Hultgren, Hunter, Käsemann, Koperski, Leenhardt, Nygren, Sanday and Headlam. Those supporting the subjective reading include K. Barth, M. Barth, Boguslawski, Campbell, Hays, Hooker, Keck, Johnson, Ljungman, Longenecker, O'Rourke, Pryor, Ramaroson, Stowers and Williams. We list the pertinent works of these scholars in the bibliography at the end of this book.

[164]See (1) Rom 3:3, (2) Rom 4:16, (3) Rom 1:12; 1 Cor 2:5; 15:14, 17; 2 Cor 1:24; 10:15; Phil 2:17; 1 Thess 1:8; 3:2, 5-7, 10, and (4) Rom 4:5, respectively. Cf. ἡ ἀπιστία αὐτῶν ("their lack of trust/unfaithfulness") in Rom 3:3.

either a clear dative or accusative,[165] or an appropriate preposition,[166] in order to signal the reader that he is discussing a particular object of trust, rather than an attitude or act of trust. When, therefore, Paul retains the genitive πίστις Ἰησοῦ Χριστοῦ in Rom 3:22 (and 26), he most likely intends for the reader to understand the phrase as "Jesus Christ's act of trust."

Third, interpreting διὰ πίστεως Ἰησοῦ Χριστοῦ as an objective genitive ("through trust in Jesus Christ") in Rom 3:22 makes the next clause (εἰς πάντας τοὺς πιστεύοντας, "toward all who trust") redundant.[167] Interpreting διὰ πίστεως Ἰησοῦ Χριστοῦ as a subjective genitive ("through Jesus Christ's act of trust") makes both this clause and the next contribute to Paul's argument. The first (διὰ πίστεως Ἰησοῦ Χριστοῦ, "through Jesus Christ's act of trust") communicates the means by which God expresses His righteousness, while the second (εἰς πάντας τοὺς πιστεύοντας, "toward all who trust") identifies the object or recipients of that righteousness.

Finally, for Paul to speak of "Jesus Christ's act of trust" conforms perfectly to his theology of the Cross, which interprets Christ's death as an expression of self-humiliation or trust in God. A detailed discussion of this aspect of Paul's thought appears in part III of chapter 4.

We conclude, on these grounds, that πίστις Ἰησοῦ Χριστοῦ in Rom 3: 22a is a subjective genitive referring to "Jesus Christ's act of trust" or, in other

---

[165]See Rom 4:3, 10:16 and Gal 3:6 for the dative, and 1 Cor 11:18 and 13:7 for πιστεύειν with the accusative.

[166]Paul marks the object of πίστις ("trust") or πιστεύειν ("to trust") with (1) εἰς ("in") in Rom 4:18; 10:14; Gal 2:16 (εἰς Χριστὸν Ἰησοῦν, "in Christ Jesus"); and Phil 1:29, (2) ἐπί ("on") in Rom 4:5, 24; 9:33; 10:11, (3) ἐν ("in") in Rom 3:25 (according to some scholars, although our translation of this verse shows that we understand it differently); Gal 3:26 (διὰ τῆς πίστεως ἐν Χριστῷ Ἰησοῦ, "by means of trust in Christ Jesus"), and (4) πρός ("toward") in 1 Thess 1:8 (ἡ πίστις ὑμῶν ἡ πρὸς τὸν θεόν, "your trust which is directed toward God"). The conjunction ὅτι ("that") introduces the content of "trust" or "belief" in Rom 6:8; 10:9; 1 Thess 4:14.

[167]A similar redundancy would likewise occur in Gal 3:22.

words, his sacrificial death on the Cross.[168] The meaning of the verse thus becomes clear: Paul is speaking of the "new covenant" (i.e., δικαιοσύνη θεοῦ, "the righteousness of God expressed"), which God established through Jesus' death on the cross (i.e., πίστις Ἰησοῦ Χριστοῦ, "Jesus Christ's act of trust"), and which He offers "to all who trust" (εἰς πάντας τοὺς πιστεύοντας), both Jews and Gentiles alike.[169]

Verses 22b-24. In v. 22b, the causal conjunction γάρ ("because") introduces the basis for Paul's contention that, by establishing the "new covenant," God has acted righteously toward "all" who trust, whether they be Jews or Gentiles. The Mosaic covenant distinguished persons under the covenant from persons outside the covenant--the "righteous" from the "unrighteous"--on the basis of the works required by the Jewish Law, or "Jewishness." The "new covenant," however, is "apart from the Law;" it differentiates between human beings only on the basis of whether or not they have entrusted themselves to the God who revealed His righteousness through the death of Jesus Christ. Under this covenant, "there is neither Jew nor Greek;"[170] "there is no distinction" based on adherence to the Jewish Law.

---

[168]In like manner, we should translate διὰ πίστεως Ἰησοῦ Χριστοῦ/Χριστοῦ as "through Jesus Christ's/Christ's act of trust" in Gal 2:16 and Phil 3:9. Ἐκ πίστεως Χριστοῦ/Ἰησοῦ Χριστοῦ means "on the basis of Christ's/Jesus Christ's act of trust" in Gal 2:16 and 3:22. (In "The Meaning of Πίστις and Νόμος in Paul: A Linguistic and Structural Perspective" [*JBL* 111 (1992): 91-103], D. A. Campbell shows that ἐκ πίστεως and διὰ τῆς πίστεως [as well as ἐκ νόμου and διὰ νόμου] "function paradigmatically in Paul; that is, they are stylistic variations of the same basic idea, allowing Paul to repeat his point without undue tedium" [96]. Habakkuk 2:4 [ὁ δὲ δίκαιος ἐκ πίστεως ζήσεται] "seems to function as the fundamental linguistic template from which the other phrases, and the structure as a whole, are derived" [101].) By τὸν ἐκ πίστεως Ἰησοῦ, in Rom 3:26, Paul means "the person grounded in Jesus' act of trust." (Pryor ["Paul's Use of *Iēsous*," 41-42] suggests "him who derives his being from the faithfulness of Jesus." Similar constructions occur in Rom 4:14, 16; and Gal 3:7, 9.) Finally, we should translate ἐν πίστει ζῶ τῇ τοῦ υἱοῦ τοῦ θεοῦ in Gal 2:20 as "I live within [the sphere] which [is determined by] the Son of God's act of trust."

[169]The content of "righteousness" under the "new covenant" is trust alone. See verse 30.

[170]Gal 3:28.

In v. 23 a second γάρ ("because") signals the grounds upon which Paul claims that the "new covenant" (i.e., "the righteousness of God expressed") makes "no distinction" between Jews and Gentiles. Since trust forms the content of its "righteousness," the "new covenant" does not recognize the Mosaic covenant's distinctively "Jewish" righteousness of works. This has a sort of leveling effect on the human race. From the perspective of the "new covenant," it is not only the Gentiles who are unrighteous "sinners;"[171] instead, "all have sinned and lack the glory of God" unless they are "freely reckoned righteous [under the 'new covenant'] by His goodwill, through the deliverance which [is] within [the sphere of] Christ Jesus[' rule]."

"All have sinned and lack the glory of God" (v. 23). The Apostle has already impressed upon his readers the universality of human sin in Rom 1:18-3:20.[172] Early in this chapter we pointed out that Paul views "sin" not so much in terms of wrong deeds, but as slavery under any "lord" other than the Creator (= participation in the "present evil age" or the Fall). Apart from the Creator's acting to restore a proper relationship with His creatures by reestablishing His lordship over them, both Jews and Gentiles are--like Adam --trapped within the dominion of "Sin." They thus lack the reflected "glory of God," or the spiritual, imperishable, immortal "image of God" now possessed by the risen Christ.[173]

Beginning in v. 24, Paul declares that, in fulfilment of His promise to Abraham, God has acted out of "goodwill" (χάρις)[174] and "righteousness" to

---

[171]See Gal 2:15-21.

[172]See esp. Rom 3:9, 12, 19-20, along with our earlier discussion of the "Context" of Rom 3:21-26.

[173]See above under (1) "Sin as a 'power,'" (2) "The 'glory' (δόξα) taken from Adam at the Fall and restored to the righteous at the Eschaton," (3) and "The 'glory of God' and the 'image (εἰκών) of God.'"

[174]The root idea conveyed by the χάρις word group is "pleasure" or "delight." The noun χάρις can denote (1) "that which causes delight"--namely, "charm" or "loveliness"--or (2) the mood or state of mind evoked by such "loveliness"--namely, "favor, appreciation, goodwill." In

reconcile "all" persons to Himself by instituting a "new covenant" based on trust in Him, or submission to His lordship. In this way, God effects "deliverance" (ἀπολύτρωσις)[175] for sinners from the dominion of Sin and places them

---

the latter case, the corresponding verb, χαρίζεσθαι, would mean "to express favor, pleasure, appreciation, goodwill, kindness." Here we find the predominant meaning for the χάρις word group in the letters of Paul, wherein the Apostle speaks often of the "favor" or "goodwill" which God has shown toward human beings. We must keep in mind, however, that Paul's God did not show "favor" to "charming" or "lovely" creatures, but to sinners (see Rom 5:6-8). Paul's concept of χάρις therefore contains a strong element of "mercy" and "love." Since the English words "favor," "appreciation," and "pleasure" tend to carry with them the idea of "approval" (which could imply that God does not take sin seriously), we have chosen to translate χάρις in most contexts with some form of the word "goodwill." This term proves capable of taking in the full range of meaning of χάρις as "favor, kindness, mercy" and "love," without necessarily implying that the objects of such "goodwill" are "lovely," or "deserving" of that "goodwill." In some contexts, Paul employs χάρις to communicate the related ideas of (1) "thanks" (i.e. an expression of appreciation), or (2) "a gift [expressing goodwill]." He uses the verb χαρίζεσθαι to mean (1) "to give thanks," (2) "to give a gift [as an expression of goodwill]" (i.e., simply to "give" without receiving anything in return, to "give freely"), or (3) "to forgive [as an expression of goodwill]."

[175]Although ἀπολύτρωσις is rare in the LXX, secular Greek writers use the term for (1) the "ransoming" or "redemption" of a slave or prisoner of war or, in a more general sense, for (2) "release" or "deliverance" from some sort of bondage. Paul seems to describe the Cross as an act of "redemption" when he reminds the Corinthians that they have been "bought with a price" (1 Cor 6:20; 7:23; cf. Gal 3:13; 4:5), and when he declares in Rom 3:25 that Christ has "purchased" Christians' righteousness "at the cost of his blood." Yet these statements, along with the three occurrences of ἀπολύτρωσις in Paul's writings (Rom 3:24; 8:23 and 1 Cor 1:30), cannot support a fully-developed "ransom theory of atonement;" for the "ransom" analogy breaks down when we ask questions such as "To whom did Christ pay the ransom?"

We therefore interpret ἀπολύτρωσις in the more general sense as "deliverance [from bondage]." From the limited evidence at our disposal, the Apostle does have in mind a specific "deliverance" each time he uses this language--namely, God's deliverance of human beings from the dominion of Sin (or the consequences of the Adamic Fall, such as mortality) through the sacrificial death of Jesus Christ. This "deliverance" bears real results for the Christian in the present, such as righteousness, transfer into the sphere of Christ's rule, and the "down-payment" of the Spirit. However, its full effect will not be felt until Christ's return, when God will overcome the "last enemy," Death. J. A. Ziesler ("Salvation Proclaimed IX: Romans 3:21-26," *ExpTim* 93 [1982]: 357) states the matter well when he writes:

> . . . [ἀπολύτρωσις] is above all a word for liberation, for change of ownership, or as in this case, of transfer from one lordship to another. Those who have been under sin's domination are redeemed, set free from that domination and transferred into the possession and lordship of Christ. Henceforth they are "in Christ" . . .

David Hill commends the same sort of interpretation in *Greek Words and Hebrew Meanings: Studies in the Semantics of Soteriological Terms* (Cambridge: The University Press, 1967), 75-76.

For a discussion of Paul's use of ἀπολύτρωσις ("deliverance") in order to express covenantal ideas, see chapter 4 under "'Deliverance,' 'Rescue' and 'Liberation.'"

"within [the sphere of] Christ Jesus" (ἐν Χριστῷ Ἰησοῦ),[176] who presently rules over Creation as the vicar of God.[177]

Verses 25-26. In v. 25a Paul tells his readers that "God's expression of His righteousness" (δικαιοσύνη θεοῦ) took the form of Jesus' dying as "a sacrifice which purifies from sin" (ἱλαστήριον).[178] It now becomes clear that

---

[176]In an essay entitled "Some Observations on Paul's Use of the Phrases 'In Christ' and 'With Christ'" (*JSNT* 25 [1985]: 83-97), A. J. M. Wedderburn describes the difficulty of interpreting the Pauline phrase ἐν Χριστῷ, since it is syntactically capable of communicating so many different ideas. For example, we could read ἐν Χριστῷ instrumentally ("by Christ" or "through Christ"), temporally ("at the time of Christ"), modally ("in the manner of Christ"), as a dative of respect ("with respect to Christ"), as a locative ("within Christ"), or in a number of other ways. (See also B. B. Colijn, "Paul's Use of the 'In Christ' Formula," *ATJ* 23 [1991]: 9-26.) On the basis of Paul's use of ἐν with "Abraham" in Gal 3, Wedderburn argues that ἐν Χριστῷ is near in sense to "through Christ," but possibly carries the additional nuance of "association with Christ." David Hill ("Liberation," 40-41) argues that "there is nothing really analogous to the phrase 'in Christ' except . . . the phrase 'in Adam.'" He then proceeds to describe ἐν Χριστῷ as "the locus of justification." Both these writers approach the mind of Paul. However, we suggest that, in most contexts, Paul uses this phrase predominantly as a locative of sphere (of dominion). In other words, ἐν Χριστῷ is the language of lordship and is therefore analogous to ἐν ἁμαρτίᾳ ("within [the sphere ruled/determined by] Sin"--see above under "Sin as a 'power'"). To be "in Christ" (ἐν Χριστῷ), then, is to be "a slave of Christ" (δοῦλος Χριστοῦ), or to have one's existence "ruled" or "determined" by the person and actions of Christ (just as Adam's sin determines the existence of the person "in Adam"--see chapter 3). Such a reading of ἐν Χριστῷ seems especially attractive in Rom 6:11; 8:1-2; 12:5; 15:17; 16:3, 7, 9, 10; 1 Cor 3:1; 4:10, 15, 17; 15:18, 22; 2 Cor 5:17; 12:2; Gal 1:22; 2:4; 3:26-28; Phil 1:1, 13; 2:1, 5; 4:21; 1 Thess 2:14; 4:16; 5:18; and Phlm 23, where Paul describes being "in Christ" in terms of freedom from Sin and membership in his Body or the Christian community. Ἐν Χριστῷ could likewise function as "domain language" in every other context in which Paul employs this phrase (Rom 3:24; 6:23; 8:39; 9:1; 1 Cor 1:2, 4, 30; 15:31; 16:24; 2 Cor 2:14, 17; 3:14; 5:19; 12:19; Gal 2:17; 3:14; Phil 1:26; 3:3, 14; 4:7, 19; Phlm 8, 20), with the exception of 1 Cor 15:19, where ἐν Χριστῷ must identify the object of hope.

[177]See the discussion of "'The Name which is above every name'" in chapter 5.

[178]The term ἱλαστήριον appears only here in the writings of Paul. The basic idea expressed by the word group to which it belongs is that of "showing mercy." Where sin is concerned (as in this context), such "mercy" takes the form of "forgiveness"--or, in light of some of the Hebrew words translated into Greek by this word group (e.g., כָּפַר, "to rub off"), it would probably be more accurate to think in terms of "purifying from sin." An ἱλαστήριον, then, is an "expression of mercy," or "a means by which one is purified from sin."

The LXX uses the noun ἱλαστήριον almost exclusively of the "mercy seat" (כַּפֹּרֶת, i.e. the "place of mercy/purification from sin"), or the slab of gold which rested on the ark of the covenant in the Jewish Holy of Holies. This "mercy seat" acted as a sort of "magnet" by attracting to itself all the sins of Israel throughout the course of the year. On the Day of Atonement (יוֹם כִּפֻּרִים, described in Lev 16), the high priest sprinkled the blood of a sacrifice on the "mercy

"Jesus Christ's act of trust" (πίστις Ἰησοῦ Χριστοῦ, vv. 22, 26) was his trustful, obedient acceptance of "the death which is the cross."[179] God established the "new covenant[180]--i.e., He acted to "deliver" (ἀπολύτρωσις, v. 24) those who trust Him from the lordship of Sin and to bring them "within [the sphere of] Christ Jesus[' rule]" (ἐν Χριστῷ Ἰησοῦ, v. 24)--through Jesus' bloody sacrificial

---

seat," and thus "rubbed out" the nation's sin, so that God would continue to dwell in Israel's midst (see J. Milgrom, "Atonement in the OT," *IDBSup*, 78-79). Some have suggested that Paul intends for ἱλαστήριον to carry this meaning in Rom 3:25. In support of this interpretation, they point to the fact that Paul refers to "blood" in v. 25 (where his usual term is "the Cross"), and to the "glory of God" (which may be a reference to the visible manifestation of God's presence which dwelt over the "mercy seat" in the Temple--see above under "Δόξα ['glory'] as the visible, radiant presence of God") in v. 23. Yet Paul probably does not intend to say that Christ is simply a "mercy seat;" for, as we have seen, the "mercy seat" was something that attracted sin to itself and was then in need of cleansing. Paul clearly views the crucified Christ as the one who effects cleansing from sin, rather than as one who was himself cleansed (unless the Apostle somehow conceives of Christ as both "mercy seat" and sacrifice which purifies from sin).

Others have noted that, in some septuagintal contexts, the ἱλαστήριον word group seems to carry the idea of "propitiation," or the averting of divine wrath. Since Paul describes the present revelation of God's "wrath" in Rom 1:18-32, they suggest that the Apostle intends his readers to understand ἱλαστήριον as "propitiation" in Rom 3:25. Yet it is difficult to conceive of God (who "publicly displays" this ἱλαστήριον) as having to appease Himself. Furthermore, in this immediate context, Paul speaks not of "deliverance" from "wrath," but of "deliverance" (ἀπολύτρωσις) from universal bondage to Sin (see note 175) through God's public display of Christ as an ἱλαστήριον.

We therefore conclude (along with Barrett, Dodd, Hunter, Käsemann, Keck and Furnish, Zeisler, and others) that ἱλαστήριον in Rom 3:25 probably functions as a neuter, singular, substantized form of the adjective ἱλαστήριος, meaning "something which effects mercy/ forgiveness of sins." Since Paul mentions Christ's "blood" (which for him, like other NT writers, evokes the idea of a sacrificial death or, more accurately, of a life poured out completely to God--see Rom 5:8-9; 1 Cor 10:16, 18; 11:25-27; cf. Lev 17:11), he probably conceives of Christ's death on the cross as a blood-sacrifice. He could rightly characterize such a sacrifice as an ἱλαστήριον in the sense that it effects mercy/purifies from sins. (We will offer a complete discussion of the idea of "sacrifice" in the Pauline writings in part I of chapter 4.) 4 Macc 17:22 offers something of a parallel in that it speaks of the ἱλαστήριος θάνατος ("purifying death") of seven martyred Jewish brothers which purified Israel from sin. On these grounds, we have chosen to translate ἱλαστήριον in Rom 3:25 as "a sacrifice which purifies from sin."

For further discussion, see (1) Nico S. L. Fryer, "The Meaning and Translation of *Hilasterion* in Romans 3:25," *EvQ* 59 (1987): 99-116, (2) Hill, *Greek Words*, 23-48, and (3) the portion of chapter 4 marked "Christ's death as 'a sacrifice which purifies from sin.'"

[179]See Phil 2:8.

[180]Compare 1 Cor 11:25-26.

70

death or, in other words, "at the cost of his blood" (ἐν τῷ αὐτοῦ αἵματι, v. 25).[181]

Paul takes great care to emphasize the public nature of "God's expression of His righteousness" in the Cross of Christ. In v. 21, he says that God's righteousness "has been revealed" (φανεροῦν). Here in vv. 25-26 he declares that God "publicly displayed" (προτιθέναι) Christ, in his death on the cross, as the "demonstration" (ἔνδειξις) of His righteousness. Paul's gospel is not an abstract philosophy, but the proclamation of a series of concrete, historical events of ultimate significance for all Creation. Paul proclaims that God long ago gave promises to Abraham, and that He recently acted publicly--in the presence of many witnesses--to fulfil those promises by first sending Jesus to die on the cross, and then three days later raising him from the dead.[182]

Paul identifies the crucified Christ as God's "demonstration of His righteousness" (ἡ ἔνδειξις τῆς δικαιοσύνης αὐτοῦ) for two reasons. First, Christ's death serves as "the demonstration of His righteousness because of the remission of the former sins [committed] during the period of God's forbearance" (διὰ τὴν πάρεσιν τῶν προγεγονότων ἁμαρτημάτων ἐν τῇ ἀνοχῇ τοῦ θεοῦ, vv. 25b-26a).[183] In all likelihood, "the period of God's forbearance" refers to the interval preceding "the Day of Wrath and the revelation of God's righteous judgment," during which God's "kindness" and "forbearance" (in

---

[181]On the phrase ἐν τῷ αὐτοῦ αἵματι ("at the cost of his blood"), compare Rom 5:9.

[182]See Paul's summary of his gospel in 1 Cor 15:1-11.

[183]Werner Georg Kümmel ("Πάρεσις und ἔνδειξις: Ein Beitrag zum Verständnis der paulinischen Rechtfertigungslehre," in *Heilsgeschehen und Geschichte* [Marburg: N. G. Elwert Verlag, 1965], 1:260-70), Ernst Käsemann (*Commentary on Romans* [Grand Rapids: William B. Eerdmans Publishing Company, 1980], 91), John Reumann ("The Gospel of the Righteousness of God: Pauline Reinterpretation in Romans 3:21-31," *Int* 20 [1966]: 436), and others argue correctly that πάρεσις here means "remission" of sins, rather than "passing over" sins. Advocates of the alternative view include Barrett (*Romans,* 79-80), Hunter (*Romans,* 47), and Sanday and Headlam (*Romans,* 90).

delaying this judgment) are intended to lead sinners to repentance.[184] Within this span of time, God put forth Christ as "a sacrifice which purifies from sin" (v. 25). Christ's death "purifies from sin," or effects "the remission of the former sins," by establishing the "new covenant" under which "sinners" (i.e., persons outside the "new covenant") become "righteous" (i.e., participants in the "new covenant") through trust in Him.[185] Christ's sacrificial death thus serves as "the demonstration of [God's] righteousness" (toward both Abraham and all nations), inasmuch as it embodies God's commitment to fulfil His covenant-promise to Abraham by giving the "new covenant" of "blessing" (in effect, "the remission of the former sins [committed] during the period of God's forbearance") to Jews and Gentiles alike.

Second, Paul identifies the crucified Christ as "the demonstration of [God's] righteousness" (ἡ ἔνδειξις τῆς δικαιοσύνης αὐτοῦ, v. 26b) because Christ's sacrificial death offers public proof--in "the present time" (see above) --that God Himself is "righteous," inasmuch as He "reckons righteous the person grounded in Jesus' act of trust." Here Paul once again makes reference to the fact that, under His covenant with Abraham, God obligated Himself to establish a "new covenant" with Jews and Gentiles based on trust. God acted publicly, in recent history, to fulfil His "righteous" promise through the Cross of Christ, or "Jesus' act of trust." The Cross "demonstrates" that God is "righteous" toward Abraham inasmuch as it is the means by which God fulfilled his covenantal promise to Abraham. At the same time, the Cross "demonstrates" that God is "righteous" toward all nations inasmuch as it is the means by which God establishes a covenant with (i.e., "reckons righteous") Jews and Gentiles who put their trust in Him (i.e., persons "grounded in Jesus' act of

---

[184]See Rom 2:4-5. For a discussion of the Day of Judgment in Paul's thought, see part I of chapter 8.

[185]For a more complete discussion of how Christ's death purifies from sin (i.e., the *modus operandi* of the atonement), see parts I and II of chapter 4.

trust," or persons who participate in the "new covenant" based on trust established through Christ's sacrificial death).

Conclusion. Romans 3:21-26 has introduced us to a number of important components of Paul's thought. These include sin (ἁμαρτία) and glory (δόξα), righteousness (δικαιοσύνη) and trust (πίστις), the Abrahamic covenant and the "new covenant" (ἡ καινὴ διαθήκη), "God's expression of His righteousness" (δικαιοσύνη θεοῦ) and "Jesus Christ's act of trust" (πίστις Ἰησοῦ Χριστοῦ), "the present time" (ὁ νῦν καιρός) and "[the sphere of] Christ Jesus[' rule]" (ἐν Χριστῷ). Each occupies a place within the "coherent center" of Paul's theology. By defining how the Apostle understands these ideas, we have begun to lay the foundation for a precise delineation of the fourteen "core convictions" which together form that center. We will take up the task of systematically reconstructing Paul's theological center in chapter 4, but we must first pause to consider one more feature of the Apostle's thought--namely, the Adam-Christ typology of Romans 5 and 1 Corinthians 15.

CHAPTER THREE

THE ADAM-CHRIST TYPOLOGY
OF ROMANS 5 AND 1 CORINTHIANS 15

I. PORTRAITS OF ADAM INHERITED BY PAUL

Paul's thought concerning Adam was shaped not only by the ancient account of his creation and fall in Genesis 1-3, but also by the variety of Jewish interpretations of Adam which sprang up between the second century B.C. and the second century A.D.[1] The Pauline portrait of Adam most closely resembles those of two writings within the apocalyptic tradition, namely, 4 Ezra (late first century A.D.) and 2 (Syriac Apocalypse of) Baruch (early second century A.D.). The parallels between their conception of Adam and that of

---

[1]John R. Levison's recent contribution to our understanding of Jewish backgrounds is *Portraits of Adam in Early Judaism: From Sirach to 2 Baruch, Journal for the Study of the Pseudepigrapha* Supplement Series, 1 (Sheffield: Sheffield Academic Press, 1988). On pp. 14-23, Levison offers an essay on "The Inadequacy of Studies of Adam as a Background for Pauline Theology," wherein he criticizes earlier studies (i.e. those by W. D. Davies, Jacob Jervell, C. K. Barrett, Egon Brandenburger, Robin Scroggs, James D. G. Dunn, and N. T. Wright--see the bibliography) primarily because, in their efforts to illuminate Pauline thought, they tend to force earlier texts into Pauline categories and thus fail to do justice to the diversity of portraits of Adam existing in early Judaism. He then proceeds to analyze the "portraits" found in Ecclesiasticus, the Wisdom of Solomon, Philo, Jubilees, Josephus, 4 Ezra, 2 Baruch, and the [Greek and Latin] Life of Adam and Eve. The chapters on 4 Ezra (pp. 113- 27) and 2 Baruch (pp. 129-44) proved particularly helpful in preparing this study.

the Apostle suggest that Jewish apocalyptic (1) served as the dominant influence behind Paul's understanding of Adam, and (2) shaped Adam into a figure Paul found useful for expressing certain of his "core convictions" concerning Christ.

The Figure of Adam in Genesis 1-3 (LXX)

Adam's creation. Genesis recounts how God made man, both male and female, "according to the image of God."[2] God formed Adam, the first man, from the dust of the earth and "breathed into his face the breath of life," so that "the man became a living psyche (ψυχή)."[3] He then formed Eve, the first woman, from material taken from Adam's side and placed her in a beautiful garden with Adam.[4]

Genesis does not state that Adam and Eve were immortal by nature. Instead, God placed the "tree of life" in the center of the garden so that, by eating its fruit, the man and the woman could live forever.[5]

Adam's sin. According to Gen 2:16-17, God had issued one command to Adam:

> You may eat from every tree which is in the garden, but you shall not eat from the tree of the knowledge of good and evil. In whatever day you eat from it, you will die.

Chapter 3 tells how the serpent deceived Eve, so that she and Adam disobeyed God, ate the forbidden fruit, and thus introduced what Paul calls "sin" into the human race.[6]

---

[2]Gen 1:27. All quotations in this section are translations of the Greek (LXX) version of Genesis.

[3]Gen 2:7. On the term ψυχή, see below under "The risen Christ."

[4]Gen 2:8, 18-24.

[5]Gen 2:9; 3:23.

[6]Gen 3:2-14; cf. Rom 5:12; 2 Cor 11:3. On the nature of Adam's "sin," see chapter 2 under "Sin as a 'power.'"

Adam's death. In accordance with God's word, sin led to death. After Adam sinned, God drove him out of the garden and away from the tree of life, so that "nature" took its course and Adam eventually died.[7]

Unlike the later writings examined below, the Genesis account does not specifically address the question of the relationship between the sin of Adam and Eve and the sin of their descendants. It never identifies Adam and Eve as the direct cause of every human sin. However, Genesis does point to the sin of the first human pair as the cause for universal death, inasmuch as their sin led God to deny access to the tree of life not only to Adam and Eve, but to their children as well.

The Figure of Adam in 4 Ezra

Occasion. Although set in the fifth century B.C., "in the reign of Artaxerxes, king of the Persians,"[8] 4 Ezra responds to the crisis of faith sparked within Judaism by the destruction of Jerusalem and the Jewish Temple in A.D. 70. The book consists of seven visions,[9] in which the angel Uriel appears to Ezra and speaks to his concerns. Uriel probably represents the viewpoint of the writer, while the figure of Ezra gives voice to the doubts and frustrations of angry and disillusioned Jews, who had seen their nation's hopes dashed once again. The first man, Adam, plays a prominent role in their discussions.

Adam as the source of the "evil heart." In the first vision (3:1-5:20), Ezra recalls how God gave His Law to the Israelite nation.[10] Israel then transgressed God's commandments, so that the Lord punished the nation by

---

[7]Gen 3:23-25; 5:5; cf. Wis 1:13-16; 2:23-24.

[8]4 Ezra 1:3.

[9]Chapters 3-14, to which a Christian introduction and conclusion (chs. 1-2 and 15-16) were later added.

[10]4 Ezra 3:19.

giving Jerusalem over to the Romans. Are, then, the Jews themselves at fault for the loss of their city? In one sense, they are; but Ezra here speaks for Jews seeking to relieve Israel of responsibility by blaming God for their sin:

> Yet you did not take away from them their evil heart, so that your Law might bring forth fruit in them. For the first Adam, burdened with an evil heart, transgressed and was overcome, as were also all who were descended from him. Thus the disease became permanent; the Law was in the people's heart along with the evil root, but what was good departed, and the evil remained . . . you raised up . . . David. And you commanded him to build a city [i.e., Jerusalem] for your name . . . but the inhabitants of the city transgressed, in everything doing as Adam and all his descendants had done, for they also had the evil heart. So you delivered the city into the hands of your enemies. (4 Ezra 3:20-27)

Ezra shares the conviction of many Jews of the early Christian era, who believed that God had created within Adam an "evil heart,"[11] which the first man then passed on to his descendants as part of their biological inheritance. Although God graciously gave Israel the Law, He declined to remove from them their "evil inclination." So the Jews, like Adam, found it difficult to obey God's commands, or to "do righteousness," and thus fell victim to the "disease" of the "evil heart," which led them into sin. Ezra here serves as spokesman

---

[11]I.e., הַיֵּצֶר הָרָע or "the evil inclination." The translation is somewhat misleading, for the rabbis do not consider הַיֵּצֶר הָרָע to be evil in and of itself; it is not an "evil nature." Instead, the term denotes the human instinct toward survival and self-propagation. If men and women do not rein in this instinct (by, for example, submitting to the Law of God), then it can lead to numerous sins. However, properly controlled and directed, הַיֵּצֶר הָרָע can be a good thing--the very foundation of civilization. As the fourth century Rabbi Samuel ben Nahman says,

> ["]Behold, it was very good["] [i.e., God's words in Gen 1:31] refers . . . [also] to the Evil Desire . . . But for the Evil Desire, however, no man would build a house, take a wife and beget children; and thus said Solomon: Again, I considered all labour and all excelling in work, that it is a man's rivalry with his neighbour (Eccl. 4:4). (Gen. Rab. I. ix. 7)

In *Judaism in the First Centuries of the Christian Era: The Age of the Tannaim* (Cambridge: Harvard University Press, 1927), 1:474-96, George Foot Moore discusses "The Origin of Sin" in Tannaitic Judaism. He gives particular attention to 4 Ezra and early rabbinic teaching concerning הַיֵּצֶר הָרָע ("the evil inclination"). For further discussion of the "evil inclination," see (1) W. D. Davies, *Paul and Rabbinic Judaism: Some Rabbinic Elements in Pauline Theology*, 4th ed. (Philadelphia: Fortress Press, 1980), 20-23, and (2) C. G. Montefiore and H. Loewe, *A Rabbinic Anthology: Selected and Arranged With Comments and Introductions* (London: Macmillan and Co., 1938), 295-314.

for those Jews who sought to blame Adam's "evil heart"--and thus to blame God, its Creator--for their sin and the consequent loss of their city.

Adam as initiator of the present evil age. Like other apocalyptic writings, 4 Ezra looks upon human history since Adam's Fall as the "evil age." Nevertheless, it anticipates the establishment of a "new age," at some point in the future, when God will overcome all evil and inaugurate His eschatological Reign.[12] Those who have not scorned God's Law, but who have been faithful to His covenant, will share in that new age. It is the righteous "to whom the age belongs and for whose sake the age was made."[13]

Uriel agrees with Ezra that Adam did possess the "evil heart," that he did pass it on to his descendants, and that this "evil inclination"--which infects the entire human race--has been the source of much sorrow and wickedness down through the centuries. Therefore, in the sense that the "evil heart" found in all human beings may be traced back to Adam, Uriel holds the father of the human race responsible for making this present age an "evil age." As the angel says in 4:27b, 30,

> . . . this age is full of sadness and infirmities . . . For a grain of evil seed was sown in Adam's heart from the beginning, and how much ungodliness it has produced until now, and will produce until the time of threshing comes!

In seeking to explain why God has permitted such evil, Uriel, in 7:3-16, sets the age to come in relationship to the present age by comparing it to a wide sea that can only be entered through a narrow channel, or a fair city that can only be approached through a dangerous pass, flanked by fire and water. The angel declares:

---

[12]See part I of chapter 2.

[13]4 Ezra 9:13b. Since only Jews possess the Law, only Jews can do "righteousness." This means, then, that only Law-abiding Jews may participate in God's coming eschatological Rule.

So also is Israel's portion. For I made the world for their sake, and when Adam transgressed my statutes, what had been made was judged. And so the entrances of this world were made narrow and sorrowful and toilsome; they are few and evil, full of dangers and involved in great hardships. But the entrances of the greater world are broad and safe, and really yield the fruit of immortality. Therefore unless the living pass through the difficult and vain experiences, they can never receive those things that have been reserved for them. (4 Ezra 7:10-14)

4 Ezra, then, portrays Adam as the initiator of "the present evil age," the ultimate (human) cause of the suffering of mankind. In *Portraits of Adam in Early Judaism*, John R. Levison makes this important observation:

By aligning Adam with sinners and the present age, Uriel implicitly excludes him from obtaining a share in the world to come, in the company of the righteous. Adam neither possesses a share in nor exercises any influence upon the age to come. (119)

Adam and individual responsibility for sin. Even though the Creator placed the "evil inclination" within Adam and thus within the entire human race, and even though Adam succumbed to it and thus initiated "the present evil age," Uriel refuses to relieve sinners of responsibility for their own actions. Instead, he maintains that it is possible for a person to overcome the "evil inclination" within him/herself, so as to "keep the Law of the Lawgiver perfectly."[14] When Ezra takes pity on the unrighteous because they endure difficulties in the present age, and yet have no hope for relief in the age to come, the angel rebukes him with these words:

You are not a better judge than God, or wiser than the Most High! Let many perish who are now living, rather than that the Law of God which is set before them be disregarded! For God strictly commanded those who came into the world, when they came, what they should do to live, and what they should observe to avoid punishment. Nevertheless they were not obedient . . . They scorned His Law, and denied His covenants; they have been unfaithful to his statutes and have not performed his

---

[14]See 4 Ezra 7:89, 92.

works. Therefore, Ezra, empty things are for the empty, and full things for the full. (4 Ezra 7:19-22a, 24-25)

Ezra makes several statements which, at first, appear to blame Adam for the sins his offspring commit and for the punishment they consequently endure. Yet, in the end, even he upholds a certain tension between Adamic responsibility for sin and eschatological judgment (inasmuch as Adam is the source of the "evil inclination," which leads his descendants into sin and thus results in condemnation) and individual responsibility for one's own sins (in the sense that human beings are not forced into sin by Adam, but freely choose--like Adam--to surrender to the "evil inclination" their forefather passed on to them). For example, in 7:46-48 [116-18], Ezra seems to identify Adam as the direct cause of all human sin and all human suffering, both in the present age and in the age to come:

> It would have been better if the earth had not produced Adam, or else, when it had produced him, had restrained him from sinning. For what good is it to all that they live in sorrow now and expect punishment after death? O Adam, what have you done? For though it was you who sinned, the fall was not yours alone, but ours also who are your descendants.

Yet the words that follow shift the focus to the liability of individual sinners:

> For what good is it to us, if an eternal age has been promised to us, but we have done deeds that bring death? . . . For while we lived and committed iniquity we did not consider what we should suffer after death. (4 Ezra 7:49 [119], 56 [126].

In the final analysis, then, 4 Ezra portrays Adam as the ultimate (human) source of the "evil inclination," but not the cause of all human sin. He was the first to succumb to the promptings of an "evil heart," but he did not thereby become responsible for the unrighteousness of others. 4 Ezra finds a correspondence, but not a causal connection, between the sin and condemnation of Adam and the sin and condemnation of his offspring. We should, therefore, not interpret this apocalypse in a way that destroys the tension between Adamic responsibility for human sin and the individual sinner's responsibility for his/her own actions and their consequences. In 4 Ezra 7:57-59 [127-29], the angel Uriel removes any uncertainty regarding the author's position with this strong affirmation of individual responsibility for sin:

> This is the meaning of the contest which every man who is born on earth shall wage, that if he is defeated [by succumbing to the "evil inclination," as Adam did,] he shall suffer what you have said, [namely, eschatological punishment,] but if he is victorious he shall receive what I have said, [namely, a place in the new age to come]. For this is the way of which Moses, while he was alive, spoke to the people, saying, "Choose for yourself life, that you may live!"

Adam as the cause of universal death. Although the author of 4 Ezra refuses to hold Adam responsible for all human sins, he does not hesitate to blame the father of humankind for universal death:

> And you laid upon him [i.e., Adam] one commandment of yours; but he transgressed it, and immediately you appointed death for him and for his descendants. (4 Ezra 3:7a)

Levison[15] objects to this interpretation by citing 3:7b-10 as evidence that death is not "hereditary," but that each sinner's demise is ultimately his/her own responsibility:

> From him there sprang nations and tribes, peoples and clans, without number. And every nation walked after its own will and did ungodly things before you and scorned you, and you did not hinder them. But again, in its time you brought the flood upon the inhabitants of the world and destroyed them. And the same fate befell them: As death came upon Adam, so the flood upon them.

In support of this view, Levison observes that Noah, who was not a sinner but a righteous man, "escaped the punishment of the flood and continued to live" (3:11). He therefore concludes that "Ezra draws only a correspondence, not a causal connection, between the death of Adam and the sinful nations."

---

[15]*Portraits of Adam*, 116.

Levison is correct to find an element of individual liability for death in 4 Ezra, for this writer does not look upon the unrighteous as innocent victims. Rather, they deserve to die because, like Adam, they "have done deeds that bring death."[16]

However, Dr. Levison fails to appreciate the sharp distinction 4 Ezra draws between the "unrighteous" (i.e., Law-less Gentiles and unfaithful Jews) and the "righteous" (i.e., the few Law-abiding Jews).[17] While the former have done "deeds that bring death" and are thus responsible, in some sense, for their own demise; the latter, who have "overcome the evil thought," are innocent of such wrongdoing.

If, as Levison suggests, there is only a correspondence--but not a causal connection--between Adam's death and the death of his descendants, then we would assume that the righteous would not die. Nevertheless, in 4 Ezra, both the righteous (including Noah) and the unrighteous do eventually die "when the decisive decree has gone forth from the Most High."[18] After death, the righteous receive a reward of glory, while the unrighteous endure torment; but both must first pass through death. Why do the righteous experience death along with the sinners? Because 4 Ezra does indeed see a causal connection between the death of Adam and the death of all his descendants!

Exactly how did the author of 4 Ezra maintain this tension, within his mind, between Adamic and individual responsibility for death? While he may not have been concerned with such questions, it seems reasonable to suppose

---

[16]4 Ezra 7:49 [119] b. In this context, what the author means by "death" is eschatological punishment. In his study of the relationship between death, resurrection and eschatological life in Jewish apocalyptic and in Paul (*The Defeat of Death: Apocalyptic Eschatology in 1 Corinthians 15 and Romans 5, Journal for the Study of the New Testament* Supplement Series, 22 [Sheffield: Sheffield Academic Press, 1988]), Martinus C. de Boer distinguishes three meanings of "death" common to this literature--namely, (1) "bodily or physical demise," (2) "moral death," and (3) "perdition," all of which are held together by the notion of "death" as separation from God (see esp. pp. 83-84).

[17]See, e.g., 4 Ezra 7: [45-48], [76-77]; 9:36.

[18]See 4 Ezra 7:[75-99].

that this writer followed the Genesis account in viewing death as the penalty ordained by God for any sin.[19] Thus, all sinners are guilty of bringing about their own deaths. At the same time, this writer was well-acquainted with the story of how, after Adam transgressed, God barred Adam and his children from the tree of life and thereby "appointed death for him and his descendants."[20] Thus, both sinners and the righteous die because of Adam's transgression. The author may have concluded, then, that both the righteous and the unrighteous share equally the penalty of death, but they do not share equally the burden of responsibility for their deaths. When a sinner dies, both s/he (because s/he sinned) and Adam (because he caused all his descendants to be cut off from the tree of life) bear responsibility for his/her death; but when a righteous person dies, only Adam is responsible. This would explain how 4 Ezra can simultaneously hold up Adam as the ultimate cause of death for all humans, and yet, at the same time, blame individual sinners for their own destruction. In short, 4 Ezra draws both a causal connection and a correspondence between the death of Adam and the death of sinners, but only a causal connection between the death of Adam and the death of the righteous.

The Figure of Adam in 2 Baruch

Occasion. Like 4 Ezra, 2 Baruch responds to the first century devastation of Jerusalem and its Temple by the Roman army. In the face of such adversities, Baruch asks the Lord,

> What have they [i.e., the Jews] profited who have knowledge before you, and who did not walk in vanity like the rest of the nations, . . . but always feared you and did not leave your ways? (2 Apoc. Bar. 14:5)

---

[19]See Gen 3:17.

[20]See Gen 3:23-25; 4 Ezra 3:7.

The Lord speaks to His servant, explaining why such trials are necessary and offering reassurance that, in the end, all will be well for the righteous. Again, the figure of Adam plays an important role in the writer's theodicy.

Adam as the first sinner. 2 Baruch does not identify Adam as the source of the "evil inclination," but it does portray him as the first sinner.[21] The writer repeatedly characterizes sin as the refusal of the creature to subject him/herself to the Creator.[22] Since the Creator has expressed His will in the Mosaic Law, 2 Baruch also describes sin, or the lack of submission to God, as "unrighteousness," or refusal to observe the Law.[23]

Adam as the initiator of death and the trials of the present age. The writer agrees with 4 Ezra that Adam's transgression brought terrible results for his offspring. First, 2 Baruch blames Adam for universal human death: ". . . Adam sinned first and has brought death upon all who were not in his own time."[24]

Second, Adam's transgression unleashed the woes of the present evil age:

> For when he trangressed, untimely death came into being, mourning was mentioned, affliction was prepared, illness was created, labor accomplished, pride began to come into existence, the realm of death[25] began to ask to be renewed with blood, the conception of children came about, the

---

[21]See 2 Apoc. Bar. 54:15; 56:5.

[22]See, e.g., 2 Apoc. Bar. 48:46; 54:14-15; cf. 17:2, 4; 54:5.

[23]See, e.g., 2 Apoc. Bar. 17:4-18:2; 48:39, 47; 51:4; 54:5, 14-15. Once again, this means that only Jews may qualify as "righteous" since they alone possess the Law.

[24]2 Apoc. Bar. 54:15; cf. 17:2-3; 23:4; 56:6. While 2 Baruch focuses primarily on Adam as the ultimate cause of human death, this book also resembles 4 Ezra in that it sees a correspondence between the death of Adam and the deaths of guilty sinners. Two important passages in this regard are (1) 2 Apoc. Bar. 19:8, which speaks of "the day death was decreed against those who trespassed," and (2) 2 Apoc. Bar. 54:14, which declares that Law-breakers are "justly perishing."

[25]On the "realm of death," see 23:4-5.

passion of the parents was produced, the loftiness of men was humiliated, and goodness vanished. (2 Apoc. Bar. 56:6)

Both righteous and unrighteous alike must endure these two consequences of Adam's sin; but Baruch urges the righteous to take heart, for they hold God's promise of resurrection and glorification in the new age to come.[26] To Law-abiding Jews he says,

Enjoy yourselves in the suffering which you suffer now . . . Prepare your souls for that which is kept for you, and make ready your souls for the reward which is preserved for you. (2 Apoc. Bar. 52:6a, 7; cf. 19:7)

Adam and individual responsibility for sin. While 2 Baruch categorically blames Adam for earthly suffering and death, the book stands with the angel Uriel of 4 Ezra in placing responsibility for sin, and whether or not one receives a place in the new age, squarely upon the shoulders of the individual. In 2 Apoc. Bar. 17:2-18:2, the author describes the Jewish Law as a "lamp" which illuminates Israel. Moses, who "took from the light" in that "he subjected himself to Him who created him," is contrasted to Adam, who remained in "darkness" because he "transgressed that which he was commanded." All human beings, says Baruch, "imitate" either Moses or Adam by obeying or rejecting God's Law. Thus, Moses and Adam serve as paradigms for the fundamental human decision--namely, the decision to submit to one's Creator by observing His Law, or to rebel against Him by transgressing His commandments.

Adam is not answerable for the sins of his descendants. Instead, the Law holds accountable every individual for the choices s/he makes.[27] Baruch declares in chapter 54 that

---

[26]See, e.g., 2 Apoc. Bar. 48:48-51:16; cf. 15:7-8; 73:1-74:3, which describes the "new age" as restoration of the primeval bliss enjoyed by Adam before the Fall and curses of Genesis 3.

[27]See, e.g., 2 Apoc. Bar. 15:5-6; 19:3; 48:46-47.

Those who do not love your Law are justly perishing. And the torment of judgment will fall upon those who have not subjected themselves to your power. For, although Adam sinned first and has brought death upon all who were not in his own time, yet each of them who has been born from him has prepared for himself the coming torment. And further, each of them has chosen for himself the coming glory . . . Adam is, therefore, not the cause [of "destruction," or "retribution"], except only for himself, but each of us has become our own Adam.[28]

In summary, 2 Baruch's portrait of Adam follows the Genesis account in identifying Adam (along with Eve) as the first to sin. It follows the portrait found in 4 Ezra when it maintains that, because of Adam's transgression, all human beings must endure the evils of the present age and, finally, death. Nevertheless, Adam does not cause his descendants to sin. Rather, each person decides for him/herself whether to imitate Moses by choosing the righteousness which leads to resurrection and eschatological glory, or to imitate Adam by choosing disobedience which results in condemnation.

---

[28]2 Apoc. Bar. 54:14-15, 19. Levison (*Portraits of Adam*, 138) observes that the polemical nature of Baruch's statements ("although Adam sinned first"; "Adam is, therefore, not the cause") suggests "that the author is responding to a view according to which hereditary sinfulness was attributed to Adam's transgression." In 48:42-43, Baruch himself appears to blame Adam and Eve for their wicked descendants when he asks,

> O Adam, what did you do to all who were born after you? And what will be said of the first Eve who obeyed the serpent, so that this whole multitude is going to corruption? And countless are those whom the fire devours.

The context, however, prohibits us from interpreting Baruch's inquiry in a manner which relieves individuals from responsibility for their own sins. Verse 40 affirms that "each of the inhabitants of the earth knew when he acted unrighteously, and they did not know my Law because of their pride." Furthermore, vv. 46-47 hold all Adam's children accountable before God:

> . . . those who are born from him . . . sinned before you, those who existed and did not recognize you as their Creator. And concerning all of those, their end will put them to shame, and your Law which they transgressed will repay them on your day. (See Levison's discussion of this text in *Portraits of Adam*, 135-36.)

II. ADAM AND CHRIST
IN ROMANS 5:12-21 AND 1 CORINTHIANS 15:20-23, 44-49

Paul mentions Adam by name in only two passages--namely, Rom 5:12-21 and 1 Cor 15:20-23, 44-49.[29] We will briefly examine each passage in its context before turning to a discussion of how Paul uses the figure of Adam to illuminate the person and work of Christ.[30]

Context of Romans 5:12-21[31]

Relationship to Romans 1:18-5:11. Earlier in Romans, Paul has sought to defend his gospel of righteousness "apart from the Law" by arguing that, in the past, all Jews have been trapped--along with all Gentiles--under the dominion of Sin, in spite of the Jews' possession of the Mosaic covenant and its Law.[32] However, God has acted to release humankind from Sin by (1) promising to Abraham a "new covenant" for all nations, which would be based on trust and thus independent of the Mosaic covenant's racial limitations, and

---

[29]Paul also has Adam in mind in Phil 2:5-8, which we will discuss in chapter 4. A. J. M. Wedderburn ("Adam in Paul's Letter to the Romans," in *Studia Biblica 1978: III. Papers on Paul and Other New Testament Authors. Sixth International Congress on Biblical Studies: Oxford, 3-7 April 1978*, ed. E. A. Livingstone, *Journal for the Study of the New Testament* Supplement Series, 3 [Sheffield: JSOT Press, 1980], 413-30) sees Adam in Rom 1:18-32 and 7:7-11. D. J. W. Milne ("Genesis 3 in the Letter to the Romans," *RTR* 39 [1980]: 10-18) discusses these same texts, adding Rom 8:19-22 (along with the obvious 5:12-19). James D. G. Dunn (*Christology in the Making: A New Testament Inquiry Into the Origins of the Doctrine of the Incarnation* [Philadelphia: The Westminster Press, 1980], 101-102) adds Rom 3:23. Michael Neary contributes an essay on "Creation and Pauline Soteriology" in *ITQ* 50 (1983/84): 1-34.

[30]Some ancient Jewish writings stress the role Eve played in bringing sin and death into the world over that of Adam. For example, in Greek Life of Adam and Eve 32:2, Eve offers up this lament: "I have sinned, O God; . . . and all sin in creation has come about through me" (cf. 10:2; 14:2; Sir 25:24). Paul focuses on Adam, rather than Eve, because (1) he is following certain well-established traditions, from the apocalyptic genre, which were built more around Adam than around Eve, and (2) directing his readers' attention to the male partner in the first human couple proves most helpful in setting forth the meaning and significance of the "one man," Jesus Christ.

[31]See chapter 2 for a more complete discussion of Paul's purpose in writing his epistle to the Romans.

[32]See Rom 1:18-3:20.

then (2) acting to establish that "new covenant" through the sacrificial death of Jesus Christ.[33]

Beginning in Rom 4:23, Paul turns to "the present time,"[34] which has been shaped by God's immeasurable "goodwill" (χάρις) in that, "while we were yet sinners, Christ died for us." Those who trust in Him are now rejoicing in their reconciliation with God under the "new covenant" and looking forward to their future salvation when Christ returns.[35]

Chapter 5, verses 12-21, form an important transition within Romans. By beginning this section of his epistle with διὰ τοῦτο ("therefore"), Paul notifies his readers that, in the subsequent verses, he will present the conclusion to be drawn from what he has said thus far.

Drawing upon resources from his Jewish past, Paul sets forth Adam as a "type" (τύπος, v. 14) of the Christ "who was to come."[36] Summing up all human existence in these two pivotal figures, Paul contrasts humanity's past under the dominion of Sin and Death (i.e., the human sphere as determined by Adam, described in 1:18-3:20) with the believers' present under the dominion of God's goodwill (i.e., the human sphere as determined by [God through] Christ, Paul's focus in 4:23-5:11), which is characterized by the righteousness

---

[33]See Rom 3:21-4:22.

[34]See part I of chapter 2.

[35]See Rom 4:23-5:11; cf. 5:20.

[36]A cognate of τύπτειν ("to strike"), the term τύπος ("type"), in ancient Greek, most often referred to the "mark," or "stamp," or "impression" left when one object--the ἀντίτυπος or "antitype" (e.g. a signet ring)--struck another object (e.g. the wax seal on a letter). The "type" was, by no means, identical to its "antitype;" but there was a correspondence between the two which enabled the "type" to "witness" to the nature and characteristics of the "antitype." This is most likely the sense in which Paul views Adam as serving as a "type" of Jesus Christ in Romans 5. For Paul, the story of Adam serves as one more example of how the Law and the Prophets "witness" to God's righteous action in Christ (see Rom 3:21).

However, τύπος can express a number of other ideas as well. Paul himself uses the term to speak of a "standard" of teaching in Rom 6:17, or an "example" in 1 Cor 10:6, 11; Phil 3:17; and 1 Thess 1:7. For a more comprehensive study of the τύπος word group, see TDNT, 8:246-59.

and sure hope of "eschatological life" effected through the Cross of Christ (as described in 3:21-4:22).

Structure of Romans 5:12-21. In Rom 5:12-14, Paul describes how "the transgression of Adam" (v. 14) caused the human past to be shaped by Sin and Death. Verse 12 contains Paul's thesis, which reads as follows:

> Therefore, just as sin came into the world through one man, [Adam,] and death [came into the world] through [Adam's] sin, so also did death spread to all persons because all sinned.

Some of Paul's Jewish readers may object to this statement because they define "sin" as breaking an express command of God. According to this line of reasoning, God had expressly forbidden Adam from eating the fruit of the tree of knowledge of good and evil, and He had given His Law to Moses and Israel in the wilderness. Since many who lived between the time of Adam and Moses received no commandments, they could not disobey--they could not "sin." Paul therefore errs when he says that "all sinned."

The Apostle answers this possible objection in vv. 13-14. He insists that "sin," as he conceives of it,[37] was indeed "in the world before the time of the Law" (v. 13). Therefore "death reigned from the time of Adam to the time of Moses--even over those who did not commit a sin like the transgression of Adam" (v. 14) by breaking an express command of God.

In vv. 15-17, Paul shifts his gaze from humanity as shaped by Adam to humanity as shaped by Christ. What God has accomplished through the Cross of Jesus Christ is much greater than what Adam brought upon humanity through his sin. Christ did not merely "inaugurate a new race of humanity," free from Sin and Death. Instead, "in response to many trespasses," he reached back into Adam's fallen race and effected righteousness for sinners who

---

[37]See chapter 2 under "Sin as a 'power.'" Paul follows 2 Baruch in defining "sin" as the refusal of the creature to submit to the Creator as Lord (see above under "Adam as the first sinner").

trust in him. "His role was that of obedience, not merely in place of disobedience but in order to undo that disobedience."[38]

In vv. 18-21, Paul sums up ("so then" [ἄρα οὖν], v. 18) everything he has said concerning the work of Adam ("trespass," "disobedience"), the work of Christ ("righteous deed," "obedience"), and what each has brought to Adam's race ("sin" and "condemnation" vs. "the righteousness [which means 'eschatological] life'"). Verses 20-21 contain a note (inspired by vv. 13-14) explaining the Law's function of "increasing the trespass" of Adam and his descendants (see below). The Apostle concludes by once again reminding his readers (after the manner of vv. 15-17) of the overwhelming greatness of God's act of goodwill in comparison with the trespasses of Adam and his offspring: "But where sin has increased, [God's] goodwill has overflowed all the more."

Relationship to the chapters which follow. By presenting Adam as a "type" of Christ, the Apostle reinforces a point he has already made--namely, that God has acted to establish a "new covenant," or "righteousness," through the "one man" Jesus Christ. This man's sacrificial death (rather than, for example, the Law) serves as the bridge--for those who trust--from the past under Sin to a present (and future) under God's goodwill (χάρις).[39]

At the same time, Paul's Adam-Christ typology enables him to lay the groundwork for several themes he develops in chapter 6 and in succeeding chapters of this letter: First, the story of Adam's "disobedience" allows the Apostle to cast Christ's going to the Cross--and thus our "death with Christ"--in terms of "obedience."[40] Second, Jewish tradition tends to view "all

---

[38]See N. T. Wright, "Adam in Pauline Christology," in *Society of Biblical Literature 1983 Seminar Papers* (Chico, CA: Scholars Press, 1983), 372. In like manner, Barrett (*Romans*, 113) writes: "The act of grace does not balance the act of sin; it overbalances it."

[39]See, e.g., Rom 3:24-31; 4:6-8; 5:6-11.

[40]See, e.g., Rom 6:12, 16-18 (cf. 1:5; 16:26), along with chapter 6.

persons" as participating, with Adam, in sin.[41] This gives Paul an opening for dividing the human race into two groups--namely, (1) those who remain, with Adam, under the dominion of Sin, and (2) those who are released, through Christ, into the dominion of God.[42] Finally, since his Jewish contemporaries interpreted universal human death as the penalty for sin (whether it be the sin of Adam, or Eve, or of each individual), Paul is able to contrast the dominion of Sin with the dominion of God (with its promise of resurrection "with Christ") as leading, respectively, to death or "eschatological life."[43]

Translation of Romans 5:12-21[44]

(12) Therefore, just as sin came into the world through one man, [Adam,] and death [came into the world] through [Adam's] sin, so also did

---

[41]See, e.g., the string of OT passages Paul quotes in Rom 3:9-18.

[42]See, e.g., Rom 6:17-18, 22. A similar division of Adam's offspring is made in Sir 36:10-15, where God separates the pious from the sinners.

[43]See, e.g., Rom 6:4-11, 13-14, 21-23.

[44]Paul's compact style makes an adequate English translation of Rom 5:12-21 difficult. The rendering of the New English Bible is much better than most. C. E. B. Cranfield (*A Critical and Exegetical Commentary on the Epistle to the Romans*, The International Critical Commentary [Edinburgh: T. & T. Clark, 1975], 269-95) has also proven quite helpful on several points--particularly the opening statements of vv. 15 and 16.

The Apostle has constructed this text using a number of aural signals, which help the reader/hearer to follow his argument: First, the passage contains six comparisons (vv. 12, 15, 16, 18, 19, 21). The writer consistently opens the comparison with ὥσπερ ("just as") or ὡς ("as"), and then completes it (with the exception of v. 16, where the reader must supply the appropriate terms) with οὕτως καί or καὶ οὕτως ("so also").

Second, this passage sets forth a great number of contrasts between what Adam did and what God/Christ did, and the respective results of each action. After choosing a word to express some aspect of Adam's work, Paul takes great care (wherever possible) to use a word with a similar sound or ending to express the contraposing aspect of Christ's work (e.g., παράπτωμα ["trespass"] versus χάρισμα ["act of goodwill"], and παραπτώματι ["trespass"] versus χάριτι ["goodwill (expressed)"] in v. 15, κρίμα ["judgment"] versus χάρισμα ["act of goodwill"], and κατάκριμα ["condemnation"] versus δικαίωμα ["righteousness"] in v. 16, παραπτώματος ["trespass"] versus δικαιώματος ["righteous deed"] in v. 18, and παρακοῆς ["disobedience"] versus ὑπακοῆς ["obedience"], and ἁμαρτωλοί ["sinners"] versus δίκαιοι ["righteous"] in v. 19). This built-in aid to interpretation cannot be captured in an English translation, but careful attention to these matters proves quite helpful in discerning Paul's meaning.

death spread to all persons (ἄνθρωποι) because (ἐφ᾿ ᾧ)[45] all sinned. (13) [I can rightfully say that "all" humans sinned--including those who lived before the giving of the Law--]because sin was [already] in the world before the time of the Law, but sin is not [formally] charged [to one's "account"] (ἐλλογεῖν) when there is no Law. (14) Nevertheless, death reigned from the time of Adam to the time of Moses--even over those who did not commit [a] sin like the transgression of Adam, who was a type (τύπος) of the [man] who was to come.

(15) But [it is] not [a mere case of] "As [is Adam's] trespass, so also [is God's] act of goodwill (χάρισμα)."[46] [God's act of goodwill is infinitely greater than Adam's trespass] because if the many died because of the one [man Adam]'s trespass, [then it is a] much greater [thing that] God's expression of His goodwill (ἡ χάρις τοῦ θεοῦ)--even the gift [of being] within [the sphere determined by] the goodwill [expressed] through the one man

---

[45]Most scholars now agree that, by ἐφ᾿ ᾧ, Paul here means "because" (cf. 2 Cor 5:4; Phil 3:12; 4:10). For detailed discussions of this matter, see (1) Cranfield, *Romans*, 1:274-79, and (2) S. Lewis Johnson, Jr., "Romans 5:12--An Exercise in Exegesis and Theology," in *New Dimensions in New Testament Study*, ed. Richard N. Longenecker and Merrill C. Tenney (Grand Rapids: Zondervan Publishing House, 1974), 303-305.

Through an article entitled "The Consecutive Meaning of ἐφ᾿ ᾧ in Romans 5:12" (*NTS* 39 [1993]: 321-39), Joseph A. Fitzmyer nearly persuades us that ἐφ᾿ ᾧ here communicates the idea of result:

Therefore, just as sin entered the world through one man, and death came through sin; so death spread to all human beings, *with the result that* all have sinned.

This translation is certainly plausible--especially if we understand "all sinned" (or "death spread to all") in terms of universal participation in the "present evil age" (see part II of chapter 2). It falls short, however, by not fully taking into account the nature of the comparison, structured around ὥσπερ and καὶ οὕτως, within which ἐφ᾿ ᾧ appears. In the five other comparisons Paul makes in this context, the idea introduced by ὥσπερ or ὡς is directly analogous to that introduced by οὕτως καί or καὶ οὕτως (the *greatness* of "Adam's trespass" versus the *greatness* of "[God's] act of goodwill" in v. 15, the *result* of Adam's "sinning" or "trespass" or "disobedience" versus the *result* of God's "gift" or Christ's "righteous deed" or "obedience" in vv. 16, 18 and 19, and the *"reign"* of "Sin" versus the *"reign"* of God's "goodwill" in v. 21). Rendering ἐφ᾿ ᾧ as "because" enables Rom 5:12 to function in the same way as a comparison (the *"sin"* of Adam *resulting in "death"* versus the *sin* of "all" *resulting in "death"*). Fitzmyer's *translation* (the *"sin"* of Adam *resulting in "death"* versus *"death" resulting in "sin"*) destroys the comparison Paul apparently intends to make. Fitzmyer's *interpretation* of this verse ("the ἐφ᾿ ᾧ clause expresses a result of the sin of Adam" [339]--i.e. Fitzmyer understands Paul to be making the following comparison: "Just as Adam effected sin and death, so also do all humans effect sin and death as a result of Adam's sin") is more acceptable, but does not do justice to the *position* of the ἐφ᾿ ᾧ "result" clause within the text. The context therefore leads us to understand ἐφ᾿ ᾧ in Rom 5:12 to mean "because," rather than "with the result that."

[46]Benedict Englezakis ("Rom 5:12-15 and the Pauline Teaching on the Lord's Death: Some Observations," *Bib* 58 [1977]: 233) appropriately renders this verse: "But what a difference between the trespass and the gift of the grace!"

Jesus Christ (ἡ δωρεὰ ἐν χάριτι τῇ τοῦ ἑνὸς ἀνθρώπου Ἰησοῦ Χριστοῦ)--has overflowed toward the many! (16) And [it is] not [a case of] "As [is that which came about] through the one [man Adam]'s sinning, [so also is] the gift (δώρημα)." [God's gift is infinitely greater than that which came about through Adam's sinning] because the judgment issued in response to [Adam's] one [trespass led] to condemnation, but [God's] act of goodwill (χάρισμα), given in response to many trespasses, [led] to righteousness. (17) [God's gift is infinitely greater than that which came about through Adam's sinning] because if, because of the trespass of the one [man, Adam], death reigned through [that] one [man]; [then it is a] much greater [thing that] those who are receiving the overflow of [God's] goodwill--even the gift of righteousness--will reign within [the sphere where "eschatological] life" [is the rule] (ἐν ζωῇ) through the one [man] Jesus Christ.

(18) So then, as all persons [enter] into condemnation through the trespass of the one [man Adam], so also [do] all persons [enter] into the righteousness [which means "eschatological] life" (δικαίωσις ζωῆς) through the righteous deed of the one [man Jesus Christ]. (19) [I can rightfully say that persons enter into condemnation through Adam, while they enter into righteousness through Christ,] because just as, through the disobedience of the one man, [Adam,] the many became sinners; so also, through the obedience of the one [man, Jesus Christ,] the many will become righteous. (20) Now the Law crept in for the purpose of increasing the trespass [formally charged to one's account].[47] But where sin has increased, [God's] goodwill has overflowed all the more, (21) in order that, just as Sin reigned within [the sphere where] death [is the rule] (ἐν τῷ θανάτῳ), so also may [God's] goodwill reign, through righteousness, toward the end of "eschatological life" (ζωὴ αἰώνιος), through Jesus Christ our Lord.

Context of 1 Corinthians 15:20-23, 44-49

In 1 Cor 7:1-16:4, Paul addresses, one by one, several issues raised in a letter from the church at Corinth.[48] Chapter 15 deals with questions concerning the Resurrection. "Some" within the Corinthian congregation had been saying that "there is no Resurrection of the dead."[49] Since this church

---

[47]See v. 13.

[48]See 1 Cor 7:1, 25; 8:1; 12:1; 16:1.

[49]See 1 Cor 15:12. For discussion and bibliography on the meaning of this phrase, see (1) Hermann Binder, "Zum geschichtlichen Hintergrund von 1 Kor 15:12," *TZ* 46 (1990): 193-201, (2) Ralph P. Martin, *The Spirit and the Congregation: Studies in 1 Corinthians 12-15* (Grand Rapids: William B. Eerdmans Publishing Company, 1984), (3) Gerhard Sellin, "'Die Auferstehung ist schon geschehen': Zur Spiritualisierung apokalyptischer Terminologie im Neuen

probably included a number of Greeks who thought of life after death in terms of release from the body, at least part of the problem may have been their difficulty with understanding or accepting the Jewish idea of the bodily Resurrection of the dead.[50] Some were ridiculing this notion, asking "how" the dead could be so raised, since there seemed to be no "sort of body" to clothe them.[51]

Paul lays the foundation for his rebuttal in 15:1-11, where he recalls the testimony of the gospel that God has raised Christ from the dead, and that there are many eyewitnesses to that reality. Then, in 15:12-34, he refutes those who deny the Resurrection: First, he points out that such a teaching is inconsistent with the historical fact of Christ's resurrection, the apostolic witness, and the Corinthians' own confession and hope (vv. 12-19). Second, he relates Christ's resurrection to the general Resurrection of the righteous, God's victory over His enemies, and the establishment of His Rule (all anticipated in apocalyptic writings) by identifying Christ as "the first-fruits of those who have fallen asleep" (vv. 20-28).[52] At this point, the Apostle contrasts Christ to Adam as a way of shedding light on the nature of Christ's role as "first-fruits." Third, he calls upon the erring Christians to "come to their senses" in light of the incongruity between a denial of the Resurrection and the Corinthians' (and certainly Paul's) own practice (vv. 29-34).

Testament," *NovT* 25 (1983): 220-37, and (4) A. J. M. Wedderburn, "The Problem of the Denial of the Resurrection in 1 Corinthians 15," *NovT* 23 (1981): 229-41.

[50]Paul's words in 2 Cor 5:1-4 (discussed in chapter 8) suggest that the concept of a bodily resurrection from the dead did meet with some resistance among the Corinthians. For a discussion of the separation of the ψυχή ("psyche") from the σῶμα ("body") as a common Greek understanding of death, see chapter 5, along with the article by C. Clifton Black, II, entitled "Pauline Perspectives on Death in Romans 5-8," *JBL* 103 (1984): 418.

[51]See 1 Cor 15:35.

[52]On Christ as "first-fruits," see chapter 5, along with the discussion which follows.

Finally, in 15:35-58, Paul takes up the matter of the resurrection body: First, he establishes that God has proven capable of creating many different types of bodies, so that "there is [such a thing as] a spiritual body"[53] characteristic of the Resurrection (vv. 35-49). Here again Paul sets Adam alongside Christ as a means of highlighting certain differences between the "earthly" bodies we now enjoy and the "heavenly" bodies we will receive in the transformation that will occur when Christ comes again (vv. 50-58).

Translation of 1 Corinthians 15:20-23, 44-49

(20) But now Christ has been raised from the dead [as] the firstfruits of those who have fallen asleep. (21) [I can rightfully set apart Christ from the remainder of the dead as the first of many to share in the Resurrection] because since death [became a reality] through a [single] man, [Adam,] the Resurrection from the dead also [has become a reality] through a [single] man, [Jesus Christ]. (22) [I can rightfully say that both death and the Resurrection from the dead have become realities through a single man] because just as, within [the sphere determined by] Adam, all [persons] die; in the same way also, within [the sphere determined by] Christ, all [persons] will be made alive. (23) But each is made alive in its own order:[54] Christ, the first-fruits, [is made alive]; then those who belong to Christ [will be made alive] at the time of his coming.

(44) It is sowed a psychical body; it is raised a spiritual body. If there is [such a thing as] a psychical body [(and there is)]; [then] there is also [such a thing as] a spiritual [body]. (45) Just as it has been written [that] "The" first "man," Adam, "became a living psyche;" [so also has] the last Adam, [Jesus Christ, become] a life-giving Spirit.[55] (46) But the spiritual [body is] not first; instead, the psychical [body comes first, and] then the spiritual [body]. (47) The first man [Adam was] from [the] earth, [and was] earthly;

---

[53]See 1 Cor 15:44.

[54]The Greek noun τάγμα ("order") usually refers to a "group," or "class," or "rank" of persons--often to a military unit (see *TDNT*, 8:31-32). Therefore when Paul says "each is made alive in its own order," he is not--with the word τάγμα--setting forth a temporal "order," but dividing the totality of those who participate in the Resurrection into two groups: (1) Christ, who makes up a group of one, whom he designates "the first-fruits;" and (2) all other persons raised from the dead, whom the Apostle identifies as "those who belong to Christ."

[55]I.e., a spiritual being (πνεῦμα), as opposed to a psychical being. On the relationship between Christ and the Holy Spirit, see chapter 7, note 40.

the second man [Christ is] from heaven. (48) As [was] the earthly [man Adam], so also [are] the earthly [persons]; and as [is] the heavenly [man Christ], so also [will] the heavenly [persons be]. (49) And just as we have worn the image of the earthly [man Adam], we will also bear the image of the heavenly [man, Jesus Christ].

The Figure of Adam in Paul

Paul's heritage. In Romans 5 and 1 Corinthians 15, Paul expresses only one thought concerning Adam that did not originate within the non-Christian Jewish milieu described above--namely, his assertion in Rom 5:14 that Adam "was a type of the [Christ] who was to come." A close examination of Paul's portrait of Adam reveals that the remainder of the Apostle's statements concerning the father of humankind were grounded either in the Old Testament (LXX), or in discussions being carried on in apocalyptic circles during Paul's lifetime.[56]

The creation of Adam. Paul makes two statements concerning God's creation of Adam: First, in 1 Cor 15:47, the Apostle says, "The first man [was] from [the] earth, [and was] earthly." This is a reference to Gen 2:7 (LXX),[57] which relates how God formed Adam from the dust of the earth. Second, Paul directly quotes Gen 2:7 (LXX)[58] when he says to the Corinthians, in 1 Cor 15:45, ". . . it has been written [that] 'The' first 'man,' Adam, '[became] a living psyche.'"

Two statements in 1 Corinthians 15 demonstrate the Apostle's belief that, during the "present time," all Adam's descendants share in their

---

[56]This statement is not intended to rule out the influence upon Paul of other early Christians, who likewise drew upon the Adam-traditions in order to set forth the meaning of Christ. That the figure of Adam occupied an important place in the christological reflections of early believers is shown by Harald Sahlin ("Adam-Christologie im Neuen Testament," *StTh* 41 [1987]: 11-32), who detects Adam-christology not only in Paul's writings, but also in, e.g., Mark 1:12-13; 2:10-12; 2:27-28; 6:35-44; John 1:1-18; 1:29, 36; 11:50; Col 1:15-20; and Heb 1:3, 6-14; 2:6.

[57]Cf. Gen 3:20; 4 Ezra 3:4-5; 7:46 [116]; 2 Apoc. Bar. 48:46.

[58]Cf. 4 Ezra 3:5.

forefather's earthly, psychical nature: (1) 1 Cor 15:48, where Paul says, "As [was] the earthly [man, Adam], so also [are] the earthly [persons],"[59] and (2) 1 Cor 15:49, which reads, in part, "we have worn the image of the earthly [man, Adam]."[60]

Adam as the first sinner. Paul refers to the events of Gen 3:2-7, wherein Adam ate fruit from "the tree of knowing good and evil,"[61] as Adam's (1) "sinning" (ἁμαρτάνειν), (2) "transgression" (παράβασις), (3) "trespass" (παράπτωμα), or (4) "disobedience" (παρακοή).[62] Paul's notion of "sin" resembles that found in 2 Baruch, insofar as both authors define sin as refusing to submit oneself to the Creator.[63] Each writer, however, holds a different view of the content of such "submission": On the one hand, 2 Baruch (along with 4 Ezra) looks upon God primarily as the One who gave the Law to Moses. Consequently, he describes submission to God in terms of "doing righteousness" under the Mosaic covenant by keeping the Law. Paul, on the other hand, has come to know God as the One who acted in Jesus Christ for the salvation of the world. Hence, he views submission to the Creator as "doing righteousness" under the "new covenant" by trusting in Christ.

In short, Paul appears to have adopted apocalyptic traditions, similar to those preserved in 2 Baruch, which paint a portrait of Adam as the first "sinner," or the first human to rebel against God's lordship. Yet, to some extent, the meaning of these traditions has changed; for Paul's experience with

---

[59]See Job 34:15; Ps 103 (102):14; 103 (104):29; Eccl 3:20; 12:7.

[60]A probable reference to Gen 5:3.

[61]Cf. 4 Ezra 3:7, 21; 7:46 [116], 48 [118]; 2 Apoc. Bar. 23:4; 48:42; 54:15; 56:5-6.

[62]See (1) Rom 5:16; (2) 5:14; (3) 5:15, 17, 18; and (4) 5:19, respectively.

[63]See chapter 2 under "Sin as a 'power,'" along with our earlier discussion of "Adam as the first sinner" in 2 Baruch.

Christ has taught him that a "sinner" is not so much a Law-breaker as s/he is someone outside the "new covenant."

Adam as initiator of the "present evil age". In Rom 8:18-22, Paul speaks of "the sufferings of the present time" and how "the entire Creation groans together and suffers labor pains together to the present [time]." Furthermore, he anticipates "the glory which is going to be revealed in us" and the liberation of Creation "from the slavery which is corruption to the freedom [from corruption] which is the glory of the children of God." Paul was obviously influenced by a doctrine of the "two ages" something like that found in the apocalyptic writings examined above. As we saw in chapter 2, Paul's encounter with the risen Christ led him to alter this doctrine in several important ways. Yet the Apostle clearly believes that, in some sense, he and his contemporaries are experiencing the "futility" of "the present evil age."

When, for Paul, did this "evil age" begin? What led God to subject His Creation to "corruption" and "futility"? The most probable answer is that Paul followed apocalyptic tradition (along with Gen 3:15-25) in identifying Adam, in his sin, as the initiator of "the present evil age."

Adam as the cause of universal death. Paul clearly follows his traditions when he affirms that, because of Adam's sin, both he and his descendants (have been cut off from the "tree of life," and thus) endure the penalty of death. This theme appears frequently in Romans 5 and 1 Corinthians 15, wherein the Apostle writes: (1) "death [came into the world] through [Adam's] sin," (2) "death reigned from the time of Adam," (3) "many died because of the one [man, Adam]'s trespass," (4) "because of the trespass of the one [man, Adam], death reigned through [that] one man," (5) "death [became a reality] through a [single] man," and (6) "within [the sphere determined by] Adam, all [persons] die."[64] Thus, Paul finds a causal connection between Adam's death

---

[64]See (1) Rom 5:12a, (2) 5:14a, (3) 5:15b, (4) 5:17a, (5) 1 Cor 15:21a, and (6) 15:22a, respectively.

98

and universal human death. He states the matter well in the last passage cited: By bringing death upon himself and his descendants, Adam made the human sphere a sphere ruled by death.[65] In other words, "within the [human] sphere [as it has been determined by] Adam, all [humans] die."

When Paul says, in Rom 5:12, that "death spread to all persons because all sinned," he appears to abandon the idea of Adam's responsibility for human death in favor of holding each individual accountable for his/her own demise. Yet, here again, Paul simply follows the apocalyptic traditions in finding a correspondence between the death of Adam and the deaths of unrighteous persons.[66] He departs from his Jewish contemporaries only over the question of who is reckoned "righteous" and who is not. Since Paul believes that "a person is not reckoned righteous [under the 'new covenant'] on the basis of the works of the Law [required by the 'old covenant'], but only by means of trust in Jesus Christ,"[67] he maintains that there were "none righteous--not even one"[68]--before the death and resurrection of Christ. Therefore, outside of Christ (i.e., under the dominion of Sin, the focus of Paul's remarks in Rom 5:12), "all persons" shared responsibility with Adam for their own deaths "because all sinned."

Adam and individual responsibility for sin. We have already established that Paul views all persons outside the "new covenant" as unrighteous "sinners." Does he, in Romans 5, assign responsibility to Adam for the sins (i.e. wrong deeds) committed by his many descendants? The Apostle had no intention of providing a detailed answer to this question, for his great concern

---

[65]See Rom 5:14a, 17a; cf. 21a.

[66]See also Rom 1:29-32, where the Apostle describes sinners, who are guilty of "every sort of unrighteousness," as persons "deserving of death."

[67]Gal 2:16a.

[68]Rom 3:10b.

is holding Christ responsible for the righteousness of the many who trust in him. Paul certainly leaves us with very little evidence upon which to base a judgment concerning his views; but since this issue has played such an important role in the development of Christian theology, we will attempt to discern his thoughts on this matter.

In Rom 5:19a, the Apostle identifies Adam as the direct cause of all human sin when he writes: ". . . through the disobedience of the one man, [Adam,] the many became sinners."[69] He makes a similar statement in v. 12a: ". . . sin came into the world through one man, [Adam]." Is Paul saying that Adam caused "many" to become "sinners" in the sense that he forces them to commit wrong deeds? Three considerations lead us to understand Paul's statements differently.

First, an alternative interpretation is possible. When Paul says that "sin came into the the world through one man, [Adam,]" he may mean no more than that Adam was the first sinner and the initiator of the "present evil age." In other words, since Adam (along with Eve) was the first human to sin, it was he who introduced, into the human sphere, the "Sin" that has plagued humankind from that day forward.[70] Accordingly, Paul's statement in Rom 5:19 ("through the disobedience of the one man, [Adam,] the many became sinners") may likewise mean that Adam inaugurated the "present evil age" and introduced his descendants to the possibility (not the necessity) of committing sinful deeds. The sad outcome has been universal sin "because all sinned."[71]

---

[69]Since, in this context, Paul uses "condemnation" (κατάκριμα) as an antonym for "righteousness" (δικαίωμα ["pronouncement of righteousness"] or δικαίωσις ["pronouncing of righteousness"], see vv. 16, 18)--i.e., as a synonym for "unrighteousness," or "sinfulness" (see v. 19, where he contrasts "sinners" with the "righteous")--vv. 18a ("all persons [enter] into condemnation through the trespass of the one [man, Adam]") and 16b ("the judgment issued in response to [Adam's] one [trespass led] to condemnation") should be read as virtually equivalent to v. 19a ("through disobedience of the one man, [Adam,] the many became sinners").

[70]See chapter 2 under "Sin as a 'power.'"

[71]See Rom 5:12b. For Paul there are, of course, exceptions to the general rule that "all" have "sinned" in the sense of committing wrong deeds. See chapter 6, note 28.

If this is the case, then Paul--like the authors of 4 Ezra and 2 Baruch--intends to highlight the correspondence between Adam's sin and the sins of his descendants without making Adam personally responsible for every individual's fall into sinful behavior. Why, then, does Paul's statement in Rom 5:19 give the appearance of saying something more? The Apostle's phraseology must be explained on the basis of his desire to set Adam alongside Christ who, as initiator of the "new covenant," is indeed personally responsible for the righteousness of "the many" who put their trust in him.

Second, the traditions themselves support that reading of Paul which upholds individual responsibility for sin. We have already observed how Paul seems to have closely followed Genesis 1-5 (LXX), along with apocalyptic traditions similar to those preserved in 4 Ezra and 2 Baruch, when he painted his portrait of Adam as (1) the creation of God, (2) the first sinner,[72] (3) the initiator of the present evil age, and (4) the cause of universal death. It would be logical to assume--apart from any compelling evidence to the contrary[73]--

---

[72]Note that Paul never identifies Adam as the source of the "evil inclination," after the manner of 4 Ezra. In an essay on "The Pauline Concept of Original Sin" (*TB* 41 [1990]: 3-30), Stanley E. Porter shows that "Paul is independent of the rabbinic formulation and conceptualisation of the origin of sin" (p. 30)--including the concept of הַיֵּצֶר הָרָע, or "the evil inclination."

[73]While there were some in Paul's day who tried to assign to Adam and/or Eve a measure of liability for the sins of their descendants, none seem to go so far as to say that--because of Adam's sin--human beings cannot possibly refrain from sinning. For example, Ezra blames Adam for humanity's "evil inclination" in 4 Ezra 3:20-26, but the author of the book (speaking through the angel Uriel) continues to hold sinners accountable for their actions by arguing that the "evil heart" can be overcome (see above).

Likewise, the first century [Greek] Life of Adam and Eve describes how "Eve rose and went out and fell on the ground and said, 'I have sinned, O God; . . . I have sinned, LORD, I have sinned much; I have sinned before you, and all sin in creation has come about through me.'" (32:1-2; cf. [Latin] Life of Adam and Eve 44:2; Sir 25:24) Yet Eve probably means no more than that she introduced the possibility of sin into the world, for she still maintains that if her children guard themselves against Satan's deceptions, they will not "forsake the good" (30:1).

In contrasting the teaching of the early rabbis to later Christian interpretations of Paul, Moore (*Judaism*, I, 479) writes:

. . . to such speculations, which have been rife in the Christian theology of the West since Augustine [whose Latin Vulgate translation incorrectly rendered the ἐφ' ᾧ ("because") of Rom 5:12 as *in quo* ("in whom"), leading him to put forward what became the classical

that Paul would follow his inherited traditions in upholding individual responsibility for sin as well. Such an interpretation of Paul is possible and, in light of the evidence, is to be preferred.

Third, this interpretation of Paul's portrait of Adam is strengthened by the fact that, elsewhere in his epistles, Paul consistently holds persons accountable for their own sin. Indeed, the wilful sin of individuals is a major complaint throughout Rom 1:18-3:20. Of the Gentiles, Paul writes:

> . . . the wrath of God is being revealed from heaven against all the godlessness and unrighteousness of persons who, by [their] unrighteousness, suppress the truth [about God]. For what can be known about God is manifest to them . . . they are without excuse. (Rom 1:18, 19, 20b)

Of both Gentiles and Jews, he says:

> Do you not know that God's kind[ness is meant to] lead you to repentance? In accordance with your hardness and [your] unrepentant heart, you are storing up for yourself wrath on the Day of Wrath--even the revelation of the righteous judgment of God, who will recompense each [person] according to his/her deeds. (Rom 2:4b-6)[74]

Here, once again, we discover a parallel between Paul's epistles and the traditions of the apocalypticists preserved in 4 Ezra and 2 Baruch. While he may make certain statements concerning Adam that appear to find a causal connection between Adam's sin and the sins of all humanity, Paul, in the end, refuses to surrender individual responsibility for sinful deeds.

The limited evidence we possess from his epistles points to the conclusion that, while the Apostle did blame Adam for introducing the human race to the possibility of sinful behavior, Paul would not have accused Adam of forcing his descendants to commit sinful deeds like himself. Instead, he would

---

doctrine of "original sin"], there is no parallel in Judaism . . . there is no notion that the original constitution of Adam underwent any change in consequence of the fall, so that he transmitted to his descendants a vitiated nature in which the appetites and passions necessarily prevail over reason and virtue, while the will to good is enfeebled or wholly impotent.

[74]On the "Day of Wrath," see chapter 8.

have agreed with 2 Baruch that "each of us has become our own Adam." Adam rebelled against the Creator; it was he who first made the realm of humanity the realm of Sin and Death. All his descendants followed Adam in his rebellion; all chose to live within the human sphere as determined by Adam, rather than in this sphere as it was originally determined by the Creator.[75] "There is no one who seeks God; they have all turned away."[76] Only "the one man Jesus Christ" was "obedient." Through him God broke the power of Sin and Death over humankind.[77] He is the real focus of Paul's concern. Adam is only "a type of the [man] who was to come."

Paul's Adam-Christ Typology

By juxtaposing Adam to Christ in Romans 5 and 1 Corinthians 15 as "type" to "antitype," Paul underscores certain convictions concerning Christ's past death on the cross, his present existence as the "first-fruits" of those raised from the dead, and the present and future results of his death for those who trust in him.[78]

---

[75]In light of the traditions which influenced him, the Apostle most likely intended for his readers to understand his statements concerning the relationship between Adam's sin and the sin of his posterity in this way. However, others have reached different conclusions. Johnson ("Romans 5:12") summarizes the various possible interpretations of Romans 5:12 (for which he offers a bibliography on p. 299, note 6) and settles on the doctrine of "immediate imputation" as best capturing Paul's meaning. Recently, Brendan Byrne has taken up this issue in "'The Type of the One to Come' (Rom 5:14): Fate and Responsibility in Romans 5:12-21," *AusBR* 36 (1988): 19-30.

[76]Rom 3:11b-12a.

[77]See chapter 2 under "Sin as a 'power.'"

[78]Seyoon Kim (*The Origin of Paul's Gospel*, Wissenschaftliche Untersuchungen zum Neuen Testament, Reihe 4, 2 [Tübingen: J. C. B. Mohr, 1981], 162-93) surveys a number of "Hypotheses on the Origin of Adam-Christology," paying special attention to the work of (1) the Religionsgeschichtliche Schule represented by Brandenburger, and (2) A. J. M. Wedderburn. In the bibliography, we list additional studies on this subject by Barrett, Barth, Brandenburger, W. D. Davies (*Paul and Rabbinic Judaism*, 36-57), Dunn (*Christology*, 98-128), Jervell, Kreitzer, Lombard, Quek, Scroggs, Weder and Wright.

The death of Christ and its results. We find Paul employing Adam-Christ typology in Rom 5:12-21 primarily to illuminate certain key convictions concerning Christ's death and its results for humankind. Earlier in Romans, Paul has described Christ's sacrificial death on the cross primarily as an act of God: First, the Cross is "God's expression of His righteousness"[79] in that, through the sacrificial death of Christ, God righteously fulfilled His promise under the Abrahamic covenant to "bless" all nations with a "new covenant" based on trust.[80] Second, Paul describes the Cross as motivated by God's "goodwill" (χάρις), so that Christ's death may be conceived of as an act of God's "mercy," or "kindness," or even as a divine "gift."[81] This terminology dominates Rom 5:15-17, where Paul stresses the surpassing greatness of "God's expression of His goodwill . . . through the one man Jesus Christ."[82] Third, Paul defines the Cross in terms of God's "love" (ἀγάπη): "God demonstrated His own love toward us, [in] that while we were still sinners, Christ died for us."[83]

Paul shifts the focus from the Cross as an act of God to the Cross as an act of Christ in Rom 3:22 and 26, where the Apostle speaks of "Jesus Christ's act of trust."[84] Likewise, in Rom 5:18-19, he concentrates on Christ's deed and Christ's motivation out of a desire to compare "the one man Adam" with "the one man Jesus Christ." Here Paul breaks new ground (at least as far as the epistle to the Romans is concerned) by presenting the Cross not as

---

[79]See Rom 3:21, 22, 25, 26, interpreted in chapter 2.

[80]See chapter 2 under "Verse 21."

[81]See Rom 3:24. Note 174 of chapter 2 contains a detailed discussion of the χάρις ("goodwill") word group.

[82]See Rom 5:15, 16, 17; cf. 5:20, 21.

[83]See Rom 5:8.

[84]See chapter 2 under "Verse 22a." We will examine this idea more closely in part III of chapter 4.

"God's expression of His righteousness," but as (1) "the righteous deed of the one [man Jesus Christ]," and (2) "the obedience of the one [man Jesus Christ]."

What does Paul mean when he calls Christ's death a "righteous deed" in Rom 5:18? In chapter 2, we saw that a "righteous deed" is an action performed in fulfilment of the demands of a covenant. Christ did not go to the cross out of any obligation laid upon him by the Mosaic Covenant, for Paul himself knows that the Law curses "every one who hangs on a tree."[85] Instead, Christ died as a sacrifice for sins because the Abrahamic covenant required it.[86] On the Cross, Jesus served as the agent through whom God fulfilled His promise to Abraham of a "new covenant" under which "all" could be reckoned righteous before God. (Note: Christ's death may also be viewed as an act of "new covenant" righteousness in the sense that it brought that covenant into existence [see chapter 4].)

Paul highlights this intended result of Christ's death by comparing his "righteous deed" (δικαίωμα) with Adam's "trespass" (παράπτωμα) in Rom 5:12-21. On the one hand, by committing the first trespass, Adam introduced his offspring to the possibility of "Sin" (both in the sense of committing wrong deeds and participating in the "present evil age"). The entire race responded by sinning, so that, "through the trespass of the one [man Adam]," his descendants experience two terrible results: First, "all persons [enter] into condemnation" or, in other words, "the many" become unrighteous "sinners."[87]

---

[85]See Gal 3:13, discussed in part II of chapter 4.

[86]See chapter 2 under "Η καινὴ διαθήκη ('the new covenant')" and part II of chapter 4.

[87]See Rom 5:12, 16, 18, 19, 21. That Paul here uses the terms "all" (οἱ πάντες) and "the many" (οἱ πολλοί) interchangeably is shown, for example, by the fact that whereas "the many" die in v. 15, Paul says "all" die in v. 12. Yet this does not mean, as some have suggested, that Paul is a universalist, who believes that eventually "all" Adam's descendants will enter "into the righteousness [which means 'eschatological] life.'" Instead, when Paul uses the term "all" (πάντες) in Rom 5:12-21, he is employing the language of potentiality rather than of actuality, in an effort to set forth the universal significance of Christ for the human race. When the first man Adam sinned, he opened up the potential for "all" humans to enter into sin and death. This

Second, they die as the penalty both for their own sin and because of the sin of their ancestor.[88]

On the other hand, Christ's death on the cross--coming as the response of God's goodwill ($\chi \acute{\alpha} \rho \iota \varsigma$) to the "many trespasses" committed by Adam and his descendants[89]--overcomes the effects of Adam's sin by making it possible for "all persons" (1) to "become righteous,"[90] in the present, through trust in him,[91] and thus (2) to attain to the Resurrection of the dead, or "eschatological life," reserved for the righteous in the future.[92] Whereas Adam's deed leads to unrighteousness and death through sin, Christ's deed leads to righteousness and "life" through trust. Hence, Paul refers to the Cross as "the righteous deed of the one [man Jesus Christ]."

Why does Paul refer to Christ's death as an act of "obedience" in Rom 5:19? This description of the Cross was inspired by the contrast between Adam's refusal to submit to his Creator as Lord and Christ's willingness to

---

potential was fully realized "because all sinned." When Christ went to the cross and thus instituted the "new covenant," he opened up the potential for "all" sinners to be delivered from the dominion of Sin and Death and to enter into the dominion of the God of goodwill ($\chi \acute{\alpha} \rho \iota \varsigma$). This potential is being realized only by "those who are receiving the overflow of [God's] goodwill--even the gift of righteousness." If there is one point that Paul has made clear in the early chapters of Romans, it is that, under the "new covenant," God does not reckon "all" Adam's descendants "righteous," but only those who trust in Him.

On this subject, see (1) M. Eugene Boring, "The Language of Universal Salvation in Paul," *JBL* 105 (1986): 269-92; and (2) William V. Crockett, "The Ultimate Restoration of All Mankind: 1 Corinthians 15:22," in *Studia Biblica 1978: III. Papers on Paul and Other New Testament Authors. Sixth International Congress on Biblical Studies: Oxford, 3-7 April 1978*, ed. E. A. Livingstone, *Journal for the Study of the New Testament* Supplement Series, 3 (Sheffield: JSOT Press, 1980), 83-87. We will discuss the ultimate end of both the "righteous" and the "unrighteous" in chapter 8.

[88]See Rom 5:12, 15, 17, 21.

[89]See Rom 5:16b.

[90]I.e., to participate in the "new covenant," or to live "within [the sphere determined by] the goodwill [expressed] through the one man Jesus Christ" (Rom 5:15).

[91]See Rom 5:16, 17, 18, 19, 21.

[92]See Rom 5:17, 18, 21; cf. 1 Cor 15:22.

surrender himself to God's purpose by going to the Cross as His agent for the deliverance of sinners.[93] When viewed in these terms, Paul's description of the Cross as Christ's "obedience" (ὑπακοή) in Rom 5:19 is virtually equivalent to his designation of Jesus' death as his "act of trust" (πίστις Ἰησοῦ/Ἰησοῦ Χριστοῦ) in Rom 3:22 and 26. In going to the cross, Jesus displayed the same kind of "obedience which proceeds from trust" (ὑπακοὴ πίστεως) that Paul hopes all nations will emulate as a result of his ministry.[94]

The only other passage in which Paul describes Christ's death in terms of "obedience" is Phil 2:8, where he recalls how Christ "humbled himself by being obedient to the point of death--even [the] death which is the cross." In that particular context, Paul concentrates primarily on Christ's attitude of "obedience" in an effort to inspire his readers to adopt the same "mind-set" of humility and self-denial in their relationships with one another.[95] However, in Romans 5 the focus is once again on the result of Christ's act of "obedience" as it compares with the result of Adam's "disobedience." Adam, by his "disobedience," introduced his descendants to the possibility of sin--a possibility which they embraced and in which they became enslaved under Sin and Death. Christ, however, obeyed God by dying on the cross as the sacrifice which instituted the "new covenant."[96] He thereby made it possible for "the many" sinners, through trust in Him, to enjoy "righteousness, toward the end of 'eschatological life.'"[97]

---

[93]See chapter 2 under "Sin as a 'power,'" along with the discussion of Philippians 2:6-8 which will appear in part III of chapter 4.

[94]See Rom 1:5; 16:26.

[95]See the discussion of Phil 2:3-5 in chapter 4.

[96]See part I of chapter 4.

[97]See Rom 5:19, 21.

The risen Christ. When we shift our focus to 1 Corinthians 15, we find Paul employing his Adam-Christ typology toward ends quite different from those in Romans 5. Here the subject of discussion is the Resurrection of the dead. The Apostle contrasts Christ with Adam in order to highlight his convictions concerning (1) the role played by Christ in the Resurrection of the dead, and (2) the nature of the resurrection body.

Paul derived his idea of the bodily Resurrection of the righteous from Jewish apocalyptic.[98] At some future time, God was expected to bring "the present evil age" to a close by subduing all his enemies, and then raising the righteous from the dead so that they might enjoy "eschatological life" in the "new age" of glory.

When the risen Christ "was seen" (ὤφθη)[99] by Paul, the Apostle could only conclude that the promised Resurrection had begun.[100] When some at Corinth doubt this fundamental element of the faith, Paul uses his Adam-Christ typology in order to impress this truth of the gospel upon them.

Drawing upon his traditions, Paul reminds the Corinthians that "death [became a reality] through a [single] man, [Adam]," and that "within [the sphere determined by] Adam, all [persons] die."[101] Just as the one man Adam bears responsibility for universal death, so also does the one man Jesus Christ bear responsibility for the Resurrection from the dead.

Jesus has made the Resurrection a human reality in two senses: First, it is a future reality for believers because Christ died on the cross as a sacrifice for sins, so that sinners may be reckoned "righteous" under the "new covenant" through trust in him. As "righteous" persons, they enjoy the sure

---

[98]See chapter 5, along with part I of chapter 2.

[99]See, e.g., 1 Cor 15:8.

[100]For further discussion of this point, see part III of chapter 5.

[101]See 1 Cor 15:21a, 22a.

hope of participation in the promised Resurrection of the "righteous" to glory. Paul states the matter in this way: "Within [the sphere determined by] Christ,[102] all [persons] will be made alive."[103] Second, Christ has made the Resurrection a present human reality inasmuch as he is the "first-fruits" (ἀπαρχή),[104] or the first of that multitude of the "righteous" which the traditions predicted would be raised by God to "eschatological life."[105]

Finally, in 1 Cor 15:44-49 Paul sets the risen Christ alongside Adam in order to contrast the "psychical body" (σῶμα ψυχικόν) of the present age with

---

[102]I.e., under Christ's lordship, or within the bounds of the "new covenant" which Christ effected through his Cross and under which persons become "righteous" through trust in him. On the phrase ἐν τῷ Χριστῷ, see chapter 2, note 176.

[103]See 1 Cor 15:22b. It is important to note here the future tense of the verb ζωοποιηθήσονται ("will be made alive"). Christ has been made alive in the present, but Christians will only be raised in the future.

[104]See 1 Cor 15:20, 23; cf. 16:15; Rom 8:23; 11:16; 16:5. The term "first-fruits" (ἀπαρχή) refers to the first part of a crop harvested, which indicates that the remainder of the harvest will soon be ready. Robert G. Bratcher (A Translator's Guide to Paul's First Letter to the Corinthians, Helps for Translators [New York: United Bible Societies, 1982], 147) rightly notes that a "modern equivalent [for the term 'first-fruits'] would be 'first installment,' which implies that there is more to come." Paul uses the term πρωτότοκος ("firstborn") in Rom 8:29 to express essentially the same idea--namely, Christ as the first of a large group of persons to bear the "image" which is glory.

[105]By calling Jesus "first-fruits" (ἀπαρχή), Paul is not saying that his resurrection, in and of itself, somehow "guarantees" the resurrection of others (as F. F. Bruce suggests in 1 and 2 Corinthians, New Century Bible Commentary [Grand Rapids: Wm. B. Eerdmans Publ. Co., 1971], 146-47). The resurrecton of believers is not effected by Christ's resurrection, but by the God who effected Christ's resurrection (see chapter 5 under ". . . he is alive because of God's strength")--the "God who makes the dead alive and who calls into existence things which had no existence" (Rom 4:17; see also the section of chapter 8 on "Resurrection as God's gift of 'goodwill'"). Christ's resurrection "guarantees" the general Resurrection of the righteous in the sense that it is God's "pledge," or "down-payment," on His promise to raise the righteous (see Gordon D. Fee, The First Epistle to the Corinthians, The New International Commentary on the New Testament [Grand Rapids: William B. Eerdmans Publishing Company, 1987], 748-49)--but not in the sense that our resurrection "depends" on the resurrection of Christ (Bruce, 146), or that there is a "causal connection between the resurrection of Christ and that of believers" (Hans Conzelmann, 1 Corinthians: A Commentary on the First Epistle to the Corinthians, Hermeneia--A Critical and Historical Commentary on the Bible [Philadelphia: Fortress Press, 1975], 270).

the "spiritual body" (σῶμα πνευματικόν) enjoyed by the righteous at the Resurrection.[106] In response to the doubtful inquiry of v. 35 ("With what

---

[106]Rudolf Bultmann gives us the classic treatment of the Pauline anthropological terms "body" (σῶμα), "psyche" (ψυχή, often translated "soul"), and "spirit" (πνεῦμα) in *Theology of the New Testament*, trans. Kendrick Grobel (New York: Charles Scribner's Sons, 1951-55), 2:192-209. It is somewhat misleading to translate the Greek noun σῶμα as "body;" for while the term does denote corporeal existence (so that Paul occasionally employs σῶμα in order to refer specifically to the outward physical form of a person--see, e.g., Rom 4:19, which speaks of Abraham's aged "body," and 2 Cor 12:2, where Paul considers the possibility of an out-of-body experience), the Apostle almost always uses σῶμα to represent the human being in his/her totality. In other words, Paul views human beings as psychosomatically indivisible; he calls a man or woman σῶμα because s/he is "[some]body" (and, more precisely, "[some]body" having "a relationship to himself," or "able to control himself and be the object of his own action," as Bultmann explains on pp. 195-96). For this reason, the term is best rendered "self," or "person," in most Pauline contexts.

However, in 1 Cor 15:35-49, the Apostle responds to "someone" concerned not with the whole person, but with the outward frame. Skeptical of the Resurrection, he asks, "With what sort of body (σῶμα) will those raised from the dead come?" Adopting, for the moment, this narrower meaning of σῶμα, Paul responds with a discussion of the various kinds of outward forms, or "bodies" (σώματα), possessed by kernels of grain, birds and animals, sun and moon (vv. 36-41). Since, in this context, Paul focuses primarily on the outward forms of persons and things, it seems best to translate σῶμα with "body" for the sake of consistency. Yet, even here, when Paul speaks of the resurrection of human σώματα ("bodies"), he means more than simply trading one "shell" for another; he envisions the renewal of the whole person, the transformation of human existence.

The term "psyche" (a transliteration of the Greek ψυχή) is likewise difficult to translate. Bultmann shows that, whereas Paul sometimes uses psyche to mean simply "person," or "self," or even "life" (p. 204), he most often employs "psyche" when he wishes to focus on "the self that lives in a man's attitude, in the orientation of his will" (p. 206).

In 1 Cor 15:44-49 the context clearly shows that what Paul means by "psyche" is the human being in his/her "earthly" state--i.e., human existence in the present age as shared by Adam and all his descendants, in contrast with human existence in the "new age" to come as experienced by Christ and the righteous. Accordingly, the "psychical body" (a rendering of σῶμα ψυχικόν suggested by Conzelmann in *1 Corinthians*, 280) is the "earthly" body of the present age as opposed to the transformed, "heavenly," "spiritual body" (σῶμα πνευματικόν) of the Resurrection (see Fee, *First Corinthians*, 791-93).

Paul employs "spirit" (πνεῦμα) in a manner similiar to the way he uses "psyche"--namely, in order to refer to a "person" or "self." The Apostle seems to prefer this term when he focuses on the "self" as "a willing and knowing self" (Bultmann, 207). In Paul's letters, πνεῦμα ("spirit") designates both human "persons" and the "Person" or "Spirit of God" (or "Spirit of Christ"), whom Paul envisions not as a mindless force, but as a willing and knowing "Person" (see chapter 7, note 40).

In 1 Cor 15:45, Paul says that Christ, the "last Adam," has become "a life-giving Spirit" (πνεῦμα ζῳοποιοῦν). Earlier in this study, we discussed how Christ--by going to the Cross as "God's expression of His righteousness" toward all nations--brings resurrection and eschatological "life" to those who trust in him. When Paul, in this same context, speaks of the "spiritual body," he means the "resurrection body," or the transformed σῶμα of the "new age," which Christ himself has already received, and which Christ--as God's "life-giving Spirit/Person"--will

sort of body [σῶμα] will [those raised from the dead] come?"), Paul cites many examples from nature (vv. 36-41) to show that God is perfectly capable of (1) creating various types of bodies suitable for various purposes, and (2) radically transforming bodies, as in the case of the kernel of grain which becomes a blade of wheat. Paul thinks it quite reasonable to suppose that God could prepare a body suitable for those raised from the dead for "eschatological life" in glory. That this is indeed the case has been shown by Christ himself, who was raised from the dead and then "seen" (ὤφθη) in bodily form by a great number of witnesses, including Paul himself (vv. 4-8). So "if there is [such a thing as] a psychical body [(and there is)]; [then] there is also [such a thing as] a spiritual [body]."

In order to shed light on the relationship between the human body (σῶμα) of the present and the human body of the future Resurrection, Paul again employs the representative figures of Adam and Christ. On the one hand, Genesis testifies that Adam's body was "psychical" and "earthly." On the other hand, the body of the risen Christ is "spiritual" and "heavenly"--i.e., radically different from the Adamic body.[107] In v. 19, Paul offers his Christian readers this assurance: "Just as we have worn the image of the earthly [man Adam], we will also bear the image of the heavenly [man, Jesus Christ]." How can this be so?

Adam was created "a living psyche,"[108] and so all human beings--by virtue of their physical descent from him--now bear "earthly," "psychical"

---

effect for the righteous when he returns in glory. The Apostle contrasts this Christ-like "spiritual body" with the Adam-like "psychical body" as a "heavenly body" to an "earthly body." This contrast will be explored more fully in chapters 5 and 8.

[107]In and of themselves, the adjectives "psychical," "spiritual," and "heavenly" tell us little about the nature of the resurrection body, other than that it is different from our present bodies (see the preceding note). Much more helpful on this point are vv. 42-43, where Paul contrasts the two kinds of bodies using terms such as "corruption/incorruption," "dishonor/glory," "weakness/strength." These matters will be explored more fully in chapters 5 and 8.

[108]Paul quotes from Gen 2:7.

bodies in the "image" of Adam.[109] In contrast to Adam, Jesus bears the "resurrection body"--the "spiritual," "heavenly" body which enjoys "eschatological life." How do we who bear the "image" of the first Adam come to bear the "image" of the "last Adam" since we are not physically descended from him?

Paul gives his reply in v. 45: "Just as it has been written [that] 'The' first 'man,' Adam, [became] a living psyche;' [so also has] the last Adam, [Jesus Christ, become] a life-giving Spirit." By dying on the cross as a sacrifice for sins, Christ has made it possible for all Adam's "psychical" descendants to be reckoned "righteous" through trust in him. As a result, they will participate in the Resurrection of the "righteous," in which they will be transformed into Christ-like, "heavenly" bodies (σώματα), fit for eschatological "life."[110] Paul thus gives a compact summary of both the nature of human existence in the present age and the age to come (i.e., "psyche" versus "life"), and the roles played by Adam and Christ in shaping the two ages (i.e., "living psyche" versus "life-giving Spirit").

Verse 46 ("the spiritual [body of Christ is] not first; instead, the psychical [body of Adam comes first and] then the spiritual [body]") sharply differentiates between the past (i.e., the period from Adam to the death and resurrection of Christ), present (i.e., the period between Christ's resurrection and his Parousia) and future (i.e., the consummated "new age" following the Resurrection of the righteous at Christ's return), between history and eschatology, in order to guard the temporal sequence so central to Paul's thought. In the past Christ bore a "psychical" body like that of Adam; in the present he bears the "spiritual" body of the "new age." In the present Christians bear a "psychical" body like that of Adam; in the future they will bear a "spiritual" body like that of Christ. The sequence is the same for both Christians and

---

[109]See Gen 5:3.

[110]See chapter 8.

their Lord: "The spiritual [is] not first, but the psychical and then the spiritual."

Against the background of Rom 3:21-26 (chapter 2) and the Adam-Christ typology of Romans 5 and 1 Corinthians 15 (chapter 3), we will now explore the fourteen "core convictions" (chapters 4, 5, 7, 8) that together make up the "coherent center" of Paul's theology.

CHAPTER FOUR

PAUL'S INTERPRETATION OF CHRIST'S DEATH

For Paul, Jesus' death on the cross was, first and foremost, an historical event; for "the Jews . . . killed . . . the Lord Jesus"[1] at a particular place and time in the past. However, this historical event did not occur in a vacuum, but within the context of early first-century Judaism, as it was reflected in and/or shaped by the Old Testament and other early Jewish literature--much of which we still possess. Like other first-century Jewish Christians, Paul interpreted Jesus' history against this background. Thus, when the Apostle summarizes his gospel in 1 Cor 15:3-8, he does not merely recite the historical fact that "Christ died;" he also insists upon a correct interpretation of that event by placing it within its proper context: "Christ died . . . in accordance with the Scriptures."[2]

This hermeneutic led Paul to three "core convictions" concerning Christ's death.[3] The Apostle interprets the Cross as (1) the sacrifice for sins

---

[1] 1 Thess 2:14-15.

[2] 1 Cor 15:3.

[3] On Paul's understanding of Christ's death, see the pertinent studies in the bibliography by Donge, Hoskyns and Davey, Cousar, Dunn, Käsemann, Léon-Dufour, McLean, Maillot, I. H.

which established the "new covenant," (2) God's expression of His righteousness toward both Abraham and all nations, and (3) Christ's expression of trust in, or self-humiliation before God. In this chapter, we will examine how Paul applies these central elements of his theology within a variety of contexts.

I. "A SACRIFICE WHICH PURIFIES FROM SIN"-- CHRIST'S DEATH AS SACRIFICE[4] (CORE CONVICTION 1)

Christ's Death "For Sins."

Four Pauline formulae. The Apostle Paul makes heavy use of formulaic statements concerning the purpose of Christ's death built around the prepositions ὑπέρ ("for") and διά ("for" or "because"). We may divide these formulae into four categories on the basis of which preposition Paul employs and whether the object of that preposition is a person(s) or some word representing the idea of "sin." Paul says that Christ's death was (1) "for" (ὑπέρ) sins,[5] (2) "for" (διά) sins,[6] (3) "for" (ὑπέρ) person(s),[7] or (4) "for" (διά) persons(s).[8] From where does Paul derive these formulae, and what do they mean?

Church tradition and the Septuagint. 1 Corinthians 15:3 indicates that Paul adopted at least part of this language for describing the purpose of Christ's death from those who were believers before him. Using terms

---

Marshall, Merklein, Minear, Morris, Osten-Sacken, Ridderbos, Shin, Travis, Vassiliadis, Weder and Whiteley.

[4]Daly, Kidner, Sykes, and F. M. Young provide helpful background studies on the subject of "sacrifice" in early Christian literature. See the bibliography.

[5]1 Cor 15:3; Gal 1:3-4.

[6]Rom 4:25.

[7]See Rom 5:6-8; 8:32; 14:15; 1 Cor 11:24; 2 Cor 5:14-15, 21; Gal 2:20; 1 Thess 5:9-10; cf. 1 Cor 1:13.

[8]1 Cor 8:11.

associated with the handing-down of established traditions, he recalls a formula from category 1 that he had earlier "delivered" (παραδιδόναι) to the Corinthians (namely, "Christ died for our sins," Χριστὸς ἀπέθανεν ὑπὲρ τῶν ἀμαρτιῶν ἡμῶν), and then states that he himself had "received" (παραλαμβάν-ειν) this tradition from others--presumably Greek-speaking Christians with whom he had contact during his early days in Palestine or Syria.[9]

Where did those earlier believers derive this unusual way of describing what was, in many respects, a typical first-century crucifixion? The evidence points to the Septuagint (LXX), which contains three of the four categories of statements described above. In other words, Paul and other early Christians say that Christ died "for our sins" because they are convinced that his death was "in accordance with the Scriptures."[10]

Below, we will examine how the various types of formulae are used in the LXX in an attempt to gain insight into their meaning in Paul.

Category 1--Dying "for" (ὑπέρ) sins. One LXX text describes a person's dying "for" (ὑπέρ) his own sins, or as the just reward for his own crimes--namely, 3 Kgs 16:18-19, which explains that Zambri "died for his own sins which he committed" (ἀπέθανεν ὑπὲρ τῶν ἀμαρτιῶν αὐτοῦ ὧν ἐποίησε). In contrast to Zambri, Paul maintains that Christ "never knew sin,"[11] and so he

---

[9]In an article entitled "The Expiatory Sacrifice of Christ" (*BJRL* 62 [1980]: 454-75), Martin Hengel traces the origin of the Greek formula Χριστὸς ἀπέθανεν ὑπὲρ τῶν ἀμαρτιῶν ἡμῶν ("Christ died for our sins") back through the Hellenists as represented by Stephen, to the earliest Aramaic-speaking Palestinian church, and ultimately to Christ himself, when he interpreted his own impending death as he instituted the Eucharist.

[10]1 Cor 15:3.

[11]2 Cor 5:21. Christ "never knew sin" in the sense of committing wrong deeds, but he did "know sin" in the sense that he became incarnate and participated in the "present evil age" marred by sin and death (see part II of chapter 2, along with chapter 6, note 28). For discussion of Christ's "sinfulness," see (1) Vincent P. Branick, "The Sinful Flesh of the Son of God [Rom 8:3]: A Key Image of Pauline Theology," *CBQ* 47 [1985]: 246-62, and (2) Florence Morgan Gillman, "Another Look at Romans 8:3: 'In the Likeness of Sinful Flesh,'" *CBQ* 49 [1987]: 597-604.

does not describe the Lord as dying for his own sins, but only "for" (ὑπέρ) the sins of others.

Jewish practice did not include putting human beings to death "for the sins" (ὑπὲρ ἁμαρτιῶν) of others. The LXX employs such language only with regard to animals slaughtered in sacrifice,[12] and only in two contexts--namely, the Temple Vision of Ezek 40-48,[13] and the parallel accounts of the dedication of the Temple rebuilt at the time of Ezra and Nehemiah in Ezra 6:17 and 1 Esdr 7:8. Sacrifices "for sins" could involve several different kinds of animals[14] and were offered on a number of different occasions.[15] Three texts indicate that the blood of such sacrifices was shed--i.e., their "life" was poured out--for the purpose of "making purification" (ἐξιλάσκειν) for sins: The offerings "for sins" purify the altar in Ezek 43:22, 26, and they purify the Temple in 45:17.[16]

Against this background, we may draw the following preliminary conclusion: Paul echoes other early Christians in saying that "Christ died for our sins" (Χριστὸς ἀπέθανεν ὑπὲρ τῶν ἁμαρτιῶν ἡμῶν) in 1 Cor 15:3, or that Jesus "gave himself for our sins" (τοῦ δόντος ἑαυτὸν ὑπὲρ τῶν ἁμαρτιῶν ἡμῶν) in Gal 1:4, because he is convinced that the Lord's death on the cross is analogous to certain animal sacrifices described in Scripture, in that it somehow "makes purification" for sins.

---

[12]Micah 6:7 raises the possibility of offering human sacrifices--as the pagans did--only to reject it. See the discussion of this text in James Luther Mays, *Micah: A Commentary,* The Old Testament Library (Philadelphia: The Westminster Press, 1976), 140-41.

[13]See Ezek 44:29; 45:17, 22, 23, 25; 46:20.

[14]I.e., male goats in Ezra 6:17 and 1 Esdr 7:8, kids of goats in Ezek 43:22, 25, and calves in 45:22, 23.

[15]I.e., Passover and the Feast of Unleavened Bread in Ezek 45:22, 23, the Feast of Booths in 45:25, and the dedication of the new Temple in 1 Esdr 7:7-8.

[16]For a discussion of the ἱλασ- word group and the "purifying" of objects from sins, see chapter 2, note 178. For blood as the seat of life and God-given means of purification (ἐξιλάσκειν) from sins, see Lev 17:11.

Category 2--Dying "for" (διά) sins. The LXX speaks of persons dying "for" (διά)--or "because of"--their own sins in, for example, (1) Lev 26:39, which also mentions Israelites dying "because of the sins of their fathers" (διὰ τὰς ἁμαρτίας τῶν πατέρων αὐτῶν), (2) Num 27:3, (3) Ps 72:19, (4) Isa 64:6-7, which tells of God's "delivering up" (παραδιδόναι) Judah because of the nation's sins, (5) Ezek 33:6, and (6) 2 Macc 12:42. Similarly, 2 Macc 7:32-33 maintains that God disciplines even His covenant people by causing them to suffer "for" (διά) their sins.

In contrast to these writers, Paul says in Rom 4:25 that Christ was "delivered over [to death] (παραδιδόναι)" by God not because of his own sins, but "for our trespasses" (διὰ τὰ παραπτώματα ἡμῶν). A single LXX text speaks of one person's dying "for" (διά) the sins of others in this manner--namely, Second Isaiah's fourth "Song"[17] concerning the "Servant of the Lord" (Isa 52:13-53:12). In this passage, God's "Servant"[18] endures humiliation,[19] suffering,[20] and death,[21] as a "sacrifice"[22] for the sins of the Gentiles,[23] but then

---

[17]Bernhard Duhm (*Die Theologie der Propheten als Grundlage für die innere Entwicklungsgeschichte der israelitischen Religion* [Bonn: Adolph Marcus, 1875]) was the first to call the excerpts from Isaiah known as the "Servant Songs" by that title.

[18]I.e., ὁ παῖς--see Isa 52:13; 53:2.

[19]See Isa 52:14; 53:2-3, 8.

[20]See Isa 53:3-5, 7.

[21]See Isa 53:7-8, 12.

[22]That Isaiah intends to interpret the Servant's suffering and death as a "sacrifice," or as one person's saving others from the consequences of their sins by enduring God's punishment for those sins, is shown by (1) his calling the Servant "an offering for sin" (περὶ ἁμαρτίας--see the discussion of the meaning of this phrase below) in 53:10, (2) his comparing the Servant in 53:7 to a "sheep," which was an animal often "slaughtered" in sacrifice, and (3) his insisting that the Servant "bears" (φέρειν or ἀναφέρειν) the sins and consequential punishment of others in 53:3, 4, 11, 12, or suffers vicariously for others in 53:4-8, 10-12.

It is difficult to discern exactly what the prophet means by "bearing sins" (ἀναφέρειν ἁμαρτίας), for this phrase appears nowhere else in pre-Christian Jewish literature. However, at least two factors indicate that we should interpret "bearing sins" as a "sacrificial" idea, denoting one person's doing away with the sins of others through his own death--namely, (1) the context of sacrifice in which this phrase appears in Isa 53 (see above), and (2) the fact that the Servant seems to live again, for God exalts and greatly glorifies him.[24] This sudden and unexpected exaltation of the Servant causes the Gentile kings to shut their mouths in amazement[25] and to realize that he had not suffered for his own sins[26] but for the sins of the Gentiles.[27]

Apparently, the second Isaiah intends for his hearers to understand that the "Servant" is Israel,[28] which has suffered, "died" as an independent nation, and been "buried"[29] in Babylon, where it languishes in captivity. Isaiah anticipates that God will soon use Cyrus to release the Jews and to restore their nation and their dignity[30]--i.e., to give them "life from the dead" and highly exalt them among the other nations of the earth. When Israel's God brings this about, Isaiah expects the Gentiles to realize suddenly that--

---

the author of Hebrews says in 9:25-28 that "bearing sins" (ἀναφέρειν ἁμαρτίας) was something done by Christ, who was "offered" (προσφέρειν) as a blood-"sacrifice" (θυσία) for the purpose of "removing sin" (ἀθετεῖν ἁμαρτίαν). On the Servant's death as an "expiatory sacrifice," see the comments by Claus Westermann in *Isaiah 40-66: A Commentary,* The Old Testament Library (Philadelphia: The Westminster Press, 1969), 268-69, which are, of course, based on the MT rather than the LXX.

[23]See Isa 53:4-6, 11-12.

[24]See Isa 52:13; 53:11-12, along with the cryptic reference to the Servant's seeing a "long-lived seed" in 53:10.

[25]See Isa 52:14-53:1.

[26]See Isa 53:9. If the Servant is Israel (see discussion of this question below), then the prophet probably means not that Israel was entirely sinless, but that the nation had suffered more than what was required for its sins alone. Tryggve N. D. Mettinger (*A Farewell to the Servant Songs: A Critical Examination of an Exegetical Axiom,* Scripta Minora, Regiae Societatis Humaniorum Litterarum Lundensis 1982-83: 3 [Lund: CWK Gleerup, 1983], 42) cites the reference in Isa 40:2 to Jerusalem's suffering "double [for] her sins" in support of this interpretation.

[27]See Isa 53:4-6.

[28]See, e.g., Isa 41:8-9; 42:1; 43:1, 10; 44:1-2, 21; 45:4; cf. 49:3. In refuting the dominant view of the twentieth century as set forth by Bernhard Duhm (*Die Theologie der Propheten*), Mettinger correctly argues that the four "Servant Songs" do not portray a different "Servant of the Lord" than that presented in the remainder of Second Isaiah.

[29]See Isa 53:9.

[30]See Isa 44:28; 45:1-6.

contrary to appearances--the Lord had not forsaken His Servant; He had not caused Israel to suffer and "die" in exile because of its *own* sins. Instead, the Lord had "offered up" Israel as a "sacrifice" for the sins of the *nations*. The Gentile kings will thus confess:

> We have all gone astray like sheep; each has gone astray in his/her own path. And the Lord delivered him [i.e., Israel, God's Servant] over [to suffering and "death" as a "sacrifice"] for our sins. (Isa 53:6)

Second Isaiah anticipates that, in the face of this act of unspeakable mercy, the Gentiles will gratefully submit to Israel's God. Thus, through its suffering and sacrificial death "for" (διά) the sins of others, Israel--God's "Servant"--will accomplish its mission of being "the light for the nations," of effecting a "covenant" between them and the Lord, and of thereby bringing "salvation to the end of the earth."[31]

Paul knows Jesus Christ as one who suffered and died, but who has now been raised to life and highly exalted by God.[32] Thus, like many of his Christian contemporaries, the Apostle sees in the Isaianic "Servant Songs" another example of the Law and the Prophets' "witness" to "God's expression of His righteousness" toward all nations in Jesus Christ.[33] His statement in

---

[31]See Isa 49:6.

[32]See, e.g., Phil 2:6-11.

[33]See Rom 3:21. The great number of Pauline quotations from, or allusions to, the Fourth Servant Song and its immediate context (see E. Earle Ellis, *Paul's Use of the Old Testament* [Edinburgh: Oliver and Boyd, 1957; reprint, Grand Rapids: Baker Book House, 1981], 150-54) testify to the Apostle's familiarity with this text and to its importance for Paul's understanding of Christ. In a chapter entitled "The Use of the Isaianic Servant Songs in the Gospel Passion Texts," Douglas J. Moo (*The Old Testament in the Gospel Passion Narratives* [Sheffield, England: The Almond Press, 1983]) examines how certain other first-century Christian writers interpreted the second Isaiah's prophecy in relationship to Jesus. Roy A. Rosenberg ("The Slain Messiah in the Old Testament," *ZAW* 99 [1987]: 259-61) hypothesizes that the primitive Church built upon a foundation laid earlier by certain Jewish sectarians who, in the light of Zech 3:8 and Jer 23:5, understood Isa 52-53 to predict the suffering and death of the Messiah. However, after examining the evidence from pre-Christian times, Sydney H. T. Page ("The Suffering Servant Between the Testaments," *NTS* 31 [1985]: 481-97) concludes that--even though "some initial steps had been taken in that direction" (p. 493)--Jesus and the early Christians

Rom 4:25--namely, that Christ was "delivered over [to death] for (διά) our trespasses, and he has been raised for (διά) our righteousness"--is best explained as an allusion to Second Isaiah's "Servant theology."[34] Against this background, the Apostle here interprets Christ's crucifixion as a sacrifice offered by God ("[he was] delivered over") for the purpose of removing the sins of all nations ("for our trespasses"). He sets forth Christ's resurrection ("he has been raised") as the event which reveals Jesus' death to be such a "sacrifice," so that the Gentiles might know to seek a new covenant-"righteousness" ("for our righteousness")[35] in him.

Category 3--Dying "for" (ὑπέρ) persons. The LXX uses formulae from category 3 to express two distinct ideas: First, they appear in contexts that speak of animals dying as sacrifices "for" (ὑπέρ) human beings.[36] This suggests that the interpretive key for understanding Paul's description of Christ's death as "for (ὑπέρ) persons" may be located in the same place where we found the key to understanding his dying "for sins" (i.e. the category 1 formulations)--namely, within the sacrificial sphere. The Apostle definitely describes Christ's crucifixion as a "sacrifice" for persons in 2 Cor 5:21, where he writes that God made Christ "a sin[-offering] for us (ὑπὲρ ἡμῶν ἁμαρτίαν)."[37] His other category 3 formulations[38] could reasonably be interpreted in sacrificial terms as well. Therefore it is quite possible that

---

were probably the first to interpret Isaiah's "Servant Songs" as prophecies of a Messiah who would atone for sins through his suffering and death.

[34]Hengel argues likewise in "Expiatory Sacrifice," 458.

[35]For a more complete discussion of Christ's death as it relates to the "covenant" idea, see below.

[36]See Ezra 6:17; 1 Esdr 8:65-66; 2 Macc 1:26; 3:32.

[37]See the discussion of this text which appears below.

[38]I.e., Rom 5:6, 8; 8:32; 14:15; 1 Cor 11:24; 2 Cor 5:14-15; Gal 2:20; and 1 Thess 5:10.

when Paul says, "Christ died for (ὑπέρ) persons," he means that "Christ died--as a sacrifice--for persons."

Second, there are a number of LXX texts in which dying "for" a person means to endure capital punishment for that person's crimes. The holy priest Eleazar petitions God for this harsh privilege in 4 Macc 6:28-29, where he prays that the Lord will show mercy to Israel by letting him die "for them" (ὑπὲρ αὐτῶν[39]). Eleazar wants God to make his blood "the purification of them" (καθάρσιος αὐτῶν) by allowing him to endure the Lord's "just punishment" (δίκη) in Israel's place, thus relieving the nation of the necessity of perishing for its sins. This account of Eleazar's murder demonstrates that, by the time of Paul,[40] at least some Jews could conceive of God's accepting the death of one human being "for" (ὑπέρ) others.

We should recognize, however, that Eleazar's prayer goes against the main stream of Jewish tradition as expressed in Deut 24:18:

> Fathers shall not be put to death for the children (ὑπὲρ τέκνων); sons shall not be put to death for the fathers (ὑπὲρ πατέρων). Each shall be put to death because of his/her own sin (ἐν τῇ ἑαυτοῦ ἁμαρτίᾳ).[41]

While the Jews, during the hellenistic period, came to admire martyrs who died for a noble cause,[42] they generally looked upon one human being's suffering the death penalty for the sins of another as an injustice contrary to the Law of God. Figures such as Eleazar in 4 Maccabees--and the Servant of the Lord in Second Isaiah--were shocking exceptions to the general rule.

---

[39]This is the text as it appears in Codex Sinaiticus. Codex Alexandrinus reads περὶ αὐτῶν.

[40]4 Maccabees dates to the late first century B.C. or the early first century A.D. The events it describes occurred during the second century B.C.

[41]Cf. 4 Kgs 14:6 // 2 Chr 25:4.

[42]E.g., seven Jewish brothers and their mother die "for virtue" (ὑπὲρ ἀρετήν) in 4 Macc 1:8 (cf. 11:15), or "for" God's "laws" (ὑπὲρ τῶν αὐτοῦ νόμων) in 2 Macc 7:9, while Mattathias and his sons die "for the covenant of our fathers" (ὑπὲρ διαθήκης πατέρων ἡμῶν) in 1 Macc 2:50. Cf. 4 Macc 16:25, which speaks of Jewish martyrs dying "for God" (διὰ τὸν θεόν).

122

All this suggests that, when Paul speaks of Christ's dying "for" (ὑπέρ) persons, he is not saying that the Lord's execution was simply a miscarriage of justice, or a mere case of one person's wrongfully enduring a punishment deserved by others. The Apostle would have found it difficult to describe such a death as being "in accordance with the Scriptures." Rather, it is becoming increasingly clear that Paul can describe Christ's death as being both "for" persons/sins and "in accordance with the Scriptures" only because he (1) interprets that historical event in "sacrificial" terms, and thus (2) sets Christ apart from other human beings who have been unjustly executed by attaching special purificatory significance to his death--much as the LXX singles out the deaths of the Servant of the Lord and Eleazer as somewhat unique and unprecedented events.[43]

Category 4--Dying "for" (διά) persons. Paul employs a category 4 formula only in 1 Cor 8:11, where he speaks of "the brother for (διά) whom Christ died."[44] Since the LXX never speaks of one person's dying "for" (διά) another in this manner, it offers us no assistance in determining Paul's meaning. However, it seems reasonable to suppose that when Paul uses a formula from category 4, he is not communicating something radically different from formulae in categories 1, 2 and 3.

Conclusions. The preceding discussion leads to several conclusions: First, when Paul says that Christ died "for" (ὑπέρ or διά) sins, or "for" (ὑπέρ) persons, he follows other early Christians in applying to Jesus language from the LXX.

Second, by using such formulae, the Apostle most probably intends to evoke sacrificial ideas. Jesus, of course, was not an animal; he was not

---

[43]We have seen that Isaiah describes the death of the Suffering Servant as a sacrifice. 4 Maccabees probably intends to present Eleazer's death in sacrificial terms also.

[44]Paul may also intend δι' ὑμᾶς ("for you") in 2 Cor 8:9 to function as such a formula. See below, under "Philippians 2:6-8."

slaughtered according to prescribed Jewish ritual. His body was not burned, nor was his blood sprinkled on an altar or temple. The Pauline formulae, in and of themselves, do not associate Christ's death with any one type of sacrifice or Jewish feast. However, by adopting the language of Scripture, the Apostle does indicate that Christ's death is analogous to that of certain sacrificial animals described in the LXX, inasmuch as this death also purifies from sin through the shedding of blood, or the giving up of life to God.

Unlike some Jews before him, Paul does not view sin as a "substance," attracted like a magnet to an altar or temple or "mercy-seat," where it is then "rubbed out" through the application of blood.[45] Instead, Paul portrays Sin as a "power," or participation in the "present evil age," or the state of being under the lordship of something or someone other than God, the Creator of the universe and the Father of Jesus Christ.[46] This means that, when Paul adopts the terminology of the cult, he transforms its meaning. When he says that Christ died as a sacrifice "for sins," or "for persons," he does not mean that, by shedding his blood, Jesus removed sin from an altar or temple (as the writer to the Hebrews pictures Christ cleansing the heavenly Temple with his blood in Heb 9:11-12). Rather, Paul employs his four formulae to communicate the idea that Christ's crucifixion somehow effects the transfer of persons out from under the lordship of Sin and into the dominion of God. We will see exactly how Christ accomplishes this "deliverance"-- i.e., Paul's conception of the *modus operandi* of the atonement--later in this chapter.

Third, the LXX frequently uses the same language employed by Paul to express the idea of suffering the death penalty for sins--whether it be for one's own sins or for the crimes of someone else. Thus the Pauline formulae

---

[45]See Milgrom, "Atonement," *IDBSup*, 78-79.

[46]See chapter 2 under "Sin as a 'power.'"

may contain faint echoes of the idea of vicarious suffering, or substitutionary atonement. However, the Apostle himself does not stress these ideas.[47]

Finally, the category 2 formula in Rom 4:25 alludes to a particular "sacrificial" death--namely, that of the Suffering Servant of the Lord, as described in Isa 52:13-53:12. The Church's early linking of Christ with the Servant probably provided Paul with an impetus to interpret Christ's death in terms of (1) humiliation, suffering and servanthood, (2) a purificatory sacrifice for the sins of others, and (3) establishment of a covenant-righteousness involving Gentiles as well as Jews.

The nature of Christ's "sacrifice".

If Paul interprets the Lord's death as a "sacrifice," then what sort of sacrifice is it? At first glance, the Apostle appears to give a number of conflicting answers to this question. In one passage Paul describes Christ's death using the rather general term ἱλαστήριον ("a sacrifice which purifies from sin," Rom 3:25). In three other texts he is more specific and identifies the Lord's crucifixion with two types of Jewish sacrifices mentioned in the Old Testament --namely, (1) the "passover" (πάσχα, 1 Cor 5:7),[48] and (2) the "sin-offering" (περὶ ἁμαρτίας, Rom 8:3; ἁμαρτία, 2 Cor 5:21).[49] However, the very fact that Paul links Christ's death with two different kinds of Jewish sacrifices clearly indicates that he will allow neither the "passover" nor the "sin-offering" to

---

[47]Ernst Käsemann makes this observation on p. 162 of "The Pauline Theology of the Cross," *Int* 24 (1970): 151-77. D. E. H. Whiteley does likewise in "St. Paul's Thought on the Atonement," *JTS* 8 (1957): 240-55.

[48]Tibor Horvath, in *The Sacrificial Interpretation of Jesus' Achievement in the New Testament: Historical Development and Its Reasons* (New York: Philosophical Library, 1979), 82, points out that "there is a Jewish tradition which called the Passover a 'sacrifice'" (θυσία in the LXX translation) in Exod 12:27 and Deut 16:2, 5, 6, as well as in Josephus and the rabbis.

[49]Some scholars have also argued that Paul--particularly in Rom 8:32--interprets Christ's death along the lines of the rabbinical notion of the "Aqedah," or "Binding of Isaac." This idea has rightly fallen out of favor, but our bibliography includes studies on this subject by Dahl, Daly (*Christian Sacrifice*, 175-86), P. R. Davies, Hayward, Hedderich, Leaney and Segal.

define completely the meaning of the Cross.[50] Instead, the Apostle mentions these sacrifices only for purposes of comparison, in order to highlight some particular aspect of the significance of Christ's death. Finally, there is a fifth passage, in 1 Cor 11:24-25, where Paul sets the Cross apart as a unique event in history by identifying Christ's death as the sacrifice which established the "new covenant." Below, we will examine each of these five texts in an effort to discern Paul's views concerning the exact nature of Christ's "sacrificial" death.

Christ's death as "a sacrifice which purifies from sin." In our earlier treatment of Paul's category 1 formulae, we saw that certain Jewish sacrifices were offered for the purpose of "making purification" (ἐξιλάσκειν) for sins. Paul likens Jesus' death to such sacrifices in Rom 3:25, where he calls it an ἱλαστήριον . . . ἐν τῷ αὐτοῦ αἵματι ("a sacrifice which purifies from sin . . . at the cost of his blood"). We find the closest parallel to Paul's language in 4 Macc 17:22, which speaks of the "purifying death" (ἱλαστήριος θάνατος) of seven Jewish martyrs; but, as we have seen, the idea of blood-sacrifices effecting "purification" from sin appears throughout the Old Testament. Paul employs this kind of terminology in Rom 3:25 because, in this context, he wants to impress upon his readers that (1) God's response of righteousness and goodwill to the human reality that "all have sinned"[51] has taken the form of a death, namely, the crucifixion of Jesus Christ, and (2) this death is "sacrificial" in that it effects "deliverance"[52] or "purification"[53] from, or

---

[50]C. William Swain ("'For Our Sins': The Image of Sacrifice in the Thought of the Apostle Paul," *Int* 17 [1963]: 134) states the matter in this way: "There seems to be no rigid system involved in Paul's various uses of sacrificial imagery . . . The key is indeed the connection between Christ's death and the forgiveness of sin, but there is a great deal of freedom regarding how this connection is to be conceived."

[51]Rom 3:23.

[52]Ἀπολύτρωσις, Rom 3:24.

[53]Ἱλαστήριον, Rom 3:25.

"remission"[54] of, those sins. For a more detailed discussion of this text, see chapter 2.

Christ's death as a "passover." In 1 Cor 5:1-13, Paul commands the church at Corinth to expel from their fellowship a man who has established a sexual relationship with his father's wife. Comparing this "sexually immoral person" with leaven, which he here employs as a symbol for "evil and wickedness" (κακίας καὶ πονηρίας),[55] the Apostle warns against the corrupting influence this man will likely have on the Corinthian church by reciting a proverb: "A little leaven leavens the whole lump [of dough]."[56] Then Paul continues the analogy, while at the same time grounding his instructions in the Cross,[57] by (1) comparing Christ's death with the sacrifice of the paschal lamb, and (2) comparing the Corinthians' present life under Christ with the Jewish Passover Feast, celebrated in conjunction with the Feast of Unleavened Bread.[58] Just as the sacrifice of the passover lamb was accompanied by the Jews' removing all leaven from their houses, so also should the sacrificial death of Christ, "our passover [lamb]" (τὸ πάσχα ἡμῶν), be accompanied by the church's removing the "leaven" of an immoral man from its midst. So even though Paul refuses to allow the Jewish Passover to define fully the meaning and significance of Christ's death, he compares the Cross with the Passover--in this context--because it helps him to set forth Christ's sacrificial death as the basis for purity of life among believers.

---

[54]Πάρεσις, Rom 3:25.

[55]1 Cor 5:8.

[56]1 Cor 5:6; cf. Gal 5:9.

[57]Note how γάρ ("because") introduces Christ's "sacrifice" as the grounds for the removal of "leaven"/the sexually immoral man in v. 7.

[58]See, e.g., Exod 12:1-28; Lev 23:5-6; Num 28:16-17; Deut 16:1-8.

Christ's death as a "sin-offering." Paul characterizes Christ's death as a "sin-offering" in two passages--namely, Rom 8:3 and 2 Cor 5:21.

In Rom 8:3, Paul says that God sent Christ περὶ ἁμαρτίας. Scholarly opinion has been sharply divided over whether, by this phrase, Paul means "for sin" or "[as a sacrificial offering] for sin" (i.e., "as a sin-offering").[59] In an article entitled "The Meaning of περὶ ἁμαρτίας in Romans 8:3," N. T. Wright sets forth two lines of argument in support of the latter view: First, the LXX provides Paul with ample precedents for using the phrase περὶ ἁμαρτίας to express the idea of "a sin-offering."[60] Second, Wright points out that, according to Leviticus and Numbers, the "sin-offering covers sinful actions which the sinner either did not know he was committing, or did not know were sinful."[61] Paul has been speaking of a sort of unwitting sin in Romans 7, where he places these words in the mouth of the Jew who desires to serve God, but who is led by the "Law [as determined by] Sin" (νόμος ἁμαρτίας) to reject God's Son: "I do not know what I am doing; for I am doing not what I want, but what I hate."[62] Now, in Rom 8:3, Paul wishes to set forth Christ's crucifixion as the sacrifice which "condemns" that very sin to death--i.e., as the act of God which does "what the Law could not do." So it would be quite appropriate for him to describe the Cross here as "a sin-offering."[63] In short,

---

[59]For a list of proponents for each view, see p. 457, notes 1 and 2, of N. T. Wright's essay on "The Meaning of περὶ ἁμαρτίας in Romans 8:3" (in *Studia Biblica 1978: III. Papers on Paul and Other New Testament Authors. Sixth International Congress on Biblical Studies: Oxford, 3-7 April 1978,* ed. E. A. Livingstone, *Journal for the Study of the New Testament* Supplement Series, 3 [Sheffield: JSOT Press, 1980], 453-59). M. Dwaine Greene argues for the translation "sin offering" in "A Note on Romans 8:3," *BZ* 35 (1991): 103-106.

[60]See Wright, "περὶ ἁμαρτίας," 454-55. Wright lists the pertinent LXX texts on p. 458, notes 8-13.

[61]Wright, "περὶ ἁμαρτίας," 455.

[62]Rom 7:15.

[63]See Wright, "περὶ ἁμαρτίας," 455-57. Earlier in this epistle, the Apostle has explained that God intends the Law to perform the dual function of (1) making known universal human bondage to Sin (see Rom 7:7, 13; 5:13, 20; 3:19; cf. Gal 3:22) and (2) witnessing to God's efforts to

both LXX usage and the context support our interpreting περὶ ἁμαρτίας in Rom 8:3 to mean "as a sin-offering."

Paul also calls Christ's death a "sin-offering" in 2 Cor 5:21, where he writes:

> He [i.e., God] made the one who never knew sin (ἁμαρτία) [i.e., Christ] a sin[-offering] (ἁμαρτία) for us (ὑπὲρ ἡμῶν), in order that we might become God's expression of His righteousness within [the sphere ruled by] him [i.e., Christ].

The category 3 formula ὑπὲρ ἡμῶν ("for us") offers strong evidence that, in this context, Paul intends his readers to understand the second ἁμαρτία as a reference to Christ's sacrificial death.[64] In other words, Paul here portrays Christ's crucifixion as a "sin-offering."[65] Why does Paul do this? Robert J. Daly sees in 2 Cor 5:21 a play on words "suggested by the Hebrew *chatta't* [חַטָּאת] which means both sin and sin-offering (cf. Lev 4)."[66] Through this device, Paul highlights the striking contrast between Christ's own sinlessness

---

deliver His creatures from Sin by establishing a covenant-righteousness, based on trust in Him, through the sacrificial death of Jesus Christ (see Rom 3:21, 31; cf. 10:4). In the case of Christians, for whom the Law successfully carries out this God-given function, Paul says that the Law is "determined by the Spirit" of God (ὁ νόμος τοῦ πνεύματος, Rom 8:2). In the case of unbelieving Jews, who desire to please God but are misled by the Law into rejecting his Son, Paul says that the Law is "determined by Sin" (ὁ νόμος τῆς ἁμαρτίας, Rom 8:2). It is the plight of the unbelieving Jew under the Law as determined by Sin that Paul describes in Rom 7:7-25. It is the sacrificial death of Christ which breaks the power of Sin over the Law (in the manner described later in this chapter), so that "the righteous action performed by the Law might be completed in us, who no longer live in accordance with the flesh [i.e., under the lordship of Sin], but in accordance with the Spirit" (Rom 8:4).

[64]Compare Paul's use of such a formula earlier the letter, in 2 Cor 5:15.

[65]For ἁμαρτία used as "sin-offering" in the LXX, see Wright, "περὶ ἁμαρτίας," 454 and 458, note 9.

[66]Robert J. Daly, *Christian Sacrifice: The Judaeo-Christian Background Before Origen*,, The Catholic University of America Studies in Christian Antiquity, 18 (Washington, D.C.: The Catholic University of America Press, 1978), 239. Since the LXX often translates חַטָּאת with ἁμαρτία, this play on words occurs in Paul's "biblical" Greek as well. In addition to 2 Cor 5:21 and Rom 8:3, Daly (pp. 237-40) detects the idea of a "sin-offering" in Rom 3:24-25; 5:6-11 and Gal 3:13. This part of his argument is unconvincing.

and the sin of those for whom he died, our unrighteousness and "God's expression of His righteousness" in the sacrificial death of Christ.

In conclusion, Paul does not allow the Old Testament "sin-offering" to define fully the meaning of the Cross any more than he allowed the sacrifice of the passover lamb to do that. He describes Christ's sacrificial death as a "sin-offering" in Rom 8:3 and 2 Cor 5:21 only for the purpose of emphasizing particular aspects of the significance of that death relevant to those contexts.

Christ's death as the sacrifice which established the "new covenant." In 1 Cor 11:24-25 Paul recalls the tradition in which Jesus himself interprets his impending death as the sacrifice which will establish the "new covenant":

> This is my body, which [is sacrificed] for you (ὑπὲρ ὑμῶν)[67] . . . This cup is the new covenant [effected] by (ἐν) my blood[y sacrificial death] . . . .

The Old Testament describes several covenants established through a blood sacrifice, including the covenants between (1) God and Abraham in Gen 15:9-10, 17-18, (2) Jacob and Laban in Gen 31:54, and (3) God and Israel (the "Mosaic covenant") in Exod 24:1-11.[68] In 1 Cor 11:24-25, Jesus declares that his death should be understood as such a sacrifice.[69] Here we find the key to the sacrificial interpretation of Christ's death in Paul.

In our earlier discussion of "Δικαιοσύνη ('Righteousness') in the Writings of Paul" (chapter 2), we saw that God made a covenant with Abraham under which He promised to give a "blessing" to all nations through Abraham and his descendants. Paul believes that, in recent history, God acted righteously--through Jesus Christ--in order to fulfil that covenant

---

[67]A category 3 formula, indicating that Paul is here expressing a sacrificial idea.

[68]Note that the Mosaic covenant and the covenant between Jacob and Laban included a meal in which the participants in the covenant ate part of the meat of the sacrificial animals. Paul may understand the Lord's Supper in similar terms--i.e., as a participation in the sacrifice of Christ and in the "new covenant" which it instituted (see 1 Cor 10:16-21).

[69]Daly, *Christian Sacrifice*, 221, finds in 1 Cor 11:25 "an obvious reference to the institution of the covenant sacrifice in Exod 24:4-8."

obligation. The promised "blessing" has taken the form of a "new covenant," under which both Jews and Gentiles are transferred from the dominion of Sin into the dominion of God through trust in Him. Jesus' death on the cross was the "sacrifice" which established that covenant. This is the *modus operandi* of the atonement for Paul.

This "core conviction" concerning the meaning of Christ's death consistently underlies Paul's use of sacrificial terminology to describe that death. The Apostle is able to use such a variety of sacrificial images because they do not conflict with, but in fact highlight important aspects of, his basic understanding of the Cross as the sacrifice which established the "new covenant." Three passages, already discussed above, serve to illustrate this point: First, in 1 Cor 15:3 the Apostle says that "Christ died for our sins (ὑπὲρ τῶν ἁμαρτιῶν ἡμῶν, a category 1 formula) in accordance with the Scriptures" because (1) Christ's death is the sacrifice ("for our sins") which established the "new covenant," in fulfilment of God's promise to Abraham, as described in the Scriptures ("in accordance with the Scriptures"), and (2) his death thereby effects "purification" from sins ("for our sins"), inasmuch as, under the "new covenant," all persons may exit the dominion of Sin and enter the dominion of God through trust in Him. Second, Paul feels free to refer to the crucified Christ as "our passover lamb" in 1 Cor 5:7 because, by establishing the "new covenant," Christ releases persons from Sin, with the result that they should no longer have anything to do with "the leaven which is evil and wickedness." Finally, Paul can properly characterize Christ's death as a "sin-offering" in Rom 8:3 only because, by establishing the "new covenant," Christ reveals the "goal" (τέλος) toward which the Law is directed--namely, "righteousness for all who trust" in him.[70] His death thus "condemns" the sin of ignorance, which thinks that the Law is opposed to Christ. In other words, it sets persons free from "the Law [as determined by] Sin," and thus enables "the Law [as

---

[70]See Rom 10:4.

determined by] the Spirit" to perform the "righteous action" of (1) "condemning sin" and (2) witnessing to "God's expression of His righteousness" in the Cross of Christ. The result is that those who heed the Law's witness by trusting in Christ "no longer live in accordance with the flesh, but in accordance with the Spirit."[71]

To say that Paul primarily understands Christ's death as the sacrifice which established the "new covenant" may, at first, seem too great a weight for the "thread" of 1 Cor 11:24-25 to bear. After all, this is the only passage in his letters where the Apostle interprets the meaning of the Cross using the term "covenant" (διαθήκη). Yet the fact that this tradition was "received from the Lord"[72] must have given it a place of special importance in Paul's thought. Furthermore, while he employs the phrase "new covenant" only in 1 Cor 11:25 and 2 Cor 3:6,[73] Paul links Christ's death with the idea of "righteousness" throughout his epistles. We must not forget that "righteousness" (δικαιοσύνη), for Paul, is predominantly a "covenantal" term.[74] A close examination of the many Pauline texts which describe the Cross in terms of "God's expression of His righteousness" will confirm that the idea of Jesus' crucifixion as the sacrifice which established the "new covenant" does stand at the center of Paul's theology as one of his "core convictions" concerning Christ's death.

---

[71]See Rom 8:2-4; 3:21.

[72]1 Cor 11:23. Otfried Hofius ("Τὸ σῶμα τὸ ὑπὲρ ὑμῶν 1 Kor 11:24," *ZNW* 80 [1989]: 80-88) assembles evidence supporting the view that τὸ σῶμα τὸ ὑπὲρ ὑμῶν in 1 Cor 11:24b is a Greek translation of a word originally spoken in Aramaic by Jesus himself.

[73]See also Gal 4:21-31, where Hagar and Sarah represent "two covenants" (v. 24)--namely, the Mosaic covenant based on the works of the Law and the "new covenant" based on trust.

[74]See chapter 2 under "Δικαιοσύνη ('Righteousness') in the Writings of Paul."

132

II. "GOD'S EXPRESSION OF HIS RIGHTEOUSNESS"--
CHRIST'S DEATH AS AN ACT OF GOD (CORE CONVICTION 2)

An Act of God

Paul acknowledges that, in a sense, the crucifixion of Christ was a terrible crime committed by "the Jews,"[75] or even by the demonic "rulers of this age."[76] However, he most often describes the Lord's death as an act of God Himself,[77] motivated by His "righteousness" (δικαιοσύνη),[78] "goodwill" (χάρις),[79] "love" (ἀγάπη),[80] or "forbearance" (ἀνοχή).[81]

"God's Expression of His Righteousness"

Earlier in this chapter, and in chapter 2, we have argued at some length that Paul interprets God's sending Christ to the Cross primarily as an act of "righteousness," wherein He simultaneously fulfils His covenant obligations under the Abrahamic and "new" covenants. This is the Apostle's second "core conviction" concerning the meaning of the Cross, and it is closely related

---

[75]See 1 Thess 2:14-15.

[76]See 1 Cor 2:8.

[77]See, e.g., (1) Rom 8:32, in which Paul says, "[God] did not spare even His own Son, but handed him over [to death] for us all," (2) 2 Cor 5:19, which reads "God was reconciling the world to Himself by means of Christ," and (3) Gal 4:4-5, where Paul writes, "God sent forth His Son . . . in order that we might receive the adoption."

[78]See, e.g., Rom 3:21, 22; 10:3; 2 Cor 5:21 (which describe the Cross as ἡ δικαιοσύνη θεοῦ, "God's expression of His righteousness"); Rom 3:25, 26 (ἡ ἔνδειξις τῆς δικαιοσύνης θεοῦ, "the demonstration of His righteousness").

[79]See, e.g., Rom 3:24; 5:15-17 (τὸ χάρισμα, "[God's] act of goodwill"); Gal 2:21 (ἡ χάρις τοῦ θεοῦ, "God's expression of His goodwill"); 2 Cor 12:9; Gal 5:4. For a discussion of the χάρις word group, see chapter 2, note 174.

[80]See. e.g., Rom 5:8; 8:37-39 (ἡ ἀγάπη τοῦ θεοῦ, "God's expression of His love").

[81]See Rom 3:26. For a discussion of the meaning of this text, see chapter 2 under "Verses 25-26."

to the first.[82] Paul views Christ's death as "God's expression of His righteousness" toward Abraham in that, by establishing the "new covenant," God fulfilled His promise of bringing a "blessing" to all nations through Abraham's "seed"--i.e., through Jesus Christ.[83] Thus Paul says, in 2 Cor 1:20, that "however many promises God may have made to us, they are all of them assured to us in Christ with His affirming 'Yes': He is their fulfilment."[84]

Furthermore, the Cross was "God's expression of His righteousness" toward all nations in that Christ's sacrifice established a "new covenant," under which both Jews and Gentiles may enjoy a covenant relationship with God--or be "reckoned righteous" by God--through trust in Him. In other words, the Cross is God's act of "righteousness," through which He effected "righteousness" for those who trust. God has made Christ "our righteousness."[85]

In addition to "righteousness" (δικαιοσύνη), or participation in the "new covenant," Paul employs a number of other images to communicate what God accomplished through Christ's sacrificial death, including (1) "reconciliation" (καταλλαγή), (2) "purchase" (ἀγοράζειν) or "redemption" (ἐξαγοράζειν), and (3) "deliverance" (ἀπολύτρωσις or ἐξαιρεῖν), "rescue" (ῥύεσθαι), or "liberation" (ἐλευθεροῦν). These terms--along with "righteousness"--have often proved to be a source of confusion to Pauline scholars, who tend to see in them at least four independent interpretations of Christ's death, or four competing theories

---

[82]We may distinguish between the two by saying that Paul's first "core conviction" is that Christ's death was the "sacrifice for sins" which established the "new covenant," while his second "core conviction" is that this "sacrifice" was offered by God Himself, in righteous fulfilment of His promise to Abraham.

[83]See Gal 3:16; cf. Rom 9:5.

[84]This is Alfred Plummer's paraphrase of 2 Cor 1:20, as it appears in *A Critical and Exegetical Commentary on the Second Epistle of St. Paul to the Corinthians,* The International Critical Commentary (New York: Charles Scribner's Sons, 1915), 30. On the "new covenant" as the fulfilment of God's "promise" to Abraham, see Rom 4:1-24; 9:8-9; 15:8-12; Gal 3:1-29; 4:21-28.

[85]1 Cor 1:20.

of the Atonement.[86] However, we must not allow the Apostle's variety of expression to obscure the fact that, for him, all these images communicate what is basically a covenantal idea. The "new covenant" is Paul's unifying concept; it provides the broad framework within which his use of all these terms may be understood. Each image expresses a different aspect of what participation in the "new covenant" involves and thus helps the Apostle to give voice to his "core conviction" that Christ's sacrificial death was "God's expression of His righteousness."

"Reconciliation"

The two most important passages for Paul's doctrine of "reconciliation" (καταλλαγή) are Rom 5:10-11 and 2 Cor 5:18-20, but the term also appears in Rom 11:15 and 1 Cor 7:11. We must briefly examine each of these texts.[87]

---

[86]To illustrate: Charles Cousar maintains that "the Pauline language for the atonement is so diverse that it is well nigh impossible for a single theory to account for its variety . . . The search for coherence in the theology of Paul must not do violence to the richness of the language of the letters themselves" (*A Theology of the Cross: The Death of Jesus in the Pauline Letters,* Overtures to Biblical Theology [Minneapolis: Fortress Press, 1990], 87). In like manner, Petros Vassiliadis ("Your Will Be Done: Reflections from St Paul," *IRM* 75 (1986): 376-82) notes Paul's use of "ransom," "sacrificial," "juridical," and "conciliatory" terminology in order to give voice to a variety of interpretations of Christ's death, including (1) "prophetic," (2) "dialectic," (3) "apocalyptic" (or "eschatological"), and (4) "eucharistic" (or "covenantal") interpretations. He then concludes that "St Paul's real contribution to the early Christian soteriology" is "the above sketched variety of interpretations of Jesus' death." "Our great apostle," he writes, "preserves, and to a certain extent accepts, all the traditional interpretations . . . he does not even show his preference for any of them" (pp. 378-79).

[87]I. Howard Marshall provides a very helpful study on the subject of "reconciliation" in Paul's epistles entitled "The Meaning of 'Reconciliation,'" which appears in *Unity and Diversity in New Testament Theology: Essays in Honor of George E. Ladd,* ed. Robert A. Guelich (Grand Rapids: William B. Eerdmans Publishing Company, 1978), 117-32. Marshall briefly surveys the range of meaning for "reconciliation" terminology in biblical and extra-biblical literature (particularly 2 and 4 Maccabees) before turning to the Pauline texts (in which he includes Col 1:20 and Eph 2:16). A second study containing many important observations comes from Paul Michael Hedquist ("The Pauline Understanding of Reconciliation in Romans 5 and 2 Corinthians 5: An Exegetical and Religio-Historical Study" [Th.D. diss., Union Theological Seminary in Virginia, 1979]), who offers a careful exegesis of Rom 5:1-11 and 2 Cor 5:11-6:2, along with an examination of the religio-historical background for Paul's understanding of "reconciliation" and its place within Pauline soteriology. The fact that both Marshall and Hedquist interpret "righteousness" as a juridical term prevents them from discerning the exact relationship between

1 Corinthians 7:11. Καταλλάσσειν ("to reconcile") is a relational term. In 1 Cor 7:10-11 we find a use of this verb drawn from the social sphere:

> To those who have married I command--not I but the Lord--[that] a wife never separate from [her] husband (but if she ever does separate, [then] let her remain unmarried or [else] let her be reconciled [καταλλαγήτω] to [her] husband) and [that] a husband never divorce [his] wife.

I. Howard Marshall observes that "since the discussion is about a wife who takes the initiative in leaving her husband, it is to be presumed that she feels offended by him and in her indignation separates from him."[88] The passive form of the verb καταλλαγήτω indicates that, in this case, "reconciliation" involves the wife's "laying aside her feeling of offense," giving up her anger against her husband, and "seeking the restoration of friendly relations and the resumption of the marriage relationship."[89] Marshall acknowledges that this may also involve "persuading the husband to lay aside any hard feelings he may have," but the initiative still lies with the wife. The action of reconciliation "is complete only when friendly mutual relations are restored."[90]

2 Corinthians 5:18-21. In 2 Cor 2:14-7:4, we find Paul defending his apostolic ministry against attacks from certain opponents within the church at Corinth. During the course of this apology--namely, in 5:18-21--the Apostle borrows the term "reconciliation" from the sphere of human relationships and uses it to describe the change effected by Christ's death in the relationship between God and human beings. He writes:

"reconciliation" and "righteousness" in Paul's thought, but Marshall comes closest to overcoming this obstacle. See also the pertinent studies in the bibliography by Anne-Etienne, Beale, Buchanan, Evans, Fryer, Thrall, Fitzmyer, Käsemann and Gloer.

[88]Marshall, "Reconciliation," 121. For the possibility that no indignation is involved, see p. 132, note 16.

[89]Marshall, "Reconciliation," 121, 127.

[90]Marshall, "Reconciliation," 121.

(18) Now all [these things are] from God, who acted to reconcile (τοῦ καταλλάξαντος) us to Himself by means of Christ, and who gave to us the ministry of reconciliation (ἡ διακονία τῆς καταλλαγῆς)--(19) [namely, the task of proclaiming the message] that God, by means of Christ, was acting to reconcile (ἦν καταλλάσσων) the world to Himself by not reckoning their trespasses to them and by appointing to us the word concerning reconciliation (ὁ λόγος τῆς καταλλαγῆς). (20) Therefore we serve as ambassadors on behalf of Christ, as God makes [His] appeal by means of us. We ourselves beg [persons] on behalf of Christ: "Be reconciled (καταλλάγητε) to God! (21) He made the [one who] never knew sin a sin[-offering] for us, in order that we might become God's expression of His righteousness by means of him."

When we examine the structure of this text, we note that the Apostle begins by describing God's past act of "reconciliation" as something He carried out in two stages:

A(1) God . . . acted to reconcile us to Himself by means of Christ (v. 18a), and

B(1) [God] gave to us the ministry of reconciliation (v. 18b).

Next, Paul gives content to "the ministry of reconciliation" by describing it as the task of proclaiming the act of God just mentioned in v. 18. In the process, he begins to reveal exactly what the first stage of God's act of "reconciliation" (marked A) was.

A(2) God, by means of Christ, was acting to reconcile the world to Himself by not reckoning their trespasses to them (v. 19a), and

B(2) [God, by means of Christ, was acting to reconcile the world to Himself] by appointing to us the word concerning reconciliation (v. 19b).

Finally, the Apostle declares that it is this God-ordained ministry in which he and his associates are involved, and this God-ordained message that they preach. Note that in v. 21 Paul casts additional light on the first stage of God's activity, and in v. 20b he indicates for the first time what the proper human response to God's act of "reconciliation" is.

B(3)   Therefore we serve as ambassadors on behalf of Christ, as God makes [His] appeal by means of us. We ourselves beg [persons] on behalf of Christ (v. 20a):

C(1)   "Be reconciled to God (v. 20b)!
A(3)   He made the [one who] never knew sin a sin[-offering] for us, in order that we might become God's expression of His righteousness by means of him (v. 21)."

This structural analysis of 2 Cor 5:18-21[91] yields several important insights concerning what Paul means by "reconciliation." First, it is God who takes the initiative to effect reconciliation between Himself and humankind, as the following phrases clearly show: (1) "all [these things are] from God," (2) "[He] acted to reconcile us to Himself, (3) "[He] gave to us the ministry of reconciliation," (4) "God . . . was acting to reconcile the world to Himself by not reckoning their trespasses to them and by appointing to us the word concerning reconciliation," (5) "God makes [His] appeal by means of us," (6) "He made . . . a sin[-offering] for us," and (7) "God's expression of His righteousness."

Second, God's initiative occurred in the past, was executed through Jesus Christ, and took the form of Christ's sacrificial death on the Cross, as seen in the words (1) "by means of Christ" (διὰ Χριστοῦ, v. 18), (2) "by means of Christ" (ἐν Χριστῷ, v. 19), (3) "He made the [one who] never knew sin a sin[-offering] for us," and (4) "by means of him."

Third, as Marshall notes,

> There are . . . three stages in the [total] process of reconciliation [marked A, B, and C above]. First, there is the reconciling act of God in the death of Jesus. Second, there is the proclamation of reconciliation by the "servants" of reconciliation . . . Third, there is the acceptance of God's message by men, when they accept his act of reconciliation by faith, putting away any feelings that they hold against God. The process is not

---

[91]Compare (1) Marshall's slightly different analysis in "Reconciliation," 122, along with (2) that of Otfried Hofius in "'Gott hat unter uns aufgerichtet das Wort von der Versöhnung' (2 Kor 5:19)," *ZNW* 71 (1980): 3-20.

complete until all three stages have taken place and people have entered into peace with God.[92]

Finally, Paul invites us to equate "reconciliation" with "righteousness" when he (1) explains "reconciliation" in v. 19a as God's "not reckoning their trespasses to them," which, for Paul, is equivalent to God's "reckoning" persons "righteous" under the "new covenant,"[93] and (2) identifies the means of "reconciliation" in v. 21 as the "sin-offering" of Christ--i.e. as the sacrifice that established the "new covenant" under which all "the world" may become "God's expression of His righteousness" through trust in Him (see above). For Paul, then, "reconciliation" and "righteousness" (both relational terms, the first drawn from the social sphere and the second from the covenantal sphere) are two different ways of expressing the same basic reality--namely, the new relationship with God enjoyed by human beings through the sacrificial death of Jesus Christ. What Paul normally calls "God's expression of His righteousness" toward both Jews and Gentiles,[94] he here describes as God's initiative

---

[92]Marshall, "Reconciliation," 128. Hedquist completely ignores this third stage of "reconciliation" (i.e., the positive human response to God's initial act of "reconciliation") when he asserts that "the author of reconciliation is God alone" ("Reconciliation," 114) and then suggests that the aorist passive imperative καταλλάγητε, in v. 20b, carries the force of "live as reconciled persons!" (p. 122), or, in other words, "live as persons already reconciled!" He takes 2 Cor 5:18-19 (along with Rom 5:10) to mean that God's "reconciliation" of all human beings to Himself was completed in the past, through the Cross, but that only Christians--or those who trust--realize that fact in the present. This interpretation stretches the meaning of the term καταλλαγή ("reconciliation") beyond the breaking point; for while one person may indeed take the initiative and "act to reconcile" a hostile enemy to him/herself, it is ridiculous to speak of a completed "reconciliation" as long as that other person still lives as an enemy, estranged from the would-be reconciler. It is true that God is solely responsible for "reconciliation" in the sense that, apart from His "acting to reconcile the world to Himself" by sending Christ to the Cross, no such "reconciliation" could ever take place. However, now that God has acted, human beings must give up their enmity against their Creator in order for the "reconciliation" intended by God to be complete. Thus Paul commands persons, in light of the Cross, to themselves "be reconciled to God" (καταλλάγητε, an aorist passive imperative), just as he commands the woman in 1 Cor 7:11 (with the aorist passive imperative καταλλαγήτω--see above) to "be reconciled to [her] husband." See also note 109.

[93]See Rom 4:7.

[94]See, e.g., Rom 3:21-22.

"to reconcile the world to Himself." What the Apostle here terms "the ministry of reconciliation," he speaks of elsewhere as the "apostleship aimed at the obedience which proceeds from trust among all the nations."[95] "The word concerning reconciliation" in 2 Cor 5:19 becomes "the word which calls for trust" in Rom 10:8.[96] Paul's appeal to "be reconciled to God" becomes the command to "trust" in the Lord Jesus Christ and thus to enter into the "righteousness" of the "new covenant."[97]

Why does Paul choose the language of "reconciliation" over the language of "righteousness" in 2 Cor 5:18-21? First, the term "reconciliation" expresses the change in the quality of personal relationship between God and sinners (namely, a shift from a relationship of the wrathful Judge toward His rebellious enemies, to a relationship of the gracious Creator and Lord toward His submissive "new creatures") effected by their trustful entrance into the "new covenant" He has established through the sacrificial death of Jesus Christ.[98] Second, and most important for this context, Paul here characterizes his work as "the ministry of reconciliation" in an effort to persuade the Corinthians to be reconciled to him. If the world may be reconciled to God only by His sending Christ to the cross and by His appointing messengers to carry the word of the Cross, and if Paul and his associates are such "ambassadors on behalf of Christ" who bear "the word concerning reconciliation;" then how can the Corinthians reject God's appointed messengers without, at the same time, rejecting God Himself? How can they be reconciled to God and not be reconciled to His "ministers"?

---

[95]Rom 1:5.

[96]Cf. Rom 10:17 ("the word concerning Christ") and Phil 1:27 ("[that] trust which has its source in the gospel").

[97]Paul calls the person who enters into this new relationship with God "a new creation" (καινὴ κτίσις) in 2 Cor 5:17.

[98]This thought plays a key role in Rom 5:10-11, which we will examine below.

140

Paul here employs the language of reconciliation "in order to call members of the church to welcome him back personally as their spiritual father."[99]

Romans 5:10-11. In Rom 3:21-4:22, Paul describes how God, in the past, sent Christ to die on the Cross in order to establish the "new covenant" in fulfilment of His promise to Abraham. Then, in Rom 4:23-5:11, Paul turns to a discussion of how that covenant shapes the present. From the time of Christ's death and resurrection forward, anyone who trusts "in the One who raised Jesus our Lord from the dead"--whether s/he be Jew or Greek--will be "reckoned" by God as "righteous," or as participating in the "new covenant" with Him.[100] Under this "new covenant," the "righteous" now enjoy (1) a new relationship with God, which Paul characterizes as "peace with God,"[101] or "standing" within the sphere of God's "goodwill,"[102] (2) the gift of "the Holy Spirit,"[103] and (3) the confident "hope" that, in the future, we will receive "the glory of God,"[104] "salvation" from the "Wrath" of God's eschatological Judgment,[105] and eschatological "life."[106]

In the course of this discussion, Paul once again describes "righteousness" under the "new covenant" in terms of being "reconciled to God." In Rom 5:10-11 he writes:

---

[99]Marshall, "Reconciliation," 129.

[100]Rom 4:24.

[101]Rom 5:1.

[102]Rom 5:2.

[103]Rom 5:5.

[104]Rom 5:2.

[105]See Rom 5:9-10.

[106]Rom 5:10. Note that, in Rom 1:17, Paul recalls the promise of Habakkuk that the "righteous" person will, on the basis of his/her "trust" (or participation in the "new covenant" established by God through Christ), "live ['eschatological life']."

(10) [I can rightfully declare that we will be saved from God's Wrath by means of Christ's blood-sacrifice] because (γάρ) if, while we were enemies, we have been reconciled to God by means of the death of His Son [(and we have been)]; [then how] much more--since we have been reconciled--will we be saved within [the sphere where] his "life" [is the rule]! (11) But not only [this]--Instead, we also express confidence in God, by means of our Lord Jesus Christ, by means of whom we have now received the reconciliation.

The word γάρ ("because") indicates that Paul, in v. 10, is offering the grounds or basis for his statements in vv. 8-9. In order to strengthen his case, the Apostle essentially repeats what he said in those earlier verses using different terms. The close parallelism between the two statements[107] shows that, in this context, Paul again uses "reconciliation" to express a covenantal idea, much as he did in 2 Cor 5:18-21. Verse 10a ("while we were enemies, we have been reconciled to God by means of the death of His Son") is parallel to v. 8 ("God demonstrated His own love toward us, in that, while we were still sinners, Christ died for us").[108] The causal clause from v. 10b ("since we have been reconciled") finds its counterpart in v. 9a ("since we have now been reckoned righteousness by means of his blood[y sacrificial death]").[109] Paul's strong assurance in v. 10c ("[how] much more . . . will we

---

[107]Marshall notes this parallelism in "Reconciliation," 124.

[108]With these phrases, Paul recalls stage A of the total process of "reconciliation"--namely, Christ's sacrificial death (see the preceding discussion of 2 Cor 5:18-21). God carried out this initial stage of His "act of reconciliation" "while we were still sinners."

[109]In these clauses, Paul gathers up all three stages in the process of "reconciliation" and speaks of them as a single event. As we observed in note 92, Hedquist ("Reconciliation," 227-32) argues that Christ's death reconciles all human beings--or all God's "enemies" (ἐχθροί)--to God, but that only those who trust have "apprehended" this totally objective reality. If this were the case, then God would have no more "enemies"--unless we empty the term of all meaning and speak of persons who are both "enemies" of God and "reconciled to God" at the same time. Paul does not do this; for in spite of the fact that Christ has been crucified, he maintains, throughout his epistles, that many persons continue to live as "enemies" (ἐχθροί) of the Cross of Christ" (Phil 3:18; cf. Rom 11:28; 1 Cor 15:25-26). Once again, Hedquist overlooks the fact that, for this Apostle, a trusting human response to "the word of reconciliation" is itself the third stage in the total process of reconciliation, without which "the reconciliation" cannot be complete. God's demonstration of love, or His act of reconciliation in the Cross of Christ, is

be saved within [the sphere where] his 'life' [is the rule]!") is parallel to v. 9b ("[how] much more, then, will we be saved from the Wrath [of God] by means of it!"). Barrett draws the correct conclusion when he says that "Justification [or 'righteousness'] and reconciliation are different metaphors describing the same fact."[110]

Why does Paul here describe "righteousness" under the "new covenant" as "reconciliation" with God? The Apostle's main purpose in Rom 5:5-11 is to give his readers assurance that, in the future, God will indeed grant to those presently participating in the "new covenant" the "salvation" and eschatological "life" promised to the "righteous." Toward this end, Paul reminds the Roman Christians of the extraordinary love God demonstrated toward His fallen creatures in that, while they were still His "enemies" and "sinners," God sacrificed Christ in order to establish the "new covenant" for their benefit. If God, in the past, showed such love toward His "enemies;" then "how much more" will He, in the future, keep His promises to those who now enjoy "peace with God" through Jesus Christ!

In this kind of an argument, the more Paul emphasizes the deep rift which existed between God and sinful humanity, the better he is able to impress upon his readers the magnitude of God's love in sending Christ to die for them.[111] The more they realize the depths of God's love, the greater

---

potentially efficacious for all human beings, so that Paul can say that God acted in the past (stage A) to reconcile all His "enemies." However, the Cross is practically efficacious "now" only for the "we"--i.e., only for Christians, for the "righteous," for participants in the "new covenant," for those who trust in Christ. All others have "rejected God's expression of His goodwill" (Gal 2:21), or refused to "be reconciled to God" (2 Cor 5:20).

[110]Barrett, *Romans,* 108.

[111]Thus Paul says that, when God sent Christ to the cross, we were not "righteous" (δίκαιος) or "good" (ἀγαθός), but "weak" (ἀσθενής) and "impious" (ἀσεβής) "sinners" (ἁμαρτωλοι)--the "enemies" (ἐχθροί) of God.

their "confidence" will be in His promises for the future.[112] The term "reconciliation" is better suited than "righteousness" for highlighting these particular points--namely, (1) the idea of hostility or disharmony between God and humankind, and (2) the depth of love required to forge a new relationship of "peace." Therefore, in this context, Paul characterizes the new relationship enjoyed between God and His creatures under the "new covenant" as a "reconciliation;" for this terminology best suits his immediate purpose of assuring his readers that they will certainly receive the "salvation" and "glory" and "life" for which they hope.

Romans 11:15. Paul employs the term "reconciliation" (καταλλαγή) in one other passage--namely, in Romans 11:15. Concerning Israel the Apostle writes:

> . . . if their rejection (ἡ ἀποβολὴ αὐτῶν[113]) [means] reconciliation (καταλλαγή) of the world, [then] what [will their] acceptance (ἡ πρόσλημψις) [mean] if not life from the dead?

Chapters 9-11 reflect Paul's struggle to understand why so many Jews have refused to trust in Christ,[114] and thus do not participate in the "new covenant" which God promised to their ancestor.[115] The Apostle suggests that God has used Israel's rejection to bring many of the Gentiles into His

---

[112]Note that Paul makes the same point in Rom 8:32, where he writes: "[He] who did not spare His very own Son, [but] instead handed him over [to death] for us all--how could He not also give us all [things] along with him [as an expression of His goodwill] (πῶς οὐχὶ καὶ σὺν αὐτῷ τὰ πάντα ἡμῖν χαρίσεται)?"

[113]Note that ἀποβολή ("rejection") is here used as an antonym of πρόσλημψις ("acceptance"). Note also that ἡ ἀποβολὴ αὐτῶν probably functions as a subjective genitive ("their rejection") rather than as an objective genitive ("[God's] rejection of them") in light of (1) the parallelism with v. 12, where the actions of the Jews are under consideration, and (2) the denial in vv. 1-2 that God has "rejected" (ἀπωθεῖν) His elect people. However, a case could be made for the other view on the basis of God's "breaking off" and "grafting in" the "branches" of Israel in vv. 17-24. Of course, God takes this action only in the face of Israel's lack of trust in Christ.

[114]See, e.g., Rom 9:30-32; 10:3-4, 16-17, 21; 11:20, 23.

[115]See Rom 9:4-5; 11:1, 27

covenant. He will then use the Gentiles' acceptance to provoke jealousy among the Jews, thereby bringing many more Israelites into that covenant.[116] His point in 11:15 is that, if Israel's rejection brought the wonderful result of "reconciliation" of the Gentiles; then Israel's acceptance will surely bring an even more glorious result--namely, the long-awaited Resurrection of the dead.

In 11:15, the Apostle employs the term καταλλαγή to refer to all three stages in the process of "reconciliation"--namely, (1) God's sending Christ to the Cross, (2) God's establishing the "ministry of reconciliation," in which Paul shares as "Apostle to the Gentiles,"[117] and (3) a trustful human response to the gospel.[118] Yet his primary focus is stage 3; for this is the point at which the Gentiles have proven "successful," while so many Jews have produced only "failure" (ἥττημα).[119] Paul here chooses the term καταλλαγή ("reconcilia-tion")--rather than "righteousness"--in "conscious contrast" to the thought of Israel's "rejection" of "God's expression of His righteousness" in Christ.[120]

Paul's use of the language of "reconciliation." In conclusion, Paul employs the language of "reconciliation" (καταλλαγή) to express what God accomplished through the death of Christ in three passages: 2 Cor 5:18-21, Rom 5:10-11, and Rom 11:15. In each passage, "reconciliation" does not communicate an idea radically different from what Paul normally means by "righteousness." Instead, the Apostle consistently uses "reconciliation" as a virtual synonym for "righteousness," or in order to highlight some particular aspect of what life under the "new covenant" involves. In other words, the

---

[116]See Rom 11:11-16, 25-32.

[117]See Rom 11:13.

[118]See above under "2 Cor 5:18-21."

[119]See Rom 11:12; cf. v. 7.

[120]Marshall makes a similar point in "Reconciliation," 125. However, he interprets ἡ ἀποβολὴ αὐτῶν as an objective genitive, rather than a subjective genitive.

"new covenant" remains Paul's unifying concept; but he employs the terminology of "reconciliation," in some contexts, because it proves more suitable for expressing certain implications of his "core conviction" that Christ's death was "God's expression of His righteousness" toward all nations.

"Purchase" or "Redemption"[121]

Paul borrows two terms from the marketplace in order to communicate what God accomplished through the sacrifice of Christ--namely, the verbs ἀγοράζειν ("to purchase") and ἐξαγοράζειν ("to redeem"). The first term appears in 1 Cor 6:20 and 7:23, while Paul employs the second in Gal 3:13 and 4:5.

1 Corinthians 7:23. In the seventh chapter of 1 Corinthians, Paul advises that every Christian should "lead the life which the Lord has assigned to him/her" or, in other words, "remain in the state in which s/he was called,"[122] whether it be as a Jew or Greek, married or unmarried, slave or free. With regard to slaves, however, he issues a partial retraction of this advice in vv. 21-23 by suggesting that, in their case, there may be a better alternative. He writes:

> (21) Have you been called [as] a slave? Never let it bother you! But if you are indeed able to become free, [then] by all means do it (μᾶλλον χρῆσαι)! (22) [I say that, if you have been called as a slave, you should not let it bother you] because the person who, [as] a slave, has been called into [the sphere where the] Lord [rules] is the Lord's freed-[person]. Likewise, the person who has been called [as] a free [person] is Christ's slave. (23) You have been purchased with a price (τιμῆς ἠγοράσθητε). Never become slaves of human beings!

---

[121] I. Howard Marshall traces the development of the concept of "redemption" (ἀγοράζειν, ἐξαγοράζειν, ἀπολύτρωσις) in Paul and other New Testament writings in "The Development of the Concept of Redemption in the New Testament," which appears in *Reconciliation and Hope: New Testament Essays on Atonement and Eschatology Presented to L. L. Morris on His 60th Birthday,* ed. Robert Banks (Exeter: The Paternoster Press, 1974), 153-69.

[122] 1 Cor 7:17, 20 (RSV); cf. v. 24.

Paul repeatedly insists that the Christian--whether s/he be slave or free in the reckoning of this world--ultimately belongs to the Lord Jesus Christ. This is seen in the very fact that Christ is called "Lord," and also in Paul's description of the believer as "Christ's slave," or as a person within "the sphere where the Lord rules." Even the "freed-person" does not belong to him/her- self; s/he is "the Lord's."

Paul most likely urges Christians who are slaves to "become free" be- cause he fears it may be difficult for them to serve two masters, to be "slaves of human beings" and slaves of Christ at the same time.[123] His reminder to the Corinthians that "you have been purchased with a price" serves to empha- size this point: Christ has "purchased" them; they are now his property. Therefore, if at all possible, they should not "be slaves of human beings," the property of wo/men.

Paul can readily refer to Christians as "slaves of Christ" because this is the nature of their relationship to Christ under the "new covenant," into which they enter through entrusting (πιστεύειν) themselves to him as Lord.[124] Therefore, when Paul employs the verb ἀγοράζειν to tell the Corinthians, "You have been purchased with a price," he is not setting forth some sort of "ransom theory of atonement." Instead, the Apostle is simply communicating a covenantal idea, using an image drawn from the slave-market that is particu- larly appropriate for this context.

1 Corinthians 6:20. In 1 Cor 6:12-20, Paul once again cites Christ's lordship over those under the "new covenant" as grounds for a certain pattern

---

[123]Compare 1 Cor 7:32-35, where Paul fears that marriage may interfere with a Christian's "undivided devotion to the Lord" (εὐπάρεδρον τῷ κυρίῳ ἀπερισπάστως).

[124]Paul also describes Christian existence in terms of being "slaves of God" (rather than slaves of some other "lord"--i.e., "slaves of Sin") in, for example, Rom 6:16-22.

of behavior among Christians. He commands the Corinthians to "flee immorality"[125] because "the body [σῶμα] [is] not for immorality [πορνεία], but for the Lord, and the Lord [is] for the body."[126] In vv. 19b-20 he writes:

> You are not your own, for you have been purchased with a price [ἠγοράσ- θητε γὰρ τιμῆς]. Glorify God in your bodies!

Here, as in 1 Cor 7:23, we fail to understand fully Paul's use of the verb ἀγοράζειν ("to purchase") if we do not interpret it against the background of his "core conviction" that the Cross is the "sacrifice" by which God established the "new covenant." Paul is not saying that Christ's death was literally some sort of "payment" by which he "purchased" the Corinthian Christians from someone else. Instead, he is using an image from the commercial sphere to communicate the fact that, within the bounds of the "new covenant," God--through Christ--rules as Lord. This new reality has important implications for the Corinthians' behavior.

Galatians 3:13. The verb ἐξαγοράζειν (ἐκ + ἀγοράζειν) literally means "to purchase out from." Hence, this term moves beyond the idea of a simple "purchase" (ἀγοράζειν) in order to convey the "ransoming" or "redeeming" of one person (or thing) out of another's ownership or sphere of control. Paul uses ἐξαγοράζειν ("to redeem") only in his epistle to the Galatians.

A careful reading of this letter suggests that a group of itinerant Jewish-Christian missionaries from the "Circumcision" party[127] are seeking

---

[125]1 Cor 6:18.

[126]1 Cor 6:13.

[127]See Gal 2:12. In an article entitled "Who Were Paul's Opponents in Galatia?" (*BSac* 147 [1990]: 329-50), Walt Russell describes three major views concerning the identity of Paul's opponents in Galatia--namely, (1) the "traditional view" (held, e.g., by Calvin, Luther, Baur, Munck and Harvey), which holds that the opponents were Judaizers, (2) the "two-opponent view" (held, e.g., by Lütgert and Ropes), which sees Paul responding to both Judaizers and antinomians, and (3) the "Gnostic/syncretistic Jewish Christian view" (held in one form or another by Crownfield, Schlier, Brinsmead, Georgi, Wegenast and Betz). Russell himself defends the "traditional view." For a more extended treatment, see George Howard, *Paul: Crisis in Galatia. A Study in Early*

to persuade Paul's Galatian converts that his "gospel for the Uncircumcision"[128] (or "Gentiles") is deficient, that he is preaching a watered-down message designed to please human beings rather than God.[129] According to Paul's gospel, the God of Jesus Christ reckons both Jews and Gentiles righteous solely on the basis of their trust in Him. The "Apostle to the Gentiles" does not require circumcision or Torah-observance from Gentile believers; for they are not entering the "old," exclusively "Jewish" covenant of Moses, but a "new," universal covenant, under which God accepts Gentiles as "Gentiles."

The Judaizers agree with Paul that Gentiles should put their trust in Christ, but they are alarmed at his apparent attempt to push aside the Mosaic covenant and its Law, a gift to the Jews from God Himself. They claim that the benefits brought by the "Jewish" Messiah are only for Jews--i.e., only for "the children (υἱοί) of Abraham."[130] Therefore any Gentiles who wish to become Christians must first become "children of Abraham" by accepting circumcision (the outward sign of "Jewishness") and the "yoke" of the Torah.[131]

Christian Theology, Society for New Testament Studies Monograph Series, 35 (Cambridge: Cambridge University Press, 1979).

[128]Gal 2:7.

[129]See Gal 1:10.

[130]See Gal 3:7. The Judaizers may have claimed that Abraham himself entered the Mosaic covenant when he was circumcised, with the result that no persons are truly "sons" or "daughters" of Abraham unless they, too, submit to the "yoke" of the Law. George Foot Moore gathers evidence for such an interpretation of Abraham from rabbinic writings which maintain that Abraham "was thoroughly versed in both the written and the unwritten law, and kept them both" (*Judaism,* I, 275-76 and III, 86, under "I, 276 N46"). In answer to the question of why circumcision, the sign of the covenant, is not mentioned in the Decalogue, R. Eliezer replies that "it had already been given [to Abraham], and is presumed in Exod 19:5, or in the repeated mention of 'the *ger* (circumcised proselyte) who is in thy towns'" (II, 18).

[131]These were the same conditions placed upon Gentile proselytes to the Jewish religion. The Judaizers could have made a strong scriptural case for their views by appealing to such texts as (1) Gen 17:9-16, in which God tells Abraham that he, his descendants, and any foreigners attached to his household, must be circumcised, and that any male who is not circumcised will be cut off from his people as a covenant-breaker, (2) Gen 17:26-27, in which

Apparently the Judaizers' "other gospel"[132] was well received in Galatia; for, throughout his epistle, Paul expresses great anger and disappointment over the fact that some Galatians are seeking to gain the "benefits" of Christ by accepting circumcision,[133] the Jewish religious calender,[134] and the other works required by the Law.[135]

Paul agrees with the Judaizers that the benefits brought by Christ come only to "the children of Abraham." However, in Gal 3:1-14 he appeals to the Galatians' experience of the Holy Spirit (which, for Paul, clearly identifies them as "children of Abraham"[136]) in order to demonstrate that the "children of Abraham" are not persons who participate in the Mosaic covenant based on works. Instead, the true "children of Abraham" are persons who participate in the "new covenant" based on trust. In vv. 6-14 he writes:

Abraham himself receives circumcision, along with his son and his household, (3) Exod 12:48-49, in which God requires any alien who wants to celebrate the Lord's Passover with Israel to have all the males in his household circumcised, and (4) Isa 56:6-8, in which all foreigners who bind themselves to the Lord are expected to hold fast to the covenant and to keep the Sabbath.

[132]Gal 1:6.

[133]See Gal 5:2-4; 6:12-13; cf. 2:3-4.

[134]See Gal 4:8-10.

[135]See Gal 3:2, 5; 4:21. Note the strict dietary laws mentioned in 2:11-14.

[136]Genesis describes how God promised to give Abraham (1) "children" as numerous as the stars in the heavens (Gen 15:5; cf. Rom 4:18), along with (2) "the earth" (ἡ γῆ, Gen 13:15; 17:8 [LXX]; cf. Rom 4:13). In an excellent article entitled "'Promise' in Galatians: A Reading of Paul's Reading of Scripture" (*JBL* 107 [1988]: 709-20), Sam K. Williams argues persuasively that Paul interprets Christians' receiving the Holy Spirit as God's fulfilment of these promises; for (1) "the Spirit begets true sons of Abraham," who are characterized by trust (p. 714; see Gal 4:4-6, 28-29), and (2) the "earth" is becoming the domain of "the children of Abraham" because "the peoples of the earth [both Gentiles and Jews], by the miraculous power of God's Spirit, are being begotten as children of God" (p. 719) and are already beginning to exercise authority as "heirs" over "all things" (pp. 718-19; see Gal 4:1-7, 21-31; cf. Rom 8:32; 1 Cor 6:2). Thus τὴν ἐπαγγελίαν τοῦ πνεύματος in Gal 3:14 functions as a genitive of apposition ("the promise which is the Spirit"). Furthermore, when Paul asks "Did you receive the Spirit by means of the works of the Law or by means of the message [which calls for] trust (ἀκοὴ πίστεως)?" in Gal 3:2 (cf. v. 5), he is, in effect, inquiring as to whether the Galatians became "children of Abraham" through participation in the Mosaic covenant or participation in the "new covenant."

(6) [It is] just as [it is written]: "Abraham trusted in God, and it [i.e., his trust] was reckoned to him as righteousness."[137] (7) Consequently [i.e., since "Abraham trusted in God"], you know that those [who live] on the basis of trust (οἱ ἐκ πίστεως)--they are the children (υἱοί) of Abraham.

(8) The scripture foresaw that God would reckon the Gentiles righteous on the basis of trust (ἐκ πίστεως), and it proclaimed the gospel to Abraham in advance (προευηγγελίσατο τῷ Ἀβραάμ): "All the Gentiles within [the sphere of] you (ἐν σοί, i.e., within the sphere of "trusting Abraham" [v. 9], or within the sphere of Abraham's trust [vv. 6-7]) will be blessed."[138] (9) Therefore those [who live] on the basis of trust (οἱ ἐκ πίστεως) are blessed along with trusting Abraham.[139] (10) [I can rightfully say that it is those who live on the basis of trust, rather than on the basis of the works of the Law, who are blessed] because as many as are [living] on the basis of the works of the Law (ἐξ ἔργων νόμου) are under a curse. [I can rightfully say that those who live on the basis of the works of the Law are under a curse] because it has been written: "Every [person is] under a curse who does not continue in all the [things which] have been written in the book which is the Law, with the result that s/he does them."[140] (11) That no one within [the sphere of] the Law (ἐν νόμῳ) is reckoned righteous before God [(toward the goal of "eschatologi- cal life") is] evident, for "the [person reckoned] righteous on the basis of trust (ἐκ πίστεως) will live ['eschatological life']."[141] (12) But the Law is not based on trust (ἐκ πίστεως). Instead, "the [person who] has done these [works of the Law] will live within [the sphere of] them (ἐν αὐτοῖς)."[142] (13) Christ has redeemed (ἐξαγοράζειν) us from the Law's curse by be- coming a curse for us (ὑπὲρ ἡμῶν) (For it has been written: "Cursed [is]

---

[137]The Apostle here quotes from Gen 15:6.

[138]Gen 12:3.

[139]Paul here alludes to Gen 12:2-3, where God promises Abraham that He will (1) "bless" Abraham himself, and (2) "bless" all the Gentiles who are "within" him (ἐν σοί)--i.e., within the sphere of Abraham's trust (see our translation of Gal 6:8). Since the Apostle interprets this latter "blessing" for the nations as an "advance" proclamation of the "gospel" (cf. Paul's similar use of Ps 32 [31]:1-2 in Rom 4:6-8)--i.e., as God's promise of the "new covenant" which is based on trust--he concludes that it is "those [who live] on the basis of trust" who "are blessed along with trusting Abraham."

[140]Deut 27:26; cf. 28:58-68.

[141]Hab 2:4.

[142]Lev 18:5.

every one who hangs on a tree."[143]), (14) in order that the blessing [promised to] Abraham might be [given] to the Gentiles [who are] within [the sphere of] Christ Jesus (ἐν Χριστῷ Ἰησοῦ), in order that we might receive the promise, which is the Spirit, by means of trust (διὰ τῆς πίστεως).

Do persons become "children of Abraham" through participation in the Mosaic covenant or participation in the "new covenant"? Since Paul's opponents view Abraham primarily as a Law-keeper, they identify the "children of Abraham" as persons under the Mosaic covenant who perform the works required by the Law. Paul argues from the Law itself that Abraham was instead distinguished by his trust in God (vv. 6, 9 ["trusting Abraham"]).[144] "Consequently," the Galatians must acknowledge that the true "children of Abraham" are those persons who participate in the "new covenant;" for they-- like Abraham--live "on the basis of trust" in Abraham's God (v. 7).

Pressing his advantage, Paul contrasts the "new covenant" with the Mosaic covenant, in vv. 8-14, in terms of "blessing" and "curse." Paul views the "new covenant," under which God reckons "the Gentiles righteous on the basis of trust," as the fulfilment of God's promise to bring "blessing" to persons from all nations who live within the sphere of Abraham's trust (vv. 8-9). If this "blessing" is based on trust, then the Law cannot give the Gentiles access to God's "blessing;" for "the Law is not based on trust," but on works (vv. 11-12). Far from offering a "blessing," the Law can only bring "curse;" for the Law curses every person who does not fulfil all the Law's demands (v. 10). However, Paul declares in vv. 13-14 that

(13) Christ has redeemed (ἐξαγοράζειν) us from the Law's curse by becoming a curse for us (ὑπὲρ ἡμῶν) (For it has been written: "Cursed [is] every one who hangs on a tree."), (14) in order that the blessing [promised to] Abraham might be [given] to the Gentiles [who are] within [the sphere

---

[143]Deut 21:23.

[144]In Gal 3:17, Paul questions whether Abraham could have kept the Law at all since the Mosaic covenant, with its Law, was not even given until "four hundred and thirty years later."

of] Christ Jesus (ἐν Χριστῷ Ἰησοῦ), in order that we might receive the promise, which is the Spirit, by means of trust (διὰ τῆς πίστεως).

When Paul here speaks of Christ's "becoming a curse," he is not making a vague reference to the *modus operandi* of the atonement, as so many scholars have suggested.[145] Instead, the Apostle is simply stating the fact that Jesus was "crucified" using the striking language of the "curse" evoked by his discussion of "the Law's curse" in vv. 10 and 13. Paul clearly reveals his intended meaning through a parenthetical reference to Deut 21:23, which he introduces with the causal conjunction γάρ ("because"): Jesus became a "curse" in the sense that he was "hanged on a tree." In other words, when Paul says,

---

[145]See, for example, the work of (1) John W. Bailey ("Gospel for Mankind: The Death of Christ in the Thinking of Paul," *Int* 7 [1953]: 163-74), who says that Paul here interprets the Cross as "the clear revelation of the truth that God does not deal with men on the basis of the law at all, but on the basis of their faith only" (p. 166), (2) Hans Dieter Betz (*Galatians: A Commentary on Paul's Letter to the Churches in Galatia*, Hermeneia--A Critical and Historical Commentary on the Bible [Philadelphia: Fortress Press, 1979]), who sees in Gal 3:13 "an underlying concept of Jesus' death interpreted by means of the Jewish concept of the meritorious death of the righteous and its atoning benefits" (p. 151), (3) F. F. Bruce (*The Epistle to the Galatians: A Commentary on the Greek Text*, The New International Greek Testament Commentary [Grand Rapids: William B. Eerdmans Publishing Company, 1982]), who argues that "the curse which Christ 'became' was his people's curse, as the death which he died was their death" (p. 166), (4) Martin Luther (*Commentary on Saint Paul's Epistle to the Galatians*, corrected and revised by Erasmus Middleton [Grand Rapids: Wm. B. Eerdmans Publishing Company, 1930]), who maintains that "because he [i.e., Christ] had taken upon him our sins, it behoved him to bear the punishment and wrath of God: not for his own person . . . but for our person . . . [thus] making a happy change with us" (p. 249), (5) I. Howard Marshall ("The Death of Jesus in Recent New Testament Study," *WW* 3 [1983]: 12-21), who writes: "Here, if anywhere in the New Testament, we have the thought of a penalty for not abiding by all the things written in the law, and this penalty has been borne by Christ . . . The language is plainly that of substitution" (p. 18), and (6) Daniel R. Schwartz ("Two Pauline Allusions to the Redemptive Mechanism of the Crucifixion," *JBL* 102 [1983]: 259-68), who argues that "Paul's thought behind Gal 3:13; 4:4-5 is as follows: Christ was hung on a tree, and so became a curse, and so could become a scapegoat which, by being sent forth to its death, redeemed the Jews from their curse" (p. 263). See also the five possible interpretations of Christ's "becoming a curse for us" discussed by Ernest De Witt Burton in *A Critical and Exegetical Commentary on the Epistle to the Galatians*, The International Critical Commentary (Edinburgh: T. & T. Clark, 1920), 172. C. M. Tuckett offers a strong critique of such interpretations of Gal 3:13 in "Deuteronomy 21:23 and Paul's Conversion," in *L'apôtre Paul: Personalité, Style et Conception du Ministère*, ed. A. Vanhoye, 345-50, Bibliotheca Ephemeridum Theologicarum Lovaniensium, 73 (Leuven: University Press, 1986).

in Gal 3:13, that Jesus "became a curse," he means no more and no less than that Jesus "died on a cross."

Paul's interpretation of Christ's crucifixion begins with his addition of the category 3 formula ὑπὲρ ἡμῶν ("for us," v. 13). This sets Christ's death apart from other executions as a "sacrifice." What kind of sacrifice was it? The sacrifice which gave "to the Gentiles" the "blessing [promised to] Abraham." What is this "blessing"? The "new covenant," under which God "reckons the Gentiles righteous on the basis of trust" (v. 8) and gives to them "the promise which is the Spirit" (v. 14).[146]

Finally, we come to the phrase that initiated this discussion of Galatians 3. What does Paul mean when he says that Christ "redeemed (ἐξα-γοράζειν) us from the Law's curse"? Whereas the Judaizers offer the Galatians only the "tyranny" of the Law, Christ went to the Cross for the very purpose of securing their release. His sacrifice removes those who trust in him from the sphere of "the Law's curse" by establishing the sphere of "blessing," the "new covenant." Thus, when Paul employs the language of "redemption" in Gal 3:13, he is not setting forth a theory of the Atonement at odds with his usual covenantal interpretation of the Cross. Instead, he is simply restating his "core conviction" that Christ's death was the sacrifice which established the "new covenant," using terminology appropriate for this context. In light of the Scriptures' testimony to the "gospel" (v. 8), along with their own experience of the Spirit through trust, Paul hopes that his Galatian readers will abandon the "old" covenant with its "curse" and firmly embrace the "new covenant" of "blessing."

Galatians 4:5. If God gives the "blessing" of the "new covenant" apart from the Mosaic covenant and its Law, then Paul's readers might very well

---

[146]I.e., they become "children of Abraham," and thus "heirs" of all things--see note 136.

ask: "Why, then, [did God give] the Law?"[147] In the course of offering a reply, Paul says that--before the "new covenant" was given--human beings (and particularly Jews) were "confined under the Law,"[148] "enslaved under the elemental powers of the world" (τὰ στοιχεῖα τοῦ δόσμου),[149] and "imprisoned under Sin."[150] Now that the "new covenant" has been given, the Apostle characterizes those who participate in it not as "slaves," but as (1) "Abraham's seed,"[151] (2) the "adopted"[152] "sons of God"[153] who have received "the Spirit of His Son,"[154] and (3) "heirs in accordance with the promise."[155]

What effected this "redemption" of sinners from "slavery" and their elevation to the status of "heirs"? Paul points to a specific act of God, carried out in history through His Son Jesus Christ:

> But when the fulness of time came, God sent forth His Son, who had been born of a woman, born under the Law, in order that he might redeem (ἐξαγοράζειν) those under the Law, in order that we might receive the adoption.[156]

---

[147]Gal 3:19.

[148]Gal 3:23.

[149]Gal 4:3.

[150]Gal 3:22. Paul is able to equate being "under the Law" with being "under Sin" or "under the (presumably demonic) elemental powers of the world" because "righteousness," or freedom from the power of Sin, comes only through trust in Christ--i.e., only through participation in the "new covenant." Before the "new covenant" was given, then, "everyone"--including the Law-abiding Jew--was "a prisoner under Sin" (Gal 3:22).

[151]Gal 3:29.

[152]Gal 4:5.

[153]Gal 3:26; 4:6, 7.

[154]Gal 4:6.

[155]Gal 3:29; cf. 4:7. On the relationship between the three, see note 136.

[156]Gal 4:4-5.

After Christ entered the human sphere, he died on the cross as the sacrifice which established the "new covenant." He thereby made possible the transfer of persons, through trust, out from the dominion of Sin and into the sphere of divine "sonship." Behind Paul's "redemption" language we detect, once again, his basic "core conviction" that the Cross of Christ was "God's expression of His righteousness."

"Deliverance," "Rescue" and "Liberation"[157]

Christ's death not only effects "reconciliation," "purchase" and "redemption." In a number of passages scattered throughout the Pauline corpus, the Apostle says that the Cross also accomplishes some sort of "rescue" (ῥύεσ-θαι) or "deliverance" (ἀπολύτρωσις or ἐξαιρεῖν) or "liberation" (ἐλευθεροῦν). Christ frees those who trust him from the dominion of Sin (ἐλευθεροῦν, Rom 6:18, 22; cf. 8:2 ["the Law as determined by Sin and Death"]; ἀπολύτρωσις, Rom 3:24; cf. 1 Cor 1:30; ἐξαιρεῖν, Gal 1:4 ["the present evil age," in which the powers of evil hold sway]; ῥύεσθαι, Rom 11:26), from the consequences of the Adamic Fall, such as corruption and death (ἀπολύτρωσις, Rom 8:23;[158] cf. ἐλευθεροῦν, Rom 8:21 [liberation of Creation from "slavery to corruption"]; ῥύεσθαι, Rom 7:24 ["this body determined by death"]), and from "the coming Wrath [of God]" (ῥύεσθαι, 1 Thess 1:10). In those few passages specifically stating how Christ accomplishes such acts of "deliverance," the Apostle points us to the Lord's death and interprets it as the sacrifice which established the "new covenant." To illustrate: (1) It is the Lord's "sacrifice which purifies from sin" (ἱλαστήριον, discussed earlier in this chapter) which

---

[157]See note 121.

[158]In an essay entitled "Greco-Roman Slave Terminology and Pauline Metaphors for Salvation" (in *Society of Biblical Literature 1987 Seminar Papers,* ed. Kent Harold Richards [Atlanta: Scholars Press, 1987], 100-110), Wayne G. Rollins focuses on "Paul's use of servile metaphors [including ἀπολύτρωσις, 'deliverance'] for the salvation event" (p. 102) in Rom 8:18-25.

156

effects "deliverance" (ἀπολύτρωσις[159]) from Sin in Rom 3:25. (2) It is Christ's "sin-offering" (also discussed earlier in this chapter) which "liberates" (ἐλευθεροῦν) from "the Law as determined by Sin and Death" in Rom 8:2. (3) Finally, in Rom 11:26-27, Paul cites Isa 59:20 and 27:9 in order to speak of God as "the Deliver" (ὁ ῥυόμενος) who will "banish godlessness from Jacob" and "remove their sins" by making a "covenant" with them.

Conclusion

There is no need to belabor a point that is becoming quite clear: Paul does not vacillate between competing theories of the Atonement, as many scholars have supposed. Instead, he consistently interprets the Cross as "God's expression of His righteousness"--i.e., as the sacrifice which established the "new covenant" in fulfilment of God's promise to Abraham in Gen 12:3. The Apostle does employ a wide variety of images in describing what God accomplished through the Cross, but both the metaphors he chooses and the content with which he fills them are determined by his fundamental beliefs concerning the meaning of Christ's death. Paul is able to speak of that death as, for example, a "passover" or "sin-offering," effecting "reconciliation" or "deliverance," only because these ideas are compatible with, or express aspects of, his "core convictions" concerning the Cross.

III. "JESUS' ACT OF TRUST"--
CHRIST'S DEATH AS AN ACT OF CHRIST (CORE CONVICTION 3)

An Act of Christ

As we have seen, Paul interprets the Cross as ultimately an act of God; it was God Himself who "handed [Christ] over [to death] for us all."[160] Yet this does not mean that Christ was a helpless pawn in God's hand; for the

---

[159]See chapter 2, note 175, on this term.

[160]Rom 8:32. See above under "An Act of God."

Apostle insists that Jesus went to the cross willingly, as God's agent.[161] In this sense, the Cross was also an act of Christ. He "delivered himself over [to death];" he "gave himself for our sins."[162]

Paul maintains that, as God's agent, the crucified Jesus was united with the Father in his aim. God promised Abraham that He would bless all nations with the gift of the "new covenant,"[163] and so Christ acted "for the sake of God's truthfulness, in order to confirm [God's] promises to the fathers."[164] Romans 3:21-26 refers to Christ's crucifixion as "God's expression of His righteousness" (δικαιοσύνη θεοῦ), and Rom 5:18 describes that death as "the righteous deed of the one [man Jesus Christ] (ἑνὸς δικαίωμα)."

The Apostle likewise portrays the Son as united with the Father in his motives. Whereas Romans 5, for example, describes the Cross as an expression of God's "goodwill" (χάρις),[165] 2 Cor 8:9 speaks of that same event (see below) as "our Lord Jesus Christ's expression of goodwill" (ἡ χάρις τοῦ κυρίου ἡμῶν Ἰησοῦ Χριστοῦ). Furthermore, while Rom 5:8 describes God's demonstration of "His own love (ἀγάπη) toward us, in that, while we were still sinners, Christ died for us," Paul elsewhere speaks of "the Son of God, who loved (ἀγαπᾶν) me and who delivered himself over [to death] for me."[166]

"Jesus' Act of Trust"

While Paul attributes "righteousness," "love," and "goodwill" to both God and His Son, he employs another complex of ideas only when focusing

---

[161]See the thought-provoking article by C. A. Wanamaker entitled "Christ as Divine Agent in Paul" (*SJT* 39 [1986]: 517-28).

[162]Gal 2:20; 1:4; cf., e.g., 2 Cor 8:9; Phil 2:5-8.

[163]See Gal 3:8.

[164]Rom 15:8.

[165]See vv. 2, 15, 16, 17, 20, 21.

[166]Gal 2:20; cf. Rom 8:35, 37.

158

on the Cross as an act of Christ. When the Apostle reflects upon Jesus'
willing acceptance of the cross, we find him speaking, for example, of Christ's
"self-humiliation," his "self-denial," and his "obedience."[167] The single term
which most effectively captures this multi-faceted understanding of Christ's act
is πίστις ("trust"). Paul's third "core conviction" concerning the death of Christ
is that his going to the cross was "Jesus' act of trust" (ἡ πίστις Ἰησοῦ)[168] in
God.

Romans 5:19. By "trust," Paul means commitment to God--the Creator
and Giver of the covenants--as Lord.[169] Christ exhibits this kind of submission to the Father in a number of Pauline passages, one of the most important
being Rom 5:19, where Paul contrasts the "obedience" (ὑπακοή) of Christ with
the "disobedience" (παρακοή) of Adam. (For a complete discussion, see chapter 3.) Whereas Adam refused to entrust himself to God as his Creator and
Lord, but instead seized the knowledge of good and evil so as to become like
God,[170] Jesus displayed "the obedience which proceeds from trust"[171] when

---

[167]Francis H. Agnew discusses (1) "The New Testament Concept of Obedience," (2) "The
Obedience of Jesus," and (3) "The Obedience of the Christian," in "Obedience: A New Testa-
ment Reflection," *RevR* 39 (1980): 409-18. The article focuses on the "Kenosis Hymn" of Phil
2 (see below) on p. 414. For a discussion of "obedience" as the content of Christ's "trust," see
Markus Barth, "'The Faith' of the Messiah," *HeyJ* 10 [1969]: 366-67. In "The Obedience of
Christ in the Theology of the Early Church" (in *Reconciliation and Hope: New Testament Essays
on Atonement and Eschatology Presented to L. L. Morris on His 60th Birthday,* ed. Robert Banks
[Exeter: The Paternoster Press, 1974]), Richard N. Longenecker traces the development of the
theme of Christ's obedience throughout the New Testament and the patristic writings of the
first four centuries. He organizes his discussion around four headings: (1) Christ's "Passive
Obedience," (2) Christ's "Active Obedience," (3) Christ's "Obedience Perfected," and (4) "Obedience and Ontology."

[168]Rom 3:26; cf. 3:22; Gal 2:16; 3:22; Phil 3:9. On this phrase, see chapter 2 under "Verse
22a."

[169]See chapter 2 under "Ἡ καινὴ διαθήκη ('the new covenant')."

[170]See Gen 3:6.

[171]See Rom 1:5.

he surrendered to God's will by going to the cross as the sacrifice through which "the many" become "righteous."[172]

Philippians 2:5-8.[173] Many scholars discern the same contrast between Christ's "obedience" and Adam's "disobedience" behind the first part of the "Kenosis Hymn"[174] (from the verb κενοῦν ["to empty"]) Paul quotes in Phil 2:6-8.[175] In vv. 5-8 the Apostle writes:

---

[172]See chapter 3 under "The death of Christ and its results." Paul also has Christ's "trust" in mind when he says that Jesus "died as far as Sin is concerned" in Rom 6:10 (see chapter 6), and that he "was crucified because of weakness" in 2 Cor 13:4 (an idea which we will fully explore in chapter 7).

[173]This passage has been the object of intense scholarly scrutiny. In the bibliography, see the studies by Feinberg, Fee, Fitzmyer, Grundmann, Hofius, R. P. Martin, Moule, Rousseau and Strimple.

[174]We will analyze the second part of the "Hymn" (vv. 9-11), concerning Christ's exaltation, in chapter 5.

[175]Scholars who interpret the "Hymn" against the background of an early Adam christology include: (1) Hans Werner Bartsch (*Die Konkrete Wahrheit und die Lüge der Spekulation: Untersuchung über den vorpaulinischen Christ-hymnus und seine gnostische Mythisierung,* Theologie und Wirklichkeit, ed. Hans-Werner Bartsch, Gerhard Dauzenberg, Friedrich Hahn, and Hans Wolfgang Offele, no. 1 [Frankfurt: Verlag Peter Lang GmbH, 1974]), and (2) James D. G. Dunn (*Christology,* 113-25, and *Unity and Diversity in the New Testament: An Inquiry Into the Character of Earliest Christianity* [Philadelphia: The Westminster Press, 1977], 134-36). Opposing views are offered by, for example, (1) L. Cerfaux (*Christ in the Theology of St. Paul,* trans. Geoffrey Webb and Adrian Walker [New York: Herder and Herder, 1959]) and Guy Wagner ("Le Scandale de la Croix Explique par le Chant du Serviteur d'Esaie 53: Reflexion sur Philippiens 2:6-11," *ETR* 61 [1986]: 177-87), who find the main background for the "Kenosis Hymn" in the Isaianic "Servant Songs" (although Wagner also acknowledges that the "Hymn" draws a contrast between Christ and Adam), (2) Jerome Murphy-O'Connor ("Christological Anthropology in Phil 2:6-11," *RB* 83 [1976]: 25-50) and Jack T. Sanders (*The New Testament Christological Hymns: Their Historical Religious Background* [Cambridge: The University Press, 1971]), who interpret the "Hymn" against the background of certain Wisdom traditions, (3) Otfried Hofius (*Der Christushymnus Philipper 2:6-11: Untersuchungen zu Gestalt und Aussage eines urchristlichen Psalms,* Wissenschaftliche Untersuchungen zum Neuen Testament, ed. Martin Hengel, Joachim Jeremias, and Otto Michel, no. 17 [Tübingen: J. C. B. Mohr, 1976]), who argues for the Old Testament Psalms as the primary background for the "Hymn," and (4) C. A. Wanamaker ("Philippians 2:6-11: Son of God or Adamic Christology?," *NTS* 33 [1987]: 179-93), who classifies Phil 2:6-11 among such "Son-of-God texts" as Gal 4:4-5; Rom 1:3-4; 8:3-4; and 1 Cor 15:24-28.

(5) Have this mind-set in you which [was] also in Christ Jesus,

  (6) Who, although [he] was in the form of God,
      did not consider equality with God something to be seized
      (ἁρπαγμός).[176]
  (7) Instead, he emptied himself
      by taking the form of a slave,
      by being [born] in the likeness of men.
      And after he was found in outward form as a man,
  (8) he humbled himself by being obedient to the point of death--
      even the death which is the cross.

The Apostle mentions Christ's preexistence[177] (v. 6), during which he was "in the form of God" (ἐν μορφῇ θεοῦ),[178] enjoying "equality with God" (ἴσα θεῷ), solely for the purpose of emphasizing the incredible depth of Christ's self-humiliation.[179] This single act of "self-humiliation" took place in two stages[180]--namely, (1) Christ's incarnation (v. 7), in which he "emptied himself" of divine glory and took "the form of a slave" (μορφὴ δούλου, i.e., the

---

[176]N. T. Wright ("ἁρπαγμός and the Meaning of Philippians 2:5-11," *JTS* 37 [1986]: 321-52) argues that ἁρπαγμός here refers to Christ's refusal to use his divine glory for his own advantage. R. W. Hoover ("The *Harpagmos* Enigma: A Philogical Solution," *HTR* 64 [1971]: 95-119) likewise argues for the meaning "an estimate of the situation as exploitable" (p. 106), "as something to take advantage of" or "as something to use for [one's] own advantage" (pp. 445-46). J. C. O'Neill ("Notes and Observations: Hoover on *Harpagmos* Reviewed, With a Modest Proposal Concerning Philippians 2:6," *HTR* 81 [1988]: 445-49) criticizes Hoover's conclusions, but is unable to reach a satisfactory solution of his own. His "own suggestion is that the text is corrupt. The original ran . . . 'who being in the form of God thought it not robbery not to be equal with God'" (p. 448).

[177]Scholars who interpret v. 6 to refer to Christ's preexistence include Dunn (*Unity and Diversity,* 135-36), Hurst, Lightfoot, Lohmeyer, R. P. Martin, Wanamaker and Wong. Scholars who judge v. 6 to refer only to the earthly Jesus include Howard and Talbert. See the pertinent entries in the bibliography.

[178]In an article entitled "The Case Against the Synonymity of *Morphē* and *Eikōn*" (*JSNT* 34 [1988]: 77-86), Dave Steenburg draws a distinction between the μορφὴ θεοῦ ("form of God") held by the pre-existent Christ and the εἰκὼν θεοῦ ("image of God") enjoyed by Adam and all human beings (see Gen 1:26).

[179]See Teresia Yai-Chow Wong, "The Problem of Pre-existence in Philippians 2:6-11," *ETL* 62 (1986): 281.

[180]See Ulrich B. Müller, "Der Christushymnus Phil 2:6-11," *ZNW* 79 (1988): 17-44.

form of a "man," a human creature of God[181]), and (2) Christ's crucifixion (v. 8), in which he suffered[182] the most painful and humiliating of deaths.[183] Adam, in his pride and disobedience, attempted to seize the "equality with God" not given to him; but Christ freely surrendered the glory he already possessed (ἴσα θεῷ, v. 6). He "humbled himself (ἐταπείνωσεν ἑαυτόν) by being obedient (ὑπήκοος);" he went to the cross willingly, in order to fulfil God's righteous purpose.

Other texts. Because God's attitude toward His fallen creatures was one of "love" (ἀγάπη) and "goodwill" (χάρις), He acted in our best interest by sending Christ to die as the sacrifice which frees from Sin. Because Christ's attitude toward God was one of "trust" (πίστις), he denied himself, took God's purpose for his own purpose, put our interests before his own interests, and willingly accepted the cross. Paul focuses on how Christ's trust in God made him not only a "slave" (δοῦλος) of God,[184] but also a "servant" (διάκονος) of humankind,[185] in several passages concerned with Christian behavior. For example, in Phil 2:3-8 (see above) Christ becomes a model for "paying attention to the interests of others." In 2 Cor 8:9, the Apostle encourages the Corinthians to share in the contribution for the Jerusalem saints by reminding them of "Jesus Christ's expression of goodwill:" "Although he was rich, he

---

[181]In an article entitled "Erwägungen zu Phil 2:6-7b" (*ZNW* 78 [1987]: 230-43), Hermann Binder argues that the term "slave" does not here express Christ's relationship to God, but his relationship to other human beings. In other words, the thought is the same as that of Mark 10:45 // Matt 20:28: "The Son of Man did not come to be served but to serve, and to give his life [as] a ransom for many."

[182]Paul focuses on Christ's "suffering" (πάσχειν), apart from his death, only in Rom 8:17.

[183]A brief survey of Martin Hengel's *Crucifixion in the Ancient World and the Folly of the Message of the Cross* (Philadelphia: Fortress Press, 1977) should convince anyone of the truth of this point.

[184]See Phil 2:7.

[185]See Rom 15:8.

became poor for you (δι' ὑμᾶς, a possible category 4 formula),[186] in order that you, by means of his poverty, might become rich." In Rom 15:3, Paul urges consideration for the "weak" by saying, "Christ did not try to please himself. Instead, [it was] just as it has been written: 'The reproaches of those who reproach you fell upon me.'" We will explore further Paul's idea of Christ's self-denial as a model for Christian behavior[187] in chapter 7.

Christ's "Body of Humiliation"

In 1 Cor 15:42-53, Paul contrasts the "earthly" (χοϊκός), "psychical" (ψυχικός), "perishable" (ἄφθαρτος), "mortal" (θνητός), "flesh and blood" (σὰρξ καὶ αἷμᾶ) bodies (σώματα) of "corruption" (φθορά), "dishonor" (ἀτιμία), and "weakness" (ἀσθένεια), possessed by Adam and his descendants, with the "heavenly" (ἐπουράνιος), "spiritual" (πνευματικός), "imperishable" (ἄφθαρτος), bodies of "immortality" (ἀθανασία), "incorruption" (ἀφθαρσία), "glory" (δόξα), and "strength" (δύναμις) possessed by the risen Christ.[188] Since his "Kenosis Hymn" describes the Christ of the incarnation and crucifixion as one who "emptied himself" of "glory," and who perished on the cross as a "mortal," we may assume that Paul understands the historical Jesus to have borne the same "image of the earthly man," Adam (v. 49)--or the same "body of our humiliation" (τὸ σῶμα τῆς ταπεινώσεως ἡμῶν, Phil 3:21)--which all human beings (including Christians) presently bear. The full significance of this fact will become clear in the following chapters.

---

[186]Leander E. Keck and Victor Paul Furnish (*The Pauline Letters,* Interpreting Biblical Texts [Nashville: Abingdon Press, 1984], 81) note that "this is Paul's way of interpreting the incarnation into the human condition, understood here as 'poverty' just as in Phil 2:7 it is characterized as 'slavery.'" For Paul, of course, the incarnation cannot be separated from Christ's sacrificial death.

[187]On this subject, see the studies in the bibliography by Giles, Hurtado (who provides a survey of the major studies on this topic), Patitsas, Stanley and Webster.

[188]On these terms, see chapter 3 under "The risen Christ," esp. note 106.

IV. SUMMARY

In summary, Paul's interpretation of Christ's death rests upon three "core convictions" concerning the meaning of that death.

First, the Apostle firmly believes that Christ died on the cross as a sacrifice. This "core conviction" finds expression in (1) Paul's free use of sacrificial formulae from the LXX in interpreting that death, and (2) his evoking the Old Testament ideas of the ἱλαστήριον ("sacrifice which purifies from sin"), "passover lamb," and "sin-offering," in order to highlight certain aspects of its meaning. Specifically, Christ's death is the sacrifice which established the "new covenant." This is shown by (1) the Apostle's mention of that covenant in 1 Cor 11:25 and 2 Cor 3:6, and (2) his frequent use of the language of covenant "righteousness" in association with that death. Here we find the *modus operandi* of the atonement for Paul.

The Apostle's second "core conviction" concerning the Cross is that Jesus' death was an act of God, carried out in righteous fulfilment of His promise to Abraham that He would bring the "blessing" of righteousness to all nations. In other words, "God's expression of His righteousness" toward Abraham took the form of the "new covenant," or "God's expression of His righteousness" toward all nations. While the Apostle's variety of expression has invited scholars to find several competing theories of the Atonement in his epistles, a closer examination reveals that, for Paul, terms such as "reconciliation," "redemption" and "deliverance" convey what are essentially covenantal ideas.

Finally, Paul's third "core conviction" concerning Christ's death is that Jesus went to the cross in "trust" (πίστις), as the willing agent of God. The idea of the crucifixion as "Jesus' act of trust" in God lies behind Paul's characterization of that event in terms of Jesus' self-humiliation, self-denial and obedience.

CHAPTER FIVE

PAUL'S INTERPRETATION OF
CHRIST'S RESURRECTION TO "LIFE"

For Paul, Christ's resurrection from the dead--like his death itself--was an historical event, effected by God in a particular place (i.e., the site where Jesus was "buried") and time (i.e., "on the third day").[1] No human being was present at that event; but Paul counted himself among those who, with their own eyes, had witnessed its results in the person of the risen Christ:

> . . . he was seen (ὤφθη) by Cephas, [and] then by the Twelve. Afterwards he was seen (ὤφθη) by more than five hundred brothers at the same time-- most of whom are still living, although some have fallen asleep. After- wards he was seen (ὤφθη) by James, then by all the apostles. Last of all he was seen (ὤφθη) by me also . . . .[2]

The meaning of a particular historical act largely depends on the con- text in which that act is performed. To illustrate: Raising a closed fist with

---

[1]See 1 Cor 15:4.

[2]1 Cor 15:5-8; cf. 9:1 ("I have indeed seen [ὤφθη] Jesus our Lord, haven't I?"). Note that Paul here describes his encounter with the risen Christ using the same language (ὤφθη) he em- ploys when speaking of earlier post-resurrection appearances; he does not look upon his own experience as completely unprecedented. Note further that when Paul, in Gal 1:12 (cf. v. 16), speaks of how he received his gospel "through a revelation which is Jesus Christ" (δι' ἀποκα- λύψεως Ἰησοῦ Χριστοῦ), he is most likely recalling the risen Christ's appearance to him.

extended thumb signifies an "out" within the context of a baseball game; but the same action, performed on the roadside, communicates the hitchhiker's request for transportation. The interpreter must take into account the context within which a given action was carried out in order to understand the true meaning and significance of that action.

God raised Christ from the dead within a first-century Jewish context, which was largely reflected in and/or shaped by the Jewish Scriptures. Paul recognizes not only the divine act itself, but also the context within which God chose to perform that act, when he testifies that Christ "has been raised on the third day in accordance with the Scriptures."[3] Below, we will first examine the context of Christ's resurrection--i.e., how "resurrection" was understood in the "Scriptures" of Paul's day. Next, we will turn to a discussion of how those Scriptures, combined with the Lord's post-resurrection appearance to Paul, led the Apostle to certain "core convictions" concerning the new "life" now enjoyed by Jesus Christ.

I. VIEWS OF THE RESURRECTION PRIOR TO PAUL

Life After Death

The traditional Jewish view.[4] During Paul's lifetime, the question of whether or not human beings would enjoy life after death was hotly debated in Jewish circles. Traditionally, the Jews had believed that God created

---

[3]1 Cor 15:4.

[4]See Bernhard Lang, "Afterlife: Ancient Israel's Changing Vision of the World Beyond," *BibR* 4 (1988): 12-23. By speaking of "The traditional Jewish view" and "The classical Greek view" (see below) of life after death, we do not mean to imply that every ancient Jew or Greek held the beliefs described. For purposes of convenience, we are simply comparing two basic ways of understanding life after death that even the ancients themselves tended to associate with one group or the other (see, e.g., Josephus' reference to "the belief of the sons of Greece" in the quote given below under "Greek influence on the Jews").

human beings mortal, subject to death.[5]   Furthermore, they had understood human beings to be psychosomatically indivisible. In Greek terms, this meant that a human being consisted of both a ψυχή ("psyche") and a σῶμα ("body"), which were inseparable from one another.[6] According to this view, there was no life after death; for the death of the body (σῶμα) necessarily involved the death of the psyche (ψυχή) as well.

Sheol. The oldest Jewish Scriptures described death as entrance into "Sheol" (שְׁאוֹל, often translated in the LXX as ᾅδης ["Hades"]), by which they meant either (1) simple annihilation, or (2) continuing (bodily) existence as a "shade" in the subterranean abode of the dead.[7] These writings did not present Sheol as "life after death," but as "death." They offered no hope of regaining any kind of meaningful existence after death; for, as Job 7:9 said, "the person who goes down to Sheol will not come up."[8]

---

[5]See chapter 3 under "Adam's creation."

[6]For purposes of comparison, we are here using Greek words in order to express a Hebrew idea. The ancient Hebrews did not draw the sharp distinction between "body" and "psyche" characteristic of the Greeks. The two were "inseparable" in thought.

[7]One of the most detailed descriptions of Sheol appears in Isa 14:9-19, where the prophet describes the "shade" (v. 9) of the king of Babylon as "weak" (v. 10) and humbled (vv. 11-17), a pale reflection of what he had once been. See also (1) 1 Sam 28:11-15, where Saul commands the medium at Endor to bring up Samuel's "shade" from Sheol, (2) Eccl 9:10, which says that there is no work, reason, knowledge or wisdom in Sheol, (3) Ps 6:5 and Isa 38:18, which state that those in Sheol neither praise God, thank God, hope in God, nor even remember God (cf. Sir 17:27-28), and (4) Ps 88:12, which likewise characterizes Sheol as "the land of forgetfulness." The latter three passages could be interpreted in terms of annihilation--i.e., the dead simply cease to exist. Lang explains the relationship between Sheol and ancient Semitic ancestor worship in "Afterlife," 12-17. In an essay entitled "Life After Death in the Prophetic Promise" (in *Congress Volume: Jerusalem, 1986,* ed. J. A. Emerton, Supplements to *Vetus Testamentum,* 40 [Leiden: E. J. Brill, 1988], 144-56), he discusses "three themes: (1) ancestor worship in the ritual universe of the ancient Semites; (2) the emergence of the Sadducean view [see below] as a consequence of the exclusive worship of Israel's God; and (3) the emergence of resurrection belief in Ezekiel [esp. the vision of dry bones in ch. 37] and related prophetic sources [Isaiah 26, Daniel 12, 2 Maccabees 7]" (p. 145).

[8]Cf. Ps 89:48.

Resuscitation of corpses. The Jewish Scriptures did contain several accounts of persons being delivered from Sheol through the resuscitation of their corpses.[9] Yet this proved to be only a temporary reprieve from the inevitability of death, for those restored to life did not gain immortality. Instead, they simply resumed their normal, earthly existence, until Sheol claimed them once again.

The classical Greek view.[10] During the Hellenistic and Roman periods, the Jewish people were exposed to Greek ideas concerning life after death. The Greeks tended to view the human being as essentially a divine, immortal psyche (ψυχή) encased in a material, mortal body (σῶμα). Death, for the Greek, did not mark the end of all existence, but only the end of bodily (or "somatic") existence as the immortal psyche gained release from the limitations of the mortal body.

Punishment and reward. What became of the psyche after death? Plato (4th century B.C.) offered a typical Greek response to this question in "The Myth of Er,"[11] which related how the psyche of the slain warrior Er left his body, witnessed the fate of other departed psychai, and was then sent back to the living in order to give an account of what he had seen. Er spoke of punishment for the wicked and reward for the good:

> For all the wrongs they [i.e., the psychai of the dead] had ever done to anyone and all whom they had severally wronged they had paid the penalty in turn tenfold for each, . . . and again if any had done deeds of

---

[9]Examples appear in (1) 1 Kgs 17:21-22, where Elijah revives the dead child of the widow of Zarephath (cf. Prop. 10:6; 21:7), (2) 2 Kgs 4:33-35, in which Elisha revives the son of the Shunammite woman (cf. Prop. 22:9), and (3) T. Abra. (rescension A) 18:9-11 (cf. 14:6 in resc. B), in which God sends "a spirit of life" back into seven thousand servants of Abraham who "died untimely" when Death showed its "ferocious" face to the patriarch.

[10]See note 4.

[11]*The Republic*, X, xiii-xvi (pp. 490-521).

kindness and been just and holy men they might receive their due reward in the same measure . . . .[12]

Greek influence on the Jews. The Jews, as a whole, rejected the Gentile "blasphemy" of attributing divinity to the human psyche and chose, instead, to maintain the sharp, biblical distinction between Creator and creation. At the same time, some Jewish thinkers began to appropriate--in one form or an-other--Greek notions of the immortality of the psyche, and of reward and punishment in the afterlife.[13]

---

[12]*The Republic,* X, xiii (pp. 495, 97). Note that, after receiving their just deserts, all psychai choose a new body and a new "pattern of life" for the next "cycle of mortal generation" on earth (see X, xv-xvi [pp. 504-21]).

[13]To illustrate: (1) A Jewish poet, writing under the name of Phocylides, composed these lines during either the first century B.C. or the first century A.D.:

For the psychai remain unharmed in the deceased.
For the spirit is a loan of God to mortals, and (his) image.
For we have a body (σῶμα) out of earth, and when afterward we are resolved again into earth
we are but dust; and then the air has received our spirit . . .
Hades is (our) common eternal home and fatherland, . . .
We humans live [a bodily existence] not a long time but for a season.
But (our) psyche is immortal and lives ageless forever (Pseudo-Phoc. 105-08, 112, 114-15).

Note that, in this same context (lines 102-04), Pseudo-Phocylides seems also to entertain the thought of a future bodily resurrection from the dead (on this idea, see below). Yet this is dif-ficult to reconcile with his statements concerning the "air" receiving "our spirit" and "Hades" being our "eternal home." P. W. van der Horst appears to be correct when he says (in *The Old Testament Pseudepigrapha,* 2:571) that Pseudo-Phocylides "has no logically thought-out system" with regard to life-after-death.

(2) Wisdom of Solomon (first century B.C.-first century A.D.) maintains that God created human beings to be immortal like Himself (1:13-14; 2:23), but "impious persons" have lost their immortality by making a "covenant" with death (1:16; cf. 2:24; 15: 17). Although the righteous appear to die (i.e., their σώματα ["bodies"] die), God preserves their psychai immortal and causes them to reign in glory (3:1-9; 5:15-16; cf. 1:15).

(3) "The Book of the Epistle of Enoch" (i.e., chs. 91-107 of 1 Enoch, discussed below) maintains that the psychai of both the righteous and the wicked are preserved after death. While the former "rejoice" (1 Enoch 103:4) and "shine like the lights of heaven" (104:2; cf. 108: 12-15), the latter "experience evil and great tribulation--in darkness, nets, and burning flame" (103:7; cf. 108:5-6).

(4) In contrast to the three works discussed above, 4 Maccabees (first century A.D.) does not view immortality as part of the natural created order, but as a gift given by God to His servants. Thus, the book describes seven martyred Jewish brothers as "running on the high-way to immortality" (14:5; cf. 7:19; 9:22; 15:3; 16:13, 25; 17:12), so that they receive "pure and deathless psychai from God" (18:23).

Flavius Josephus (a Jewish historian of the first century A.D.) informs us that, by Paul's day, the party of the Essenes could be counted among those who had embraced the hellenistic influence:

> . . . it is a fixed belief of theirs that the body (σῶμα) is corruptible and its constituent matter impermanent, but that the psyche (ψυχή) is immortal and imperishable . . . Sharing the belief of the sons of Greece, they maintain that for virtuous psychai there is reserved an abode beyond the ocean, a place which is not oppressed by rain or snow or heat, but is refreshed by the ever gentle breath of the west wind coming in from the ocean; while they relegate base psychai to a murky and tempestuous dungeon, big with never-ending punishments. (*The Jewish War,* II, viii, 11 [pp. 380-83])

In contrast to the Essenes, Josephus says that the Sadducees continued to hold more closely to the traditional Jewish view of death as the end of life:

> As for the persistence of the psyche (ψυχή) after death, penalties in the underworld (ἅδης), and rewards, they will have none of them.[14]

Resurrection of the body (σῶμα). Alongside the Sadducees and Essenes, certain New Testament writers testify that a third party, the Pharisees, held still a different opinion concerning life after death. The author of Acts writes:

> Sadducees say there is no resurrection (ἀνάστασις), nor angel, nor spirit; but Pharisees acknowledge [them] all.[15]

---

[14]*The Jewish War,* II, viii, 14 (pp. 386-87).

[15]Acts 23:8; cf. Matt 22:23 // Mark 12:18 // Luke 20:27. Josephus offers this description of Pharisaic belief in *The Jewish War,* II, viii, 14 (pp. 384-87):

> Every psyche (ψυχή), they maintain, is imperishable, but the [psyche] of the good alone passes into another body (σῶμα), while the psychai of the wicked suffer eternal punishment.

The phrase concerning the psyche's passing "into another body" suggests that Josephus--like the New Testament writers--does associate the idea of a bodily resurrection with the Pharisees. Yet, as we will see, some parts of this statement (i.e., his description of the psyche as "imperishable," his characterization of the new body as "another body," and his insistence that the "good" receive a new body while the "wicked" do not) raise doubts concerning whether he fully understands what "resurrection" means. In his autobiography, Josephus recalls that, at the age of sixteen, he acquainted himself with the teachings of the Pharisees, Sadducees and Essenes. At age nineteen, he "began to govern [his] life by the rules of the Pharisees" (see Josephus, *The Life,* 2 [pp. 4-7]). In later life, however, he may have been drawn to the more characteristically

The idea of a bodily "resurrection" (ἀνάστασις or ἔγερσις) from the dead originated in Persia, and then spread to Palestine through Jewish apocalyptic circles.[16] Below, we will trace how this notion developed in Jewish literature leading up to the time of Paul.[17]

Isaiah 26:19 and Daniel 12:2-3 (MT)

Belief in the resurrection of the dead appears only "at the very limits of the Old Testament."[18] The Hebrew canon makes explicit reference to the idea in only two passages, both belonging to the apocalyptic genre. First, the "Isaiah Apocalypse" of Isa 24-27 promises that

> Your dead [nation (see v. 15)] will live; my corpse [i.e., the dead "body" of the nation[19]] will arise. Awaken and shout aloud, you who rest in the

---

Greek ideas of the Essenes. He seems most familiar with the "philosophy" of this sect, to which he devotes eight times as many lines as to that of the Pharisees and Sadducees together. Furthermore, he states in *The Jewish War* that the Essenes "irresistibly attract all who have once tasted their philosophy" (*The Jewish War*, II, viii, 11 [pp. 382-83]).

[16]Diogenes Laertius (in *Lives of Eminent Philosophers*, I, i, 9 [pp. 10-11, see also note a]) recalls the Greek historian Theopompus as saying that "according to the [Persian] Magi persons will live in a future life and be immortal, and that what exists now will exist hereafter under its own present name." He further notes that some trace the beliefs of the Jews back to these same Magi. See also Lang, "Afterlife," 19, which notes that "the concept of bodily resurrection . . . first appears in the teachings of the Iranian prophet Zoroaster (about 1500 B.C.)."

[17]Helpful studies on this subject have been written by (1) R. H. Charles (*Eschatology: The Doctrine of a Future Life in Israel, Judaism and Christianity. A Critical History*, with an Introduction by George Wesley Buchanan [New York: Schocken Books, 1963]), who discusses the eschatology of the Old Testament, apocryphal and apocalyptic literature (second century B. C. through the first century A.D.), and New Testament, including the development of the idea of the Resurrection, (2) W. D. Davies (*Paul and Rabbinic Judaism*), who provides a chapter (pp. 285-320) on "The Old and the New Hope: Resurrection," and (3) George W. E. Nickelsburg, Jr. (*Resurrection, Immortality, and Eternal Life in Intertestamental Judaism*, Harvard Theological Studies, 26 [Cambridge: Harvard University Press, 1972]), who treats most of the writings discussed in this chapter.

[18]Otto Kaiser, *Isaiah 13-39: A Commentary*, The Old Testament Library (Philadelphia: The Westminster Press, 1974), 218.

[19]Note that editors of the *BHS* propose the reading נְבֵלָתָם, "their corpses."

dust! For the dew of light[20] [is] your dew; the earth will give birth to the shades[21] (Isa 26:19[22]).

Second, the apocalypse of Daniel 7-12 anticipates that

Many of those who sleep in the dust of the earth will awaken (יָקִיצוּ), some to eternal life (לְחַיֵּי עוֹלָם) and some to reproaches, to eternal abhorrence (לְדִרְאוֹן עוֹלָם). Those who enlighten [others] will shine like the shining of the firmament; those who cause many persons to be righteous [will shine] like the stars forever and ever (לְעוֹלָם וָעֶד). (Dan 12:2-3)

From these two passages[23] we gain several important insights into what the earliest apocalypticists mean when they speak of the "Resurrection:"

(1) The concept of the "Resurrection" is understood against the background of the "two ages" (in Greek, αἰῶνες), which forms its original apocalyptic framework (see our discussion of "the present time" in chapter 2). The "Resurrection" is an event which will occur at the end of the present historical age and which will mark the beginning of the coming eschatological age. Chronologically speaking, "resurrection" life is life in the eschatological age.

(2) "Resurrection" must be distinguished from the Greek notion of the immortality of the psyche for two reasons: First, each person is not "raised" individually at the time of his/her death, as would be the case if "resurrection" referred to the mere release of an immortal psyche from a mortal body.

---

[20]BDB, 21, suggests that the writer is thinking of the "light of life"--i.e., "light that quickens dead bodies as dew the plants."

[21]The phrase וָאָרֶץ רְפָאִים תַּפִּיל literally means "And the earth will cause the shades to fall." BDB, 657-58, suggests that the prophet here employs an idiom for "dropping" or "casting" one's young--i.e., for "giving birth." The appearance of the image of childbirth in vv. 17-18 lends strength to this view.

[22]See the comments on this verse by Kaiser (*Isaiah 13-39*, 215-20), which appear under the heading "Chapter 26:19: The Resurrection of the Dead."

[23]Gerhard F. Hasel focuses on Isa 26:19 and Dan 12:1-4 in "Resurrection in the Theology of Old Testament Apocalyptic," *ZAW* 92 (1980): 267-84. He includes a bibliography on the subject in note 1 on p. 267.

Instead, the dead remain "dead" (i.e., they either cease to exist or they remain as "shades" in Sheol, the place of the dead) until the Eschaton, when all who participate in the Resurrection (whether they be all people, as in Dan 12,[24] or only God's people, as in Isa 26) are raised together as a group. The first apocalypticists do not conceive of an individual "resurrection" apart from the "general Resurrection." Second, early apocalyptic writers base their idea of the "Resurrection" on the "Jewish" assumption that human beings are psychosomatically indivisible; for they indicate that what will "arise" in the "Resurrection" are (in Greek terms) σώματα ("bodies"), which presently lie buried "in the dust of the earth." Anthropologically speaking, "resurrection" existence is somatic (bodily) existence.

(3) Yet "resurrection" must not be confused with simple reanimation of corpses; for those who "arise" from the dead do not resume the normal, earthly existence they enjoyed before death. Instead, their persons are somehow transformed; they are re-created by God in a form suitable for the eschatological age, whether it be characterized, for example, in terms of "reproaches" and "eternal abhorrence," or in terms of shining "like the shining of the firmament" and "like the stars forever and ever." Qualitatively speaking, "resurrection" life is "eschatological life."

In short, Isaiah 26 and Daniel 12 illustrate how the first apocalypticists chart a third course between the traditional Jewish and Greek views concerning life after death. By "resurrection" they mean transformed, somatic existence in the coming eschatological age.

The Septuagint

Isaiah 26:19 and Daniel 12:2-3 (LXX). An examination of the Septuagint versions of Isa 26:19 and Dan 12:2-3 yields three observations:

---

[24]For a discussion of this point, see Hasel, "Resurrection," 277-81.

First, in the case of both passages, the transformation from Hebrew to Greek involves a shift in meaning. The Hebrew version of Isa 26:19 (see above) indicates that it is the Jewish nation--i.e., the people of God ("your dead [nation]"), who are presently "shades" in Sheol--which will eventually participate in the Resurrection. The LXX preserves the idea of "God's people" by speaking of the "pious" (in contrast to the "impious" mentioned at the end of the verse), but it eliminates the reference to "shades":

> The [pious] dead will rise (ἀνιστάναι); those in the tombs will be raised (ἐγείρειν). Those in the earth will rejoice, for the dew from you [i.e., from God] is healing them. But the land of the impious will be destroyed.

The contrast between the Hebrew and Greek versions of Dan 12:2-3 is even more striking. While the Hebrew (see above) indicates that only the teachers of the Law ("those who enlighten others," "those who cause many persons to be righteous") will "shine" like the firmament and like the stars, the Greek maintains that all the righteous (i.e., all Law-abiding Jews) will share in this glory:

> Many of those who sleep in the dust of the earth will be raised (ἐξεγείρειν), some to eschatological life (ζωὴ αἰώνιος) and some to reproach and eschatological shame (αἰσχύνη αἰώνιος). Those who are enlightened will shine like the shining of the firmament; [those] from the multitude of the righteous [will shine] like the stars for ever and ever (εἰς τοὺς αἰῶνας, καὶ ἔτι) (Dan 12:2-3).

Second, Isa 26:19 (LXX) and Dan 12:2-3 (LXX)--like their Hebrew counterparts--represent two different views concerning whom God will raise from the dead. On the one hand, Isaiah envisions a "limited Resurrection," in which only "pious" Jews will participate. The "impious" Gentiles remain in the grave. Daniel, on the other hand, anticipates a "general Resurrection" involving reward for the righteous and punishment for the unrighteous. As we will see, both views continue to attract adherents until Paul's day.

Finally, the LXX versions of Isa 26:19 and Dan 12:2-3 introduce us to a vocabulary that will become standard in Greek apocalyptic. The verbs

174

ἀνιστάναι ("to raise," or "to rise"), εγείρειν ("to raise") and ἐξεγείρειν ("to raise")--along with the corresponding nouns ἀνάστασις ("resurrection") and ἔγερσις ("resurrection")--are used to speak of the coming "Resurrection." The noun αἰών ("age") and its corresponding adjective αἰώνιος ("of the [eschatological] age"--i.e., "eschatological") call to mind the coming eschatological age of apocalyptic expectation. The phrase ζωὴ αἰώνιος ("age-life," or "eschatological life"), or simply ζωή ("life") alone, refers to the quality of life enjoyed by those raised up in the eschatological age--i.e., "eschatological life."[25]

Job 42:17 (LXX). Turning to the Greek translation of the book of Job, we find that "righteous" man doubting whether there is such a thing as life after death:

A person who has fallen asleep will certainly not rise. Till the heavens come apart at the seams (ἕως ἂν ὁ οὐρανὸς οὐ μὴ συρραφῇ) they will not awaken from their sleep (Job 14:12, LXX).

Apparently, the editors of the LXX find Job's attitude intolerable, for they add a word of hope, at the end of the book, absent from the Hebrew text:

Job died, old and full of days; but it has been written that he will rise again with those whom the Lord raises (Job 42:17; cf. T. Job 4:9, which may be an interpolation in light of 52:10).

This expansion witnesses to a growing belief in the resurrection during the final centuries of the pre-Christian era.[26]

---

[25]Hill discusses "The Background and Biblical Usage of ζωή and ζωὴ αἰώνιος" in *Greek Words*, chapters V and VI (pp. 163-201).

[26]Belief in the Resurrection is also taken for granted in (1) The Lives of the Prophets (first century A.D.), which says that "in the Resurrection the ark [of the covenant] will be the first to be resurrected" (2:15), and that "in the wonder of the dead bones [see Ezek 37:1-14]" Ezekiel "persuaded them that there is hope for Israel both here and in the coming [age]" (3:12), and (2) 4 Baruch (first or second century A.D.), which cites the miraculous preservation of Abimelech's figs as evidence that God can indeed raise the righteous (6:6-10).

Testaments of the Twelve Patriarchs

In the Testaments of the Twelve Patriarchs (second century B.C.), we find two different views of the Resurrection. On the one hand, T. Jud 25:1-4 and T. Zeb 10:1-3 (like Isa 26) speak of a Resurrection limited to righteous Jews[27] (notably the patriarchs).[28] On the other hand, T. Benj 10:6-11 (like Dan 12) anticipates a "general Resurrection" followed by God's judgment of all nations:

> And then you will see Enoch and Seth and Abraham and Isaac and Jacob being raised up (ἀνιστάναι) at the right hand in great joy. Then shall we [i.e., the twelve patriarchs] also be raised (ἀνιστάναι), each of us over our tribe, and we shall prostrate ourselves before the heavenly King. Then all shall be raised (ἀνιστάναι), some destined for glory (δόξα), others for dishonor (ἀτιμία), for the Lord first judges Israel for the wrong she has committed and then He shall do the same for all the nations . . . You, therefore, my children, may your lot come to be with those who fear the Lord. Therefore, my children, you shall again dwell with me in hope; all Israel will be gathered to the Lord.

Note that Benjamin characterizes eschatological existence for "those who fear the Lord" as "glory" and "great joy," while those who do not fear the Lord are destined for "dishonor."

2 Maccabees

2 Maccabees (late second century B.C.) tells of seven Jewish brothers who, along with their mother, are tortured to death during Antiochus Epiphanes' attempt to hellenize the Jews by force.[29] Refusing to abandon God's laws,[30] the family suffers bravely, all the while expressing hope in the

---

[27]I.e., "those who died in sorrow . . . those who died in poverty for the Lord's sake . . . those who died on account of the Lord" (T. Jud 25:4), or "as many as keep the Law of the Lord and the commandments of Zebulon, their father" (T. Zeb 10:2).

[28]See also T. Asher 5:2: "Righteous actions [lead] to life (ζωή), unrighteous actions to death, since eschatological life (ἡ αἰώνιος ζωή) wards off death."

[29]Antiochus reigned from 175 to 164 B.C.

[30]2 Macc 7:2, 9.

Resurrection[31] "to an eschatological return to life" (εἰς αἰώνιον ἀναβίωσιν ζωῆς[32]). Like the author of Isa 26, they seem to believe in only a "limited Resurrection;" for the fourth son says to the king: "There will be no resurrection to life for you."[33] Like the author of Daniel 12, they anticipate that those who will participate in the "Resurrection to life" are the "righteous"--i.e., those Jews who fulfil the demands of the Mosaic Covenant.

Sibylline Oracles

The Sibylline Oracles contain two references to the Resurrection of the dead which pre-date Paul. The first is found in Book 4, lines 179-92 (second century B.C.), while the second appears in Book 2, lines 221-37 (probably late first century B.C., although the lines immediately following belong to a later Christian redaction).

Book 4. Book 4 threatens that, if sinners do not repent, then God Himself will come, "gnashing His teeth in wrath and destroying the entire race of men at once by a great conflagration."[34] Afterwards will follow a "general Resurrection" of the dead, in which God re-creates all those who once lived on the earth:

> God Himself will again fashion the bones and ashes of persons
> and He will raise up mortals again as they were before.[35]

---

[31]2 Macc 7:9, 11, 14, 23; cf. 12:43-45; 14:46.

[32]2 Macc 7:9.

[33]2 Macc 7:14. It may be, however, that the author expects the enemies of God to be raised to eschatological punishment, or "death;" for the fifth son issues this threat: "Wait awhile, and see His great power, how he will torment you and your descendants.

[34]Sib. Or. 4:160-61.

[35]Sib. Or. 4:181-82.

Those raised will then be judged. The impious will be covered over with "a mound of earth," and will endure "broad Tartarus and the repulsive recesses of Gehenna."[36]

> But as many as are pious, they will live on earth again when God gives spirit and life (ζωή) and favor to these pious ones. Then they will all see themselves beholding the delightful and pleasant light of the sun. (Sib. Or. 4:187-91)

Book 2. Book 2 also anticipates the fiery destruction of the heavens and the earth, and the "general Resurrection" of the dead. In 2:221-26, the sibyl describes the latter event either as release from the "murky dark" of "Hades,"[37] or in terms reminiscent of Ezek 37:1-14:

> Then the heavenly one will give psychai and breath and voice to the dead and bones fastened with all kinds of joinings . . . flesh and sinews and veins and skin about the flesh, and the former hairs. Bodies of humans, made solid in heavenly manner, breathing and set in motion, will be raised on a single day.

All those raised from the dead will then be led "to judgment, to the tribunal of the great immortal God."[38]

Psalms of Solomon

Only two of the Psalms of Solomon (a collection which was completed in the first century B.C.) make explicit reference to the Resurrection of the dead, and both reflect essentially the same understanding of that event. Psalm 3 declares that

> The destruction (ἀπώλεια) of the sinner is forever (εἰς τὸν αἰῶνα),
> and s/he will not be remembered when [God] looks after the righteous.
> This is the share of sinners forever (εἰς τὸν αἰῶνα),

---

[36]Sib. Or. 4:185-86.

[37]Sib. Or. 2:217, 227-30.

[38]Sib. Or. 2:18-19.

but those who fear the Lord shall rise up (ἀνιστάναι) to eternal life
(ζωὴ αἰώνιος),
and their life (ζωή) shall be in the Lord's light (φῶς), and it shall
never end." (Ps. Sol. 3:11-12)

In like manner, the psalmist says in Ps. Sol. 2 that

[God] is king over the heavens,
  judging even kings and rulers,
Raising (ἀνιστάναι) me up to glory (δόξα),
  but putting to sleep the arrogant for eternal destruction (ἀπώλεια αἰῶνος)
  in dishonor (ἀτιμία),
because they did not know Him.
And now, officials of the earth, see the judgment of the Lord,
  that He is a great and righteous King, judging what is under heaven.
Praise God, you who fear the Lord with understanding,
  for the Lord's mercy is upon those who fear him with judgment.
To separate between the righteous and the sinner
  to repay sinners forever (εἰς τὸν αἰῶνα) according to their actions
And to have mercy on the righteous [keeping him/her] from the humiliation (ταπείνωσις) of the sinner,
  and to repay the sinner for what s/he has done to the righteous."
(Ps. Sol. 2:30-35)

Both psalms anticipate that the Resurrection will occur at a particular
point in the future--namely, the time "when [God] looks after the righteous,"
or the time of "the Judgment of the Lord."[39] Both speak of a "limited Resurrection" involving only the "righteous," or "those who fear the Lord"[40]--i.e.,
Law-abiding Jews.[41] While God "mercifully" raises up the "righteous" to the
honor[42] of "eternal life"[43] in the "light" of His "glory,"[44] He "repays" the

---

[39]Pss. Sol. 3:11; 2:32; cf. 14:9 ("the day of mercy for the righteous"); 15:12 ("the Day of the
Lord's Judgment, when God oversees the earth at His Judgment").

[40]Pss. Sol. 3:12; 2:33; cf. 15:13.

[41]This last statement is based on the fact that, elsewhere in the Psalms of Solomon, those
persons who inherit eschatological life are characterized as "the Lord's devout" (12:6; 14:3, 10),
"those who truly love Him," who "endure His discipline," and who "live in the righteousness of
His commandments, in the Law, which He has commanded for our life" (14:1-3).

[42]See Ps. Sol. 2:35.

"unrighteous" for their sins[45] by leaving them in the grave, where they endure the "dishonor" and "humiliation"[46] of "eternal destruction."[47]

Jewish versus Greek anthropology. All of the writings discussed thus far (Isaiah, Daniel, Testaments of the Twelve Patriarchs, 2 Maccabees, Sibylline Oracles, and Psalms of Solomon--along with The Lives of the Prophets and 4 Baruch, considered in note 26) conceive of the Resurrection in terms of a traditional Jewish anthropology. They give no clear indication of belief in the immortality of the psyche, but instead anticipate God's re-creation of human beings as psychosomatically indivisible wholes. Beginning in the first century B.C., this stream of Jewish thought divides into two branches. While some writers (1 Enoch and 2 Baruch) continue to uphold the traditional understanding of resurrection as "re-creation," others (Apocryphon of Ezekiel, [Greek] Life of Adam and Eve, and 4 Ezra--along with Testament of Abraham, discussed in note 48) adopt a more characteristically Greek anthropology which transforms resurrection into the "reunion" of departed psychai with their entombed σώματα ("bodies").

Apocryphon of Ezekiel

Fragment 1 of the Apocryphon of Ezekiel (first century B.C. or first century A.D.) tells the story of a lame man and a blind man who conspire together to trespass in the king's garden. Riding on the shoulders of his

---

[43]See Ps. Sol. 3:12; cf. 12:6 ("the salvation of the Lord"); 13:11; 14:3-4, 10 ("life in happiness"); 15:13.

[44]See Pss. Sol. 2:31; 3:12.

[45]See Ps. Sol. 2:34-35.

[46]See Ps. Sol. 2:31, 35.

[47]See Pss. Sol. 2:31; 3:11-12; cf. 12:6 ("may the wicked perish once and for all"); 13:6, 11 ("no memory of them will ever be found"); 14:9 ("their inheritance is in Hades, and darkness [σκότος, which contrasts with the 'glory' (δόξα) or 'light' (φῶς) enjoyed by the righteous] and destruction"); 15:10-13 ("the inheritance of sinners is destruction and darkness (σκότος) . . . Hades . . . inheritance shall not be found for their children"); 16:2, 5.

accomplice, the lame man serves as the blind man's eyes, while the blind man's legs give the lame man mobility. When the two are captured, each denies that he is capable of committing such a crime because of his handicap; but the king places the lame man on the blind man's shoulders and punishes them together.

The parable is designed to make a point concerning the Resurrection of the dead and God's final Judgment. It presents the Resurrection--in Greek anthropological terms--as God's reunion of each human psyche with his/her corresponding body. The whole person then stands before the judgment seat of God in order to receive punishment or reward for his/her deeds.[48]

1 (Ethiopic Apocalypse of) Enoch[49]

1 Enoch is a composite work, consisting of five primary books dating from the second century B.C. to the first century A.D.[50] The idea of a bodily "resurrection" from the dead appears only in "The Book of the Similitudes" (chs. 37-71), which dates to the first century A.D.[51] Chapters 50-51 predict

---

[48]Testament of Abraham (resc. B) 7:16 (first to second century A.D.) likewise views the Resurrection as the reunion of psychai taken up into the "heavens" with their bodies buried on earth.

[49]For bibliography on 1 Enoch, see F. Garcia Martinez and E. J. C. Tigchelaar, "1 Enoch and the Figure of Enoch: A Bibliography of Studies 1970-1988," RevQ 14 (1989): 149-74.

[50]See the discussion by E. Isaac, which appears in The Old Testament Pseudepigrapha, 2:6-7.

[51]Isaac (in The Old Testament Pseudepigrapha, 1:9) says that the "Resurrection" also plays a role in "The Book of the Watchers" (chs. 1-36, late first century B.C. or early first century A.D.), "The Book of Dream Visions" (chs. 83-90, ca. 165-161 B.C.) and "The Book of the Epistle of Enoch" (chs. 91-107, first century A.D.); but a close examination reveals that he has read more into these texts than is justified:
"The Book of Watchers" opens with an apocalyptic vision of the end of the historical age and the beginning of the eschatological age. Enoch foresees that God "will arrive with ten million of the holy ones in order to execute judgment upon all" (1 Enoch 1:9). He will "destroy the wicked" (1:9), and will make their names "an eternal execration to all the righteous" (5:6). Yet there is no promise that the righteous who have already died will be raised to live again. Instead, "the elect and the righteous" who remain alive on the earth at the time of "the removal of all the ungodly ones" (1:1) will simply "complete the [designated] number of the days of their life" in "gladness and peace" (5:9-10). We find essentially the same idea in chapter 25, which predicts that, after "the great Judgment" (25:4), God will give fruit from the tree of life (see

a "general Resurrection" of the dead, in which "Sheol will return all the depos-
its which she had received and hell will give back all that which it owes."[52]
"The Lord of the Spirits" will "choose the righteous and the holy ones from
among [the risen dead]."[53] They will live upon the earth, enjoying "glory and
honor," "mercy," salvation and victory.[54] As for the sinners, they must either
repent or perish.[55]

The (Greek) Life of Adam and Eve[56]

Like the Apocryphon of Ezekiel, the (Greek) Life of Adam and Eve
(first century A.D.) conceives of death as the separation of the psyche (or
spirit[57]) from the body; for when Adam dies, his psyche is taken up "into
Paradise, to the third heaven,"[58] while his body (σῶμα) remains buried in the

---

Gen 3:22-24) to "the righteous and the pious" (25:5), so that they will live "long life" on "earth,
such as your fathers lived in their days" (25:6).

"The Book of Dream Visions" likewise speaks of a final Judgment in which the wicked
(including the unfaithful Jews--i.e., the "blinded sheep") will be annihilated (90:26-27), and the
righteous (including both Jews [the "snow-white" sheep, 90:32] and Gentiles ["the beasts of the
field and the birds of the sky," 90:30, 33], with the latter subordinate to the former) will live out
their lives in the "house" of the Lord (90:33-36). Again, there is no mention of God's raising
up those who die before the Day of Judgment comes.

Finally, "The Book of the Epistle of Enoch" speaks not of "resurrection" of the dead,
but of the immortality of psychai, as seen in note 13.

[52]1 Enoch 51:1.

[53]1 Enoch 51:2.

[54]1 Enoch 50:1-3; 51:2, 5. 1 Enoch 62:14-16 adds:

The Lord of the Spirits will abide over them; they shall eat and rest and rise with that Son
of Man [i.e., the Messiah] forever and ever. The righteous and elect ones shall rise from
the earth and shall cease being of downcast face. They shall wear the garments of glory
. . . the garments of life from the Lord of the Spirits.

[55]1 Enoch 50:2-5.

[56]This work is otherwise known as the "Apocalypse of Moses."

[57]Ψυχή and πνεῦμα are used interchangeably in 42:8.

[58]See (Greek) Life of Adam and Eve 37:5; cf. (1) 13:6, where the archangel Michael says
to Seth and Eve: "And as his [i.e., Adam's] psyche departs, you are sure to witness its fearful
upward journey," (2) 31:1, which mentions Adam's "going out of his body (σῶμα)," (3) 31:4,

ground.[59]   Death, however, is not God's final word to His creation; for in 41:2-3 He addresses Adam's buried body (σῶμα):

> I told you that you are dust and to dust you shall return. Now I promise to you the Resurrection (ἡ ἀνάστασις); I shall raise (ἀνιστάναι) you on the last day in the Resurrection[60] with every person of your seed.

Although nowhere explicitly stated, the writer seems to envision the "Resurrection" as the reunion of human psychai with their entombed bodies.[61]

Who will participate in the Resurrection? Chapter 41, verse 3, suggests a "general Resurrection" in which God raises "every person" of Adam's "seed." However, 28:4 seems to limit the scope of this promise to those who "guard" themselves "from all evil, preferring death to it."[62]

What will be the nature of "resurrection" existence for such persons? The author emphasizes the restoration to humankind of the blessings lost in Adam's Fall, including "the oil of mercy" which gives healing,[63] the "glorious

---

where Adam says, "I shall give back my spirit (πνεῦμα) into the hands of the One who has given it," (4) 32:4, where an angel says to Eve: "Adam your husband has gone out of his body (σῶμα). Rise and see his spirit (πνεῦμα) borne up to meet its Maker," (5) 42:8, where the dying Eve petitions God to "receive" her "spirit (πνεῦμα), and then gives "up her psyche (ψυχή) to God" (note that her body is buried in 43:1), and (6) 43:3, which speaks of "the psyche's (ψυχή) migration from the earth."

[59]See (Greek) Life of Adam and Eve 38-42.

[60]Cf. (Greek) Life of Adam and Eve 28:4; 10:2 and 43:2 ("the Day of the Resurrection," ἡ ἡμέρα τῆς ἀναστάσεως); 12:1 ("the Day of Judgment"); 37:5 ("that great and fearful day which I am about to establish for the world").

[61]See (Greek) Life of Adam and Eve 43:2.

[62]The fact that (Greek) Life of Adam and Eve makes no mention whatsoever of an afterlife for the wicked probably means that the author intends to leave such persons in the grave. Chapter 13, verse 3 (which does not appear in most manuscripts) also reinforces the idea of a "limited Resurrection" by saying that God will raise only "such as shall be the holy people."

[63]See (Greek) Life of Adam and Eve 13:1-2; cf. 9:3.

throne" of "dominion" usurped by Satan,[64] and "the tree of life" with the immortality it brings.[65]

4 Ezra

The Fourth Book of Ezra (dating, in its final form, to the late first century A.D.) consists of a Jewish apocalypse (chs. 3-14) to which a Christian framework (chs. 1-2, 15-16) was later added. The Jewish portion of 4 Ezra contains a series of seven visions purportedly given to Ezra during his years in Babylonian captivity.[66] The third vision (4 Ezra 6:35-9:25) is most important for our purposes inasmuch as it contains a detailed description of the Resurrection, the Judgment, and the final destination of the wicked and the righteous.

The "righteous" and the "unrighteous." Like so many other Jewish writings of the time, 4 Ezra divides human beings into two groups on the basis of whether or not they embrace God's Law. The vast majority have "scorned His Law, and denied His covenants;"[67] but a few "righteous" persons have kept "the Law of the Lawgiver perfectly" and therefore have "a treasure of works laid up with the Most High."[68]

Death and the state of the dead before the Judgment. Both the righteous and the unrighteous experience death, which the author of 4 Ezra understands

---

[64]See (Greek) Life of Adam and Eve 39:2-3.

[65]See (Greek) Life of Adam and Eve 28:4. Note that 13:4-5 (absent from many manuscripts) also adds "every joy of Paradise," the presence of God, and replacement of "the evil heart" (ἡ καρδία ἡ πονηρά--i.e., הַיֵּצֶר הָרָע, the "evil inclination") with "a heart that understands the good and worships God alone."

[66]See 4 Ezra 3:1.

[67]See 4 Ezra 7:24. For 4 Ezra's characterization of the "unrighteous," see 7:21-24; 8:56-60.

[68]See 4 Ezra 7:[77], [89].

as the "spirit's" (or "psyche's"[69]) leaving "the body to return again to Him who gave it."[70] After death, the spirits of the unrighteous do "not enter into habitations," but "immediately wander about in torments, ever grieving and sad;" for they know that "they have scorned the Law of the Most High" and must soon face "the torment laid up for themselves in the last days."[71] In contrast with the wicked, the spirits of the righteous enjoy seven days of "freedom," during which they contemplate both the punishment of the ungodly and their own future reward. Afterwards, these righteous spirits are gathered into "chambers," or "habitations," where they are "guarded by angels in profound quiet" until the Day of Resurrection.[72]

The Resurrection, the Judgment, and its consequences. Like other apocalyptic writers, the author of 4 Ezra views reality in terms of two "ages." The present historical "age is hastening swiftly to its end."[73] It will be followed by "the Day of Judgment," which will mark "the end of this age and the beginning of the immortal age to come."[74] On that day,

> the earth shall give up those who are asleep in it; and the chambers shall give up the psychai which have been committed to them. And the Most High shall be revealed upon the seat of judgment . . . And recompense shall follow, and the reward shall be manifested; righteous deeds shall awake, and unrighteous deeds shall not sleep. Then the pit of torment shall appear, and opposite it shall be the place of rest; and the furnace of Hell shall be disclosed, and opposite it the Paradise of delight. Then the Most High will say to the nations that have been raised from the dead,

---

[69]The terms are used interchangeably in 4 Ezra 7:[75], [78].

[70]See 4 Ezra 7:[78]; cf. 7:[88] ("when they shall be separated from their mortal body").

[71]See 4 Ezra 7:[75-87].

[72]See 4 Ezra 7:[88-101]; cf. 4:35 ("the psychai of the righteous in their chambers"), 42 ("in Hades the chambers of the psychai").

[73]See 4 Ezra 4:26.

[74]4 Ezra 7:43 [113]; cf. 7:49 [119] ("an eternal age").

'Look now, and understand whom you have denied, whom you have not served, whose commandments you have despised! Look on this side and on that; here are delight and rest, and there are fire and torments!' Thus He will speak to them on the Day of Judgment. (4 Ezra 7:32-33a, 35-[38])

This passage offers several important insights into 4 Ezra's conception of the Resurrection and its aftermath:

First, the author envisions a "universal Resurrection" ("the nations that have been raised from the dead") involving both Jews and Gentiles, righteous and unrighteous.[75] He seems to view "resurrection" itself as the reunion of departed psychai/spirits ("the chambers shall give up the psychai") with their own bodies now buried in the earth ("the earth shall give up those who are asleep in it").

Second, all those raised from the dead will stand before God's "seat of judgment,"[76] and the criterion for judgment will be the Law ("righteous deeds . . . and unrighteous deeds," "commandments").[77]

Third, those judged by the Law to be "unrighteous" (including many Jews, along with all of the Gentiles, whom God declares in 6:56 to be "nothing," "like spittle") will receive eschatological "punishment,"[78] which the author variously describes as "suffering,"[79] "recompense,"[80] "perishing,"[81]

---

[75]Cf. 4 Ezra 5:45.

[76]Cf. 4 Ezra 4:30, 39 ("the time of threshing").

[77]Cf. 4 Ezra 7:[72]-[73], which reads:

For this reason, therefore, those who dwell on earth shall be tormented, because though they had understanding they committed iniquity, and though they received the commandments they did not keep them, and though they obtained the Law they dealt unfaithfully with what they received. What, then, will they have to say in the Judgment, or how will they answer in the last times?

[78]See 4 Ezra 7:21; 7:47 [117] ("punishment after death"); 9:13.

[79]See 4 Ezra 7:56 [126].

[80]See 4 Ezra 7:35.

"fire and torments,"[82] "the furnace of Hell (Lat. *gehenna*)"[83] and "damnation."[84]

Fourth, those judged by the Law to be "righteous"[85] will receive eschatological "reward."[86] They will shine with the light of "glory;"[87] they will enjoy "rest"[88] and "plenty,"[89] "salvation"[90] and "immortality,"[91] in "the Paradise of delight."[92]

Eschatological "life" in the Law. Finally, it is important to note that the author of 4 Ezra grounds his statements concerning eschatological reward and punishment in the Jewish Scriptures--particularly in the Law:

---

[81]See 4 Ezra 7:[61]; 8:55; cf. 7:43 [113]-44 [114] ("corruption has passed away, sinful indulgence has come to an end, unbelief has been cut off").

[82]See 4 Ezra 7:[38]; cf. 7:[66], [99] and 9:12 ("torment"); 7:[47] and 9:9 ("torments"); 7:[36] ("the pit of torment").

[83]See 4 Ezra 7:[36].

[84]See 4 Ezra 7:61 [131]; 8:38.

[85]Note that such persons are described in 4 Ezra 8:30 as "those who have always put their trust in [God's] glory." Cf. 4 Ezra 9:7.

[86]See 4 Ezra 7:35, [98]; 8:39.

[87]See 4 Ezra 7:[95], [98]; 8:51; cf. 7:[97] ("their face is to shine like the sun, . . . they are to be made like the light of the stars"), 55 [125] ("the faces of those who practiced self-control shall shine more than the stars but [the unrighteous persons'] faces shall be blacker than darkness").

[88]See 4 Ezra 8:52; cf. 7:[36] ("the place of rest").

[89]See 4 Ezra 8:52.

[90]See 4 Ezra 7:[66], 61 [131]; 8:39; cf. 7:[60]; 9:7-8, 13.

[91]See 4 Ezra 7:[97]; cf. 7:13 ("the fruit of immortality"), [97] ("incorruptible"), 50 [120] ("an everlasting hope"); 8:52 ("the tree of life"), 53-54 ("the root of evil is sealed up from you, illness is banished from you, and death is hidden; hell has fled and corruption has been forgotten; sorrows have passed away, and in the end the treasure of immortality is made manifest").

[92]See 4 Ezra 7:[36]; cf. 7:[47] ("delight"), 51 [121] ("safe and healthful habitations"), 53 [123] ("a paradise . . . whose fruit remains unspoiled and in which are abundance and healing"); 8:52 ("Paradise," "a city").

O sovereign Lord, behold, you have ordained in your Law that the righteous shall inherit these things, but that the ungodly shall perish. (4 Ezra
7:17)

Since the notions of resurrection, judgment, and a coming eschatological age did not enter Jewish circles until long after the Law had achieved its
fixed form, what passage(s) of scripture could 4 Ezra possibly have in mind?
Chapter 7, verses 59 [129]-60 [130] point to Deut 30:19:

For this is the way of which Moses, while he was alive, spoke to the people, saying, "Choose for yourself life, that you may live!" But they did not
believe him, or the prophets after him, or even myself who have spoken
to them.

The author of 4 Ezra here reinterprets a biblical statement concerning the
"good life"[93] to refer to "eschatological life." Below, we will see that 2
Baruch makes a similar hermeneutical move.

2 (Syriac Apocalypse of) Baruch

We find one of the most detailed descriptions of the Resurrection in
2 Baruch (early second century A.D.). Even though this book was not written
until several decades after Paul's death, we have already seen that it contains
a number of ideas which were in circulation during the Apostle's lifetime and
which clearly influenced his thought.[94] For this reason, 2 Baruch is worthy
of careful consideration here.

The "lamp" of the Law. At the center of 2 Baruch's theology lies "the
lamp of the eternal Law which exists forever and ever."[95] Before Moses, "the

---

[93]Note that, in this context, the Lord speaks of how He has set before Israel "life and good,
death and evil" (Deut 30:15, MT), or "life and death, good and evil" (LXX).

[94]See chapter 3.

[95]2 Apoc. Bar. 59:2.

188

unwritten Law was in force."[96] Beginning with Moses, the written Law "illuminated all those who sat in darkness."[97]

The "righteous" and the "unrighteous." 2 Baruch divides the human race into two groups on the basis of their relationship to the Law. The first group, the "righteous," is made up of those Jews[98] who "sow into" their minds "the fruits of the Law," those who are "spotless," who "fear" God and "subject themselves" to Him and His Law "in faith."[99] Conversely, the second group, the "unrighteous," consists of Gentiles and "unfaithful" Jews who have "despised" their Creator, who have "separated themselves" from His "statutes and who have cast away from themselves the yoke" of His "Law."[100]

The coming "reversal." In this present life, the "unrighteous" often prosper, while the "righteous" suffer humiliation and defeat.[101] However, the Law reveals that, at "the end of times,"[102] God will bring about a great reversal; it announces "to those who believe the promise of their reward and

---

[96]2 Apoc. Bar. 57:2.

[97]2 Apoc. Bar. 59:2.

[98]See, e.g., 2 Apoc. Bar. 48:23-24, where Baruch says that the people who "received one Law from the One [God]" did not "mingle with the nations."

[99]2 Apoc. Bar. 32:1; 54:4-5; cf. 41:4; 44:3, 7, 14; 46:5; 48:22-24. Note that "faith," or "belief," or "trust," in the Second Apocalypse of Baruch, means strict adherence to the Law. Baruch's prayer makes this clear in 48:22: "In you we have put our trust, because, behold, your Law is with us, and we know that we do not fall as long as we keep your statutes." See also 42:2; 51:7; 54:16, 21; 59:2.

[100]2 Apoc. Bar. 42:2; 41:3; cf. 48:46-47; 54:14, 17-18, 21-22; 55:2, 7.

[101]See, e.g., 2 Apoc. Bar. 14:2-19.

[102]2 Apoc. Bar. 30:3.

to those who deny the punishment of the fire which is kept for them."[103]
How will this come about?

Death and the Resurrection of the dead. The author of 2 Baruch
believes that, after death, all persons enter "the realm of death," or "the treasuries of the psychai."[104] These terms do not refer to the dwelling places of
immortal psychai, but to the grave; for this writer views death as "sleep in the
earth,"[105] or the end of existence.

Yet the Lord promises Baruch that, "in the future," He will "renew His
Creation."[106] "The dust will be called, and told, 'Give back that which does
not belong to you and raise up all that you have kept until its own time.'"[107]
When Baruch asks, "In which shape will the living live in your day?,"[108] the
Lord responds that He will carry out His creative activity in two stages: First,
all the dead--both the "righteous" and the "unrighteous"--will be raised up in
exactly the same form they enjoyed in their former life:

> For the earth will surely give back the dead at that time; it receives them
> now in order to keep them, not changing anything in their form. But as
> it has received them so it will give them back. And as I have delivered
> them to it so it will raise them. For then it will be necessary to show
> those who live that the dead are living again, and that those who went
> away have come back. (2 Apoc. Bar. 50:2-3)

---

[103] 2 Apoc. Bar. 59:2. Since the Law contains this revelation, 2 Baruch says that to "investi-
gate the Law" is to "distinguish between life and death" (46:3). With regard to which passages
in the Law promise such eschatological reward and punishment, we have already seen how 4
Ezra interprets Deut 30:19 along these lines.

[104] 2 Apoc. Bar. 21:23; cf. 11:6; 23:4-5; 30:2; 48:16; 52:2. Compare 24:1 ("the treasuries in
which are brought together the righteousness of all those who have proven themselves to be
righteous").

[105] 2 Apoc. Bar. 11:4.

[106] 2 Apoc. Bar. 32:5-6.

[107] 2 Apoc. Bar. 42:8; cf. 21:23.

[108] 2 Apoc. Bar. 49:2.

190

Once "they have recognized each other,"[109] the Lord will implement the second stage of His plan: "Both the shape of those who are found to be guilty as also the glory of those who have proved to be righteous will be changed."[110] By this transformation of their σώματα ("bodies"), the Lord will "reward" the righteous and bring "punishment" on the unrighteous.[111]

The reward of the righteous. What will be the shape of God's "reward"[112] for the righteous? In chapter 51, the Lord tells Baruch that in "the coming world"[113]--or "Paradise"[114]--the righteous will

> be glorified by transformations, and the shape of their face will be changed into the light of their beauty so that they may acquire and receive the undying world which is promised to them . . . [The righteous will] be more exalted and glorified than [the unrighteous] . . . they will be changed into any shape which they wished, from beauty to loveliness, and from light to the splendor of glory." (2 Apoc. Bar. 51:3, 5, 10)

In these verses, the author of 2 Baruch gives voice to his three most central convictions concerning the nature of "resurrection" existence for the righteous. First, the transformed bodies of the righteous will shine with the radiant "light"[115] of eschatological "glory."[116] Not only will God's faithful

---

[109]2 Apoc. Bar. 50:4.

[110]2 Apoc. Bar. 51:1.

[111]See 2 Apoc. Bar. 59:2.

[112]See 2 Apoc. Bar. 52:7; 54:16; 59:2.

[113]See 2 Apoc. Bar. 44:15; cf. 15:7-8; 14:13 ("the world which you have promised to them"); 44:12 ("the new world"); 51:8 ("that world which is now invisible to them, . . . a time which is now hidden to them").

[114]See 2 Apoc. Bar. 51:11.

[115]See 2 Apoc. Bar. 48:50; 51:3, 10.

[116]See 2 Apoc. Bar. 48:49; 51:5, 10, 16; 54:16, 21; cf. 15:8 ("a crown with great glory"). Note also the discussion of this topic found in chapter 2 under "The 'glory' (δόξα) taken from Adam at the Fall and restored to the righteous at the Eschaton."

ones see "the beauty of the majesty of the living beings under the throne, as well as all the hosts of the angels;"[117] they themselves "will be like the angels" and "equal to the stars."[118] The Lord even says that "the excellence of the righteous" will be "greater than that of the angels."[119]

Second, the "new world"[120] promised to the righteous will be "undying."[121] Everything in this life is transitory,[122] but the righteous will inherit "that world which has no end."[123] The present life is stained by "corruption," "polluted by the great wickedness in this world;"[124] but the righteous will receive "the new world which does not carry back to corruption,"[125] and God "will purge them from sins."[126] "Everything" in this world "is in a state of dying,"[127] but the righteous will enjoy "the undying world which is promised

---

[117]See 2 Apoc. Bar. 51:11.

[118]See 2 Apoc. Bar. 51:10; cf. v. 5.

[119]See 2 Apoc. Bar. 51:12.

[120]See 2 Apoc. Bar. 44:12.

[121]See 2 Apoc. Bar. 51:3.

[122]See 2 Apoc. Bar. 83:10-22.

[123]See 2 Apoc. Bar. 48:50; cf. 44:11-12 ("a time that does not pass away," which "will remain forever").

[124]See 2 Apoc. Bar. 21:19; cf. 40:3 ("the world of corruption"); 44:9 ("the present time which is polluted by evils"); 85:5.

[125]See 2 Apoc. Bar. 44:12; cf. 85:5 ("that which we receive will not be corruptible").

[126]See 2 Apoc. Bar. 85:15.

[127]See 2 Apoc. Bar. 21:22.

to them."[128]   "Time will no longer make them older;"[129] their "life"[130] will be "preserved"[131] forever.

Third, the righteous will be "exalted."[132] In this life, they have "profited" little from their "diligence" and "good works;" they have been "treated shamefully" in spite of their refusal to "walk in vanity like the rest of the nations."[133] However, since the righteous have not "lost their life" and "exchanged their psyche"[134] for "nothing," God has promised them a future which will be "very great."[135] They will be "saved from this world of affliction" and will "put down the burden of anguishes."[136] 2 Baruch promises that, at "the consolation of Zion,"[137] the "present time will be forgotten"[138] and the righteous will receive "good things"[139]--"everything which we lost again by many times" (including the prophets, the land, and Zion).[140]

---

[128]See 2 Apoc. Bar. 51:3; cf. 44:9.

[129]See 2 Apoc. Bar. 51:9; cf. v. 16.

[130]See 2 Apoc. Bar. 42:7.

[131]See 2 Apoc. Bar. 48:6.

[132]See 2 Apoc. Bar. 51:5.

[133]See 2 Apoc. Bar. 14:5-7, 14.

[134]See 2 Apoc. Bar. 51:15.

[135]See 2 Apoc. Bar. 44:8.

[136]See 2 Apoc. Bar. 51:14; cf. v. 7.

[137]See 2 Apoc. Bar. 44:7.

[138]See 2 Apoc. Bar. 44:9.

[139]See 2 Apoc. Bar. 55:8.

[140]See 2 Apoc. Bar. 85:4.

Glory, an incorruptible life, and exaltation--such will be the "blessed-ness"[141] of God's "own" people[142] when He grants them "rest"[143] and causes them "to rejoice"[144] under His eschatological "Rule."[145]

The punishment of the unrighteous. The "resurrection" existence of the unrighteous will be quite different from that of the righteous, for they will be "blotted out" from God's own people[146] and "excluded" from the world to come.[147]

Whereas the resurrection bodies of the righteous will be transformed into glorious shapes, "the shape of those who now act wickedly will be made more evil than it is (now)."[148] The unrighteous will be changed "into startling visions and horrible shapes."[149]

Whereas the righteous will enjoy "life" that lasts forever, the un-righteous will "waste away."[150] Throughout all eternity, they will know only "corruption"[151] and "destruction;"[152] for "there will not be an opportunity

---

[141]See 2 Apoc. Bar. 48:49.

[142]See 2 Apoc. Bar. 54:22.

[143]See 2 Apoc. Bar. 85:11.

[144]See 2 Apoc. Bar. 55:8.

[145]See 2 Apoc. Bar. 54:22.

[146]See 2 Apoc. Bar. 54:22.

[147]See 2 Apoc. Bar. 83:8.

[148]See 2 Apoc. Bar. 51:2; cf. 51:16.

[149]See 2 Apoc. Bar. 51:5.

[150]See 2 Apoc. Bar. 30:4; cf. 48:6, which describes how the unrighteous "will pass away" and not be "preserved."

[151]See 2 Apoc. Bar. 42:7; 85:13.

[152]See 2 Apoc. Bar. 54:17; cf. 54:14 ("those who do not love your Law are justly perishing"); 85:15.

to repent anymore, nor a limit to the times,...nor supplicating for offenses,... nor help of the righteous."[153]

The unrighteous will witness the vindication and joyful exaltation of the righteous,[154] but they themselves will experience only the "shame"[155] and "sadness"[156] of God's "judgment."[157] The Lord will "convict" them of their sins[158] and will "condemn"[159] them to "punishment"[160] and "retribution,"[161] to "torment"[162] and "perdition"[163] in eternal "fire."[164]

Summary

We may summarize the results of our inquiry as follows: The idea of a bodily resurrection from the dead entered Jewish thought through apocalyptic circles. By the end of the second century B.C., it had gained acceptance among significant numbers of Jews. In accordance with traditional Jewish

---

[153]See 2 Apoc. Bar. 85:12.

[154]See 2 Apoc. Bar. 51:6.

[155]See 2 Apoc. Bar. 48:47.

[156]See 2 Apoc. Bar. 51:4.

[157]See 2 Apoc. Bar. 50:4; 55:5; 85:13; cf. 24:1, which describes how "the books will be opened in which are written the sins of all those who have sinned," and 83:1-3, which says that God "will truly inquire into everything with regard to all their works which were sins . . . he will make them manifest in the presence of everyone with blame."

[158]See 2 Apoc. Bar. 55:8.

[159]See 2 Apoc. Bar. 85:11.

[160]See 2 Apoc. Bar. 55:2, 7; 59:2.

[161]See 2 Apoc. Bar. 54:21; cf. 48:47 ("your Law which they transgressed will repay them on your day").

[162]See 2 Apoc. Bar. 30:5; 44:12; 46:6; 51:2, 6; 54:14-15; 83:8.

[163]See 2 Apoc. Bar. 30:5; 44:12.

[164]See 2 Apoc. Bar. 59:2; cf. 44:15 ("the habitation . . . in the fire"); 85:13 ("the way to the fire and the path that leads to the glowing coals").

anthropology, the Resurrection was at first envisioned as God's "re-creation" of the dead (Isaiah, Daniel, Books 2 and 4 of the Sibylline Oracles, the "Book of the Similitudes" in 1 Enoch, Psalms of Solomon, 2 Baruch). However, beginning in the first century B.C., some Jewish writers adopted a more characteristically Greek anthropology. This led them to transform the concept of "resurrection" into God's "reunion" of departed spirits/psychai with their entombed bodies (Apocryphon of Ezekiel, [Greek] Life of Adam and Eve, 4 Ezra, Testament of Abraham).

All Jewish writers who believed in the Resurrection expected the "righteous" to share in it. Furthermore, they consistently identified the "righteous" as Law-abiding Jews, or those persons who participated in the Mosaic covenant (see esp. Daniel [MT, teachers of the Law only], Daniel [LXX], Lives of the Prophets, Testament of Judah, Testament of Benjamin, Testament of Zebulon, 2 Maccabees, Psalms of Solomon, 4 Ezra, 2 Baruch). While some spoke of a "limited Resurrection" involving only these "righteous" persons (Isaiah, Job [LXX, "those whom the Lord raises"], Lives of the Prophets, 4 Baruch, Testament of Judah, Testament of Zebulon, 2 Maccabees, Psalms of Solomon, [Greek] Life of Adam and Eve), others anticipated a "general Resurrection" in which the "unrighteous" would also take part (Daniel, Testament of Benjamin, the "Book of the Similitudes" in 1 Enoch, Books 2 and 4 of the Sibylline Oracles, 4 Ezra, 2 Baruch). The resurrection existence of the "unrighteous" was variously described as some sort of punishment for their sins. While many different images were used to characterize the transformed existence of the "righteous," the three ideas appearing most frequently were (1) the light of "glory" (Daniel, Testament of Benjamin, the "Book of the Similitudes" in 1 Enoch, Psalms of Solomon 2 and 3, [Greek] Life of Adam and Eve, 4 Ezra, 2 Baruch), (2) immortality or incorruptibility (Daniel, Psalm of Solomon 3, [Greek] Life of Adam and Eve, 4 Ezra, 2 Baruch), and (3) exaltation (The "Book of the Similitudes" in 1 Enoch, Psalm of Solomon 2,

[Greek] Life of Adam and Eve [the "glorious throne" of "dominion"], Testament of Benjamin, 2 Baruch).

II. THE VIEW OF THE RESURRECTION
HELD BY PAUL THE PHARISEE

Before Paul came to know Christ, he was a dedicated Pharisee.[165] We have already seen that first-century Pharisees were known for their belief in the coming Resurrection of the dead. Therefore Paul probably possessed a well-developed notion of the Resurrection, grounded in the Scriptures, even before the Eschaton invaded his own experience with the appearance of the risen Christ.[166]

What was the view of the Resurrection held by Paul the Pharisee? If we assume that beliefs Paul shared in common with his Jewish contemporaries (as described in chapters 2, 3, 5 and 8) were inherited from the tradition, then the following portrait emerges: First, Paul the Pharisee was an apocalypticist; he numbered himself among those of his contemporaries who anticipated that God would soon bring to an end "the present evil age" (ὁ αἰὼν ὁ ἐνεστηκὼς πονηρός)[167] and inaugurate the eschatological age of His "Rule" (βασιλεία).[168] For Paul, the Resurrection of the dead had meaning only within this apocalyptic framework. This event would mark the arrival of the new age.

---

[165]See Phil 3:5; Gal 1:14; cf. Acts 23:6; 26:5.

[166]Anthony J. Saldarini discusses the problems involved in discerning the beliefs of first-century Pharisees in *Pharisees, Scribes and Sadducees in Palestinian Society: A Sociological Approach* (Wilmington, DE: Michael Glazier, 1988).

[167]See Gal 1:4; cf. Rom 12:2.

[168]See esp. 1 Cor 6:9, 10; 15:24, 50; Gal 5:21; 1 Thess 2:12.

Second, Paul the Pharisee expected the Resurrection to be limited to the "righteous."[169] Who were these "righteous" persons God would raise from the dead? Paul the Pharisee still held to the traditional Jewish understanding of "righteousness" as acceptance of the Mosaic covenant and the "yoke" of its Law.[170] He therefore must have anticipated that only Law-abiding Jews would share in the Resurrection.

Third, Paul understood "resurrection" in traditional Jewish anthropological terms as God's "re-creation"[171] of psychosomatically indivisible persons.[172]

Finally, he expected resurrection existence, or "eschatological life" ($\zeta\omega\grave{\eta}$ $\alpha\grave{\iota}\acute{\omega}\nu\iota o\varsigma$),[173] to be characterized by glory, immortality and exaltation.[174]

Paul the Pharisee's notion of the Resurrection most closely resembles the view put forward by the Psalms of Solomon[175]--a collection thought by many scholars to represent the thinking of the Pharisees.[176] We also note

---

[169]Throughout his epistles, the Apostle gives no clear indication that he expects the "unrighteous" to participate in the Resurrection. Instead, he appears to leave them in the grave (see chapter 8 under "A Resurrection/transformation for the unrighteous?"). This suggests that Paul the Pharisee was at home in the stream of tradition (represented, for example, by the "Isaiah Apocalypse") which anticipated a "limited Resurrection," involving only the "righteous."

[170]See Phil 3:5, 6, 9.

[171]See, e.g., Rom 4:17 ("the God who makes the dead alive and who calls into existence things which had no existence").

[172]See chapter 3, note 106.

[173]Like other apocalypticists before him, Paul uses $\zeta\omega\grave{\eta}$ ("life") to refer to both physical life and "eschatological life." See Hill, *Greek Words,* 189-91.

[174]See below, and also in chapter 8.

[175]Like Paul himself, Pss. Sol. 2 and 3 look forward to the day when God will "re-create" the righteous only, granting them glory, immortality and exaltation (see above).

[176]See R. B. Wright's discussion of this matter in *The Old Testament Pseudepigrapha,* 2:641-42.

strong similarities between Paul's views and those found in Daniel,[177] 1 Enoch, and 2 Baruch (which, in chs. 50-51, contains the most detailed description of the Resurrection in Jewish literature), with the major difference being that these three apocalypses anticipate a "general Resurrection" of the dead rather than one involving the righteous only.[178] In short, the evidence suggests that, before he became the Apostle of Christ, Paul was a Pharisee of the apocalyptic persuasion, who held the sort of opinions concerning the Resurrection which would be expected in such a man.

III. PAUL THE CHRISTIAN'S "CORE CONVICTIONS" CONCERNING CHRIST'S RESURRECTION AND "LIFE"[179]

Paul the Pharisee's face to face encounter with the risen Jesus left many of his ideas concerning the Resurrection intact. At the same time, this new reality led the Apostle to alter his views at several significant points, thus transforming him into Paul the Christian.[180] We will postpone discussion of the Apostle's new understanding of the general Resurrection of the righteous until chapter 8. In the remainder of this present chapter, we will narrow our focus to the resurrection of one particular man--namely, Jesus Christ.

---

[177]Harald Sahlin sets forth Daniel as the possible source for many elements of Paul's apocalyptic eschatology, including his concept of the Resurrection, in "Paulus och Danielsboken," *SEA* 46 (1981): 95-110.

[178]Like Paul, the [Greek] Life of Adam and Eve anticipates that only the righteous will be raised, and that eschatological life will be characterized by glory, immortality and exaltation. However, this writer ascribes to an entirely different anthropology than does Paul--namely, a more characteristically Greek anthropology which views the Resurrection as God's reunion of departed psychai with their entombed bodies.

[179]J. Christiaan Beker offers an excellent discussion of Paul's understanding of Christ's resurrection in chapter 8 (pp. 135-81) of *Paul the Apostle,* which he titles "Paul's Apocalyptic Theology: Apocalyptic and the Resurrection of Christ."

[180]See Leander E. Keck's excellent discussion of the ex post facto thinking prompted in Paul by Christ's resurrection in "Paul as Thinker," *Int* 47 (1993): 27-38.

Paul interpreted the historical event of Christ's resurrection against the background of the Jewish Scriptures and thereby arrived at four "core convictions" concerning its meaning. The Apostle viewed Christ's resurrection as (1) an act of God, (2) the beginning of the eschatological age and the general Resurrection of the righteous, (3) Christ's entrance into "eschatological life" characterized by glory and immortality, and (4) God's exaltation of the humble, trusting Jesus. Below, we will trace the *probable* route by which Paul arrived at these convictions.[181] Along the way, we will examine how these central elements of his theology manifest themselves within a variety of contexts.

". . . he is alive because of God's strength"--Christ's Resurrection to "Life" as an Act of God (Core Conviction 4)

For Paul, the Pharisee and apocalypticist, the mere sight of the risen Lord immediately confirmed that there was such a thing as "resurrection," that the scriptural promises concerning the Resurrection had been grounded in God's truth. This, in turn, served to increase Paul's confidence in those same Scriptures as the key to understanding the meaning of Christ's resurrection from the dead.

The Apostle's first "core conviction" concerning the Lord's resurrection came in response to the question of "Who raised Jesus from the dead?" We have already seen that, whenever Jewish writings dating to Paul's time mention the Resurrection, they consistently and without exception describe that event as an act of God. There apparently was no precedent for speaking of a person's rising from the dead, and thus entering into "eschatological life," by his/her own power. Thus, when the risen Christ appeared to Paul, the

---

[181]For a more extensive treatment of Paul's conversion experience, see Alan F. Segal, *Paul the Convert: The Apostolate and Apostasy of Saul the Pharisee* (New Haven, CT: Yale University Press, 1990).

200

Apostle concluded that God was "the One who raised Jesus from the dead."[182] In his defense against the Corinthian "super apostles" (discussed more fully in chapter 7), Paul expresses this same "core conviction" using the language of "power" or "strength" (δύναμις): "[Christ] is alive because of God's strength."[183]

"The first-fruits of those who have fallen asleep"--Christ's Resurrection as the Beginning of the Eschatological Age and the General Resurrection of the Righteous (Core Conviction 5)

"The present time." The Scriptures had also declared that God's raising the dead would mark the end of history and the beginning of the eschatological age.[184] Thus, his encounter with the risen Christ drove Paul to conclude that the Eschaton had already come. At the same time, Paul's own experience showed that God had not yet subdued all His enemies, that humanity's "history" of rebellion continued (as seen, for example, in Paul's own persecution of Christ's Church[185]), that "the present evil age" had not entirely passed away.

In order to hold these two undeniable realities together, Paul was led to alter slightly his views concerning the temporal relationship of the "two

---

[182]See Rom 8:11a; cf. Rom 4:24 ("the One who raised Jesus our Lord from the dead"); 6:4 ("Christ has been raised from the dead by the Glory who is the Father"); 8:11b ("the One who raised Christ from the dead"); Rom 10:9 ("God raised him from the dead"); 1 Cor 6:14 ("God raised the Lord"); 1 Cor 15:15 ("God . . . raised Christ"); 2 Cor 4:14 ("the One who raised the Lord Jesus"); Gal 1:1 ("God the Father . . . raised him from the dead"); 1 Thess 1:10 ("His Son . . . whom He raised from the dead"). Note also (1) the many "divine passive" forms of ἐγείρειν ("to raise") which appear with Christ as subject in the Pauline correspondence (Rom 4:25; 6:4, 9; 7:4; 8:34; 1 Cor 15:4, 12, 13, 14, 16, 17, 20; 2 Cor 5:15), along with (2) Paul's description of God as "the One who makes the dead alive" (ὁ ζῳοποιῶν) in Rom 4:17 (cf. 8:11; 1 Cor 15:22, 36).

[183]See 2 Cor 13:4; cf. Rom 1:4 ("designated Son of God in power [δύναμις] . . . by his resurrection from the dead" [RSV]); 1 Cor 6:14 ("God raised the Lord and He will also raise us by means of His strength [δύναμις]"); Phil 3:10-11 ("the strength [δύναμις] [of God which effected] his resurrection").

[184]For a discussion of Paul's eschatological scenario, see chapter 2 under "The present time."

[185]See Gal 1:13; Phil 3:6; cf. Acts 8:1-3; 9:1-2.

ages" to one another. Instead of there being a sharp break between the historical age and the eschatological age, it was clear that--at least for a short time--the two ages would "overlap." The eschatological age had already arrived--but not yet in all its fullness. The days of the historical age were numbered--but it had not entirely faded away.[186]

In his epistles, Paul refers to this "time between the times" as ὁ νῦν καιρός, "the present time."[187] "Christ died" in the past, at the "time" (καιρός) of God's choosing.[188] Three days later, God raised him from the dead and thereby inaugurated "the present time" (ὁ νῦν καιρός), the dawning of the eschatological age. Yet there still remains a future "time" (καιρός)--"when the Lord comes"[189]--marked by the final defeat of all God's enemies and the final end of the historical age. The appearance of the risen Christ led Paul to mesh history with eschatology, to view "the present time" as the beginning of the eschatological age.

"The first-fruits of those who have fallen asleep." Did the fact that only Jesus had been raised from the dead mean that he alone would participate in the Resurrection? Paul did not draw such a conclusion; for the prophets had not predicted that God would raise only one individual, but that He would raise the whole multitude of the righteous. For this reason, the Apostle could not conceive of the resurrection of Jesus apart from the Resurrection of the

---

[186]We see this gradual turning of the ages in, for example, Rom 13:12, where Paul writes: "the night is far gone, the day is at hand" (RSV).

[187]See Rom 3:26; 8:18; 11:5; 13:11 (τὸν καιρόν . . . νῦν); 2 Cor 6:2; 8:14. Sometimes the Apostle refers to this same period using only ὁ καιρός ("the time," see 1 Cor 7:29, and possibly Gal 6:10) or νῦν ("now," see Rom 3:21; 5:9, 11; 6:19, 21, 22 (νυνί); 7:6 (νυνί); 8:1, 22; 11:30, 31; 16:26; 1 Cor 7:14; 13:13 (νυνί); 15:20 (νυνί); 2 Cor 5:16; Gal 2:20; 4:9; Phil 1:30). For further discussion of "the present time," see part I of chapter 2.

[188]See Rom 5:6.

[189]See 1 Cor 4:5; cf. Gal 6:9; 1 Thess 5:1.

whole company of God's servants.[190]   He therefore viewed the risen Christ
not as a mere anomaly, but as "the first-fruits (ἀπαρχή) of those who have fall-
en asleep,"[191] the first of many to be raised from the dead.[192]

To summarize: Paul's second "core conviction" is that the resurrection
of Jesus marked the start of the eschatological age and the general Resurrection of the righteous.   The Apostle began with the Scriptures, saw the risen
Christ, and then most likely followed the line of reasoning described above in
order to arrive at this interpretation of what he had seen.

"The body of his glory"--The Nature of Christ's Resurrection "Life"
(Core Conviction 6)

Paul's third "core conviction" has to do with the nature of the Lord's
resurrection existence, or "eschatological life."   The Apostle indicates in 1 Cor

---

[190]J. M. Ross (in "Does 1 Corinthians 15 Hold Water?," *IBS* 11 [1989]: 69-72) writes: "It
does not necessarily follow from the resurrection of Jesus that disbelief in the bodily resurrection of others is illogical. Christ was unique" (pp. 70-71). This may be true in Ross' twentieth
century European context, but it does not appear to have been the case for a first century Pharisaic Jew of the apocalyptic persuasion like Paul. Note how the two ideas are inseparable in
1 Cor 15:13, 20, 21, where the Apostle writes: "Now if there is no Resurrection from the dead,
then neither has Christ been raised . . . But in the present time Christ has been raised from the
dead . . . the Resurrection from the dead [has become a reality] through a [single] man." One
resurrection meant "the Resurrection." Absolutely no precedent for thinking otherwise existed.

[191]See 1 Cor 15:20, 23. Compare "the first-born among many brothers" (ὁ πρωτότοκος ἐν
πολλοῖς ἀδελφοῖς) in Rom 8:29 (cf. Col 1:18 ["the first-born from the dead"]).

[192]Some commentators on 1 Corinthians 15 suggest that, when Paul speaks of Christ as
"first-fruits," he means that Jesus' resurrection somehow "guarantees" the Resurrection of others
(e.g., Bruce, *1 and 2 Corinthians,* 145: "as surely as the first fruits guarantee the coming harvest,
so surely does his resurrection guarantee theirs"). Since Christ's resurrection is the first act in
the general Resurrection of the righteous, it does hold a certain "promise" of resurrection for
all God's people--just as the first ripe head of grain offers "promise" for a larger harvest to
come. However, Christ's resurrection does not "effect" the Resurrection of the righteous any
more than the "first-fruits" of grain "effect" the successful harvest of the rest of the crop. As
we saw above, the "power" behind the Resurrection is neither Christ nor the resurrection of
Christ; instead, the Resurrection is an act of God. Human beings will live again not simply
because Christ lives again, but because God chooses to give them new life. To whom has God
chosen to give "eschatological life"? Paul's answer is "Those whom He reckons 'righteous.'"
And whom does He reckon "righteous"? Those who entrust themselves to the One who sent
Jesus to die on the cross as the sacrifice which established the "new covenant." "The person
[reckoned] righteous on the basis of trust will live ['eschatological life']" (Rom 1:17; cf. Hab
2:4).

15:42-58 that the risen Christ now enjoys the same kind of "spiritual" (πνευμα-τικός), "heavenly" (ἐπουράνιος) existence God will one day give to all the righteous[193]--namely, a bodily (somatic) existence characterized by "glory" (δόξα) and "immortality" (ἀθανασία[194]). The Apostle draws attention to these same two qualities of Christ's "eschatological life" in other contexts as well. For example, he speaks of the Lord's "immortality" in Rom 6:9 ("since Christ has been raised from the dead, he dies no more; death is his lord no longer"), while "the body of his glory" (τὸ σῶμα τῆς δόξης αὐτοῦ) becomes the pattern for the Christian's future existence in Phil 3:21.[195]

What led Paul to believe that the risen Christ possessed an immortal "body of glory"? First, as we have already seen, the Scriptures of Paul's day typically described resurrection existence in such terms.[196] The Fourth Book of Ezra (dating roughly to Paul's time), for example, predicts that the right-eous will "escape what is mortal" when they are "glorified."[197] Likewise, 2 Baruch maintains that the righteous will be "glorified by transformations" when they "receive the undying world which is promised to them."[198] Once Paul became convinced that Christ had indeed risen from the dead, he

---

[193]See the discussion of this text in chapters 3 and 8.

[194]In this context, the terms ἀφθαρσία ("incorruption") and δύναμις ("strength") are synonyms for ἀθανασία ("immortality").

[195]Cf. 1 Cor 2:8 ("the Lord of glory"); 2 Cor 3:18 ("the glory of the Lord").

[196]In an article entitled "Firstborn of Many Brothers: A Pauline Notion of Apotheosis" (in Society of Biblical Literature 1984 Seminar Papers, ed. Kent Harold Richards [Chico, CA: Schol-ars Press, 1984], 295-303), James Tabor explores how the notion of "'mass apotheosis' might be set in the context of various hellenistic ways of understanding divinity" (p. 295). He includes in this discussion "a host of Jewish texts in and around the Second Temple period which speak of the destiny of both individuals and select groups in terms of heavenly transformation, glorifi-cation, or even enthronement" (p. 302). Most of these texts received careful consideration earlier in this chapter.

[197]See 4 Ezra 7:[96, 98].

[198]See 2 Apoc. Bar. 51:3.

probably assumed that the Lord's resurrection existence could be accurately described using the traditional language of the Scriptures.

However, there is a second consideration that should not be passed over lightly. Paul told the Corinthians that the risen Christ "was seen by me also."[199] What, exactly, did Paul see?[200] The Book of Acts repeatedly mentions "a light from heaven" (φῶς ἐκ τοῦ οὐρανοῦ),[201] but we hear nothing of this "light" from the Apostle himself (unless 2 Cor 4:4, 6 is a reference to this reality). Paul says only that he saw "Jesus our [risen] Lord."[202] Since he elsewhere describes this same Jesus as having a "body of glory," it would not be unreasonable to suppose that what Paul saw, with his own eyes, was the radiant[203] "body of [Christ's] glory."[204] If this was indeed the case, then Christ appeared to Paul in exactly the form in which a first century Pharisee and apocalypticist would expect to see someone whom God had raised from the dead. (This, of course, would have important implications for how the Lord intended his chosen Apostle to interpret his resurrection.) Furthermore, it would mean that Paul's third "core conviction"--like the others--was erected upon the double foundation of the Jewish Scriptures and his own encounter with the risen Christ.

---

[199]See 1 Cor 15:8.

[200]Apart from what the Apostle may have heard, he repeatedly insists that he did "see" something.

[201]See Acts 9:3; 22:6, 9, 11 (ἡ δόξα τοῦ φωτὸς ἐκείνου, "the glory of that light"); 26:13 (οὐρανόθεν ὑπὲρ τὴν λαμπρότητα τοῦ ἡλίου . . . φῶς, "a light from heaven, brighter than the sun").

[202]See 1 Cor 9:1; cf. 15:8.

[203]If this was the case, then the bright "light" mentioned in the Book of Acts had some basis in Paul's history.

[204]See Phil 3:21. At the very least, we know that Paul saw nothing which prevented him from describing the risen Jesus using this traditional terminology for resurrection existence.

"The Name which is above every name"--Christ's Resurrection to "Life" as God's Exaltation of the Humble, Trusting Jesus (Core Conviction 7)

In chapter 4, we saw how Paul interprets Christ's death as his act of obedience, or trust, or self-humiliation before God. This idea is prominent, for example, in the "Kenosis Hymn" Paul quotes in Phil 2:5-11. The first part of the "Hymn" reads:

(5) Have this mind-set in you which [was] also in Christ Jesus,

    (6) Who, although [he] was in the form of God,
      did not consider equality with God something to be seized.
    (7) Instead, he emptied himself
      by taking the form of a slave,
      by being [born] in the likeness of men.
    And after he was found in outward form as a man,
    (8) he humbled himself by being obedient to the point of death--
      even the death which is the cross.

The latter portion of the "Hymn" describes how God responded to Christ's humility by highly exalting His obedient servant:

    (9) For this very reason (διὸ καί) God super-exalted him
      and gave to him the Name[205] which is above every name,
    (10) in order that, at the nam[ing] of Jesus,
      every knee should bow--
      of heavenly [beings] and of earthly [beings] and of [beings] under
      the earth--
    (11) and every tongue should confess, "Jesus Christ [is] Lord,"
      to the glory of God the Father.

The "Hymn" does not explicitly mention God's raising Christ from the dead, but we may be sure that--at least in Paul's mind--Christ's exaltation to lordship cannot be separated from his resurrection. The Apostle holds the two ideas together in, for example, (1) Rom 15:12, which describes Jesus as "the one who rises (ἀνιστάναι) to rule over the Gentiles," (2) Rom 14:9, which maintains that "Christ died and lived [again] in order that he might rule as

---

[205]Paul is referring to the Name κύριος ("Lord," see v. 11), which is used throughout the Septuagint in place of יהוה, the Name of God Himself.

Lord over both the dead and the living," (3) Rom 8:34, where the Christ "at the right [hand] of God" is the same Christ who "has been raised," (4) 1 Cor 15:24-28, where the risen Christ "reigns" as God's vicar over "every ruler and every authority and power," and (5) 2 Cor 5:10, where the risen Christ is described as eschatological Judge. Paul's fourth "core conviction" is that, by raising Jesus from the dead, God elevated him from a state of humiliation to an exalted status as cosmic Ruler and Lord.

Resurrection as exaltation. Unfortunately, in this case, it is easier to discern what Paul believed than how he came to believe it. We have already seen that the idea of resurrection as God's exaltation of the righteous was quite common in the Scriptures of Paul's day. The Apostle stands firmly on this tradition when, for example, he (1) describes resurrection as movement from "dishonor" (ἀτιμία) to "glory" (δόξα, here carrying connotations of "honor"[206]),[207] and (2) says to the Corinthians, "You know, don't you, that the saints will judge the world?"[208] When Paul viewed it against the background of the Jewish Scriptures, the mere fact of Christ's resurrection signified that he had been exalted by God.

Yet Paul does not simply say that Christ has been exalted; he insists that the Lord has been exalted above all others, that he has been given "the Name which is above every name." What was the source for this belief? Several statements made by the Apostle suggest that his fourth "core conviction" concerning Christ's resurrection was probably rooted in two of the earliest christological speculations of the Church--namely, those interpreting the risen Christ as the "last Adam" and promised "Davidic king." We will explore both these possibilities in the following paragraphs.

---

[206]See chapter 2 under "Basic meanings of δόξα ('glory')."

[207]See 1 Cor 15:43.

[208]See 1 Cor 6:2.

The "last Adam." First, Paul was not alone in his understanding of Christ as "the last Adam;" other early Christians also drew a contrast between Jesus and the father of humankind.[209] They were familiar with Gen 1:26-28 (LXX), which described how God made man (ἄνθρωπος) in His own image, both male and female, and then commanded him to "exercise lordship" (κατα-κυριεύειν) over the earth--to "rule (ἄρχειν) over the fish of the sea, the birds of heaven, and all creatures." They knew how Adam lost his dominion over the earth through disobedience--i.e., through trying to be "like God."[210] Some first-generation Christians erected a meaningful interpretation of Christ's death and resurrection upon this foundation.

To illustrate: The author of the "Kenosis Hymn" (apparently with Paul's approval) drew a contrast between Adam's action and that of Christ by saying that Christ did not--like Adam--view "equality with God" (which Christ already possessed) as "something to be seized" (ἁρπαγμός) and exploited. Instead, "he humbled himself by being obedient to the point of death." In the face of Christ's subsequent resurrection, the hymnwriter seems to have concluded that God granted to Jesus' obedience the "rule," or "lordship," previously forfeited through Adam's disobedience.

Other early Christians found scriptural warrant for such an interpretation of Christ's resurrection in Ps 8:4-6 (LXX):

What is man (ἄνθρωπος, which was taken to refer to Jesus Christ, the "representative man," or "last Adam"), that you should be mindful of him? or the Son of Man (another title applied to Christ), that you should be concerned about him? You made him a little lower than the angels; you crowned him with glory and honor, and set him over the works of your hands. You have put all things in subjection under his feet.

---

[209]See chapter 3, note 56.

[210]See Gen 3:6, 18-20; cf. [Greek] Life of Adam and Eve 39:2-3 (the "glorious throne" of "dominion" (ἀρχή).

The author of Ephesians applies v. 6b ("you have put all things in subjection under his feet") to the risen Christ in Eph 1:20-22, while the writer to the Hebrews uses this same text to prove that God has subjected "the world to come" (ἡ οἰκουμένη ἡ μέλλουσα) to the risen Lord.[211]

Paul himself makes use of the Psalm in 1 Corinthians 15, where he speaks of the eschatological reign of the risen Christ, the "last Adam." The Apostle writes:

> . . . it is necessary [that the risen Christ] rule until the time when [God] will have put all "enemies" under his "feet."[212] The last enemy rendered powerless [will] be Death. [I can rightfully predict that even Death will be rendered powerless] because [Psalm 8:7 says that] "[God] has put all [things] in subjection under his feet." (1 Cor 15:25-27a)

This passage, along with the "Kenosis Hymn" of Philippians 2, suggests that Paul's interpretation of Christ's resurrection as his exaltation to lordship was partly grounded in an "Adam christology" developed (with Paul's participation) during the first decades of the Church's existence.

Before leaving Paul's interpretation of Christ as the "last Adam," we must stress one further point: Paul, by means of the "Kenosis Hymn," does not simply draw a contrast between Christ's death as humiliation and his resurrection as exaltation; instead, he makes a causal connection between the two. After describing Jesus' self-humiliation, his obedience, his acceptance of the status of a "slave," the Apostle declares that it was "for this very reason" (διὸ καί) that God "super-exalted" Jesus and made him "Lord." In other words, God's decision to raise Christ from the dead and exalt him was made on the basis of Christ's attitude of humility and servanthood and obedience "to the point of death"--i.e., on the basis of his "trust" in God.[213] For Paul, then, the

---

[211]See Heb 2:5-9.

[212]Paul here alludes to Ps 110:1, discussed below.

[213]For further discussion of this point, see chapter 6 under "Christ's death."

meaning of Christ's resurrection is found not only in the fact that God did raise the dead, but also in the particular person whom God raised from the dead. The Jesus who presently lives and reigns is the person who first submitted to "the death which is the cross." The full significance of this observation will be seen in chapters 6 and 7.

The "Son of God." Paul's understanding of Jesus' resurrection as his exaltation to Rule also seems to be grounded in a second branch of early christology which viewed the risen Christ as Davidic King, or "Son of God." In 2 Kings 7 (LXX, 2 Samuel 7 in the MT), God promised that He would "raise up" (ἀνιστάναι) one of David's descendants and establish his rule (βασιλεία) forever (ἕως αἰῶνος[214]).[215] Psalm 2 (one of the "Royal Psalms") calls the Davidic king God's "Christ" (Χριστός),[216] and describes him as the "Son" of God, who exercises authority over all nations as God's vicar. The king declares in vv. 6-9 (LXX):

> I have been set up as king by Him on Zion, His holy mountain, and I issue the command of the Lord. The Lord has said to me, "You are my Son; today I have begotten you. Ask of me, and I will give to you the nations as your inheritance, and the ends of the earth as your possession. You will rule them with a rod of iron; you will shatter them like a potter's vessel."

In like manner, another psalmist writes:

> The Lord (i.e., God) said to my lord (i.e., the Davidic king), "Sit at my right [hand] until I make your enemies a footstool for your feet." (Ps 110 [109]:1 [LXX])

Some of the first Christians saw in these scriptures a witness to the risen Christ. For example, Luke-Acts identifies Jesus as that descendant of

---

[214]To a person with Paul's apocalyptic mind-set, this phrase could possibly be understood to mean "until the eschatological age" comes in all its fullness (see 1 Cor 15:24-28).

[215]See 2 Kgs 7:12, 16 (LXX).

[216]See Ps 2:2 (LXX).

David to whom God has given "the throne of his father" and an everlasting Rule, thus making him the "begotten" one, the "Son of the Most High."[217] The writer to the Hebrews likewise maintains that it is the risen Jesus who "has sat down at the right [hand] of the Majesty on high," who has been "appointed heir of all things," and to whom God has said, "You are my Son; today I have begotten you."[218]

The Apostle Paul was also acquainted with this line of interpretation, for he employs it on a number of occasions in order to shed light on the meaning of Christ's resurrection from the dead. Perhaps, after seeing the risen Jesus, the attention of the newly ordained "Apostle to the Gentiles" was first captured by a prophecy he cites in Rom 15:12--namely, Isa 11:10 (LXX), which identifies "the one who rises" (ὁ ἀνιστάμενος) as "the root of Jesse" (ἡ ῥίζα τοῦ Ἰεσσαί, i.e., the descendant of David's father, or the Davidic king) and the one who will "rule over the Gentiles" (ἄρχειν ἐθνῶν).[219] Paul opens his epistle to the Romans with a proclamation of this same idea--namely, that Jesus was "from the seed of David according to the flesh" (i.e., he was from "the root of Jesse"), and that he was designated "Son of God" (i.e., the Davidic king who rules over all nations as God's vicar[220]) "in power" (ἐν δυνάμει) by his "resurrection from the dead" (ἀνάστασις νεκρῶν).[221]

---

[217]See Luke 1:31-33; Acts 13:23, 33.

[218]Heb 1:2-3, 5; cf. 5:5.

[219]Cf. 2 Kgs 7:12 (LXX), where God promises to "raise up" (ἀνιστάναι) David's descendant and establish his "rule" (βασιλεία) forever" (see above).

[220]See the passages from Psalm 2 and Psalm 110 (109) discussed above.

[221]See Rom 1:3-4.

Once Paul identified the risen one with the promised "Son of God" and descendant of David,[222] he would have immediately recognized Jesus to be the second "Lord" of Ps 110 (109):1. Thus, he positions the risen Christ "at the right [hand] of God," where he rules as God's vicar, in Rom 8:34. Furthermore, this same Psalm is clearly the source for Paul's views concerning the temporal (until "the end") and authoritative (excepting God) limits of Christ's eschatological reign in 1 Cor 15:24-25, 27b-28:

> Then [will come] the end, when [the risen and exalted Christ] will hand over the Rule (βασιλεία) to God--even to the Father--after [God] has rendered powerless every ruler and every authority and power. [I can rightfully say that he will hand over the Rule to God only after He has rendered powerless every ruler and every authority and power] because [Psalm 110 (109):1 says that] it is necessary [that] he rule until the time when [God] will have put all "enemies" under his "feet" . . . (Now when it is said that all things have been put in subjection, [it is] evident that the One who put all things in subjection to him is excepted.) But after all things have been subjected to him, then even the Son himself will be subject to the One who subjected all things to him,[223] in order that God may be all in all.[224]

Conclusion

In conclusion, Paul arrived at his views concerning Christ's resurrection and "eschatological life" by interpreting that reality--which he himself had

---

[222]Note also that Psalm 72 (71):17b ("All the tribes of the earth will be blessed in him [i.e., the Davidic king]") appears to set forth the Davidic king as that "offspring" of Abraham through whom the "blessing" promised to Abraham (which Paul understands to be the "new covenant"-- see chapter 4 under "Galatians 3:13") would come to all nations (compare Gen 12:3b, 18:18b, and 22:18). If Paul knew this "royal psalm," he may have interpreted it as a prophetic witness to the sacrificial death of Christ (the "Son of God," or Davidic King) through which God brought the "blessing" of the "new covenant" based on trust to all nations.

[223]Cf. 1 Cor 3:23 ("you are Christ's, Christ is God's"); 11:3 ("the head of every man is Christ, the head of woman is man, the head of Christ is God").

[224]Psalm 110 (109):1 portrays God as the One who enables the Davidic king to subdue his enemies. Thus, Paul can speak of Christ's "reigning" and of God's putting his enemies under Christ's feet at the same time. On the relationship between God and Christ in Paul's eschatology, see Joseph L. Kreitzer, *Jesus and God in Paul's Eschatology, Journal for the Study of the New Testament* Supplement Series, 19 (Sheffield, England: JSOT Press, 1987).

seen--against the background of the Jewish Scriptures. Certain primarily Pharisaic and apocalyptic descriptions of the final Resurrection of the righteous led the Apostle to view Christ's own resurrection as (1) an act of God, (2) the beginning of the eschatological age and general Resurrection of the righteous, and (3) Jesus' entrance into the glory and immortality of "eschatological life." Another group of texts, identifying the risen Christ as "last Adam" and Davidic "Son of God," convinced Paul (along with other first-century Christians[225]) that, by raising the humble Jesus from the dead, God had exalted him to the status of eschatological Ruler over all His Creation.

---

[225]For a more detailed discussion of the development of these early christologies, see (1) Oscar Cullmann, *The Christology of the New Testament,* 1st ed., rev., trans. Shirley C. Guthrie and Charles A. M. Hall (Philadelphia: The Westminster Press, 1963), (2) Dunn, *Christology,* and (3) Reginald H. Fuller, *The Foundations of New Testament Christology* (New York: Charles Scribner's Sons, 1965).

CHAPTER SIX

ROMANS 6:1-14

In the previous two chapters, we examined Paul's interpretation of the
death and resurrection of Jesus Christ. Yet Jesus is not the only one who
emerges from the grave to enjoy "eschatological life." Throughout his epistles,
Paul maintains that Christians "die" and will rise "with Christ." This idea
appears, for example, in Rom 6:1-14, one of the most controversial and often-
discussed passages in the Pauline corpus.[1] In the following pages, we will
examine this key text in the light of our new-found insight into Christ's Cross
and resurrection. Romans 6:1-14 will thus serve as the introduction to a more
comprehensive study of the Christian's "death" and resurrection with Christ in
chapters 7 and 8. We begin with an examination of the context and structure
of this important text.

---

[1]Recent exegetical studies of Rom 6:1-14 include: (1) James D. G. Dunn, "Salvation Proclaimed VI. Romans 6:1-11: Dead and Alive," *ExpTim* 93 (1982): 259-64, (2) Douglas J. Moo,
"Exegetical Notes: Romans 6:1-14," *TJ* 3 n.s. (1982): 215-20, (3) G. M. M. Pelser, "The Objec-
tive Reality of the Renewal of Life in Romans 6:1-11," *Neot* 15 (1981): 101-17, and (4) James
L. Price, "Romans 6:1-14," *Int* 34 (1980): 65-69. For further bibliography on this important text,
see the articles listed above, along with (1) James D. G. Dunn, *Romans,* Word Biblical
Commentary (Dallas: Word Books, Publisher, 1988), 1:303-04, and (2) Käsemann, *Romans,* 160.
Robert Schlarb summarizes early patristic interpretations of these verses in "Röm 6:1-11 in der
Auslegung der frühen Kirchenväter," *BZ* 33 (1989): 104-13.

I. CONTEXT, STRUCTURE, AND TRANSLATION OF ROMANS 6:1-14

Context and Structure of Romans 6:1-14

Romans 5:12-21. In Rom 5:12-21, Paul describes human reality, as shaped by Adam, in terms of bondage under Sin and Death. He maintains that introduction of the Mosaic covenant did not fundamentally change that reality; for the Jewish Law could not break the power of Sin, but served only to "increase the trespass."[2] However, "where sin has increased, [God's] goodwill has overflowed all the more."[3] God acted to effect deliverance--or to transform human reality--through the sacrificial death of Jesus Christ, which brings "the righteousness [which means] 'eschatological life'"[4] to those who trust in him. Sin, the Jewish Law, and God's expression of His goodwill (χάρις) in Christ--these have become the focus of Paul's concern at the end of Romans 5.[5]

Romans 6:1-7:25.[6] The Apostle further explores the relationship between sin, the Law, and God's goodwill in Romans 6 and 7. He neatly organizes his remarks into three main arguments ([1] Rom 6:1-14, [2] Rom 6:15-7:6, and [3] Rom 7:7-25), each introduced by a rhetorical question ("What shall we say then?" [Τί οὖν ἐροῦμεν;] or simply "What then?" [Τί οὖν;]), along with a possible response ([1] "Shall we remain within the sphere where Sin rules in order that goodwill may increase?" in Rom 6:1, [2] "Shall we sin

---

[2]See Rom 5:20.

[3]See Rom 5:20.

[4]See Rom 5:18.

[5]For a more detailed discussion of the content and context of Rom 5:12-21, see chapter 3.

[6]We owe the following insights into the structure of Romans 6-7 to Paul J. Achtemeier. See *Romans,* Interpretation: A Bible Commentary for Teaching and Preaching (Atlanta: John Knox Press, 1985), 102.

because we are not under the Law but under goodwill?" in Rom 6:15, and [3] "Is the Law sin?" in Rom 7:7) which Paul emphatically rejects ("Certainly not!" [μὴ γένοιτο]). Romans 6:1-14 unfolds the relationship between God's goodwill (as expressed in the Cross) and sin. Romans 6:15-7:6 and 7:7-25 deal, respectively, with (1) the relationship between God's act of goodwill and the Jewish Law, and (2) the relationship between the Jewish Law and Sin.

Romans 6:1-14. The point of departure for Paul's discussion of human sin in relation to God's goodwill (Rom 6:1-14) lies in Rom 5:15-21, where the Apostle declares that, in the face of human sin, "God's expression of His goodwill . . . has overflowed toward the many!"[7] From statements such as this, some who heard Paul inferred that God's act of goodwill in Christ functions as an incentive for unbridled sin. The Apostle mentions these persons in Rom 3:8: ". . . some say that we say, 'Let us do evil so that good may result.'"[8]

Paul returns to this issue in Rom 6:1, where he asks, "Shall we remain within [the sphere where] Sin [rules] in order that [God's] goodwill may increase?" His reply in v. 2 is "Certainly not! How can we who have died to Sin still live within [the sphere where] it [rules]?" Paul defends this thesis in vv. 3-11 by showing that God's expression of His goodwill in the Cross of Christ does not promote sin. Instead, it releases human beings from Sin's power and thus demands an end to sinning. In an exhortatory conclusion (vv. 12-14), Paul urges his readers to act accordingly: "Therefore continue not to let Sin reign."[9]

---

[7]See Rom 5:15.

[8]Paul is probably responding to Jewish critics who argue that God's goodwill toward human beings increases not within the context of human sin, but within the context of human obedience to God's Law.

[9]See Rom 6:12a.

216

Summary. In summary, Rom 6:1-14 consists of an introduction (v. 1), a thesis (v. 2), an argument supporting that thesis (vv. 3-11), and an exhortatory conclusion (vv. 12-14). In these verses, Paul discusses the relationship between human sin and God's act of goodwill in Christ. He thus draws out some of the implications of statements he made in Rom 5:12-21.

Translation of Romans 6:1-14

Romans 6:1-14 may be translated as follows:

(1) What shall we say then? Shall we remain within [the sphere where] Sin [rules] (τῇ ἁμαρτίᾳ) in order that [God's] goodwill (χάρις) may increase? (2) Certainly not! How can we who have died to Sin (τῇ ἁμαρτίᾳ) still live within [the sphere where] it [rules] (ἐν αὐτῇ)? (3) Or do you not realize that as many of us as have been baptized into Christ Jesus have been baptized into his death? (4) We, then, have been buried together with him, by means of baptism, into "death," in order that, just as Christ has been raised from the dead by the Glory who is the Father (ἡ δόξα τοῦ πατρός),[10] so might we also live a new life (ἐν καινότητι ζωῆς περιπατήσωμεν). (5) [I can rightfully say that, having been baptized into Christ's death, we will also rise to live a new life] because if we have been planted together [with one another][11] in [a "death"] like his death, [then] we will certainly also [participate in a resurrection like his] resurrection (εἰ γὰρ σύμφυτοι γεγόναμεν τῷ ὁμοιώματι τοῦ θανάτου αὐτοῦ, ἀλλὰ καὶ τῆς ἀναστάσεως ἐσόμεθα).[12] (6) This we know: Our old self (ἄνθρωπος) has been

---

[10]Ἡ δόξα τοῦ πατρός ("the Glory who is the Father") most likely refers to God in His power. See chapter 2, note 55.

[11]For a list of those who interpret σύμφυτος in Rom 6:5 as a botanical metaphor ("planted together with"), see James D. G. Dunn, *Baptism in the Holy Spirit: A Re-examination of the New Testament Teaching on the Gift of the Spirit in Relation to Pentecostalism Today* (Philadelphia: The Westminster Press, 1970), p. 141, note 5.

[12]Florence Morgan Gillman discusses the context, grammar, and 20th century interpretation of Rom 6:5a in (1) "Romans 6:5a: United to a Death Like Christ's," *ETL* 59 (1983): 267-302, and (2) *A Study of Romans 6:5a: United to a Death Like Christ's* (San Francisco: Mellen Research University Press, 1992). Dr. Morgan convincingly argues several points worthy of mention here:

First, τὸ ὁμοίωμα τοῦ θανάτου αὐτοῦ refers to "the believer's (not Christ's) death to sin." Paul is "making a comparison between Christ and believers;" he is not "speaking of a direct union between Christ or his death and believers." Τὸ ὁμοίωμα τοῦ θανάτου αὐτοῦ is a reference to the believer's death insofar as it is a copy, likeness or image of Christ's" (see Morgan, "Romans 6:5a," 300). (Bo Frid argues likewise in "Römer 6:4-5: Εἰς τὸν θάνατον und τῷ ὁμοιώματι

crucified together with [Christ], in order that the body [ruled by] Sin (τὸ σῶμα τῆς ἁμαρτίας)[13] might pass away (καταργεῖν), with the result that we are no longer enslaved to Sin. (7) [I can rightfully say that the crucified self is no longer enslaved to Sin] because the person who has [thus] died has been reckoned righteous (δικαιοῦν); [s/he is] apart from Sin (ἀπὸ τῆς ἁμαρτίας).[14] (8) Now if we have died with Christ, [then] we trust that we will also come to life with him (συζήσομεν αὐτῷ).[15] (9) [We] know that since Christ has been raised from the dead, he dies no more. Death is his lord no longer (θάνατος αὐτοῦ οὐκέτι κυριεύει). (10) [I can rightfully say that Death no longer rules over Christ] because [the death] which [Christ] died he died to Sin (τῇ ἁμαρτίᾳ), once for all time (ἐφάπαξ); but [the life]

τοῦ θανάτου αὐτοῦ als Schlüssel zu Duktus und Gedankengang in Röm 6:1-11," *BZ* 30 [1986]: 188-203. Dunn [*Baptism*, 142] adds: "ὁμοίωμα ... signifies neither complete identity ['that which is'] nor mere similarity ['that which is similar to'] but a very close likeness ['that which is precisely like'].")

Second, σύμφυτος is not part of the σὺν Χριστῷ ("with Christ") terminology so prominent in Rom 6:4-8. The Apostle is not saying that Christians have--together with Christ--been "planted in/united to" a death like his death, but that they have--together with one another--been "planted in/united to" a Christ-like "death" (see pp. 268-76).

Third, ἐσόμεθα is a temporal rather than a logical future. Paul promises that Christians will participate in a resurrection like Christ's resurrection not in the present, but in the eschatological future (see pp. 301-302).

Fourth, Morgan concludes that Rom 6:5 should be "taken to mean: If we have been united to the same form of death which Christ died (i.e. received in ourselves a death to sin like his), we will certainly also be united to the same form of resurrection (i.e. receive in ourselves a resurrection like his)" (p. 301).

[13]Σῶμα (here translated "body") refers not simply to the physical body, but to the human "person" in his/her totality (see chapter 3, note 106). When Paul here speaks of "the body [ruled by] Sin" (τὸ σῶμα τῆς ἁμαρτίας; cf. Rom 7:24, "this body [ruled by] Death [τὸ σῶμα τοῦ θανάτου]"), his focus is probably on individual sinners ("in order that the [individual] body [ruled by] Sin might pass away"), as in v. 12 ("continue not to let Sin reign within [the sphere of] your mortal body, so that [you] obey its evil desires"--i.e., continue not being sinners). However, the Apostle may be focusing on the community of sinful individuals as a whole ("in order that the [whole] Body [ruled by] Sin might pass away")--i.e., "the Body [ruled by] Sin" (τὸ σῶμα τῆς ἁμαρ- τίας) as opposed to "the Body [ruled by] Christ" (τὸ σῶμα Χριστοῦ--see 1 Cor 12:27), humanity as determined by the "first Adam" as opposed to humanity as determined by the "last Adam" (see 1 Cor 15:45 and the discussion of Paul's Adam-Christ typology in chapter 3). This is more a question of focus than of meaning, for Paul would consider Rom 6:6 to be a true statement regardless of whether "body" (σῶμα) is understood individually or collectively.

[14]For a similar construction, see Sir 26:29: ". . . a salesman will not be reckoned righteous [i.e.,] apart from sin (οὐ δικαιωθήσεται ... ἀπὸ ἁμαρτίας)."

[15]Συζήσομεν ("we will come to life with") here represents an instance of the inceptive aoristic future, as discussed by Ernest De Witt Burton in *Syntax of the Moods and Tenses in New Testament Greek*, 2d ed. (Chicago: University Press of Chicago, 1893), 31.

which [Christ] lives he lives to God (τῷ θεῷ). (11) In the same way, reckon yourselves to be dead to Sin (τῇ ἁμαρτίᾳ), but alive to God (τῷ θεῷ) within [the sphere where] Christ Jesus [rules] (ἐν Χριστῷ Ἰησοῦ).

(12) Therefore continue not to let Sin reign within [the sphere of] your mortal body (σῶμα),[16] so that [you] obey its evil desires (ἐπιθυμίαι). (13) And continue not to yield your members (τὰ μέλη) to Sin as instruments [working] unrighteousness. Instead, yield yourselves to God as persons who are alive from the dead, and [yield] your members to God [as] instruments [working] righteousness. (14) [I can urge you to yield yourselves to God rather than to Sin] because Sin will continue not to exercise lordship over you (ἁμαρτία γὰρ ὑμῶν οὐ κυριεύσει).[17] [I can rightfully say that Sin will continue not to exercise lordship over you] because you are not under the Law, but under [God's act of] goodwill.

II. KEY ISSUES IN THE INTERPRETATION OF ROMANS 6:1-14

An accurate interpretation of Rom 6:1-14 requires that we first address three important questions: (1) What is the relationship between "the sphere where Sin rules" and "the sphere where Christ Jesus rules"? (2) What does the Apostle mean by "dying with Christ"? and (3) What is the place of baptism in Pauline theology?

The Sphere of Sin Versus the Sphere of Christ

Paul's conception of sin. We saw in chapters 2 and 3 that Paul holds essentially the same conception of "sin" (ἁμαρτία) as the author of 2 Baruch: "Sin" is the refusal to acknowledge God as God--the refusal of the creature

---

[16]See note 13.

[17]Κυριεύσει ("it will continue to exercise lordship") here represents an instance of the progressive future, as discussed by James A. Brooks and Carlton L. Winbery in *Syntax of New Testament Greek* (New York: University Press of America, 1979), 87-88. The term could also be taken as an imperative future ("Sin must not lord it over you," the reading preferred by Brooks and Winbery [p. 88]), but this might lead the reader to interpret v. 14b to mean that "the Law is sin"--an idea which Paul rejects in Rom 7:7. The Apostle is definitely not predicting that, at some time in the *future*, Sin will cease to exercise lordship over Christians (a predictive future); for, according to vv. 12-13, Sin's reign over believers has *already* ended. Cf. chapter 2 under "'Sinners' and 'saints.'"

to subject him/herself to the Creator as his/her rightful Lord.[18] To be a "sinner" is to be under the lordship of some person or some thing other than God.[19]

The lordship of Sin and the lordship of God. In his letters, Paul often personifies human "sinfulness," or rebellion against God, as a "power" which exercises lordship--i.e., as "Sin."[20] The Apostle describes "sinners" as persons who are "within the sphere where Sin rules" (ἐν ἁμαρτία or τῇ ἁμαρτία, a locative of sphere). In other words, they are persons who serve a lord--any lord --other than the God who has acted in Jesus Christ. In Paul's eyes, every human being is either "within the sphere where God rules" or "within the sphere where Sin (i.e., some lord other than God) rules;" s/he is either under the lordship of the Creator or under the lordship of "Sin."[21] This belief underlies Paul's words in Rom 6:1-14.

The reign of God and the reign of Christ. The Apostle here describes those under the lordship of the Creator as persons who "live to God" (v. 10). In other words, they "yield" themselves "to God" and yield their "members to God as instruments working righteousness" (v. 13). Since God has chosen--for "the present time" (ὁ νῦν καιρός)--to exercise His lordship through His Son,[22]

---

[18]See chapter 2 under "Sin as a 'power'" and chapter 3 under "Adam as the first sinner." 2 Baruch's understanding of "sin" is based, of course, on a particular interpretation of Genesis 3.

[19]Compare Rom 1:18-28 with 2 Bar 48:46; 54:14-15 (cf. 17:2, 4; 54:5).

[20]See chapter 2 under "Sin as a 'power.'"

[21]Against the background of Rom 5:12-21 (discussed in chapter 3), we could also state the matter in this way: Every human being either remains within the human sphere as it has been determined by Adam (i.e., the sphere of Sin and Death) or embraces the new possibilities for humanity effected through the death of Christ (i.e., "new covenant" righteousness in the present and "eschatological life" in the future).

[22]See, e.g., 1 Cor 15:24-28; Phil 2:9-11 (discussed in chapter 5).

the Apostle views being "within the sphere where God rules" as equivalent to being "within [the sphere where] Christ Jesus [rules]" (ἐν Χριστῷ Ἰησοῦ, v. 11).

The reign of Sin and the reign of Death. Paul characterizes those under the lordship of Sin as persons who live "to Sin."[23] In other words, they "yield" their "members to Sin as instruments working unrighteousness" (v. 13). They exist "within [the sphere where] Sin [rules]" (vv. 1-2), so that they are "[ruled by] Sin" and "enslaved to Sin" (v. 6). Sin "exercises lordship over" them (v. 14); it "reigns within the sphere of their mortal body," so that they "obey its evil desires" (v. 12). Since "the wages [paid by] Sin [is] death,"[24] Paul quite naturally considers those under the lordship of Sin to be also enslaved under the lordship of "Death" (personified as a "power" in v. 9).

Transfer from lordship to lordship. Paul's argument in Rom 6:1-14 ("continue not to let Sin reign") rests on the assumption that Christians have been transferred from the sphere ruled by Sin and Death to the sphere ruled by God through Christ. This transfer from lordship to lordship involves the believer's "death with Christ."[25]

"Dying With Christ"

Christ's death. Paul speaks of Christ's own death in Rom 6:9-10:

> (9) [We] know that since Christ has been raised from the dead, he dies no more. Death is his lord no longer. (10) [I can rightfully say that Death no longer rules over Christ] because [the death] which [Christ] died he died to Sin (τῇ ἁμαρτίᾳ), once for all time; but [the life] which [Christ] lives he lives to God (τῷ θεῷ).

Verse 9 recalls the historical events of Christ's death and resurrection. Personifying death as a "power," Paul characterizes Christ's execution as

---

[23] I.e., they have not "died to Sin" (see vv. 2, 10, 11).

[24] See Rom 6:23, along with the portion of chapter 3 marked "Adam as the cause of universal death."

[25] See, e.g., vv. 6-7.

slavery under the lordship of Death. Accordingly, Christ's emergence from the tomb to the immortality ("he dies no more") of "eschatological life" constitutes release from that lordship, so that "Death is his lord no longer."

Verse 10 maintains that Christ, in his death, "died to Sin" (ἀποθνῄσκειν τῇ ἁμαρτίᾳ). What does the Apostle mean? If living "to Sin" (v. 6) involves submitting oneself to a lord other than God (see above), then "dying to Sin" must certainly involve forsaking all false lords in order to entrust oneself fully to the true Creator and Lord of all.[26] When Paul says that "the death which Christ died he died to Sin," he is simply expressing his "core conviction" that Christ's death on the cross was an act of "trust" (πίστις) in God, or an act of total self-surrender to God as Lord (see part III of chapter 4). When he says that "the life which Christ lives he lives to God," the Apostle is affirming that the risen Christ continues to submit himself to God as ultimate Lord.[27] In both his past death on the cross and his present "life" as the risen Lord, Jesus has fully entrusted himself to God. To display such trust (πίστις) is what Paul means by "dying to Sin."[28]

---

[26]In chapter 7, we will demonstrate that this is indeed what Paul means by "dying with Christ."

[27]Note that, for Paul, "dying to Sin" is equivalent to "living to God." The contrast in Rom 6:10 (marked by δέ, "but") is not between "dying to Sin" and "living to God," but between "dying" and "living." On the risen Christ's eternal subjection to God, see 1 Cor 15:24-28.

[28]This idea appears in 2 Cor 5:21, where Paul affirms that Christ "never knew sin." Yet how can Paul speak of Christ's "death to Sin"/sinlessness while, at the same time, speaking of Christ's death? If Paul considers death to be the "wages paid by Sin" (see above), then how could Christ die if he "never knew sin"?

The answer lies with Paul's understanding of Adam as the first sinner and the cause of universal death (discussed in chapter 3). Like the authors of 4 Ezra and 2 Baruch, Paul views death as the penalty ordained by God for sin (a belief grounded in Gen 2:17). Adam committed the first sin and thereby brought the penalty of death upon himself and all his descendants (see, e.g., Rom 5:12 ["Sin came into the world through one man, Adam, and death came into the world through Adam's sin"], 15 ["many died because of the one man Adam's trespass"], 17 ["because of the trespass of the one man, Adam, death reigned through that one man"]). At the same time, Adam's descendants have sinned (see, e.g., Rom 3:23: "All have sinned"), thereby "earning" death for themselves (see, e.g., Rom 6:23 ["the wages paid by Sin is death"], and Rom 5:12 ["death spread to all persons because all sinned"]). (note continued on next page)

222

The conjunction γάρ ("because") indicates that v. 10 provides the basis for Paul's statement in v. 9. The logical structure of the Apostle's argument may therefore be represented as follows:

God raised Christ from the dead, so that he now enjoys freedom from the lordship of Death (v. 9)

because (γάρ)

Christ "died to Sin" in the past, so that (having been raised from the dead) he continues to "live to God" in the present (v. 10).

Paul here draws a causal connection between Christ's "death to Sin" (= his trust in God displayed on the cross) and Christ's release from the lordship of Death (= God's raising him from the dead). He thus gives expression to his "core conviction" that the Jesus whom God has raised from the dead and exalted to the highest place is the same humble, trusting (πίστις) Jesus, who was "obedient to the point of death--even the death which is the cross"[29] (see chapter 5 under "The 'last Adam'").

To summarize: Paul, in Rom 6:9-10, describes Jesus' death on the cross as a "death to Sin," or an act of trust in God (= "core conviction" 3 in the thesis statement given in chapter 1). Furthermore, he draws a causal connection between Christ's trust/death to Sin and God's decision to raise him from the dead/release him from the lordship of Death (= "core conviction" 7 in our

---

Against this background, Paul's interpretation of death becomes quite clear (for a more complete explanation, see chapter 3 under "Adam as the cause of universal death" [in 4 Ezra], "Adam as the cause of universal death" [in Paul], and "Adam and individual responsibility for sin"): Those descendants of Adam who "remain within the sphere where Sin rules" (see Rom 6:1) die (i.e., Death rules over them) because of both Adam's sin and their own sin (i.e., because of their slavery under Sin, which brings death). Those descendants of Adam who are freed from Sin through the Cross of Christ still die (i.e., Death rules over them); but their death is due to their ancestor's sin, rather than to their own sin. (They themselves have been "reckoned righteous, apart from Sin;" "Sin will continue not to exercise lordship over" them [see Rom 6:7, 14, discussed below].) Likewise, Jesus Christ--that one descendant of Adam who "never knew sin"--died on the cross ("Death is his lord," Rom 6:9) not because of his own sin, but because of the sin of Adam. (Presumably, Paul would explain the deaths of innocent babies along the same lines.)

[29]See Phil 2:8.

thesis statement). Against this background, we now turn to the question of the Christian's "death with Christ."

The Christian's "death with Christ." Throughout Rom 6:1-14, Paul employs a number of different images in order to express the idea that Christians have somehow "died with Christ" (v. 8). He says that believers have been "crucified together with [Christ]" (v. 6), "buried together with him . . . into 'death'" (v. 4), and "planted together [with one another] in [a 'death'] like his death" (v. 5).[30]

How should we interpret these metaphors? What idea does Paul intend for them to convey? Verse 5 provides an important clue: For Paul, "dying with Christ" does not mean participating in Christ's own death, but participating in "[a 'death'] like his death" (τὸ ὁμοίωμα τοῦ θανάτου αὐτοῦ).[31] If the Apostle views Christ's own death as "death to Sin," or an expression of trust (πίστις) in God (see above), then it would be quite logical to suppose that "dying with Christ" (ἀποθνήσκειν σὺν Χριστῷ) refers to a similar "death to Sin"--or attitude of trust (πίστις)--on the part of the Christian. A careful reading of Rom 6:1-14 confirms that this is indeed what Paul has in mind.

According to v. 6, "dying with Christ" (or being "crucified together with [Christ]") involves release from slavery to Sin ("we are no longer enslaved to Sin"), or the "passing away" (καταργεῖν) of "the body ruled by Sin" (τὸ σῶμα τῆς ἁμαρτίας).[32] Verses 2 and 11 identify those who have "died with Christ"

---

[30]John D. Harvey investigates "The 'With Christ' Motif in Paul's Thought" in *JETS* 35 (1992): 329-40.

[31]See note 12.

[32]Scholarly analysis of Rom 6:7 has yielded a harvest of confusion. Robin Scroggs ("Romans 6:7: ὁ γὰρ ἀποθανὼν δεδικαίωται ἀπὸ τῆς ἁμαρτίας, *NTS* 10 [1963]: 104-108) represents one group of scholars who argue that ὁ ἀποθανών ("the person who has died") refers primarily to Jesus, and only secondarily to Christian believers. He writes:

[Jesus'] death, because it is a martyr's death, has atoning significance [since 'rabbinic theology postulated atoning significance to the death of the righteous,' p. 106]. It is a death that can justify one from sin. The believer, by participating through baptism in his death,

(i.e., Christians) as persons who are "dead to Sin, but alive to God;" they exist "within the sphere where Christ Jesus rules" (ἐν Χριστῷ Ἰησοῦ), rather than "within the sphere where Sin" rules (ἐν αὐτῇ). Verses 12-13 likewise describe those who have "died with Christ" as persons who do not "let Sin reign," but who instead "yield" themselves "to God." In short, "dying with Christ" means "dying to Sin" just as Christ himself "died to Sin." "Dying with Christ" means forsaking the lordship of Sin and embracing the lordship of God, just as Christ himself embraced the lordship of God when he accepted death on the cross.

How does a person "die to Sin" or embrace the lordship of God? If Christ "died to Sin" by entrusting himself to God (see above), then it would be reasonable to assume that Christians "die to Sin" by making a similar commitment of trust (πίστις). That this was Paul's own view is shown by Rom 6:7: "The person who has [thus] died has been reckoned righteous (δικαιοῦν); [s/he is] apart from Sin (ἀπὸ τῆς ἁμαρτίας)."[31] Paul here identifies the "righteous" as persons who have "died with Christ."[33] Elsewhere in his letters, he repeatedly insists that the only persons "reckoned righteous" by God under the "new covenant" are those who put their "trust" in Him. "Trust" (πίστις) and

---

appropriates for himself the atonement achieved by the death of the Martyr . . . the death of the Righteous One (p. 107).

Conleth Kearns reaches a similar conclusion in "The Interpretation of Romans 6:7," *AnBib* 17 [1961]: 301-307.

James D. G. Dunn (*Romans*, 1:320-21) represents another large group of scholars who interpret δεδικαίωται ἀπὸ τῆς ἁμαρτίας ("s/he has been reckoned righteous, apart from Sin") to mean "s/he is declared free from sin." They understand the verse as a whole to be echoing a Jewish "proverbial principle like 'death pays all debts.'"

Scroggs' interpretation of Rom 6:7 must be rejected on the grounds that believers participate not in Christ's own death, but in "the likeness of his death," or "[a 'death'] like his death" (v. 5). Dunn's reading of the verse must be rejected on the grounds that Paul consistently uses δικαιοῦν as a covenantal term (see chapter 2) meaning "to reckon righteous," rather than as a legal term meaning "to declare free." Furthermore, the Apostle views death not as a release from Sin, but as the very mark of Sin's reign (see above under "The reign of Sin and the reign of Death"). Below, we will offer an interpretation of Rom 6:7 that is both attractive in its simplicity and consistent with Paul's theology.

[33]See also vv. 12-13, where Paul describes those who have "died with Christ" (i.e., those over whom Sin has ceased to reign) as persons who yield their "members to God as instruments working righteousness."

"dying with Christ" (ἀποθνῄσκειν σὺν Χριστῷ) are two different terms by which the Apostle expresses a single idea--namely, trustful commitment to God as Lord! The former calls to mind the attitude of "trust" itself, while the latter stresses the fact that "Christian trust" is "Christ-like trust"--the kind of "trust" Jesus himself displayed in going to his death on the cross. (The reader is reminded that Christians are able to "trust," able to embrace "new covenant" righteousness, able to escape the power of Sin, only because Christ first died on the cross to make such trust, such righteousness, such an escape possible.[34])

We may sum up the results of our inquiry as follows: In Rom 6:9-10, Paul interprets Christ's death on the cross as a "death to Sin," or an expression of trust in God. A careful reading of the remainder of Rom 6:1-14 suggests that, when the Apostle reminds his readers that they have "died with Christ," he is speaking of their own "death to Sin," or their own Christ-like trust in God. Further evidence in support of this thesis will be provided in chapter 7. For now, we will proceed on the assumption that Paul does indeed understand the Christian's "death with Christ" to be his/her trustful commitment to God as Lord.

The Place of Baptism in Paul's Theology

A third issue of crucial importance for the interpretation of Rom 6:1-14 concerns the place of baptism in Paul's theology.[35] The Apostle mentions baptism only in a few passages, and only in the service of addressing other concerns.[36] We therefore possess very little evidence upon which to base a

---

[34]See chapter 4.

[35]Scholarship on this subject includes the studies in the bibliography by Beasley-Murray, Carlson, Frankemölle, Légasse, Schnackenburg, Schweizer and Tannehill.

[36]I.e., (1) the relationship between sin and God's act of goodwill in Rom 6:3-4, (2) schisms within the Body of Christ in 1 Cor 1:13-17, (3) the dangers of doing evil in 1 Cor 10:2, (4) the interdependence of believers in 1 Cor 12:13, (5) the Resurrection of the dead in 1 Cor 15:29, and (6) the Christian's freedom from the Law in Gal 3:27.

judgment concerning Paul's views. This problem has been compounded by the tendency to read Paul's words through the lens of 2000 years of sacramental theology--including the theologies of New Testament writers dating to the post-Pauline period. We will briefly review the Apostle's own statements concerning baptism in an attempt to distinguish Paul's voice from those of his interpreters.

Baptism in Galatians 3:23-29. In Gal 3:23-29, Paul argues that the blessing of "righteousness" promised to Abraham and his offspring comes through the "new covenant" based on trust, rather than through the "old covenant" based on the Law. The Apostle writes:

(23) Before [the "new covenant" based on] trust (πίστις) came, we were confined under the Law, imprisoned until the coming trust was revealed. (24) So the Law was our pedagogue until [the time when] Christ [came] for the purpose of our being reckoned righteous on the basis of trust (εἰς Χριστὸν ἵνα ἐκ πίστεως δικαιωθῶμεν).[37] (25) Now that trust has come, we are no longer under a pedagogue. (26) [I can rightfully say that we are no longer under the pedagogue of the Law] because [now] you are all the sons of God by means of trust in Christ Jesus. (27) [I can rightfully say that you are all the sons of God by means of trust in Christ Jesus] because as many of you as have been baptized into Christ (εἰς Χριστόν) have put on Christ (Χριστὸν ἐνδύειν). (28) There is neither Jew nor Greek; there is neither slave nor free; there is neither male nor female. [I can rightfully say that there is neither Jew nor Greek, slave nor free, male nor female] because you are all one within [the sphere where] Christ Jesus [rules] (ἐν Χριστῷ Ἰησοῦ). (29) If you [are] Christ's (Χριστοῦ) [(and you are)], then you are Abraham's seed--heirs in accordance with the promise.

According to v. 27, the Galatians were baptized "into Christ" (εἰς Χριστόν). What does this mean? G. M. M. Pelser (discussing Rom 6:3) offers a convenient summary of the two leading interpretations of this formula:

The one is that the formula *eis Christon* should be interpreted in a local sense (i.e. the believer is baptized "into Christ"). Christ in this context is understood as corporate personality in whom all the believers are

---

[37]The conjunction ἵνα ("for the purpose of") introduces the purpose of Christ's coming, rather than the purpose of the Law's pedagogical activity.

included. The other approach is to take the formula as an abbreviated form of the longer baptismal formula *eis to onoma tou Christou* ["into the name of Christ"], which in turn is interpreted as a formula for transfer of ownership, or as an indication of the constitutive factor for the nature of the baptismal act, or an indication of the goal of this act.[38]

Pelser observes that the first interpretation operates on the "mystical" level, the second on the "juristical."

Paul's words in Gal 3:23-29 suggest that each of these interpretations of εἰς Χριστόν ("into Christ") is partly correct and partly incorrect. Observe how the Apostle describes those who have been "baptized into Christ" (εἰς Χριστὸν βαπτίζειν): They are persons "within the sphere where Christ Jesus rules" (ἐν Χριστῷ Ἰησοῦ, v. 28). They belong to Christ (i.e., they are "Christ's," Χριστοῦ, v. 29). They participate in the "new covenant" based on "trust" (πίστις, vv. 23-26), which means that they have "entrusted" themselves to Christ as Lord. Furthermore, Paul says that being "baptized into Christ" involves one's "putting on Christ" (Χριστὸν ἐνδύειν, v. 27). The Apostle employs this same image in Rom 13:14 to express the idea of "putting off the works of darkness" and adopting behavior appropriate to those who serve Christ.

Every verse in this pericope leads to one conclusion: Those who have been baptized "into Christ" have entered into the sphere where Christ rules. Paul uses the εἰς Χριστόν ("into Christ") formula in order to characterize baptism as an entrance into the sphere of Christ's rule. The "mystical" approach correctly interprets εἰς Χριστόν ("into Christ") in the local sense; but Paul "locates" baptized believers within the sphere of Christ's rule, rather than within Christ himself as some sort of "corporate personality." The "juristical" approach rightly understands baptism "into Christ" as involving a "transfer of ownership" or lordship, but it is not necessary to read εἰς Χριστόν ("into Christ") as an abbreviated form of the longer baptismal formula εἰς τὸ ὄνομα τοῦ Χριστοῦ ("into the name of Christ").

---

[38]Pelser, "The Objective Reality," 105.

Baptism in 1 Corinthians 1:12-17. Alongside Gal 3:23-29, there are three passages in 1 Corinthians which shed light on Paul's understanding of the baptismal rite.[39] The first appears early in the letter, where Paul urges the Corinthians to put an end to factionalism within the church. He writes:

> (12) Each of you is saying "I belong to Paul," or "I belong to Apollos," or "I belong to Cephas," or "I belong to Christ" (Χριστοῦ). (13) Has Christ been divided? Paul was not crucified for you, was he? Or were you baptized into the name of Paul (εἰς τὸ ὄνομα Παύλου)? (14) I thank God that I baptized none of you except Crispus and Gaius, (15) so that no one may say that you were baptized into my name (εἰς τὸ ἐμὸν ὄνομα). (16) (I also baptized the household of Stephanus. Beyond that I do not know whether I baptized anyone else.) (17) [I am thankful that no one can say that you were baptized into my name] because Christ did not send me in order to baptize, but in order to preach the gospel[40]--[and to preach it] not in wisdom of word, in order that the Cross of Christ may never be nullified. (1 Cor 1:12-17)

Paul rebukes certain of the Corinthian Christians for acting as if they were baptized "into the name of Paul" (εἰς τὸ ὄνομα Παύλου) (vv. 13, 15), rather than "into the name of Christ." We have already seen that the εἰς τὸ ὄνομα Χριστοῦ ("into the name of Christ") formula interprets baptism in terms of transfer into Christ's ownership. This is confirmed by v. 12; for if baptism "into the name of Paul" identifies the baptized as one who "belongs to Paul," then baptism "into the name of Christ" identifies that person as one who "belongs to Christ." Paul's words in 1 Cor 1:12-17 therefore reflect the same basic understanding of baptism found in Gal 3:23-29: Baptism is an entrance "into" the sphere of Christ's rule or the sphere of Christ's ownership.

Baptism in 1 Corinthians 10:1-13. A second passage relevant to our discussion is 1 Cor 10:1-13. Here the Apostle recalls how the ancient Israelites

---

[39]We will pass over the obscure reference to "baptism for the dead" in 1 Cor 15:29.

[40]On the interpretation of this statement, see Mauro Pesce, "'Christ did not send me to baptize, but to evangelize' (1 Cor 1:17a)," in *Paul de Tarse: Apôtre du Notre Temps,* ed. Lorenzo De Lorenzi (Rome: Abbaye de S. Paul h.l.m., 1979), 339-62.

were "baptized into Moses (εἰς τὸν Μωυσῆν) in the cloud and in the sea" (v. 2), only to be "overthrown in the wilderness" (v. 5) because of their idolatry and immorality. Paul's purpose is to warn the Corinthian believers that their own baptism "into Christ" will not save them from destruction if they follow Israel's example of wickedness.

In what sense were the Israelites "baptized into Moses" (εἰς τὸν Μωυσῆν)? Paul probably refers to their entrance into the "old covenant" God established through Moses. If so, this serves as a further indication (along with Gal 3:23-29) that Paul views baptism "into Christ" as entrance into the "new covenant" established through Christ. Since this "new covenant" is based on trust in Christ as Lord, baptism "into Christ" involves one's entrance into the sphere of Christ's kingly rule.[41] Such submission to Christ would, of course, rule out the kind of rebellion against God displayed by Israel in the wilderness.

Baptism in 1 Corinthians 12:13. Finally, in 1 Cor 12:13, Paul states that "we have all been baptized into one Body (εἰς ἓν σῶμα), whether [we are] Jews or Greeks, slaves or free." The Apostle here describes baptism as entrance into the Church, the "Body of Christ" (see vv. 27-28), the company of those who trust in him and submit to his rule.

Baptism as initiation rite. In the four texts discussed above, Paul says very little about Christian baptism. Nevertheless, a definite pattern seems to emerge: The Apostle consistently portrays baptism as an initiation rite--as an entrance into the sphere of Christ's rule ([Gal 3] = the sphere of Christ's ownership [1 Cor 1] = the sphere of trust in God [Gal 3] = the company of those who trust in God [1 Cor 12] = the "new covenant" based on trust in

---

[41]In an article entitled "Baptised into Moses--Baptised into Christ: A Study in Doctrinal Development" (*EvQ* 88 [1988]: 23-29), William B. Badke agrees: "In 1 Corinthians 10:1ff., allegiance is the only link between Moses and baptism that makes sense in Paul's use of baptismal terminology" (p. 28).

God [Gal 3, 1 Cor 10]). Against this background, we now turn to the discussion of baptism found in Rom 6:3-4.

Baptism in Romans 6:3-4. In these verses, Paul describes Christians as persons who have been (1) "baptized into Christ Jesus" (εἰς Χριστὸν Ἰησοῦν), (2) "baptized into his death" (εἰς τὸν θάνατον αὐτοῦ), and (3) "buried together with him, by means of baptism, into 'death'" (συνθάπτειν αὐτῷ διὰ τοῦ βαπτίσματος εἰς τὸν θάνατον). How should we interpret the first formula? We have already seen that Paul employs the phrase "baptism into Christ" in order to characterize baptism as an entrance into the sphere of Christ's lordship or rule.[42]

How should we interpret the third formula? We have already identified "burial together with Christ into 'death'" as one of the many metaphors by which Paul expresses the idea of "dying with Christ," "dying to Sin," entrusting oneself to God/Christ as Lord, or entering into the sphere of God's/ Christ's rule.[43] The third formula describes baptism as the means--the "initiation rite"--by which persons enter into "death with Christ," or the sphere of his rule.

Both the first and the third baptismal formulae in Rom 6:3-4 clearly express an understanding of baptism identical to that found in Paul's letters to the Galatians and the Corinthians. Both portray baptism as an initiation rite through which persons enter into the sphere of Christ's rule. How should we interpret the second formula? What does Paul mean by "baptism into Christ's death"?

Many scholars understand the Apostle to be saying that baptized persons participate in Christ's own death on the cross; they enjoy sacramental

---

[42]See above under "Baptism in Galatians 3:23-29."

[43]See above under "The Christian's 'death with Christ.'"

union with Christ and thus "die" Christ's death. We find a typical expression of this view in Rudolf Schnackenburg's *Baptism in the Thought of St. Paul*:[44]

> In baptism the believer in Christ is drawn into the Christ event; he accompanies his Lord through death to resurrection . . . It is not simply a question of remembrance and becoming like Him, but rather a participation in Christ's cross and resurrection, so that everything that Christ went through for our salvation also happens to the baptized, and he thus obtains the fruit of Christ's dying. These statements . . . are founded on a Semitic idea, according to which the founder of a people is inseparably bound up with those who are joined to him; he represents and takes the place of his followers, and these again share his destiny. Baptism is the place where the union of believers with Christ, the founder of a new humanity, is established, and therefore they die "with him" and live "with Him." The entire process takes place in them sacramentally by grace. (pp. 205-206)[45]

---

[44]Rudolf Schnackenburg, *Baptism in the Thought of St. Paul: A Study in Pauline Theology*, trans. G. R. Beasley-Murray (New York: Herder and Herder, 1964).

[45]The history of religions school popularized the similar notion that Paul's idea of baptismal union with Christ was derived from the mystery cults of his day. According to this view, the deities of the mystery religions suffered, died, and were then raised to new life. By participating in a cultic drama portraying the deity's fate, worshippers were incorporated into the destiny of the deity so that they, too, passed through suffering and death into life. Eduard Lohse (among others) argues that this

> was also the interpretation given to the Christian baptism. Anyone who is baptized into Christ is incorporated into his death and resurrection, so that the powers of immortality flow through him. (*The New Testament Environment*, trans. John E. Steely [Nashville: Abingdon, 1976], 242)

Other scholars have severely criticized this view, arguing that the mystery model presumably behind the Pauline doctrine of baptism appears in no known cult. See, for example, the work of Günter Wagner (*Das religionsgeschichtliche Problem von Römer 6:1-11* [Zürich: Zwingli Verlag, 1962]) and A. J. M. Wedderburn (*Baptism and Resurrection: Studies in Pauline Theology against Its Graeco-Roman Background* [Tübingen: J. C. B. Mohr, 1987], and "The Soteriology of the Mysteries and Pauline Baptismal Theology," *NovT* 29 [1987]: 53-72). After examining the cults of Isis and Osiris, Cybele and Attis, the Eleusinian mysteries and the Dionysiac rites, Wedderburn concludes that

> Even if many (but not all) of the mysteries did worship a hero or deity who was thought to have died and to have come to life again in some form or other, we have found no evidence that the initiates in any of their rites believed that in their initiations they were experiencing in themselves the death and resurrection of their deity, let alone that this idea was common to all or many of them. (*Baptism and Resurrection*, 394)

See also the article by Morton Smith ("Pauline Worship as Seen By Pagans," *HTR* 73 [1980]: 241-49), in which he argues that Paul's contemporaries would have interpreted various aspects of Christian worship (baptism, the Lord's Supper, spirits, tongues) as "magical rites."

This interpretation of "baptism into Christ's death" must be rejected for two primary reasons: First, it is grounded in an understanding of the *modus operandi* of the atonement different from that held by Paul. Schnackenburg assumes that a person must somehow participate in "everything that Christ went through for our salvation" before s/he can "obtain the fruit of Christ's dying" (see above). In order to make this possible, Christ died "vicariously" as our "substitute" or "representative."[46] By becoming one with Christ through baptism, believers are able to participate not only in his death, but in his resurrection (his "destiny") as well.

Such "substitutionary" theories of the atonement command widespread support, but not from the Apostle Paul. We saw in chapter 4 that Paul interprets Christ's cross as the sacrifice for sins by which God, in His right-eousness, established the "new covenant" promised to Abraham. Persons participate in this "new covenant" ("the fruit of Christ's dying") not through sharing in Christ's own death, but through Christ-like trust in God (i.e., through "dying with Christ"). In Paul's way of thinking, there is no need for persons to share in "everything that Christ went through for our salvation." We are urged not to die "in" Christ, but to "die" along with Christ.

Our second objection to Schnackenburg's interpretation of "baptism into Christ's death" is closely related to the first. According to Dr. Schnackenburg, Christ functions as the "second Adam" in the sense that he is "inseparably bound up with those who are joined to him; he represents and takes the place of his followers, and these again share his destiny" (see above).

---

[46]Professor Schnackenburg writes:

Christ is the one great Representative of mankind; God reckons his death as an atonement for the sins of all and so effects the "reconciliation" of all with Himself . . . Christ (as cor-porate personality) includes, represents and takes the place of us all . . . We do not die "mystically" on the cross of Christ on Golgotha; rather the death of the one in God's eyes passes for the death of all . . . this is not simply a juristic fiction or arrangement, as if God simply reckoned the death of Christ to our account; rather Christ's death really becomes our death, so soon as we die "with Him" in baptism. (*Baptism,* p. 120)

We saw in chapter 3 that Paul's Adam-Christ typology does not portray Christ as this sort of "corporate personality." Instead, Christ became "the founder of a new humanity" by establishing a new human reality (namely, righteousness under the "new covenant" in the present, which holds the promise of "eschatological life" in the future) through his sacrificial death on the cross. Human beings participate in this new reality not through sacramental union with Christ, but through trust in him as Lord.

If Christians do not participate in Christ's own death, then in what sense have they been "baptized into his death"? For the answer to this question, we must examine Paul's words within their context.

In Rom 6:2, the Apostle lays down the following thesis: Persons who have "died to Sin" must not continue to "live within the sphere where it rules." In other words, persons who have entrusted themselves to God as Lord must not live as if He were not their Lord.[47]

Paul introduces his next statement with the phrase ἤ ἀγνοεῖτε ὅτι ("Or do you not realize that . . . ?"), which indicates that vv. 3 and 4 are intended to lend support to the thesis set down in v. 2. The content of that supporting statement reads as follows:

> (3) As many of us as have been baptized into Christ Jesus have been baptized into his death. (4) We, then, have been buried together with him, by means of baptism, into "death," in order that, just as Christ has been raised from the dead by the Glory who is the Father, so might we also live a new life.

Paul here speaks of (1) "baptism into Christ Jesus," (2) "baptism into his death," and (3) "burial together with him, by means of baptism, into 'death.'" Both the first and the third formulae characterize baptism as an entrance into the sphere of Christ's rule (see above). Can we assign to the second formula ("baptized into his death") an interpretation that (1) does

---

[47]See above under "The Sphere of Sin Versus the Sphere of Christ" and "Dying With Christ."

justice to Paul's language, (2) accords with what we know of his theology, and
(3) suits the context, inasmuch as it supports Paul's thesis statement in verse
2? Indeed we can.

It seems quite likely, in this context, that Paul employs the formula
"baptism into Christ's death" in order to describe baptism as an entrance into
the sphere "ruled," or determined, by Christ's sacrificial death on the cross.[48]
In other words, this formula sets forth baptism as an initiation into the new
reality established by Christ's death--the new reality which has taken the form
of a "new covenant" based on trust (πίστις) in God/Christ as Lord. If this is
the case, then Paul's argument in Rom 6:2-4 is structured as follows:

Thesis (v. 2): Persons who have entrusted themselves to God as Lord
must not live as if He were not their Lord.

("We who have died to Sin" cannot "live within the sphere
where it rules.")

Proof (v. 3): Our baptism signifies that we have entered into the sphere
ruled by "Christ Jesus,"

("baptized into Christ Jesus")

which means that

our baptism signifies that we have entered into the "new
covenant" based on trust in God/Christ as Lord, established
through "his death."

("baptized into his death")

(v. 4): [The fact that our baptism signifies that we have entered
into the "new covenant" established through Christ's death
(= trust in God/Christ as Lord) means], then,

("then," οὖν)

that our baptism signifies that we have "died with Christ," or
entrusted ourselves to God as Lord,

("buried together with him, by means of baptism, into
'death'")

---

[48]On Christ's death as "sacrifice," see part I of chapter 4.

toward the end that we might one day be raised from the dead as Christ was raised from the dead.

("in order that" [ἵνα] . . .")[49]

The force of the argument is clear: Paul finds it inconceivable that Christians should live as if God were not their Lord (v. 2) in view of the fact that their baptism signifies (1) submission to God's rule in Christ (v. 3a), (2) participation in the "new covenant" established through Christ's death, which is based on trustful submission to God as Lord (v. 3b), and (3) Christ-like trust in God as Lord (v. 4).

This interpretation of Rom 6:3 satisfies all three criteria laid down above: First, it accords with the language and structure of the verse, which seem to equate "baptism into Christ Jesus" with "baptism into his death," thus making the two inseparable from one another. Second, it is consistent with Paul's theology--particularly (1) his understanding of baptism as an entrance into the "new covenant" or the sphere of God's rule in Christ, (2) his "core conviction" that Christ's death was an expression of trust in God,[50] and (3) his "core convictions" concerning the Christian's "death with Christ" as his/her participation in the "new covenant" through trust in God (discussed in the next chapter). Finally, the proposed interpretation of Rom 6:3 is appropriate to this context in that it enables verse 3--in conjunction with verse 4--to support the thesis Paul presents in verse 2.

Paul's understanding of baptism. To summarize: Paul provides us with very little information concerning his views on Christian baptism. However, all the evidence we possess (including Rom 6:3-4) points in one direction: The Apostle looks upon baptism as an "initiation rite"--a means of entrance into

---

[49]Behind v. 4b lies the Pauline conviction that those who are reckoned righteous under the "new covenant" through trust in God/"dying with Christ" will participate in the promised Resurrection of the righteous. See note 59.

[50]On Christ's sacrificial death as his act of trust in God, see part III of chapter 4.

the "new covenant" based on trust, or the sphere of God's rule in Christ, or "the Body of Christ" (τὸ σῶμα Χριστοῦ, "the Body [ruled by] Christ"[51]).

The relationship between baptism and trust. Yet this raises an important question: Throughout his letters, Paul repeatedly insists that persons enter the "new covenant," or the sphere of God's rule, only through trust (πίστις) in Him. What, then, are we to make of the handful of Pauline texts which identify not trust, but baptism, as the means of entering that covenant or rule? In other words, what is the relationship between baptism and trust in Paul's thought?

The most probable answer is that baptism, for Paul, does not have an independent significance apart from trust. Baptism, for Paul, is the initial, outward manifestation of that Christ-like trust--that "death" with Christ--which God reckons "righteousness" under the "new covenant." Paul does not view baptism as a "sacrament" in the traditional sense of the word: God has chosen to exercise His "life"-giving power not within the context of the baptismal act itself, but within the context of the attitude of trustful, Christ-like submission to God which baptism signifies and celebrates. Paul views baptism as an "initiation rite" marking one's entrance into trustful commitment to God. When he speaks of "the baptized," he speaks of Christians--the community of trust.

III. INTERPRETATION OF ROMANS 6:1-14

Our examination of key issues in the interpretation of Rom 6:1-14 has yielded the following results: First, when Paul speaks of "the sphere of Sin and Death" versus "the sphere of God in Christ," he is contrasting persons under God's lordship with persons under some lordship other than God's (the lordship of "Sin"). Second, Paul employs the metaphor "dying with Christ" in

---

[51]See note 13.

order to refer to the kind of trust (πίστις) in God as Lord which Christ displayed in his death on the cross. Those who display such trustful submission to God have entered into (1) the sphere of God's lordship, and (2) the "new covenant" based on trust. Finally, Paul views baptism as an "initiation rite," a public confession of the kind of trust in God through which persons enter into His lordship and His "new covenant." We will now apply these insights to the interpretation of Rom 6:1-14.

God's Goodwill and Sin (vv. 1-2)

(1) What shall we say then? Shall we remain within [the sphere where] Sin [rules] in order that [God's] goodwill may increase? (2) Certainly not! How can we who have died to Sin still live within [the sphere where] it [rules]?

Verse 1. The subject of Rom 6:1-14 is the relationship between sin and God's concrete expression of His goodwill (χάρις) in the Cross of Jesus Christ. Paul begins with a rhetorical question that sets forth a possible misunderstanding of what he said in Rom 5:15-21. This question may be paraphrased as follows: "If God's goodwill increases to include those outside His lordship, then should we not remain outside His lordship to allow His goodwill to increase?"

Verse 2. In v. 2, the Apostle soundly rejects this proposition ("Certainly not!") on the grounds that the whole purpose of God's act of goodwill was to bring sinners under His lordship. God sent Christ to die a sacrificial death on the cross in order to establish a "new covenant" based on trust in God as Lord.[52] Paul reminds his Christian readers that they themselves have responded to this expression of divine goodwill by "dying to Sin." In other words, they have been removed from the lordship of Sin and transferred to the lordship of God through trustful commitment to God as Lord. If the

---

[52]See part I of chapter 4.

Roman believers have entrusted themselves to God as Lord, then Paul finds it inconceivable that they should behave as if He were not their Lord.

Appeal to Baptism (vv. 3-5)

> (3) Or do you not realize that as many of us as have been baptized into Christ Jesus have been baptized into his death? (4) We, then, have been buried together with him, by means of baptism, into "death," in order that, just as Christ has been raised from the dead by the Glory who is the Father, so might we also live a new life. (5) [I can rightfully say that, having been baptized into Christ's death, we will also rise to live a new life] because if we have been planted together [with one another] in [a "death"] like his death, [then] we will certainly also [participate in a resurrection like his] resurrection.

Verses 3-4a. In order to prove that his readers have made such a commitment of trust, Paul appeals to their baptism in vv. 3-5. He reminds the Roman believers ("do you not realize?") that baptism signifies both (1) entrance into the rule of God in Christ ("baptism into Christ Jesus") and (2) entrance into the "new covenant," based on trustful surrender to God's lordship, which was established through Christ's sacrificial death ("baptism into his death"). The fact that Christians have been baptized signifies, then, that they have "died with Christ" ("buried together with him, by means of baptism, into 'death,'" or "planted together with one another in a 'death' like his death"); they have entrusted themselves to God as Lord, just as Jesus did when he went to the cross in humble obedience to God's will (vv. 4-5).[53] Christians cannot "remain within the sphere where Sin rules" (v. 1), for they behave consistently with their baptism/trust only insofar as they forsake the rule of Sin and embrace the Rule of God.

Verses 4b-5. Paul indicates in vv. 4b-5 that the end result of the Christian's "death with Christ," or trust in God, will be resurrection from the dead and "eschatological life" with Christ. Participation in "life" is conditioned ("if"

---

[53]See, e.g., Phil 2:8.

[εἰ], v. 5; cf. "in order that" [ἵνα], v. 4) upon one's first entering into "death."[54] In vv. 6-11, the Apostle appeals to this basic affirmation of the gospel in order to strengthen his case against Christian indifference toward Sin.

Dying and Rising With Christ (vv. 6-11)

> (6) This we know: Our old self has been crucified together with [Christ], in order that the body [ruled by] Sin might pass away, with the result that we are no longer enslaved to Sin. (7) [I can rightfully say that the crucified self is no longer enslaved to Sin] because the person who has [thus] died has been reckoned righteous; [s/he is] apart from Sin. (8) Now if we have died with Christ, [then] we trust that we will also come to life with him. (9) [We] know that since Christ has been raised from the dead, he dies no more. Death is his lord no longer. (10) [I can rightfully say that Death no longer rules over Christ] because [the death] which [Christ] died he died to Sin, once for all time; but [the life] which [Christ] lives he lives to God. (11) In the same way, reckon yourselves to be dead to Sin, but alive to God within [the sphere where] Christ Jesus [rules].

Verses 6-7. Paul begins, in vv. 6-7, by reminding his readers of their "death with Christ" ("crucified together with [Christ]," "the person who has [thus] died"), or their Christ-like trust in God as Lord. Since trust in God involves the repudiation of all other would-be "lords" (here referred to collectively as "Sin"), the Romans' "death with Christ" marked the "passing away" of their "old self"--"the person ruled by Sin"[55]--and the end of their being "enslaved to Sin." Furthermore, since trust forms the content of righteousness under the "new covenant," the Romans' "death with Christ" marked their entrance into that "new covenant." God no longer reckons them among the "sinners" ("apart from Sin"), but among the "righteous."

Verses 8-11. Next, the Apostle invites his readers to consider the future promised to those who "die with Christ" by participating in the "new covenant" based on trust. He reminds them that God's decision to raise Christ from the

---

[54]This Pauline "core conviction" will be discussed in chapter 8.

[55]See note 13.

dead came in response to Jesus' own decision to "die to Sin" and "live to God" (vv. 9-10).[56] In other words, God granted "eschatological life" to the Jesus who first entrusted himself to God as Lord.[57]

As it was with Christ, so will it be with Christians:[58] "Dying with Christ" in the present brings "eschatological life" with him in the future. Participation in the "new covenant" of trust in the present brings participation in the Resurrection of the righteous in the future.[59] "If we have died with Christ" in the present, then "we will also come to life with him" in the future (v. 8).

Since participation in the Resurrection is promised only to the "righteous"--only to those who trust in God and submit to His lordship--the Roman believers cannot afford to be indifferent to sin. They must not "remain within the sphere where Sin rules" (v. 1); they must not behave as if they were still "enslaved to Sin" (v. 6). Instead, Christians must reckon themselves "to be dead to Sin, but alive to God;" they must fully entrust themselves to God as Lord "in the same way" that Jesus did when he went to the cross in trustful obedience to God's will (v. 11). The goodwill of God in the Cross of Jesus Christ functions not as an invitation to sin but as an invitation to righteousness and "eschatological life" through trustful submission to God as the true Creator and Lord of all.

---

[56]See above, under "Christ's death."

[57]This Pauline "core conviction" was discussed in chapter 5.

[58]Paul expresses this idea in terms of Christ's role as the "last Adam" in Rom 5:12-21 (discussed in chapter 3).

[59]This Pauline "core conviction" (discussed in chapter 8) rests upon the scriptural promise (discussed in chapter 5) that the "righteous" will have a share in the coming Resurrection and eschatological Rule of God. Paul, of course, understands the "righteous" to refer to those who participate in the "new covenant" based on trust. Earlier in Romans, he cites Hab 2:4 (LXX) in support of this view: "The [person reckoned] righteous on the basis of trust will live ['eschatological life']" (see Rom 1:17; cf. Gal 3:11).

Exhortatory Conclusion (vv. 12-14)

(12) Therefore continue not to let Sin reign within [the sphere of] your mortal body (σῶμα), so that [you] obey its evil desires. (13) And continue not to yield your members to Sin as instruments [working] unrighteousness. Instead, yield yourselves to God as persons who are alive from the dead, and [yield] your members to God [as] instruments [working] righteousness. (14) [I can urge you to yield yourselves to God rather than to Sin] because Sin will continue not to exercise lordship over you. [I can rightfully say that Sin will continue not to exercise lordship over you] because you are not under the Law, but under [God's act of] goodwill.

Having established the thesis laid down in v. 2, Paul concludes his discussion of the relationship between sin and God's goodwill by urging his readers to behave accordingly. They are not to act as if they were still under the lordship of Sin, doing deeds of "evil" and "unrighteousness." Instead, they are to behave in a manner appropriate for those whom God will one day make "alive from the dead." Their conduct should be characterized by trustful submission to God, or "righteousness" (v. 13).

Conclusion

Romans 6:1-14 introduces us to three Pauline "core convictions" concerning the Christian's "death" and resurrection with Christ: First, Paul understands the Christian's "death with Christ" as his/her Christ-like trust in God ("core conviction" 8 in the thesis statement given in chapter 1). Second, the Apostle conceives of "death with Christ" in terms of participation in the "new covenant," or the "righteousness" based on trust ("core conviction" 9). Finally, he links the believer's future resurrection with Christ to his/her present "death" with Christ ("core conviction" 14). We will explore further these essential elements of Paul's gospel in chapters 7 and 8.

CHAPTER SEVEN

PAUL'S INTERPRETATION OF
THE CHRISTIAN'S "DEATH" WITH CHRIST

We saw in chapter 4 that Paul interprets Christ's past death on the cross as the sacrifice for sins which established the "new covenant." The Apostle likewise employs the language of "death" and "sacrifice" to describe the present existence of Christians.[1] Paul says that Christians have "died with Christ"[2] and "died to Sin."[3] Their "old self has been crucified together with Christ, in order that the body (σῶμα) [ruled by] Sin might pass away."[4] Christians have been "planted together [with one another] in [a 'death'] like

---

[1]For a comprehensive treatment of Paul's theology of sacrifice, see Raymond Corriveau, *The Liturgy of Life: A Study of the Ethical Thought of St. Paul in His Letters to the Early Christian Communities,* Studia, 25 (Montreal: Les Éditions Bellarmin, 1970).

[2]See Rom 6:8; cf. v. 7 ("the person who has [thus] died"); 2 Cor 5:14 ("all have died").

[3]See Rom 6:2; cf. v. 11 ("reckon yourselves to be dead to Sin").

[4]See Rom 6:6 (discussed in chapter 6); cf. 8:13 ("you are putting to death the deeds of the body [as determined by the flesh]"); Gal 5:24 ("Those who belong to Christ Jesus have crucified the flesh, along with the passions and desires").

[Christ's] death" and "buried together with him . . . into 'death.'"[5] They continually present themselves to God as "a living sacrifice."[6]

Paul sets forth both himself and the other apostles as persons who exemplify the sort of self-sacrifice, or cruciform existence, characteristic of all Christians. He tells the Galatians that "The world has been crucified to me, and I [have been crucified] to the world."[7] In his letter to the Philippians, Paul speaks of his being "poured out [as a drink-offering] upon the sacrifice and ministry [which is] your trust."[8] To the Corinthians, he writes: "We [apostles] are always carrying about in [our] body (σῶμα) the death of Jesus;" "we who are alive are continually being delivered over to death for the sake of Jesus;" "death itself is continually at work in us."[9]

Paul and his fellow apostles are "poured out" as a "sacrifice" toward the end that their converts might also become an "offering" presented to the Lord. Paul and his fellow apostles "die" with Christ toward the end that their converts might also taste of this "death." Paul's mission as an Apostle is to

---

[5]See Rom 6:4-5, discussed in chapter 6.

[6]See Rom 12:1; cf. Phil 2:17 (discussed below).

[7]See Gal 6:14.

[8]See Phil 2:17; cf. 4:18.

[9]See 2 Cor 4:10-12. Note also 1 Cor 4:9 ("God has displayed us apostles last [of all], like [persons] condemned to death," i.e., like the condemned prisoners of war paraded at the end of a Roman general's "triumph"); 15:31 ("I die every day!"); 2 Cor 1:9 ("[We thought] within ourselves, 'We have received the ruling [ἀπόκριμα] which is death'" [On the meaning of ἀπόκρι-μα ("ruling"), see C. J. Hemer, "A Note on 2 Corinthians 1:9," *TB* 23 (1972): 103-107. John E. Wood ("Death at Work in Paul," *EvQ* 54 [1982]: 151-55) maintains that Paul's account of his difficulties in Asia "is coloured by the passion narratives" (p. 152) and that "the ruling which is death" recalls the cry of the Jewish crowd that Jesus should be crucified. We find this argument unconvincing.]); and Gal 6:17 ("I bear the marks of Jesus upon my body [σῶμα]"). In these passages, Paul's primary focus is the suffering and the repeated threat of physical death he has endured while carrying out his apostolic commission. However, the language Paul chooses also reflects a secondary concern--namely, the Christian's continuing obligation to "die" (metaphorically) with Christ. We will explore this matter further in part III of this chapter.

prepare a "sacrifice," to bring about "death."[10] He describes himself in Rom 15:16 as "a minister (λειτουργός) of Christ Jesus to the Gentiles, serving the gospel of God as a priest (ἱερουργοῦντα τὸ εὐαγγέλιον τοῦ θεοῦ), in order that the offering (προσφορά) which is the Gentiles may be acceptable, sanctified in the Holy Spirit." To the Corinthians he writes: "You are continually in our hearts, toward the end of our dying together."[11]

What are we to make of all this? What does Paul mean by "dying with Christ"? Why does he characterize present Christian existence as "a living sacrifice"? In this chapter, we will uncover the meaning of these metaphors (which we will collectively refer to as "'death' with Christ") and thereby penetrate further the "coherent center" of Paul's theology. We will discover that Paul understands the Christian's "death" with Christ to be his/her (1) trust in,

---

[10]Anthony Tyrrell Hanson (*The Paradox of the Cross in the Thought of St Paul, Journal for the Study of the New Testament* Supplement Series, 17 [Sheffield: JSOT Press, 1987]) notes this relationship between the suffering and death of the apostles and the suffering and death of their converts in (1) 1 Cor 4:10-13; (2) 2 Cor 4:7-15; (3) 2 Cor 6:1-10; Rom 8:35-37; 15:3; (4) Phil 3:2-16; Gal 6:17; and (5) 2 Cor 10:2-6; 2:14; 1 Cor 4:9; 15:32; 2 Cor 6:7. He argues that

> Paul, in describing the life of the apostolic community, has in mind the tradition he knew of Jesus' teaching about the life and characteristics of the citizens of the kingdom, that he consciously modelled this description on the pattern of the sufferings and death of Jesus Christ, and that in doing so he was frequently inspired by his interpretation of scripture (p. 36).

According to Hanson, Paul presents "God's saving activity" as "taking place at three levels":

> [Jesus,] in his suffering, death, and resurrection . . . gives the perfect pattern [of that "suffering, dying life which God can use for" His "redemptive purposes"] which itself effects the salvation. Then the apostolic community, heirs of the kingdom in the new age, manifest the same pattern of life, and, because Christ lives in them, continue God's saving activity based on the once-for-all events of Jesus Christ's career. Finally this pattern of life is to be reproduced in every generation of Christians (pp. 36-37).

Hanson performs a great service by pointing out these "three levels" of thinking in Paul's letters. However, we are not convinced that the Apostle draws his description of Christian existence from the Jewish scriptures and the teachings of Jesus to the extent Hanson claims. Nor are we convinced that "Paul regarded the sufferings and possible death of the apostles as possessing an atoning, reconciling, salvific value" (p. 36). We will offer a different interpretation of the Pauline data in the pages that follow.

[11]See 2 Cor 7:3.

or self-humiliation before God, (2) participation in the "new covenant," or in the "righteousness" that is based on trust, and (in the case of many Christians) (3) suffering for Christ's sake.

I. "THE SACRIFICE AND SERVICE WHICH IS YOUR TRUST"-- THE CHRISTIAN'S "DEATH" WITH CHRIST AS HIS/HER TRUST IN, OR SELF-HUMILIATION BEFORE GOD (CORE CONVICTION 8)

Christ's death and the Christian's "death" with Christ

Jesus' trusting death. Earlier in this study, we observed that Paul characterizes Christ's sacrificial death--the death by which God established the "new covenant"--as πίστις Ἰησοῦ Χριστοῦ, "Jesus Christ's act of trust."[12] Paul interprets Christ's obedient acceptance of the cross as an expression of his trust in, or self-humiliation before God.[13]

The Christian's "death" of trust. Throughout his epistles, Paul maintains that Christians display this same attitude of trust toward God--this same Christ-like commitment to God as Creator and Lord of all.[14] When Paul refers to this Christian stance toward God, he normally employs the term πίστις ("trust"). However, there are a number of texts in which the Apostle speaks of Christ-like "trust" using metaphors of "sacrifice" or "death." When Paul characterizes present Christian existence as "crucifixion with Christ," or "death with Christ," or "a living sacrifice," he is calling attention to the fact that Christians trust in God just as Christ did when he went to his crucifixion, his death, his sacrifice for sins on the cross. Paul uses such metaphors of "death"

---

[12]See Rom 3:22, 26; Gal 2:16; 3:22; Phil 3:9.

[13]For further discussion of this Pauline "core conviction," see chapter 2 under "Verse 22a" and chapter 4 under "Jesus' Act of Trust."

[14]On "trust" (πίστις) as commitment to God as Lord, see chapter 2 under "Ἡ καινὴ διαθήκη ('the new covenant')."

and "sacrifice" in order to define Christian "trust" as Christ-like "trust." Three texts from three different Pauline letters illustrate this point.

Trust as "Sacrifice" and "Death" in Three Pauline Texts

Philippians 2:17. First, Paul employs a sacrificial metaphor in Phil 2:17:

> But even if I am being poured out [as a drink-offering] (σπένδειν) upon the sacrifice (θυσία) and ministry (λειτουργία) [which is] your trust (πίστις), I rejoice; I rejoice together with you all.

The Apostle here characterizes the present existence of the Philippian Christians as a "sacrifice and ministry." What idea does Paul intend for this metaphor to communicate? He provides a definition: The Philippians' "sacrifice and ministry" is their "trust." Paul's Philippian converts possess the same attitude of "trust" in God that Christ Jesus displayed as he went to the cross in humble submission to God's will.[15] They possess the same attitude of "trust" Christ displayed when he died as a "sacrifice" for sins.

Galatians 2:19b-20. A second text providing insight into the Pauline imagery of "death" and "sacrifice" is Gal 2:19b-20.[16] The Apostle writes:

> (19b) I have been crucified with Christ. (20) I myself no longer live. Instead, Christ lives in me. The life which I am now living in the flesh, I am living within [the sphere where] trust [is the rule--namely], the [trust] of the Son of God, who loved me and who delivered himself over [to death] for me.

Paul here describes "the life which" he is "now living in the flesh"--i.e., his present existence as a Christian. The Apostle characterizes this present life as "death." He "no longer lives;" he has been "crucified with Christ." In what sense has Paul's life become "death"? He tells us in v. 20b: "The life which I am now living in the flesh, I am living within [the sphere where] trust

---

[15]Note the exhortation to Christ-like obedience and humility that appears earlier in this chapter, in Phil 2:5-8.

[16]Gal 2:19b-20 will be discussed more fully in part II of this chapter.

[is the rule--namely], the [trust] of the Son of God, who loved me and who delivered himself over [to death] for me."[17] Since Christ's going to the cross was an "act of trust" in God, Paul speaks of his own Christ-like trust as "crucifixion with Christ," or "death" ("I myself no longer live"). "Death" and "crucifixion with Christ" are metaphors by which Paul refers to the life of "trust." Paul favors such metaphors because they highlight the correspondence between the Christian's attitude toward God and the attitude displayed by the dying Christ.

2 Corinthians 4:10-14. A third text shedding light on the Christian's "death" with Christ is 2 Cor 4:10-14.[18] Paul writes:

(10) [We apostles] are always carrying about in our body (σῶμα) the "death" of Jesus, in order that the "life" of Jesus might also be manifested in our body (σῶμα). (11) For we who are alive are continually being delivered over to "death" for the sake of Jesus, in order that the "life" of Jesus might also be manifested in our mortal flesh.[19] (12) So then, "death" is

---

[17]For a discussion of Christ's death on the cross as his act of obedient "trust" (πίστις) in God, see part III of chapter 2, along with the portion of that chapter marked "Verse 22a."

[18]2 Cor 4:10-14 will be discussed more fully in parts II and III of this chapter.

[19]In the light of v. 14 ("the One who raised the Lord Jesus will also raise us along with Jesus, and will bring us into His presence along with you"), Paul is probably not speaking of a proleptic manifestation of Christ's resurrection "life" in the "mortal flesh"/"body"/*present* existence of Christians. Instead, he most likely refers to the fact that, in the *future* Resurrection of the righteous, "this mortal" body will "put on immortality" (see 1 Cor 15:53-54). For the alternative view, see (1) Norbert Baumert, *Täglich Sterben und Auferstehen: Der Literalsinn von 2 Kor 4:12-5:10,* Studien zum Alten und Neuen Testament, 34 (München: Kösel-Verlag, 1973), (2) Richard B. Gaffin, "The Usefulness of the Cross," *WTJ* 41 (1979): 228-46, and (3) Jerome Murphy-O'Connor, "Faith and Resurrection in 2 Cor 4:13-14," *RB* 95 (1988): 543-50.

In "The Nekrosis ['Death'] of Jesus: Ministry and Suffering in 2 Cor 4:7-15" (in *L'apôtre Paul: Personnalité, Style et Conception du Ministère,* Bibliotheca Ephemeridum Theologicarum Lovaniensium, 73, ed. A. Vanhoye [Leuven: University Press, 1986], 120-43), J. Lambrecht (responding to Baumert and Erhardt Güttgemanns [*Der leidende Apostle und sein Herr: Studien zur paulinischen Christologie,* Forschungen zur Religion und Literatur des Alten und Neuen Testaments, 90 (Göttingen: Vandenhoeck & Ruprecht, 1966)]) concludes that "one has to interpret Paul carrying in his body the *nekrōsis* ['death'] of Jesus and the twofold mention of Jesus' life manifested in the apostle (2 Cor 4:10-11) in terms of participation, the natural result or effect of his union with Christ" (p. 137). We have criticized the "participationist" interpretation of Paul's writings in chapter 6 under "Baptism in Romans 6:3-4."

continually at work in us, but "life" [is continually at work] in you.[20] (13) The scripture [says]: "I trusted; therefore I spoke out." Since we have the same Spirit of trust, we also trust; therefore we also speak out. (Ἔχοντες δὲ τὸ αὐτὸ πνεῦμα τῆς πίστεως κατὰ τὸ γεγραμμένον· ἐπίστευσα, διὸ ἐλάλησα, καὶ ἡμεῖς πιστεύομεν, διὸ καὶ λαλοῦμεν.) (14) For we know that the One who raised the Lord Jesus will also raise us along with Jesus, and will bring us into [His] presence along with you.

Paul here quotes from the Septuagint version of Ps 116:10 (Ps 115:10, LXX), which begins with the words: "I trusted; therefore I spoke out" (Ἐπίστευσα, διὸ ἐλάλησα). Who is the speaker in this psalm? If Paul divides Ps 116:1-9 (Ps 114, LXX) and Ps 116:10-19 (Ps 115, LXX) into two separate psalms (as the LXX does), then he most probably understands the speaker in 116 (115):10 to be David. In this case, Paul's point is that he and his fellow ministers possess the same kind of "trust" David wrote about in "the scripture" (τὸ γεγραμμένον)--namely, the kind of "trust" that compels a person to "speak out."

If, however, Paul reads Ps 116:1-9 (Ps 114, LXX) and Ps 116:10-19 (Ps 115, LXX) as a single psalm (as in the Hebrew Masoretic Text)--or as two closely related psalms in which we hear the voice of a single speaker--then the Apostle probably interprets Ps 116 (115):10 christologically. The expanded context describes the speaker as one who died, and who was then delivered from death. In 116 (114):3a he says, "The pains of death have seized me; the perils of Hades have come upon me" (περιέσχον με ὠδῖνες θανάτου, κίνδυνοι ᾅδου εὕροσάν με). Then later, in 116 (114):8a, he says: "[God] has rescued me from death" (ἐξείλετο τὴν ψυχήν μου ἐκ θανάτου). If Paul interprets Ps 116 (115):10 as a constituent part of Ps 116:1-19 (Pss 114-115, LXX), then he probably hears in this inspired word from scripture the voice of Jesus, who went to his death "trusting" in God, and who was then raised up to "eschatological

---

[20]The Apostle here employs sarcasm. Verse 12a ("'death' is continually at work in us") represents Paul's understanding of present Christian existence, while 12b ("'life' [is continually at work] in you") represents the Corinthians' misguided understanding. See below under "Paul's Defense Against the 'Super Apostles.'"

life."[21] In this case, Jesus is the one who "trusted" (in his being "obedient to the point of death") and therefore "spoke out" (presumably the gospel--as, e.g., in 1 Cor 11:23-25, where the Lord interprets his own impending death as the sacrifice for sins which will establish the "new covenant"). Paul's point is that he and his fellow ministers possess the same kind of "trust" seen in Jesus-- namely, the kind of "trust" which compels a person to "speak out."

Since the subject of 2 Cor 4:10-12 is the "manifestation" of Christ's death (i.e., his act of "trust") and resurrection "life" in the person of Christians, Paul most probably cites Ps 116 (115):10 in v. 13 as a word from the Christ who "trusted," died and rose again.[22] Paul's claim in v. 13b is that he and the other apostles possess "the same Spirit of trust" seen in Jesus, who died because he "trusted" in God. Paul refers to such Christ-like trust in vv. 10-12 using the metaphor of "death"--the same basic metaphor he employed in Phil 2:17 (which refers to Christian trust as a sacrificial "death") and Gal 2:19b-20 (which speaks of Christian trust in terms of "death" by crucifixion). "'Death' is continually at work" in Paul and his companions in the sense that they continually display the same attitude of "trust" in God which Jesus displayed in his death on the cross.

God responded to Jesus' death/"act of trust" by raising him to "eschatological life." Verses 10, 11 and 14 show that Paul fully expects the same divine response to the "death"/Christ-like trust of Christians. (We will return to 2 Corinthians 4 and explore the basis for Paul's confidence later in this chapter.) For this reason, Paul and his fellow missionaries "trust" in God as

---

[21]Hanson (*The Paradox of the Cross*, 51-54) argues that Paul views Jesus as the speaker in Ps 116 (115):10-19 even if these verses are separated from 116 (114):1-9. His evidence, however, is not compelling.

[22]Even if he understands the speaker in Ps 116 (115):10 to be David, Paul is still describing "Christian trust," and he still conceives of "Christian trust" as "Christ-like trust," or "death with Christ." The meaning of 2 Cor 4:10-14 does not change significantly.

Jesus himself trusted in God. For this reason, Paul and his companions "speak out" the gospel calling for trust on the part of all nations (v. 13b).

We have examined three different texts, addressing three different subjects, from three different Pauline letters. Together they demonstrate that Paul has a penchant for using metaphors of "death" and "sacrifice" in order to express the idea of Christian "trust." Paul favors such metaphors because they highlight the correspondence between the Christian's attitude toward God and the attitude displayed by Christ when he embraced his sacrificial death on the cross. In parts II and III of this chapter we will examine additional Pauline texts that lend support to this interpretation of the Apostle's language. For now, it is important to note that Paul understands the Christian's "death" with Christ to be his/her Christ-like trust in, or self-humiliation before God. This is Paul's first "core conviction" concerning the Christian's "dying" with Christ.

II. "THE PERSON WHO HAS THUS DIED HAS BEEN RECKONED RIGHTEOUS"--THE CHRISTIAN'S "DEATH" WITH CHRIST AS HIS/HER PARTICIPATION IN THE "NEW COVENANT," OR IN THE "RIGHTEOUSNESS" THAT IS BASED ON TRUST (CORE CONVICTION 9)

The texts examined above show that Paul sometimes employs "death" as a metaphor for Christ-like trust in God. Earlier in this study, we observed that "trust" is the content of righteousness under the "new covenant" effected by Christ's sacrifice on the cross.[23] If "death" is a metaphor for trust, and trust is equivalent to righteousness, then it would be no great surprise to find "death" also serving as a metaphor for "new covenant" righteousness in the epistles of Paul. Three texts show that the Apostle does, indeed, understand the Christian's "death" with Christ to be his/her participation in the "new covenant," or in the "righteousness" that is based on trust.

---

[23]See, e.g., chapter 2 under "Η καινὴ διαθήκη ('the new covenant')."

Righteousness as "Death" in Three Pauline Texts

Romans 6:1-14. We begin with Rom 6:1-14, which was discussed in detail in chapter 6. In that chapter, we observed how Paul repeatedly characterizes present Christian existence as "death." Believers have "died with Christ" (v. 8) and "died to Sin" (vv. 2, 11). They have been "crucified together with [Christ]" (v. 6), "buried together with him, by means of baptism, into 'death'" (vv. 3, 4), and "planted together [with one another] in [a 'death'] like his death" (v. 5).

The Apostle declares in v. 7 that "the person who has [thus] died has been reckoned righteous." The meaning of this statement becomes perfectly clear once we realize that "death" (here, as in the other Pauline passages discussed above) is a metaphor communicating the idea of Christ-like trust in God, or Christ-like commitment to God as Lord.[24] "The person who has died has been reckoned righteous" because "dying with Christ," or trust, forms the content of righteousness under the "new covenant." What the Apostle says plainly in Rom 5:1 ("we have been reckoned righteous on the basis of trust"), he here repeats with a metaphor. To "die with Christ," then, means not only to trust in God as Lord, but also to participate in the "new covenant" based on such trust. This is Paul's second "core conviction" concerning the Christian's "death" with Christ.

Philippians 3:6b-11. The Apostle expresses this same "core conviction" in Phil 3:6b-11:

(6b) . . . with regard to the righteousness which [is] within [the sphere determined by] the Law, [I was] faultless. (7) But what used to be gain, I have come to consider loss because of Christ. (8) Indeed, I consider all things loss because of the superior thing, [which is] knowing Christ Jesus my Lord. Because of him, I have been caused to lose all things. I consider [them mere] dung, in order that I may gain Christ, (9) and may be found within [the sphere determined by] him (ἐν αὐτῷ)--not having my own

---

[24]See chapter 6 under "The Christian's 'death with Christ.'"

righteousness [under the Mosaic covenant], which [is] based on the Law, but that which [is] through Christ's act of trust (πίστις Χριστοῦ),[25] [namely,] the righteousness from God [under the "new covenant"] based on trust. (10) [I have been caused to lose all things] in order that I may know him, and the strength [of God which effected] his resurrection (ἡ δύναμις τῆς ἀναστάσεως αὐτοῦ), and fellowship [with him] in his sufferings,[26] being conformed with [him] in his death (συμμορφιζόμενος τῷ θανάτῳ αὐτοῦ), (11) [so that] if at all possible I may attain to the Resurrection of the dead.

Paul here speaks of his experience under two different covenants--namely, (1) the Mosaic covenant under which the content of righteousness is the works required by the Law, and (2) the "new covenant" under which the content of righteousness is trust ("the righteousness from God based on trust," v. 9). Before he became a Christian, Paul believed that it was those reckoned "righteous" under the Mosaic covenant (i.e., Law-abiding Jews) who would participate in the coming Resurrection of the "righteous."[27] Therefore he zealously--and successfully--worked to fulfil righteousness under that covenant. "With regard to the righteousness which [is] within [the sphere determined by] the Law," Paul says that he was "faultless" (v. 6).

After becoming a Christian, Paul believed that it was those reckoned "righteous" under the "new covenant" (i.e., Jews and Gentiles who trust in the God who acted to establish that "new covenant" through Christ's sacrificial death/"Christ's act of trust" [v. 9, see below]) who would receive a place in the promised Resurrection of the "righteous."[28] He considered the Mosaic

---

[25]"Christ's act of trust" is his sacrificial death on the cross, by which he established the "new covenant." See the portion of chapter 2 marked "Verse 22a," along with parts I and III of chapter 4.

[26]On the meaning of the phrase "fellowship with [him] in his sufferings," see part III of this chapter.

[27]See chapter 5 under "The View of the Resurrection Held by Paul the Pharisee."

[28]See chapter 8 under "The Resurrection of the righteous dead" and "The future Resurrection of the righteous."

covenant "loss" (at least for purposes of attaining "eschatological life") and wholeheartedly embraced the "new covenant" as "gain" (v. 8, "that I may gain Christ")--i.e., as the only means by which persons will one day experience "the strength [of God which effected Christ's] resurrection" (v. 10).[29]

In Phil 3:10b-11, the Apostle gives voice to this hope using a metaphor of "death:" "[I am] conforming with [Christ] in his death, [so that] if at all possible I may attain to the Resurrection of the dead." What does Paul mean by "conforming with [Christ] in his death"? Earlier in this same context, the Apostle refers to Christ's death on the cross as "Christ's act of trust" (v. 9).[30] It would be reasonable to suppose, then, that "conforming with [Christ] in his death" involves exercising the same kind of trust in God which Jesus displayed in his own death, or his own "act of trust" on the cross. Since Christ-like trust is "righteousness" under the "new covenant," "conforming with [Christ] in his death" also serves as a metaphor for "righteousness" within the parameters of that covenant. This interpretation makes good sense in the context and accords well with Paul's use of "death" metaphors elsewhere in his letters (see above). Philippians 3:6b-11 thus provides further evidence that Paul's statements concerning the Christian's Christ-like "death" are references to his/her Christ-like "trust," or his/her fulfilment of "righteousness" under the "new covenant."

Galatians 2:19b-20. Let us now return to Gal 2:19b-20 and examine this text in its larger context. In 2:11-14 Paul recounts how he had opposed Cephas and certain other Jewish Christians who insisted that participants in the "new covenant" must also perform the works of the Law required under

---

[29]See chapter 5 under "'. . . he is alive because of God's strength'--Christ's Resurrection to 'Life' as an Act of God."

[30]For further discussion of this Pauline "core conviction," see chapter 2 under "Verse 22a" and chapter 4 under "Jesus' Act of Trust."

the Mosaic covenant.[31] Paul responds to these Judaizers by pointing out that the works of the Law have nothing to do with "righteousness" under the "new covenant;" for the "new covenant" is based not on the Law, but on trust. In vv. 15-16 he writes:

(15) We [are] Jews by nature, and not "Gentile sinners."[32] (16) But since we [Jews] have come to realize that a person is not reckoned righteous [under the "new covenant" which holds the promise of "eschatological life"] on the basis of the works of the Law [required under the Mosaic covenant], but only by means of Jesus Christ's act of trust (πίστις Ἰησοῦ Χριστοῦ),[33] even we [Jews living under the Mosaic covenant] have put our trust in Christ Jesus, in order that we might be reckoned righteous [under the "new covenant"] on the basis of Christ's act of trust (πίστις Χριστοῦ)[34] and not on the basis of the works of the Law [required under the Mosaic covenant]. For no flesh will be reckoned righteous [under the "new covenant"] on the basis of the works of the Law [required under the Mosaic covenant].

Paul declares that he himself has abandoned the Law in order to embrace the "new covenant" in vv. 19b-20--a passage similar, in many respects, to Phil 3:6b-11 (discussed above):

(19b) . . . I have died to the Law [which embodies the Mosaic covenant], in order that I may live to God [under the "new covenant" based on Christ-like trust in God as Lord].[35] I have been crucified with Christ. (20) I myself no longer live. Instead, Christ lives in me. The life which I am now living in the flesh, I am living within [the sphere where] trust [is the rule--namely], the [trust] of the Son of God, who loved me and who delivered himself over [to death] for me.

---

[31]On the situation at Galatia, see chapter 4 under "Galatians 3:13."

[32]"Gentile sinners" was a typically Jewish designation for non-Jews, or "Gentiles," who were called "sinners" because they stood outside the Mosaic covenant and therefore did not uphold its "righteousness" by doing the works of the Law. See Dunn, *Romans*, lxix-lxx.

[33]"Jesus Christ's act of trust" is his sacrificial death on the cross, by which he established the "new covenant." See the portion of chapter 2 marked "Verse 22a," along with parts I and III of chapter 4.

[34]See the preceding note.

[35]Compare Rom 6:10-11 (discussed in the last chapter) and 7:4.

In our earlier discussion of this text,[36] we saw that "crucifixion with Christ" (v. 19b) is a metaphor by which Paul communicates the idea of Christ-like trust in God as Lord. An examination of the larger context reminds us once again that such trust forms the content of righteousness under the "new covenant." When, therefore, Paul speaks of being "crucified with Christ," he means not only that he has put his trust in God, but also that he has thereby entered into the "new covenant," or the "righteousness" based on trust.

Metaphors of "Sacrifice" and "Death" in Other Pauline Texts

So far in this chapter we have examined five Pauline texts in which the Apostle employs the language of "death" and "sacrifice" in order to describe Christian existence during "the present time."[37] Taken together, these texts show that Paul has a penchant for speaking of the Christian's Christ-like trust in God (Paul's first "core conviction" concerning present Christian existence), or his/her righteousness under the "new covenant" (Paul's second "core conviction" concerning present Christian existence), using a variety of metaphors ("death," "death with Christ," "death to Sin," "burial into death," "deliverance over to death," "dying together," "dying every day," "[death by] crucifixion with Christ," "[death by] sacrifice," and so forth) which we have collectively labeled "'death' with Christ." In the following paragraphs, we will bring this insight to bear upon several additional Pauline texts which characterize the Christian's present life as a "sacrifice" or "death."

Galatians 6:11-17. Paul closes his letter to the Galatians with these words:

> (11) Look! I have written to you with large letters, in my own hand! (12) As many as are desiring to make a good appearance in the flesh--these [persons] are compelling you to be circumcised. [They are

---

[36]See part I of this chapter.

[37]Ὁ νῦν καιρός ("the present time") refers to the period between Christ's resurrection and his Parousia. See chapter 2 under "The present time."

doing it] only so that they may never be persecuted on account of the Cross of Christ. (13) [I can rightfully say that they compel you to be circumcised in order to avoid persecution, rather than out of any great concern for the Law,] because not even those who are themselves circumcised observe the Law. Instead, they desire for you to be circumcised so that they may boast in your flesh. (14) But, for my part, [I say] let there be no boasting if [it is] not within [the sphere where] the Cross of our Lord Jesus Christ [rules] (ἐν τῷ σταυρῷ τοῦ κυρίου ἡμῶν Ἰησοῦ Χριστοῦ). Through [the Cross of our Lord Jesus Christ], the world has been crucified to me and I [have been crucified] to the world (ἐμοὶ κόσμος ἐσταύρωται κἀγὼ κόσμῳ). (15) [Our existence should be determined by the Cross, and not the world,] because neither circumcision nor uncircumcision matters, but [only] a new creation (καινὴ κτίσις). (16) As many as follow this rule-- [may] peace and mercy [rest] upon them, even upon the [true] Israel of God.

(17) Henceforth, let no one cause troubles for me. [No one should trouble me] because I bear the marks of Jesus (τὰ στίγματα τοῦ Ἰησοῦ) on my body (σῶμα).

Paul's "death" metaphor in v. 14 has proven to be something of an enigma. What does the Apostle mean when he says "Through [the cross of our Lord Jesus Christ], the world has been crucified to me and I [have been crucified] to the world"? In order to arrive at an accurate interpretation of this verse, we must first determine what Paul means by "a new creation" (καινὴ κτίσις) in v. 15.

In our earlier discussion of Paul's apocalyptic scenario, we described how the Apostle thinks in terms of the past, the "present time," and the future. The "past" refers to that portion of the historical age (or "present evil age"[38]) when God's enemies (collectively personified as "Sin") are at the height of their power, when Creation is held in the bonds of decay, sin and death. The "future" refers to that portion of the eschatological age when these demonic "powers" are completely nullified or destroyed, when God renews His Creation, releases it from futility and decay, and raises up the righteous to glorious "eschatological life." "The present time" (ὁ νῦν καιρός) refers to the

---

[38]The term "present evil age" (ὁ αἰὼν ὁ ἐνεστηκὼς πονηρός) appears in Gal 1:4.

"intermediate period" between the two ages. It is the "time between the times" in which the historical age has already begun to fade away, but the eschatological age has not yet fully arrived.[39]

Paul employs the phrase "new creation" (καινὴ κτίσις) to refer to the transformed reality of the eschatological age, already proleptically present during "the present time." He speaks of this emerging new reality in Rom 8: 18-23:

> (18) . . . I consider the sufferings of "the present time" (ὁ νῦν καιρός) [to be] nothing compared to the glory [which] is going to be revealed in us. (19) [I can rightfully anticipate that we Christians will participate in the glory of the eschatological age] because the Creation's eager longing expectantly awaits the revealing of the children (υἱοί) of God. (20) [I can rightfully say that the Creation is eagerly awaiting a change--namely, the revealing of the children of God--]because the Creation has been subjected to futility not of [its] own will, but by [the will of] the One who subjected it in the hope (21) that the Creation itself will also be liberated from the slavery which is corruption to the freedom [from corruption] which is the glory of the children (τέκνα) of God. (22) [I can rightfully say that the Creation has been subjected to futility] because we know [from experience] (εἰδέναι) that the entire Creation groans together and suffers labor pains together to "the present [time]" (ὁ νῦν [καιρός]). (23) But [it is] not only [the Creation]. Instead, [we] ourselves, who possess the down-payment (ἀπαρχή) which is the Spirit, also [groan]. We groan within ourselves as we expectantly await adoption--[namely,] the deliverance of our bodies (σώματα) [from the slavery which is corruption to the freedom from corruption which is the glory of the children of God].

Note how Paul describes "the present time:" Creation has not yet been "liberated" from futility and corruption (vv. 20-21), but the "labor pains" marking the beginning of the end of its ordeal have already commenced (v. 22). Christians are likewise suspended between a dying "past" and the birth

---

[39]On the past, "the present time," and the future, see chapter 2 under "The present time."

of a new eschatological "future." They have already received the "down-payment which is the Spirit"[40] (v. 23); but they have not yet received the

---

[40]The Spirit is a Person whom Paul identifies as "the Holy Spirit" (Rom 5:5; 9:1; 14:17; 15:13, 16; 1 Cor 2:13; 12:3; 2 Cor 6:6; 13:14; 1 Thess 1:5-6; 4:8; cf. Rom 1:4 ["the Spirit of holiness"]), "the Spirit of God" (1 Cor 2:11, 14; 6:11; 7:40; 12:3; cf. Rom 8:11 ["the Spirit of the One who raised Jesus from the dead"]; 2 Cor 3:3 ["the Spirit of the living God"]; 1 Thess 4:8 ["His Holy Spirit"]), or "the Spirit of Christ" (Rom 8:9; cf. 1 Cor 15:45 ["the last Adam . . . has become a life-giving Spirit"]; 2 Cor 3:17-18 ["the Spirit is the Lord," "the Spirit of the Lord," "the Lord (who is) the Spirit"]; Gal 4:6 ["the Spirit of His Son"]; Phil 1:19 ["the Spirit of Jesus Christ"]).

The Spirit comes from God (1 Cor 2:12; 6:19). He is given by God to Christians (Rom 5:5; Gal 3:5; 4:6; 1 Thess 4:8; cf. 2 Cor 11:4), to those who trust in God/Christ as Lord (1 Cor 12:3 ["no one can say 'Jesus is Lord' except by the Holy Spirit"]; Gal 3:2 ["receive the Spirit . . . by means of the hearing which is trust"], 5 ["the One who gives you the Spirit . . . by means of the hearing which is trust"], 14 ["in order that we might receive . . . the Spirit by means of trust"]) and who thereby enter into the "new covenant" based on trust as opposed to the "old" Mosaic covenant based on the works of the Law (Rom 7:6 ["we serve in the newness of the Spirit and not in the oldness of the written (Law)"]; 2 Cor 3:6-8 ["a new covenant . . . the ministration of the Spirit"]; Gal 4:29 ["the one who has been fathered according to the Spirit"--i.e., Isaac, who here serves as an allegory for participants in the "new covenant"]; Gal 5:18 ["if you are led by the Spirit, then you are not under the Law"]; Phil 3:3 ["we are the (true) circumcision, who worship God in the Spirit . . . and put no confidence in the flesh"]). The Spirit dwells within Christians (Rom 8:9, 11; 1 Cor 3:16; 6:19; 2 Cor 1:22 ["in our hearts"]), binding them to one another (1 Cor 12:13 ["in one Spirit we have all been baptized into one Body--whether Jews or Greeks, slaves or freepersons--all have been given to drink of the one Spirit"]; 2 Cor 13:13 ["the fellowship of the Holy Spirit"]; Phil 2:1 ["fellowship of the Spirit"]), and setting them apart as the adopted children of God (Rom 8:14-17 ["the Spirit of adoption (υἱοθεσία)"], 23; Gal 4:6) and persons who belong to Jesus Christ (Rom 8:9; cf. 1 Cor 6:17 ["the one who is united to the Lord is one Spirit (with him)"]).

The Spirit is the personal presence of the risen Lord within his Body, the Church (Rom 8:9-10 ["the Spirit of Christ . . . Christ (is) in you"]). During "the present time" (ὁ νῦν καιρός), the Spirit cares for the Church, making intercession before God (Rom 8:26-27) and providing spiritual gifts which ensure the continual upbuilding of the Body (1 Cor 2:14; 12:1, 4-11; 14:1, 12; cf. Rom 1:11; 15:19; 1 Cor 2:4, 13; 2 Cor 6:6; and 1 Thess 1:5, which show the Spirit to be effective in Paul's apostolic ministry). He reveals to Christians the things of God/Christ (1 Cor 2:10-16; 7:40) and works to transform the person and behavior of believers so that they conform to God's emerging eschatological "Kingdom" or "Rule." (See, e.g., Rom 8:4-9 ["you are not within (the sphere where) the flesh (rules), but within (the sphere where) the Spirit (rules)"], 12-13 ["by means of the Spirit, you are putting to death the deeds of the body"]; Gal 5:16-26; and 6:8.) Life "in the Spirit" is characterized by love [Rom 15:30; Gal 5:22], joy [Rom 14:17 ["the Rule of God is . . . righteousness and peace and joy in the Holy Spirit"); Gal 5:22; 1 Thess 1:6], peace [Rom 8: 6; 14:17; Gal 5:22], patience [Gal 5:22], kindness [Gal 5: 22], goodness [Gal 5:22], trust [Gal 5:22; cf. 2 Cor 4:13], gentleness [Gal 5:23; 6:1], self-control [Gal 5:23], righteousness [Rom 14:17], holiness [1 Thess 4:7-8; cf. Rom 15:16], freedom [2 Cor 3:17], hope [Rom 15:13; Gal 5:5] and glory [2 Cor 3:18].) In this way, the Spirit serves as the "first-fruits" (ἀπαρχή, Rom 8:23) or "down payment" (ἀρραβών, 2 Cor 1:22; 5:5; cf. Eph 1:13-14) on the coming eschatological age, when Christians will be "with the Lord" (1 Thess 4:17; 5:10; cf. Phil 1:23), when they will know as they are known (1 Cor 13:9, 12), and when they will be fully conformed to the image of

glorious, incorruptible resurrection body promised to "the children of God" (vv. 18, 21, 23).[41] Christians already belong to the eschatological age, but the eschatological age has not yet been fully "revealed" (vv. 18-19). Christians already belong to the "new creation,"[42] but they must "expectantly await" its final consummation. The Galatians' participation in the emerging "new creation" (καινὴ κτίσις) "matters" a great deal to the Apostle Paul (Gal 6:15).

Next, we turn to the question of what Paul means by "the world" (ὁ κόσμος) in Gal 6:14. In his other letters, Paul employs the term κόσμος ("world") to refer to (1) the "natural" Creation of the present historical age,[43] (2) the "supernatural" "new creation" of the dawning eschatological age (see above),[44] (3) the human community in its totality,[45] or (4) those "powers"-- both human and angelic--who oppose God and who exercise their baneful influence during this "present evil age" (see above).[46] Elsewhere in Galatians, κόσμος ("world") appears only in 4:3, where the Apostle speaks of "the elemental powers of the world" (τὰ στοιχεῖα τοῦ κόσμου). This usage of the term belongs to category 4 and may shed light on Paul's meaning in Gal 6:14.

Christ (Rom 8:29; 1 Cor 15:49; 2 Cor 3:18). These promises will be fully realized at Christ's future Parousia (discussed in chapter 8), when "the Spirit of life" (Rom 8:2) grants resurrection and "eschatological life" to those reckoned righteous under the "new covenant" (Rom 8:6, 10-11, 13, 23 ["the deliverance of our bodies"]; 1 Cor 15:44-46 ["a life-giving Spirit"]; 2 Cor 3:6; Gal 6:8).

[41]The nature of the resurrection body will be discussed more fully in chapter 8.

[42]See 2 Cor 5:17: "So then, if someone [is] within [the sphere where] Christ [rules] (ἐν Χριστῷ), [s/he is] a new creation (καινὴ κτίσις); the old [things] have passed away, behold, [the] new have come."

[43]See Rom 1:20; 1 Cor 8:4.

[44]See Rom 4:13; 1 Cor 3:22.

[45]See Rom 1:8; 3:6, 19; 5:12, 13; 11:12, 15; 1 Cor 4:13; 7:33, 34; 14:10; 2 Cor 1:12; 5:19.

[46]See 1 Cor 1:20, 21, 27, 28; 2:12; 3:19; 4:9; 5:10; 6:2; 7:31; 11:32; 2 Cor 7:10; Phil 2:15.

260

In Gal 4:1-11, Paul refers to God's enemies as "the elemental powers of the world" (τὰ στοιχεῖα τοῦ κόσμου, v. 3), "those [beings] who are not by nature gods" (αἱ φύσεις μὴ ὄντες θεοί, v. 8), and "the weak and inferior elemental powers" (τὰ ἀσθενῆ καὶ πτωχὰ στοιχεῖα, v. 9). These demonic "powers" resist the Rule of God; they make slaves of human beings and prevent them from serving the true and living God, the Creator of heaven and earth.[47]

The Apostle seems to identity the Law itself as one of these "powers" opposed to God in Gal 4:3-4:

When we were minors, we ourselves were enslaved under the elemental powers of the world. But when the fullness of time came, God sent forth His Son . . . in order that he might redeem those under the Law . . . .[48]

However, in the light of Paul's other statements concerning the Law, it is probably more accurate to say that the Apostle does not view the Law as inherently "demonic."[49] Instead, evil "powers" sometimes exercise their influence through the Law; they twist God's good gift, transforming it into "the Law [as determined by] Sin" (ὁ νόμος ἁμαρτίας, to borrow a phrase from Rom 7:25), as opposed to "the Law [as determined by] God" (ὁ νόμος θεοῦ, Rom 7:25; 8:7), or "the Law [as determined by] Christ" (ὁ νόμος τοῦ Χριστοῦ, Gal

---

[47]See, e.g., Gal 4:3 ("we ourselves were enslaved under the elemental powers of the world"), 8 ("Formerly, when you did not know God, you served those beings"), 9 ("Do you desire to serve them once again?").

[48]Compare Gal 3:23-24.

[49]Paul envisions a positive role for the Law in, e.g., Gal 3:21-22 ("[Is] the Law, then, against God's promises? Certainly not! . . . the Scripture made everyone a prisoner under Sin, in order that the promise [of a 'new covenant' for all nations (see 3:8)] based on Jesus Christ's act of trust [ἐκ πίστεως Ἰησοῦ Χριστοῦ, i.e., his sacrificial death on the cross, which established this 'new covenant'] might be given to those who trust") and 24 ("the Law was our pedagogue until Christ [came] for the purpose of our being reckoned righteous on the basis of trust" [cf. Rom 10:4: "Christ is the goal (τέλος) of the Law, directed toward righteousness for all who trust"]).

6:2), or "the Law [as determined by] the Spirit of life" (ὁ νόμος τοῦ πνεύματος τῆς ζωῆς, Rom 8:2).[50]

Paul sees the Law functioning against the purposes of God in the hands of the Galatian Judaizers. How is this so? According to Paul's gospel, God showed goodwill to all nations by sending Christ to die on the cross as the sacrifice that established the "new covenant."[51] This "new covenant" is "apart from the Law;"[52] persons enter into it through trust (πίστις) alone. Those who participate in the "new covenant" based on trust will one day be raised to "eschatological life" with Christ in glory.[53] Although Paul acknowledges that the Mosaic Law and the Mosaic covenant are "holy and righteous and good,"[54] he insists that they are not "able to make alive."[55] A place in the emerging "new creation" (see above) and the future Resurrection of the righteous comes only through participation in the "new covenant" based on trust.

Paul maintains that the Judaizers at Galatia are preaching "another gospel" (1:6), "a gospel contrary to that which we have already preached to

---

[50]See Rom 7:7, 11-13:

[Is] the Law sin? Certainly not! . . . Sin, taking advantage of the opportunity, led me astray by means of the commandment and, by means of it, put [me] to death. So the Law is holy; the commandment is holy and righteous and good. Did, then, [that which is] good become death for me? Certainly not! Instead, [it was] Sin bringing about death for me by means of the good [Law or commandment] . . . .

[51]See part I of chapter 4.

[52]See, e.g., Rom 3:21.

[53]See chapter 8 under "The Resurrection of the righteous dead" and "The future Resurrection of the righteous." The coming Resurrection is not Paul's primary focus in Galatians, but the idea does appear in Gal 3:11 ("The [person reckoned] righteous on the basis of trust will live [eschatological life]"), 21 ("able to make alive"); and 6:8 ("the one who sows toward the end of fulfilling the purpose of the Spirit will, from the Spirit, reap eschatological life"). Cf. 1:4 ("rescue from out of the present evil age") and 5:21 ("God's Rule" [ἡ βασιλεία θεοῦ]).

[54]See Rom 7:12.

[55]See Gal 3:21.

you" (1:8-9). According to this judaizing gospel, persons do not enjoy righteousness and "eschatological life" through trust in Christ alone,[56] but through trust combined with the works of the Jewish Law.[57] These include circumcision for males, observing certain "days and months and times and years" (4:10), and keeping all the other commandments set forth in the Mosaic Law.[58]

Paul angrily denounces the Judaizers' message as no gospel at all, but rather an attempt to "pervert the gospel about Christ" (1:7). He warns that those who seek "righteousness by means of the Law" reject the righteousness-- and the resurrection "life"--which come only through trust. They "reject God's expression of His goodwill" (ἡ χάρις τοῦ θεοῦ) which has taken the form of the "new covenant" established through Christ's sacrificial death (see 2:21). In Gal 5:2 and 4 he says:

> Listen closely! I, Paul, tell you that if you should ever accept circumcision, then Christ will be of no benefit to you at all . . . You have been cut off from Christ, you who are trying to be reckoned righteous [so as to gain "eschatological life"] by means of the Law; you have fallen away from [God's/Christ's expression of] goodwill (χάρις).

The Judaizers are using the Mosaic Law--God's good gift to the Jewish people--to turn the Galatian Christians away from the "life" that is found only through participation in the "new covenant." They thwart God's saving purpose by blinding the Gentiles to the gospel which calls only for trust. If Paul uses the term "world" (κόσμος) to refer to the totality of those "powers" who

---

[56]Jews and judaizing Christians denounced this feature of Paul's gospel as a "scandal" (σκάνδαλον). See Gal 5:11; cf. Rom 9:30-33; 11:9; 1 Cor 1:23.

[57]On the situation at Galatia, see chapter 4 under "Galatians 3:13."

[58]In Gal 5:3 Paul reminds his readers that any man who accepts circumcision (the sign of the Mosaic covenant) is "under obligation to do the whole Law" (which spells out the content of righteousness under the Mosaic covenant).

oppose God and who resist the coming of His eschatological Rule, then the Judaizers are a manifestation of "the world" (ὁ κόσμος) in Galatia.

Against this background, the meaning of Gal 6:14-15 becomes clear. Paul is urging his converts to reject the Judaizers' false gospel (i.e., "the world") and to boast only "within [the sphere where] the Cross of our Lord Jesus Christ [rules]" (v. 14a). In other words, they should place their confidence not in the Mosaic covenant based on the works of the Law, but in the "new covenant" based on trust--the "new covenant" established through Christ's sacrificial death ("the Cross of our Lord Jesus Christ").

What is important for Paul is a place in the "new creation" (καινὴ κτίσις). This comes only through participation in the "new covenant" of trust, under which "neither circumcision [i.e., 'Jewishness'/the righteousness of the Law] nor uncircumcision [i.e., the lack of 'Jewishness'/righteousness under the Law] matters" (v. 15). To participate in the "new covenant" based on trust is to embrace God's emerging "new creation;" to participate in the "new covenant" based on trust is to reject "the world."

Paul expresses this same idea using a metaphor of "death" in v. 14b:

> Through [the Cross of our Lord Jesus Christ], the world has been crucified to me and I [have been crucified] to the world (v. 14b).[59]

The Apostle has "died" to "the world" (ὁ κόσμος). He repudiates everyone and everything (including the Judaizers and their false gospel) opposing God's saving purpose of bringing resurrection, "eschatological life," and a "new creation" to all nations, both Jews and Gentiles alike.[60] This "death"--this "crucifixion"

---

[59]Cf. Gal 5:24: "Those who belong to Christ Jesus have crucified the flesh, along with [its] passions and desires."

[60]Paul Sevier Minear ("The Crucified World: The Enigma of Galatians 6:14," in *Theologia Crucis--Signum Crucis: Festschrift für Erich Dinkler zum 70. Geburtstag,* ed. Carl Andresen and Günter Klein, 395-407 [Tübingen: J. C. B. Mohr, 1979]) describes "that κόσμος ['world'] which had been crucified to Paul" as follows:

> Positively it is constituted by reliance on circumcision, on the flesh, on the Law, and on the covenant community which is bound by those standards. Negatively, this κόσμος ["world"]

--has occurred "through [the Cross of our Lord Jesus Christ]." In other words, Paul has been "crucified to the world," and "the world has been crucified to" Paul, by virtue of the fact that he has embraced the "new covenant" of trust established by Christ's sacrificial death. To trust, to participate in the "new covenant"--this is what it means to be "crucified to the world." Paul once again employs a metaphor of "death" in order to express the idea of "trust" in God within the bounds of the "new covenant."

Paul concludes his defense against the Judaizers with these words:

> Henceforth, let no one cause troubles for me. [No one should trouble me] because I bear the marks of Jesus (τὰ στίγματα τοῦ Ἰησοῦ) on my body (σῶμα). (Gal 6:17)[61]

The "marks of Jesus" may be literal, physical wounds which Paul has suffered in the course of carrying out his apostolic ministry.[62] These call to mind the wounds of the crucified Christ and show that the Apostle has shared in the sufferings of his Lord.[63] Furthermore, they serve as visible proof that Paul has not followed the Judaizers' example of seeking never to be "persecuted on

---

is constituted by its opposition to the new creation, its avoidance of persecution for the sake of Christ, and its rejection of "the Israel of God" that walks by the new rule. When we allow this context to define the κόσμος ["world"] there is nothing inherently enigmatic about Paul's use of the term. What makes the sentence puzzling is our own habit of using the term world to refer to other entities (p. 398).

[61]The term stigma ("mark" [from στίζειν, "to prick"]) was used to refer to (1) a brand or tattoo placed on a slave, an animal, or some other piece of property, as a sign of ownership, (2) a similar mark placed, for example, on a criminal or soldier as a sign of identification, or (3) any kind of mark (usually) made with a sharp instrument. (See TDNT, s.v. "Στίγμα," by Otto Betz, 7:657-64.) When Paul says, "I bear the marks of Jesus upon my body," he may be identifying himself as a "slave" of Christ--i.e., one who has received the "mark of Christ." However, two considerations lead us to believe that Paul is instead thinking of the nailprints left in Jesus' wrists and feet when he was hung on the cross: First, Paul uses the plural στίγματα ("marks"), rather than the singular στίγμα ("mark"). Second, the immediate context contains references to Jesus' crucifixion in v. 12 and to Paul's own "crucifixion to the world" in v. 14.

[62]Paul describes the severe persecution he has endured in 2 Cor 11:23-33, discussed later in this chapter.

[63]Compare Rom 8:17; cf. Col 1:24.

account of the Cross of Christ."[64] Paul's interpretation of Christian suffering will be discussed further in part III of this chapter.

"The marks of Jesus" may also be a striking metaphor through which Paul communicates the idea of his "death" with Christ, his "crucifixion to the world," his Christ-like trust in God. The Apostle points to these "marks" (i.e., his trust) as proof that his apostleship and his gospel are valid, inasmuch as they uphold the "new covenant" God established through Christ's sacrificial death. Those who "cause troubles for" Paul are resisting God Himself.

Romans 12:1-2 and 15:14-18. Next, we examine Paul's use of sacrificial metaphors in Rom 12:1-2 and Rom 15:14-18. These verses frame the parenesis, or hortatory section of the epistle, found in 12:1-15:13. The Apostle begins his appeal with these words:

> (1) I therefore urge you, brothers [and sisters], by the mercies of God (διὰ τῶν οἰκτιρμῶν τοῦ θεοῦ), to offer your bodies [as] a living sacrifice (παραστῆσαι τὰ σώματα ὑμῶν θυσίαν ζῶσαν), holy and pleasing to God, [which is] your logical service (ἡ λογικὴ λατρεία ὑμῶν). (2) Continue not to be conformed to the pattern of this age (μὴ συσχηματίεσθε τῷ αἰῶνι τούτῳ). Instead, continue to be transformed by the renewal of [your] mind, so that you may discern what the will of God [is--what is] good and pleasing and perfect [in His sight]. (Romans 12:1-2)

Paul then proceeds to address a number of specific issues pertaining to the day-to-day conduct of the Roman believers, including the use of spiritual gifts (12:3-8), subjection to the governing authorities (13:1-7), relationships between the "weak" and the "strong" in the church (14:1-15:13), and the kind of behavior appropriate for servants of Christ (12:9-21; 13:8-14). Afterwards, he reminds the Romans of the responsibility he bears for them as Christ's appointed Apostle to the Gentiles:[65]

---

[64]See Gal 6:12.

[65]Compare Rom 1:1, 5-6, 14-15; 11:13.

(14) I have confidence in you, my brothers [and sisters], that you are full of goodness, [that you] have been filled with all knowledge, and [that you] are able to give guidance to (νουθετεῖν) one another. (15) But on some points I have written to you very boldly, as a reminder to you, because of the [gift expressing His] goodwill (χάρις[66]) which has been given to me by God.[67] (16) [God gave me this gift] so that I might be a minister (λειτουργός) of Christ Jesus to the Gentiles, serving the gospel of God as a priest (ἱερουργοῦντα τὸ εὐαγγέλιον τοῦ θεοῦ), toward the end that the offering (προσφορά) which is the Gentiles may be acceptable [to God], sanctified in the Holy Spirit. (17) I therefore have this boast within [the sphere where] Christ Jesus [rules] (ἐν Χριστῷ); [I am speaking of] the [things] of God (τὰ πρὸς τὸν θεόν[68]). (18) [I limit my boast to the sphere of Christ's lordship, to the things of God,] because I will not presume (τολμᾶν) to speak of anything except what Christ has accomplished through me[69] toward the goal of obedience on the part of the Gentiles . . . (Rom 15:14-18)

Paul opens the parenesis by urging the Roman Christians to "offer" their "bodies as a living sacrifice (θυσία ζῶσα, Rom 12:1);" he closes with a reference to "the offering (προσφορά) which is the Gentiles" (15:16). A comprehensive treatment of Pauline ethics is beyond the scope of this study.[70] What is important to note, however, is that Paul here employs "sacrifice" as his controlling metaphor for discussing the nature of present Christian

---

[66]For χάρις as a gift expressing the giver's goodwill, see chapter 2, note 174.

[67]Paul here refers to the gift of apostleship. See Rom 1:5.

[68]The phrase τὰ πρὸς τὸν θεόν ("the things pertaining to God") also appears in Heb 2:17 and 5:1.

[69]Οὐ γὰρ τολμήσω τι λαλεῖν ὧν οὐ κατειργάσατο Χριστὸς δι᾽ ἐμοῦ, literally "I will not presume to say anything about [things] which Christ did not accomplish through me."

[70]For further discussion of Pauline ethics, see the studies in the bibliography by Collange, Corriveau, Furnish, Hasenstab and Meeks. All contain extensive bibliographies.

existence.[71] What is the content of this metaphor? How does a person "offer" him/herself to God?

The entire parenesis reflects a great concern for "discerning" and doing "the will of God" (12:2), for yielding oneself to the God who exercises His lordship through the gifts He gives (see 12:3), through Scripture (see, e.g., 13:9), through the governing authorities (13:1-7), and through Jesus Christ, the "root of Jesse" who "rises [from the dead] to rule the Gentiles" (15:12).[72] Such self-surrender, or self-humiliation before God, is the essence of "trust" (πίστις)--the essence of "new covenant" righteousness (δικαιοσύνη, 14:17)--for Paul.[73] The exhortation to be "a living sacrifice" in Rom 12-15 represents one more instance in which Paul uses a metaphor of "sacrifice" or "death" in order to communicate the idea of Christ-like trust in God.

Two observations lend support to this reading of the text: First, the Apostle begins his ethical appeal by urging the Romans to act in accordance with "trust" (12:3); he ends by asking God to "fill" them "with all joy and peace in [their] trusting" (15:13). Midway through the parenesis, Paul reminds his readers that "anything not grounded in trust is sin" (πᾶν δὲ ὃ οὐκ ἐκ πίστεως ἁμαρτία ἐστίν, 14:23). The Christian life is portrayed as an "offering" (προσφορά, 15:16), or "sacrifice" (θυσία, 12:1), in the sense that it is grounded in the same kind of trust in God that Christ displayed in his own "sacrificial" death on the cross.

Second, Calvin Roetzel correctly observes that Paul links "the offering which is the Gentiles" with "obedience on the part of the Gentiles" in Romans

---

[71]Calvin J. Roetzel makes this observation in "Sacrifice in Romans 12-15," *WW* 6 (1986): 410-19. Roetzel goes on to argue that "Sacrifice and obedience are synonymous . . . Paul is building a case with the emphasis on sacrificial obedience to refute the charge that his gospel is antinomian and his apostleship unworthy of support" (pp. 417-18).

[72]See chapter 5 under "The 'Son of God.'"

[73]See chapter 2 under "Η καινὴ διαθήκη ('the new covenant')."

268

15:16 and 18.[74] This "obedience" is nothing less than "the obedience which proceeds from trust" (ὑπακοὴ πίστεως), of which Paul speaks in Rom 1:5 and 16:26. It is the same kind of "obedience" Christ himself displayed in his going to the cross out of trust in God.[75]

Christian ethics begins, for Paul, with the ethic displayed by Christ at the cross.[76] The Christian's attitude and behavior are shaped, in a word, by "trust" (πίστις) in God--i.e., by his/her Christ-like commitment to God as Lord. In Rom 12:1 and 15:16, Paul once again chooses to express this "core conviction" concerning the nature of present Christian existence through the metaphor of "[death by] sacrifice."[77]

---

[74]Both the "offering" and the "obedience" are presented as the goal of Paul's apostolic ministry. Roetzel maintains that "sacrifice and obedience are synonymous" ("Sacrifice," 417).

[75]On Christ's "obedience," see Rom 5:19 ("the obedience of the one [man Jesus Christ]"); cf. Phil 2:8 ("obedient to the point of death--even the death which is the Cross"). On the Roman Christians' Christ-like "obedience," see Rom 6:16 ("obedience [which leads] to righteousness"); cf. 16:19.

[76]See, e.g., (1) Rom 3:22, 26; Gal 2:16; 3:22; Phil 3:9 (the Cross as an act of trust), (2) Rom 5:19; Phil 2:8 (the Cross as an act of obedience), (3) Phil 2:3-8 (the Cross as an act of humility), (4) Rom 15:8; cf. Phil 2:7 (the Cross as an act of servanthood [see Dale B. Martin, *Slavery as Salvation: The Metaphor of Slavery in Pauline Christianity* (New Haven and London: Yale University Press, 1990)]), (5) 2 Cor 5:14; Gal 2:20; cf. Rom 8:35, 37 (the Cross as an act of love), and (6) Rom 15:3; 1 Cor 10:32-11:1; 2 Cor 8:9; Phil 2:3-5 (the Cross as an act of selflessness carried out for the benefit of others). Christ's "trust" (πίστις) is primary for Paul. The Lord expressed obedience, humility, servanthood, love and selflessness in the course of carrying out "his act of trust" (πίστις Ἰησοῦ) on the cross. For further discussion, see part III of chapter 4.

[77]Compare the sacrificial metaphor contained in 2 Cor 2:15, where Paul describes himself and his fellow-workers as "the aroma (εὐωδία) of Christ [ascending] to God among those who are being saved and those who are perishing." Stephen B. Heiny ("2 Corinthians 2:14-4:6: The Motive for Metaphor," in *Society of Biblical Literature 1987 Seminar Papers,* ed. Kent Harold Richards [Atlanta: Scholars Press, 1987], 1-22) maintains that this metaphor of the apostles as "the aromatic smoke emanating from a sacrifice to God" expresses the idea of "a person so utterly selfless and faithful [i.e., 'trusting'] that he or she sacrifices himself or herself to show others what is expected of human beings" (p. 15). Daniel Patte ("A Structural Exegesis of 2 Corinthians 2:14-7:4 With Special Attention on 2:14-3:6 and 6:11-7:4," in *Society of Biblical Literature 1987 Seminar Papers,* ed. Kent Harold Richards [Atlanta: Scholars Press, 1987], 23-49) similarly argues that "the metaphor of the 'acceptable burnt-offering'" communicates the idea that ministers of Christ "must be oriented toward God, as a burnt-offering goes up to God" (p. 34). "Paul defends his ministry against his antagonistic Corinthian readers by attempting to convince them that what they viewed as detrimental effects of a false ministry on their

2 Corinthians 5:11, 14-15; 4:10-14; and 7:3b. Finally, we must briefly examine three texts from 2 Corinthians, all of which were identified as Pauline "summary statements" in chapter 1. All contain metaphors of "death" which have tended to obscure Paul's meaning. However, the task of interpretation is greatly simplified when we remember that Paul regularly employs such metaphors to communicate the idea of "trust" or "new covenant" righteousness.

The first text is 2 Cor 5:11, 14-15:

(11) . . . we try to persuade[78] men [and women] . . . (14) Christ's expression of his love (ἀγάπη τοῦ Χριστοῦ) compels us, since we have judged this--[namely,] that one has died for all; therefore all have died. (15) And he died for all in order that those who are alive might no longer live for themselves, but for the one who died for them, and who was raised.

Christ is the "one" who "has died for all," and "who was raised." Through his sacrificial death, Christ established the "new covenant." Persons enter into this "new covenant" through Christ-like "trust" (πίστις) or, in other words, through "dying" with Christ. This is what Paul means in v. 14 when he says, "One has died for all; therefore all have died." Christ established the "new covenant" based on trust; therefore all should respond in trust.

The Apostle repeats the same idea in v. 15 using different words: "[Christ] died for all" (i.e., he established the "new covenant") "in order that

---

experience (death-like situations) should in fact be viewed as marks of faithfulness [i.e., 'trust']" (p. 49). A discussion of "The Apostle Paul as the Sacrificial Aroma of Christ (2 Cor 2:14-16a)" also appears in Scott J. Hafemann, *Suffering and the Spirit: An Exegetical Study of 2 Cor 2:14-3:3 Within the Context of the Corinthian Correspondence,* Wissenschaftliche Untersuchungen zum Neuen Testament, Reihe 2, 19 (Tübingen: J. C. B. Mohr, 1986), 41-87. A revised version of this book was published in 1990 under the title *Suffering and Ministry in the Spirit: Paul's Defense of His Ministry in 2 Corinthians 2:14-3:3* (Grand Rapids: Eerdmans, 1990). Calvin J. Roetzel examines Paul's "death" and "resurrection" metaphors in 2 Cor 1:3-11, 2:14-17, 4:7-18, and 5:1-15, in "'As Dying, and Behold We Live': Death and Resurrection in Paul's Theology," *Int* 46 (1992): 5-18.

[78]The verb πείθομεν ("we try to persuade") here represents an instance of the "tendential present."

those who are alive[79] might no longer live for themselves, but for the one who died for them, and who was raised" (i.e., so that persons might entrust themselves to Christ as Lord [πίστις] and thus fulfil "righteousness" under the "new covenant"). "Christ's expression of his love" (i.e., his sacrificial death which established the "new covenant" based on trust) demands a response of trust from all nations. It "compels" Paul and the apostolic company to "try to persuade men [and women]" to trust in Christ as Lord, to participate in the "new covenant," to "live no longer for themselves, but for the [one] who died for them."

2 Corinthians 4:10-14 and 7:3b are two more texts in which Paul employs the metaphor of "death" in order to explain his conduct as an Apostle of Christ. In the first passage, Paul writes:

(10) [We apostles] are always carrying about in our body the "death" of Jesus, in order that the "life" of Jesus might also be manifested in our body.[80] (11) For we who are alive are continually being delivered over to "death" for the sake of Jesus, in order that the "life" of Jesus might also be manifested in our mortal flesh. (12) So then, "death" is continually at work in us, but "life" [is continually at work] in you. (13) The scripture [says]: "I trusted; therefore I spoke out." Since we have the same Spirit of trust, we also trust; therefore we also speak out. (14) For we know that the One who raised the Lord Jesus will also raise us along with Jesus, and will bring us into [His] presence along with you.

In the second passage, Paul assures the Corinthians that

. . . you are continually in our hearts, toward the end of our "dying" together and our living together.

In our earlier discussion of 2 Cor 4:10-14 (see part I of this chapter), we saw that "death" serves as a metaphor for Christ-like "trust" (πίστις) in

---

[79]Note that Paul is describing present Christian existence, or Christian existence during "the present time" (ὁ νῦν καιρός).

[80]In "Apostolic Suffering and the Language of Processions in 2 Corinthians 4:7-10" (*BTB* 21 [1991]: 158-65), Paul Brooks Duff argues that Paul here employs a metaphorical allusion to the "carrying about" of sacred objects in Greco-Roman epiphany processions.

God. Paul is describing present Christian existence ("we who are alive," v. 11) as a life characterized by the same kind of submission to God's lordship that Jesus displayed in going to the cross.

Paul is confident that those who embrace "death" (trust) in the present will be raised to "eschatological life" in the future. What is the basis for this confidence? The Apostle believes that, at the time of Christ's Parousia (i.e., his "Second Coming"), God will raise to "eschatological life" those reckoned "righteous" under the "new covenant."[81] Since the content of "righteousness" under the "new covenant" is "trust," it is those who trust--those in whom "'death' is continually at work" (to use the metaphor found in 2 Cor 4:12)-- who will one day participate in the promised Resurrection of the "righteous." Paul and his companions "speak out" (v. 13) the gospel which calls for trust, in the hope that the Corinthians will respond in trust, so that they too might participate in the coming Resurrection of the righteous. 2 Corinthians 7:3b expresses the same concern: ". . . you are continually in our hearts, toward the end of our 'dying' together [i.e., toward the end of our sharing together in the 'new covenant' based on trust] and our living ['eschatological life'] together [in the future Resurrection of the righteous]." In both texts, "death" serves as a metaphor not only for Christ-like trust in God, but for the "new covenant" righteousness which leads to "eschatological life."[82]

Let us now pause to summarize the results of our investigation: The Christian's "death" with Christ represents the third of four ideas (along with Christ's death, Christ's resurrection, and the Christian's resurrection with Christ) which together form the "coherent center" of Paul's theology. We have examined a variety of ways Paul expresses this idea in his letters to

---

[81]See (1) chapter 1 under "The present time," (2) chapter 3 under "The risen Christ," (3) chapter 5 under "The View of the Resurrection Held by Paul the Pharisee" and "'The first-fruits of those who have fallen asleep,'" and (4) the more complete discussion found in chapter 8 under "The Resurrection of the righteous dead" and "The future Resurrection of the righteous."

[82]We will have more to say about 2 Cor 4:10-14 in part III of this chapter.

Corinth, Galatia, Philippi and Rome. We have discovered that "death with Christ"[83] is a metaphor through which Paul expresses two "core convictions" concerning the nature of Christian existence during "the present time:"[84] First, the Christian has adopted an attitude of "trust" (πίστις) in, or self-humiliation before God, which informs his/her day-to-day conduct. Second, the believer has embraced the "new covenant" established by God through Christ's sacrificial death; s/he seeks to fulfil the "righteousness" based on trust.

If "death with Christ" is only a metaphor pointing beyond itself to the ideas of trust, or "new covenant" righteousness, then why should we identify the Christian's "death with Christ" as part of the Pauline center? Why not say that "trust," or "righteousness," is the third idea in Paul's fourfold center? We have retained the metaphor because Paul himself does so in most of the "summary statements" discussed in chapter 1. When Paul summarizes the "co-herent center" of his theology, or "the truth which is the gospel," he prefers to speak of "death with Christ" rather than simply "trust" or "righteousness." The metaphor draws a connection between the attitude of the Christian and the attitude of the dying Christ which the terms "trust" and "righteousness" cannot, in and of themselves, convey. "Death with Christ" identifies the Christian's "trust," or the Christian's "righteousness," as specifically "Christ-like trust" in God as Lord.

---

[83]Again, we are using this phrase to refer to the whole range of images Paul evokes through terms such as "death," "crucifixion," "burial," "sacrifice," and "offering."

[84]See chapter 2 under "The present time."

III. "FELLOWSHIP WITH HIM IN HIS SUFFERINGS"--
THE CHRISTIAN'S "DEATH" WITH CHRIST AS HIS/HER
SUFFERING FOR CHRIST'S SAKE (CORE CONVICTION 10)

Christ's trust in God led to a violent death, a death of much suffering and pain. Christ's death on the cross was a manifestation of his trust in, or complete self-humiliation before God.[85] Paul believes that the Christian's Christ-like trust in God--his/her "death with Christ"--may also lead to pain, suffering, persecution, or even a violent death. The person who "conforms with [Christ] in his death" may also endure "fellowship [with him] in his sufferings."[86] The person who "dies with Christ" may also be required to "suffer together with him."[87] The Christian's "death with Christ" (i.e., trust, or participation in the "new covenant") may become manifest in his/her suffering for Christ's sake.[88] We will examine this third Pauline "core conviction" concerning the nature of present Christian existence in the following paragraphs.[89]

Christian Suffering in Paul's Thought

   Suffering as the Christian norm. Nothing in Paul's theology says that Christians, of necessity, must suffer.[90] Paul is no Ignatius of Antioch, who

---

[85]We discussed this Pauline "core conviction" in part III of chapter 4.

[86]See Phil 3:10-11.

[87]See Rom 8:17.

[88]See, e.g., Phil 1:29.

[89]For scholarship on Paul's interpretation of suffering and "weakness," see the pertinent studies in the bibliography by Baasland, Beker, Bloomquist, Hamerton-Kelly, Pobee, Proudfoot, Sumney and Wolter.

[90]In other words, Paul would not deny that a person is a Christian solely on the grounds that s/he has never suffered for Christ's sake. For Paul, the mark of the Christian is trust in God, the Father of Jesus Christ. Suffering may be evidence of such trust, but suffering alone does not set a person apart as a child of God or a servant of Christ (see below).

actively seeks out persecution and martyrdom.[91] However, the Apostle's own experience showed him that trust in God, or "dying with Christ," often leads to intense suffering. Paul provides a catalogue of the hardships he himself endured as a servant of Christ in 2 Cor 11:23-33 (discussed below). His letters include numerous references to the persecution that pursued him and his companions as they carried the gospel throughout the eastern half of the Roman empire. Paul narrowly escaped arrest in Damascus;[92] he faced a test of "endurance" (ὑπομονή) in Corinth.[93] Paul "fought with wild beasts at Ephesus;"[94] he speaks of the "suffering" he and his companions "endured in Asia."[95] Paul and the apostolic company experienced "suffering of all sorts" in Macedonia,[96] "suffering" and "shameful treatment" in Philippi,[97] and "great opposition" in Thessalonica.[98]

---

[91]Ignatius was the third bishop of Antioch in Syria, who was condemned to die in the arena at Rome during the reign of the emperor Trajan (A.D. 98-117). In his epistle to the Christians at Rome, he begged that church not to interfere, but to allow him to achieve martyrdom: "Suffer me to be eaten by the beasts, through whom I can attain to God" (Kirsopp Lake, trans., *The Apostolic Fathers,* The Loeb Classical Library [New York: G. P. Putnam's Sons, 1930], 231). Walter Rebell contrasts Ignatius' understanding of suffering with that of Paul in "Das Leidensverständnis bei Paulus und Ignatius von Antiochien," *NTS* 32 (1986): 457-65.

[92]See 2 Cor 11:32-33.

[93]See 2 Cor 12:12 (discussed below).

[94]See 1 Cor 15:32. The Apostle may have been literally forced to fight wild animals in the arena, or he may be likening human opponents to such beasts.

[95]See 2 Cor 1:8-9. Paul says, "We were weighed down to an extraordinary degree, beyond [the limits of our] strength, so that we despaired even of living [itself]. [We thought] within ourselves, 'We have received the ruling (ἀπόκριμα, see note 9) which is death.'" Paul may be referring to his struggle with the "wild beasts at Ephesus," for Ephesus was located in the province of Asia.

[96]See 2 Cor 7:5.

[97]See 1 Thess 2:1.

[98]See 1 Thess 2:2.

Such difficulties were not limited to the apostles but were common to the Christian community as a whole. Epaphroditus drew "near to [the point of] death because of the work of Christ,"[99] while Prisca and Aquila "risked their necks" in aiding Paul.[100] The Corinthians are Paul's "partners in suffering,"[101] while the Philippians are engaged in "the same sort of struggle" they witnessed in Paul himself.[102] "The churches of Macedonia" undergo "a great test of suffering,"[103] while the Roman believers must "endure suffering" and "bless those who persecute" them.[104] The Thessalonians suffer "at the hands of [their] own people,"[105] while both the Galatians and "the churches of God which are in Judea" are persecuted by the Jews.[106] Paul freely acknowledges that, before he became a Christian, he himself "was severely persecuting God's Church and was trying to destroy it."[107]

Christian suffering may not be a divine necessity, but it was certainly the norm for Paul and the first-century Church. The Apostle's own experience, along with that of his converts, could only strengthen Paul's conviction that persecution, suffering, and perhaps even martyrdom, would distinguish

---

[99]See Phil 2:30, along with the discussion of Epaphroditus and Timothy that appears in R. Alan Culpepper, "Co-Workers in Suffering: Philippians 2:19-30," *RevExp* 77 (1980): 349-58.

[100]See Rom 16:3-4.

[101]See 2 Cor 1:7.

[102]See Phil 1:29-30.

[103]See 2 Cor 8:1-2.

[104]See Rom 12:12, 14.

[105]See 1 Thess 2:14; cf. 1:6; 3:3-4.

[106]See 1 Thess 2:14; Gal 4:29; cf. 5:11; 6:12; and possibly 3:4 ("Have you experienced/suffered so many things in vain?").

[107]See Gal 1:13; cf. 1:23; 1 Cor 15:9; Phil 3:6.

276

Christian existence during "the present time" (ό νῦν καιρός).[108] How did Paul interpret this aspect of the Christian life?

Human suffering versus Christian suffering. The Apostle believes that Christians are subject to two different kinds of suffering: First, they endure the kind of suffering common to all human beings during the "present evil age."[109] During this age, the whole Creation has been "subjected to futility;" "the entire Creation groans together," longing to "be liberated from the slavery which is corruption."[110] During this age, Christians--like all human beings-- possess a weak, mortal, corruptible body,[111] and are, therefore, subject to pain, sickness and death. God has not yet fully established His eschatological Rule, and so Christians--like all human beings--are subject to the harmful forces of nature and to mistreatment by other persons.

Christians may also endure a second kind of suffering--a specifically "Christian" kind of suffering--which Paul variously refers to as "fellowship [with Christ] in his sufferings,"[112] suffering "for Christ's sake,"[113] or suffering "for the Cross of Christ."[114] Paul employs such terms in order to speak of perse- cution aimed at Christians solely because they are Christians, or hardships Christians endure solely because of their commitment to Christ as Lord. What meaning does Paul attach to this distinctly "Christian" kind of suffering?

---

[108]On "the present time," see above under "Galatians 6:11-17." Paul speaks of "the sufferings of the present time" (ό νῦν καιρός) in Rom 8:18, 22. See also 1 Cor 7:26 ("the present distress," RSV) and Gal 4:29 ("As at that time the one fathered according to the flesh kept on persecut- ing the [one fathered] according to the Spirit, so [is it] now (νῦν)."

[109]See above under "Galatians 6:11-17."

[110]See Rom 8:20-22.

[111]See, e.g., 1 Cor 15:42-43, 53.

[112]See Phil 3:10; cf. Rom 8:17 ("suffering together with [Christ]").

[113]See 2 Cor 12:10; Phil 1:29-30.

[114]See Gal 6:12.

Christian suffering as a manifestation of trust. Paul interprets the Christian's "suffering for Christ's sake" as an outward manifestation of his/her Christ-like trust in God--a visible proof that s/he has "died with Christ" by embracing the "new covenant" based on trust. The Apostle gives voice to this "core conviction" in Phil 3:9-11, where he expresses a desire to

> be found within [the sphere determined by Christ]--not having my own righteousness [under the Mosaic covenant], which [is] based on the Law, but that which [is] through Christ's act of trust [i.e., Christ's sacrificial death, through which God established the "new covenant"[115]], [namely,] the righteousness from God [under the "new covenant"] based on trust. [I have been caused to lose all things] in order that I may know him, and the strength [of God which effected] his resurrection (ἡ δύναμις τῆς ἀναστάσεως αὐτοῦ), and fellowship [with him] in his sufferings (ἡ κοινωνία τῶν παθημάτων αὐτοῦ), being conformed with [him] in his death (συμμορφιζόμενος τῷ θανάτῳ αὐτοῦ), [so that] if at all possible I may attain to the Resurrection of the dead.

Paul has entrusted himself to God; he has embraced the "new covenant" with its righteousness based on trust; he has "conformed" to the attitude of trust displayed by Christ "in his death" (i.e., he has "died with Christ"). The result has been "fellowship" with Christ "in his sufferings." In other words, the Apostle's Christ-like trust in God has led to the same kind of persecution and hardship Christ himself endured because of his trust in God.[116] Christian suffering is an outward manifestation of Christ-like trust in God, or of participation in the "new covenant" based on trust. To accept the gift of God's goodwill in the Cross of Christ (i.e., the "new covenant") is also to accept the possibility--if not the probability--of suffering for Christ's sake. As Paul says in Phil 1:28b-30,

---

[115]For a discussion of the Cross as "Christ's act of trust," see chapter 2 under "Verse 22a," along with part III of chapter 4. For a discussion of the Cross as the sacrifice by which God established the "new covenant" based on trust, see parts I and II of chapter 4.

[116]Paul therefore reckons his scars to be "the marks of Jesus" (τὰ στίγματα τοῦ Ἰησοῦ) upon his body. See Gal 6:17, discussed in part II of this chapter.

278

(28b) This [is] from God--(29) [namely,] that it has been given to you [as an expression of God's goodwill] (χαρίζεσθαι[117]), [and] for the sake of Christ, not only to trust in him, but also to suffer for his sake, (30) by having the same sort of struggle which you have seen in me, and [which] you are now hearing [to be] in me [still].

Philippians 3:10-11 also links "fellowship [with Christ] in his sufferings" to participation in "the Resurrection of the dead," or "the strength [of God which effected Christ's] resurrection." Paul is able to draw such a connection between the Christian's present suffering and his/her future "eschatological life" only because he interprets such suffering as a manifestation of Christ-like trust in God, or of "death with Christ." Suffering represents trust. Trust forms the content of "righteousness" under the "new covenant." It is those reckoned "righteous" under the "new covenant" based on trust whom God will raise from the dead to participate in "eschatological life" in glory.[118] This same Pauline "core conviction" lies behind Rom 8:17, in which the Apostle affirms that Christians will "be glorified together with" Christ in the future, "provided that" they first "suffer together with him" in the present. It also forms the basis for 2 Cor 4:17, in which Paul assures his readers that "our momentary, insignificant suffering is preparing for us an eternal weight of eschatological glory (αἰώνιος βάρος δόξης[119]), transcendent beyond measure."

We may summarize Paul's interpretation of Christian suffering as follows: The Apostle views suffering on the part of Christians not as a necessity but as the norm. Like other human beings, Christians endure "the sufferings of 'the present time'"--the weakness, pain, and adversity common to mortals during "the present evil age." Unlike other human beings, they are often required to suffer "for Christ's sake"--to endure hardships, persecution, and perhaps even martyrdom, in the course of carrying out the Lord's will. Paul

[117]See chapter 2, note 174.

[118]See above under "2 Corinthians 5:11, 14-15; 4:10-14; and 7:3b."

[119]See chapter 8, note 15.

interprets this specifically "Christian" kind of suffering as a manifestation of Christ-like trust in God, or evidence that a person has "died with Christ."

In the following pages, we will examine how these beliefs come to expression in two very different sets of circumstances: First, we will focus on Paul's interpretation of the persecution suffered by the church at Thessalonica. Afterwards, we will explore how Paul interprets his own suffering as an Apostle of Christ in his defense against the "super apostles" of Corinth.

The Case of the Thessalonians[120]

Suffering as norm. The Thessalonian Christians were persecuted from the moment they first embraced the gospel of Christ.[121] Paul recalls that event in 1 Thess 1:6-7:

> (6) You became imitators of us and of the Lord; for you received the word in much suffering, with joy from the Holy Spirit, (7) so that you became an example to all those who trust in Macedonia and Achaia.

The Apostle returns to this subject in 2:13-15a:

> (13) We continually thank God for this: When you received the word of God, heard from us, you accepted [it] not [as] the word of human beings, but as [what] it truly is--[namely,] the word of God which is indeed working in you who trust. (14) [I can rightfully say that the word of God is working in you who trust] because you, brothers [and sisters], have become imitators of the churches of God which are in Judea, within [the sphere of] Christ Jesus' [rule]. You have suffered the same things at the hands of your own people as they [suffered] at the hands of the Jews, (15) who killed both the Lord Jesus and the prophets, and who drove us out. [They] are not pleasing to God and [are] hostile toward all people, for they hinder us from speaking to the Gentiles in order that they might be saved . . . .

---

[120]For a survey of current scholarship on Thessalonians, see Earl Richard, "Contemporary Research on 1 (& 2) Thessalonians," *BTB* 20 (1990): 107-15. Page 109 describes the scholarly debate between "Persecution versus Alienation" as the "likely context for the reading of the letter."

[121]Acts 17:1-9 describes how Paul's preaching at Thessalonica incited a riot among the Jews.

The Thessalonian believers have suffered at the hands of their "own people" (2:14). Paul does not view such persecution as unusual or unexpected, but as typical of Christians all over the world. The Thessalonians have become "imitators" of the apostles and of "the churches of God which are in Judea" (1:6; 2:14-25), following in the blood-stained footsteps of those who knew Christ before them. They have become "an example to all those who trust in Macedonia and Achaia," showing their brothers and sisters in the faith how to accept suffering "with joy from the Holy Spirit" (1:6-7). Paul's letter to the saints at Thessalonica reflects his belief that suffering is the Christian norm.

Suffering as trust. The Thessalonians' pain is the direct result of their having "received the word" of the gospel through "trust" in God as Lord (1:6-7; 2:13-14). They have become "imitators of the Lord" (1:6) inasmuch as they suffer because of their trust in God, just as Jesus himself suffered and died because of his trust in God (see part III of chapter 4). Paul highlights the link between Christian suffering and Christian trust in 1 Thess 3:2-8:

> (2) We sent Timothy, our brother and God's fellow-worker within [the sphere of] the gospel about Christ, in order to strengthen and encourage you in your trust, (3) that no one should be shaken (σαίνειν) in these sufferings. [No one should be shaken in these sufferings] because you yourselves know that this is what God has appointed for us.[122] (4) [You should not be surprised to hear that God has appointed sufferings for Christians] because when we were with you, we warned you in advance that we are going to suffer--just as it has happened, and [as] you [now] know [from experience] (εἰδέναι). (5) For this reason, when I could bear [it] no longer, I sent [Timothy] so that [I could] find out about your trust, for fear that somehow (μή πως) the tempter had tempted you and our labor had been in vain.
>
> (6) Now Timothy has returned to us from you and has brought us good news concerning [your] trust and your love. [He has told us] that you have fond memories (μνεία ἀγαθή) of us [and that you] are always longing

---

[122]This is a paraphrase of εἰς τοῦτο κείμεθα ("we are appointed to this"). The verb κεῖσθαι ("to lay down, appoint") here functions as a "divine passive," inasmuch as it describes an action performed by God.

to see us, just as we also [long to see] you. (7) For this reason, brothers [and sisters], we have been encouraged about you, in all our want and suffering, by your trust; (8) for now we live, if you continue to stand firm within [the sphere of] the Lord's [rule].

God "appointed" (κεῖσθαι) Jesus to put his trust in God, to suffer and die on the cross as the sacrifice which established the "new covenant" based on trust (see 1 Cor 3:11).[123] God "appointed" (κεῖσθαι) Paul and the other apostles to proclaim what God has done--to preach the gospel calling for trust (see Phil 1:16).[124] Those who respond to the gospel by embracing the "new covenant" of trust are often required to suffer for Christ's sake. Their suffering serves as visible proof that "the word of God" is "indeed working in [those] who trust" (1 Thess 2:13-14)--that they "continue to stand firm within [the sphere of] the Lord's [rule]" (1 Thess 3:8). God has "appointed" (κεῖσθαι) suffering for Christians (1 Thess 3:3-4) in the sense that He has "appointed" the covenant of trust in which they share.[125] Paul's letter to the saints at Thessalonica reflects his "core conviction" that Christian suffering is a manifestation of Christ-like trust in God, or "death with Christ." It reflects his "core

---

[123]Paul here identifies Jesus as the "foundation" which has been "appointed" (κεῖσθαι) by God.

[124]Compare Rom 1:1, 5; 1 Cor 1:1; Gal 1:15-16.

[125]Compare (1) Phil 1:28b-29:

(28b) This [is] from God--(29) [namely,] that it has been given to you [as an expression of God's goodwill] (χαρίζεσθαι--see chapter 2, note 174), [and] for the sake of Christ, not only to trust in him, but also to suffer for his sake.

and (2) Rom 8:35-37:

(35) What will separate us from Christ's love? [Will] suffering or pressure or persecution or famine or nakedness or danger or sword [separate us from Christ's love]? ((36) [I have no difficulty implying that a person loved by Christ could endure trouble, or persecution, or even a violent death; for scripture itself indicates that this will be our experience as Christians.] Just as it has been written,

For your sake are we killed the whole day [long];
We have been reckoned as sheep of the slaughter.)

[None of these things will be able to separate us from Christ's love!] (37) In all these [hardships] we are completely victorious by means of the one who loved us.

conviction" that trust in God, or participation in the "new covenant," involves a willingness to suffer for Christ's sake in the face of the high probability that such suffering will indeed be required.

Paul's Defense Against the "Super Apostles"

Paul's most profound treatment of Christian suffering appears in 2 Corinthians 10-13, in which he defends his apostolic ministry against a group of critics whom he calls the "super apostles" (ὑπερλίαν ἀπόστολοι[126]).[127] The precise identity of these "super apostles" has been the subject of much debate.[128] Efforts to reconstruct their history and their theological views are

---

[126]See 2 Cor 11:5; 12:11.

[127]Hans Dieter Betz examines Paul's defense in the context of ancient philosophy and rhetoric in *Der Apostel Paulus und die sokratische Tradition: Eine exegetische Untersuchung zu seiner "Apologie" 2 Korinther 10-13,* Beiträge zur historischen Theologie, 45 (Tübingen: J. C. B. Mohr, 1972). Georg Strecker analyzes Paul's defense in "Die Legitimität des paulinischen Apostolates nach 2 Korinther 10-13," *NTS* 38 (1992): 566-86.

[128]The "super apostles" have been variously identified as (1) "Jews, Jerusalem Jews, Judaizing Jews, . . . a rival apostolate to Paul's, backed by all the prestige of the mother church" (C. K. Barrett, "Paul's Opponents in 2 Corinthians," *NTS* 17 [1971]: 251; reprinted in C. K. Barrett, *Essays on Paul* [Philadelphia: The Westminster Press, 1982], 60-86. See also the essay entitled "Ψευδαπόστολοι [2 Cor 11:13]," which appears on pp. 87-107 of the same volume.), (2) the Jerusalem Apostles, who were being represented at Corinth by associates of Peter who were-- like Peter himself--both "servants of Christ" and "servants of Satan" (Margaret E. Thrall, "Super-Apostles, Servants of Christ, and Servants of Satan," *JSNT* 6 [1980]: 42-57. Scott E. McClelland rejects Thrall's thesis in "'Super-Apostles, Servants of Christ, Servants of Satan': A Response," *JSNT* 14 [1982]: 82-87. See also the next note.), (3) Jews in some way related to Stephen and the circle of hellenistic Jews described in Acts 6 (Gerhard Friedrich, "Die Gegner des Paulus im 2. Korintherbrief," in *Abraham unser Vater: Juden und Christen im Gespräch über die Bibel. Festschrift für Otto Michel zum 60. Geburtstag,* ed. Otto Betz, Martin Hengel, and Peter Schmidt, Arbeiten zur Geschichte des Spätjudentums und Urchristentums, 5 [Leiden/Köln: E. J. Brill, 1963], 181-215), (4) "migrant preachers of Jewish origin who were working for the early church," who "came from the world of Hellenistic-Jewish Apologetics," and who presented themselves as θεῖοι ἄνδρες ("divine men") (Dieter Georgi, *The Opponents of Paul in Second Corinthians* [Philadelphia: Fortress Press], 315), (5) "Hellenistic Jews who were preaching another gospel and another Jesus based on syncretic gnostic principles," who were "propagating what we call 'spiritual gnosticism'" (Doyle Kee, "Who Were the 'Super-Apostles' of 2 Corinthians 10-13?" *RestQ* 23 [1980]: 72, 69), (6) "pneumatics" (πνευματικοί) (Jerry L. Sumney, *Identifying Paul's Opponents: The Question of Method in 2 Corinthians, Journal for the Study of the New Testament* Supplement Series, 40 [Sheffield, England: JSOT Press, 1990]), and (7) "shameful hybrists" (Peter Marshall, "Hybrists not Gnostics in Corinth," in *Society of Biblical Literature 1984 Seminar Papers,* ed. Kent Harold Richards [Chico, CA: Scholars Press, 1984], 285. Marshall

hindered by uncertainty over whether Paul's remarks in 2 Cor 10-13 are directed toward only one group of opponents, or two or more different groups of opponents.[129] The problem is further complicated by the lack of scholarly consensus concerning whether or not the "super apostles" should be identified with critics of Paul's apostolic ministry mentioned elsewhere in the Corinthian correspondence (e.g., the Apollos-, or Cephas-, or Christ-faction of 1 Cor 1:12; the group denying the Resurrection from the dead mentioned in 1 Cor 15:12; those who caused Paul's "pain" in 2 Cor 1:23-2:11).[130] A detailed discussion

---

develops his argument in much greater detail in *Enmity in Corinth: Social Conventions in Paul's Relations with the Corinthians,* Wissenschaftliche Untersuchungen zum Neuen Testament, Reihe 2, 23 [Tübingen: J. C. B. Mohr, 1987].). Wayne A. Meeks offers many helpful insights into the "super apostles'" identity and behavior, as well as Paul's response to them, in *The First Urban Christians: The Social World of the Apostle Paul* (New Haven and London: Yale University Press, 1983).

[129]To illustrate: Ferdinand Christian Baur (*Paul the Apostle of Jesus Christ, His Life and Works, His Epistles and Teachings: A Contribution to a Critical History of Primitive Christianity,* 2d ed., trans. E. Zeller [London: Williams and Norgate, 1873]), Ernst Käsemann ("Die Legitimität des Apostels: Eine Untersuchung zu 2 Korinther 10-13," *ZNW* 41 [1942]: 33-71), P. W. Barnett ("Opposition in Corinth," *JSNT* 22 [1984]: 3-17), and Ralph P. Martin (in [a] "The Setting of 2 Corinthians," *TB* 37 [1986]: 3-19, [b] "The Opponents of Paul in 2 Corinthians: An Old Issue Revisited," in *Tradition and Interpretation in the New Testament: Essays in Honor of E. Earle Ellis for His 60th Birthday,* ed. Gerald F. Hawthorne with Otto Betz [Grand Rapids: William B. Eerdmans Publishing Company, 1987], 279-89, and [c] "Theological Perspectives in 2 Corinthians: Some Notes," in *Society of Biblical Literature 1990 Seminar Papers,* ed. David J. Lull [Atlanta: Scholars Press, 1990], 240-56) all distinguish between the "super apostles" of 2 Cor 11:5 and the "false apostles" of 11:13. The former they identify as the Jerusalem Apostles under the leadership of James and Cephas; the latter represent a group of Judaizers acting as their emissaries.

[130]To illustrate: Georgi maintains that "the adversaries in 1 Cor were Gnostics, and those of 2 Cor were shaped by Hellenistic-Jewish Apologetics" (*The Opponents,* 317). Marshall ("Hybrists Not Gnostics") examines the same evidence and concludes that both letters are directed against a single group of opponents. Jerome Murphy-O'Connor ("*Pneumatikoi* and Judaizers in 2 Cor 2:14-4:6," *AusBR* 34 [1986]: 42-58, and "Pneumatikoi in 2 Corinthians," in *Proceedings of the Irish Biblical Association,* 11, ed. Martin McNamara [Dublin: Irish Biblical Association Publications, 1987], 59-66) understands 2 Corinthians to be concerned with two different groups--namely, (1) the Judaizing "super apostles," and (2) a group of hellenistic-Jewish pneumatics (= the Apollos-group) who brought a Philonic perspective to the preaching of the gospel. Sumney (*Identifying Paul's Opponents*) reads the same text and discovers only one group of opponents, whom he characterizes as "pneumatics."

In an essay entitled "Paul and His Opponents: Trends in the Research" (in *Christianity, Judaism and Other Greco-Roman Cults: Studies for Morton Smith at Sixty. Part One: New Testament,* ed. Jacob Neusner, Studies in Judaism in Late Antiquity, 12 [Leiden: E. J. Brill, 1975],

of these issues is beyond the scope of this study. However, we will proceed on the basis of the following assumptions: First, 2 Cor 10:1-13:10 is a unity, addressed by Paul to the church at Corinth, whether it was originally attached to chapters 1-9 or not.[131] Second, the Apostle's words are primarily directed against a single group of opponents (hereafter referred to as the "super apostles"), although he does, of course, have the entire Corinthian situation in mind. Below, we will offer a few observations (primarily from 2 Cor 10-13) concerning the "super apostles'" identity and the kinds of criticisms they leveled against Paul. Afterwards, we will examine Paul's defense, paying close attention to how he interprets his suffering as a Christian and Apostle of Christ.

The "super apostles" of Corinth. It appears that the "super apostles" were a group of Christians[132] of Jewish descent.[133] They were not native

---

264-98), E. Earle Ellis describes the state of scholarly inquiry into the identity of the "super apostles" of Corinth (pp. 285-92), and also of Paul's opponents in Philippians 3, Galatians, Colossians, and the Pastoral Epistles. See also Michel Quesnel, "Paul en Conflit avec les Chrétiens de Son Temps," *FV* 84 (1985): 57-64. Quesnel argues that the teaching of Paul's opponents in Galatia, Colossae and Corinth was marked by a common denial of the Cross or at least a reduction of its importance.

[131]Frances Young and David F. Ford (*Meaning and Truth in 2 Corinthians* [Grand Rapids: William B. Eerdmans Publishing Company, 1987]) join Werner Georg Kümmel (*Introduction to the New Testament,* rev. ed., trans. Howard Clark Kee [Nashville: Abingdon, 1975], 287-93) in arguing for the unity of 2 Corinthians 1-13. However, many scholars view 2 Cor 1-9 (with or without 6:14-7:1 and chapters 8-9) and 10-13 as two (or more) separate letters which were joined together after Paul's death. To illustrate: James Houghton Kennedy (*The Second and Third Epistles of St. Paul to the Corinthians with Some Proofs of Their Independence and Mutual Relation* [London: Methuen & Co., 1900]) put forth the classic hypothesis (later strengthened by Francis Watson in "2 Cor 10-13 and Paul's Painful Letter to the Corinthians," *JTS* 35 [1984]: 324-46) that chapters 10-13 pre-date 1-9 (a letter of reconciliation) and are identical to the "painful letter" mentioned by Paul in 2 Cor 2:4 and 7:8. Jerome Murphy-O'Connor refutes this theory in "The Date of 2 Corinthians 10-13," *BR* 39 (1991): 31-43. For a survey of scholarship on the unity of 2 Corinthians, see Watson, "2 Cor 10-13," 325-31.

[132]2 Cor 10:7 indicates that the "super apostles" claim to "represent Christ."

[133]See 2 Cor 11:22, where Paul describes the "super apostles" as "Hebrews," "Israelites," and "descendants of Abraham." That the "super apostles" took pride in their Jewish roots is shown by 2 Cor 11:21b-22, where Paul identifies "Jewishness" as one sphere in which the "super

to Corinth, but came to the city from some other part of the Roman Empire.[134] They presented themselves to the Corinthians as "apostles sent by Christ"[135] and proceeded to exercise their apostolic authority within the Christian community founded by Paul.[136]

In the past, Paul had shown himself more than willing to work alongside other apostles for the good of the Body of Christ.[137] However, the "super apostles" proclaimed "another Jesus" and "a different gospel" than that which the Corinthians had received from Paul.[138] Furthermore, they tried to turn the church against Paul by calling into question his legitimacy and his qualifications as an Apostle of Christ.[139] This led Paul to reject their apostleship as "false"[140] and to condemn the "super apostles" for "boasting . . . in another person's labors."[141]

---

apostles" "demonstrate boldness." This may also be the thought behind 11:18, where Paul describes his opponents as "boasting in accordance with the flesh."

[134]2 Cor 10:12-18 implies that the "super apostles" have overstepped their bounds by invading the territory which the "God of Measure" had already "allotted" to Paul (see below).

[135]See 2 Cor 11:13; cf. 10:7 ("someone has convinced himself [that he] represents Christ").

[136]Paul says that the "super apostles" desire an opportunity for being exactly like us in what they are boasting" (see 2 Cor 11:12).

[137]Note the spirit of cooperation between Paul and Apollos displayed in 1 Cor 3:5-10: "I planted, Apollos watered, but God makes [the church] grow . . . we are God's fellow-workers."

[138]See 2 Cor 11:4.

[139]The "super apostles" "set themselves forth as approved" by the Lord (2 Cor 10:12, 18); but they have caused the Corinthians to doubt whether Paul is approved (see 13:6: "I hope that you will know that we are not unapproved"), to doubt that Paul "represents Christ" (see 10:7), to seek "proof of Christ's speaking through" him (see 13:3).

[140]See 2 Cor 11:13-15, where Paul describes the "super apostles" as "deceitful laborers who are disguised as apostles sent by Christ," servants of Satan who are "disguised as servants characterized by righteousness."

[141]See 2 Cor 10:15 (discussed below).

The "super apostles'" attack on Paul seems to have centered around his "inferiority" and their own "superiority"[142] (hence Paul's sarcastic references to them as "super apostles"). The "super apostles" possess "knowledge" (γνῶσις) gained through "visions and revelations from the Lord"[143] but claim that Paul lacks "knowledge."[144] The "super apostles" are spiritual[145] but charge that Paul "walks after the manner of the flesh."[146] The "super apostles" display "wisdom" (σοφία) not only in the content of their gospel but also in the skill of their preaching[147] and in its effects--they make the Corinthians "wise."[148] Paul, on the other hand, can offer only "foolishness" (ἀφροσύνη);[149] he is "unskilled as far as speaking is concerned"[150] and his

---

[142]See 2 Cor 12:11: "I was in no respect inferior to [those] 'super apostles'--even if I am nothing." Cf. 11:5-6.

[143]Note that Paul states his intention in 2 Cor 11:21 to "demonstrate boldness" in "whatever [sphere]" the "super apostles" "demonstrate boldness." He then proceeds to boast not only in his Jewish heritage (11:22) and his service to Christ (11:23), but in his "visions and revelations from the Lord (12:1-4). For further discussion, see below.

[144]See 2 Cor 11:6.

[145]They help the Corinthians to "receive" the "Spirit" (see 2 Cor 11:4).

[146]See 2 Cor 10:2.

[147]C. K. Barrett ("Christianity at Corinth," *BJRL* 46 [1964]: 269-97; reprinted in *Essays on Paul*, 1-27) points out that, in the Greek world, σοφία ("wisdom") can denote "a kind of eloquence, a technique for persuading the hearer" (p. 278). Yet "σοφία ('wisdom') is more than technique; it has come to be a way of estimating and assessing life . . . [a] philosophy" (p. 279). For a discussion of the link between "wisdom" and "power" in Jewish thought, see Celine Mangan, "Christ the Power and the Wisdom of God: The Semitic Background to 1 Cor 1:24," in *Proceedings of the Irish Biblical Association, 4 (1980),* ed. Martin McNamara (Dublin: The Irish Biblical Association, 1980), 21-34.

[148]See 2 Cor 11:19.

[149]See, e.g., 2 Cor 11:16: "Let no one reckon me to be a fool. But even if [you do], [then] at least accept me as a fool." This is a present particular conditional statement in which Paul is describing reality as he sees it. The Apostle believes that at least some of the Corinthians actually do consider him to be a "fool."

[150]See 2 Cor 11:6.

"word is counted as nothing."[151] The self-proclaimed "superiority" of Paul's opponents is further exhibited in the way they relate to the Corinthian believers. The "super apostles" "exalt" themselves by treating the Corinthians as slaves and requiring payment for their services.[152] Paul, however, does the opposite: he "humbles himself"[153] and "exalts" the Corinthians by preaching "the gospel about God" to them "free of charge" (see below).[154]

Here we find the key to understanding the conflict between Paul and the "super apostles" of Corinth. Paul came to that city determined to preach "nothing but Jesus Christ, and him crucified."[155] He interpreted Christ's death on the Cross as both (1) Jesus' act of trust in God,[156] and (2) the sacrifice through which God established the "new covenant" based on such trust.[157] Paul called on the Corinthians to respond to God's action in Christ by embracing this "new covenant" righteousness--i.e., by "entrusting" (πιστεύειν) themselves to God as Lord, or "dying with Christ."[158] In both his preaching and his manner of life, Paul demonstrated that such Christ-like

---

[151]See 2 Cor 10:10.

[152]See 2 Cor 11:20: "If someone makes slaves of you, if someone devours [you], if someone takes from [you], if someone arrogantly exalts [him/herself], if someone strikes you upon the face, [then] you put up with it!"

[153]See 2 Cor 11:7; cf. 10:1.

[154]See 2 Cor 11:7-11; cf. 12:14-18 ("I am not seeking your things. Instead, [I am seeking] you."). For further discussion, see below.

[155]See 1 Cor 2:2. For a discussion of this phrase within the context of 1 Cor 1-4, see E. Earle Ellis, "Christ Crucified," in *Reconciliation and Hope: New Testament Essays on Atonement and Eschatology Presented to L. L. Morris on His 60th Birthday*, ed. Robert Banks (Exeter: The Paternoster Press, 1974), 69-75. For a discussion of Christ's Cross as the theological center by which Paul interprets the world, the Christian community in its present cruciform existence, and all humanity, see Ulrich Luz, "Theologia crucis als Mitte der Theologie im Neuen Testament," *EvT* 2 (1974): 116-41.

[156]See part III of chapter 4.

[157]See parts I and II of chapter 4.

[158]See parts I and II of the present chapter.

"trust" takes the form of obedience and self-sacrifice, hard work and suffering, humility and servanthood, selflessness and love[159]--the very kind of love and self-humiliation and self-sacrifice seen, for example, in Paul's decision to preach to the Corinthians "free of charge."[160] Paul proclaimed that those who display such "trust" in the present will be raised to "eschatological life" in the future, when Christ comes again.[161]

Paul portrayed present Christian existence in terms of humility and servanthood, suffering and "death;" but the Apostle's letters reveal a tendency on the part of the Corinthian believers to reject this aspect of his gospel in favor of a more comfortable, a more exalted way of life.[162] If the "super apostles"

---

[159]See above under "Romans 12:1-2 and 15:14-18."

[160]See 2 Cor 11:7, 11 ("Or did I [commit] sin by humbling myself in order that you might be exalted, since I preached to you the gospel about God free of charge? . . . [It is] because I do love you, [is it] not? God knows [I do]!"); 12:14-15 ("I will not be a [financial] burden . . . most gladly will I spend--and be spent fully--for your sakes. If I love you more, then am I loved less?"). Note that, in 2 Cor 11:6-7, Paul identifies the decision to preach to the Corinthians "free of charge" as a manifestation of his "knowledge" (γνῶσις).

[161]See above under "2 Corinthians 5:11, 14-15; 4:10-14; and 7:3b," along with the more detailed discussion of this aspect of Paul's gospel found in chapter 8.

[162]Paul contrasts the life sought by the Corinthians with the life actually lived by himself and his fellow apostles in 1 Cor 4:8-13:

> (8) Already you are filled! Already you have become rich! You have begun to reign without us! Would that you did reign, so that we might reign together with you! (9) [I wish that we could reign now] because I think [that] God has displayed us apostles last [of all], like [prisoners] condemned to death [at the end of a Roman general's "triumph"]; for we have become a spectacle in the eyes of the world, in the eyes of angels, and in the eyes of wo/men. (10) Because of Christ, we [are] fools; but you [are] wise within [the sphere where] Christ [rules]. We [are] weak, but you [are] strong. You [are honored] glorious[ly], but we [are] dishonored. (11) To the present hour we continue to be hungry and thirsty and naked and beaten and homeless. (12) We labor and work with [our] own hands. Although [we] are reviled, we bless. Although [we] are persecuted, we endure. (13) Although [we] are defamed, we speak words of encouragement. We have become like [the] offscouring of the world--[like the] filth which is wiped off all [things]--[even] until now. (On this text, see Karl A. Plank, *Paul and the Irony of Affliction,* The Society of Biblical Literature Semeia Studies [Atlanta: Scholars Press, 1987].)

Paul draws the same sort of contrast in 2 Cor 4:8-12, which highlights the tension between the "overlapping" ages of "the present time":

did not plant this tendency in Corinth, then they at least capitalized on it by preaching "another Jesus"[163]--probably "Jesus Christ, and him glorified," as opposed to Paul's "Jesus Christ, and him crucified." Their "different gospel"[164] called for the Corinthians to show "strength" (δύναμις), as opposed to the contemptible "weakness" (ἀσθένεια) displayed by Paul.[165] The "super apostles" seduced the Corinthians,[166] leading them away from Paul and from the Christ he proclaimed, by advancing what appeared to be a "superior" gospel and a "superior" way of life.

Paul's defense. Paul's defense against the "super apostles" in 2 Cor 10: 1-13:10 consists of an introduction (10:1-6), thesis (10:7-11), three arguments supporting that thesis (10:12-18; 11:1-15; 11:16-12:13), and a lengthy conclusion (12:14-13:10).

The introduction serves to frame Paul's defense as the personal appeal of Christ's Apostle to the Corinthian church. The stated goal of Paul's appeal is to prevent his having to "act boldly against certain [persons]" when he

---

(8) [We apostles] are squeezed (θλίβειν) in every [way], but [we] are not crushed. [We] are uncertain, but [we] do not despair. (9) [We] are persecuted, but [we] are not forsaken. [We] are knocked down, but [we] are not destroyed. (10) [We] are always carrying about in our body (σῶμα) the "death" of Jesus, in order that the "life" of Jesus may also be manifested in our body. (11) For we who are alive are continually being delivered over to "death" for the sake of Jesus, in order that the "life" of Jesus might also be manifested in our mortal flesh. (12) So then, "death" is continually at work in us, but "life" [is continually at work] in you.

[163]See 2 Cor 11:4.

[164]See 2 Cor 11:4.

[165]See, e.g., 2 Cor 10:10-11 ("It is said that 'The letters [are] weighty and powerful, but the coming of the person is weak . . . [he is merely] frightening you with the letters'"); 11:20-21a ("someone makes slaves of you . . . someone devours [you] . . . someone arrogantly exalts [him/herself] . . . To [my own] shame I say that we have certainly been very 'weak' [by not doing likewise]!"); 13:9 ("we rejoice whenever we are 'weak,' but you were being 'strong'").

[166]Paul himself employs this metaphor in 2 Cor 11:1-4.

returns to Corinth for the "third time"[167] and, thereby, to ensure that the Corinthians' "obedience may be made complete."[168]

Paul presents the basic content of his appeal in 10:7-11. He calls into question the criteria by which the Corinthians are discerning who is, and who is not, a legitimate apostle of Christ.[169] Then he puts forward the thesis he intends to prove in the remainder of the letter: "So also [do] we [represent Christ]."[170]

In 10:12-12:13, Paul sets down three arguments supporting this thesis. All three are intended to demonstrate that Paul has "entrusted" himself to God as Lord--he has "died with Christ"--while the "super apostles" have not. "Trust" (πίστις), or "dying with Christ," is the mark of a true Christian and the sign of a true apostle of Christ for Paul (see below).

The initial argument (10:12-18) is grounded in the historical fact that Paul was the first Christian missionary to preach the gospel at Corinth, whereas the "super apostles" did not arrive until later. Paul interprets his temporal precedence as evidence of God's will--as proof that God has appointed him to be Apostle to the Corinthians. When, therefore, Paul exercises apostolic authority over the Corinthian believers, he is not "overextending" (ὑπερεκ-τείνειν) himself (v. 10); he is not going beyond the limits which God has set; he is not "boasting about what is unmeasured" (vv. 13a, 15). Paul is instead boasting "in accordance with the measure--even the limit--which the God of Measure (ὁ θεὸς μέτρου) has allotted to us, so that [it] reaches even as far as

---

[167]See 2 Cor 10:2; 13:1-3, 10.

[168]See 2 Cor 10:6; cf. 13:9.

[169]See 2 Cor 10:7a: "You are looking at things according to [their] outward appearance. If someone has convinced himself [that he] represents Christ, [then] let that [person] re-consider himself."

[170]2 Cor 10:7b.

you" (v. 13b).[171] In other words, he is "trusting" (πιστεύειν) in God; he is submitting to the Lord's revealed will; he is boasting "within [the sphere of] the Lord's [rule]" (v. 17) and thereby proving himself to be a true servant of Christ.

In contrast to Paul, the "super apostles" are interlopers with no respect for the will of God. They have elbowed their way into Paul's appointed field of ministry and are now "boasting about what is unmeasured--[that is, boasting] in other [person]s' labors . . . in [labors] already completed" (vv. 13a, 15-16). They claim to be apostles "approved" by God, but they do not submit to "the God of Measure"--they do not "trust" (πιστεύειν) in Him as Lord. Paul declares that the "super apostles" are "lacking in insight when they measure themselves by themselves and when they compare themselves with themselves" (v. 12b). He warns that the person who "sets him/herself forth as approved--that [person] is not approved. Instead, [it is the person whom] the Lord sets forth as approved [who is approved]" (v. 18). Paul's "trust" (πίστις) in God--displayed in his respect for the "limits" measured out by God--sets him apart from the "super apostles" as a true representative of Christ.

The second portion of Paul's defense (11:1-15) focuses on his "knowledge" (γνῶσις) of Christ (v. 6). What is the content of this "knowledge"? Elsewhere in 2 Corinthians, Paul makes Christ "known" to his converts as one whose "trust" (πίστις) in God[172] led him to express great "love" (ἀγάπη)[173]

---

[171]Paul's respect for the ethnic, geographical, and ministerial limits assigned by God is seen, for example, in (1) Gal 2:7, where Paul says that he has been "entrusted with the gospel for the uncircumcision, just as Peter [has been entrusted with the gospel] for the circumcision," (2) Rom 15:20-21, where Paul writes, "I aspire to preach the gospel where Christ has not been named," and (3) 1 Cor 3:5-6, where the Apostle declares that he "plants" churches, while Apollos "waters" them, because those are the tasks which God "assigned" to each.

[172]On the Cross as "Christ's act of trust," see chapter 4, part III.

[173]See 2 Cor 5:14, where Paul sees "Christ's expression of his love" (ἡ ἀγάπη τοῦ Χριστοῦ) in his having "died for all."

and "goodwill" (χάρις)[174] toward all nations through his sacrificial death on the cross.[175] This "knowledge" has "compelled" Paul to adopt the same kind of trust in God[176] and to make that trust "manifest" in a similar act of "love" and "goodwill" toward the Corinthians--namely, the act of preaching "the gospel about God" to them "free of charge" (v. 7).[177] Paul declares that

> Even during [the time] I was present with you, and when I was in need, I was not a [financial] burden to anyone . . . In every [respect] I have kept myself a "light [load]" for your benefit, and I will continue to do [so]. Christ's truthfulness is in me [when I declare] that this boast will not be silenced in me throughout the regions which make up Achaia. Why [will I continue to keep myself a light load for your benefit]? [It is] because I do love (ἀγαπᾶν) you, is it not? God knows [I do]! (2 Cor 11:9-11)

Paul preaches the gospel "free of charge" as an expression of his "love" (ἀγάπη) for the Corinthians. This "love" is evidence of his Christ-like "trust" (πίστις) in God, and this "trust" sets him apart as one who possesses "knowledge" of Christ--a true Apostle and servant of the Lord.[178] The fact that the "super apostles" do collect payment for their services indicates that they

---

[174]See 2 Cor 8:9: "You know our Lord Jesus Christ's expression of his goodwill (ἡ χάρις τοῦ κυρίου ἡμῶν Ἰησοῦ Χριστοῦ): Although rich, he became poor for us, in order that you yourselves, by means of his poverty, might become rich." Compare 2 Cor 6:10 (discussed in note 186), in which Paul characterizes himself and his fellow apostles "as [persons who are] poor, but who enrich many."

[175]See also note 76.

[176]See 2 Cor 4:13 ("we have the same Spirit of trust") and 5:14 ("Christ's expression of his love compels us . . . one has died for all [an act of trust]; therefore all have died [i.e., they embrace Christ-like trust]"), discussed earlier in this chapter.

[177]Compare Paul's action with the action of Christ as described in 2 Cor 8:9 (translated in note 174). E. A. Judge discusses the possible social implications of Paul's refusal to accept monetary support from the Corinthians in "Cultural Conformity and Innovation in Paul: Some Clues From Contemporary Documents," *TB* 35 (1984): 3-24.

[178]That Paul does not oppose payment for ministers in principle is shown by the fact that he accepted financial assistance from "other churches"--including "the brothers who came from Macedonia" (2 Cor 11:8-9; see also 1 Cor 9:3-18; Phil 2:25, 30; 4:10-18). Paul chose not to receive support from the Corinthians because this enabled him to highlight the differences between himself and his opponents, and to "cut off the opportunity from [those 'super apostles' who] desire an opportunity for being exactly like us in what they are boasting" (v. 12).

lack such "knowledge" (They proclaim "another Jesus," a "different gospel" [v. 4].); they do not "love" the Corinthians and do not "trust" in God. Paul therefore condemns them as "false apostles--deceitful laborers who are disguised as apostles sent by Christ," servants of Satan who are "disguised as servants characterized by righteousness (= trust[179])" (vv. 13, 14). He does not "consider [himself] to be inferior, in any way, to the 'super apostles'" (v. 5).

Paul's third argument in defense of his apostleship (11:16-12:13) centers around his suffering for Christ's sake. The "weakness" which the "super apostles" have criticized in Paul is seen most clearly in his suffering, and so Paul's strongest, most effective line of defense consists of turning this weapon back on his opponents. We will examine this third argument in some detail.

The "super apostles" portray Paul as "weak" and "foolish," while they themselves are "strong" and "wise." Paul believes that the reverse is true--that the "super apostles" are "fools" because they refuse to embrace the "wisdom" of God which Paul displays in his so-called "foolishness" and "weakness." Nevertheless, Paul is willing, for the moment, to play the part of a "fool"--to adopt the misdirected values of the "super apostles," to "boast" (καυχᾶσθαι) as they boast--in order to demonstrate his ability to compete with them on their own terms.[180] In 2 Cor 11:16-23a he says:

> (16) I repeat: Let no one reckon me to be a fool. But even if [you do],[181] [then] at least accept me as a fool, so that I too may boast[182] a

---

[179]On "trust" (πίστις) as the content of "new covenant" righteousness, see part II of the present chapter.

[180]Josef Zmijewski provides a close analysis of Paul's "foolish discourse" (2 Cor 11:1-12:10) in *Der Stil der paulinischen "Narrenrede": Analyse der Sprachgestaltung in 2 Kor 11:1-12:10 als Beitrag zur Methodik von Stiluntersuchungen neutestamentlicher Texte,* Bonner Biblische Beiträge, 52 (Köln--Bonn: Peter Hanstein Verlag GmbH, 1978).

[181]This RSV rendering of εἰ δὲ μή γε accurately conveys Paul's meaning. A more literal translation of the phrase would read "but if [this is] indeed not [the case]."

294

little bit. ((17) I am not saying this in accordance with the Lord; instead, I am speaking as a fool on account of the plan behind the boasting (ἐν ταύτῃ τῇ ὑποστάσει τῆς καυχήσεως)[183]--(18) [namely, that] since many [persons] are boasting in accordance with the flesh, I too will boast [in accordance with the flesh].) (19) [I can ask you to accept me as a fool] since you willingly put up with fools, although [you] are "wise." (20) [And I can rightfully say that you willingly put up with fools] because if someone

---

[182]C. K. Barrett ("Boasting [καυχᾶσθαι, κτλ.] in the Pauline Epistles," in *L'apôtre Paul: Personnalité, Style et Conception du Ministère*, ed. A. Vanhoye, Bibliotheca Ephemeridum Theologicarum Lovaniensium, 73, [Leuven: University Press, 1986], 363-68) correctly notes that the Pauline "theme of καυχᾶσθαι ['boasting']" is "bound up with that of πεποιθέναι ['to express confidence in someone/something']" (pp. 367-68). Paul is not against "boasting" in principle but follows the LXX in speaking of this practice "in both bad and good senses" (p. 363), depending on the ground or object of one's "boast." Barrett criticizes both (1) C. H. Dodd's "psychological interpretation" (see "The Mind of Paul: I," in *New Testament Studies* [Manchester: University Press, 1953], 67-82), which defines Paul's "boast" as "intense national feeling" (p. 364) "replaced by pride in the cross" (p. 365), and (2) Rudolf Bultmann's "theological interpretation" (see *TDNT*, 3:645-54), in which "Paul's fundamental attitude to boasting is that καυχᾶσθαι ['to boast'] means self-confidence before God and is, therefore, the opposite of πίστις ['trust']" (p. 366).

[183]The phrase ἐν ταύτῃ τῇ ὑποστάσει τῆς καυχήσεως ("on account of the plan behind the boasting") is difficult. The key to discerning Paul's meaning lies with the word ὑπόστασις, which is almost impossible to translate. The term seems to refer to a "transcendent reality," or the "reality behind the appearance" of some person or thing. To illustrate: Hebrews 1:3 describes Jesus as the "radiance of [God's] glory (δόξα) and the exact representation of His reality (ὑπόστασις)." God is the glorious "Light," the Source of the "radiance" who is Jesus; God is the invisible "reality" (ὑπόστασις) behind His visible "representation," who is Jesus. God is the "reality behind the appearance" (the ὑπόστασις), who is Jesus Christ.

In 2 Cor 11:17, the noun ὑποστάσει ("the reality behind the appearance") functions as an instrumental of cause, modified by the demonstrative adjective ταύτῃ ("that"), and governed by the causal preposition ἐν ("because of," "on account of"). Καυχήσεως ("boasting") is an adjectival genitive modifying ὑποστάσει ("the reality behind the appearance"). The clause may be literally translated: "on account of that reality [which is] behind the boasting." What "reality" (ὑπόστασις) does Paul have in mind? The Apostle is speaking of his stated intention to boast as a fool ("accept me as a fool, so that I too may boast a little bit," v. 16)--the same plan referred to in v. 18:

(17) I am not saying this in accordance with the Lord; instead, I am speaking as a fool on account of that reality [which is] behind the boasting--(18) [namely, that] since many [persons] are boasting in accordance with the flesh, I too will boast [in accordance with the flesh].

Since the "reality" (ὑπόστασις) behind Paul's boasting is his plan to boast as a fool, the phrase ἐν ταύτῃ τῇ ὑποστάσει τῆς καυχήσεως in 2 Cor 11:17 is best rendered: "on account of the plan behind the boasting."

2 Corinthians 9:4 provides a nearly exact parallel, involving only a slight shift in word order (ἐν τῇ ὑποστάσει ταύτῃ τῆς καυχήσεως as opposed to ἐν ταύτῃ τῇ ὑποστάσει τῆς καυχήσεως). In this context, the "plan behind [Paul's] boasting" is his long-standing promise to deliver a collection for the poor Judean saints.

makes slaves of you, if someone devours [you], if someone takes from [you], if someone arrogantly exalts [him/herself], if someone strikes you on the face, [then] you put up with it! (21) To [my own] shame I say that we have certainly been very "weak" [by not doing likewise]![184]

In whatever [sphere] someone may demonstrate boldness (I am speaking foolishly.), I also will demonstrate boldness. (22) Are they Hebrews? I [am] also. Are they Israelites? I [am] also. Are they descendants of Abraham? I [am] also. (23a) Are they Christ's servants? (I am speaking in the manner of a fool.) I [am] more so.

At this point in the argument, the reader expects Paul the "fool" to provide proofs of his "strength" and his "wisdom" which demonstrate to the "super apostles'" satisfaction that he, too, is an exalted "servant of Christ"--their equal, or even their "superior" ("I am more so") in "knowledge," ability and power. Instead, Paul suddenly begins to boast in his "weaknesses" (ἀσθε-νείαι)--to boast in those very aspects of his ministry that his enemies cite as proof that he does not represent Christ:

(23b) [I have been involved] in labors even more so. [I have been] in prisons even more so. [I have suffered] with beatings much more severely. [I have] repeatedly [been] in danger of death. (24) Five times have I received forty [lashes]-less-one[185] from Jews. (25) Three times have I been beaten with rods. Once have I been stoned. Three times have I been shipwrecked; a day and a night have I spent in the open sea. (26) [I have been] on journeys often. [I have been] in dangers from rivers, in dangers from bandits, in dangers from [my own] people, in dangers from Gentiles, in dangers in the city, in dangers in the country, in dangers at sea, in dangers among false brothers. (27) [I have experience] with labor and toil, with frequent sleeplessness, with hunger and thirst, with frequent fasting, with cold and the lack of sufficient clothing. (28) Apart from [these] external [things], [there rests] upon me, from day to day, the burden of concern for all the churches. (29) Who is weak and I am not weak? Who is caused to stumble and I am not burning [with anger]? ((30) If boasting becomes necessary, [then] I will boast in those things which spring from my "weakness." (31) The God and Father of the Lord Jesus, who is

---

[184]Paul here employs biting sarcasm in an effort to loosen the "super apostles'" grip on the Corinthian church.

[185]On the "forty [lashes]-less-one from Jews," see S. Gallas, "'Fünfmal vierzig weniger einen . . .': Die an Paulus vollzogenen Synagogalstrafen nach 2 Kor 11:24," *ZNW* 81 (1990): 178-91.

blessed forever, knows that I am not lying.) (32) In Damascus, king Aretas' governor was guarding the city of the Damascenes in order to arrest me. (33) But I was let down through a window--through the wall--in a rope-basket, and I escaped from his clutches. (2 Cor 11:23b-33)[186]

When Paul is not playing the part of a "foolish" "super apostle"--when he speaks as a true Apostle of Christ--then he boasts only "in those things which spring from [his] 'weakness'" (v. 30). The "tribulation list"[187] in 2 Cor 11:23b-33 shows that "those things which spring from [Paul's] 'weakness'" consist largely of sufferings and hardships endured in the course of carrying out

---

[186]Compare 2 Cor 6:4-10:

(4) We commend [our]selves as God's servants in every [circumstance]: in great patience, in sufferings, in wants, in pressures, (5) in strokes [of the whip], in imprisonments, in disturbances, in labors, in wakefulness, in fastings, (6) in purity, in knowledge, in forbearance, in kindness, in the Holy Spirit, in love without hypocrisy, (7) in [the] word [which is] truth, in [the] strength of God; through the weapons of righteousness for the right [hand] and for the left; (8) through ill repute and good repute; as deceitful [persons] and truthful [persons]; (9) as [persons who] are not known and [persons who] are [well-]known; as [persons who] are dying and, behold, we live; as [persons who] are disciplined and not killed; (10) as [persons who] are grieving but [who] rejoice forever; as [persons who are] poor, but who enrich many; as [persons who] have nothing and who possess all [things].

[187]Robert Hodgson ("Paul the Apostle and First Century Tribulation Lists," *ZNW* 74 [1983]: 59-80) builds upon the work of (1) Rudolf Bultmann (*Der Stil der paulinischen Predigt und die kynisch-stoische Diatribe*, Forschungen zur Religion und Literatur des alten und neuen Testaments, 13 [Göttingen: Vandenhoeck & Ruprecht, 1910]), who stresses the Stoic influence on Paul, and (2) Wolfgang Schrage ("Leid, Kreuz und Eschaton: Die Peristasenkataloge als Merkmale paulinischer theologia crucis und Eschatologie," *EvT* 34 [1974]: 141-75), who stresses Jewish apocalyptic, in order to set forth "a history of religions background for Paul's tribulation lists" (p. 59). Hodgson shows that Josephus, the Nag Hammadi Library (gnostic), the Mishnah (Pharisaic Judaism), and Plutarch and Arrian (especially in the Twelve Labors of Heracles) further illumine the tribulation lists in Paul.

John T. Fitzgerald (*Cracks in an Earthen Vessel: An Examination of the Catalogues of Hardships in the Corinthian Correspondence*, Society of Biblical Literature Dissertation Series, 99 [Atlanta: Scholars Press, 1988]) argues that Paul's "tribulation lists" most closely resemble those used in the Graeco-Roman world to describe the wise man as the "suffering sage." His sufferings serve "as a depiction and demonstration of the sage's various qualities as the ideal philosopher" (p. 203). They "show him to be virtuous because *peristaseis* ('hardships') have a revelatory and probative function in regard to character . . . [they serve as] proof that he is a man of genuine worth and/or a true philosopher" (p. 203). "Hellenistic philosophers use the figure of the suffering sage in order to admonish their students and set before them the proper model for their conduct. Similarly, in 1 Cor 4 [and here in 2 Cor 11] Paul presents himself as a model and admonishes his young converts by means of the catalogue that he compiles" (p. 204).

his ministry as an Apostle of Christ. What exactly does Paul mean by "weakness" (ἀσθένεια)?[188] and what is the relationship between Paul's "weakness" and his suffering for Christ's sake?

In the context of his defense against the "super apostles," Paul employs the term "weakness" (ἀσθένεια) in order to speak of "trust" (πίστις). Paul normally describes the Lord's death on the cross as "Christ's act of trust" (πίστις Ἰησοῦ Χριστοῦ),[189] but here he maintains that Christ was "crucified because of 'weakness'" (2 Cor 13:4, discussed below). Paul normally speaks of his own Christ-like "trust" in God, or "death with Christ;"[190] but here he speaks of his "weakness." Paul normally speaks of suffering brought on by "trust" in God,[191] but here he speaks of hardships "which spring from [his] 'weakness.'" The "super apostles" are aware of Paul's suffering, and they interpret it as "weakness"--as proof that he does not represent Christ. Paul accepts his opponents' terminology, but he rejects their interpretation of the suffering--or "weakness"--he endures in the course of carrying out his apostolic commission. Paul believes that what the "super apostles" perceive to be "weaknesses" are actually manifestations of his "trust" in God and sure proof that he is a true Apostle and representative of Christ. Paul will press this point later in his argument, but he first returns to the "foolishness" of boasting in "strengths" in

---

[188]David Alan Black (in [1] "*Paulus Infirmus*: The Pauline Concept of Weakness," *GTJ* 5 [1984]: 77-93, and [2] *Paul, Apostle of Weakness: Astheneia and its Cognates in the Pauline Literature* [New York: Peter Lang, 1984]; see also "Weakness Language in Galatians," *GTJ* 4 [1983]: 15-36) argues that "the central idea in the Pauline weakness motif is that the greatest revelation of divine power has occurred in the person and work of Jesus Christ in the midst of his human and earthly existence" (*Apostle of Weakness*, 250). In other words, Paul's focus is human weakness as "the showplace of God's might" ("*Paulus Infirmus*," 86-89). Michael L. Barré ("Qumran and the 'Weakness' of Paul," *CBQ* 42 [1980]: 216-27) offers an alternative view--namely, that ἀσθένεια ("weakness"), in 2 Cor 10-13, "describes the condition of Paul caused by the 'thorn in the flesh'" (see below), which Barré understands to be "persecution by adversaries" (p. 225).

[189]See above under "Jesus' trusting death."

[190]See parts I and II of the present chapter.

[191]See our earlier discussions of "Christian suffering as a manifestation of trust" and "Suffering as trust (among the Thessalonians)."

order to heighten further the contrast between himself and the "super apostles" of Corinth.

> (1) [I] must go on boasting--even though [I] certainly do not gain [anything by it]. But I will go on to visions and revelations from the Lord.[192] (2) I know a man within [the sphere of] Christ['s rule] (ἐν Χριστῷ) who, fourteen years ago (Whether [it was] in the body, I do not know; whether [it was] outside of the body, I do not know. God knows.), was caught up (this same man) as far as the third heaven. (3) And I know that this same man (Whether [it was] in the body or apart from the body, I do not know. God knows.) (4) was caught up into Paradise, and [that] he heard inexpressible things--[things] which a human being is not permitted to speak. (2 Cor 12:1-4)

Verse 7 (see below) makes it evident that Paul is speaking of himself, but the Apostle is so reluctant to participate in this kind of "foolish" boasting that he speaks of his "visions and revelations from the Lord" in the third person. The "real" Paul, who will boast only in his "weaknesses" (i.e., his "trust"), emerges once again in the parenthetical statement found in vv. 5-6:

> ((5) I will boast on behalf of this man, but I will not boast on behalf of myself--unless [I am boasting] in "weaknesses." (6) [I will only boast in "weaknesses"] because if I should ever desire to boast, [then] I will not be a fool. [I will not be a fool] because I will speak truth. But I am presently holding back [from speaking truth]. Let no one consider me [to be] more than what s/he [actually] sees me [to be], or [more than] what s/he [actually] hears from me.)

In other words, the Corinthians must take care not to confuse the "real" Paul, who boasts only in his "weakness," with the "foolish" Paul who, for the sake of

---

[192]In an article entitled "'Paul the Visionary': The Setting and Significance of the Rapture to Paradise in 2 Corinthians 12:1-10" (*NTS* 25 [1979]: 204-20), A. T. Lincoln sees "no necessity for treating this visionary experience of Paradise as an event which was unique to Paul and happened only this once in the life of the church . . . it can be seen as part of the manifestation of the Spirit in the Christian community" (p. 219). Lincoln correctly observes that "Paul will not use such an experience as evidence for his apostleship, and, since for him the question of apostleship is integrally related to that of the nature of Christian existence, neither will he use it as evidence for his belonging to Christ" (p. 219). See also Russell P. Spittler, "The Limits of Ecstasy: An Exegesis of 2 Corinthians 12:1-10," in *Current Issues in Biblical and Patristic Interpretation: Studies in Honor of Merrill C. Tenney Presented by His Former Students,* ed. Gerald F. Hawthorne (Grand Rapids: William B. Eerdmans Publishing Company, 1975), 259-66.

argument, boasts in his Jewish heritage and in "visions and revelations from the Lord." The Corinthians must not fail to see the difference between the "super apostles" and one who truly "represents Christ."

Paul gives the reason for his resolve to boast only in "weaknesses" in 12:7-10. Here we find the heart of Paul's argument, the core of his defense, and the "coherent center" of his theology. The Apostle begins, in vv. 7-8, with a reference to what he calls his "thorn in the flesh":

(7) Now for this reason--[even] because of the outstanding quality of [these] revelations--a "thorn in the flesh (σκόλοψ τῇ σαρκί)[193] was given to me so that I might never become haughty. [This] messenger from Satan (ἄγγελος σατανᾶ) [was given to me] in order that it might buffet me, so that I might never become haughty. (8) I made appeal to the Lord three times concerning this ["thorn in the flesh"], that it might depart from me.

The exact nature of Paul's "thorn in the flesh" remains a mystery. "Thorn in the flesh" (like "messenger from Satan") is a figure of speech which could refer to virtually anything that affected Paul in an adverse manner (including a literal "thorn in the flesh" or "angel from Satan"). Most scholars speculate that the Apostle is thinking of (1) some sort of physical ailment,[194]

---

[193]David M. Park ("Paul's Σκόλοψ τῇ σαρκί: Thorn or Stake? [2 Cor 12:7]," NovT 22 [1980]: 179-83) shows that the Greek word σκόλοψ was most often used of a "thorn," a "stake" (an instrument used in war or torture), or a "cross." "The noun was not imputed with the connotation of 'cross' until the time of Origen, almost two hundred years after the death of Paul" (p. 180). However, "the definitions 'stake' and 'thorn' appear equally valid" as possible interpretations for the term in 2 Cor 12:7. "The meaning 'stake' is suggestive of the intensity of the Apostle's suffering. The definition 'thorn' emphasizes the superficiality of the affliction" (pp. 182-83). Since Park assumes that Paul's σκόλοψ was a "severe" physical malady "inflicting extreme pain and discomfort," he prefers to translate the term as "stake" (p. 183).

[194]Alan Hisey and James S. P. Beck ("Paul's 'Thorn in the Flesh': A Paragnosis," JBR 29 [1961]: 125-29) go so far as to suggest "subarachnoid hemorrhage occurring first in the occipital lobe of one of the cerebral hemispheres, then spreading into the adjacent auditory receptive areas of the temporal lobe," resulting in "hemianopsia and/or aphasia," possibly accompanied by "minor epileptiform attacks" (p. 129).

(2) one or more of his adversaries, or (3) the temptation to engage in sinful behavior.[195]

Perhaps the best way to approach this problem would be to ask: What would the "thorn in the flesh" have to be in order for Paul to see fit to mention it at this point in his defense against the "super apostles"? The most probable answer is that Paul's "thorn in the flesh" was something preventing him from boasting in his "strength," as the "super apostles" would expect a true apostle to do. It was something preventing Paul from being "haughty," as the "super apostles" were "haughty." The "thorn in the flesh" was some sort of "weakness," from which Paul could find no release, and on account of which the "super apostles" would reject him as a true, authoritative representative of Christ.

Paul "made appeal to the Lord three times concerning this ['thorn in the flesh'], that it might depart" from him; but the Lord reassured his chosen Apostle that, in truth, he lacked nothing. In 2 Cor 12:9a Paul writes:

> Then He has said to me, "My expression of my goodwill (ἡ χάρις μου) is enough for you, for strength (δύναμις) achieves its intended end (τελεῖ-ται[196] within [the sphere where] 'weakness' [is the rule] (ἐν ἀσθενείᾳ)."

---

[195]In "The Thorn that Stayed: An Exposition of 2 Corinthians 12:7-9" (*Int* 13 [1959]: 409-16), Neil Gregor Smith provides a brief historical survey of some of the major theories:

> Tertullian had heard that the apostle suffered from a severe pain in the head or ears, and assumed that this was his thorn in the flesh. Chrysostom thought that the reference was not to a physical infirmity, but to the opposition of adversaries such as Alexander the Coppersmith, or Hymenaeus of Philetus . . . Many of the mediaeval commentators assumed that the "thorn in the flesh" was a temptation to lust, an interpretation encouraged by the Vulgate rendering, *stimulus carnis*. Calvin, who rejected this interpretation as a preposterous fancy, put forward a suggestion, equally fanciful, that the reference was to all sorts of temptations which assailed him in the flesh. Later scholars have suggested epilepsy (Lightfoot), a malady of the eyes, or a tendency to contract malarial fever (p. 410).

For further discussion of Paul's "thorn in the flesh," see the studies in the bibliography by Goddard and Cummins, Heckel, Leary, McCant, Mullins, R. M. Price, and Woods.

[196]As the noun τέλος is often used of the intended "end" or "goal" or "outcome" of a given action, so does the verb τελεῖν ("achieves its intended end") express the "fulfilment" or "achievement" or "completion" of a given end. Barré ("Qumran," 222) suggests that the verb should here be rendered "is accomplished" or "achieves its purpose."

What is the meaning of this word from the Lord? We know from our earlier discussion that "[Christ]'s expression of [his] goodwill" (ἡ χάρις μου) is a reference to his sacrificial death on the cross,[197] through which God gave the "blessing" of the "new covenant" to all who trust in Him. "Strength" (δύναμις) is a term used by Paul to refer to the power by which God raises the dead to "eschatological life."[198] "Weakness" (ἀσθένεια) is employed, in the Corinthian context, to speak of "trust" (πίστις) in God, or "dying with Christ" (see above). Against this background, the Lord's word to Paul may be paraphrased as follows:

> Your participation in the "new covenant" based on trust ("my expression of my goodwill") is sufficient, for God exercises His power to raise the dead ("strength achieves its intended end") within the context of trust in Him ("within the sphere of 'weakness'").

The "super apostles" reject Paul's displays of trust--particularly his willingness to suffer--as "weakness" unbecoming of a "strong" representative of Christ. However, the Lord has reaffirmed for Paul that such "weakness" marks the arena within which true "strength" will be exercised--namely, the "strength" (δύναμις) of God which raises the dead. Since Paul's deepest desire is to "attain to the Resurrection of the dead,"[199] he is content to endure the "super apostles'" scorn and to remain within the sphere of "weakness." Since those reckoned "righteous" under the "new covenant" are promised a place in God's coming eschatological Rule,[200] Paul is content to embrace "the righteousness based on trust." Since those who "die with Christ" will also "live"

---

[197]See note 174, along with the portion of chapter 4 marked "An Act of Christ."

[198]See chapter 5 under ". . . he is alive because of God's strength," along with the discussion of "Resurrection as God's act of 'strength'" in chapter 8.

[199]See Phil 3:11.

[200]See above under "2 Corinthians 5:11, 14-15; 4:10-14; and 7:3b."

with him,[201] Paul is content to suffer as a servant of the Lord. In 12:9b-10
he writes:

> (9b) Most gladly, therefore, will I boast all the more within [the sphere
> where] my "weaknesses" [are the rule] (ἐν ταῖς ἀσθενείαις μου), so that the
> strength [which is] Christ (ἡ δύναμις τοῦ Χριστοῦ) may "pitch its tent" upon
> me. (10) For this reason, I am delighted [to be] within [the sphere where]
> "weaknesses" [are the rule] (ἐν ἀσθενείαις)--[that is,] within [the sphere
> where] indignities, needs, persecutions and pressures [suffered] for the
> sake of Christ [are the rule]. [I am delighted to be within the sphere
> where "weaknesses" are the rule] because whenever I am "weak," then am
> I "strong"!

Here we have the unchanging "truth which is the gospel," the "coherent
center" of Paul's theology, expressed in terms of "weakness" and "strength"[202]
--in language ideally suited to the contingent situation the Apostle faced at
Corinth.[203] Paul's ultimate defense against the "super apostles" is the gospel
of Christ--the gospel which gives the promises of God not to the "wisdom" and
"strength" and self-aggrandizement of the "super apostles," but to the "foolishness" and "weakness" and self-humiliation of trusting, suffering Christians like
Paul.[204]

---

[201]See note 203.

[202]Gerald G. O'Collins focuses on Paul's use of these terms in 2 Cor 12:9-10 in "Power
Made Perfect in Weakness: 2 Cor 12:9-10," *CBQ* 33 (1971): 528-37.

[203]Compare (1) 2 Cor 12:9a and (2) 2 Cor 12:10b with, for example, (3) Rom 1:17 and (4)
Rom 6:8:

(1) Within [the sphere where] "weakness" [is the rule]	[God's] strength achieves its intended end.
(2) Whenever I am "weak,"	then am I "strong"!
(3) The [person reckoned] righteous on the basis of trust	will live ["eschatological life"].
(4) Now if we have "died" with Christ,	[then] we trust that we will also come to "life" with him.

See also the Pauline "summary statements" discussed in chapter 1.

[204]Compare 1 Cor 1:17-3:23.

The third portion of Paul's defense against the "super apostles" ends with these words:

> (11) I have become a fool; you have driven me to it. [I can rightfully say that you have driven me to foolishness] because I ought to have been set forth as approved by you. [I can rightfully say that I ought to have been set forth as approved by you] because I was in no respect inferior to [those] "super apostles"--even if I am nothing. (12) The signs distinguishing an apostle were exhibited among you in every [kind of] endurance (ἐν πάσῃ ὑπομονῇ), [and they were] even accompanied by signs and wonders and exhibitions of strength (σημείοις τε καὶ τέρασιν καὶ δυνάμεσιν).[205] (13) [I speak the truth when I say that the signs distinguishing an apostle were exhibited among you in every kind of endurance,] for what is there with respect to which you have been treated worse than the other churches--unless it [is] that I have not been a [financial] burden to you? [Please] forgive me this injustice![206] (2 Cor 12:11-13)

God has designated Christ-like "trust" (πίστις) in Him as the mark of a Christian, the "sign" of a true apostle of the Lord. Paul has consistently exhibited such trust among the Corinthians--most notably in his "endurance" of financial restraint for the sake of that church, and in his persecution for the sake of Christ. On these grounds, Paul maintains that he "ought to have been set forth as approved;" he ought to be recognized by the Corinthians as a true representative of Christ.

---

[205]Paul points to his "endurance" (ὑπομονή) of suffering for Christ's sake as the first and foremost "sign" (σημεῖον) of his apostleship. Σημείοις ("signs"), τέρασιν ("wonders") and δυνάμεσιν ("exhibitions of strength") function here as instrumentals of accompaniment. Margaret E. Thrall (The First and Second Letters of Paul to the Corinthians, The Cambridge Bible Commentary [Cambridge: The University Press, 1965], 180) correctly notes that "the constant fortitude displayed by the apostles is just as much an indication of their genuineness as are their more obviously unusual actions." C. K. Barrett ("Paul's Opponents," 73) agrees:

[T]hough σημείοις τε καὶ τέρασιν καὶ δυνάμεσιν ["signs and wonders and exhibitions of strength"] must refer to the working of miracles, Paul is careful to place such signs in a context determined by ἐν πάσῃ ὑπομονῇ ["every (kind of) endurance"]; that is, the stress lies not on miracles as such but on the fact that they are integrated into the apostolic ministry of service and suffering, in which they play only a subordinate part.

[206]Once again, the Apostle employs stinging sarcasm.

Confidence in his gospel and his apostleship radiates from the conclusion of Paul's defense in 2 Cor 12:14-13:10. Paul is unapologetic about his refusal to accept monetary support from the Corinthians,[207] and he boldly exerts his apostolic authority over that congregation. He informs the Corinthians that he is about to make a third visit to their city,[208] and he demands that they put their house in order. In 13:2b-5a he issues this warning to "those who have sinned, along with all the rest":

> (2b) If I should ever come to [you] again, I will not hold back. (3) Since you are seeking proof of Christ's speaking through me, he will not show weakness to you; instead, he will demonstrate strength among you. (4) [I can rightfully say that Christ will demonstrate strength] because he was indeed crucified because of "weakness," but he is alive because of God's strength. And [I can rightfully say that he will exercise this strength among you through our apostolic ministry (rather than that of the "super apostles")] because we ourselves are now "weak" within [the sphere ruled by] him--but we will live along with him because of the strength God [will demonstrate] toward you. (5) Test yourselves [to determine] whether you are within [the sphere where] trust [is the rule] (ἐν τῇ πίστει)!

Verse 4 is a Pauline "summary statement," in which the Apostle sets forth, in abbreviated fashion, the four ideas which together form the "coherent center" of his gospel:[209]

(1) "[Christ] was crucified because of 'weakness'"--i.e., he accepted death on the cross because of his trust (πίστις) in, or self-humiliation before God.[210] Through Christ's sacrificial death, God established the "new covenant" under which God has promised to raise to "eschatological life" those who trust (πιστεύειν) in Him.[211]

---

[207]See 2 Cor 12:14-19.

[208]See 2 Cor 12:14; 13:1.

[209]See chapter 1 under "Pauline 'summary statements.'"

[210]See part III of chapter 4.

[211]See parts I and II of chapter 4.

(2) "He is alive because of God's strength." God raised Christ from the dead and exalted him to the highest place as the Second Adam and the Davidic King--the one who rules over all Creation as God's vicar, the one who exercises God's kingly power or "strength."[212]

(3) "We ourselves are now 'weak' within [the sphere ruled by] him." Christians are persons who submit to Christ's kingly Rule, who embrace the "new covenant," who exercise the same sort of "weakness"--or trust (πίστις) in God (through Christ)--which Christ himself displayed in accepting "the death which is the cross."[213]

(4) "We will live along with him because of the strength God [will demonstrate]." Christians who entrust (πιστεύειν) themselves to God--who participate in the "new covenant" based on trust--will be raised to "eschatological life" in the future, just as Christ was raised in the past.[214]

Paul is convinced that Christ will "demonstrate strength" among the Corinthians because God has raised him from the dead and made him Lord of all. Paul is convinced that Christ will exercise his "strength" through him and his fellow-workers (rather than through the "super apostles") because they submit to the Lord's Rule in the "weakness" of trust--they are true servants and apostles of Christ. Paul is convinced that he and his companions will "live along with" Christ in the coming Resurrection of the "righteous" because they participate in the "new covenant" under which persons are reckoned "righteous" on the basis of trust. Paul knows that the Corinthians will share in the Resurrection only through embracing this same "weakness," this same Christ-like trust. He therefore commands his erring converts, in v. 5, to "test" themselves to determine whether they "are within [the sphere of] trust."

---

[212]See parts I and III of chapter 5.

[213]See parts I and II of the present chapter.

[214]See above under "2 Corinthians 5:11, 14-15; 4:10-14; and 7:3b," along with the more complete discussion of these matters in chapter 8.

Later, in v. 9, Paul offers his own judgment: "We rejoice whenever we are 'weak,' but you were being 'strong.'" Nevertheless, Christ's appointed Apostle to the Gentiles continues to pray for the Corinthian's "completion."

Suffering as a manifestation of trust. His defense against the "super apostles" provides an excellent example of how Paul was able (in Beker's terms) to "incarnate" the "coherent center" of his gospel into "the particularity of historical occasions and contexts," so that "in each new situation the gospel comes to speech again" as a "word on target" for that situation.[215] Paul normally speaks of "trust" (πίστις) and "righteousness" (δικαιοσύνη) and "dying with Christ" (ἀποθνῄσκειν σὺν Χριστῷ), of "resurrection" (ἀνάστασις) and "eschatological life" (ζωὴ αἰώνιος) and the coming "Rule of God" (βασιλεία τοῦ θεοῦ). Here in 2 Cor 10-13, however, he expresses these same ideas in the language of the "super apostles"--i.e., the language of "weakness" (ἀσθένεια) and "strength" (δύναμις).

Paul's discussion of "weakness" in these chapters reinforces our earlier findings concerning his understanding of Christian suffering: First, Paul views suffering as the Christian norm. He expects that Christians will not be "strong,"[216] but that they will live "within [the sphere where] 'weaknesses' [are the rule]--[that is,] within [the sphere where] indignities, needs, persecutions and pressures [suffered] for the sake of Christ [are the rule]."[217] Second, Paul interprets such sufferings as manifestations of Christ-like "trust" (πίστις) in God, as evidence that a person has embraced the "new covenant" and thus "died with Christ."

---

[215]See chapter 1 under "The 'coherent center' of Paul's 'theology.'"

[216]See 2 Cor 13:9.

[217]See 2 Cor 12:10a.

Conclusion

In this chapter we have seen that Paul characterizes Christian existence during the period between Christ's resurrection and Parousia ("the present time") as a "sacrifice," or "death with Christ." Paul employs such metaphors in order to express three "core convictions" concerning what it means to be a Christian: First, Christians have adopted an attitude of Christ-like trust in God, which informs their day-to-day conduct. Second, Christians have embraced the "new covenant" based on trust, which holds the promise of a future Resurrection for the "righteous." Third, Christians have willingly accepted the probability that, like Christ, they too will endure hardship, persecution, or even martyrdom, in the course of carrying out their trustful commitment to God.

Paul devotes more lines to the Christian's "death with Christ" than to any other subject, for this is his "present" concern--both for himself and for his churches. We will examine the Apostle's "core convictions" concerning the Christian's future "resurrection existence" in chapter 8.

CHAPTER EIGHT

PAUL'S INTERPRETATION OF
THE CHRISTIAN'S RESURRECTION TO "LIFE" WITH CHRIST

Earlier in this study we showed that Paul thinks in terms of (1) the past, (2) "the present time" (ὁ νῦν καιρός), and (3) the future.[1] The "past" refers to that portion of the present historical age (or "present evil age," ὁ αἰὼν ὁ ἐνεστηκὼς πονηρός) during which Sin and Death were at the pinnacle of their power. It began with Adam's Fall[2] and ended with Christ's resurrection from the dead. "Jesus' act of trust" (πίστις Ἰησοῦ)--his sacrificial death through which God established the "new covenant" based on trust--took place in the "past" and was the focus of our discussion in chapter 4.

"The present time" refers to the period during which the historical age and the eschatological age "overlap." God has already begun to subdue His enemies, to put an end to Sin and Death; but He has not yet consummated His eschatological Rule (ὁ βασιλεία τοῦ θεοῦ). "The present time" began with Christ's resurrection from the dead and will continue to his "Second Coming," or Parousia (παρουσία). During this interval, the risen Christ enjoys "eschatological life" and reigns as Lord over all Creation. At the same time,

---

[1]See chapter 2 under "'The present time.'"

[2]See chapter 3 under "Adam as initiator of the 'present evil age.'"

Christians embrace God's emerging eschatological Rule by "dying with Christ," or participating in the "new covenant" based on Christ-like trust in God. Christ's present "life" and the Christian's present "death" were discussed in chapters 5 and 7.

The "future" refers to the period when the historical age has completely passed away, so that only the eschatological age remains--the period when God has totally destroyed Sin and death and has established His eschatological Reign in all its fullness. The "future" will begin with Christ's Parousia and will continue forever without end. Christians who welcomed God's Rule during "the present time," who embraced the "new covenant" based on trust, will be raised from the dead to enjoy "eschatological life" with Christ.

In this chapter we will focus on Paul's understanding of the eschatological "future." Part I examines the Apostle's views concerning what will happen at Christ's Return. Part II explores his "core convictions" concerning the Christian's resurrection to "eschatological life" with Christ. The Christian's "life" with Christ (the "future") joins Christ's death (the "past"), Christ's resurrection, and the Christian's "death" with Christ ("the present time"), to form the "coherent center" of Paul's theology.

I. PAUL'S UNDERSTANDING OF THE ESCHATOLOGICAL "FUTURE"

Paul's letters do not provide us with a complete picture of his "future" hope. The Apostle's precise views on a number of issues (particularly the questions of the "intermediate state" and the nature of the Judgment, both discussed below) remain open to debate. Nevertheless, the main features of Paul's eschatology appear to be (1) the Day of the Lord, (2) the Resurrection of the righteous, (3) the Judgment of the righteous and the unrighteous, and (4) the consummated Rule of God. We will trace the contour of Paul's eschatological expectation in the following paragraphs.

The Living and the Dead

Death of the righteous and the unrighteous. Paul saw with his own eyes that Jesus had been raised from the dead, and he inferred that the eschatological age and the promised Resurrection of the righteous had begun in him. Yet he also witnessed the fact that Sin and Death continue to exercise a degree of lordship over human beings during "the present time."[3] Both Christians[4] and non-Christians, the "righteous" (under the "new covenant") and the "unrighteous," continue to die. The "unrighteous" enter the grave because of their own sin and the sin of Adam; the "righteous" (who are "apart from Sin"[5]) taste of death because of Adam's sin alone.[6] Throughout his letters, Paul acknowledges that Death, "the last enemy," has not yet been completely destroyed.[7]

How does Paul conceive of death? What happens to those who pass from this life? The Apostle's letters seem to indicate that the dead cease to exist. To illustrate: 1 Cor 15:12-19 suggests that, apart from the promised "Resurrection" (see below), those who have died--including Christians "who have fallen asleep[8] within [the sphere of] Christ['s rule]"--have simply

---

[3]See chapter 5 under "'The present time.'"

[4]See, e.g., Rom 14:7-9; 1 Cor 15:6, 18, 51; Phil 1:21; 1 Thess 4:13-16; cf. 1 Cor 11:30.

[5]See Rom 6:7, discussed in chapter 6. See also the portion of chapter 2 marked "'Sinners' and 'saints.'"

[6]See chapter 3 under "Adam as the cause of universal death" (in 4 Ezra) and "Adam as the cause of universal death" (in Paul). See also note 28 in chapter 6.

[7]See, e.g., 1 Cor 15:26.

[8]1 Cor 15:6 ("five hundred brothers [and sisters]--most of whom are still living, although some have fallen asleep") shows that Paul employs "sleep" (κοιμᾶν) as a euphemism for death. For further discussion, see note 22.

"perished" (ἀπολλύειν, v. 18).[9] They have no "hope" for any life other than "this life" (v. 19).[10] Such an understanding of death as annihilation, or nothingness,[11] accords well with two features of Paul's thought discussed in chapter 3. First, the Apostle believes that Adam and his descendants were created mortal--that, without access to the "tree of life," all human beings will eventually die.[12] Second, Paul views human beings as psychosomatically indivisible.[13] If the body dies, then the whole person dies with it.

An intermediate state? A number of scholars reject the notion that Paul views death as annihilation on the grounds that certain Pauline passages appear to describe an "intermediate" form of existence between death and the Resurrection.[14] One such passage is 2 Cor 4:16-5:10:

---

[9]See also 1 Cor 1:18 ("the word concerning the Cross is foolishness in the eyes of those who are perishing"); 2 Cor 2:15-16 ("we are the aroma of Christ [ascending] to God among . . . those who are perishing . . . a fragrance from death to [greater] death" [see note 196 on Rom 1:16-17]); 4:3 ("our gospel . . . is hidden among those who are perishing"). Compare Rom 4:17 (God's "making the dead alive" as His "calling into existence things which do not exist" [καλοῦν-τος τὰ μὴ ὄντα ὡς ὄντα]); 8:20-21 ("the Creation has been subjected to futility . . . the slavery which is corruption"), 38-39 ("death . . . will [not] be able to separate [Christians] from God's love"--as it does separate non-Christians?); 1 Cor 6:9 and Gal 5:19-21 ("the unrighteous will not inherit God's [eschatological] Rule," which Paul elsewhere [e.g., in 1 Cor 3:21-23 and Phil 2:9-11] describes as all-inclusive); 2 Cor 4:16 ("our outer person is being destroyed [διαφθείρειν]"); 5:17 and Gal 6:15 (Christians as part of a "new creation"--a re-creation from nothing?); Gal 6:8 ("corruption" as the alternative to "eschatological life"); Phil 1:28 ("destruction" [ἀπώλεια] as the alternative to "salvation"); 3:18-19 ("destruction" [ἀπώλεια] as the "end" awaiting "enemies of the Cross of Christ").

[10]Compare 1 Cor 15:32, where Paul writes: "If the dead are not raised, [then] 'Let us eat and drink, for tomorrow we will surely die.'"

[11]For further discussion of death as annihilation, see below under "Judgment and condemnation for the unrighteous."

[12]See chapter 3 under "Adam's creation" and "Adam's death."

[13]See chapter 3, note 106.

[14]For discussion of the "intermediate state," see (1) Karel Hanhart, *The Intermediate State in the New Testament* (Franeker: T. Wever, 1966), (2) Murray J. Harris, *Raised Immortal: Resurrection and Immortality in the New Testament* (Grand Rapids: William B. Eerdmans Publishing Company, 1983), 133-42, (3) Herman Ridderbos, *Paul: An Outline of His Theology* (Grand Rapids: William B. Eerdmans Publishing Company, 1975), "Section 75. Death Before

312

(16) Therefore we do not lose heart. Although our outer person (ἔξω ἄνθρωπος) is being destroyed, our inner [person] (ἔσω [ἄνθρωπος]) is being renewed daily. (17) [I can rightfully say that our outer person is being destroyed, while our inner person is being renewed,] because our momentary, insignificant suffering (τὸ παραυτίκα ἐλαφρὸν τῆς θλίψεως ἡμῶν) is preparing for us an eternal weight of eschatological glory (αἰώνιος βάρος δόξης[15]), transcendent beyond measure (καθ᾽ ὑπερβολὴν εἰς ὑπερβολήν). (18) [We know this] because we do not focus [our] attention on the [things which] are seen, but [on] the [things which] are not seen. [We focus our attention on the things which are not seen, rather than on the things which are seen,] because the [things which] are seen [are] transitory (πρόσκαιρος), but the [things which] are not seen [are] eternal (αἰώνιος).

(5:1) [I can rightfully say that our outer person is being destroyed, while our inner person is being renewed,] because we know that if our earthly "house" (ἡ ἐπίγειος ἡμῶν οἰκία)--[which is a temporary shelter, a mere] "tent" (τοῦ σκήνους)--should ever be destroyed, [then] we have a "building" (οἰκοδομή) from God, a "house" (οἰκία) not made by [human] hands, eternal [and] eschatological (αἰώνιος)[16] in the heavens. (2) [I speak of our anticipating a permanent, heavenly "house" to replace this temporary, earthly "house"] because, in this ["tent"] (ἐν τούτῳ),[17] we are groaning because we long to clothe ourselves with our "dwelling" (οἰκητήριον) which [is] from heaven. (3) If we have [thus] clothed ourselves, [then] we will certainly not be found naked (γυμνός)! (4) [I can rightfully say that we will not be without a body, or "naked,"] because we who are presently in the "tent" are continually groaning because [we] are weighed

---

the Parousia: The 'Intermediate State'" (pp. 497-508; includes bibliography on p. 497, note 20), and (4) Rudolf Schnackenburg, *New Testament Theology Today* (New York: Herder and Herder, 1963), 89 (includes bibliography in note 2).

[15]The adjective αἰώνιος can communicate both (1) duration ("eternal"), and (2) quality ("eschatological"--see chapter 5 under "Isaiah 26:19 and Daniel 12:2-3 [LXX]"). Both ideas play an important role in this context, inasmuch as Paul focuses on (1) the length of future "eschatological life" in 2 Cor 4:17-5:2, 4, and (2) the "glorious," "heavenly" quality of future "eschatological" existence in 4:17 and 5:1-2, 4. Paul probably intends for his readers to "hear" both connotations of αἰώνιος--especially when they read 2 Cor 4:17 and 5:1. We have therefore translated the single Greek term αἰώνιος with two different English words ("eternal" and "eschatological") in those verses.

[16]Compare v. 4.

[17]See verse 4 and the comment in note 18.

down; for (ἐφ' ᾧ) we do not desire to strip ourselves [of the body],[18] but to clothe ourselves [with the glorious heavenly body], so that the mortal [body] may be swallowed up by "[eschatological] life." (5) The One who has prepared us for this very [event is] God, who has given to us the down-payment [which is] the Spirit (ὁ ἀρραβὼν τοῦ πνεύματος). (6) Therefore [we] are always confident. We know that as long as we are housed (ἐνδημεῖν) in the [mortal] body (σῶμα), we are away (ἐκδη‐μεῖν) from the Lord. (7) [I say that we are not yet with the Lord] because we are presently walking by means of trust (πίστις), not by means of sight. (8) But we are confident and would rather (εὐδοκοῦμεν μᾶλλον) be away (ἐκδημεῖν) from the [mortal] body (σῶμα) and housed (ἐνδημεῖν) with the Lord (πρὸς τὸν κύριον). (9) We therefore have [it] as [our] ambition, whether (εἴτε) we are housed (ἐνδημεῖν) [with the Lord] or (εἴτε) away (ἐκδημεῖν) [from the Lord], to be pleasing in his sight.[19] (10) [We want to be pleasing in the Lord's sight] because all of us must appear before the judgment seat (βῆμα) of Christ, so that each [person] may receive the [judgments appropriate] to the [things] which s/he did while [in] the [mortal] body (διὰ τοῦ σώματος),[20] whether good or bad.

Some scholars[21] understand the Apostle to be speaking of three differ-ent states of being or modes of existence: (1) present bodily existence in the "earthly" body or "house" (5:1), (2) an intermediate "disembodied" state (i.e., the separation of one's psyche [ψυχή] or spirit [πνεῦμα] from his/her body

---

[18]If Paul believes that there is an intermediate, bodiless form of existence between death and the Resurrection, then he "groans" at the thought of it (an attitude toward death quite different from that found in Phil 1:21-23 ["to die is gain"], discussed below). If he does not believe in an intermediate state, then he "groans" at the thought of death/annihilation itself, in which he will be "stripped" of the body (σῶμα)--i.e., "stripped" of himself. The Apostle would rather survive to the Parousia, be transformed and "swallowed up by '[eschatological] life'" (see below), and thus avoid death entirely.

[19]Verse 9 could also be understood as follows: "We therefore have [it] as [our] ambition, whether we are housed [in the mortal body] or away [from the mortal body], to be pleasing in his sight."

[20]The phrase διὰ τοῦ σώματος ("while [in] the [mortal] body") should here be read as an adverbial genitive of time.

[21]These include, for example, (1) C. K. Barrett in *A Commentary on the Second Epistle to the Corinthians,* Harper's New Testament Commentaries (New York: Harper & Row, Publish-ers, 1973), 153-55, 159, (2) Ralph P. Martin, *2 Corinthians,* Word Biblical Commentary (Waco, TX: Word Books, Publisher, 1986), 105-106, (3)Ben F. Meyer, "Did Paul's View of the Resur-rection Undergo Development?" *TS* 47 (1986): 379-82, and (4) Alfred Plummer, *Corinthians,* 153-54.

[σῶμα]), immediately following the Christian's death (i.e., "being destroyed," 4:16), which Paul describes as "nakedness" (γυμνός, 5:3)[22] or being "away

---

[22]In "Some Remarks on the γυμνός in 2 Cor 5:3" (in *Studia Paulina in honorem Johannis de Zwaan septuagenarii,* ed. J. N. Sevenster and W. C. van Unnick [Haarlem: Erven F. Bohn N. V., 1953], 202-14), J. N. Sevenster shows that the term γυμνός ("naked") was sometimes used in the Greek-speaking world to describe the disembodied souls of the dead. Barrett cites several examples of this usage from classical texts in *A Commentary on the Second Epistle to the Corinthians,* 153-54. Rudolf Bultmann (*The Second Letter to the Corinthians,* ed. Erich Dinkler [original German edition], trans. Roy A. Harrisville [Minneapolis: Augsburg Publishing House, 1985], 135-37) does likewise, adding examples from gnostic texts. T. Francis Glasson ("2 Corinthians 5:1-10 versus Platonism," *SJT* 43 [1990]: 145-55) denies the gnostic influence, but finds "many points of contact with Platonism" (p. 155).

Oscar Cullmann (*The Immortality of the Soul or Resurrection of the Dead? The Witness of the New Testament* [London: The Epworth Press, 1958], 48-57) equates the "naked" state referred to in 2 Cor 5:3 with the "sleep" of the departed saints which Paul mentions, for example, in 1 Cor 15:6 and 1 Thess 4:13. However, Ridderbos refutes the "sleep" theory in *Paul,* 497.

Some scholars (e.g., Barrett, 155; Martin, *2 Corinthians,* 106) find a parallel to 2 Cor 5:3 in 1 Cor 15:37, where the Apostle writes:

And what you sow [is] not the body (σῶμα) which will be. Instead, you sow a bare kernel (γυμνὸς κόκκος) of grain, whether it be [a kernel] of wheat, or of some other [grain].

Paul here likens the transformation by which a weak, mortal human "body" (σῶμα) becomes a powerful, immortal "resurrection body" to the metamorphosis by which a "bare kernel" becomes a fully-grown, fully-developed blade of "wheat, or of some other grain." At issue is whether the Apostle's description of a "kernel of grain" as "bare" (γυμνός) reflects a belief that human beings continue to exist in some sort of "bare," or "naked," or disembodied state, during the interval between death and the promised Resurrection of the dead.

1 Corinthians 15:37 should not be interpreted in this way for three primary reasons: First, if the "bare kernel of grain" in this verse refers to something which has no body (a bodiless kernel? a disembodied human psyche?), then it cannot be buried or "sown."

Second, the whole thrust of vv. 35-49 is that God makes different kinds of bodies (σώματα) and that, in some cases, He replaces an old body with a new. In the case of kernels of grain, "[the body] which you sow [is] not the body which will be . . . But God gives it a [new] body as He sees fit" (vv. 37-38). In the case of Christians, "it is sowed a psychical body; it is raised a spiritual body" (v. 44). The "bare kernel of grain" in v. 37 compares to the "psychical body" of v. 44 insofar as both are "bodies" (σώματα), both are "sown," and both receive a new "body" (σῶμα) from God. If the "bare kernel of grain" in v. 37 refers to something which has no body, then it contributes nothing to Paul's argument.

Third, the Apostle plainly states that the "bare kernel" of which he speaks is not a dead, disembodied human being, but "[a kernel] of wheat, or of some other [grain]." If Paul is speaking of a kernel of wheat, then why does he describe it as "naked" or "bare" (γυμνός)? A clue may be found in Matt 6:28-30, where Jesus speaks of the bloom of the wildflower, the mature "body" of the grass, as "clothing":

Why do you worry about clothing? Consider the lilies of the field, how they grow . . . not even Solomon in all his glory was clothed like one of these. If God so clothes the grass of the field . . . , [will He] not much more [clothe] you?

(note continued on next page)

from the body and housed with the Lord" (5:8), and (3) future bodily exist-ence in a new body or "'dwelling' which is from heaven" (5:2).

A closer examination of the text reveals that Paul mentions the theo-retical possibility of a disembodied state[23] only to deny it. He says in 5:3-4 that Christians "will certainly not be found naked!" They "do not desire to strip" themselves of the body completely (i.e., to be "naked" or disembodied), "but to clothe [them]selves [with the glorious heavenly body], so that the mor-tal [body] may be swallowed up by '[eschatological] life.'" Likewise, in 5:8, the phrase "away from the body" does not mean "without a body" or (to use Paul's metaphor) "unhoused." Instead, to be "away from the [mortal] body" (ἐκδημεῖν ἐκ τοῦ σώματος) is to be "housed" (ἐνδημεῖν)--"with the Lord"--in a new body. The Christian's firm hope and sure expectation is not to be rid of the body entirely, but to "trade" the inferior, mortal, earthly body for the superior, immortal, body "from heaven."

2 Corinthians 4:16-5:10 describes only two states of being, two modes of existence for Christians.[24] (Death itself is non-being, non-existence.) Paul

---

When Paul describes a kernel of wheat as "naked," he probably means that it lacks the "cloth-ing" of the full-grown head of grain. In other words, the adjective γυμνός ("naked," "bare") serves to contrast the relatively small, humble, unimpressive body of the "kernel" with the larger, more "glorious" body "God gives" (v. 38) to the mature grain. This interpretation of γυμνός ("naked," "bare") makes good sense in the context of 1 Cor 15:35-49, where Paul's concern is to contrast the Christian's present body of "dishonor" with the coming body of "glory" (v. 43).

In light of these considerations, Victor Paul Furnish (2 *Corinthians: Translated with Introduction, Notes, and Commentary,* The Anchor Bible [Garden City, NY: Doubleday & Com-pany, Inc., 1984], 298) is almost certainly correct when he says:

> The "naked kernel" mentioned in 1 Cor 15:37 is not [or better, "it does not compare to"] the "soul" stripped of its body, but the present, death-ridden body, the person who dies and is buried without yet having received the body to come.

[23]Many in Paul's time understood death as the separation of psyche from body. See chapter 5 under "The classical Greek view" and "Greek influence on the Jews."

[24]Scholars who argue that there is no intermediate state in 2 Cor 4:16-5:10 include (1) Bruce (*1 and 2 Corinthians,* 203-204), (2) Bultmann (*The Second Letter to the Corinthians,* 133 [esp. note 120], 137-38, 140), (3) E. Earle Ellis ("The Structure of Pauline Eschatology [2 Corinthians 5:1-10]," in *Paul and His Recent Interpreters* [Grand Rapids: William B. Eerdmans Publishing

calls the first "our outer person" (ἔξω ἡμῶν ἄνθρωπος, 4:16)[25] because it is visible; it is "seen" (4:18) during "the present time." It is a bodily (i.e., somatic) existence, lived out in a "house" (5:1, 6) or "tent" (5:1, 4) made of flesh and blood. It is temporary, "transitory" (4:18), "momentary" (4:17), because our present bodies are "earthly" (5:1) and "mortal" (5:4), capable of "suffering" (4:17; 5:4) and death ("destroyed," 4:16; 5:1). Paul says that Christians, in their present existence, "walk by means of trust" (πίστις, 5:7). They have not yet gained "sight" of God's eschatological Rule (see below), but they order their lives according to its emerging reality. They are "away from the Lord" (5:6, 9), but they nevertheless "have [it] as [their] ambition . . . to be pleasing in his sight" (5:9). Christians, in other words, "die with Christ."[26]

Paul calls the second form of existence "our inner [person]" (ἔσω ἡμῶν [ἄνθρωπος], 4:16) because--even though it is proleptically present in "the down-payment [which is] the Spirit" (5:5)[27]--it remains "not seen" (4:18); it belongs to the future Resurrection of the righteous (see below). It, too, will be a bodily (i.e., somatic) existence; but the future "resurrection body" will be qualitatively different from the "earthly house" of the present. It will be a "'building' from God," a "'dwelling' which [is] from heaven" (5:1-2, 8-9). It will be "an eternal weight of eschatological glory, transcendent beyond measure (4:17-18; 5:1)--a body "swallowed up by ['eschatological] life'" (5:4). Christians

---

Company, 1961]), and (4) C. F. D. Moule ("St Paul and Dualism: The Pauline Conception of Resurrection," *NTS* 12 [1966]: 120-21).

[25]Barrett (*A Commentary on the Second Epistle to the Corinthians,* 146) correctly observes that "'Inward' and 'outward man' are not the elements of a psychological dualism (of which hardly any trace is to be found in Paul's writing as a whole) but refer to the man of this age and the man of the age to come (cf. the natural body and the spiritual body of 1 Cor 15:44)." (For a survey of opposing views, see p. 147.) Bruce (*1 and 2 Corinthians,* 199) adds: "This 'inner man' is the 'new creation' of 5:17, which will be consummated in the immortal nature to be put on at the resurrection."

[26]See chapter 7.

[27]It is in this hopeful sense that "our inner [person]" is "renewed daily" (2 Cor 4:16). On the Spirit as "down-payment," see chapter 7, note 40.

will be "with the Lord" and they will still seek "to be pleasing in his sight" (5:8-9), for God's eschatological Rule will have come in its fullness and "every knee"[28] will have bowed to Christ (see below).

To summarize: 2 Corinthians 4:16-5:10 contrasts the Christian's present, "earthly" bodily existence with his/her future, "heavenly" bodily existence. Paul mentions the hellenistic notion of the "naked" or disembodied state of the dead only to deny that it plays any role in God's design for His saints.

A second Pauline text which appears to describe an "intermediate" form of existence between death and the Resurrection is Phil 1:18b-26. Paul writes from prison,[29] facing a possible sentence of death.[30] Yet he tells the Philippians:

(18b) I will continue to rejoice. (19) [I predict that I will continue to rejoice] because I know that, through your prayer and the support of the Spirit of Jesus Christ, this will end in my salvation (τοῦτό μοι ἀποβήσεται εἰς σωτηρίαν), (20) in accordance with my eager expectation and hope. [Furthermore, I continue to rejoice because I know] that I will be in no way disgraced,[31] but [that] in all boldness, now as always, Christ will be magnified in my body (σῶμα), whether by means of [my] life or by means of [my] death. (21) [I say that Christ will be magnified whether I live or die] because, for me, living [means] Christ and dying [means] gain (κέρδος). (22) If [I continue] to live in the flesh, [then] this [means] fruitful labor for me. Yet which I will choose I cannot tell (γνωρίειν).[32] (23) I am torn between the two;[33] for I have the desire to depart and be with Christ (σὺν Χριστῷ) ([which would be] much, much better), (24) but [it is]

[28] See Phil 2:10.

[29] See Phil 1:7, 13-14, 17.

[30] See Phil 1:19-23; cf. 2:17.

[31] Gerald F. Hawthorne defends the thesis that Paul's successful avoidance of "disgrace" is the content of his "knowledge" (see v. 19), rather than of his "hope" (v. 20), in *Philippians,* Word Biblical Commentary (Waco, TX: Word Books, Publisher, 1983), 42.

[32] On the meaning of this verb, see Hawthorne, *Philippians,* 47.

[33] "I am torn between the two" is a paraphrase of συνέχομαι ἐκ τῶν δύο, which could be translated more literally as "I am distressed because of the two."

necessary [for me] to remain (ἐπιμένειν) in the flesh for your sake. (25) Convinced of this, I know that I will remain (μένειν) and will continue to stay (παραμένειν) with you all, toward the end of your progress and joy which spring from trust. (26) [I will remain] in order that your boasting in me, within [the sphere ruled by] Christ Jesus (ἐν Χριστῷ Ἰησοῦ), may overflow because of my coming to you again.

Many scholars[34] cite v. 23 ("I have the desire to depart and be with Christ") as proof that Paul expects to enjoy some form of conscious existence immediately following his death. If this is the case, the verse tells us nothing about the nature of the "intermediate" existence apart from its being "with Christ" (σὺν Χριστῷ). Furthermore, Phil 1:23 is the only explicit reference to the "intermediate state" in the Pauline corpus.

Such an understanding of Paul's words is difficult to reconcile with important elements of his thought discussed elsewhere in this study--most notably an anthropology that views human beings as psychomatically indivisible[35] and an eschatology that anticipates a future Day of Resurrection for all the righteous dead (see below). If Paul is a mortal "body" (σῶμα), and the Resurrection of dead "bodies" (σώματα) does not take place until Christ's future Parousia (see below), then how can Paul possibly expect to survive "with Christ" during the interval between his death and the promised Resurrection of the dead? Is Phil 1:23 a mere incidental remark, which should not be taken very seriously?[36] Must we posit some sort of "intermediate" bodily

---

[34]These include, for example, (1) F. W. Beare (*A Commentary on the Epistle to the Philippians*, 3d ed., Black's New Testament Commentaries [London: Adam & Charles Black, 1973], 64-65), (2) Thomas F. Dailey ("To Live or Die: Paul's Eschatological Dilemma in Philippians 1:19-26," *Int* 44 [1990]: 18-28), who envisions "a new mode of consciousness prior to the final resurrection" (p. 28), (3) Gerald F. Hawthorne (*Philippians*, 49-51), who argues for an "intermediate state" followed by the Resurrection, and (4) Ralph P. Martin (*Philippians*, New Century Bible Commentary [Grand Rapids: Wm. B. Eerdmans Publ. Co., 1976], 77-79).

[35]See chapter 3, note 106.

[36]Marvin R. Vincent (*A Critical and Exegetical Commentary on the Epistles to the Philippians and to Philemon*, The International Critical Commentary [Edinburgh: T. & T. Clark, 1897], 29) maintains that

(somatic) existence of the dead? Must we conclude--along with Bruce, Dodd, and others--that Paul's eschatology and/or anthropology have undergone change or development since he wrote his earlier letters?[37] Has Paul, for example, surrendered the idea of a future Day of Resurrection in favor of a series of individual "resurrections" occurring immediately after death?[38] Has

---

> The passage does not lend itself to controversies on the condition of the dead in Christ. It is not probable that the dogmatic consciousness enters at all into this utterance of the apostle . . . Paul throws out, almost incidentally, the thought that death implies, for him, immediate presence with Christ.

[37]Ben F. Meyer conducts a critical examination of this approach to Pauline eschatology in an article titled, "Did Paul's View of the Resurrection Undergo Development?" He describes, for example, the once influential view of Ernst Teichmann (*Die paulinische Vorstellungen von Auferstehung und Gericht und ihre Beziehungen zur jüdischen Apokalyptik* [Freiburg-Leipzig: J. C. B. Mohr, 1896]) and Otto Pfleiderer (*Primitive Christianity: Its Writings and Teachings in Their Historical Connections*, 4 vols., trans. W. Mongomery, ed. W. D. Morrison [Clifton, NJ: Reference Book Publishers, Inc., 1965]), who maintain that the "evolution" of "Paul's thought on the resurrection of the dead" can be "traced through three stages":

> In the first stage (1 Thess 4:13-17) Paul affirmed a resurrection of the dead in the sense of a resuscitation of the corpses of the faithful, an event to take place at the Parousia. In a second, mediating stage (1 Cor 15:50 ff.) he affirmed the annihilation of everything earthly, including the earthly body, and the appropriation of a new, spiritual body--still, however, to take place at the Parousia. In a third and final phase, represented by 2 Cor 5:1 ff. and, still better, by Phil 1:21 ff., resurrection has been abandoned, or abandoned in all but name, in favor of the bestowal of a new body at the moment of death. (p. 367)

Meyer rightly concludes that "there is a total lack of persuasive evidence that Paul's teaching on the resurrection of the dead underwent significant development either between 1 Thess 4 and 1 Cor 15, or between 1 Cor 15 and 2 Cor 5" (p. 382). Ellis makes the same judgment in "The Structure of Pauline Eschatology" (see p. 48), which focuses primarily on 2 Cor 5:1-10. Both writers do, however, find a place for the "intermediate state" in Paul's thought--particularly in Phil 1:23.

[38]W. D. Davies (*Paul and Rabbinic Judaism*, 317-18), Murray J. Harris (*Raised Immortal*, 98-101), and Jac[obus] J. Müller (*The Epistles of Paul to the Philippians and to Philemon*, The New International Commentary on the New Testament [Grand Rapids: Wm. B. Eerdmans Publishing Company, 1955], 63) interpret Phil 1:23 along these lines. Yet D. W. Palmer ("'To Die Is Gain' [Philippians 1:21]," *NovT* 17 [1975]: 203-18) destroys this line of argument with a simple observation:

> Taken in isolation, Phil 1:21-24 might seem capable of such an interpretation; but in the light of other passages in the letter this view is not plausible. For references to the "day of Christ" in Phil 1:6, 10-11, and 2:16 involve an eschatological climax for believers at the parousia. Moreover, although Phil 3:2 is ambivalent, the wording suggests that the resurrection is a definite event, in which Paul hopes to be one participant. Again, Phil 3:20-21 refers to a single act of transformation of the earthly body at the coming of the saviour who is awaited from heaven. These passages [discussed later in this chapter] are consistent with

320

his missionary activity among the Gentiles led Paul to adopt a more characteristically Greek anthropology which holds that each human being possesses an
immortal psyche (ψυχή) that survives the death of his/her body (σῶμα)?[39]
Or can we arrive at an understanding of Phil 1:23 that is both faithful to the
text and consistent with the beliefs expressed in Paul's other writings?

An accurate interpretation of Phil 1:23 begins with three observations.
First, Paul expresses a desire to be "with Christ" (σὺν Χριστῷ). Elsewhere in
his letters, the Apostle employs the phrase "with Christ" (σὺν Χριστῷ) to
describe not an "intermediate" existence between one's death and the Resurrection, but the future, eschatological existence Christians will enjoy after
Christ's Return and the general Resurrection of the righteous.[40] This observation raises the possibility--if not the probability--that Phil 1:23 describes
post-Resurrection existence, rather than an "intermediate state."

Second, Paul says: "I have the desire to depart (ἀναλύειν) and be with
Christ." A striking parallel appears in 2 Cor 5:8, where the Apostle says:
"[We] would rather be away (ἐκδημεῖν) from the [mortal] body (σῶμα) and
housed (ἐνδημεῖν) with the Lord (πρὸς τὸν κύριον)." In the latter text, Paul
describes the Christian's movement from the earthly, mortal bodily existence
of "the present time" to the heavenly, immortal bodily existence of the future
Resurrection (see above). This again raises the possibility--if not the

---

Paul's earlier views, and show that, in Philippians also, an eschatological general resurrection has not been displaced by immediate individual union with Christ at death. (p. 204)

[39]This is the view of C. J. de Vogel ("Reflexions on Phil 1:23-24," *NovT* 19 [1977]: 262-74),
who maintains that "Paul did distinguish between soul and body, . . . he regarded death as leaving the body while the conscious subject, say 'the soul', is living on and entering a new and
more blessed state of life" (p. 273).

[40]See 2 Cor 13:4 ("we will live along with him [σὺν αὐτῷ] because of the strength God [will
demonstrate] toward you" [see the discussion of this verse in chapter 7 under "Paul's defense"]);
1 Thess 4:17 ("Thus will we always be with the Lord [σὺν κυρίῳ]"); 5:10 ("who died for us so
that, whether we are awake or asleep, we might live ['eschatological] life' together with him [σὺν
αὐτῷ]"); cf. 2 Cor 5:8 ("[we] would rather be away from the [mortal] body and housed with the
Lord [πρὸς τὸν κύριον]"); Rom 6:8 ("we will also come to life with him [συζήσομεν αὐτῷ]").

probability--that Phil 1:23 describes post-Resurrection existence, rather than a disembodied "intermediate state."

Third, we must place Phil 1:23 within its larger context. Paul knows that his imprisonment will end in either release and life, or execution and martyrdom. If, on the one hand, the Apostle is released, then he will have two reasons to "rejoice" (v. 18b): First, Christ will continue to "be magnified" in his "body" (i.e., "magnified" in his σῶμα, his person, his life "in the flesh" [v. 24], his present bodily existence; v. 20) because, for Paul, "living [means] Christ" (v. 21).[41] Second, his release from prison and restoration to the churches will allow the Apostle to continue his "fruitful labor" (v. 22) among the Gentiles.

If, on the other hand, Paul should be executed, he would still have reason to rejoice. He says, "Christ will be magnified . . . by means of [my] death" (v. 20). "Dying [means] gain" (v. 21). "To depart" would be "much, much better" (v. 23). How can death be "better" than life in Phil 1:23 when Paul calls it "the wages [paid by] Sin" in Rom 6:23? How can death "magnify" Christ in Phil 1:20 when it is linked with the "fleshly orientation" which opposes Christ in Rom 8:6? How can death be "gain" in Phil 1:21 when Paul calls it an "enemy" in 1 Cor 15:26? The answer becomes clear once we realize that Phil 1:20-23 does not describe every death, but only one particular kind of "death" --namely, the death which Paul may have to endure as a Christian martyr.

---

[41]Paul acknowledges that Christ is Lord (see Phil 2:9-11) and shapes his present bodily existence accordingly (see chapter 7). Hawthorne (*Philippians,* p. 45) comments:

To say "living is Christ" is to say that for him "life means Christ." Life is summed up in Christ. Life is filled up with, occupied with Christ, in the sense that everything Paul does-- trusts, loves, hopes, obeys, preaches, follows, and so on--is inspired by Christ and is done for Christ. Christ and Christ alone gives inspiration, direction, meaning and purpose to existence. Paul views his life in time as totally determined and controlled by his own love for and commitment to Christ . . . Paul can see no reason for being except to be "for Christ."

Paul is in chains because he "trusts" (πιστεύειν) in Christ--because he chooses to live "within [the sphere of] Christ's [rule] (ἐν Χριστῷ)."[42] If Paul dies in prison, it will be because he trusts (πιστεύειν) in Christ--because he chooses to live "within [the sphere of] Christ's [rule] (ἐν Χριστῷ)." His death will be an act of trust (πίστις) culminating a life of trust (πίστις) in God.[43]

In chapter 7 we saw that Paul often refers to such "trust" (πίστις) as "dying with Christ" because it involves the same sort of humble, obedient surrender to God's will which Jesus himself displayed in accepting "the death which is the cross."[44] This Christ-like "trust" in God--this "death with Christ"-- is the content of "righteousness" under the "new covenant."[45] Those who participate in the "new covenant" based on "trust" (πίστις) will be raised from the dead, at the future Resurrection, in fulfilment of the promise of scripture: "The [person reckoned] righteous on the basis of trust (ἐκ πίστεως) will live ['eschatological life']."[46]

The upshot of all this is that Paul believes that suffering and/or dying for Christ's sake is a sure sign of one's "trust" (πίστις) in God, and that such "trust" receives the sure promise of a place in the coming Resurrection to "eschatological life." Paul draws this connection between his own "trust"/ "dying with Christ"/righteousness/suffering/potential martyrdom and his anti-cipated resurrection from the dead in Phil 3:7-11:

---

[42]See Phil 1:13; cf. 1:7 ("my chains . . . [my] verbal defense and establishment of the gospel"), 16 ("for the verbal defense of the gospel"), 29 ("for his sake").

[43]For a full discussion of this Pauline interpretation of Christian suffering and death, see part III of chapter 7.

[44]See Phil 2:8, along with part III of chapter 4 and part I of chapter 7.

[45]See part II of chapter 7, along with the portion of chapter 2 marked "Ἡ καινὴ διαθήκη ('the new covenant')."

[46]See (1) Rom 1:17 and Gal 3:11, in which Paul quotes from Hab 2:4, (2) the portion of chapter 7 marked "2 Corinthians 5:11, 14-15; 4:10-14; and 7:3b," and (3) the discussion of "The righteousness which means 'life'" appearing later in this chapter.

(7) But what used to be gain (κέρδος), I have come to consider loss because of Christ. (8) Indeed, I consider all things loss because of the superior thing, [which is] knowing Christ Jesus my Lord. Because of him, I have been caused to lose all things. I consider [them mere] dung, in order that I may gain (κερδαίνειν) Christ, (9) and may be found within [the sphere determined by] him (ἐν αὐτῷ)--not having my own righteousness, which [is] based on the Law, but that which [is] through Christ's act of trust (πίστις Χριστοῦ), [namely,] the righteousness from God based on trust (πίστις). (10) [I have suffered the loss of all things] in order that I may know him, and the strength [of God which effected] his resurrection, and fellowship [with him] in his sufferings, being conformed with [him] in his death, (11) [so that] if at all possible I may attain to the Resurrection of the dead.

This same view of Christian martyrdom lies behind Paul's words in Phil 1:18b-26. Paul's execution would "magnify" Christ (v. 20) because the Apostle would be dying for Christ's sake--dying because of his commitment and witness to Christ as Lord.[47] "Dying [means] gain (κέρδος)" for Paul (v. 21) not because death itself is a "gain,"[48] but because the particular death he contemplates--the martyr's death resulting from "trust" (πίστις) in Christ--will receive the promised "gain" (κέρδος) of resurrection and "eschatological life" with Christ in glory.[49]

When Paul speaks of "departing and being with Christ (σὺν Χριστῷ) ([which would be] much, much better)" (v. 23), he is not portraying death as immediate entrance into some sort of "better," "intermediate" fellowship with the Lord. Once again, Paul is speaking of a particular "departure"--namely, his own (potential) death as a "trusting" martyr for Christ. He links this particular "departure"--this particular act of "trust" (πίστις)--to being "with

---

[47]For a full discussion of this Pauline interpretation of Christian suffering and death, see part III of chapter 7.

[48]On the contrary, Paul considers Death an "enemy" which God will one day destroy (see 1 Cor 15:26). For an alternative view, see the article by Palmer ("'To Die Is Gain'") in which he argues that Paul is citing a "commonplace of Greek literature" which views death as gain "because it brings release from earthly troubles" (p. 218).

[49]Note that this is the same "gain" (κέρδος) of which Paul speaks in Phil 3:7-11, 20-21.

324

Christ" (σὺν Χριστῷ) after the Parousia[50] because he knows that persons who display such "trust"--who thereby embrace God's "new covenant" based on "trust"--are promised "eschatological life" "with Christ" (σὺν Χριστῷ) on the Day when God raises the dead. It is this new "life" in the future resurrection body (σῶμα) that Paul judges to be "much, much better" than life in the present psychical body (σῶμα), which is subject to decay, suffering and death.[51]

When Paul says, "I have the desire to depart and be with Christ" (v. 23), he is not expressing a preference for death over life, for non-existence over existence, during the interval leading up to the Parousia.[52] Paul has not ceased to value life; he has not embraced the "enemy." The Apostle's "desire to depart" must be viewed in the light of his continuing resolve to remain faithful to Christ, to follow the path of "trust" (πίστις) to the end and, thereby, to "attain to the Resurrection of the dead."[53] If "trust" in Christ leads to martyrdom, then Paul "has the desire to depart and [at the Parousia] be with Christ" (v. 23). If "trust" in Christ leads to life and continued "fruitful labor" among the Philippians (v. 22), then it is Paul's "eager expectation and hope" (v. 20) that he will remain and (at the Parousia) be "with Christ." The only

---

[50]See the discussion of Paul's use of this phrase which appeared in note 40.

[51]See, e.g., Rom 8:18-23, along with the discussion of these matters which will appear below.

[52]2 Corinthians 5:4 shows that Paul would prefer to survive to the Parousia so that he could avoid death entirely (see note 18).

[53]The Apostle gives voice to this concern in Phil 3:12b and 14b:

I press forward, [in the hope] (εἰ) that I may lay hold of [my own completion in the Resurrection], because I myself have been laid hold of by Christ Jesus . . . I press forward toward the prize which is the upward calling of God within [the sphere of] Christ Jesus' [rule] (ἐν Χριστῷ).

Paul urges his readers to do the same in Phil 3:15 ("as many [of us] as [are] complete, let us think this [way]") and 2:12b-13 ("continue to work out your own salvation with fear and trembling, for God is the One who continues to work among you both the willing and the working for the sake of [His] good pleasure").

alternative to "trust" is disobedience and "destruction" (ἀπώλεια),[54] "disgrace" (αἰσχύνη)[55] and eternal death. Yet Paul is prepared to persevere in his "trust"--even if it results in martyrdom. He is confident that he "will be in no way disgraced (αἰσχύνειν), but that in all boldness, now as always, Christ will be magnified in my body (σῶμα), whether by means of [my] life or by means of [my] death" (v. 20).

In his own mind, the Apostle is "torn between the two" alternatives (v. 23); which he "will choose" he "cannot tell" (v. 22). "To depart" (v. 23) now would enable Paul to end his life in a manner singularly appropriate for a "trusting" (πιστεύειν) servant of the crucified Christ.[56] A martyr's death would be a sure sign that Paul had indeed "died with Christ"--that he had indeed (in the words of 2 Tim 4:7) "fought the good fight, finished the course," and "fulfilled trust (πίστις)." It would seal his confidence that, beginning on the future Day of Resurrection, he will at last be "with Christ" (σὺν Χριστῷ, v. 23) forever. This is the attraction of a martyr's death for Paul. It is in this sense that "to depart" now would be "much, much better" (v. 23) than life.

The Apostle is convinced, however, that it is "necessary" for him "to remain in the flesh" in order to continue his "fruitful labor" among the Philippians (vv. 24-26). He is therefore confident that the Lord will allow him to remain--that, through the Philippians' "prayer and the support of the Spirit of Jesus Christ," his imprisonment "will end in [his] salvation."[57] Persuaded that

---

[54]See Phil 1:28; 3:19.

[55]See Phil 3:19.

[56]I.e., the Christ who was "obedient to the point of death--even the death which is the cross" (see Phil 2:8). For a discussion of Christ's death as an act of obedient trust (πίστις), see part III of chapter 4.

[57]The Apostle probably means simply "salvation" (σωτηρία) from imprisonment and possible execution by the Roman authorities (see Phil 1:7, 12-17, 20-26; 4:22). However, his conviction that "trust" (whether it takes the form of life and "fruitful labor," or imprisonment and death) receives the promise of resurrection and "eschatological life" raises the possibility that Paul may here be using the term "salvation" (σωτηρία) in its broader, theological sense. This thesis is

this is the Lord's will, Paul looks forward to his release with "eager expectation and hope" (v. 20).

We have examined Phil 1:23 ("I have the desire to depart and be with Christ [σὺν Χριστῷ]") in the light of (1) its setting within Paul's discussion of his possible martyrdom, (2) the parallel text in 2 Cor 5:8, and (3) the Apostle's use of the phrase σὺν Χριστῷ ("with Christ") elsewhere in his letters. The evidence strongly suggests that what Paul "desires" is not some sort of "intermediate state," but fellowship "with Christ" in the coming Resurrection of the dead.

Ben F. Meyer speaks for many when he says that,

> On the face of it, the text of Phil 1:23 simply confirms that Paul entertained the conception of an intermediate state between the present life and the Parousia, entered into by death and aptly characterized as being "with the Lord." Those who deny that Paul harbored any such conception generally find themselves constrained to discover the Parousia motif here. But in this text, at least, there really is not so much as a hint that the Parousia is intended.[58]

Meyer fails to take into account the close connection, in Paul's thought, between "dying with Christ" and "living with Christ," "trust" (πίστις) and the Resurrection, righteousness and "eschatological life," the martyr's death and the Parousia of Christ. It is only natural for Paul to speak of "departing" and "being with Christ" in the same breath. H. A. A. Kennedy was correct when he wrote, long ago, that

> The yearning to die and be with Christ is for [Paul] the same thing as the hope of resurrection. His yearning overlaps all between death and

---

strengthened by the fact that, elsewhere in his letters, Paul consistently employs σωτηρία to speak of eschatological "salvation" (see note 140). When the Apostle is thinking of "salvation" from mortal danger, his preferred term is ῥύεσθαι (see Rom 7:24; 15:31; 2 Cor 1:10).

[58]Meyer, "Did Paul's View of the Resurrection Undergo Development?" 381.

resurrection, and hurries to its goal for reunion with Jesus"[59] . . . His thought transcends all experience of an Intermediate State, an interval between death and the full consummation of blessedness. He only sees the earthly life, on the one hand, and Christ, in whom his life is hid, on the other. What may happen between cannot interfere with his glowing conviction that his salvation is independent of death.[60]

A third text often cited as evidence for Paul's belief in an "intermediate state" is Rom 8:38-39:

I am convinced that neither death nor life . . . will be able to separate us from the love of God (ἡ ἀγάπη τοῦ θεοῦ), which [is] within [the sphere of] Christ Jesus' [rule] (ἐν Χριστῷ Ἰησου).

On the basis of this passage, some[61] have put forward (either explicitly or implicitly) the following line of reasoning:

Annihilation constitutes separation from the love of God.

Paul believes that death cannot "separate us from the love of God."

Therefore Paul does not view death as annihilation, but as entrance into some form of fellowship with (the opposite of "separation from") God/Christ--i.e., entrance into the "intermediate state" (supposedly) described in 2 Cor 5:3, 8 and Phil 1:23.

The main problem with this syllogism is that Paul does not believe the first premise ("annihilation constitutes separation from the love of God"). This is the whole point of Rom 8:38-39!

---

[59]Here Kennedy offers his own translation of a passage from Paul Wernle, *Die Anfänge unserer Religion* (Tübingen and Leipzig: J. C. B. Mohr, 1904), 207. G. A. Bienemann's two-volume translation of this work has been published under the title *The Beginnings of Christianity,* ed. with an Introduction by W. D. Morrison (New York: G. P. Putnam's Sons, 1903). The passage under discussion appears in vol. 1, p. 287.

[60]H. A. A. Kennedy, *St Paul's Conceptions of the Last Things,* 2d ed. (London: Hodder and Stoughton, 1904), 272.

[61]See, e.g., (1) Hanhart, *The Intermediate State,* 184, (2) Hawthorne, *Philippians,* 46, 50, and (3) Ridderbos, *Paul,* 507-508.

328

Those who view death as entrance into the "intermediate state" maintain that death is not really "death" (in the sense of annihilation), but only a transition into a different form of life. Paul, on the other hand, views death as a terrible reality. It is the "enemy" that claims both Christians and non-Christians alike;[62] it is the conqueror that will not be conquered until Christ's Parousia.[63] When Paul says that death cannot "separate us from the love of God," he is not saying that there is no more death (in the sense of annihilation). He is alluding to the promised Resurrection when God, in his "love," will "undo" death. Who will participate in this Resurrection? Where can this "love" be found? It is found "within [the sphere of] Christ Jesus' [rule]" (ἐν Χριστῷ Ἰησοῦ). It is given, in other words, to Christians--to those who "entrust" (πιστεύειν) themselves to Christ as Lord, who embrace the "new covenant" with its righteousness based on "trust," who "die with Christ" during "the present time" because they hope to "come to life with him" in the future.[64] Death can (temporarily) separate Christians from God, but it cannot "separate us from the love of God." God will remember His righteous servants and will raise them up on the last Day (see below).

Paul may have believed that the dead enjoy some form of conscious, "intermediate" existence between death and the promised Resurrection of the dead. There was certainly ample precedent for such a belief in the Judaism of Paul's day.[65] Yet the Apostle's letters seem to point in the opposite direction. His references to death as "perishing" or "destruction" are more indicative of annihilation than of continued life in an "intermediate state." His

---

[62]See above under "Death of the righteous and the unrighteous."

[63]See 1 Cor 15:21-26, 51-57.

[64]See Rom 6:8, discussed in chapter 6.

[65]Belief in an "intermediate state" of one sort or another appears, for example, in The (Greek) Life of Adam and Eve (departed psychai in "Paradise" or the "third heaven") and 4 Ezra (departed spirits or psychai in "habitations"), both of which were discussed in chapter 5.

convictions concerning the psychosomatic indivisibility of human beings and the future Day of Resurrection seem to rule out a belief in the immortality of the psyche (ψυχή) or the resurrection of individuals immediately after death. Finally, the three Pauline texts most often cited in support of Paul's belief in the "intermediate state" (i.e., 2 Cor 5:3, 8; Phil 1:23; and Rom 8:38-39) have, under scrutiny, proven less than compelling. We conclude, then, that Paul viewed death as annihilation and that his "hope" for the future was tied to the bodily Resurrection of the dead at the time of Christ's Parousia, rather than to some sort of conscious, "intermediate" existence beginning immediately after death. As the Apostle says in 1 Cor 15:32,

> If the dead are not raised, [then] "Let us eat and drink, for tomorrow we will surely die."

"We who remain." Paul knew from experience that many people--both Christians and non-Christians--will not live to see the Day of the Lord.[66] Many will "perish"--many will cease to exist--before Christ appears in his glory. At the same time, Paul does not expect that all will die; he does not foresee the extinction of the human race. He fully anticipates that some human beings--including a number of Christians--will be alive on the earth at the Day of Christ's Return. The Apostle speaks of "we who are alive, who remain until the Coming (or 'Parousia,' παρουσία) of the Lord," in 1 Thess 4:15 and 17, and again in 1 Cor 15:51 ("we will not all sleep"). As we enter into a discussion of the Day of the Lord, we must keep in mind the fact that Paul thinks in terms of "the living and the dead"[67]--i.e., "those who are alive, who remain,"[68] and those who have already died, who have ceased to exist.

---

[66]See above under "Death of the righteous and the unrighteous."

[67]See, e.g., Rom 14:9.

[68]See 1 Thess 4:17.

The Day of the Lord

Paul's "hope" (ἐλπίς)[69] for the future centers around an event he calls "the Day of the Lord" (ἡ ἡμέρα τοῦ κυρίου),[70] "the Day of Christ" (ἡμέρα Χριστοῦ),[71] or simply "the Day" (ἡ ἡμέρα).[72] The Day of the Lord will mark the end of "the present time" (ὁ νῦν καιρός) and the beginning of the eschatological "future," or the consummation of the "eschatological age."[73] Paul describes this event as the "time" (καιρός)[74] of Christ's Parousia (παρουσία, i.e., Christ's "Appearance" or "[Second] Coming")[75] and the "time" when God raises the dead.[76] It will be "the Day of Wrath" (ἡμέρα ὀργῆς) and "Judgment"[77] and, at the same time, "the Day of Salvation" (ἡμέρα σωτηρίας)[78]

---

[69]See Rom 5:2 ("that for which we hope, which is the glory of God"), 4-5; 8:20-21 ("the hope that the Creation itself will also be liberated from the slavery which is corruption to the freedom which is the glory of the children of God"), 24-25 ("we have been saved within [the sphere of] hope . . . we hope for what we do not see . . . we wait with perseverence"); 12:12; 15:4, 12-13 ("the root of Jesse . . . in him will the Gentiles hope"); 1 Cor 15:19 ("if we are hoping in Christ in this life only, [then] we [are] the most pitiable of all persons"); 2 Cor 3:12 ("we have such a hope [i.e., the ministration of the Spirit]"); Gal 5:5 ("that for which righteousness hopes [ἐλπίς δικαιοσύνης]"); Phil 1:20 ("my eager expectation and hope that I will be in no way disgraced"); 1 Thess 1:3 ("your endurance springing from hope in our Lord Jesus Christ"); 4:13 ("the others who have no hope"); 5:8 ("the hope of salvation").

[70]See 1 Cor 5:5; 1 Thess 5:2, 4; cf. 1 Cor 1:8 ("the Day of our Lord Jesus Christ"); 2 Cor 1:14 ("the Day of our Lord Jesus").

[71]See Phil 1:10; 2:16; cf. 1:6 ("the Day of Christ Jesus").

[72]See 1 Cor 3:13; 1 Thess 5:4, 5, 8.

[73]See chapter 2 under '"The present time."'

[74]See chapter 2 under '"The present time."'

[75]See, e.g., 1 Cor 1:7-8 ("the revelation of our Lord Jesus Christ . . . the Day of our Lord Jesus Christ").

[76]See, e.g., 1 Thess 4:16 and 5:2 ("the dead within [the sphere of] Christ's rule [οἱ νεκροὶ ἐν Χριστῷ] will rise first . . . like a thief in the night, so comes the Day of the Lord").

[77]See Rom 2:5 ("the Day of Wrath--even the revelation of the righteous judgment [δικαιοκρισία] of God"); cf. 2:16 ("the Day when, according to my gospel, God judges the secrets of human beings [ἄνθρωποι] by means of Jesus Christ"); 1 Cor 3:13-15 ("[the quality of] each [person]'s work will be made manifest . . . because the Day will show [it]"); Phil 1:10 ("pure and

and "eschatological life." We will examine all these aspects of the Day of the Lord--Parousia, Resurrection, Judgment and Salvation--in the following paragraphs.

The Parousia of Christ. Paul's most detailed description of the Parousia (παρουσία) appears in 1 Thess 4:13-5:11.[79] The Apostle addresses the time of the Lord's Coming in 5:1-2:

(1) Concerning the chronologies (χρόνοι) and the times (καιροί), brothers [and sisters], you have no need [for anything] to be written to you. (2) [You have no need for anything to be written to you] because you yourselves know very well that, like a thief in the night, so comes (ἔρχεται)[80] the Day of the Lord (ἡμέρα κυρίου).

Paul clearly believes that the Day of the Lord has not yet occurred--that it belongs to the future. Exactly when Christ will return has not been revealed;

---

innocent for the Day of Christ, filled with the fruit of righteousness"); 1 Thess 5:2, 3, and 9 ("like a thief in the night, so comes the Day of the Lord . . . sudden destruction [will] come upon them . . . [but] God has not appointed us for Wrath"). Compare 1 Cor 4:3, which speaks of a day (ἡμέρα) of human judgment.

[78]See 2 Cor 6:2 ("[the] present [time (νῦν) is] Day of Salvation"--in the sense that the decision of "trust" [πίστις], which will receive the gift of eschatological "salvation" [σωτηρία] on the future Day of the Lord, is made "now" [νῦν], during "the present time" [see chapter 2 under "'The present time'"]); 1 Cor 3:13 and 15 ("[the quality of] each [person]'s work will be made manifest . . . if someone's work should be burned up; [then] s/he will suffer a loss, but s/he him/herself will be saved"); 5:5 ("deliver this [person] to Satan for the destruction of the flesh, so that the spirit may be saved on the Day of the Lord"). Compare Rom 13:11-13 ("our salvation [is] nearer now . . . the day is dawning") and 1 Thess 5:8-9 ("we belong to the day . . . God has not appointed us for Wrath, but for attaining salvation through our Lord Jesus Christ").

[79]See also 1 Cor 1:7 ("the revelation [ἀποκάλυψις] of our Lord Jesus Christ"); 4:5 ("the time [καιρός], when the Lord comes [ἔρχεσθαι]"); 11:26 ("until he comes [ἔρχεσθαι]"); 15:23 ("at [the time of] his Coming [παρουσία]"); 1 Thess 1:10 ("to wait for His Son from the heavens, whom He raised from the dead"); 2:19 ("our Lord Jesus at the [time of] his Coming [παρουσία]"); 3:13 ("at [the time of] the Coming [παρουσία] of our Lord Jesus"); 5:23 ("at the Coming [παρουσία] of our Lord Jesus Christ").

[80]The verb ἔρχεται ("[it] comes"), like ἐφίσταται ("sudden destruction [will] come upon them") in v. 3, is a "futuristic present." See Brooks and Winbery, *Syntax,* 80-81.

332

for, as the Lord himself once said,[81] he will come suddenly and unexpectedly --"like a thief in the night."

Paul speaks of the manner of Christ's Return in 4:16:

The Lord himself will descend from heaven with a shout of command (κέλευσμα), with the voice of the archangel (φωνὴ ἀρχαγγέλου) and the sounding of the trumpet (σάλπιγξ) of God.

Two observations are in order: First, the Christ who will come on the Day of the Lord is the risen and glorified Christ whom we described in chapter 5. God has "super-exalted" him and named him "Lord" of all; God has placed him on David's throne and given him the rule over all nations.[82] Paul says that Christ will return "from heaven," where he presently sits at God's right hand, making intercession for the saints.[83]

Second, Christ's Coming will be marked by "a shout of command" (κέλευσμα), the "voice of the archangel" (φωνὴ ἀρχαγγέλου), and "the sounding of the trumpet (σάλπιγξ) of God" (which Paul also mentions in 1 Cor 15:52). Jewish prophecy associated the trumpet-blast (σάλπιγξ) with the arrival of the Day of the Lord (ἡμέρα κυρίου),[84] and this probably provided the basis for Paul's eschatological expectation here. Taken together, the "sounding of the trumpet," the "voice of the archangel," and Christ's "shout of command" also

---

[81]See Matt 24:43-44 // Luke 12:39-40; cf. 2 Pet 3:10; Rev 3:3; 16:15.

[82]See Phil 2:9-11 and 1 Cor 15:24-28, along with the portion of chapter 5 marked "'The Name which is above every name.'"

[83]See Rom 8:34; cf. Ps 110(109):1, which Paul interprets christologically in 1 Cor 15:25.

[84]See the LXX translation of Joel 2:1-11 (note that Paul quotes v. 32 of this chapter in Rom 10:13), Zeph 1:14-16 ("the Day of the Lord . . . the Day of the Lord's Wrath"), and Zech 9:14-17 (in which the LORD Himself sounds the trumpet--the "trumpet of God"?). Compare (1) Ps 47(46):5, where the trumpet-sound announces God's kingship over all nations, (2) Ps 98(97):6, where the trumpets celebrate God's judgment and salvation, (3) Sib. Or. 4:171-92, in which the trumpet announces the Resurrection and the Judgment, (4) Matt 24:31, in which the trumpet accompanies the coming of the Son of Man, and (5) Rev 11:15, in which the sounding of the seventh trumpet (the "last trumpet" of 1 Cor 15:52?) announces the consummation of God's eschatological Rule (βασιλεία).

evoke images of the battlefield.[85] Paul expects Christ to come as a conquering warrior, bringing death and destruction to God's enemies, but victory and life to those who welcome his Return (see below).

The Resurrection of the righteous dead. Christ's Return "from heaven" will immediately be followed by the Resurrection and transformation of the righteous. Paul describes these events in 1 Thess 4:13-18:

> (13) Now we do not want you to be ignorant, brothers [and sisters], concerning those who are asleep, so that you may not grieve like the others who have no hope. (14) [You need not grieve for them] because if we trust that Jesus died and rose [from the dead], [then we] certainly also [trust that] God, through Jesus, will bring along with him those who have fallen asleep. (15) [We trust that God will bring along with Jesus those who have fallen asleep] because we are telling you this by the word of the Lord (ἐν λόγῳ κυρίου). We who are alive, who remain until the Coming (παρουσία) of the Lord, will certainly not precede those who have fallen asleep. (16) For the Lord himself will descend from heaven with a shout of command (κέλευσμα), with the voice of the archangel and the sounding of the trumpet (σάλπιγξ) of God. The dead within [the sphere of] Christ's [rule] (ἐν Χριστῷ) will rise first. (17) Then we who are alive, who remain, will be taken up together with them in the clouds to meet the Lord in the air. Thus will we always be with the Lord (σὺν κυρίῳ).[86] (18) So then, comfort one another with these words.

---

[85]For the trumpet (σάλπιγξ) as a signal used in war, see Num 10:9; 31:6; Josh 6:20; Job 39:25; Jer 4:19; Ezek 33:2-6; 1 Macc 5:31-33; 9:12-13; Ps. Sol. 8:1. For the archangel (ἀρχάγγελος) Michael as the "commander-in-chief" (ἀρχιστράτηγος) of God's angelic armies, see T. Abra. (resc. A) 1:4 (cf. [Greek] Life of Adam and Eve 22:1-2, in which the archangel Michael summons the angels to witness God's judgment against Adam by sounding his trumpet). For κέλευσμα ("shout of command")--or the verb form κελεύειν ("to command")--as a military command, see Prov 30:27; Jdt 2:15; 1 Macc 11:23; 2 Macc 5:12; 13:12 (all LXX).

[86]Joseph Plevnik ("The Taking Up of the Faithful and the Resurrection of the Dead in 1 Thessalonians 4:13-18," *CBQ* 46 [1984]: 274-83) interprets vv. 16-17 in terms of resurrection of the dead (= "a return to this life," p. 282) followed by assumption of both the living and the dead (= transformation to "eschatological life"). In response to Plevnik, Ben F. Meyer ("Note: Paul and the Resurrection of the Dead," *TS* 48 [1987]: 157-58) advocates a second interpretation more compatible with 1 Corinthians 15--namely, resurrection of the dead (which is "intrinsically transformative," p. 158) and transformation of the living (= transformation to "eschatological life"--an event described in 1 Cor 15, but only assumed in 1 Thess 4), followed by assumption (= "with the Lord") of both. We find Meyer's arguments more compelling.

The Thessalonian believers thought that Christians who remained alive at the Lord's Parousia would enjoy some sort of advantage over Christians who died before Christ's Return.[87] Paul corrects this misconception by explaining that "we who are alive, who remain until the Coming (παρουσία) of the Lord, will certainly not precede those who have fallen asleep" (v. 15). Instead, "the dead within [the sphere of] Christ's [rule] (ἐν Χριστῷ) will rise first" (v. 16). They will witness everything the living believers witness; they will experience everything the living Christians experience.

Who will participate in the future Resurrection of the dead? Paul's response is "the dead within [the sphere of] Christ's [rule] (ἐν Χριστῷ)" (v. 16) or, in other words, Christians who embraced Christ's lordship, but who died before their Lord's Return. Persons who entrusted (πιστεύειν) themselves to Christ during their lifetimes--they will be raised to "eschatological life." Persons whom God reckoned "righteous" under the "new covenant" based on trust (πίστις)--they will receive the resurrection body (σῶμα).[88] When Christ appears in glory, God "will bring along with [Jesus] those [Christians] who have fallen asleep" (v. 14).[89] The Day of the Lord will thus be a Day of Resurrection and "eschatological life" for the "righteous" dead.

What is the nature of resurrection from the dead? Earlier in this chapter, we argued that Paul views death as annihilation, non-existence, nothingness. If death is nothingness, then resurrection--for Paul--is re-creation from nothingness (*creatio ex nihilo*). When the Apostle speaks of a "new creation" (καινὴ κτίσις) in 2 Cor 5:17 and Gal 6:15,[90] he means it quite literally.

---

[87]A. F. J. Klijn examines this notion against the background of Jewish apocalyptic in "1 Thessalonians 4:13-18 and its Background in Apocalyptic Literature," in *Paul and Paulinism: Essays in Honour of C. K. Barrett*, ed. M. D. Hooker and S. G. Wilson (London: SPCK, 1982), 67-73.

[88]See below under "'The righteousness which means "life."'"

[89]Cf. 1 Thess 3:13 ("the Coming [παρουσία] of our Lord Jesus with all his saints").

[90]Gal 6:11-17 was discussed in chapter 7.

Paul's concept of resurrection as re-creation is seen most clearly in Rom 4:17b, which speaks of "the God who makes the dead alive and who calls into existence things which had no existence" (θεὸς τοῦ ζῳοποιοῦντος τοὺς κεκροὺς καὶ καλοῦντος τὰ μὴ ὄντα ὡς ὄντα).[91] We will explore more fully the nature of resurrection existence, or "eschatological life," in part II of this chapter.

The transformation of the righteous who live. Christians "who are alive, who remain until the Coming (παρουσία) of the Lord" (v. 15), will not, strictly speaking, be raised from the dead. (They are not dead, so they cannot be raised "from the dead.") Instead, they will be transformed. They will receive the same sort of "resurrection body"--the same sort of immortal, incorruptible "eschatological existence"--which the risen righteous already enjoy. (It is in this sense that all Christians participate in the Resurrection.) Paul describes this miraculous transformation in 1 Cor 15:51-53:

> (51) Behold, I tell you a mystery (μυστήριον): We will not all sleep (κοιμᾶν, i.e., not all Christians will die), but we will all be transformed (ἀλλάσσειν) (52) in a moment, in the blink of an eye, at [the sounding of] the eschatological (ἐσχάτης) trumpet.[92] [I can rightfully say that we Christians will be transformed at the sounding of the eschatological trumpet] because [the trumpet] will sound, the dead will be raised incorruptible (ἄφθαρτος), and we will be transformed (ἀλλάσσειν). (53) [We Christians will be transformed] because it is necessary for this corruptible (φθαρτός) [body] to put on incorruptibility (ἀφθαρσία), and for this mortal (θνητός) [body] to put on immortality (ἀθανασία).

Again, we will examine more fully the nature of "resurrection existence" in part II of this chapter.

---

[91]Hans Conzelmann (*An Outline of the Theology of the New Testament* [New York: Harper & Row Publishers, 1969], 188-89) argues that Paul "interprets the resurrection as new creation" in 1 Corinthians 15 as well (p. 188).

[92]Paul mentions the "eschatological trumpet" in 1 Thess 4:16 also.

"Always with the Lord." Once the righteous dead have been raised and the living righteous have been transformed, they will be united with one another and united with Christ. Paul describes this union in 1 Thess 4:16b-17:

> The dead within [the sphere of] Christ's [rule] (ἐν Χριστῷ) will rise first. Then we who are alive, who remain, will be taken up together with them in the clouds to meet the Lord in the air. Thus will we always be with the Lord.[93]

A Resurrection/transformation for the unrighteous? Paul clearly believes that the "righteous" (i.e., Christians who participate in the "new covenant" based on Christ-like trust in God[94]) will be raised from the dead, or transformed, at the future Day of the Lord. What about the "unrighteous"? Will those who never confessed Christ be delivered from death when he returns? Will those who denied the Creator have a part in His "new creation"? Will those who never "died with Christ"[95] yet, somehow, "live" with him?

The book of Acts portrays Paul as a person who believed in "a resurrection of both the righteous and the unrighteous" (ἀνάστασις δικαίων τε καὶ ἀδίκων).[96] In contrast, the Apostle's own writings never mention the possibility of a resurrection/transformation for non-Christians (i.e., persons who do not fulfil "righteousness" under the "new covenant" based on "trust" [πίστις]).[97] The historical Paul appears to leave unbelievers (ἄπιστοι) in the grave; he appears to view the "unrighteous" as persons who literally "have no

---

[93]Compare 2 Cor 4:14 ("the One who raised the Lord Jesus will also raise us along with Jesus, and will bring us into [His] presence along with you") and 5:8-9 ("we would rather be away from the [mortal] body and housed with the Lord").

[94]See the portion of chapter 2 marked "Η καινὴ διαθήκη ('the new covenant')," along with parts I and II of chapter 4, and parts I and II of chapter 7.

[95]See chapter 7.

[96]See Acts 24:15.

[97]In his study of *Eschatology,* R. H. Charles suggests that Paul's description of the "resurrection body" as "spiritual" (πνευματικός) implies that "only the righteous [i.e., Christians who have received Christ's Spirit--see chapter 7, note 40] can share in the resurrection" (p. 452).

hope."[98] In Paul's mind, the Day of the Lord brings "life" and "new creation" for the "righteous," but only death and annihilation for the "unrighteous."

"The righteous judgment of God."[99] The Apostle links Christ's Coming to both death and "life" because he views the Day of the Lord as both the Day of "Judgment" and the "Day of Salvation."[100] Paul speaks of God's judgment in Rom 2:1-11, where he seeks to establish that all persons--both Jews and Gentiles alike--are "under [the dominion of] Sin" (ὑφ' ἁμαρτίαν):[101]

(1) Therefore [you]--every person who judges (ὦ ἄνθρωπε πᾶς ὁ κρίνων)--you are left without a defense (ἀναπολόγητος εἶ). [You are left without a defense] because in what[ever area] (ἐν ᾧ) you judge someone else, you are condemning (κατακρίνειν) yourself. [You are condemning yourself] because you, the judge (ὁ κρίνων), are doing the same things. (2) We know that God's judgment against persons who do such things is [always] (ἐστιν)[102] in accordance with the truth.[103] (3) Do you suppose (λογίζῃ τοῦτο) that you will escape the judgment of God--you (ὦ ἄνθρωπε) who judge those who do such things and do them [yourself]? (4) Or do you show contempt for His wealth of kindness (χρηστότης) and forbearance and patience because you do not know that God's kind[ness] (χρηστός) [is meant to] lead (ἄγει)[104] you to repentance? (5) In accordance with your hardness and [your] unrepentant heart, you are storing up for yourself wrath on the Day of Wrath (ἡμέρα ὀργῆς)--even the revelation

---

[98]See 1 Thess 4:13; cf. 1 Cor 15:14, 17-19.

[99]For a discussion of "The Judgment" and its place in Pauline theology, see Ridderbos, *Paul,* 551-56.

[100]See above under "The Day of the Lord."

[101]See Rom 3:9. For a discussion of "Sin as a 'power'" which exercises dominion, see chapter 2.

[102]The verb ἐστιν ("it is [always]") here represents an instance of the "gnomic present," which is used to express "a universal truth, a maxim, a commonly accepted fact, a state or condition which perpetually exists." See Brooks and Winbery, *Syntax,* 79.

[103]On "true" judgment, see chapter 2 under "'Righteousness' as a forensic term."

[104]This RSV translation of ἄγει ("it [is meant to] lead") captures well the tendential force of the verb. On the "tendential present," see Brooks and Winbery, *Syntax,* 78-79.

of the righteous judgment (δικαιοκρισία[105]) of God, (6) who will recompense each [person] according to his/her deeds. (7) To those who seek "eschatological life" (ζωὴ αἰώνιος), [He will give] glory and honor and immortality in accordance with [their] persistence in doing good (ὑπομονὴ ἔργου ἀγαθοῦ). (8) To those who continue to reject the truth (ἀπειθεῖν τῇ ἀληθείᾳ) out of self-centered factionalism (ἐριθεία), [He will show] wrath and terrible fury (θυμός). (9) [There will be] trouble and distress on every person (ψυχὴ ἀνθρώπου) who does evil, [on] the Jew first and also [on] the Greek. (10) But [there will be] glory and honor and peace for every [person] who does good, for the Jew first and also for the Greek. (11) [I say "the Jew first and also the Greek"] because, with God, there is no favoritism.

Paul follows the Old Testament and Jewish tradition[106] when he speaks of God as the One who judges (κρίνειν) the world.[107] In Paul's view, God judges all persons--both Jews and Gentiles, the "good" and the "evil" (vv. 9-11), Christians and non-Christians (see below).[108] Furthermore, God is a "righteous" Judge--a Judge whose judgments are just, without "favoritism," "in accordance with the truth" (vv. 2, 11).[109]

---

[105]A "righteous judgment" is a just judgment, or a judgment "in accordance with the truth" (v. 2). See chapter 2 under "'Righteousness' as a forensic term."

[106]See, e.g., Gen 18:25 ("the Judge of all the earth"); Ps 9:7-8 ("He has established His throne for judgment; He will judge the world in righteousness"); Isa 51:22 ("the Lord God who judges His people"); Ps. Sol. 2:32 ("[the Lord is] a great and righteous King, who judges what [is] under heaven"); T. Benj. 10:8-9 ("the Lord first judges Israel for the wrong she has committed and then he will do the same for all the nations").

[107]See Rom 2:2-3, 5-6, 16 ("God judges the hidden [things] of human beings"); 3:6-8 ("otherwise, how could God judge the world?"); 13:1-2; 14:10-12 ("we will all stand before the judgment seat [βῆμα] of God . . . each of us will give an account of him/herself to God"); 1 Cor 4:4-5 ("the one who judges me is the Lord"); 11:29-32; 1 Thess 4:6 ("the Lord [is] the Righteous Avenger [ἔκδικος] in all these [things]"). Note that Paul sometimes speaks of God exercising His judgment through the Lord Jesus Christ.

[108]Compare Rom 14:10 ("all will stand before the judgment seat of God"); 2 Cor 5:10 ("all of us must appear before the judgment seat of Christ").

[109]See Rom 3:5-6 and Gal 6:7 ("Do not be deceived! God is not mocked. [I can rightfully say that God is not mocked] because whatever a person sows, that [is what] s/he will also reap."), along with the discussion of "'Righteousness' as a forensic term" in chapter 2.

Paul conceives of God's judgment as both a present reality and a future promise. The Apostle speaks of God's judging activity during "the present time"[110] in Rom 1:18-31, where he describes how

> the wrath (ὀργή) of God is [presently] being revealed (ἀποκαλύπτεται) from heaven against all the godlessness (ἀσέβεια) and unrighteousness (ἀδικία) of persons who, by [their] unrighteousness (ἐν ἀδικίᾳ), suppress the truth [about God].[111] (v. 18)

Since these persons "did not glorify [God] as God" (v. 21), but instead "worshipped and served the creature rather than the Creator" (v. 25), "God gave them over to the desires of their hearts" (vv. 24-31). They "receive in their own persons"--in the present--"the necessary recompense for their error" (ἡ ἀντιμισθία ἣ ἔδει τῆς πλάνης αὐτῶν ἐν ἑαυτοῖς ἀπολαμβάνοντες, v. 27).[112]

According to Rom 13:1-5, God sometimes employs earthly rulers as the instrument of His present judgment. The Apostle writes:

> (1) Let every person (ψυχή) be subordinate to the governing authorities. [Every person must be subordinate to the governing authorities] because there is no authority except [that established] by God, and those which exist exist because they have been appointed by God. (2) Therefore the one who opposes the [governing] authority has resisted the ordinance of God, and those who resist will obtain for themselves judgment (κρίμα). (3) [I say that those who resist the governing authorities will receive judgment] because rulers are not a terror to good behavior (ἔργον), but to evil [behavior]. You do not want to fear the [governing] authority, do you? Continue to do good, and you will have its approval (ἔπαινος ἐξ αὐτῆς). (4) [The governing authority encourages good behavior and discourages evil behavior] because it is God's servant (διάκονος), [acting] for you[r benefit] (σοί[113]), [acting] for the good (εἰς τὸ ἀγαθόν). If you ever do evil, then you should be afraid. [Evildoers should be afraid] because [the

---

[110]See chapter 2 under "'The present time.'"

[111]Verse 25 shows that the "truth" of which Paul speaks is the "truth about God."

[112]For an instance of God's present judgment against Christians, see 1 Cor 11:27-32.

[113]Σοί ("for you[r benefit]") here functions as a personal interest dative of advantage. See Brooks and Winbery, *Syntax,* 30-31.

governing authority] does not bear the sword in vain. [I can rightfully say that the governing authority does not bear the sword in vain] because God's servant (διάκονος) is a just avenger (ἔκδικος), directed toward the goal of wrath (εἰς ὀργήν) for the one who practices evil. (5) Subordination [to the governing authority is] therefore necessary--not only because of the wrath (ὀργή), but also because of the conscience (συνείδησις).

Romans 1:18-31, 2:1-11, and 13:1-5 express Paul's conviction that God continually makes judgments--in the present--concerning what is "good" and what is "evil" (1:18, 25; 2:7, 9-10; 13:3-4), what is "true" and what is "false" (1:18; 2:8).[114] God has resolved to reward the "good" and the "true," and to punish or condemn what is "evil" and "false" (e.g., 2:6-10). Sometimes these divine judgments are carried out in the present--through the "governing authority," or through other "servants" (13:4) God has "appointed" (13:1-2; cf. 1:24-31) for this purpose.[115] Most of the time, however, the "good" is not praised (see 13:3) and the "truth" remains hidden (1:18-25). Wickedness abounds, and not every wrong is righted in this life. For this reason, Paul looks to the future Day of the Lord as the "Day of Wrath" (2:5) and Judgment. When Christ appears in glory, all God's judgments will be made manifest. Christ's Return (παρουσία) "from heaven" will mark the complete "revelation of the righteous judgment (δικαιοκρισία) of God" (2:5).[116]

Judgment and condemnation for the unrighteous. For the "unrighteous," who have not participated in the "new covenant" based on "trust" (πίστις), the Day of Judgment will bring "condemnation" (κατάκριμα)[117] and "wrath"

---

[114]Compare 2 Cor 13:5-7 (discussed in chapter 7), where Paul distinguishes between persons who are "approved" and persons who are "unapproved."

[115]We see the Apostle himself acting as God's "servant" for judgment in 1 Cor 5:1-5 ("a certain [man] has the wife of [his] father . . . I have already judged the one who has done this [thing]").

[116]Compare 1 Cor 3:13-15 ("[the quality of] each [person]'s work will be made manifest . . . because the Day will show [it]").

[117]See Rom 2:1; 5:16, 18; 14:23; 1 Cor 11:31-32; 2 Cor 3:9; cf. Rom 8:1, 33-34.

(ὀργή).[118]   Warnings against God's impending "wrath" (ὀργή) appear thoughout the Pauline corpus:

> (8) To those who continue to reject the truth out of self-centered factionalism, [God will show] wrath (ὀργή) and terrible fury (θυμός). (9) [There will be] trouble and distress on every person (ψυχὴ ἀνθρώπου) who does evil, [on] the Jew first and also [on] the Greek. (Rom 2:8-9)

> (9) You know, don't you, that unrighteous [persons] (ἄδικοι) will not inherit the Rule of God (θεοῦ βασιλεία)? Never be deceived! Neither sexually immoral persons (πόρνοι), nor idolators, nor adulterers, nor effeminates (μαλακοί), nor male homosexuals (ἀρσενοκοῖται), (10) nor thieves, nor covetous persons, nor drunkards, nor verbally abusive persons, nor robbers, will inherit the Rule of God (βασιλεία θεοῦ, discussed below). (1 Cor 6:9-10[119])

> (7) Do not be deceived! God is not mocked. [I can rightfully say that God is not mocked] because whatever a person sows, that [is what] s/he will also reap. (8) The [person] who sows toward [the end of fulfilling the desires[120] of] his/her own flesh (εἰς τὴν σάρκα ἑαυτου) will, from the flesh, reap corruption (φθορά). (Gal 6:7-8a)

What will be the shape of God's eschatological Wrath (ὀργή)? What form will His Judgment against the "unrighteous" take? Some interpret Paul's reference to a universal Judgment in Rom 14:10 ("all will stand before the judgment seat of God") to imply that (1) the "unrighteous" will be raised from the dead along with the "righteous," (2) all will endure a literal, face-to-face appearance before God's judgment throne, and (3) each person will receive either reward or punishment in accordance with his/her deeds.[121]   Such Judgment scenes appear often in Jewish and Christian writings from the

---

[118]See Rom 1:18; 2:5, 8; 3:5; 4:15; 9:22; 12:19; 13:4-5; 1 Thess 1:10; 2:16; cf. Rom 5:9; 1 Thess 5:9.

[119]Compare Gal 5:19-21.

[120]Compare Gal 5:16-17.

[121]Ridderbos, for example, raises this possibility in *Paul,* 554-55.

apostolic era,[122] but never in the letters of Paul. The Apostle's own words suggest that God's "condemnation" (κατάκριμα) of the "unrighteous" will take the form of death and nothingness, destruction and eternal annihilation. Paul believes that

> Many [persons] are living (περιπατεῖν) . . . [as] enemies of the Cross of Christ. Their end [is] destruction. (Phil 3:18-19)

> The [person] who sows toward [the end of fulfilling the desires of] his/her own flesh will, from the flesh, reap corruption (φθορά). (Gal 6:8)

> The wages [paid by] Sin [is] death. (Rom 6:23)

When the "Day of Wrath" finally arrives, God will destroy any "sinners" (i.e., any "unrighteous" persons who have not embraced the "new covenant" established through Christ's sacrificial death[123]) who remain alive,[124] and He will leave in the grave those of His "enemies" who have already died.[125] This, in itself, will consititute "the revelation of the righteous judgment of God"[126] against the "unrighteous."

Judgment and salvation for the righteous. The "righteous" (i.e., Christians who participate in the "new covenant") are not exempt from God's Judgment, but Paul is confident that they will be saved from "condemnation"

---

[122]See, e.g., 2 Apoc. Bar. 50-51; Test. Abra. (resc. A) 12-13; Matt 25:31-46; Rev 20:11-14.

[123]For a discussion of "sinners" as persons outside a covenant, see chapter 2 under "'Righteousness' as a covenantal term."

[124]See 1 Cor 3:16-17 ("you are God's temple . . . If someone tries to destroy God's temple, [then] God will destroy that [person]"); 6:13a ("'Food [is] for the stomach and the stomach [is] for food'--but God will destroy both the one and the other [καὶ ταύτην καὶ ταῦτα]"); cf. 1 Thess 5:3 ("When they say, '[We have] peace and security,' then sudden ruin [ὄλεθρος] will come upon them").

[125]Such persons are under God's "curse" (ἀνάθεμα), "cut off from Christ," "fallen away from [God's] goodwill (χάρις)," which has taken the form of the "new covenant" based on Christ-like "trust" (πίστις) in Him. See Rom 9:3; Gal 1:8-9; 5:4.

[126]See Rom 2:5.

(κατάκριμα) and "wrath" (ὀργή) through their covenantal relationship with Him. Paul mentions the future Judgment of Christians in 2 Cor 5:9-10:[127]

(9) We [Christians] have [it] as [our] ambition, whether we are housed [with the Lord] or away [from the Lord], to be pleasing in his sight. (10) [We want to be pleasing in the Lord's sight] because all of us must appear before the judgment seat (βῆμα) of Christ, so that each [person] may receive the [judgments appropriate] for the [things] which s/he did while [in] the [mortal] body, whether good or bad.

The idea of a future Judgment for Christians also appears in 1 Cor 3:11-15, where Paul insists that

(11) No one is able to put down another foundation beside the one which is already laid, which is Jesus Christ. (12) If someone builds upon the foundation with gold, with silver, with precious stones, with wood, with hay, with straw; (13) [then the quality of] each [Christian]'s[128] work will be made manifest. [I can rightfully say that the quality of each Christian's work will be made manifest] because the Day (ἡ ἡμέρα) will show [it], for it [will certainly] be revealed (ἀποκαλύπτεται[129]) by means of fire. The fire will test it--namely, of what sort each [Christian]'s work is. (14) If someone's work, which s/he has built upon [the foundation], should endure; [then] s/he will receive a reward. (15) If someone's work should be burned up; [then] s/he will suffer a loss, but s/he him/herself will be saved--but [it will be] as through fire.

These texts offer four important insights into Paul's thought concerning Christians and the Judgment: First, the Apostle assumes that Christian believers "have [it] as [their] ambition . . . to be pleasing in [Christ's] sight."[130] Christians, by definition, are persons who have "died with Christ," or committed themselves to God/Christ as Lord, or embraced the "new covenant" based

---

[127]For further discussion of this text, see above under "An intermediate state?"

[128]That Paul here speaks of Christians is shown by the fact that they "build" upon the "foundation" which is Christ.

[129]The verb ἀποκαλύπτεται here functions as a "futuristic present" ("it [will certainly] be revealed"). See Brooks and Winbery, *Syntax,* 80-81.

[130]See 2 Cor 5:9.

on Christ-like "trust" (πίστις) in God.[131] If Christians bow before God as Lord, then Paul takes it for granted that they are seeking to do His will.

Second, Paul recognizes that Christians--whether it be out of ignorance, or weakness, or indolence, or even momentary rebelliousness--do not always behave in a manner consistent with their confession. Some "build" on the "foundation" of Christ using "gold" or "silver;" others "build" using "hay" or "straw."[132]

Third, Paul's God is concerned with human behavior; He is the Judge of the world.[133] Everything we think, everything we do, everything we are will be exposed and scrutinized--tried by the "fire" of God's Judgment.[134] Whatever meets with God's approval will be rewarded, preserved, and incorporated into His eschatological "Rule" (βασιλεία, described below).[135] Whatever earns His disapproval will be "consumed," destroyed, banished from His presence forever.[136] This will constitute "the revelation of the righteous judgment of God"[137] with regard to the "righteous."

---

[131] On Christian "trust" (πίστις) as submission to God's lordship, see parts I and II of chapter 7, along with the portion of chapter 2 marked "Ἡ καινὴ διαθήκη ('the new covenant')."

[132] See 1 Cor 3:12.

[133] See 2 Cor 5:10; cf. Rom 3:6.

[134] See 1 Cor 3:13, 15.

[135] See also Rom 2:7, 10 (compare Gal 6:8b-9):

To those who seek "eschatological life" (through participation in the "new covenant" which holds the promise of "eschatological life"--see below, under "'The righteousness which means 'life.'"), [God will give] glory and honor and immortality in accordance with [their] persistence in doing good (ὑπομονὴ ἔργου ἀγαθοῦ) . . . [there will be] glory and honor and peace for every [person] who does good, for the Jew first and also for the Greek.

[136] See 1 Cor 3:15; 2 Cor 5:10.

[137] See Rom 2:5.

Fourth, Paul believes that even "if [a Christian]'s work should be burned up . . . , s/he him/herself will be saved"[138] from eternal destruction --saved from God's eschatological Wrath (ὀργή). How can this be? If deliverance from God's Wrath depended on one's being found faultless in the Judgment (which it does not), then few Christians--if any--would escape God's Wrath.[139] The "good news" of Paul's gospel is that "salvation" (σωτηρία) from Wrath[140] does not depend on human perfection, but on the gracious act of God. God has shown "goodwill" (χάρις) toward sinful human beings[141] by sending Christ to die as the sacrifice for sins which established the "new covenant."[142] God has promised to give salvation and "eschatological life" to sinners who embrace this covenant by "entrusting" (πιστεύειν) themselves to Him as Lord.[143] "Salvation" and "eschatological life" are not "earned" through good behavior. They are received, as a "gift of God's goodwill" (χάρισμα θεοῦ), through participation in the new, covenantal relationship with God, made possible by the Cross of Christ. Paul expresses this conviction throughout his epistles:

---

[138]See 1 Cor 3:15. Compare 1 Cor 5:5; 11:29-32.

[139]Paul does not deny the theoretical possibility that a person could live a faultless life. He describes Jesus as "one who never knew sin" in 2 Cor 5:21. He portrays himself as "faultless"--at least as far as the Law was concerned--in Phil 3:6b. As a general rule, however, Rom 3:23 applies: "All have sinned and lack the glory of God."

[140]Paul employs the language of eschatological "salvation" (σωτηρία, σώζειν) in Rom 1:16; 5:9 (salvation from "wrath" [ὀργή]), 10; 8:24 (salvation from "the slavery which is corruption," v. 21); 9:27 (salvation from God's judgment--see v. 28); 10:1, 9, 10, 13; 11:11, 14, 26; 13:11; 1 Cor 1:18 (salvation from "perishing" [ἀπολλύειν]), 21; 3:15; 5:5; 7:16; 9:22; 10:33; 15:2; 2 Cor 1:6; 2:15 (salvation from "perishing" [ἀπολλύειν]); 6:2; 7:10; Phil 1:19 (see the discussion of this text which appears above under "An intermediate state?"), 28 (salvation from "destruction" [ἀπώλεια]); 2:12; 1 Thess 2:16; 5:8, 9 (salvation from "wrath" [ὀργή]). He speaks of Jesus as "Savior" (σωτήρ) in Phil 3:20 (cf. 1 Thess 1:10: "Jesus, who rescues [ῥύεσθαι] us from the coming Wrath [ὀργή]").

[141]Paul's conception of "sin" was described in chapter 2.

[142]See parts I and II of chapter 4.

[143]See below, under "'The righteousness which means "life."'"

[There is] now no condemnation (κατάκριμα) for those [who are] within [the sphere of] Christ Jesus[' rule] (ἐν Χριστῷ Ἰησοῦ). (Rom 8:1)

... unrighteous [persons] (ἄδικοι, i.e., persons outside the "new covenant" based on trust) will not inherit the Rule of God (θεοῦ βασιλεία). Never be deceived! Neither sexually immoral persons (πόρνοι), nor idolators, nor adulterers, nor effeminates (μαλακοί), nor male homosexuals (ἀρσενοκοῖται), (10) nor thieves, nor covetous persons, nor drunkards, nor verbally abusive persons, nor robbers, will inherit the Rule of God (βασιλεία θεοῦ, discussed below). (11) Some [of you] used to be these very things. But you have been washed! But you have been sanctified! But you have been reckoned righteous (i.e., you have entered into the "new covenant" based on trust) in the name of the Lord Jesus Christ and by the Spirit of our God! (1 Cor 6:9-11)

God has not appointed us for Wrath (ὀργή), but for obtaining salvation (σωτηρία) through our Lord Jesus Christ, who died for us so that, whether we are awake (i.e., alive) or asleep (i.e., dead), we might live ["eschatological life"] together with him. (1 Thess 5:9-10)

The wages [paid by] Sin [is] death, but the gift of God's goodwill (τὸ χάρισμα τοῦ θεοῦ) [is] "eschatological life" (ζωὴ αἰώνιος) within [the sphere where] Christ Jesus our Lord [rules] (ἐν Χριστῷ Ἰησοῦ τῷ κυρίῳ ἡμῶν). (Rom 6:23)

If Christians guilty of evil deeds can still survive the Judgment, then why refrain from evil deeds? If Christians who "build" with "hay" and "straw" will, nevertheless, be "saved" from God's Wrath; then why put forth the effort and "expense" required to "build" with "gold" or "silver"? Does not the Apostle's gospel of "salvation" (σωτηρία) by God's "goodwill" (χάρις) through the "righteousness" (δικαιοσύνη) of "trust" (πίστις) promote sinning?[144] Paul's own response is:

Certainly not! How can we who have died to Sin (τῇ ἁμαρτίᾳ) still live within [the sphere where] it [rules] (ἐν αὐτῇ)? (Rom 6:2[145])

---

[144]Paul employs a similar rhetorical question in Rom 6:1: "Shall we remain within [the sphere where] Sin [rules] (τῇ ἁμαρτίᾳ) in order that [God's] goodwill (χάρις) may increase?"

[145]For an interpretation of Rom 6:1-14, see chapter 6.

If Christians (as we saw above) are committed to God as Lord, then they cannot continue "in Sin" (ἐν ἁμαρτίᾳ). If Christians are consciously seeking God's will, then they cannot persist in deliberate disobedience. Christians will instead "put off the deeds of darkness and put on the weapons of light."[146] They will discipline themselves, and "run" so as to obtain the "prize."[147] They will continually "test" themselves to determine whether they are "within the sphere of trust (πίστις)."[148] Christians will seek "to discern what the will of God [is],"[149] and will then do their best to accomplish it. To be content with anything less is to "reject the goodwill (χάρις) of God"[150]--to reject His gift of the "new covenant" based on Christ-like "trust" (πίστις) in Him. To be content with anything less is to "receive God's expression of [His] goodwill (ἡ χάρις τοῦ θεοῦ) in vain."[151] Christians pursue good works not because they must "merit" salvation, but because they are committed to Christ as Lord and must "appear before the judgment seat of Christ."[152]

To the "unrighteous," who do not participate in the "new covenant" established by Christ's sacrificial death, the Day of Judgment will bring wrath (ὀργή), condemnation (κατάκριμα) and eternal destruction (ἀπώλεια). To the "righteous," who trustfully embrace the "new covenant" established by Christ's sacrificial death, the Day of Judgment will bring resurrection (ἀνάστασις), salvation (σωτηρία) and "eschatological life" (ζωὴ αἰώνιος). The determining

---

[146]See Rom 13:12.

[147]See 1 Cor 9:24-27.

[148]See 2 Cor 13:5, discussed in part III of chapter 7.

[149]See Rom 12:2.

[150]See Gal 2:21.

[151]See 2 Cor 6:1.

[152]See 2 Cor 5:10; cf. Rom 14:10-12. In 1 Cor 1:7-8 and 1 Thess 5:23, Paul expresses confidence in God's/Christ's ability to preserve Christians "blameless" and "faultless" at the Coming (παρουσία) of the Lord. Compare Phil 1:6 and 2:13.

factor will be one's relationship to Jesus Christ. This is what Paul means, in Rom 2:16, when he speaks of "the Day when, according to my gospel, God [will] judge[153] the secrets of human beings (ἄνθρωποι) by means of Christ Jesus (διὰ Χριστοῦ Ἰησοῦ)."

Parousia, Resurrection, Judgment and Salvation. We may summarize Paul's expectation concerning the future Day of the Lord as follows: Christ will descend from heaven, as a conquering warrior, to execute God's Judgment on the "righteous" (i.e., Christians who have participated in the "new covenant" based on Christ-like trust in God as Lord) and the unrighteous (i.e., non-Christians, who have not shared in the "new covenant"). The "righteous" dead will be raised--or re-created--in a form free from impurities, having their works of "hay" and "straw" burned away in the refining "fire" of God's Judgment. The "righteous" who remain alive will be likewise purified, as their "bodies" (σώματα) are transformed and given the same sort of "resurrection existence" now enjoyed by their fellow servants of Christ. (Note that the Resurrection and the Judgment occur simultaneously.) All the "righteous" will be united with Christ, and will enjoy "eschatological life" with him forever.

At the same time, God's Judgment against the "unrighteous" will take the form of Wrath and a consuming "fire": Those who remain alive will be destroyed, while those who have already died will be left in the grave. The "unrighteous" will not share in the Resurrection and "eschatological life," but will simply cease to exist. Every person, every "power"[154] who opposes God,[155] will be condemned to eternal annihiliation and nothingness.

---

[153]The verb κρίνει ("He [will] judge") here represents an instance of the "futuristic present." See Brooks and Winbery, *Syntax,* 80-81.

[154]See chapter 2 under "Sin as a 'power.'"

[155]See Rom 16:20: "The God of peace will soon crush Satan under your feet."

The Rule of God (Ἡ βασιλεία τοῦ θεοῦ)

"That God may be all in all." When God's servants have been raised and purified, and God's enemies are no more, then the eschatological "Rule of God" (ἡ βασιλεία τοῦ θεοῦ)[156] will have arrived in all its fullness.[157] Paul describes this future Consummation in 1 Cor 15:24-28:[158]

(24) Then the end [will come], when [the risen and exalted Christ] will hand over the Rule (βασιλεία) to God--even to the Father--after [God] has rendered powerless every ruler and every authority and power. (25) [I can rightfully say that Christ will hand over the Rule to God only after God has rendered powerless every ruler and every authority and power] because [Psalm 109 (110):1 says that] it is necessary [that] he rule until the time when [God] will have put all "enemies" under his "feet." (26) The last enemy rendered powerless [will] be Death.[159] (27) [I can rightfully predict that even Death will be rendered powerless] because [Psalm 8:7 says that] "[God] has put all [things] in subjection under his feet." (Now when it is said that all things have been put in subjection, [it is] evident that the One who put all things in subjection to him is excepted.) (28) But after all things have been subjected to him, then even the Son himself will be subject to the One who subjected all things to him, in order that God may be all in all (πάντα ἐν πᾶσιν).[160]

---

[156]See Rom 14:17; 1 Cor 4:20; 6:9-10; 15:24, 50; Gal 5:21; 1 Thess 2:12. Beker properly refers to this emerging reality as "The Triumph of God" (see chapter 1, note 3).

[157]See chapter 2 under "'The present time.'"

[158]The relationship between God and Christ described in this passage was discussed in the portions of chapter 5 marked "The 'last Adam'" and "The 'Son of God.'"

[159]If the "last enemy" to be "rendered powerless" is "Death," then this serves as a further indication that (1) the "unrighteous" will not be raised, and that (2) the Resurrection and Judgment will occur simultaneously.

[160]Compare 1 Cor 3:21-23:

(21) All [things] belong to you--(22) whether [it be] Paul, or Apollos, or Cephas, or [the] world, or life, or death, or [things] present, or [things still to] come. All [things belong to] you! (23) And you [belong to] Christ. And Christ [belongs to] God.

350

The "good" and the "true." Under God's eschatological Rule, all wrongs will be righted; all "evil" and "falsehood" will cease.[161] According to 1 Cor 6:9-10,

> (9) . . . unrighteous [persons] will not inherit the Rule of God (θεοῦ βασιλεία) . . . Neither sexually immoral persons, nor idolators, nor adulterers, nor effeminates, nor male homosexuals, (10) nor thieves, nor covetous persons, nor drunkards, nor verbally abusive persons, nor robbers, will inherit the Rule of God (βασιλεία θεοῦ).

The Apostle issues a similar declaration in Gal 5:19-21:

> (19) Now the flesh's works are evident: They are fornication, impurity, licentiousness, (2) idolatry, sorcery, enmities, strife, jealousy, wrath, selfish ambitions, dissensions, factions, (21) envy, drunkenness, carousing, and things similar to these. I [now] warn you in advance about these things, just as I have warned [you in the past], that those who do such things will not inherit God's Rule (βασιλεία θεοῦ).

"Evil" and "falsehood" will have no part in God's eschatological Kingdom, but whatever is "good" and "true" will be raised and exalted and vindicated.[162] "Love, joy, peace, patience, kindness, goodness, trust (πίστις), gentleness, self-control"--these are the Spirit-borne[163] qualities that will characterize persons who share in the Rule of God.[164] As Paul says in Rom 14:17, "the Rule of God (ἡ βασιλεία τοῦ θεοῦ)" will be "righteousness (δικαιοσύνη) and peace and joy within [the sphere where] the Holy Spirit [rules] (ἐν πνεύματι ἀγίῳ)."

---

[161] On God's condemnation of what is "evil" and "false," see above under "'The righteous judgment of God.'"

[162] On God's vindication of what is "good" and "true," see above under "'The righteous judgment of God.'"

[163] See chapter 7, note 40.

[164] See Gal 5:19-23.

"A new Creation." God's salvation and Rule will not be limited to human beings but will encompass the whole of His Creation. In Rom 8:19-21, Paul writes:

> (19) The Creation's eager longing expectantly awaits the revealing of the children (υἱοί) of God. (20) [I can rightfully say that the Creation is eagerly awaiting a change--namely, the revealing of the children of God--] because the Creation has been subjected to futility not of [its] own will, but [by the will of] the One who subjected it in the hope (21) that the Creation itself will also be liberated from the slavery which is corruption to the freedom [from corruption] which is the glory of the children (τέκνα) of God.

When Christ returns in glory, to execute God's Judgment and to raise the "righteous" dead, the result will be "a new creation" (καινὴ κτίσις)[165]--a sanctified and glorious Creation, free from corruption and wholly conformed to the will of God. Great are the goodwill and the mercy of God, "who calls [us] into His own Rule and glory"![166]

II. PAUL'S "CORE CONVICTIONS" CONCERNING THE CHRISTIAN'S RESURRECTION TO "LIFE" WITH CHRIST

In part I of this chapter, we surveyed Paul's vision of the eschatological "future." Against this background, we will now describe the fourth and final component of Paul's "coherent center"--namely, the Christian's resurrection to "eschatological life" with Christ.[167] Paul understands the promised resurrection of the Christian to be (1) an act of God, (2) his/her future participation in the general Resurrection of the righteous, (3) his/her future entrance into

---

[165]See 2 Cor 5:17 and Gal 6:15, both discussed in chapter 7.

[166]See 1 Thess 2:12.

[167]The three other major components of Paul's "coherent center" are (1) Christ's death (discussed in chapter 4), (2) Christ's resurrection to "eschatological life" (discussed in chapter 5), and (3) the Christian's "death" with Christ (discussed in chapter 7). See our thesis statement in chapter 1.

"eschatological life," which is characterized by glory and immortality, and (4) God's future exaltation of the humble, trusting Christian.

"The One who raised the Lord Jesus will also raise us"--The Christian's Resurrection to "Life" as an Act of God (Core Conviction 11)

Resurrection as God's act of "strength." In accordance with Jewish tradition,[168] Paul believes that Christians will rise to "eschatological life" not by their own power, but by the power or "strength" (δύναμις) of God.[169] It is "God who raises the dead"[170] out of annihilation and nothingness. It is "God who makes the dead alive and who calls into existence things which had no existence (θεὸς τοῦ ζῳοποιοῦντος τοὺς νεκροὺς καὶ καλοῦντος τὰ μὴ ὄντα ὡς ὄντα)."[171] A clear expression of this first Pauline "core conviction" appears in 2 Cor 4:14:

> The One who raised the Lord Jesus will also raise us along with Jesus, and will bring us into [His] presence along with you.[172]

---

[168]See chapter 5 under "'. . . he is alive because of God's strength.'"

[169]See 2 Cor 12:9 ("[God's] strength [δύναμις] achieves its intended end within [the sphere where] 'weakness' [is the rule]"), 2 Cor 6:14 ("God raised the Lord and He will also raise us by means of His strength [δύναμις]"), 2 Cor 13:4 ("we will live along with [Christ] because of the strength [δύναμις] God will demonstrate toward you"), and Phil 3:10-11 ("[I have suffered the loss of all things] in order that I may know [Christ], and the strength [δύναμις] [of God which effected] his resurrection, . . . [so that] if at all possible I may attain to the Resurrection of the dead"), all discussed in chapter 7.

[170]See 2 Cor 1:9.

[171]See Rom 4:17.

[172]Compare Rom 6:4 ("in order that, just as Christ has been raised from the dead by the Glory who is the Father, so might we also live a new life"); 1 Cor 15:22 ("within [the sphere determined by] Christ, all [persons] will be made alive [ζῳοποιηθήσονται, a 'divine passive']"), 42 ("The Resurrection of the dead [is] like [this]. [The body] is sowed in corruption; it is raised [ἐγείρεται, a 'divine passive'] in incorruption"), 51 ("we will all be transformed [ἀλλαγησόμεθα, a 'divine passive']"). Paul sometimes portrays God as working through the agency of His Son (see 1 Cor 15:45 [Christ as "life-giving Spirit"] and Phil 3:21 ["(Christ) will transform our body of humiliation, so that it will be in conformity with his body of glory"]) or His Holy Spirit (see Rom 8:11 ["if the Spirit of the One who raised Jesus from the dead dwells in you; (then) the One who raised Christ from the dead will also give life to your mortal body by means of His Spirit, who is living in you"]).

Resurrection as God's gift of "goodwill." If God alone can raise the dead, then it is impossible for human beings to "save" (σώζειν) themselves from the Wrath (ὀργή) of endless annihiliation.[173] If God alone can raise the dead, then human beings cannot "achieve" eternal "life." Salvation, resurrection, and "eschatological life" are wholly the work of God. They are given at God's good pleasure as the gift of God's "goodwill" (χάρις). Paul gives voice to this truth in Rom 6:23, where he says:

The wages [paid by] Sin [is] death, but the gift of God's goodwill (τὸ χάρισμα τοῦ θεοῦ) [is] "eschatological life" (ζωὴ αἰώνιος) within [the sphere where] Christ Jesus our Lord [rules] (ἐν Χριστῷ Ἰησοῦ τῷ κυρίῳ ἡμῶν).[174]

"The righteousness which means 'life'"--The Christian's Resurrection to "Life" as Participation in the General Resurrection of the Righteous (Core Conviction 12)

The future Resurrection of the righteous. The Apostle's second "core conviction" is that the Christian's resurrection with Christ will be his/her future participation in the general Resurrection of the righteous. When Paul writes concerning the "resurrection" (ἀνάστασις, ἀνιστάναι, ἐξανάστασις, ἐγείρειν) of Christians,[175] he is not describing Christian existence during "the present time."[176] Nor is he referring to a series of individual "resurrections" occurring immediately after death. Paul employs the term "resurrection" to refer to a particular event in his eschatological scenario--namely, the Resurrection of the righteous dead. This event began in the past, when God raised up Jesus as "the first-fruits of those who have fallen asleep" (as described in

---

[173]On "salvation" (σωτηρία) as deliverance from God's Wrath (ὀργή), see above under "Judgment and salvation for the righteous."

[174]Compare Rom 7:24-25a: "I [am] a miserable man! Who will rescue me from this body [determined by] Death (σῶμα τοῦ θανάτου)? [May] goodwill (χάρις) [be attributed] to God[, who rescues me] by means of Jesus Christ our Lord!"

[175]See 1 Cor 15:12, 13, 16, 21, 29, 32, 35, 42, 43, 44, 52; 2 Cor 1:9; 4:14; Phil 3:11.

[176]See chapter 2 under "'The present time.'"

chapter 5).[177] It will be completed in the future, at the time of Christ's Parousia, when God re-creates the remainder of His servants by raising them up to "eschatological life" (as described in part I of this chapter).

It is important to note that Paul's "core" belief in the general Resurrection of the righteous presupposes the eschatological/apocalyptic scenario described earlier in this chapter. The Day of the Lord, Christ's Parousia, the Resurrection, the final Judgment, the Rule of God--all belong to the "coherent center" of Paul's theology. In our thesis statement (see chapter 1 under "Thesis"), we allow the terms "resurrection," "eschatological life," and "future" to stand for this whole complex of ideas--the whole sweep of the eschatological "future." We lay particular stress on "the Christian's resurrection with Christ"--the event which inaugurates the eschatological "future"--because Paul himself does so in the "summary statements" discussed in chapter 1.

The covenant of "life." Belief in the Resurrection was not uncommon among Jews of Paul's time. For over two centuries, prophets and visionaries had predicted that God would soon put an end to this "present evil age" and raise up the "righteous" to "eschatological life."[178] Paul differed with his contemporaries not over the fact of the Resurrection, but over which "righteous" (δίκαιος) persons would share in the Rule of God. Would it be Jews reckoned "righteous" under the Mosaic covenant based on the Law? or would it be Jewish and Gentile Christians reckoned "righteous" under the "new covenant" based on trust (πίστις)?[179]

Paul believed that the Mosaic Law was not "able to make 'alive.'"[180] He proclaimed, instead, that resurrection and "eschatological life" come only

---

[177]See the portion of chapter 5 marked "'The first-fruits of those who have fallen asleep.'"

[178]See part I of chapter 5.

[179]On "righteousness" (δικαιοσύνη) as a covenantal term, see chapter 2.

[180]See Gal 3:21.

through participation in the "new covenant" established by Christ's sacrificial death.[181] Paul sets the two covenants in opposition to one another in 2 Cor 3:6, where he maintains that the Mosaic covenant "kills," while the "new covenant" "makes 'alive.'" He finds scriptural support for this view in Hab 2:4, which identifies "the [person reckoned] righteous on the basis of trust (ἐκ πίστεως)"--not the person reckoned righteous under the Jewish Law--as the one who "will live ['eschatological life'] (ζήσεται)."[182] Paul expects the Resurrection of the "righteous" (δίκαιοι) to involve persons who share in the "new covenant," rather than persons who cling to the "old."[183]

Paul links "eschatological life" to "new covenant" righteousness throughout his letters. In Rom 5:18, "all persons [enter] into the righteousness [which means] 'life' through the righteous deed of the one [man Jesus Christ]" (i.e., through Christ's sacrificial death, by which God established the "new covenant" with its "righteousness" based on trust [πίστις]).[184] In 1 Cor 6:9-14, "unrighteous [persons] will not inherit the Rule of God" (v. 9), but Christians will be "raised up" by God's "strength" (v. 14) since they are "reckoned righteous" through trust (v. 14). Galatians 5:5 says that Christians, "by means of trust (ἐκ πίστεως), await eagerly what righteousness hopes for (ἐλπὶς δικαιο-σύνης)"--namely, the resurrection/transformation to "eschatological life." In the same way, Phil 3:8-11 identifies "the righteousness from God based on

---

[181]For a discussion of Christ's sacrifice, see part I of chapter 4.

[182]See Rom 1:17 and Gal 3:11.

[183]This statement is not intended to rule out the possibility that there may be Jewish Christians who participate in both covenants. However, "eschatological life" comes through participation in the "new covenant."

[184]Romans 5:12-21 was discussed in chapter 3. Compare Rom 8:10 ("life because of righteousness," ζωὴ διὰ δικαιοσύνην) and 8:30b ("those whom He reckoned righteous--these He also glorified"). On Christ's death as the act of "righteousness" which established the "new covenant," see parts I and II of chapter 4.

trust" (v. 9) as the means by which Paul himself will "attain to the Resurrection of the dead" (v. 11).[185]

Paul communicates the idea that "future" participation in the Resurrection depends on "present"[186] participation in "new covenant" righteousness through other means as well. Sometimes he uses the language of "salvation" (σωτηρία):[187]

(9) Since we have now been reckoned righteous by means of [Christ's] blood[y sacrificial death]; [how] much more, then, will we be saved from Wrath by means of it![188] (10) [I can rightfully declare that we will be saved from God's Wrath by means of Christ's blood-sacrifice] because if, while we were enemies, we have been reconciled to God by means of the death of His Son [(and we have been)]; [then how] much more--since we have been reconciled--will we be saved within [the sphere where] his "life" [is the rule]! (Rom 5:9-10)[189]

. . . if you confess with your mouth [that] Jesus [is] Lord and trustfully believe (πιστεύειν) with your heart that God raised him from the dead, [then] you will be saved (σώζειν). For [God's raising of Jesus] is trustfully believed (πιστεύειν) with the heart toward [the goal of] righteousness (εἰς δικαιοσύνην), and [the lordship of Jesus] is confessed with the mouth toward [the goal of] salvation (εἰς σωτηρίαν). (Romans 10:9-10)[190]

---

[185] Philippians 3:6b-11 was discussed in chapter 7.

[186] On the eschatological "future" and "the present time," see the portion of chapter 2 marked "'The present time.'"

[187] See note 140.

[188] Compare 1 Thess 5:9-10:

(9) For God has not appointed us for Wrath but for attaining salvation (σωτηρία) through our Lord Jesus Christ, (10) who died for us (ὑπὲρ ἡμῶν, one of the sacrificial formulae discussed in part I of chapter 4) so that, whether we are awake or asleep (i.e., whether we are alive or dead at his Parousia), we might live ["eschatological" life] (ζήσωμεν) together with him (σὺν αὐτῷ).

[189] Romans 5:12-21 was discussed in chapter 3.

[190] Compare Rom 11:25-27, which draws a connection between God's new "covenant" and the "salvation" of "all Israel" (= trusting Jews and trusting Gentiles, as in Gal 6:16).

On other occasions, Paul speaks of "dying" (= Christ-like trust in God, the content of "righteousness" under the "new covenant"[191]) and "living" (= resurrection existence or "eschatological life") with Christ:

> (6) Our old self has been crucified together with [Christ] (i.e., Christians have "entrusted" [πιστεύειν] themselves to God, just as Jesus "entrusted" himself to God on the cross), in order that the body ruled by Sin might pass away, with the result that we are no longer enslaved to Sin. (7) [I can rightfully say that the crucified self is no longer enslaved to Sin] because the person who has [thus] died (i.e., the Christian who displays Christ-like "trust" [πίστις] in God) has been reckoned righteous [under the "new covenant" (since "trust" is the content of "righteousness" under the "new covenant")]; s/he is apart from Sin. (8) Now if we have died with Christ (i.e., if we trust in God/participate in the "new covenant"), then we trust that we will also come to "[eschatological] life" with him. (Romans 6: 6-8)[192]

> (10) [We apostles] are always carrying about in our body (σῶμα) the "death" of Jesus (i.e., we display the same "trust" in God [= "new covenant" righteousness] seen in the dying Jesus), in order that the "[eschatological] life" of Jesus might also be manifested in our body. (11) For we who are alive are continually being delivered over to "death" for the sake of Jesus (i.e., we continually trust in God/fulfil "new covenant" righteousness--which often results in persecution or martyrdom), in order that the "[eschatological] life" of Jesus might also be manifested in our mortal flesh. (2 Cor 4:10-11)[193]

> . . . you [Corinthians] are continually in our hearts, toward the end of our "dying" (i.e., "trusting" in God, or participating in the "new covenant") together and our "living" ["eschatological life"] together. (2 Cor 7:3b)

On still another occasion--namely, his defense against the "super apostles" of Corinth--Paul expresses this same "core conviction" in terms of "weakness" (= Christ-like trust, the content of righteousness under the "new covenant" which

---

[191]See chapter 7.

[192]Romans 6:1-14 was discussed in chapters 6 and 7.

[193]2 Corinthians 4:10-14 was discussed in parts I and II of chapter 7. Compare 2 Cor 6:4, 9: "We [apostles] commend [our]selves as God's servants in every [way] . . . as [persons who] are 'dying' and, behold, we 'live.'"

Paul displays in his suffering for Christ's sake) and "strength" (= the power by which God raises the dead to "eschatological life"):

> (9) Then [God] has said to me, "My expression of my goodwill (i.e., Christ's death on the cross, by which God established the "new covenant" which holds the promise of "eschatological life" for those who trust in Him) is enough for you, for strength (i.e., the power by which God raises the dead) achieves its intended end (i.e., it raises the dead) within the sphere where 'weakness' is the rule" (i.e., it operates within the bounds of the trust Paul displays in his suffering, or within the bounds of the "new covenant" based on trust). Most gladly, therefore, will I boast all the more within the sphere where my "weaknesses" (i.e., trust/the "new covenant") are the rule, so that the strength which is Christ may "pitch its tent" upon me (i.e., so that I may participate in the promised Resurrection of the dead). (10) For this reason, I am delighted to be within the sphere where "weaknesses" are the rule (i.e., I am delighted to participate in the "new covenant" based on trust)--that is, within the sphere where indignities, needs, persecutions and pressures suffered for the sake of Christ are the rule. [I am delighted to be within the sphere where "weaknesses" are the rule (i.e., within the "new covenant" based on trust) because whenever I am "weak" (i.e., when I participate in the "new covenant" based on trust), then am I "strong" (i.e., I participate in the Resurrection of the dead effected by God's strength)! (2 Corinthians 12:9-10)

> (4) . . . [Christ] was indeed crucified because of "weakness" (i.e., trust in God), but he is alive because of God's strength (i.e., the power by which God raises the dead) . . . we ourselves are now "weak" within the sphere ruled by him (i.e., we trust; we participate in the "new covenant" righteousness based on trust in God/Christ as Lord), but we will live along with him (i.e., we will participate, along with Christ, in the general Resurrection of the righteous) because of the strength God will demonstrate toward you.[194] (5a) Test yourselves to determine whether you are within the sphere where trust is the rule (i.e., within the "new covenant" based on trust). (2 Corinthians 13:4-5a)[195]

---

[194]Compare 1 Thess 3:7-8 ("we have been encouraged . . . by your trust; for now we live, if you continue to stand firm within [the sphere of] the Lord's [rule]") and 4:16 ("the dead within [the sphere of] Christ's [rule] will rise first").

[195]Both 2 Cor 12:9-10 and 2 Cor 13:4-5a were discussed in part III of chapter 7.

"The strength of God for salvation." Paul's belief that the Resurrection will be limited to "righteous" Christians is also reflected in the way he describes his gospel. In Rom 1:16-17, the Apostle writes:

(16) [I am eager to preach the gospel to you who are in Rome] because I am not ashamed of the gospel. [I am not ashamed of the gospel] because it is the strength of God (δύναμις θεοῦ) for salvation (σωτηρία) for every [person] who trusts (πιστεύειν), for the Jew first and also for the Greek. (17) [The gospel is the strength of God for the salvation of both Jews and Greeks] because, in [the gospel] (ἐν αὐτῷ), God's expression of His righteousness (δικαιοσύνη θεοῦ) is revealed [to be] based entirely on trust (ἐκ πίστεως εἰς πίστιν).[196] [It is] just as it has been written [in Habakkuk 2:4]: "The [person reckoned] righteous on the basis of trust (ἐκ πίστεως) will live ['eschatological life']."

The content of Paul's gospel is that (1) Christ's death (i.e., "God's expression of His righteousness"[197]) was the sacrifice for sins by which God established the "new covenant" based on trust (as discussed in chapters 4 and 7), and that (2) Christ's resurrection was the beginning of the general Resurrection of those reckoned "righteous" under the "new covenant" (as discussed in chapters 5 and 8). On the basis of this proclamation, Paul urges all persons --both Jews and Gentiles--to put their trust in God, to embrace His "new

---

[196]Dunn (*Romans,* 1:43) shows that "the [ἐκ . . . εἰς . . .] idiom is clearly one denoting some sort of progression, where ἐκ refers to the starting point and εἰς the end" (see, e.g., Ps 84:7 [83:7, LXX] [πορεύσονται ἐκ δυνάμεως εἰς δύναμιν, "they will proceed from strength to (greater) strength"]; Jer 9:3 [LXX] [ἐκ κακῶν εἰς κακὰ ἐξήλθοσαν, "they have gone from evil to (greater) evil"]; 2 Cor 2:16 [ὀσμὴ ἐκ θανάτου εἰς θάνατον . . . ἐκ ζωῆς εἰς ζωήν, "a fragrance from death to (greater) death . . . from life to (greater) life"]; cf. 2 Cor 3:18 [ἀπὸ δόξης εἰς δόξαν, "from (one degree of) glory to (a greater degree of) glory"]). Here in Rom 1:17, the Apostle may intend for the phrase to express the idea of "starting with [Christ's] act of trust [i.e., his sacrificial death on the cross by which God established the 'new covenant' based on trust] and ending with the trust [of Jews and Gentiles who embrace this 'new covenant' of trust]." (The phrase would then be parallel to 2 Cor 5:14b ["One has died for all; therefore all have died"], as interpreted in chapter 7 under "2 Corinthians 5:11, 14-15; 4:10-14; and 7:3b.") However, the context suggests that Paul's immediate concern is human trust alone. Since the "new covenant" (i.e., "God's expression of His righteousness"--see the portion of chapter 2 marked "Verse 21") "starts with [human] trust and ends with [human] trust"--since it is "based entirely on trust" (ἐκ πίστεως εἰς πίστιν)--it is free from the racial limitations of the Mosaic covenant and is open to "every [person] who trusts," both Jew and Gentile alike.

[197]See the portion of chapter 2 on Rom 3:21.

covenant," to enter the sphere within which God has chosen to exercise His divine "strength" (δύναμις) to raise the dead.[198] Only because Paul links participation in the Resurrection to "new covenant" righteousness is he able to describe his gospel (which calls for such righteousness) as "the strength of God for salvation for every person who trusts" (δύναμις θεοῦ εἰς σωτηρίαν παντὶ τῷ πιστεύοντι).[199]

"An eternal weight of eschatological glory"--The Christian's Resurrection to "Life" as His/Her Future Entrance Into "Eschatological Life," Which Is Characterized by Glory and Immortality (Core Conviction 13)

Paul employs the phrase "eschatological life" (ζωὴ αἰώνιος)[200] to refer to the "righteous" Christian's post-Parousia, post-Judgment, post-Resurrection (or post-transformation) existence under the consummated Rule of God (ἡ βασιλεία τοῦ θεοῦ, discussed above). What will be the shape of "eschatological life"? What will be the nature of "resurrection existence"?

"What eye has not seen, what ear has not heard, what has not occurred to the human heart--[this is] what God has prepared for those who love Him."[201] "Now we see in a mirror dimly,"[202] but the contours of God's

---

[198]See above under "'The One who raised the Lord Jesus.'"

[199]Compare 1 Cor 1:18, 21 ("the word which concerns the cross is . . . the strength [δύναμις] of God . . . God was pleased to save those who trust by means of the foolishness which is [the content of] the proclamation"); Rom 11:15 ("if [Israel's] rejection [of the gospel (see 10:16, 21) means] reconciliation of the world, [then] what [will their] acceptance [of the gospel mean] if not '[eschatological] life' from the dead?"); 1 Thess 2:16 ("speaking to the Gentiles in order that they may be saved"). See also the discussion of Paul's "ministry of reconciliation" in chapter 4, under "2 Corinthians 5:18-21."

[200]Note Paul's use of the terms (1) ζωὴ αἰώνιος ("eschatological life") in Rom 2:7; 5:21; 6:22, 23; Gal 6:8; (2) ζωή ("[eschatological] life") in Rom 5:17, 18; 6:4; 8:2, 6, 10; 2 Cor 2:16; 4:10, 11, 12; 5:4; Phil 2:16; 4:3; and (3) ζῆν ("to live ['eschatological life']") in Rom 1:17; 6:11, 13; 8:13b; 2 Cor 4:11b; 6:9; 13:4b; Gal 3:11; 1 Thess 3:8; 5:10.

[201]See 1 Cor 2:9.

[202]See 1 Cor 13:12.

"new creation" (καινὴ κτίσις)²⁰³ have already come into view. Paul believes that Christians will be raised to the same form of somatic (i.e., bodily) existence now enjoyed by the risen Christ (described in chapter 5).²⁰⁴ This "new life" (καινὴ ζωή)²⁰⁵ will be "spiritual" (πνευματικός)²⁰⁶ and "heavenly" (ἐπουράνιος).²⁰⁷ Paul describes it as "peace" (εἰρήνη),²⁰⁸ "strength" (δύναμις),²⁰⁹ and "joy" (χαρά)²¹⁰ in the presence of the Lord.²¹¹ Two qualities of the resurrection body (σῶμα) seem most firmly fixed in the Apostle's mind: First, it will be "eternal" (αἰώνιος),²¹² "immortal" (ἀθάνατος or ἄφθαρτος),²¹³

---

²⁰³See 2 Cor 5:17 and Gal 6:15, discussed above.

²⁰⁴See, e.g., Rom 6:5 ("if we have been planted together in [a 'death'] like [Christ's] death, then we will certainly also [participate in a resurrection like his] resurrection"); 1 Cor 15:49 ("just as we have worn the image of the earthly [man Adam], we will also bear the image of the heavenly [man, Jesus Christ]"); Phil 3:21 ("[Christ] will transform our body of humiliation, so that it will be in conformity with his body of glory").

²⁰⁵See Rom 6:4.

²⁰⁶See 1 Cor 15:44, 46; cf. 2 Cor 5:5 ("[God] has given to us the down-payment which is the Spirit").

²⁰⁷See 1 Cor 15:48, 49; 2 Cor 5:1 ("we have a 'building' from God, a 'house' not made by [human] hands, eternal [and] eschatological [αἰώνιος] in the heavens"), 2 ("our 'dwelling' which is from heaven"); Phil 3:20 ("our commonwealth is in the heavens").

²⁰⁸See Rom 2:10; 8:6; 14:17 ("the Rule of God is . . . peace").

²⁰⁹See, e.g., 1 Cor 15:43.

²¹⁰See Rom 14:17 ("the Rule of God is . . . joy"); cf. 2 Cor 6:9-10 ("persons who are dying and, behold, we live [ἀεὶ χαίρειν]").

²¹¹See 2 Cor 5:8 ("away from the [mortal] body and housed with the Lord"); Phil 1:23 ("I have the desire to depart and be with Christ"); 1 Thess 4:17 ("Thus will we always be with the Lord").

²¹²See, e.g., 2 Cor 4:17 ("an eternal weight of eschatological glory" [αἰώνιος βάρος δόξης]), 18; 5:1.

²¹³See Rom 2:7; 1 Cor 15:53, 54.

"incorruptible" (ἄφθαρτος).[214]   Second, it will shine with the radiance of eschatological "glory" (δόξα).[215] Paul's "core conviction" that "eschatological life" will be characterized by "glory" and "immortality" is expressed most clearly in 1 Cor 15:42-43:

> (42) The Resurrection of the dead [is] like [this]. [The body] is sowed in corruption (φθορά); it is raised in incorruption (ἀφθαρσία). (43) It is sowed in dishonor (ἀτιμία); it is raised in glory (δόξα).

"Glory and honor and immortality"--The Christian's Resurrection to "Life" as God's Future Exaltation of the Humble, Trusting Christian (Core Conviction 14)

In chapter 5, we saw that Paul interprets Christ's resurrection from the dead as God's "super-exaltation" of the humble Jesus to the status of "Lord" (κύριος) over all.[216]   Paul does not believe that Christians will receive "the Name which is above every name,"[217] but he does view the Resurrection of the "righteous" as an exaltation to "honor" (τιμή),[218] an elevation to "reign" (βασιλεία).[219]   When Christ returns from heaven, Paul expects him to "transform our body of humiliation (τὸ σῶμα τῆς ταπεινώσεως), so that it will be in

---

[214]See Rom 8:21 ("liberated from the slavery which is corruption to the freedom [from corruption] which is the glory of the children of God"); 1 Cor 9:25 ("an incorruptible crown"); 15:42, 50, 52, 53, 54.

[215]See Rom 2:7, 10; 5:2; 8:17, 18, 21, 30; 9:23; 1 Cor 2:7; 15:43; 2 Cor 3:18; 4:17 ("an eternal weight of eschatological glory" [αἰώνιος βάρος δόξης]); Phil 3:21; 1 Thess 2:12. See also the portion of chapter 2 on "The 'glory' (δόξα) taken from Adam at the Fall and restored to the righteous at the Eschaton."

[216]See the section of chapter 5 marked "'The Name which is above every name.'"

[217]See Phil 2:9, discussed in chapter 5.

[218]See Rom 2:7 ("to those who seek 'eschatological life,' [God will give] glory and honor and immortality"), 10; 1 Cor 15:43 ("[the body] is sowed in dishonor [ἀτιμία]; it is raised in glory"); cf. Rom 10:11 ("no one who trusts in Him will be put to shame").

[219]See 1 Cor 4:8 and 11 ("You have begun to reign without us! Would that you did reign, so that we might reign together with you! . . . You [are honored] glorious[ly], but we [are] dishonored"), where Paul criticizes the Corinthians' premature celebration of the final Consummation.

conformity with his body of glory (τὸ σῶμα τῆς δόξης αὐτοῦ)."²²⁰ When God establishes His Rule (βασιλεία), Paul expects that "the saints will judge the world;" Christians "will judge angels."²²¹

---

²²⁰See Phil 3:21.

²²¹See 1 Cor 6:2-3. Fee (*First Corinthians*, 234) comments that this passage "probably reflects an apocalyptic motif as to the judgment of fallen angels" which may be seen, for example, in 2 Pet 2:4, Jude 6, and 1 Enoch 67-69.

CHAPTER NINE

"THE TRUTH WHICH IS THE GOSPEL"

Our task in this study has been to reconstruct the "coherent center" of Paul's theology, or "the truth which is the gospel"[1] (ἡ ἀλήθεια τοῦ εὐαγγελίου).[2] "Summary statements" (e.g., Rom 6:3-11; 8:17; 2 Cor 4:10-11; 13:4-5a; Phil 3: 10-11) scattered throughout the Apostle's writings suggest that (1) Christ's death, (2) Christ's resurrection, (3) the Christian's "death" with Christ, and (4) the Christian's resurrection with Christ, constitute the nucleus[3] of Paul's thought.[4] Working from this hypothesis, we have analyzed these four ideas in order to determine the "core convictions" implicit in each. The results are summarized in the thesis put forward in chapter one:

---

[1]These terms were defined in chapter 1 under "'Paul's theology' as 'the truth'" and "The 'coherent center' of Paul's theology."

[2]See Gal 2:5, 14.

[3]We are here thinking of a "nucleus" in the sense of a central network of ideas around which other ideas are organized.

[4]See the discussion of "Pauline 'summary statements'" in chapter 1.

The content of the "coherent center" of Paul's theology consists of a network of fourteen "core convictions" revolving around four ideas--namely,

(A) Christ's death, which Paul understands as
   (1) the sacrifice for sins which established the "new covenant,"
   (2) God's expression of His righteousness toward both Abraham and all nations, and
   (3) Christ's expression of trust in, or self-humiliation before God;

(B) Christ's resurrection to "eschatological life," which Paul understands as
   (4) an act of God,
   (5) the beginning of the eschatological age and the general Resurrection of the righteous,
   (6) Christ's entrance into "eschatological life," which is characterized by glory and immortality, and
   (7) God's exaltation of the humble, trusting Jesus;

(C) the Christian's "death" with Christ, which Paul understands as his/her
   (8) trust in, or self-humiliation before God,
   (9) participation in the "new covenant," or in the "righteousness" that is based on trust, and (in the case of many Christians)
   (10) suffering for Christ's sake; and

(D) the Christian's resurrection to "eschatological life" with Christ, which Paul understands as
   (11) an act of God,
   (12) his/her future participation in the general Resurrection of the righteous,
   (13) his/her future entrance into "eschatological life," which is characterized by glory and immortality, and
   (14) God's future exaltation of the humble, trusting Christian.

In earlier chapters, we examined each of these "core convictions" individually, showing what they mean and where they occur in the Pauline texts. Still, the whole of Paul's "coherent center" is greater than the sum of its parts. When we reassemble the fourteen major components of Paul's theology, placing each in its proper relationship to the others, the result is an "apocalyptic interpretation of the Christ-event,"[5] which may be summarized as follows:

---

[5]The term is Beker's (see chapter 1, note 24).

In the past, God--the God of Abraham, Isaac and Jacob, the God of Moses and Israel, the God of David and the prophets, the God and Father of Jesus Christ--created the heavens and the earth, where He reigned as Lord over all. Adam, the first man, initiated "the present evil age" (ὁ αἰὼν ὁ ἐνεστηκὼς πονηρός or αἰὼν οὗτος ["this age"])[6] by rejecting God's lordship, and thereby introducing the "powers" of Sin (ἁμαρτία) and Death (θάνατος) into the realm of God's Creation.[7]

God showed "goodwill" (χάρις) toward sinful humanity by making a covenant with Abraham and his descendants, under which He promised to "bless" (εὐλογεῖν) persons from "all nations" who adopt Abraham's "trust" (πίστις) in God (i.e., the "children of Abraham").[8] The Jewish Scriptures "proclaimed the gospel in advance" (προευαγγελίζειν)[9] by testifying that God would fulfil His covenant promise through Jesus Christ, who is both the human descendant of Abraham and David,[10] and the divine, preexistent "equal" of God.[11]

Christ fulfilled God's promise to the patriarchs[12] by "humbling himself"--by "emptying himself" of the glory he shared with the Father, and then

---

[6]See Gal 1:4, along with Rom 12:2; 1 Cor 1:20; 2:6, 8; 3:18; 2 Cor 4:4.

[7]In our thesis statement, the terms "God" and "sin" presuppose this entire complex of ideas. Adam, Sin, Death, and "the present evil age" were discussed in chapters 2 and 3.

[8]See (1) Gen 12:3 and (2) Gen 15:6, which Paul interprets in (1) Gal 3:8-9, and (2) Rom 4:1-25; Gal 3:6-9, respectively.

[9]See Gal 3:8; cf. Rom 1:1-2; 3:21; 1 Cor 15:3-4 ("according to the scriptures"). The Old Testament passage which most clearly anticipates Paul's gospel is Hab 2:4 ("The [person reckoned] righteous on the basis of trust will live ['eschatological life'].") which the Apostle cites in Rom 1:17 and Gal 3:11.

[10]See Gal 3:16 and Rom 1:3.

[11]See Phil 2:6.

[12]See Rom 15:8.

"trustfully" (πίστις Χριστοῦ, "Christ's act of trust") and "obediently" (ὑπακοή)[13] (core conviction 3) dying on the cross as the sacrifice which established the "new covenant" (καινὴ διαθήκη) (core conviction 1).[14] This "new covenant" is the "blessing" (εὐλογία) for "all nations," which God promised to Abraham. Since its "righteousness" (δικαιοσύνη) is based on Christ-like "trust" (πίστις), or Abraham-like "trust" in God, the "new covenant" is open to both Jews and Gentiles who commit themselves to Him as Lord. Since it holds the promise of resurrection (ἀνάστασις) to "eschatological life" (ζωὴ αἰώνιος) in the coming "Rule of God" (ἡ βασιλεία τοῦ θεοῦ), the "new covenant" offers a glorious future to those who fulfil its "righteousness" of "trust." In acting to establish the "new covenant" through His Son Jesus Christ, God performed covenant "righteousness" (δικαιοσύνη θεοῦ, "God's expression of His righteousness") toward both Abraham (in the sense that God gave the "new covenant" in fulfilment of His covenant obligation to Abraham) and "all nations" (in the sense that God acted to establish this "new covenant" with them) (core conviction 2).

On the third day,[15] God raised Christ to "eschatological life" (core conviction 4) and exalted him to the highest place as "the last Adam" (ὁ ἔσχατος Ἀδάμ), the Davidic "Son of God" (υἱὸς θεοῦ), and the heavenly "Lord" (κύριος)[16] (core conviction 7) who sits enthroned at God's right hand.[17] Christ's resurrection marked the beginning of the general Resurrection of the "righteous": he is "the first-fruits (ἀπαρχή) of those who have fallen asleep."[18]

---

[13]See, e.g., Phil 2:6-8.

[14]See, e.g., 1 Cor 11:24-26.

[15]See 1 Cor 15:4.

[16]See, e.g., Rom 1:4 and Phil 2:9-11.

[17]See Rom 8:34; cf. the allusion to Ps 110:1 (109:1, LXX), which appears in 1 Cor 15:25, 27.

[18]See 1 Cor 15:20, 23.

The Lord's entrance into "eschatological life" also marked the beginning of "the present time" (ὁ νῦν καιρός), in which the "present evil age" starts to fade away as the "eschatological age" starts to dawn (core conviction 5). Christ's new "resurrection existence" is characterized by "honor" (δόξα or τιμή) and "glory" (δόξα) and "immortality" (ἀθανασία or ἀφθαρσία) (core conviction 6).

During "the present time," God appoints ministers (such as Paul) to preach the "gospel" (εὐαγγέλιον)--or "good news"--concerning what God has accomplished in the person of Jesus Christ.[19] Both Jews and Gentiles are urged to respond to God's act of "goodwill" (χάρις) by "dying with Christ" (ἀποθνήσκειν σὺν Χριστῷ)--i.e., by exercising Christ-like (or Abraham-like) "trust" (πίστις) in God (core conviction 8), by fulfilling "new covenant" righteousness (core conviction 9), by "walking by the Spirit,"[20] by embracing the emerging "Rule of God" (ἡ βασιλεία τοῦ θεοῦ). Such persons may suffer persecution and martyrdom (core conviction 10); but they rejoice in the knowledge that they have been transferred from the dominion of Sin to the dominion of God in the present, and they will participate in the Resurrection to "eschatological life" in the future.

At some point in the future, Christ will return from heaven (his Parousia, παρουσία) to execute God's "Judgment" (κρίσις) on the living and the dead. "Unrighteous" persons (ἄδικοι), who have not participated in God's "new covenant," will be destroyed (if still alive) or left in the grave (if already dead). "Righteous" persons (δίκαιοι), who have embraced the "new covenant," will be raised up (if already dead) (core conviction 12) or transformed (if still alive) by God (core conviction 11) to enjoy "eschatological life" with Christ

---

[19]See, e.g., Rom 1:5; 10:8-18; 2 Cor 3:5-6; 5:18-6:2 ("the ministry of reconciliation").

[20]See, e.g., Gal 5:25.

under God's consummated Reign (βασιλεία).[21] The Christian's new "life" will be an exalted existence (core conviction 14) characterized by "honor" (δόξα or τιμή), "glory" (δόξα), and "immortality" (ἀθανασία or ἀφθαρσία) (core conviction 13).

The preceding summary describes the essential and unchanging elements of Paul's gospel in their proper relationship to one another. Out of this "coherent center," Paul speaks to the contingent situations which called forth his letters to the churches (e.g., the Judaizing heresy at Galatia, confusion concerning dead Christians in Thessalonica, the movement of the "super apostles" into Corinth). When Paul wishes to refer to this entire network of convictions, he speaks of his "gospel" (εὐαγγέλιον), or he composes a "summary statement" organized around the four fundamental components of his thought--namely, (1) Christ's death, (2) Christ's resurrection, (3) the Christian's "death" with Christ, and (4) the Christian's resurrection with Christ. These four ideas contain within themselves all fourteen of the "core convictions" which together make up the "coherent center" of Paul's theology.

Our reconstruction of Paul's "coherent center" meets the five criteria laid down in chapter 1 for determining the content of that "center":[22]

First, it is based on the seven undisputed epistles of Paul--namely, Romans, 1 Corinthians, 2 Corinthians, Galatians, Philippians, 1 Thessalonians and Philemon.

Second, it treats traditional materials employed by Paul (e.g., the "Kenosis Hymn" of Phil 2:6-11 and the summary of the gospel found in 1 Cor 15:3-7) as accurate expressions of the Apostle's own convictions.

---

[21]In our thesis statement, the terms "resurrection," "eschatological life," and "future" presuppose the apocalyptic scenario described here--namely, Christ's Parousia, the Resurrection, the final Judgment, and the consummation of God's eschatological Reign.

[22]See chapter 1 under "Criteria for identifying the 'center.'"

Third, it includes nothing that "is of merely temporal, contingent significance."[23] Everything assigned to the Pauline "center" is just as true and relevant today as it was in Paul's own time.

Fourth, it encompasses the whole "network of convictions" Paul himself (judging from his "summary statements") considers most basic and most fundamental.

Fifth, every major aspect of the Apostle's theology may be derived from the "coherent center" as we have described it. Paul's fourteen "core convictions" take in the whole sweep of time and eternity--the "present evil age" and the "eschatological age," the past, the "present time," and the eschatological "future." They include both the objective events of God's action in Christ (i.e., His covenant-promises to Abraham, His speaking through the Law and the Prophets, His sending Christ to the cross, His raising Christ from the dead, and His promise to raise the righteous to "eschatological life") and the subjective appropriation of those events by the believer (i.e., "dying with Christ," "new covenant" righteousness, "trust" in God as Lord which informs one's day-to-day conduct). They form the basis for Paul's theology (God as Creator and Lord, the God of Abraham, the God of the Old Testament, the Father of Jesus Christ, the Judge of the world, the God who raises the dead), christology (Jesus as the preexistent "equal" of God, the "trusting" Servant of God, the crucified and risen one, the "seed of Abraham," the "last Adam," the Davidic "Son of God," the "Lord" of all, the "life-giving Spirit," the eschatological Judge, the Saviour who will come again), soteriology (salvation from Sin and annihilation through participation in the "new covenant" established by Christ's sacrificial death), eschatology ("the present time" and the eschatological "future," the Day of the Lord, the "Second Coming of Christ, the Resurrection of the righteous, the final Judgment, and the eschatological Rule of God), ecclesiology (the Church as the community of "trust" (πίστις), the

---

[23]See Plevnik, "The Center," 465.

"righteous" under the "new covenant," the "children of Abraham," the "Body [ruled by] Christ" [σῶμα Χριστοῦ], the community which suffers and "dies" with Christ in the present in the confident hope of being raised to "eschatological life" with him in the future, the Body entrusted with "the ministry of reconciliation"), nomology (the Law's witness to God's expression of His righteousness in Christ, its inability to bring "eschatological life"), and ethics (Christ-like trust in God as the standard for Christian behavior)--along with both his doctrine of "righteousness" (= participation in the "new covenant" which holds the promise of "eschatological life") by God's "goodwill" (expressed in His action to [1] establish the "new covenant" by sending Christ to his death, [2] raise Christ from the dead, [3] elicit "trust," or "new covenant" righteousness, from all nations,[24] and [4] grant "eschatological life" to the righteous[25]) through "trust" in Him (= commitment to God as Lord), and his doctrine of "participation in Christ" (understood not in terms of mystically sharing in Christ's own sacrificial death and his own resurrection to "lordship," but in terms of entering "into [the sphere of] Christ's [rule]" [εἰς Χριστόν or ἐν Χριστῷ]--i.e., adopting the "trustful" attitude of the dying Christ in the confident hope of one day sharing in the general Resurrection of the righteous along with him).

On these grounds, we conclude that the "core convictions" expounded in this study do indeed represent the "coherent center" of Paul's theology. Together, they express "the truth about God"--"the truth which is the gospel."

---

[24]See, e.g., 2 Cor 5:18-20 and Phil 2:13.

[25]Note that Christ's death, Christ's resurrection, the Christian's "death" with Christ, and the Christian's resurrection with Christ are all acts of God's "goodwill" (χάρις).

BIBLIOGRAPHY

Achtemeier, Paul J. *The Quest for Unity in the New Testament Church: A Study in Paul and Acts.* Philadelphia: Fortress Press, 1987. 132 pp.

_____. *Romans.* Interpretation: A Bible Commentary for Teaching and Preaching. Atlanta: John Knox Press, 1985. 244 pp.

_____. "'Some Things in Them Hard to Understand': Reflections on an Approach to Paul." *Interpretation* 38 (1984): 254-67.

Agnew, Francis H. "Obedience: A New Testament Reflection." *Review for Religious* 39 (1980): 409-18.

Anne-Etienne, Soeur. "Réconciliation, un Aspect de la Théologie Paulinienne." *Foi et Vie* 84 (1985): 49-57.

The Apocrypha and Pseudepigrapha of the Old Testament in English. Edited by R. H. Charles. Oxford: The Clarendon Press, 1913. 2 vols.

Arndt, William F., and F. Wilbur Gingrich. *A Greek-English Lexicon of the New Testament and Other Early Christian Literature.* 4th ed. Chicago: The University of Chicago Press, 1957. 909 pp.

Baasland, Ernst. "Persecution: A Neglected Feature in the Letter to the Galatians." *Studia Theologica* 38 (1984): 135-50.

Badke, William B. "Baptised Into Moses--Baptised Into Christ: A Study in Doctrinal Development." *Evangelical Quarterly* 88 (1988): 23-29.

Bailey, John W. "Gospel for Mankind: The Death of Christ in the Thinking of Paul." *Interpretation* 7 (1953): 163-74.

Barnett, P. W. "Opposition in Corinth." *Journal for the Study of the New Testament* 22 (1984): 3-17.

Barré, Michael L. "Qumran and the 'Weakness' of Paul." *The Catholic Biblical Quarterly* 42 (1980): 216-27.

Barrett, C. K. "Boasting (καυχᾶσθαι, κτλ.) in the Pauline Epistles." In *L'apôtre Paul: Personalité, Style et Conception du Ministère,* ed. A. Vanhoye, 363-68. Bibliotheca Ephemeridum Theologicarum Lovaniensium, 73. Leuven: University Press, 1986.

_____. "Christianity at Corinth." *Bulletin of the John Rylands Library, Manchester* 46 (1964): 269-97.

_____. *A Commentary on the Epistle to the Romans.* Harper's New Testament Commentaries. New York: Harper & Row, Publishers, 1957. 294 pp.

_____. *Essays on Paul.* Philadelphia: The Westminster Press, 1982.

_____. *A Commentary on the Second Epistle to the Corinthians.* Harper's New Testament Commentaries. New York: Harper & Row, Publishers, 1973. 354 pp.

_____. *From First Adam to Last: A Study in Pauline Theology.* New York: Charles Scribner's Sons, 1962. 124 pp.

_____. "Paul's Opponents in 2 Corinthians." In *Essays on Paul.* Philadelphia: The Westminster Press, 1982.

_____. "Ψευδαπόστολοι (2 Cor 11:13)." In *Essays on Paul.* Philadelphia: The Westminster Press, 1982.

Barth, Karl. *Christ and Adam: Man and Humanity in Romans 5.* Translated by T. A. Smail. New York: The Macmillan Company, 1957. 123 pp.

_____. *The Epistle to the Romans.* Translated from the Sixth Edition by Edwyn C. Hoskyns. New York: Oxford University Press, 1933. 547 pp.

Barth, Markus. "'The Faith of the Messiah.'" *The Heythrop Journal* 10 (1969): 363-70.

Bartsch, Hans-Werner. *Die Konkrete Wahrheit und die Lüge der Spekulation: Untersuchung über den vorpaulinischen Christushymnus und seine gnostische Mythisierung.* Theologie und Wirklichkeit, ed. Hans-Werner Bartsch, Gerhard Dauzenberg, Friedrich Hahn, and Hans Wolfgang Offele, no. 1. Frankfurt: Verlag Peter Lang GmbH, 1974. 133 pp.

Bassler, Jouette M., ed. *Pauline Theology, Volume I: Thessalonians, Philippians, Galatians, Philemon.* Minneapolis: Fortress Press, 1991. 289 pp.

_____. "Paul's Theology: Whence and Whither? A Synthesis (of Sorts) of the Theology of Philemon, 1 Thessalonians, Philippians, Galatians, and 1 Corinthians." In *Society of Biblical Literature 1989 Seminar Papers,* ed. David J. Lull, 412-23. Atlanta: Scholars Press, 1989.

Baumert, Norbert. *Täglich Sterben und Auferstehen: Der Literalsinn von 2 Kor 4:12-5:10.* Studien zum Alten und Neuen Testament, 34. München: Kösel-Verlag, 1973. 462 pp.

Baur, Ferdinand Christian. *Paul the Apostle of Jesus Christ, His Life and Works, His Epistles and Teachings: A Contribution to a Critical History of Primitive Christianity.* 2d ed. Translated by E. Zeller. London: Williams and Norgate, 1873. 2 vols.

Beale, G. K. "The Old Testament Background of Reconciliation in 2 Corinthians 5-7 and Its Bearing on the Literary Problem of 2 Corinthians 6:14-7:1." *New Testament Studies* 35 (1989): 550-81.

Beare, F. W. *A Commentary on the Epistle to the Philippians.* Black's New Testament Commentaries. 3d ed. London: Adam & Charles Black, 1973. 182pp.

Beasley-Murray, G. R. *Baptism in the New Testament.* Grand Rapids: William B. Eerdmans Publishing Company, 1962. 422 pp.

Beker, J. Christiaan. "Contingency and Coherence in the Letters of Paul." *Union Seminary Quarterly Review* 33 (1978): 141-51.

_____. "The Method of Recasting Pauline Theology: The Coherence-Contingency Scheme as Interpretive Model." In *Society of Biblical Literature 1986 Seminar Papers,* ed. Kent Harold Richards, 596-602. Atlanta: Scholars Press, 1986.

_____. "Paul's Theology: Consistent or Inconsistent?" *New Testament Studies* 34 (1988): 364-77.

_____. *Paul the Apostle: The Triumph of God in Life and Thought.* Philadelphia: Fortress Press, 1980. 452 pp.

_____. "Paul the Theologian: Major Motifs in Pauline Theology." *Interpretation* 43 (1989): 352-65.

_____. "Recasting Pauline Theology: The Coherence-Contingency Scheme as Interpretive Model." In *Pauline Theology, Volume I: Thessalonians, Philippians, Galatians, Philemon,* ed. Jouette M. Bassler, 15-24. Minneapolis: Fortress Press, 1991.

_____. *Suffering and Hope: The Biblical Vision and the Human Predicament.* Philadelphia: Fortress Press, 1987. 94 pp.

_____. "Suffering and Triumph in Paul's Letter to the Romans." *Horizons in Biblical Theology* 7 (1985): 105-19.

_____. *The Triumph of God: The Essence of Paul's Thought.* Translated by Loren T. Stuckenbruck. Minneapolis: Fortress Press, 1990. 152 pp.

Best, Ernest. *The Letter of Paul to the Romans.* The Cambridge Bible Commentary. Cambridge: The University Press, 1967. 184 pp.

Betz, Hans Dieter. *Der Apostel Paulus und die sokratische Tradition: Eine exegetische Untersuchung zu seiner "Apologie" 2 Korinther 10-13.* Beiträge zur historischen Theologie, 45. Tübingen: J. C. B. Mohr, 1972. 157 pp.

_____. *Galatians: A Commentary on Paul's Letter to the Churches in Galatia.* Hermeneia--A Critical and Historical Commentary on the Bible. Philadelphia: Fortress Press, 1979. 352 pp.

Biblia Hebraica Stuttgartensia. Edited by K. Elliger and W. Rudolph. Stuttgart: Deutsche Bibelstiftung, 1977.

Biblia Sacra: Iuxta Vulgatam Versionem. 3d ed. Edited by Bonifatius, with H. I. Frede, Iohanne Gribomont, H. F. D. Sparks, and W. Thiele. Stuttgart: Deutsche Bibelgesellschaft, 1983. 2 vols.

Binder, Hermann. "Erwägungen zu Phil 2:6-7b." *Zeitschrift für die neutestamentliche Wissenschaft* 78 (1987): 230-43.

_____. "Zum geschichtlichen Hintergrund von I Kor 15:12." *Theologische Zeitschrift* 46 (1990): 193-201.

Black, C. Clifton, II. "Pauline Perspectives on Death in Romans 5-8." *Journal of Biblical Literature* 103 (1984): 413-33.

Black, David Alan. *Paul, Apostle of Weakness: Astheneia and its Cognates in the Pauline Literature.* New York: Peter Lang, 1984. 332 pp.

_____. "*Paulus Infirmus*: The Pauline Concept of Weakness." *Grace Theological Journal* 5 (1984): 77-93.

_____. "Weakness Language in Galatians." *Grace Theological Journal* 4 (1983): 15-36.

Bloomquist, L. Gregory. *The Function of Suffering in Philippians.* Journal for the Study of the New Testament Supplement Series, 78. Sheffield, England: JSOT Press, 1993. 235 pp.

Boer, Martinus C. de. *The Defeat of Death: Apocalyptic Eschatology in 1 Corinthians 15 and Romans 5.* Journal for the Study of the New Testament Supplement Series, 22. Sheffield: Sheffield Academic Press, 1988. 278 pp.

_____. "Paul and Jewish Apocalyptic Eschatology." In *Apocalyptic and the New Testament: Essays in Honor of J. Louis Martyn,* ed. Joel Marcus and Marion L. Soards, 169-90. Journal for the Study of the New Testament Supplement Series, 24. Sheffield, England: JSOT Press, 1989.

Boers, Hendrikus W. "The Foundations of Paul's Thought: A Methodological Investigation--The Problem of the Coherent Center of Paul's Thought." *Studia Theologica* 42 (1988): 55-68.

_____. *What is New Testament Theology? The Rise of Criticism and the Problem of a Theology of the New Testament.* Philadelphia: Fortress Press, 1979. 95 pp.

Boguslawski, Steven R. "Implicit Faith in Karl Rahner: A Pauline View." *The Irish Theological Quarterly* 51 (1985): 300-08.

Boring, M. Eugene. "The Language of Universal Salvation in Paul." *Journal of Biblical Literature* 105 (1986): 269-92.

Bornkamm, Günther. *Paul.* New York: Harper & Row, Publishers, 1971. 260 pp.

Bounds, Kenneth. *Addresses on the Epistle to the Romans.* London: The Epworth Press, 1953. 72 pp.

Bousset, Wilhelm. *Kyrios Christos: A History of the Belief in Christ from the Beginnings of Christianity to Irenaeus.* Translated by John E. Steely. New York: Abingdon Press, 1970. 496 pp.

Brandenburger, Egon. *Adam und Christus: exegetisch-religionsgeschichtliche Untersuchung zu Röm 5:12-21 (1 Kor 15).* Wissenschaftliche Monographien zum Alten und Neuen Testament, 7. Neukirchen: Neukirchener Verlag, 1962. 302 pp.

Branick, Vincent P. "Apocalyptic Paul?" *The Catholic Biblical Quarterly* 47 (1985): 664-75.

_____. "The Sinful Flesh of the Son of God (Rom 8:3): A Key Image of Pauline Theology." *Catholic Biblical Quarterly* 47 (1985): 246-62.

Bratcher, Robert G. *A Translator's Guide to Paul's First Letter to the Corinthians.* Helps for Translators. New York: United Bible Societies, 1982. 176 pp.

Brauch, Manfred T. "Perspectives on 'God's righteousness' in recent German discussion." In *Paul and Palestinian Judaism: A Comparison of Patterns of Religion,* by E. P. Sanders, 523-42. Philadelphia: Fortress Press, 1977.

Brooks, James A., and Carlton L. Winbery. *Syntax of New Testament Greek.* New York: University Press of America, 1979. 179 pp.

Brown, Francis, S. R. Driver, and Charles A. Briggs. *A Hebrew and English Lexicon of the Old Testament.* Oxford: The Clarendon Press, 1959. 1127 pp.

Bruce, F. F. *The Epistle to the Galatians: A Commentary on the Greek Text.* The New International Greek Testament Commentary. Grand Rapids: William B. Eerdmans Publishing Company, 1982. 305 pp.

_____. *1 and 2 Corinthians.* New Century Bible Commentary. Grand Rapids: Wm. B. Eerdmans Publ. Co., 1971. 262 pp.

_____. *Paul: Apostle of the Heart Set Free*. Grand Rapids: William B. Eerdmans Publishing Company, 1977. 491 pp.

Buchanan, George Wesley. "The Day of Atonement and Paul's Doctrine of Redemption." *Novum Testamentum* 32 (1990): 236-49.

Buck, Charles, and Greer Taylor. *Saint Paul: A Study of the Development of His Thought*. New York: Charles Scribner's Sons, 1969. 278 pp.

Bultmann, Rudolf. "Δικαιοσύνη θεοῦ." *Journal of Biblical Literature* 83 (1964): 12-16.

_____. *The Second Letter to the Corinthians*. Original German edition edited by Erich Dinkler. Translated by Roy A. Harrisville. Minneapolis: Augsburg Publishing House, 1985. 272 pp.

_____. *Der Stil der paulinischen Predigt und die kynisch-stoische Diatribe*. Forschungen zur Religion und Literatur des alten und neuen Testaments, 13. Göttingen: Vandenhoeck & Ruprecht, 1910. 110 pp.

_____. *Theology of the New Testament*. Translated by Kendrick Grobel. New York: Charles Scribner's Sons, 1951-55. 2 vols.

Burton, Ernest De Witt. *A Critical and Exegetical Commentary on the Epistle to the Galatians*. The International Critical Commentary. Edinburgh: T. & T. Clark, 1920. 541 pp.

_____. *Syntax of the Moods and Tenses in New Testament Greek*. 2d ed. Chicago: University Press of Chicago, 1893. 215 pp.

Byrne, Brendan. "'The Type of the One to Come' (Rom 5:14): Fate and Responsibility in Romans 5:12-21." *Australian Biblical Review* 36 (1988): 19-30.

Calvin, John. *Commentaries on the Epistle of Paul the Apostle to the Romans*. Grand Rapids: Wm. B. Eerdmans Publishing Company, 1947. 592 pp.

Campbell, Douglas A. "The Meaning of Πίστις and Νόμος in Paul: A Linguistic and Structural Perspective." *Journal of Biblical Literature* 111 (1992): 91-103.

_____. *The Rhetoric of Righteousness in Romans 3:21-26*. Journal for the Study of the New Testament Supplement Series, 65. Sheffield, England: JSOT Press, 1992. 272 pp.

_____. "Romans 1:17--A *Crux Interpretum* for the Πίστις Χριστοῦ Debate." *Journal of Biblical Literature* 113 (1994): 265-85.

Carlson, Richard Paul. "Baptism and Apocalyptic in Paul." Ph.D. diss., Union Theological Seminary in Virginia, 1983. 383 pp.

378

_____. "The Role of Baptism in Paul's Thought." *Interpretation* 47 (1993): 255-66.

Carter, Warren C. "Rome (and Jerusalem): The Contingency of Romans 3: 21-26." *Irish Biblical Studies* 11 (1989): 54-68.

Cerfaux, L. *Christ in the Theology of St. Paul.* Translated by Geoffrey Webb and Adrian Walker. New York: Herder and Herder, 1959. 560 pp.

Charles, R. H. *Eschatology: The Doctrine of a Future Life in Israel, Judaism and Christianity. A Critical History.* With an Introduction by George Wesley Buchanan. New York: Schocken Books, 1963. 482 pp.

Charlesworth, James H., ed. *The Old Testament Pseudepigrapha.* Garden City, NY: Doubleday & Company, Inc., 1983. 2 vols.

Colella, Pasquale. "Cristo Nostra Pasqua? 1 Cor 5:7." *Bibbia e Oriente* 28 (1986): 197-217.

Colijn, B. B. "Paul's Use of the 'In Christ' Formula." *Ashland Theological Journal* 23 (1991): 9-26.

Collange, J. F. *De Jesus à Paul: L'éthique du Nouveau Testament.* Le Champ Éthique, 3. Genève: Labor et Fides, 1980. 313 pp.

Collins, John J., ed. Apocalypse: The Morphology of a Genre. *Semeia* 14 (1979). 219 pp.

Collins, John J. *The Apocalyptic Imagination: An Introduction to the Jewish Matrix of Christianity.* New York: Crossroad, 1984. 280 pp.

Collins, John J., and James H. Charlesworth, eds. *Mysteries and Revelations: Apocalyptic Studies since the Uppsala Colloquium. Journal for the Study of the Pseudepigrapha* Supplement Series, 9. Sheffield: JSOT Press, 1991. 172 pp.

Conzelmann, Hans. "Current Problems in Pauline Research." *Interpretation* 22 (1968): 171-86.

_____. *1 Corinthians: A Commentary on the First Epistle to the Corinthians.* Hermeneia--A Critical and Historical Commentary on the Bible. Philadelphia: Fortress Press, 1975. 323 pp.

_____. *An Outline of the Theology of the New Testament.* New York: Harper & Row, Publishers, 1969.

_____. "Die Rechtfertigungslehre des Paulus: Theologie oder Anthropologie?" *Evangelische Theologie* 28 (1968): 389-404.

Corriveau, Raymond. *The Liturgy of Life: A Study of the Ethical Thought of St. Paul in His Letters to the Early Christian Communities.* Studia, 25. Montreal: Les Éditions Bellarmin, 1970. 296 pp.

Court, John M. "Paul and the Apocalyptic Pattern." In *Paul and Paulinism: Essays in Honour of C. K. Barrett,* ed. M. D. Hooker and S. G. Wilson, 57-66. London: SPCK, 1982.

Cousar, Charles B. *A Theology of the Cross: The Death of Jesus in the Pauline Letters.* Overtures to Biblical Theology. Minneapolis: Fortress Press, 1990. 194 pp.

Cranfield, C. E. B. *A Critical and Exegetical Commentary on the Epistle to the Romans.* The International Critical Commentary. Edinburgh: T. & T. Clark, 1975. 2 vols.

_____. "Giving a Dog a Bad Name: A Note on H. Räisänen's *Paul and the Law.*" *Journal for the Study of the New Testament* 38 (1990): 77-85.

Cremer, Hermann. *Die Paulinische Rechtfertigungslehre im Zusammenhange ihrer geschichtlichen Voraussetzungen.* Gütersloh: C. Bertelsmann, 1900. 448 pp.

Crockett, William V. "The Ultimate Restoration of all Mankind: 1 Corinthians 15:22." In *Studia Biblica 1978: III. Papers on Paul and Other New Testament Authors. Sixth International Congress on Biblical Studies: Oxford, 3-7 April 1978,* ed. E. A. Livingstone, 83-87. *Journal for the Study of the New Testament* Supplement Series, 3. Sheffield: JSOT Press, 1980.

Cullmann, Oscar. *Christ and Time: The Primitive Christian Conception of Time and History.* Translated by Floyd V. Filson. London: SCM Press, 1951. 253 pp.

_____. *The Christology of the New Testament.* 1st ed., rev. Translated by Shirley C. Guthrie and Charles A. M. Hall. Philadelphia: The Westminster Press, 1963. 346 pp.

_____. *The Immortality of the Soul or Resurrection of the Dead? The Witness of the New Testament.* London: The Epworth Press, 1958. 60 pp.

Culpepper, R. Alan. "Co-Workers in Suffering: Philippians 2:19-30." *Review and Expositor* 77 (1980): 349-58.

Daalen, D. H. van. "'Faith' According to Paul." *Expository Times* 87 (1975-76): 83-85.

Dahl, Nils Alstrup. "The Atonement--An Adequate Reward for the Akedah? (Rom 8:32)." In *Neotestamentica et Semetica: Studies in Honour of Matthew Black,* ed. E. Earle Ellis and Max Wilcox, 15-29. Edinburgh: T. & T. Clark, 1969.

_____. "The Particularity of the Pauline Epistles as a Problem in the Ancient Church." In *Neotestamentica et Patristica: Eine Freundesgabe, Herrn Professor Dr. Oscar Cullmann zu seinem 60. Geburtstag Überreicht,* 261-71. Leiden: E. J. Brill, 1962.

_____. Review of *Paul and Palestinian Judaism: A Comparison of Patterns of Religion,* by E. P. Sanders. In *Religious Studies Review* 4 (1978): 153-58.

_____. *Studies in Paul: Theology for the Early Christian Mission.* Assisted by Paul Donahue. Minneapolis: Augsburg Publishing House, 1977. 198 pp.

Dailey, Thomas F. "To Live or Die: Paul's Eschatological Dilemma in Philippians 1:19-26." *Interpretation* 44 (1990): 18-28.

Daly, Robert J. *Christian Sacrifice: The Judaeo-Christian Background Before Origen.* The Catholic University of America Studies in Christian Antiquity, 18. Washington, D. C.: The Catholic University of America Press, 1978. 587 pp.

Davies, Philip R. "Passover and the Dating of the Aqedah." *Journal of Jewish Studies* 30 (1979): 59-67.

Davies, W. D. *Paul and Rabbinic Judaism: Some Rabbinic Elements in Pauline Theology.* 4th ed. Philadelphia: Fortress Press, 1980. 403 pp.

Deissmann, Adolf. *Paul: A Study in Social and Religious History.* 2d ed. Translated by William E. Wilson. London: Hodder and Stoughton, 1926. 323 pp.

Denis, Albert-Marie. *Concordance Grecque des Pseudépigraphes D'Ancien Testament.* Prepared with the collaboration of Yvonne Janssens and the cooperation of CETEDOC [Centre de Traitement Electronique des Documents]. Louvain-la-Neuve: Université Catholique de Louvain, Institut Orientaliste, 1987. 925 pp.

Dinter, Paul E. "Paul and the Prophet Isaiah." *Biblical Theology Bulletin* 13 (1983): 48-52.

Diogenes Laertius. *Lives of Eminent Philosophers.* With an English Translation by R. D. Hicks. The Loeb Classical Library. Cambridge, MA: Harvard University Press, 1942. 2 vols.

Dodd, C. H. *The Epistle of Paul to the Romans.* The Moffatt New Testament Commentary. New York: Harper and Brothers Publishers, 1932.

_____. *The Meaning of Paul for To-day.* London: The Swarthmore Press, 1920. 172 pp.

_____. "The Mind of Paul: I." In *New Testament Studies.* Manchester: University Press, 1953.

Donge, Gloria van. "In What Way is Paul's Gospel *(Euangelion)* of Freedom Theology of the Cross *(Theologia Crucis)*? *Colloquium (The Australian and New Zealand Theological Review)* 21 (1988): 19-33.

Drane, John W. *Paul: Libertine or Legalist? A Study in the Theology of the Major Pauline Epistles.* London: SPCK, 1975. 194 pp.

Duff, Paul Brooks. "Apostolic Suffering and the Language of the Processions in 2 Corinthians 4:7-10." *Biblical Theology Bulletin* 21 (1991): 158-65.

Duhm, Bernhard. *Die Theologie der Propheten als Grundlage für die innere Entwicklungsgeschichte der israelitischen Religion.* Bonn: Adolph Marcus, 1875. 324 pp.

Dunn, James D. G. *Baptism in the Holy Spirit: A Reexamination of the New Testament Teaching on the Gift of the Spirit in Relation to Pentecostalism Today.* Philadelphia: The Westminster Press, 1970. 248 pp.

_____. *Christology in the Making: A New Testament Inquiry Into the Origins of the Doctrine of the Incarnation.* Philadelphia: The Westminster Press, 1980. 443 pp.

_____. "Paul's Understanding of the Death of Jesus." In *Reconciliation and Hope: New Testament Essays on Atonement and Eschatology Presented to L. L. Morris on His 60th Birthday,* ed. Robert Banks, 125-41. Exeter: The Paternoster Press, 1974.

_____. "Prolegomena to a Theology of Paul." *New Testament Studies* 40 (1994): 407-32.

_____. *Romans.* Word Biblical Commentary. Dallas: Word Books, Publisher, 1988. 2 vols.

_____. "Salvation Proclaimed VI. Romans 6:1-11: Dead and Alive." *The Expository Times* 93 (1982): 259-64.

_____. *The Theology of Paul's Letter to the Galatians.* New Testament Theology. Cambridge: University Press, 1993. 161 pp.

_____. *Unity and Diversity in the New Testament: An Inquiry Into the Character of Earliest Christianity.* Philadelphia: The Westminster Press, 1977. 470 pp.

Ellis, E. Earle. "'Christ Crucified.'" In *Reconciliation and Hope: New Testament Essays on Atonement and Eschatology Presented to L. L. Morris on His 60th Birthday,* ed. Robert Banks, 69-75. Exeter: The Paternoster Press, 1974.

_____. "Paul and His Opponents: Trends in the Research." In *Christianity, Judaism and Other Greco-Roman Cults: Studies for Morton Smith at Sixty. Part One: New Testament,* ed. Jacob Neusner, 264-98. Studies in Judaism in Late Antiquity, 12. Leiden: E. J. Brill, 1975.

_____. *Paul's Use of the Old Testament.* Edinburgh: Oliver and Boyd, 1957; reprint, Grand Rapids: Baker Book House, 1981. 204 pp.

_____. "The Structure of Pauline Eschatology (2 Corinthians 5:1-10)." In *Paul and His Recent Interpreters.* Grand Rapids: William B. Eerdmans Publishing Company, 1961.

Englezakis, Benedict. "Rom 5:12-15 and the Pauline Teaching on the Lord's Death: Some Observations." *Biblica* 58 (1977): 231-36.

Evans, David Lynn. "The Atonement-Motifs of 2 Cor 5:11-21: A Historical and Exegetical Study." Ph.D. diss., Southwestern Baptist Theological Seminary, 1984.

Fee, Gordon D. *The First Epistle to the Corinthians.* The New International Commentary on the New Testament. Grand Rapids: William B. Eerdmans Publishing Company, 1987. 880 pp.

_____. "Philippians 2:5-11: Hymn or Exalted Pauline Prose?" *Bulletin for Biblical Research* 2 (1992): 29-46.

Feinberg, Paul D. "The Kenosis and Christology: An Exegetical-Theological Analysis of Phil 2:6-11." *Trinity Journal* 1 n.s. (1980): 21-46.

Fitzgerald, John T. *Cracks in an Earthen Vessel: An Examination of the Catalogues of Hardships in the Corinthian Correspondence.* Society of Biblical Literature Dissertation Series, 99. Atlanta: Scholars Press, 1988. 289 pp.

Fitzmyer, Joseph A. "The Aramaic Background of Philippians 2:6-11." *The Catholic Biblical Quarterly* 50 (1988): 470-83.

_____. "The Consecutive Meaning of ἐφ' ᾧ in Romans 5:12." *New Testament Studies* 39 (1993): 321-39.

_____. "The Gospel in the Theology of Paul." *Interpretation* 33 (1979): 339-50.

_____. *Pauline Theology: A Brief Sketch.* Englewood Cliffs, NJ: Prentice-Hall, Inc., 1967. 88 pp.

_____. "Reconciliation in Pauline Theology." In *No Famine in the Land: Studies in Honor of John L. McKenzie,* ed. James W. Flanagan and Anita Weisbrod Robinson, 155-77. Missoula, MT: Scholars Press, 1975.

Frankemölle, Hubert. "Das Taufverständnis des Paulus: Taufe, Tod und Auferstehung nach Röm 6." *Stuttgarter Bibelstudien* 47 (1970): 1-136.

Freedman, H., trans. *Midrash Rabbah: Genesis.* London: Soncino Press, 1939. 2 vols.

Frid, Bo. "Römer 6:4-5: Εἰς τὸν θάνατον und τῷ ὁμοιώματι τοῦ θάνατου αὐτοῦ als Schlüssel zu Duktus und Gedank engang in Röm 6:1-11." *Biblische Zeitschrift* 30 (1986): 188-203.

Friedrich, Gerhard. "Die Gegner des Paulus im 2. Korintherbrief." In *Abraham unser Vater: Juden und Christen im Gespräch über die Bibel. Festschrift für Otto Michel zum 60. Geburtstag,* ed. Otto Betz, Martin Hengel, and Peter Schmidt, 181-215. Arbeiten zur Geschichte des Spätjudentums und Urchristentums, 5. Leiden/Köln: E. J. Brill, 1963.

Fryer, Nico S. L. "The Meaning and Translation of *Hilastērion* in Romans 3:25." *The Evangelical Quarterly* 59 (1987): 99-116.

_____. "Reconciliation in Paul's Epistle to the Romans." *Neotestamentica* 15 (1981): 34-68.

Fuller, Reginald H. *The Foundations of New Testament Christology.* New York: Charles Scribner's Sons, 1965. 268 pp.

Fung, Ronald Y.-K. "Justification by Faith in 1 & 2 Corinthians." In *Pauline Studies: Essays Presented to Professor F. F. Bruce on His 70th Birthday,* ed. Donald A. Hagner and Murray J. Harris, 246-61. Grand Rapids: The Paternoster Press and William B. Eerdmans Publishing Company, 1980.

_____. "The Status of Justification by Faith in Paul's Thought: A Brief Survey of a Modern Debate." *Themelios* 6 (1981): 4-11.

Funk, Robert W., ed. *Apocalypticism.* With Contributions by Hans Dieter Betz, Frank M. Cross, Gerhard Ebeling, David Noel Freedman, Ernst Fuchs, Robert W. Funk and Ernst Käsemann. *Journal for Theology and the Church,* 6. New York: Herder and Herder, 1969. 207 pp.

Furnish, Victor Paul. "Development in Paul's Thought." *Journal of the American Academy of Religion* 38 (1970): 289-303.

_____. "On Putting Paul in His Place." *Journal of Biblical Literature* 113 (1994): 3-17.

_____. *Theology and Ethics in Paul.* New York: Abingdon Press, 1968. 304 pp.

_____. *2 Corinthians: Translated with Introduction, Notes, and Commentary.* The Anchor Bible. Garden City, NY: Doubleday & Company, Inc., 1984. 619 pp.

Gaffin, Richard B. "The Usefulness of the Cross." *The Westminster Theological Journal* 41 (1979): 228-46.

Gallas, S. "'Fünfmal vierzig weniger einen . . . ': Die an Paulus vollzogenen Synagogalstrafen nach 2 Kor 11:24." *Zeitschrift für die neutestamentliche Wissenschaft* 81 (1990): 178-91.

Gamble, Harry Y. *The New Testament Canon: Its Making and Meaning.* Philadelphia: Fortress Press, 1985. 95 pp.

Garlington, D. B. "The Obedience of Faith in the Letter to the Romans, Part I: The Meaning of ὑπακοὴ πίστεως (Rom 1:5; 16:26)." *The Westminster Theological Journal* 52 (1990): 201-24.

_____. "The Obedience of Faith in the Letter to the Romans, Part II: The Obedience of Faith and Judgment by Works." *The Westminster Theological Journal* 53 (1991): 47-72.

_____. "The Obedience of Faith in the Letter to the Romans, Part III: The Obedience of Christ and the Obedience of the Christian." *The Westminster Theological Journal* 55 (1993): 87-112.

_____. "The Obedience of Faith in the Letter to the Romans, Part III: The Obedience of Christ and the Obedience of the Christian (continued)." *The Westminster Theological Journal* 55 (1993): 281-97.

Gaster, Theodore H. *The Dead Sea Scriptures.* 2d ed. Garden City, NY: Doubleday & Company, Inc., 1964. 420 pp.

Georgi, Dieter. *The Opponents of Paul in Second Corinthians.* Philadelphia: Fortress Press, 1986. 463 pp.

Giles, Kevin. "'Imitatio Christi' in the New Testament." *The Reformed Theological Review* 38 (1979): 65-73.

Gillman, Florence Morgan. "Another Look at Romans 8:3: 'In the Likeness of Sinful Flesh.'" *Catholic Biblical Quarterly* 49 (1987): 597-604.

_____. "Romans 6:5a: United to a Death Like Christ's." *Ephemerides Theologicae Lovanienses* 59 (1983): 267-302.

_____. *A Study of Romans 6:5a: United to a Death Like Christ's*. San Francisco: Mellen Research University Press, 1992. 404 pp.

Glasson, T. Francis. "2 Corinthians 5:1-10 versus Platonism." *Scottish Journal of Theology* 43 (1990): 145-55.

Gloer, William Hulitt, Jr. "An Historical Exegetical and Theological Study of 2 Corinthians 5:14-21." Ph.D. diss., The Southern Baptist Theological Seminary, 1981. 428 pp.

Goddard, A. J., and S. A. Cummins. "Ill or Ill-Treated? Conflict and Persecution as the Context of Paul's Original Ministry in Galatia (Galatians 4:12-20)." *Journal for the Study of the New Testament* 52 (1993): 93-126.

Greene, M. Dwaine. "A Note on Romans 8:3." *Biblische Zeitschrift* 35 (1991): 103-06.

Grundmann, Walter. "Der Weg des Kyrios Jesus Christus: Erwägungen zum Christhymnus Phil 2:6-11 und der mit ihm verbundenen Konzeption im Neuen Testament." In *Wandlungen im Verständnis des Heils: Drei nachgelassene Aufsätze zur Theologie des Neuen Testaments*. Arbeiten zur Theologie, Heft 65. Stuttgart: Calwer Verlag, 1980. 59 pp.

Güttgemanns, Erhardt. *Der leidende Apostel und sein Herr: Studien zur paulinischen Christologie*. Forschungen zur Religion und Literatur des Alten und Neuen Testaments, 90. Göttingen: Vandenhoeck & Ruprecht, 1966. 419 pp.

Hafemann, S. J. "The Glory and Veil of Moses in 2 Cor 3:7-14: An Example of Paul's Contextual Exegesis of the OT--A Proposal." *Horizons in Biblical Theology* 14 (1992): 31-49.

_____. *Suffering and Ministry in the Spirit: Paul's Defense of His Ministry in 2 Corinthians 2:14-3:3*. Grand Rapids: Eerdmans, 1990. 261 pp.

_____. *Suffering and the Spirit: An Exegetical Study of 2 Cor 2:14-3:3 Within the Context of the Corinthian Correspondence*. Wissenschaftliche Untersuchungen zum Neuen Testament, Reihe 2, 19. Tübingen: J. C. B. Mohr, 1986. 258 pp.

Hamerton-Kelly, Robert G. "A Girardian Interpretation of Paul: Rivalry, Mimesis and Victimage in the Corinthian Correspondence." *Semeia* 33 (1985): 65-81.

Hanhart, Karel. *The Intermediate State in the New Testament*. Franeker: T. Wever, 1966. 248 pp.

Hanson, Anthony Tyrrell. *The Paradox of the Cross in the Thought of St Paul.* Journal for the Study of the New Testament Supplement Series, 17. Sheffield: JSOT Press, 1987. 243 pp.

Hanson, Paul D. *The Dawn of Apocalyptic: The Historical and Sociological Roots of Jewish Apocalyptic Eschatology.* Philadelphia: Fortress Press, 1975. 426 pp.

Harper's Bible Dictionary. Edited by Paul J. Achtemeier. San Francisco: Harper & Row, Publishers, 1985.
S.v. "Time," by Jeremiah Unterman and Paul J. Achtemeier. 1072-73.

Harris, Murray J. *Raised Immortal: Resurrection and Immortality in the New Testament.* Grand Rapids: William B. Eerdmans Publishing Company, 1983. 304 pp.

Harrisville, Roy A., III. *The Figure of Abraham in the Epistles of St. Paul: In the Footsteps of Abraham.* San Francisco: Mellen Research University Press, 1992. 314 pp.

Harvey, John D. "The 'With Christ' Motif in Paul's Thought." *Journal of the Evangelical Theological Society* 35 (1992): 329-40.

Hasel, Gerhard. "Resurrection in the Theology of the Old Testament Apocalyptic." *Zeitschrift für die alttestamentliche Wissenschaft* 92 (1980): 267-84.

Hasenstab, Rudolf. *Modelle paulinischer Ethik: Beiträge zu einem Autonomie-Modell aus paulinischem Geist.* Tübinger theologische Studien, 11. Mainz: Matthias-Grünewald-Verlag, 1977. 336 pp.

Hawthorne, Gerald F. *Philippians.* Word Biblical Commentary. Waco, TX: Word Books, Publisher, 1983. 232 pp.

Hay, David M., ed. *Pauline Theology, Volume II: 1 & 2 Corinthians.* Minneapolis: Fortress Press, 1993. 300 pp.

_____. "*Pistis* as 'Ground for Faith' in Hellenized Judaism and Paul." *Journal of Biblical Literature* 108 (1989): 461-76.

Hays, Richard Bevan. "Crucified with Christ: A Synthesis of 1 and 2 Thessalonians, Philemon, Philippians, and Galatians." In *Society of Biblical Literature 1988 Seminar Papers,* ed. David J. Lull, 318-35. Atlanta: Scholars Press, 1988.

_____. *Echoes of Scripture in the Letters of Paul.* New Haven, CT: Yale University Press, 1989. 240 pp.

_____. *The Faith of Jesus Christ: An Investigation of the Narrative Substructure of Galatians 3:1-4:11*. Society of Biblical Literature Dissertation Series, 56. Chico, CA: Scholars Press, 1983. 305 pp.

_____. "'Have we found Abraham to be our forefather according to the flesh?' A Reconsideration of Rom 4:1." *Novum Testamentum* 27 (1985): 76-98.

_____. "Jesus' Faith and Ours: A Re-reading of Galatians 3." *TSF Bulletin* 7 (1983): 2-6.

_____. "Psalm 143 and the Logic of Romans 3." *Journal of Biblical Literature* 99 (1980): 107-15.

Hayward, Robert. "Appendix: The Aqedah." In *Sacrifice*, ed. M. F. C. Bourdillon and Meyer Fortes, 84-87. New York: Academic Press, 1980.

_____. "The Present State of Research into the Targumic Account of the Sacrifice of Isaac." *Journal of Jewish Studies* 32 (1981): 127-50.

Heckel, Ulrich. "Der Dorn im Fleisch: Die Krankheit des Paulus in 2 Kor 12:7 und Gal 4:13f." *Zeitschrift für die neutestamentliche Wissenschaft* 84 (1993): 65-92.

Hedderich, Ronald Louis. "An Investigation of the Implications of the Akedah Hypothesis for the Pauline Concept of Atonement." Ph.D. diss., Southwestern Baptist Theological Seminary, 1983.

Hedquist, Paul Michael. "The Pauline Understanding of Reconciliation in Romans 5 and 2 Corinthians 5: An Exegetical and Religio-Historical Study." Th.D. diss., Union Theological Seminary in Virginia, 1979. 405 pp.

Heiny, Stephen B. "2 Corinthians 2:14-4:6: The Motive for Metaphor." In *Society of Biblical Literature 1987 Seminar Papers*, ed. Kent Harold Richards, 1-22. Atlanta: Scholars Press, 1987.

Helmbold, Andrew K. "Redeemer Hymns--Gnostic and Christian." In *New Dimensions in New Testament Study*, ed. Richard N. Longenecker and Merrill C. Tenney, 71-78. Grand Rapids: Zondervan Publishing House, 1974.

Hemer, C. J. "A Note on 2 Corinthians 1:9." *Tyndale Bulletin* 23 (1972): 103-107.

Hengel, Martin. *Crucifixion In the Ancient World and the Folly of the Message of the Cross*. Philadelphia: Fortress Press, 1977. 99 pp.

_____. "The Expiatory Sacrifice of Christ." *Bulletin of the John Rylands University Library of Manchester* 62 (1980): 454-75.

Hill, David. *Greek Words and Hebrew Meanings: Studies in the Semantics of Soteriological Terms*. Cambridge: The University Press, 1967. 333 pp.

_____. "Liberation Through God's Righteousness." *Irish Biblical Studies* 4 (1982): 31-44.

Hisey, Alan, and James S. P. Beck. "Paul's 'Thorn in the Flesh': A Paragnosis." *The Journal of Bible and Religion* 29 (1961): 125-29.

Hodgson, Robert. "Paul the Apostle and First Century Tribulation Lists." *Zeitschrift für die neutestamentliche Wissenschaft* 74 (1983): 59-80.

Hofius, Otfried. *Der Christushymnus Philipper 2:6-11: Untersuchungen zu Gestalt und Aussage eines urchristlichen Psalms*. Wissenschaftliche Untersuchungen zum Neuen Testament, ed. Martin Hengel, Joachim Jeremias, and Otto Michel, no. 17. 2d ed. Tübingen: J. C. B. Mohr (Paul Siebeck), 1991. 170 pp.

_____. "'Gott hat unter uns aufgerichtet das Wort von der Versöhnung' (2 Kor 5:19)." *Zeitschrift für die neutestamentliche Wissenschaft* 71 (1980): 3-20.

_____. "Τὸ σῶμα τὸ ὑπὲρ ὑμῶν 1 Kor 11:24." *Zeitschrift für die neutestamentliche Wissenschaft* 80 (1989): 80-88.

Holtzmann, Heinrich Julius. *Lehrbuch der neutestamentlichen Theologie*. Edited by D. A. Jülicher and Lic. W. Bauer. Tübingen: Verlag von J. C. B. Mohr, 1911. 2 vols.

Hooker, Morna D. "Beyond the Things That Are Written? St Paul's Use of Scripture." *New Testament Studies* 27 (1981): 295-309.

_____. "Πίστις Χριστοῦ." *New Testament Studies* 35 (1989): 321-42.

Hoover, R. W. "The *Harpagmos* Enigma: A Philogical Solution." *Harvard Theological Review* 64 (1971): 95-119.

Horvath, Tibor. *The Sacrificial Interpretation of Jesus' Achievement in the New Testament: Historical Development and Its Reasons*. New York: Philosophical Library, 1979. 100 pp.

Hoskyns, Edwyn Clement, and Francis Noel Davey. *Crucifixion--Resurrection: The Pattern of the Theology and Ethics of the New Testament*. With a Biographical Introduction by Gordon S. Wakefield. London: SPCK, 1981. 383 pp.

Howard, George. *Paul: Crisis in Galatia. A Study in Early Christian Theology*. Society for New Testament Studies Monograph Series, 35. Cambridge: Cambridge University Press, 1979. 114 pp.

_____. "Phil 2:6-11 and the Human Christ." *The Catholic Biblical Quarterly* 40 (1978): 368-87.

Howell, Don N., Jr. "Pauline Eschatological Dualism and Its Resulting Tensions." *Trinity Journal* 14 (1993): 3-24.

_____. "Pauline Thought in the History of Interpretation." *Bibliotheca Sacra* 150 (1993): 303-26.

Hübner, Hans. *Das Gesetz bei Paulus: Ein Beitrag zum Werden der paulinischen Theologie.* Göttingen: Vandenhoeck & Ruprecht, 1978. 195 pp.

_____. "Methodologie und Theologie: Zu neuen methodischen Ansätzen in der Paulusforschung. Teil I." *Kerygma und Dogma* 33 (1987): 150-76.

_____. "Methodologie und Theologie: Zu neuen methodischen Ansätzen in der Paulusforschung. Teil II." *Kerygma und Dogma* 33 (1987): 303-329.

Hultgren, Arland J. "The *Pistis Christou* Formulation in Paul." *Novum Testamentum* 22 (1980): 248-63.

Hunter, A. M. *The Epistle to the Romans: Introduction and Commentary.* Torch Bible Commentaries. London: SCM Press, 1955. 134 pp.

Hurst, L. D. "Re-enter the Pre-existent Christ in Philippians 2:5-11?" *New Testament Studies* 32 (1986): 449-57.

Hurtado, L. W. "Jesus as Lordly Example in Philippians 2:5-11." In *From Jesus to Paul: Studies in Honour of Francis Wright Beare,* ed. Peter Richardson and John C. Hurd, 113-26. Waterloo, Ontario, Canada: Wilfrid Laurier University Press, 1984.

The Interpreter's Dictionary of the Bible: An Illustrated Encyclopedia. Edited by George Arthur Buttrick. New York: Abingdon Press, 1962. 4 vols. S.v. "Righteousness in the NT," by P. J. Achtemeier. 4:91-99. S.v. "Righteousness in the OT," by E. R. Achtemeier. 4:80-85.

The Interpreter's Dictionary of the Bible: An Illustrated Encyclopedia. Supplementary Volume. Edited by Keith Crim. Nashville: Abingdon, 1976. S.v. "Atonement in the OT," by J. Milgrom. 78-82. S.v. "Righteousness in the NT," by G. Klein. 750-52.

Jervell, Jacob. *Imago Dei: Gen 1:26f. im Spätjudentum, in der Gnosis und in den paulinischen Briefen.* Forschungen zur Religion und Literatur des alten und neuen Testaments, 58. Göttingen: Vandenhoeck & Ruprecht, 1960. 379 pp.

390

Johnson, H. Wayne. "The Paradigm of Abraham in Galatians 3:6-9." *Trinity Journal* 8 n.s. (1987): 179-99.

Johnson, Luke Timothy. "Rom 3:21-26 and the Faith of Jesus." *The Catholic Biblical Quarterly* 44 (1982): 77-90.

Johnson, S. Lewis, Jr. "Romans 5:12--An Exercise in Exegesis and Theology." In *New Dimensions in New Testament Study,* ed. Richard N. Longenecker and Merrill C. Tenney, 298-316. Grand Rapids: Zondervan Publishing House, 1974.

Josephus. *Works.* With an English Translation by H. St. J. Thackeray. The Loeb Classical Library. Cambridge, MA: Harvard University Press, 1976. 9 vols.

Judge, E. A. "Cultural Conformity and Innovation in Paul: Some Clues From Contemporary Documents." *Tyndale Bulletin* 35 (1984): 3-24.

Kaiser, Otto. *Isaiah 13-39: A Commentary.* The Old Testament Library. Philadelphia: The Westminster Press, 1974. 412 pp.

Käsemann, Ernst. "The Beginnings of Christian Theology." In *New Testament Questions of Today.* Philadelphia: Fortress Press, 1969.

_____. *Commentary on Romans.* Grand Rapids: William B. Eerdmans Publishing Company, 1980. 428 pp.

_____. "Erwägungen zum Stichwort 'Versöhnungslehre im Neuen Testament.'" In *Zeit und Geschichte: Dankesgabe an Rudolf Bultmann zum 80. Geburtstag,* ed. Erich Dinkler, 47-59. Tübingen: J. C. B. Mohr, 1964.

_____. "The Faith of Abraham in Romans 4." In *Perspectives on Paul.* Philadelphia: Fortress Press, 1971.

_____. "Justification and Salvation History in the Epistle to the Romans." In *Perspectives on Paul.* Philadelphia: Fortress Press, 1971.

_____. "Die Legitimität des Apostels: Eine Untersuchung zu 2 Korinther 10-13." *Zeitschrift für die neutestamentliche Wissenschaft* 41 (1942): 33-71.

_____. "On the Subject of Primitive Christian Apocalyptic." In *New Testament Questions of Today.* Philadelphia: Fortress Press, 1969.

_____. "The Pauline Theology of the Cross." *Interpretation* 24 (1970): 151-77.

_____. "'The Righteousness of God' in Paul." In *New Testament Questions of Today.* Philadelphia: Fortress Press, 1969.

_____. The Saving Significance of the Death of Jesus in Paul." In *Perspectives on Paul.* Philadelphia: Fortress Press, 1971.

_____. "Zum Verständnis von Röm 3:24-26." In *Exegetische Versuche und Besinnungen,* vol 1. Göttingen: Vandenhoeck & Ruprecht, 1960.

Kearns, Conleth. "The Interpretation of Romans 6:7." *Analecta biblica* 17 (1961): 301-307.

Keck, Leander E. "'Jesus' in Romans." *Journal of Biblical Literature* 108 (1989): 443-60.

_____. "Paul and Apocalyptic Theology." *Interpretation* 38 (1984): 229-41.

_____. "Paul as Thinker." *Interpretation* 47 (1993): 27-38.

Keck, Leander E., and Victor Paul Furnish. *The Pauline Letters.* Interpreting Biblical Texts. Nashville: Abingdon Press, 1984. 156 pp.

Kee, Doyle. "Who Were the 'Super-Apostles' of 2 Corinthians 10-13?" *Restoration Quarterly* 23 (1980): 65-76.

Kennedy, H. A. A. *St Paul's Conceptions of the Last Things.* 2d ed. London: Hodder and Stoughton, 1904. 370 pp.

Kennedy, James Houghton. *The Second and Third Epistles of St. Paul to the Corinthians With Some Proofs of Their Independence and Mutual Relation.* London: Methuen & Co., 1900. 202 pp.

Kertelge, Karl. *"Rechtfertigung" bei Paulus: Studien zur Struktur und zum Bedeutungsgehalt des paulinischen Rechtfertigungsbegriffs.* Münster: Verlag Aschendorff, 1967. 335 pp.

Kidner, Derek. "Sacrifice--Metaphors and Meaning." *Tyndale Bulletin* 33 (1982): 119-36.

Kim, Seyoon. *The Origin of Paul's Gospel.* Wissenschaftliche Untersuchungen zum Neuen Testament, Reihe 4, 2. Tübingen: J. C. B. Mohr, 1981. 391 pp.

Kirby, John T. "The Syntax of Romans 5:12: A Rhetorical Approach." *New Testament Studies* 33 (1987): 283-86.

Klijn, A. F. J. "1 Thessalonians 4:13-18 and Its Background in Apocalyptic Literature." In *Paul and Paulinism: Essays in Honour of C. K. Barrett,* ed. M. D. Hooker and S. G. Wilson, 67-73. London: SPCK, 1982.

Koch, Dietrich-Alex. "Beobachtungen zum christologischen Schriftgebrauch in den vorpaulinischen Gemeinden." *Zeitschrift für die neutestamentliche Wissenschaft* 71 (1980): 174-91.

Koperski, V. "The Meaning of *Pistis Christou* in Philippians 3:9." *Louvain Studies* 18 (1993): 198-216.

Kreitzer, L. Joseph. *Jesus and God in Paul's Eschatology.* Journal for the Study of the New Testament Supplement Series, 19. Sheffield: JSOT Press, 1987. 293 pp.

Kreitzer, Larry. "Adam as Analogy: Help or Hindrance?" *King's Theological Review* 11 (1988): 59-62.

Kümmel, Werner Georg. *Introduction to the New Testament.* rev. ed. Translated by Howard Clark Kee. Nashville: Abingdon Press, 1975. 629 pp.

_____. *The New Testament: The History of the Investigation of Its Problems.* Translated by S. McLean Gilmour and Howard C. Kee. New York: Abingdon Press, 1972. 510 pp.

_____. "Πάρεσις und ἔνδειξις: Beitrag zum Verständnis der paulinischen Rechtfertigungslehre." In *Heilsgeschehen und Geschichte,* vol. 1. Marburg: N. G. Elwert Verlag, 1965.

_____. *The Theology of the New Testament According to Its Major Witnesses: Jesus--Paul--John.* London: SCM Press, 1973. 350 pp.

Küng, Hans. *Justification: The Doctrine of Karl Barth and a Catholic Reflection.* Philadelphia: The Westminster Press, 1964. 332 pp.

Lake, Kirsopp, trans. *The Apostolic Fathers.* The Loeb Classical Library. New York: G. P. Putnam's Sons, 1930. 2 vols.

Lambrecht, J. "The *Nekrōsis* of Jesus: Ministry and Suffering in 2 Cor 4:7-15." In *L'apôtre Paul: Personnalité, Style et Conception du Ministère,* ed. A. Vanhoye, 120-43. Bibliotheca Ephemeridum Theologicarum Lovaniensium, 73. Leuven: University Press, 1986.

Lang, Bernhard. "Afterlife: Ancient Israel's Changing Vision of the World Beyond." *Bible Review* 4 (1988): 12-23.

_____. "Life After Death in the Prophetic Promise." In *Congress Volume: Jerusalem, 1986,* ed. J. A. Emerton, 144-56. Supplements to *Vetus Testamentum,* 40. Leiden: E. J. Brill, 1988.

Lategan, B. C. "Formulas in the Language of Paul: A Study of Prepositional Phrases in Galatians." *Neotestamentica* 25 (1991): 75-87.

Leaney, A. R. C. "The Akedah, Paul and the Atonement, or: Is a Doctrine of the Atonement Possible?" In *Studia Evangelica, Vol. VII: Papers Presented to the Fifth International Congress on Biblical Studies Held at Oxford, 1973,* ed. Elizabeth A. Livingstone, 307-15. Berlin: Akademie-Verlag, 1982.

Leary, T. J. "'A Thorn in the Flesh'--2 Corinthians 12:7." *The Journal of Theological Studies* 43 (1992): 520-22.

Leenhardt, Franz J. *The Epistle to the Romans: A Commentary.* London: Lutterworth Press, 1961. 389 pp.

Légasse, S. "Être baptisé dans la mort du Christ: Étude de Romains 6:1-14." *Revue Biblique* 98 (1991): 544-59.

Lemcio, Eugene E. "The Unifying Kerygma of the New Testament." *Journal for the Study of the New Testament* 33 (1988): 3-17.

_____. "The Unifying Kerygma of the New Testament (II)." *Journal for the Study of the New Testament* 38 (1990): 3-11.

Léon-Dufour, Xavier. *Face à la Mort: Jésus et Paul.* Paris: Éditions du Seuil, 1979. 322 pp.

Levison, John R. *Portraits of Adam in Early Judaism: From Sirach to 2 Baruch.* Journal for the Study of the Pseudepigrapha Supplement Series, 1. Sheffield: Sheffield Academic Press, 1988. 255 pp.

Liddell, Henry George, and Robert Scott. *A Greek-English Lexicon.* 9th ed. Oxford: The Clarendon Press, 1940. 2111 pp.

Lindsay, Dennis R. "The Roots and Development of the πιστ- Word Group as Faith Terminology." *Journal for the Study of the New Testament* 49 (1993): 103-18.

Lightfoot, J. B. *Saint Paul's Epistle to the Philippians: A Revised Text With Introduction, Notes, and Dissertations.* London: Macmillan and Co., 1913. 350 pp.

Lincoln, A. T. "'Paul the Visionary': The Setting and Significance of the Rapture to Paradise in 2 Corinthians 12:1-10." *New Testament Studies* 25 (1979): 204-20.

Ljungman, Henrik. *Pistis: A Study of Its Presuppositions and Its Meaning in Pauline Use.* Lund: C. W. K. Gleerup, 1964.

Lohmeyer, Ernst. *Kyrios Jesus: Eine Untersuchung zu Phil 2:5-11.* Heidelberg: Carl Winter, Universitätsverlag, 1961. 89 pp.

Lohse, Eduard. *Märtyrer und Gottesknecht: Untersuchungen zur urchristlichen Verkündigung vom Sühntod Jesu Christi.* Göttingen: Vandenhoeck & Ruprecht, 1955.

_____. *The New Testament Environment.* Translated by John E. Steely. Nashville: Abingdon, 1976. 300 pp.

Lombard, H. A. "The Adam-Christ 'Typology' in Romans 5:12-21." *Neotestamentica* 15 (1981): 69-100.

Longenecker, Richard N. *Biblical Exegesis in the Apostolic Period.* Grand Rapids: William B. Eerdmans Publishing Company, 1975. 246 pp.

_____. "The Obedience of Christ in the Theology of the Early Church." In *Reconciliation and Hope: New Testament Essays on Atonement and Eschatology Presented to L. L. Morris on His 60th Birthday,* ed. Robert Banks, 142-52. Exeter: The Paternoster Press, 1974.

_____. "Πίστις in Romans 3:25: Neglected Evidence for the 'Faithfulness of Christ'?" *New Testament Studies* 39 (1993): 478-80.

Lowe, John. "An Examination of Attempts to Detect the Developments in St. Paul's Theology." *The Journal of Theological Studies* 42 (1941): 129-42.

Luedemann, Gerd. *Paul, Apostle to the Gentiles: Studies in Chronology.* Translated by F. Stanley Jones. With a Foreword by John Knox. Philadelphia: Fortress Press, 1984. 311 pp.

Lührmann, Dieter. "*Pistis* im Judentum." *Zeitschrift für die neutestamentliche Wissenschaft* 64 (1973): 19-38.

Luther, Martin. *Commentary on Saint Paul's Epistle to the Galatians.* Corrected and revised by Erasmus Middleton. Grand Rapids: Wm. B. Eerdmans Publishing Company, 1930. 536 pp.

Luz, Ulrich. "Theologia crucis als Mitte der Theologie im Neuen Testament." *Evangelische Theologie* 2 (1974): 116-41.

Maillot, A. "Les Théologies de la Mort du Christ chez Paul." *Foi et Vie* 85 (1986): 33-45.

Mangan, Celine. "Christ the Power and the Wisdom of God: The Semitic Background to 1 Cor 1:24." In *Proceedings of the Irish Biblical Association, 4 (1980),* ed. Martin McNamara, 21-34. Dublin: The Irish Biblical Association, 1980.

Marshall, I. Howard. "The Death of Jesus in Recent New Testament Study." *Word & World* 3 (1983): 12-21.

_____. "The Development of the Concept of Redemption in the New Testament." In *Reconciliation and Hope: New Testament Essays on Atonement and Eschatology Presented to L. L. Morris on His 60th Birthday,* ed. Robert Banks, 153-69. Exeter: The Paternoster Press, 1974.

_____. "The Meaning of 'Reconciliation.'" In *Unity and Diversity in New Testament Theology: Essays in Honor of George E. Ladd,* ed. Robert A. Guelich, 117-32. Grand Rapids: William B. Eerdmans Publishing Company, 1978. 219 pp..

Marshall, Peter. *Enmity in Corinth: Social Conventions in Paul's Relations With the Corinthians.* Wissenschaftliche Untersuchungen zum Neuen Testament, Reihe 2, 23. Tübingen: J. C. B. Mohr, 1987. 450 pp.

_____. "Hybrists Not Gnostics in Corinth." In *Society of Biblical Literature 1984 Seminar Papers,* ed. Kent Harold Richards, 275-87. Chico, CA: Scholars Press, 1984.

Martin, Dale B. *Slavery as Salvation: The Metaphor of Slavery in Pauline Christianity.* New Haven and London: Yale University Press, 1990. 245 pp.

Martin, Ralph P. *Carmen Christi: Philippians 2:5-11 in Recent Interpretation and in the Setting of Early Christian Worship.* Grand Rapids: William B. Eerdmans Publishing Company, 1967. 367 pp.

_____. "The Opponents of Paul in 2 Corinthians: An Old Issue Revisited." In *Tradition and Interpretation in the New Testament: Essays in Honor of E. Earle Ellis for His 60th Birthday,* ed. Gerald F. Hawthorne with Otto Betz, 279-89. Grand Rapids: William B. Eerdmans Publishing Company, 1987.

_____. *Philippians.* New Century Bible Commentary. Grand Rapids: Wm. B. Eerdmans Publ. Co., 1976. 176 pp.

_____. "The Setting of 2 Corinthians." *Tyndale Bulletin* 37 (1986): 3-19.

_____. *The Spirit and the Congregation: Studies in 1 Corinthians 12-15.* Grand Rapids: William B. Eerdmans Publishing Company, 1984. 168 pp.

_____. "Theological Perspectives in 2 Corinthians: Some Notes." In *Society of Biblical Literature 1990 Seminar Papers,* ed. David J. Lull, 240-56. Atlanta: Scholars Press, 1990.

_____. *2 Corinthians.* Word Biblical Commentary. Waco, TX: Word Books, Publisher, 1986. 527 pp.

Martínez, F. Garcia, and E. J. C. Tigchelaar. "*1 Enoch* and the Figure of Enoch: A Bibliography of Studies 1970-1988." *Revue de Qumran* 14 (1989): 149-74.

Mays, James Luther. *Micah: A Commentary.* The Old Testament Library. Philadelphia: The Westminster Press, 1976. 169 pp.

McCant, Jerry W. "Paul's Thorn of Rejected Apostleship." *New Testament Studies* 34 (1988): 550-72.

McClelland, Scott E. "'Super-Apostles, Servants of Christ, Servants of Satan': A Response." *Journal for the Study of the New Testament* 14 (1982): 82-87.

McLean, Bradley H. "The Absence of an Atoning Sacrifice in Paul's Soteriology." *New Testament Studies* 38 (1992): 531-53.

Meeks, Wayne A. *The First Urban Christians: The Social World of the Apostle Paul.* New Haven and London: Yale University Press, 1983. 299 pp.

_____. *The Origins of Christian Morality: The First Two Centuries.* New Haven and London: Yale University Press, 1993. 275 pp.

Merklein, Helmut. "Die Bedeutung des Kreuzestodes Christi für die paulinische Gerechtigkeits- und Gesetzesthematik." In *Studien zu Jesus und Paulus.* Tübingen: J. C. B. Mohr, 1987.

_____. *Studien zu Jesus und Paulus.* Tübingen: J. C. B. Mohr, 1987. 479 pp.

Mettinger, Tryggve N. D. *A Farewell to the Servant Songs: A Critical Examination of an Exegetical Axiom.* Scripta Minora, Regiae Societatis Humaniorum Litterarum Lundensis 1982-83: 3. Lund: CWK Gleerup, 1983. 52 pp.

Meyer, Ben F. "Did Paul's View of the Resurrection Undergo Development?" *Theological Studies* 47 (1986): 363-87.

_____. "Note: Paul and the Resurrection of the Dead." *Theological Studies* 48 (1987): 157-58.

_____. "The Pre-Pauline Formula in Rom 3:25-26a." *New Testament Studies* 29 (1983): 198-208.

Mills, Watson E. *An Index to Periodical Literature on the Apostle Paul.* New Testament Tools and Studies, 16. New York: E. J. Brill, 1993. 345 pp.

Milne, D. J. W. "Genesis 3 in the Letter to the Romans." *The Reformed Theological Review* 39 (1980): 10-18.

Minear, Paul Sevier. "The Crucified World: The Enigma of Galatians 6:14." In *Theologia Crucis--Signum Crucis: Festschrift für Erich Dinkler zum 70. Geburtstag,* ed. Carl Andresen and Günter Klein, 395-407. Tübingen: J. C. B. Mohr, 1979.

_____. "The Truth About Sin and Death: The Meaning of Atonement in the Epistle to the Romans." *Interpretation* 7 (1953): 142-55.

Montefiore, C. G., and H. Loewe. *A Rabbinic Anthology: Selected and Arranged With Comments and Introductions.* London: Macmillan and Co., 1938. 853 pp.

Moo, Douglas J. "Exegetical Notes: Romans 6:1-14." *Trinity Journal* 3 n.s. (1982): 215-20.

_____. *The Old Testament in the Gospel Passion Narratives.* Sheffield: The Almond Press, 1983. 468 pp.

_____. "Paul and the Law in the Last Ten Years." *Scottish Journal of Theology* 40 (1987): 287-307.

Moore, George Foot. *Judaism in the First Centuries of the Christian Era: The Age of the Tannaim.* Cambridge: Harvard University Press, 1927. 3 vols.

Moore, R. K. "Issues Involved in the Interpretation of δικαιοσύνη θεοῦ in the Pauline Corpus." *Colloquium* 23 (1991): 59-70.

Morris, Leon. *The Cross in the New Testament.* Grand Rapids: William B. Eerdmans Publishing Company, 1965. 454 pp.

Morris, Leon. *Apocalyptic.* 2d ed. Grand Rapids: Wm. B. Eerdmans Publishing Co., 1972. 105 pp.

Moule, C. F. D. "Further Reflexions on Philippians 2:5-11." In *Apostolic History and the Gospel: Biblical and Historical Essays Presented to F. F. Bruce on His 60th Birthday,* ed. W. Ward Gasque and Ralph P. Martin, 264-76. Exeter: The Paternoster Press, 1970.

_____. "St Paul and Dualism: The Pauline Conception of Resurrection." *New Testament Studies* 12 (1966): 106-23.

Müller, Christian. *Gottes Gerechtigkeit und Gottes Volk: Eine Untersuchung zu Römer 9-11.* Göttingen: Vandenhoeck & Ruprecht, 1964. 116 pp.

Müller, Jac[obus] J. *The Epistles of Paul to the Philippians and to Philemon.* The New International Commentary on the New Testament. Grand Rapids: Wm. B. Eerdmans Publishing Company, 1955. 200 pp.

Müller, Ulrich B. "Der Christushymnus Phil 2:6-11." *Zeitschrift für die neutestamentliche Wissenschaft* 79 (1988): 17-44.

Mullins, Terence Y. "Paul's Thorn in the Flesh." *Journal of Biblical Literature* 76 (1957): 299-303.

Murphy-O'Connor, Jerome. "Christological Anthropology in Phil 2:6-11." *Revue Biblique* 83 (1976): 25-50.

398

_____. "The Date of 2 Corinthians 10-13." *Australian Biblical Review* 39 (1991): 31-43.

_____. "Faith and Resurrection in 2 Cor 4:13-14." *Revue Biblique* 95 (1988): 543-50.

_____. "*Pneumatikoi* and Judaizers in 2 Cor 2:14-4:6." *Australian Biblical Review* 34 (1986): 42-58.

_____. "Pneumatikoi in 2 Corinthians." In *Proceedings of the Irish Biblical Association, 11,* ed. Martin McNamara, 59-66. Dublin: Irish Biblical Association Publications, 1987.

Neary, Michael. "Creation and Pauline Soteriology." *The Irish Theological Quarterly* 50 (1983/84): 1-34.

The New English Bible With the Apocrypha: Oxford Study Edition. Edited by Samuel Sandmel. New York: Oxford University Press, 1976.

The New Jerusalem Bible. Garden City, NY: Doubleday & Company, Inc., 1985.

The New Oxford Annotated Bible With the Apocrypha: Revised Standard Version. Edited by Herbert G. May and Bruce M. Metzger. New York: Oxford University Press, 1977.

Nickelsburg, George W. E., Jr. *Resurrection, Immortality, and Eternal Life in Intertestamental Judaism.* Harvard Theological Studies, 26. Cambridge: Harvard University Press, 1972. 202 pp.

Novum Testamentum Graece: Nestle-Aland. 26th ed. Stuttgart: Deutsche Bibelstiftung, 1979.

Nygren, Anders. *Commentary on Romans.* Philadelphia: Muhlenberg Press, 1949. 457 pp.

O'Collins, Gerald G. "Power Made Perfect in Weakness: 2 Cor 12:9-10." *The Catholic Biblical Quarterly* 33 (1971): 528-37.

O'Neill, J. C. "Notes and Observations: Hoover on *Harpagmos* Reviewed, With a Modest Proposal Concerning Philippians 2:6." *Harvard Theological Review* 81 (1988): 445-49.

The Old Testament in Greek: According to the Text of Codex Vaticanus, Supplemented from Other Uncial Manuscripts . . . . Edited by Alan England Brooke and Norman McLean. Cambridge: The University Press, 1917. 2 vols.

O'Rourke, John J. "*Pistis* in Romans." *The Catholic Biblical Quarterly* 35 (1973): 188-94.

Osten-Sacken, Peter von der. "Die paulinische theologia crucis als Form apokalyptischer Theologie." *Evangelische Theologie* 39 (1979): 477-96.

Page, Sydney H. T. "The Suffering Servant Between the Testaments." *New Testament Studies* 31 (1985): 481-97.

Palmer, D. W. "'To Die Is Gain' (Philippians 1:21)." *Novum Testamentum* 17 (1975): 203-18.

Park, David M. "Paul's σκόλοψ τῇ σαρκί: Thorn or Stake? (2 Cor 12:7)." *Novum Testamentum* 22 (1980): 179-83.

Patitsas, Chrestos. "'Kenosis' According to Saint Paul." *The Greek Orthodox Theological Review* 27 (1982): 67-82.

Patte, Daniel. *Paul's Faith and the Power of the Gospel: A Structural Introduction to the Pauline Letters.* Philadelphia: Fortress Press, 1983. 408 pp.

_____. "A Structural Exegesis of 2 Corinthians 2:14-7:4 With Special Attention on 2:14-3:6 and 6:11-7:4." In *Society of Biblical Literature 1987 Seminar Papers,* ed. Kent Harold Richards, 23-49. Atlanta: Scholars Press, 1987.

Pelser, G. M. M. "The Objective Reality of the Renewal of Life in Romans 6:1-11." *Neotestamentica* 15 (1981): 101-117.

Pesce, Mauro. "'Christ did not send me to baptize, but to evangelize' (1 Cor 1:17a)." In *Paul de Tarse: Apôtre du Notre Temps,* ed. Lorenzo De Lorenzi, 339-62. Rome: Abbaye de S. Paul h.l.m., 1979.

Pfleiderer, Otto. *Der Paulinismus: Ein Beitrag zur Geschichte der urchristlichen Theologie.* Leipzig: Fues's Verlag, 1873. 518 pp.

_____. *Primitive Christianity: Its Writings and Teachings in Their Historical Connections.* Translated by W. Montgomery. Edited by W. D. Morrison. Clifton, NJ: Reference Book Publishers, Inc., 1965. 4 vols.

Piper, John. "The Demonstration of the Righteousness of God in Romans 3:25, 26." *Journal for the Study of the New Testament* 7 (1980): 2-32.

Plank, Karl A. *Paul and the Irony of Affliction.* The Society of Biblical Literature Semeia Studies. Atlanta: Scholars Press, 1987. 109 pp.

Plato. *The Republic.* With an English Translation by Paul Shorey. The Loeb Classical Library. Cambridge, MA: Harvard University Press, 1937. 2 vols.

Plevnik, Joseph. "The Center of Pauline Theology." *Catholic Biblical Quarterly* 51 (1989): 461-78.

_____. "The Taking Up of the Faithful and the Resurrection of the Dead in 1 Thessalonians 4:13-18." *Catholic Biblical Quarterly* 46 (1984): 274-83.

Plummer, Alfred. *A Critical and Exegetical Commentary on the Second Epistle of St. Paul to the Corinthians.* The International Critical Commentary. New York: Charles Scribner's Sons, 1915. 404 pp.

Pobee, John S. *Persecution and Martyrdom in the Theology of Paul.* Journal for the Study of the New Testament Supplement Series, 6. Sheffield: JSOT Press, 1985. 155 pp.

Porter, Stanley E. "The Pauline Concept of Original Sin, in Light of Rabbinic Background." *Tyndale Bulletin* 41 (1990): 3-30.

Price, James L. "God's Righteousness Shall Prevail." *Interpretation* 28 (1974): 259-80.

_____. "Romans 6:1-14." *Interpretation* 34 (1980): 65-69.

Price, Robert M. "Punished in Paradise (An Exegetical Theory on 2 Corinthians 12:1-10)." *Journal for the Study of the New Testament* 7 (1980): 33-40.

Proudfoot, C. Merrill. "Imitation or Realistic Participation? A Study of Paul's Concept of 'Suffering With Christ.'" *Interpretation* 17 (1963): 140-60.

Pryor, John W. "Paul's Use of *Iēsous*--A Clue for the Translation of Romans 3:26?" *Colloquium (The Australian and New Zealand Theological Review)* 16 (1983): 31-45.

Quek, Swee-Hwa. "Adam and Christ According to Paul." In *Pauline Studies: Essays Presented to Professor F. F. Bruce on His 70th Birthday,* ed. Donald A. Hagner and Murray J. Harris, 67-79. Grand Rapids: The Paternoster Press and William B. Eerdmans Publishing Company, 1980.

Quesnel, Michel. "Paul en Conflit avec les Chrétiens de Son Temps." *Foi et Vie* 84 (1985): 57-64.

Räisänen, Heikki. *Paul and the Law.* 2d ed. Wissenschaftliche Untersuchungen zum Neuen Testament, 29. Tübingen: J. C. B. Mohr, 1987. 320 pp.

Ramaroson, Léonard. "La Justification par la Foi du Christ Jésus." *Science et Esprit* 39 (1987): 81-92.

Rebell, Walter. "Das Leidensverständnis bei Paulus und Ignatius von Antiochien." *New Testament Studies* 32 (1986): 457-65.

Reid, Daniel G. "The Misunderstood Apostle." *Christianity Today* 34 (1990): 25-27.

Reitzenstein, Richard. *Hellenistic Mystery-Religions: Their Basic Ideas and Significance.* Pittsburgh Theological Monograph Series, 15. Translated by John E. Seely. Pittsburgh: The Pickwick Press, 1978. 572 pp.

Reumann, John. "The Gospel of the Righteousness of God: Pauline Reinterpretation in Romans 3:21-31." *Interpretation* 20 (1966): 432-52.

Reumann, John, Joseph A. Fitzmyer, and Jerome D. Quinn. *"Righteousness" in the New Testament: "Justification" in the United States Lutheran--Roman Catholic Dialogue.* Philadelphia: Fortress Press, 1982. 278 pp.

Richard, Earl. "Contemporary Research on 1 (& 2) Thessalonians." *Biblical Theology Bulletin* 20 (1990): 107-15.

Ridderbos, Herman. "The Earliest Confession of the Atonement in Paul." In *Reconciliation and Hope: New Testament Essays on Atonement and Eschatology Presented to L. L. Morris on His 60th Birthday,* ed. Robert Banks, 76-89. Exeter: The Paternoster Press, 1974.

_____. *Paul: An Outline of His Theology.* Grand Rapids: William B. Eerdmans Publishing Company, 1975. 587 pp.

Roberts, J. H. "Righteousness in Romans With Special Reference to Romans 3:19-31." *Neotestamentica* 15 (1981): 12-33.

Roetzel, Calvin J. "As Dying, and Behold We Live." *Interpretation* 46 (1992): 5-18.

_____. "Sacrifice in Romans 12-15." *Word & World* 6 (1986): 410-19.

Rollins, Wayne G. "Greco-Roman Slave Terminology and Pauline Metaphors for Salvation." In *Society of Biblical Literature 1987 Seminar Papers,* ed. Kent Harold Richards, 100-110. Atlanta: Scholars Press, 1987.

Rosenberg, Roy A. "The Slain Messiah in the Old Testament." *Zeitschrift für die alttestamentliche Wissenschaft* 99 (1987): 259-61.

Ross, J. M. "Does 1 Corinthians 15 Hold Water?" *Irish Biblical Studies* 11 (1989): 69-72.

Rousseau, François. "Une disposition des versets de Philippiens 2:5-11." *Studies in Religion/Sciences Religieuses* 17 (1988): 191-98.

Rowland, Christopher. "Books on Apocalyptic." *Epworth Review* 16 (1989): 86-90.

Russell, Walt. "Who Were Paul's Opponents in Galatia?" *Bibliotheca Sacra* 147 (1990): 329-50.

402

Sahlin, Harald. "Adam-Christologie im Neuen Testament." *Studia Theologica (Scandinavian Journal of Theology)* 41 (1987): 11-32.

_____. "Paulus och Danielsboken." *Svensk Exegetisk Årsbok* 46 (1981): 95-110.

Saldarini, Anthony J. *Pharisees, Scribes and Sadducees in Palestinian Society: A Sociological Approach.* Wilmington, DE: Michael Glazier, 1988. 325 pp.

Sampley, J. Paul. "Overcoming Traditional Methods by Synthesizing the Theology of Individual Letters." In *Society of Biblical Literature 1986 Seminar Papers,* ed. Kent Harold Richards, 603-13. Atlanta: Scholars Press, 1986.

Sanday, William, and Arthur C. Headlam. *A Critical and Exegetical Commentary on the Epistle to the Romans.* 5th ed. The International Critical Commentary. Edinburgh: T. & T. Clark, 1902. 450 pp.

Sanders, E. P. *Paul and Palestinian Judaism: A Comparison of Patterns of Religion.* Philadelphia: Fortress Press, 1977. 627 pp.

_____. *Paul, the Law, and the Jewish People.* Philadelphia: Fortress Press, 1983. 227 pp.

Sanders, Jack T. *The New Testament Christological Hymns: Their Historical Religious Background.* Cambridge: The University Press, 1971. 163 pp.

Schade, Hans-Heinrich. *Apokalyptische Christologie bei Paulus: Studien zum Zusammenhang von Christologie und Eschatologie in den Paulusbriefen.* Göttingen: Vandenhoeck & Ruprecht, 1981. 337 pp.

Schlarb, Robert. "Röm 6:1-11 in der Auslegung der frühen Kirchenväter." *Biblische Zeitschrift* 33 (1989): 104-113.

Schnackenburg, Rudolf. *Baptism in the Thought of St. Paul: A Study in Pauline Theology.* Translated by G. R. Beasley-Murray. New York: Herder and Herder, 1964. 228 pp.

_____. "Christologie des Neuen Testamentes." In *Das Christusereignis,* III/I, ed. Johannes Feiner and Magnus Löhrer, 227-388. Zürich: Benziger Verlag, 1970.

_____. *New Testament Theology Today.* New York: Herder and Herder, 1963. 133 pp.

Schnelle, Udo. "Der Erste Thessalonicherbrief und die Entstehung der paulinischen Anthropologie." *New Testament Studies* 32 (1986): 207-224.

Schrage, Wolfgang. "Leid, Kreuz und Eschaton: Die Peristasenkataloge als Merkmale paulinischer theologia crucis und Eschatologie." *Evangelische Theologie* 34 (1974): 141-75.

_____. "Jesu ureigenes Todesverständnis: Bemerkungen zur 'impliziten Soteriologie' Jesu." In *Begegnung mit dem Wort: Festschrift für Heinrich Zimmermann,* ed. Josef Zmijewski and Ernst Nellessen, 273-309. Bonn: Peter Hanstein Verlag GmbH, 1980.

Schwartz, Daniel R. "Two Pauline Allusions to the Redemptive Mechanism of the Crucifixion." *Journal of Biblical Literature* 102 (1983): 259-68.

Schweitzer, Albert. *The Mysticism of Paul the Apostle.* With a Prefatory Note by F. C. Burkitt. New York: The Seabury Press, 1931. 411 pp.

Schweizer, Eduard. "Dying and Rising With Christ." *New Testament Studies* 14 (1967): 1-14.

Scroggs, Robin. *The Last Adam: A Study in Pauline Anthropology.* Philadelphia: Fortress Press, 1966. 139 pp.

_____. "Romans 6:7 ὁ γὰρ ἀποθανὼν δεδικαίωται ἀπὸ τῆς ἁμαρτίας." *New Testament Studies* 10 (1963): 104-108.

Segal, Alan F. "'He who did not spare his own son . . .': Jesus, Paul, and the Akedah." In *From Jesus to Paul: Studies in Honour of Francis Wright Beare,* ed. Peter Richardson and John C. Hurd, 169-84. Waterloo, Ontario, Canada: Wilfrid Laurier University Press, 1984.

_____. *Paul the Convert: The Apostolate and Apostasy of Saul the Pharisee.* New Haven, CT: Yale University Press, 1990. 368 pp.

Sellin, Gerhard. "'Die Auferstehung ist schon geschehen': Zur Spiritualisierung apokalyptischer Terminologie im Neuen Testament." *Novum Testamentum* 25 (1983): 220-37.

The Septuagint With Apocrypha: Greek and English. Edited and translated by Lancelot C. L. Brenton. Grand Rapids: Zondervan Publishing House, 1851.

Septuaginta; id est Vetus Testamentum graece iuxta LXX interpretes. Edited by Alfred Rahlfs. Stuttgart: Privilegierte Württembergische Bibelanstalt, 1935. 2 vols.

Septuaginta: Vetus Testamentum Graecum Auctoritate Academiae Scientiarum Gottingensis editum. Göttingen: Vandenhoeck & Ruprecht, 1931-[86].

Sevenster, J. N. "Some Remarks on the γυμνός in 2 Cor 5:3." In *Studia Paulina in honorem Johannis de Zwaan septuagenarii,* ed. J. N. Sevenster and W. C. van Unnick, 202-14. Haarlem: Erven F. Bohn N.V., 1953.

Shin, Samuel Shahoon. "St. Paul and the Atonement." Ph.D. diss., Drew University, 1945. 488 pp.

Sinclair, Scott Gambrill. *Jesus Christ According to Paul: The Christologies of Paul's Undisputed Epistles and the Christology of Paul.* Berkeley, CA: BIBAL Press, 1988. 150 pp.

Smith, D. Moody. "The Pauline Literature." In *It is Written: Scripture Citing Scripture. Essays in Honour of Barnabus Lindars, SSF,* ed. D. A. Carson and H. G. M. Williamson, 265-91. New York: Cambridge University Press, 1988.

Smith, Morton. "Pauline Worship as Seen By Pagans." *Harvard Theological Review* 73 (1980): 241-49.

Smith, Neil Gregor. "The Thorn that Stayed: An Exposition of 2 Corinthians 12:7-9." *Interpretation* 13 (1959): 409-16.

Soards, Marion L. "Once Again 'Righteousness of God' in the Writings of the Apostle Paul." *Bible Bhashyam: An Indian Biblical Quarterly* 17 (1991): 14-44.

_____. "The Righteousness of God in the Writings of the Apostle Paul." *Biblical Theology Bulletin* 15 (1985): 104-109.

Spallek, A. J. "The Origin and Meaning of Εὐαγγέλιον in the Pauline Corpus." *Concordia Theological Quarterly* 57 (1993): 177-90.

Spittler, Russell P. "The Limits of Ecstasy: An Exegesis of 2 Corinthians 12:1-10." In *Current Issues in Biblical and Patristic Interpretation: Studies in Honor of Merrill C. Tenney Presented by His Former Students,* ed. Gerald F. Hawthorne, 259-66. Grand Rapids: William B. Eerdmans Publishing Company, 1975.

Stanley, David. "Imitation in Paul's Letters: Its Significance for His Relationship to Jesus and to His Own Christian Foundations." In *From Jesus to Paul: Studies in Honour of Francis Wright Beare,* ed. Peter Richardson and John C. Hurd, 127-41. Waterloo, Ontario, Canada: Wilfrid Laurier University Press, 1984.

Steenburg, Dave. "The Case Against the Synonymity of *Morphē* and *Eikōn.*" *Journal for the Study of the New Testament* 34 (1988): 77-86.

Stendahl, Krister. *Paul Among Jews and Gentiles, and Other Essays.* Philadelphia: Fortress Press, 1976. 133 pp.

Stewart, James S. *A Man in Christ: The Vital Elements of St. Paul's Religion.* New York: Harper and Brothers Publishers, [1935]. 332 pp.

Stowers, Stanley K. "Ἐκ πίστεως and διὰ τῆς πίστεως in Rom 3:30." *Journal of Biblical Literature* 108 (1989): 665-74.

Strecker, Georg. "Die Legitimität des paulinischen Apostolates nach 2 Korinther 10-13." *New Testament Studies* 38 (1992): 566-86.

Strimple, Robert B. "Philippians 2:5-11 in Recent Studies: Some Exegetical Conclusions." *The Westminster Theological Journal* 41 (1979): 247-68.

Stuhlmacher, Peter. *Gerechtigkeit Gottes bei Paulus.* Göttingen: Vandenhoeck & Ruprecht, 1965. 276 pp.

Sturm, Richard E. "Defining the Word 'Apocalyptic': A Problem in Biblical Criticism." In *Apocalyptic and the New Testament: Essays in Honor of J. Louis Martyn,* ed. Joel Marcus and Marion L. Soards, 17-48. *Journal for the Study of the New Testament* Supplement Series, 24, Sheffield, England: JSOT Press, 1989.

Summey, Jerry L. *Identifying Paul's Opponents: The Question of Method in 2 Corinthians. Journal for the Study of the New Testament* Supplement Series, 40. Sheffield: JSOT Press, 1990. 256 pp.

————. "Paul's 'Weakness': An Integral Part of His Conception of Apostleship." *Journal for the Study of the New Testament* 52 (1993): 71-91.

Swain, C. William. "'For Our Sins': The Image of Sacrifice in the Thought of the Apostle Paul." *Interpretation* 17 (1963): 131-39.

Sykes, S. W. "Sacrifice in the New Testament and Christian Theology." In *Sacrifice,* ed. M. F. C. Bourdillon and Meyer Fortes, 61-83. New York: Academic Press, 1980.

Tabor, James. "Firstborn of Many Brothers: A Pauline Notion of Apotheosis." In *Society of Biblical Literature 1984 Seminar Papers,* ed. Kent Harold Richards, 295-303. Chico, CA: Scholars Press, 1984.

Talbert, Charles H. "A Non-Pauline Fragment at Romans 3:24-26?" *Journal of Biblical Literature* 85 (1966): 287-96.

————. "The Problem of Pre-Existence in Philippians 2:6-11." *Journal of Biblical Literature* 86 (1967): 141-53.

Tannehill, Robert C. *Dying and Rising With Christ: A Study in Pauline Theology.* Berlin: Alfred Töpelmann, 1967. 136 pp.

Teichmann, Ernst. *Die paulinische Vorstellungen von Auferstehung und Gericht und ihre Beziehungen zur jüdischen Apokalyptik.* Freiburg-Leipzig: J. C. B. Mohr, 1896. 125 pp.

Theissen, Gerd. *Psychological Aspects of Pauline Theology.* Translated by John P. Galvin. Philadelphia: Fortress Press, 1987. 433 pp.

Theological Dictionary of the New Testament. Translated and edited by Geoffrey W. Bromiley. Grand Rapids: Wm. B. Eerdmans Publishing Company, 1964. 10 vols.
S.v. "Καιρός," by Gerhard Delling. 3:455-64.
S.v. "Καυχάομαι," by R. Bultmann. 3:645-54.
S.v. "Στίγμα," by Otto Betz. 7:657-64.

Thrall, Margaret E. *The First and Second Letters of Paul to the Corinthians.* The Cambridge Bible Commentary. Cambridge: The University Press, 1965. 198 pp.

_____. "Salvation Proclaimed V. 2 Corinthians 5:18-21: Reconciliation With God." *The Expository Times* 93 (1982): 227-32.

_____. "Super-Apostles, Servants of Christ, and Servants of Satan." *Journal for the Study of the New Testament* 6 (1980): 42-57.

Toit, A. B. du. "Faith and Obedience in Paul." *Neotestamentica* 25 (1991): 65-74.

Travis, S. H. "The Doctrine of the Atonement: A Question and an Affirmation." *Epworth Review* 20 (1993): 74-79.

Tuckett, C. M. "Deuteronomy 21:23 and Paul's Conversion." In *L'apôtre Paul: Personnalité, Style et Conception du Ministère,* ed. A. Vanhoye, 345-50. Bibliotheca Ephemeridum Theologicarum Lovaniensium, 73. Leuven: University Press, 1986.

Vassiliadis, Petros. "Σταυρός: Centre of the Pauline Soteriology and Apostolic Ministry." In *L'apôtre Paul: Personnalité, Style et Conception du Ministère,* ed. A. Vanhoye, 247-53. Bibliotheca Ephemeridum Theologicarum Lovaniensium, 73. Leuven: University Press, 1986.

_____. "Your Will Be Done: Reflections from St Paul." *The International Review of Mission* 75 (1986): 376-82.

Vermes, G. *The Dead Sea Scrolls in English.* 2d ed. New York: Penguin Books, 1975. 281 pp.

Vincent, Marvin R. *A Critical and Exegetical Commentary on the Epistles to the Philippians and to Philemon.* The International Critical Commentary. Edinburgh: T. & T. Clark, 1897. 201 pp.

Vogel, C. J. de. "Reflexions on Phil 1:23-24." *Novum Testamentum* 19 (1977): 262-74.

Wagner, Günter. *Das religionsgeschichte Problem von Römer 6:1-11.* Zürich: Zwingli Verlag, 1962. 351 pp.

Wagner, Guy. "Le Scandale de la Croix Expliqué par le Chant du Serviteur d'Esaie 53: Réflexion sur Philippiens 2:6-11." *Etudes theologiques et religieuses* 61 (1986): 177-87.

Wanamaker, C. A. "Christ as Divine Agent in Paul." *Scottish Journal of Theology* 39 (1986): 517-28.

_____. "Philippians 2:6-11: Son of God or Adamic Christology?" *New Testament Studies* 33 (1987): 179-93.

Watson, Francis. "2 Cor 10-13 and Paul's Painful Letter to the Corinthians." *The Journal of Theological Studies* 35 (1984): 324-46.

Watson, Nigel M. "'. . . To make us rely not on ourselves but on God who raises the dead': 2 Cor 1:9b as the Heart of Paul's Theology." In *Die Mitte des Neuen Testaments: Einheit und Vielfalt neutestamentlicher Theologie. Festschrift für Eduard Schweizer zum siebzigsten Geburtstag*, ed. Ulrich Luz and Hans Weder, 384-98. Göttingen: Vandenhoeck & Ruprecht, 1983.

Webster, John B. "The Imitation of Christ." *Tyndale Bulletin* 37 (1986): 95-120.

Wedderburn, A. J. M. "Adam in Paul's Letter to the Romans." In *Studia Biblica 1978: III. Papers on Paul and Other New Testament Authors. Sixth International Congress on Biblical Studies: Oxford, 3-7 April 1978*, ed. E. A. Livingstone, 413-30. *Journal for the Study of the New Testament* Supplement Series, 3. Sheffield: JSOT Press, 1980.

_____. *Baptism and Resurrection: Studies in Pauline Theology against Its Graeco-Roman Background*. Tübingen: J. C. B. Mohr, 1987. 487 pp.

_____. "The Problem of the Denial of the Resurrection in 1 Corinthians 15." *Novum Testamentum* 23 (1981): 229-41.

_____. "Some Observations on Paul's Use of the Phrases 'In Christ' and 'With Christ.'" *Journal for the Study of the New Testament* 25 (1985): 83-97.

_____. "The Soteriology of the Mysteries and Pauline Baptismal Theology." *Novum Testamentum* 29 (1987): 53-72.

Weder, Hans. "Gesetz und Sünde: Gedanken zu Einem Qualitativen Sprung im Denken des Paulus." *New Testament Studies* 31 (1985): 357-76.

_____. *Das Kreuz Jesu bei Paulus: Ein Versuch, über den Geschichtsbezug des christlichen Glaubens nachzudenken*. Göttingen: Vandenhoeck & Ruprecht, 1981. 273 pp.

Weima, Jeffrey A. D. "The Function of the Law in Relation to Sin: An Evaluation of the View of H. Räisänen." *Novum Testamentum* 32 (1990): 219-35.

Weinel, H. *Biblische Theologie des Neuen Testaments: Die Religion Jesu und des Urchristentums.* Tübingen: J. C. B. Mohr, 1911. 603 pp.

Wendland, Heinz-Dietrich. *Die Mitte der paulinische Botschaft: Die Rechtfertigungslehre des Paulus im Zusammenhange seiner Theologie.* Göttingen: Vandenhoeck & Ruprecht, 1935. 48 pp.

Wernle, Paul. *Die Anfänge unserer Religion.* Tübingen and Leipzig: J. C. B. Mohr, 1904. 514 pp.

_____. *The Beginnings of Christianity.* Translated by G. A. Bienemann. Edited, with an Introduction, by W. D. Morrison. New York: G. P. Putnam's Sons, 1903. 2 vols.

Westerholm, Stephen. *Israel's Law and the Church's Faith: Paul and His Recent Interpreters.* Grand Rapids: William B. Eerdmans Publishing Company, 1988. 238 pp.

Westermann, Claus. *Isaiah 40-66: A Commentary.* The Old Testament Library. Philadelphia: The Westminster Press, 1969. 429 pp.

Whiteley, D. E. H. "St. Paul's Thought on the Atonement." *The Journal of Theological Studies* 8 (1957): 240-55.

_____. *The Theology of St. Paul.* Oxford: Basil Blackwell, 1964. 295 pp.

Wiefel, W. "Die Hauptrichtung des Wandels im eschatologischen Denken des Paulus." *Theologische Zeitschrift* 30 (1974): 65-81.

Williams, Sam K. "Again *Pistis Christou.*" *The Catholic Biblical Quarterly* 49 (1987): 431-47.

_____. "The Hearing of Faith: ἀκοὴ πίστεως in Galatians 3." *New Testament Studies* 35 (1989): 82-93.

_____. "'Promise' in Galatians: A Reading of Paul's Reading of Scripture." *Journal of Biblical Literature* 107 (1988): 709-20.

_____. "The 'Righteousness of God' in Romans." *Journal of Biblical Literature* 99 (1980): 241-90.

Wolter, Michael. "Der Apostel und seine Gemeinden als Teilhaber am Leidensgeschick Jesu Christi: Beobachtungen zur paulinischen Leidenstheologie." *New Testament Studies* 36 (1990): 535-57.

Wong, Teresia Yai-Chow. "The Problem of Pre-existence in Philippians 2:6-11." *Ephemerides Theologicae Lovanienses* 62 (1986): 267-82.

Wood, John E. "Death at Work in Paul." *The Evangelical Quarterly* 54 (1982): 151-55.

Woods, Laurie. "Opposition to a Man and His Message: Paul's 'Thorn in the Flesh' (2 Cor 12:7)." *Australian Biblical Review* 39 (1991): 44-53.

Wrede, William. *Paul.* Translated by Edward Lummis. With a Preface by J. Estlin Carpenter. Lexington, KY: American Theological Library Association Committee on Reprinting, 1962. 183 pp.

Wright, N. T. "Adam in Pauline Christology." In *Society of Biblical Literature 1983 Seminar Papers,* ed. Kent Harold Richards, 359-89. Chico, CA: Scholars Press, 1983.

_____. "ἁρπαγμός and the Meaning of Philippians 2:5-11." *The Journal of Theological Studies* 37 (1986): 321-52.

_____. "The Meaning of περὶ ἁμαρτίας in Romans 8:3." In *Studia Biblica 1978: III. Papers on Paul and Other New Testament Authors. Sixth International Congress on Biblical Studies: Oxford, 3-7 April 1978,* ed. E. A. Livingstone, 453-59. *Journal for the Study of the New Testament* Supplement Series, 3. Sheffield: JSOT Press, 1980.

Young, Frances, and David F. Ford. *Meaning and Truth in 2 Corinthians.* Grand Rapids: William B. Eerdmans Publishing Company, 1987. 289 pp.

Young, Frances M. *The Use of Sacrificial Ideas in Greek Christian Writers From the New Testament to John Chrysostom.* Patristic Monograph Series, 5. Cambridge, MA: The Philadelphia Patristic Foundation, 1979. 317 pp.

Young, Norman H. "The Figure of the *Paidagōgos* in Art and Literature." *Biblical Archaeologist* 53 (1990): 80-86.

_____. "*Paidagōgos*: The Social Setting of a Pauline Metaphor." *Novum Testamentum* 29 (1987): 150-76.

Ziesler, J. A. *The Meaning of Righteousness in Paul: A Linguistic and Theological Enquiry.* Cambridge: The University Press, 1972. 255 pp.

_____. "Salvation Proclaimed IX: Romans 3:21-26." *The Expository Times* 93 (1982): 356-59.

Zmijewski, Josef. *Der Stil der paulinischen "Narrenrede": Analyse der Sprachgestaltung in 2 Kor 11:1-12:10 als Beitrag zur Methodik von Stiluntersuchungen neutestamentlicher Texte.* Bonner Biblische Beiträge, 52. Köln--Bonn: Peter Hanstein Verlag GmbH, 1978. 449 pp.

418

426

OLD TESTAMENT (MT and LXX)

428

430

APOCRYPHA (LXX)

PSEUDEPIGRAPHA